Analytical Perspectives

BUDGET OF THE U.S. GOVERNMENT

FISCAL YEAR 2024

OFFICE OF MANAGEMENT AND BUDGET

Bernan
Press

Lanham • Boulder • New York • London

Published by Bernan Press
An imprint of The Rowman & Littlefield Publishing Group, Inc.
4501 Forbes Boulevard, Suite 200, Lanham, Maryland 20706
www.rowman.com

86-90 Paul Street, London EC2A 4NE

ISBN 978-1-63671-398-4

∞™ The paper used in this publication meets the minimum requirements of American National Standard for Information Sciences—Permanence of Paper for Printed Library Materials, ANSI/NISO Z39.48-1992.

TABLE OF CONTENTS

LIST OF CHARTS AND TABLES

LIST OF CHARTS AND TABLES

LIST OF CHARTS

LIST OF TABLES

*Available on the internet at *http://www.whitehouse.gov/omb/analytical-perspectives/*

Management Priorities

Technical Budget Analyses

*Available on the internet at *http://www.whitehouse.gov/omb/analytical-perspectives/*

INTRODUCTION

1. INTRODUCTION

The *Analytical Perspectives* volume presents analyses that highlight specific subject areas or provide other significant data that contextualize the President's 2024 Budget and assist the public, policymakers, the media, and researchers in better understanding the Budget. This volume complements the main *Budget* volume, which presents the President's Budget policies and priorities, and the Budget *Appendix* volume, which provides appropriations language, schedules for budget expenditure accounts, and schedules for selected receipt accounts.

Presidential Budgets have included separate analytical presentations of this kind for many years. The 1947 Budget and subsequent budgets included a separate section entitled *Special Analyses and Tables* that covered four, and later more, topics. For the 1952 Budget, the section was expanded to 10 analyses, including many subjects still covered today, such as receipts, investment, credit programs, and aid to State and local governments. With the 1967 Budget, this material became a separate volume entitled *Special Analyses*, and included 13 chapters. The material has remained a separate volume since then, with the exception of the Budgets for 1991–1994, when all of the budget material was included in one volume. Beginning with the 1995 Budget, the volume has been named *Analytical Perspectives*. Marking a change from previous editions, the 2024 *Analytical Perspectives* volume reorganizes chapters into four sections: Economic Analyses, Special Analyses and Presentations, Management Priorities, and Technical Budget Analyses. In an effort to increase accessibility to supplemental chapter materials, a number of tables are now available online in Excel.

In addition to the information included in this volume, supplemental tables and other materials that are part of the *Analytical Perspectives* volume are available at *http://www.whitehouse.gov/omb/analytical-perspectives*. Tables included at this link are shown in the List of Tables in the front of this volume with an asterisk instead of a page number.

Overview of the Chapters

Economic and Budget Analyses

Economic Assumptions. This chapter reviews recent economic developments; presents the Administration's assessment of the economic situation and outlook; compares the economic assumptions on which the 2024 Budget is based with the assumptions for last year's Budget and those of other forecasters; provides sensitivity estimates for the effects on the Budget of changes in specified economic assumptions; and reviews past errors in economic projections.

Long-Term Budget Outlook. This chapter assesses the long-term budget outlook under current policies and under the Budget's proposals. It focuses on 25-year projections of Federal deficits and debt to illustrate the long-term impact of the Administration's proposed policies. It also discusses the uncertainties of the long-term budget projections and discusses the actuarial status of the Social Security and Medicare programs.

Special Analyses and Presentations

Budget Process. This chapter describes the Administration's approach and proposals related to budget enforcement, such as sequestration and Pay-As-You-Go procedures, and budget presentation, such as adjustments to the baseline to improve comparisons of the cost of policy. It discusses suggested reforms in budgeting, including for large Federal capital projects.

Federal Investment. This chapter discusses federally financed spending that yields long-term benefits. It presents information on annual spending on physical capital, research and development, and education and training.

Research and Development. This chapter presents a crosscutting review of research and development funding in the Budget.

Credit and Insurance. This chapter provides crosscutting analyses of the roles, risks, and performance of Federal credit and insurance programs and Government-sponsored enterprises (GSEs). The chapter covers the major categories of Federal credit (housing, education, small business and farming, energy and infrastructure, and international) and insurance programs (deposit insurance, pension guarantees, disaster insurance, and insurance against terrorism-related risks). Five additional tables address transactions including direct loans, guaranteed loans, and GSEs. These tables are available at the internet address cited above.

Aid to State and Local Governments. This chapter presents crosscutting information on Federal grants to State and local governments. The chapter also includes a table showing historical grant spending and a table displaying budget authority and outlays for grants in the Budget. Tables showing State-by-State spending for major grant programs are available at the internet address cited above.

Leveraging Federal Statistics to Strengthen Evidence-Based Decision-Making. This chapter discusses the role of the Federal statistical system in generating data that the public, businesses, and governments need to make informed decisions. The chapter describes how operating as a seamless Federal statistical system, with enhanced statistical capacity and infrastructure, will improve its ability to meet growing demands while addressing new and emerging challenges. The chapter also highlights

2024 Budget proposals for the Government's principal statistical agencies and units, and presents examples of innovative developments, as well as advancements in implementing the Foundations for Evidence-Based Policymaking Act of 2018.

Budget Exposure to Increased Costs and Lost Revenue Due to Climate Change. This chapter discusses the financial risks that the Federal Government faces from broad exposure to threats caused by global climate change. It summarizes recent OMB analyses of individual programmatic climate impacts that are informed by distinct climate scenarios, as well as potential impacts on revenues.

Management Priorities

Delivering a High-Performance Government. This chapter reviews the Administration's Performance Framework approach to performance management. It discusses the Federal Government's use of strategic planning and priority goal-setting to define success, and routines of data-driven performance reviews to remain on track. The chapter details actions and investments supported by the Budget to advance the Framework, and previews forthcoming efforts around "organization health" and "organization performance" to support agency decision-making related to future work environments.

Building and Using Evidence to Improve Government Effectiveness. This chapter discusses the Administration's commitment to evidence-based policymaking through its efforts to build and promote a culture of evidence and evaluation in the Federal Government. It highlights Government-wide progress and Administration accomplishments, efforts to implement Title I of the Evidence Act, and other new initiatives to advance an evidence-based Government. It also details investments in the Budget to enhance agency evaluation capacity, including qualified evaluators, and examples of other evidence investments at agencies. This chapter also provides examples of programmatic agency investments that are supported by evidence of effectiveness.

Strengthening the Federal Workforce. This chapter presents summary data on Federal employment, compensation, and personnel priorities, and discusses the Administration's strategic approach to rebuilding and investing in the Federal workforce.

Information Technology and Cybersecurity Funding. This chapter addresses Federal information technology (IT) and cybersecurity, highlighting initiatives and proposed funding levels to deliver critical citizen services, keep sensitive data and systems secure, and further the vision of modern Government. The Administration will invest in modern, secure technologies and services to drive enhanced efficiency and effectiveness. This will include undertaking complex Government-wide modernization efforts, driving improved delivery of citizen-facing services, and improving the overall management of the Federal IT portfolio. The Administration will also continue its efforts to further build the Federal IT workforce and seek to reduce the Federal Government's cybersecurity risk in order to better serve and protect the American public.

Technical Budget Analyses

Budget Concepts. This chapter includes a basic description of the budget process, concepts, laws, and terminology, and includes a glossary of budget terms.

Coverage of the Budget. This chapter describes activities that are included in budget receipts and outlays (and are therefore classified as "budgetary") as well as those activities that are not included in the Budget (and are therefore classified as "non-budgetary"). The chapter also defines the terms "on-budget" and "off-budget" and includes illustrative examples.

Governmental Receipts. This chapter presents information on estimates of Governmental receipts, which consist of taxes and other compulsory collections. It includes descriptions of tax-related legislation enacted in the last year and describes proposals affecting receipts in the 2024 Budget.

Offsetting Collections and Offsetting Receipts. This chapter presents information on collections that offset outlays, including collections from transactions with the public and intragovernmental transactions. In addition, this chapter presents information on "user fees," which are charges associated with market-oriented activities and regulatory fees. Detailed tables of offsetting receipts and offsetting collections in the Budget are available at the internet address cited above.

Tax Expenditures. This chapter describes and presents estimates of tax expenditures, which are defined as revenue losses from special exemptions, credits, or other preferences in the tax code.

Federal Borrowing and Debt. This chapter analyzes Federal borrowing and debt and explains the budget estimates. It includes sections on special topics such as trends in debt, debt held by the public net of financial assets and liabilities, investment by Government accounts, and the statutory debt limit.

Current Services Estimates. This chapter discusses the conceptual basis of the Budget's current services, or "baseline," estimates, which are generally consistent with the baseline rules in the Balanced Budget and Emergency Deficit Control Act of 1985 (BBEDCA). The chapter presents estimates of receipts, outlays, and the deficit under this baseline. Supplemental tables addressing factors that affect the baseline and providing details of baseline budget authority and outlays are available at the internet address cited above.

Trust Funds and Federal Funds. This chapter provides summary information about the two fund groups in the Budget—trust funds and Federal funds. In addition, it provides detailed information about income, outgo, and balances for the major trust funds and certain Federal fund programs.

Comparison of Actual to Estimated Totals. This chapter compares the actual receipts, outlays, and deficit for 2022 with the estimates for that year published in the 2022 Budget.

The following materials are available at the internet address cited above.

Detailed Functional Table

Detailed Functional Table. Table 24–1, "Budget Authority and Outlays by Function, Category, and Program," displays budget authority and outlays for major Federal program categories, organized by budget function (such as healthcare, transportation, or national defense), category, and program.

Federal Budget by Agency and Account

Federal Budget by Agency and Account. Table 25–1, "Federal Budget by Agency and Account," displays budget authority and outlays for each account, organized by agency, bureau, fund type, and account.

Federal Drug Control Funding

Federal Drug Control Funding. The Federal Drug Control Funding crosscut displays enacted and proposed drug control funding for Federal Departments and Agencies to implement the President's National Drug Control Strategy.

Calfed Bay-Delta Program Federal Budget Crosscut

Calfed Bay-Delta Program Crosscut. The Calfed Bay-Delta Program interagency budget crosscut report provides an estimate of Federal funding by each of the participating Federal Agencies with authority and programmatic responsibility for implementing this program, fulfilling the reporting requirements of section 106(c) of Public Law 108–361.

Columbia River Basin Federal Budget Crosscut

Columbia River Basin Federal Budget Crosscut. The Columbia River interagency budget crosscut report includes an estimate of Federal funding by each of the participating Federal agencies to carry out restoration activities within the Columbia River Basin, fulfilling the reporting requirements of section 123 of the Clean Water Act (33 U.S.C. 1275).

Lead Pipe Federal Budget Crosscut

Lead Pipe Federal Budget Crosscut. The lead pipe interagency budget crosscut report provides an estimate of Federal funding by agency that can be used for investments in lead pipe replacement and related activities, fulfilling the commitment made in the Biden-Harris Lead Pipe and Paint Action Plan.

Long Range Budget Projections for the FY 2024 Budget

Long Range Budget Projections for the FY 2024 Budget. The long range crosscut contains 25-year projections of deficits and debt as a percent of GDP under current policies, the Budget's proposals, and alternative assumptions.

ECONOMIC ANALYSES

2. ECONOMIC ASSUMPTIONS

This chapter presents the economic assumptions that underlie the Administration's 2024 Budget.[1] It provides an overview of the recent performance of the American economy, presents the Administration's projections for key macroeconomic variables, compares them with forecasts prepared by other prominent institutions, and discusses the unavoidable uncertainty inherent in providing an eleven-year forecast.

The chapter proceeds as follows. The first section provides an overview of the recent performance of the U.S. economy based on a broad array of key economic indicators. The second section presents a detailed exposition of the Administration's economic assumptions underlying the 2024 Budget and how key macroeconomic variables are expected to evolve over the years 2023 to 2033. The third section compares the forecast of the Administration with those of the Congressional Budget Office (CBO), the Federal Open Market Committee of the Federal Reserve (FOMC), and the Blue Chip Economic Indicators panel of professional forecasters. The fourth section discusses the sensitivity of the Administration's projections of Federal receipts and outlays to alternative paths of macroeconomic variables. The fifth section considers the errors in past Administrations' forecasts, comparing them with the errors in forecasts produced by the CBO and the Blue Chip Economic Indicators panel of professional forecasters. The sixth section uses information on past accuracy of Administration forecasts to provide understanding and insight into the uncertainty associated with the Administration's current forecast of the budget balance.

Recent Economic Performance

The Administration has made real progress on the President's top economic priority—transitioning to steady, stable economic growth with lower inflation and while maintaining a robust labor market—and the 2022 economy is proof that the President's plan to build an economy from the bottom up and middle out is showing results: the rate of inflation is declining, the economy is growing and adding jobs, and unemployment has fallen to a 50-year low.

The Labor Market

Employment—The labor market was a point of strength for the economy in 2022. After averaging 8.1 percent during 2020 and 5.4 percent in 2021, the unemployment rate remained at or below 4 percent for the entirety of 2022, averaging 3.6 percent for the year overall. Other metrics of labor market health also showed

signs of strength during 2022: the long-term unemployment rate steadily declined, there were fewer marginally attached and discouraged workers, and a smaller share of the labor force worked part-time for economic reasons such as not being able to find full-time employment.

The labor market also crossed an important milestone during 2022, as the total number of jobs surpassed its pre-pandemic high from early 2020. Notably, the economy added an average of 400,000 jobs per month during the 12 months of 2022. The prime-age labor force participation is now only 0.3 percentage points below its pre-pandemic rate. Looking ahead, growing the labor force, including through a range of policy measures the Administration has proposed, will remain an important economic priority.

Wages—As of 2022:Q4, average hourly earnings (AHE) increased 4.9 percent among total private workers from one year prior, while the AHE for production and nonsupervisory workers grew at an even faster rate of 5.6 percent over that same period. Between December 2021 and 2022, civilian hourly compensation as measured by the Employment Cost Index (ECI)—which adjusts for compositional effects that can arise from hiring and firing—grew by 5.1 percent. Furthermore, real wages increased over the second half of 2022, as gas prices fell, inflation moderated, and the labor market remained solid.

Gross Domestic Product

Consumption—Household consumption of goods and services accounts for two-thirds of U.S. GDP. As the largest source of spending, it greatly affects U.S. GDP growth. Real personal consumption expenditures (PCE), which adjusts for inflation, increased by 1.8 percent during the four quarters of 2022.

A prominent feature of the pandemic was the extent of the economic damage in specific sectors. While the service sector experienced the largest losses during the initial stages of the pandemic, supply-chain disruptions and reductions in purchasing power held back spending on goods over the past year. Following rapid growth during the four quarters of 2021, real spending on durable goods during 2022 grew at (a subdued) 0.5 percent, while spending on nondurable goods declined by 1.7 percent. Encouragingly, supply-chain difficulties have greatly abated over the course of 2022 according to the Federal Reserve Bank of New York's Global Supply Chains Pressure Index (see Chart 2-1). As improvements in supply chains can be expected to work through the economy with a lag, this is a promising development for the resiliency of the economy going forward.

Nonresidential Fixed Investment—After declining at an annual rate of 3.5 percent in 2020 (fourth-quarter-over-fourth-quarter), real nonresidential fixed investment increased 5.0 and 4.3 percent in 2021 and 2022, respec-

---

[1] Economic performance, unless otherwise specified, is discussed in terms of calendar years (January-December). Budget figures are discussed in terms of fiscal years (October-September).

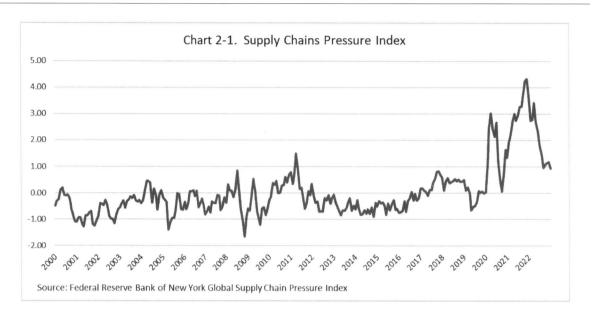

Chart 2-1. Supply Chains Pressure Index

Source: Federal Reserve Bank of New York Global Supply Chain Pressure Index

tively. Equipment and intellectual property investment increased 4.0 and 8.5 percent, respectively, during 2022, while business structures investment declined for the third consecutive year (-3.3 percent).

The Government Sector—Real Government expenditures on consumption and investment increased 0.8 percent in the four quarters ending 2022:Q4, which includes a 0.1 percent increase in Federal spending and a 1.3 percent increase in State and Local spending. Within the Federal spending category, nondefense spending increased 0.5 percent while defense spending decreased 0.2 percent.

Trade—Real exports of goods and services increased 5.2 percent in the four quarters ending 2022:Q4, generated by increases of 4.0 percent in goods and 7.8 percent in services. Real imports increased 1.8 percent over the same period, generated by increases of 0.9 percent in goods and 6.5 percent in services.

Economic Projections

The Administration's forecast was finalized in late November 2022, with the parameters of that forecast close to the consensus prevailing at that date. Since late November, data for 2022 has come in better than expected: real GDP has been higher than expected while inflation and unemployment were lower than expected. Specifically, the labor market has remained strong, with the unemployment rate falling from 3.6 percent to 3.4 percent. Economic activity has also remained solid, with upward revisions to third quarter GDP and the second estimate of fourth quarter GDP at 2.7 percent. Further, price pressures have continued to ease, with three-month annualized CPI inflation falling from 4.6 percent in October to 3.3 percent at the end of the year and three-month annualized core CPI inflation falling from 6.1 percent in October to 4.3 percent at the end of the year. In light of the new data available since these assumptions were formulated, a forecast assembled today would, of course, differ in various ways, and would likely include higher growth

rates and lower unemployment, just as many other forecasts have improved since last Fall.

The forecast informs the 2024 Budget and assumes implementation of the Administration's policy proposals. The Administration's projections are reported in Table 2-1 and summarized below. Note that, for 2022, the table reflects the projections finalized in November. As discussed below, reported data for 2022, which are available at the time of this writing, reflected better economic outcomes than the Administration's projections.

Real GDP—The Administration's economic assumptions project real GDP growth of 0.2 percent for the four quarters of 2022; subsequently released data show that actual real GDP growth over that period was 0.9 percent. Real GDP is expected to increase 0.4 percent in 2023, to average 2.1 percent growth between 2024-2028, and to average 2.2 percent growth during 2029-2033.

Unemployment—The Administration's economic assumptions project a 3.7 percent unemployment rate on average over 2022; subsequently released data show that the actual average over that period was 3.6 percent. The unemployment rate is projected to rise modestly during 2023 and 2024, before declining over the forecast horizon to a long-run rate of 3.8 percent by 2031.

Interest Rates—Interest rates are expected to rise over the near-term, a continuation of a trend started in 2022. The 91-day Treasury bill rate is expected to steadily rise from an average of 0.04 percent in 2021 to 4.9 percent in 2023. Thereafter, it is expected to gradually converge to a terminal rate of 2.5 percent. The 10-year rate follows a similar path as it is projected to increase from 1.4 percent in 2021 to 3.8 percent in 2023, reaching 3.4 percent at the end of the budget window, reflecting both the increase in expected short-term rates and an increase in the term premium.

General Inflation—The Administration's forecast reflects a background of elevated inflation during 2022, which is expected to decline through 2023 and return

Table 2–1. ECONOMIC ASSUMPTIONS[1]
(Calendar Years, Dollar Amounts in Billions)

	Actual 2021	Projections											
		2022	2023	2024	2025	2026	2027	2028	2029	2030	2031	2032	2033
Gross Domestic Product (GDP)													
Levels, Dollar Amounts in Billions:													
Current Dollars	23,315	25,409	26,544	27,523	28,750	29,981	31,224	32,516	33,884	35,342	36,880	38,483	40,157
Real, Chained (2012) Dollars	19,610	19,971	20,092	20,385	20,852	21,300	21,726	22,160	22,617	23,106	23,615	24,134	24,665
Chained Price Index (2012=100), Annual Average	119	127	132	135	138	141	144	147	150	153	156	160	163
Percent Change, Fourth-Quarter-over-Fourth-Quarter:													
Current Dollars	12.2	6.7	3.2	4.3	4.6	4.1	4.1	4.1	4.2	4.3	4.4	4.3	4.3
Real, Chained (2012) Dollars	5.7	0.2	0.4	2.1	2.4	2.0	2.0	2.0	2.1	2.2	2.2	2.2	2.2
Chained Price Index (2012=100)	6.1	6.6	2.8	2.1	2.1	2.1	2.1	2.1	2.1	2.1	2.1	2.1	2.1
Incomes, Billions of Current Dollars													
Domestic Corporate Profits	2,359	2,576	2,626	2,533	2,576	2,702	2,879	3,040	3,183	3,310	3,445	3,592	3,747
Employee Compensation	12,538	13,582	14,312	14,989	15,694	16,419	17,161	17,936	18,736	19,583	20,481	21,419	22,401
Wages and Salaries	10,290	11,205	11,812	12,358	12,938	13,532	14,136	14,768	15,424	16,118	16,850	17,634	18,484
Nonwage Personal Income	5,680	6,055	6,593	6,596	6,814	7,123	7,455	7,794	8,145	8,537	8,914	9,335	9,849
Consumer Price Index (All Urban)[2]:													
Level (1982–1984=100), Annual Average	271.0	293.0	305.7	313.0	320.3	327.6	335.2	342.9	350.7	358.8	367.1	375.5	384.2
Percent Change, Fourth-Quarter-over-Fourth-Quarter	6.7	7.6	3.0	2.3	2.3	2.3	2.3	2.3	2.3	2.3	2.3	2.3	2.3
Unemployment Rate, Civilian, Percent													
Annual Average	5.4	3.7	4.3	4.6	4.4	4.3	4.2	4.1	4.0	3.9	3.8	3.8	3.8
Q4 Level	4.2	3.8	4.6	4.5	4.4	4.3	4.2	4.1	4.0	3.8	3.8	3.8	3.8
Interest Rates, Percent													
91-Day Treasury Bills	0.0	2.0	4.9	3.8	3.0	2.5	2.3	2.2	2.3	2.4	2.4	2.5	2.5
10-Year Treasury Notes	1.4	3.0	3.8	3.6	3.5	3.4	3.4	3.4	3.4	3.4	3.4	3.4	3.4

[1] Based on information available as of November 2022.
[2] Seasonally Adjusted

to a rate consistent with the Federal Reserve target in 2024. Specifically, the assumptions anticipate that, after peaking at a projected 7.6 percent rate on a fourth quarter-over-fourth quarter basis in 2022, the Consumer Price Index for all Urban Consumers (CPI-U) is forecasted to increase 3.0 percent in 2023 and 2.3 percent in 2024. For context, the forecast was finalized before the release of November and December CPI data. The Administration's CPI inflation forecast for 2022 (7.6 percent) turned out higher than what was later reported (7.1 percent). Note that 2.3 percent is the rate of CPI-U inflation that is consistent with the Federal Reserve's 2.0 percent inflation target for the Personal Consumption Expenditures Price Index.

Changes in Economic Assumptions from Last Year's Budget—Table 2-2 compares the Administration's forecast for the 2024 Budget with that from the 2023 Budget. Compared with the 2023 Budget forecast, the Administration's expectations for the outyears of the forecast are little changed. Revisions to the near-term largely reflect the economic data at the time these assumptions were finalized. As noted above, a forecast formulated today would likely look different along several dimensions.

Comparison with Other Forecasts

This section compares the Administration's forecast with the then-available forecasts from CBO, the FOMC, and the Blue Chip panel of professional forecasters.

There are important methodological differences across these forecasts. The most important difference is that different forecasts make different assumptions about the implementation of the Administration's proposed policies. As already noted, the Administration's forecast assumes impacts of proposed Administration policies. In contrast, the CBO forecast assumes no changes to current law. It is not clear to what extent FOMC participants and Blue Chip panelists incorporate policy implementation expectations in their respective outlooks. The Blue Chip panel, in particular, comprises a large number of private-sector forecasters, who have different expectations about the enactment of the Administration's proposed policies and different views about how those policies might affect economic growth.

A second key difference is that the various forecasts were published on different dates. For example, while the forecast published by the Administration is based on data available as of late November 2022, the Blue Chip forecasts are drawn from a survey administered in early November. In addition, the Federal Reserve's FOMC projections were released in mid-September and the CBO forecast was published in May 2022.

Table 2–2. COMPARISON OF ECONOMIC ASSUMPTIONS IN THE 2023 AND 2024 BUDGETS

	2022	2023	2024	2025	2026	2027	2028	2029	2030	2031	2032
(fourth-quarter-over-fourth-quarter percent change)											
Real GDP:											
2023 Budget Assumptions	3.8	2.5	2.1	2.0	2.0	2.0	2.1	2.2	2.3	2.3	2.3
2023 MSR Assumptions	1.4	1.8	2.0	2.0	2.0	2.0	2.1	2.2	2.3	2.3	2.3
2024 Budget Assumptions	0.2	0.4	2.1	2.4	2.0	2.0	2.0	2.1	2.2	2.2	2.2
GDP Price Index:											
2023 Budget Assumptions	2.4	2.0	2.0	2.0	2.0	2.0	2.0	2.0	2.0	2.0	2.0
2023 MSR Assumptions	6.3	2.6	2.1	2.1	2.1	2.1	2.1	2.1	2.1	2.1	2.1
2024 Budget Assumptions	6.6	2.8	2.1	2.1	2.1	2.1	2.1	2.1	2.1	2.1	2.1
Consumer Price Index (All-Urban):											
2023 Budget Assumptions	2.9	2.3	2.3	2.3	2.3	2.3	2.3	2.3	2.3	2.3	2.3
2023 MSR Assumptions	6.6	2.8	2.3	2.3	2.3	2.3	2.3	2.3	2.3	2.3	2.3
2024 Budget Assumptions	7.6	3.0	2.3	2.3	2.3	2.3	2.3	2.3	2.3	2.3	2.3
(calendar year average)											
Civilian Unemployment Rate:											
2023 Budget Assumptions	3.9	3.6	3.7	3.8	3.8	3.8	3.8	3.8	3.8	3.8	3.8
2023 MSR Assumptions	3.7	3.7	3.8	3.8	3.8	3.8	3.8	3.8	3.8	3.8	3.8
2024 Budget Assumptions	3.7	4.3	4.6	4.4	4.3	4.2	4.1	4.0	3.9	3.8	3.8
91-Day Treasury Bill Rate:											
2023 Budget Assumptions	0.2	0.9	1.6	1.9	2.1	2.2	2.3	2.3	2.3	2.3	2.3
2023 MSR Assumptions	1.6	3.0	2.9	2.7	2.6	2.5	2.5	2.4	2.4	2.4	2.4
2024 Budget Assumptions	2.0	4.9	3.8	3.0	2.5	2.3	2.2	2.3	2.4	2.4	2.5
10-Year Treasury Note Rate:											
2023 Budget Assumptions	2.1	2.5	2.7	2.8	3.0	3.1	3.1	3.2	3.2	3.2	3.3
2023 MSR Assumptions	2.7	3.2	3.2	3.2	3.2	3.3	3.3	3.3	3.3	3.3	3.4
2024 Budget Assumptions	3.0	3.8	3.6	3.5	3.4	3.4	3.4	3.4	3.4	3.4	3.4

Real GDP—The Administration forecasts an average real GDP growth rate of 2.0 percent (fourth-quarter-over-fourth-quarter) during the 11 years 2023-2033, modestly higher than the 1.7 percent average for each of Blue Chip, CBO, and the FOMC over the same window. Over the near term, the Administration forecasts an average growth rate of 1.3 percent during 2023-2024, which is above the 0.8 percent average for Blue Chip and below the 1.9 and 1.5 percent forecast average from CBO and the FOMC, respectively.

Unemployment—The Administration, Blue Chip, and FOMC all forecast that the average unemployment rate during 2023 will be slightly elevated compared with 2022, while the CBO forecast from May 2022 projects a mild decrease in unemployment for 2023. Over the near-term (2023-2025), the Administration forecasts that the unemployment rate will average 4.4 percent, compared with CBO, Blue Chip, and Federal Reserve averages of 3.7, 4.3, and 4.4 percent during that window, respectively. Over the long run, the Administration projects a terminal unemployment rate 3.8 percent, compared with 4.1 percent for Blue Chip, 4.0 percent for the FOMC, and 4.5 percent for CBO.

Interest Rates—The Administration's 91-day interest rate forecast is qualitatively consistent with the Blue Chip forecast over the forecast horizon, though modestly higher in magnitude during most years. The Administration, CBO, and Blue Chip all expect short-term rates to rise meaningfully over the 2023-2025 period, with the Administration forecasting a faster rise over the coming few years than CBO and Blue Chip. Short-term rates are then expected to plateau in the 2.3-2.5 percent range over the remainder of the horizon. For 10-year rates, the Administration forecasts a gradual fall to a 3.4 percent terminal rate, compared with Blue Chip and CBO forecasts of 3.1 and 3.8 percent, respectively.

General Inflation—The Administration's forecast for CPI-U inflation (on a fourth-quarter-over-fourth-quarter basis) is broadly consistent with outside forecasters throughout the budget window. The Administration, CBO, Blue Chip, and the FOMC all project that inflation will continue to moderate over the course of 2023 and into 2024. The Administration's projection for the long-term CPI inflation rate of 2.3 percent equals CBO's long-term projection, is 0.1 percentage points higher than Blue Chip's long-term projection, and is consistent with the FOMC's 2.0 percent target for PCE inflation.

Table 2–3. COMPARISON OF ECONOMIC ASSUMPTIONS [1]

	2022	2023	2024	2025	2026	2027	2028	2029	2030	2031	2032	2033
(fourth-quarter-over-fourth-quarter percent change)												
Real GDP:												
2024 Budget (November 2022)	0.2	0.4	2.1	2.4	2.0	2.0	2.0	2.1	2.2	2.2	2.2	2.2
Blue Chip [2] (November 2022)	0.2	0.1	1.5	2.1	2.1	1.9	1.9	1.9	1.9	1.9	1.9	1.9
CBO (May 2022)	3.1	2.2	1.5	1.6	1.4	1.7	1.8	1.8	1.8	1.7	1.7	....
Federal Reserve [3] (September 2022)	0.2	1.2	1.7	1.8	1.8	1.8	1.8	1.8	1.8	1.8	1.8	1.8
Consumer Price Index (CPI-U):												
2024 Budget (November 2022)	7.6	3.0	2.3	2.3	2.3	2.3	2.3	2.3	2.3	2.3	2.3	2.3
Blue Chip [2] (November 2022)	7.6	3.0	2.4	2.2	2.2	2.2	2.2	2.2	2.2	2.2	2.2	2.2
CBO (May 2022)	4.7	2.7	2.3	2.3	2.3	2.3	2.4	2.4	2.4	2.3	2.3	....
Federal Reserve [3,4] (September 2022)	5.4	2.8	2.3	2.0	2.0	2.0	2.0	2.0	2.0	2.0	2.0	2.0
(calendar year average)												
Unemployment Rate:												
2024 Budget (November 2022)	3.7	4.3	4.6	4.4	4.3	4.2	4.1	4.0	3.9	3.8	3.8	3.8
Blue Chip [2] (November 2022)	3.7	4.4	4.5	4.1	4.1	4.1	4.1	4.1	4.1	4.1	4.1	4.1
CBO (May 2022)	3.8	3.5	3.7	3.9	4.0	4.2	4.5	4.5	4.6	4.5	4.5	....
Federal Reserve [3,5] (September 2022)	3.8	4.4	4.4	4.3	4.0	4.0	4.0	4.0	4.0	4.0	4.0	4.0
91-Day Treasury Bills (discount basis):												
2024 Budget (November 2022)	2.0	4.9	3.8	3.0	2.5	2.3	2.2	2.3	2.4	2.4	2.5	2.5
Blue Chip [2] (November 2022)	2.2	4.5	3.2	2.6	2.4	2.4	2.4	2.3	2.3	2.3	2.3	2.3
CBO (May 2022)	0.9	2.0	2.5	2.6	2.5	2.3	2.3	2.3	2.3	2.3	2.3	....
10-Year Treasury Notes:												
2024 Budget (November 2022)	3.0	3.8	3.6	3.5	3.4	3.4	3.4	3.4	3.4	3.4	3.4	3.4
Blue Chip [2] (November 2022)	3.1	3.8	3.3	3.2	3.1	3.2	3.1	3.1	3.1	3.1	3.1	3.1
CBO (May 2022)	2.4	2.9	3.1	3.2	3.5	3.7	3.8	3.8	3.8	3.8	3.8	....

Sources: Administration; CBO, The Budget and Economic Outlook: 2022 to 2032, May 2022; October 2022 and November 2022 Blue Chip Economic Indicators, Aspen Publishers, Inc.; Federal Reserve Open Market Committee, September 22, 2022

[1] Calendar Year
[2] Values for 2022–2023 based on November survey, and 2024–2033 based on October survey. Values for 2029–2033 are 5 year averages.
[3] FOMC Median Projection
[4] PCE Inflation
[5] Average rate during 4th quarter.

Sensitivity of the Budget to Economic Assumptions

Federal spending and tax collections are heavily influenced by developments in the economy. Income tax receipts are a function of growth in incomes for households and firms. Spending on social assistance programs may rise when the economy enters a downturn, while increases in nominal spending on Social Security and other programs are dependent on consumer price inflation. A robust set of projections for macroeconomic variables assists in budget planning, but unexpected developments in the economy have ripple effects for Federal spending and receipts. This section seeks to provide an understanding of the magnitude of the effects that unforeseen changes in the economy can have on the budget.

To make these assessments, the Administration relies on a set of heuristics that can predict how certain spending and receipt categories will react to a change in a given subset of macroeconomic variables, holding almost everything else constant. These sensitivity analyses provide a sense of the broad changes one would expect after a given development, but they cannot anticipate how policy makers would react and potentially change course in such an event. For example, if the economy were to suffer an unexpected recession, tax receipts would decline and spending on programs such as unemployment insurance would rise. In such a situation, however, policy makers might enact policies that stimulate the economy, leading to secondary and tertiary changes that are difficult to predict. Another caveat is that it is often unrealistic to suppose that one macroeconomic variable might change while others would remain constant. Most macroeconomic variables interact with each other in complex and subtle ways. These are important considerations to bear in mind when examining Table 2-4.

For real GDP growth and employment:

- The first panel in the table illustrates the effect on the deficit resulting from a one percentage point reduction in real GDP growth, relative to the Administration's forecast, in 2022 that is followed by a subsequent recovery in 2023 and 2024. The unemployment rate is assumed to be half a percentage

Table 2–4. SENSITIVITY OF THE BUDGET TO ECONOMIC ASSUMPTIONS

(Fiscal Years; In Billions Of Dollars)

Budget Effect	2023	2024	2025	2026	2027	2028	2029	2030	2031	2032	2033	Total of Budget Effects: 2023–2033
Real Growth and Employment:												
Budgetary effects of 1 percentage point lower real GDP growth:												
(1) For calendar year 2023 only, with real GDP recovery in 2024–2033: [1]												
Receipts	−19.3	−30.3	−15.4	−2.7	−0.2	−0.2	−0.2	−0.2	−0.2	−0.2	−0.3	−69.2
Outlays	13.5	26.1	13.4	3.4	2.7	2.5	2.5	2.6	2.7	2.8	2.8	74.9
Increase in deficit (+)	32.8	56.4	28.9	6.0	2.9	2.7	2.7	2.8	2.9	3.0	3.1	144.2
(2) For calendar year 2023 only, with no subsequent recovery:												
Receipts	−19.3	−40.2	−46.6	−49.1	−51.4	−53.4	−55.5	−57.8	−60.1	−62.6	−65.3	−561.4
Outlays	13.5	31.6	34.9	38.6	41.8	45.3	50.3	56.9	63.2	68.1	73.6	517.8
Increase in deficit (+)	32.8	71.8	81.5	87.6	93.1	98.7	105.8	114.7	123.4	130.7	138.9	1,079.2
(3) Sustained during 2023–2033, with no change in unemployment:												
Receipts	−19.3	−59.7	−107.7	−160.8	−217.8	−277.6	−341.6	−409.8	−483.0	−561.2	−645.7	−3,284.3
Outlays	0.2	1.5	3.1	5.0	7.2	10.0	14.5	20.1	26.6	33.4	40.9	162.6
Increase in deficit (+)	19.5	61.2	110.9	165.8	225.0	287.6	356.1	429.9	509.6	594.7	686.6	3,446.9
Inflation and Interest Rates:												
Budgetary effects of 1 percentage point higher rate of:												
(4) Inflation and interest rates during calendar year 2023 only:												
Receipts	20.1	39.2	41.0	41.4	43.3	44.9	46.7	48.6	50.6	52.6	54.9	483.3
Outlays	34.7	73.0	61.5	62.8	62.6	65.0	62.9	66.1	66.7	70.0	73.6	698.9
Increase in deficit (+)	14.5	33.8	20.5	21.4	19.3	20.1	16.2	17.6	16.1	17.4	18.7	215.7
(5) Inflation and interest rates, sustained during 2023–2033:												
Receipts	20.1	60.5	105.2	153.6	206.2	262.1	322.6	388.0	459.4	536.1	620.2	3,134.0
Outlays	39.1	141.5	231.8	318.6	405.6	504.1	591.4	701.0	812.0	933.7	1,078.2	5,757.1
Increase in deficit (+)	19.0	81.0	126.6	165.0	199.3	242.0	268.7	312.9	352.6	397.7	458.1	2,623.1
(6) Interest rates only, sustained during 2023–2033:												
Receipts	1.6	3.7	4.5	4.8	5.1	5.4	5.6	5.8	6.1	6.3	6.7	55.5
Outlays	21.8	92.7	146.5	190.4	229.6	269.8	308.8	346.3	383.6	423.4	462.4	2,875.3
Increase in deficit (+)	20.1	89.0	142.0	185.6	224.5	264.5	303.3	340.5	377.5	417.1	455.7	2,819.8
(7) Inflation only, sustained during 2023–2033:												
Receipts	18.5	56.8	100.6	148.6	200.9	256.4	316.7	381.8	452.8	529.2	612.8	3,075.0
Outlays	17.4	49.1	85.9	129.0	177.1	235.8	284.4	357.0	431.2	513.4	619.0	2,899.3
Decrease in deficit (−)	−1.1	−7.7	−14.7	−19.6	−23.8	−20.7	−32.3	−24.8	−21.6	−15.8	6.2	−175.8
Interest Cost of Higher Federal Borrowing:												
(8) Outlay effect of 100 billion increase in borrowing in 2023	2.5	4.7	3.8	3.2	2.9	2.8	2.9	3.1	3.3	3.5	3.6	36.4

[1] The unemployment rate is assumed to be 0.5 percentage points higher per one percent shortfall in the level of real GDP.

point higher in 2022 before returning to the baseline level in 2023 and 2024.

- The next panel in the table reports the effect of a reduction of one percentage point in real GDP growth in 2022 that is not subsequently made up by faster growth in 2023 and 2024. Consistent with this output path, the rate of unemployment is assumed to rise by half a percentage point relative to that assumed in the Administration's forecasts.

- The third panel in the table shows the impact of a GDP growth rate that is permanently reduced by one percentage point, while the unemployment rate is not affected. This is the sort of situation that would arise if, for example, the economy was to experience a permanent decline in productivity growth.

For inflation and interest rates:

- The fourth panel in Table 2-4 shows the effect on the budget in the case of a one percentage point higher rate of inflation and a one percentage point higher nominal interest rate in 2022. Both inflation and interest rates return to their assumed levels in 2023. This would result in a permanently higher price

Table 2–5. FORECAST ERRORS, 2002-PRESENT

REAL GDP ERRORS			
2-Year Average Annual Real GDP Growth	Administration	CBO	Blue Chip
Mean Error	1.1	0.5	0.7
Mean Absolute Error	1.2	0.8	0.8
Root Mean Square Error	1.5	1.1	1.2
6-Year Average Annual Real GDP Growth			
Mean Error	1.5	1.3	1.2
Mean Absolute Error	1.6	1.3	1.2
Root Mean Square Error	1.6	1.4	1.3
INFLATION ERRORS			
2-Year Average Annual Change in the Consumer Price Index	Administration	CBO	Blue Chip
Mean Error	-0.1	-0.2	-0.0
Mean Absolute Error	0.6	0.6	0.6
Root Mean Square Error	0.7	0.8	0.7
6-Year Average Annual Change in the Consumer Price Index			
Mean Error	0.1	0.1	0.3
Mean Absolute Error	0.4	0.3	0.5
Root Mean Square Error	0.5	0.4	0.5
INTEREST RATE ERRORS			
2-Year Average 91-Day Treasury Bill Rate	Administration	CBO	Blue Chip
Mean Error	0.6	0.6	0.8
Mean Absolute Error	0.8	0.8	0.9
Root Mean Square Error	1.1	1.1	1.2
6-Year Average 91-Day Treasury Bill Rate			
Mean Error	2.0	2.1	2.2
Mean Absolute Error	2.0	2.1	2.2
Root Mean Square Error	2.2	2.6	2.4

level and nominal GDP level over the course of the forecast horizon.

- The fifth panel in the table illustrates the effects on the budget deficit of a one percentage point higher inflation rate and interest rate than projected in every year of the forecast.

- The sixth panel reports the effect on the deficit resulting from an increase in interest rates in every year of the forecast, with no accompanying increase in inflation.

- The seventh panel in the table reports the effect on the budget deficit of a one percentage point higher inflation rate than projected in every year of the forecast window, while the interest rate remains as forecast.

- The table also shows the effect on the budget deficit if the Federal Government were to borrow an additional $100 billion in 2022, while all of the other projections remain constant.

- These simple approximations that inform the sensitivity analysis are symmetric. This means that the effect of, for example, a one percentage point higher rate of growth over the forecast horizon would be of the same magnitude as a one percentage point reduction in growth, though with the opposite sign.

Forecast Errors for Growth, Inflation, and Interest Rates

As with any forecast, the Administration's projections are inherently uncertain because they are based on underlying assumptions about social, political, and global conditions. It is impossible to foresee every eventuality over a one-year horizon, much less over ten or more years. This section evaluates the historical accuracy of the past Administrations' forecasts for real GDP growth, inflation, and short-term interest rates from 2002 to the present day, especially relative to the accuracy of forecasts produced by the CBO and Blue Chip panel. For this exercise, forecasts produced by all three entities are compared with realized values of these variables.

The results of this exercise are reported in Table 2-5 and contain three different measures of accuracy. The first is the average forecast error. When a forecaster has an average forecast error of zero, it may be said that the forecast has historically been unbiased, in the sense that realized values of the variables have not been systematically above or below the forecasted value. The second is

Table 2–6. DIFFERENCES BETWEEN ESTIMATED AND ACTUAL SURPLUSES OR DEFICITS FOR FIVE-YEAR BUDGET ESTIMATES SINCE 1985

	Current Year Estimate	Budget Year Estimate	Estimate for Budget Year Plus:			
			One Year (BY + 1)	Two Years (BY + 2)	Three Years (BY + 3)	Four Years (BY + 4)
Mean Error	−0.5	0.7	1.6	2.2	2.6	2.9
Mean Absolute Error	1.5	1.9	2.6	3.1	3.6	3.9
Root Mean Squared Error	2.4	3.0	3.6	4.3	4.7	4.8

the average absolute value of the forecast error, which offers a sense of the magnitude of errors. Even if the past forecast errors average to zero, the errors may have been of a very large magnitude, with both positive and negative values. The table also reports the square root of the mean of squared forecast error (RMSE). This metric applies a harsher penalty to forecasts exhibiting large errors. The table reports these measures of accuracy at both the 2-year and the 6-year horizons, thus evaluating the relative success of different forecasts in the short run and in the medium run.

Past Administrations have forecast 2-year real GDP growth and average annual interest rates that were higher than actually realized, on average, by 1.1 percentage points and 0.6 percentage points, respectively. This is partly due to the assumption that Administration policy proposals contained in the Budget will be enacted, which has not always come to pass. The 2-year average forecast error for inflation is smaller, -0.1 percentage points, and similar to other forecasts.

Uncertainty and the Deficit Projections

This section assesses the accuracy of past budget forecasts for the deficit or surplus, measured at different time horizons. The results of this exercise are reported in Table 2-6, where the average error, the average absolute error, and the RMSE are reported.

In Table 2-6, a negative number means that the Federal Government ran a larger surplus or a smaller deficit than was expected, while a positive number in the table indicates a smaller surplus or a larger deficit. In the current

year in which the budget is published, the Administration has tended to understate the surplus (or, equivalently, overstate the deficit) by an average of 0.5 percent of GDP. For the budget year, however, the historical pattern has been for the budget to understate the deficit by an average of 0.7 percent of GDP.[2] One possible reason for this is that past Administrations' policy proposals have not all been implemented. The forecast errors tend to grow with the time horizon, which is not surprising given that there is much greater uncertainty in the medium run about both the macroeconomic situation and the specific details of policy enactments.

A probabilistic range of outcomes for the deficit over the budget window can be calculated by building off of the historical forecast errors summarized in Table 2-6. This is accomplished by taking the RMSE of previous forecast errors and assuming that these errors are drawn from a normal distribution. This exercise is undertaken at every forecast horizon from the current year through fours year after the budget year. Chart 2-2 displays the projected range of possible deficits. In the chart, the middle line represents the Administration's expected fiscal balance and represents the 50th percentile outcome. The rest of the lines in the chart may be read in the following fashion. The top line reports the 95th percentile of the distribution of outcomes over 2023 to 2028, meaning that there is a 95 percent probability that the actual balance in those years will be more negative than expressed by the line. Similarly, there is a 95 percent probability that the balance will be more positive than suggested by the bottom line in the chart.

---

[2] Additionally, the CBO has historically forecasted smaller deficits, on average, than actually materialized.

Chart 2-2. Range of Uncertainty for the Budget Deficit

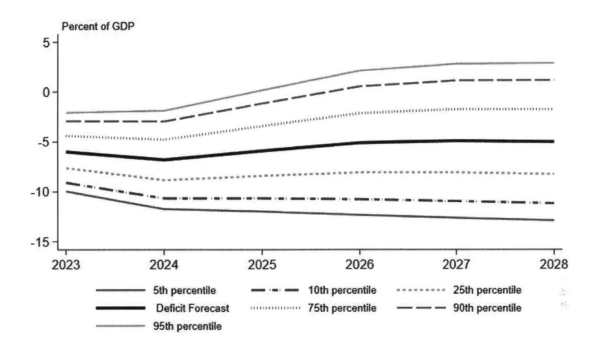

3. LONG-TERM BUDGET OUTLOOK

The horizon for most of the analysis in this Budget is ten years. This ten-year horizon reflects a balance between the importance of considering both the current and future implications of budget decisions made today and a practical limit on the construction of detailed budget projections for years in the future.

Nonetheless, it can be informative to look further into the future, despite the uncertainty surrounding the assumptions needed for such estimates. This chapter begins by discussing the fiscal outlook under current law over the next 25 years. The second section discusses the fiscal impact of the Administration's policies, finding they will cut deficits and debt, compared to the baseline. In the third section, alternative assumptions about the evolution of key variables and uncertainties in the projections are discussed, including the macroeconomic risks of climate change. The fourth section discusses the actuarial projections for Social Security and Medicare. The *technical note* to this chapter provides further detail on data sources, assumptions, and other methods for estimation.

Long-Run Projections under Continuation of Current Policies

The baseline long-term projections assume that current policy continues for Social Security, Medicare, Medicaid, other mandatory programs, and revenues.[1] Projections for all mandatory programs and revenues maintain consistency with other Federal agency projections. From 2034-2048, total mandatory spending grows by 0.2 percentage points as a share of gross domestic product (GDP), while revenues increase by 0.4 percentage points. The Budget provides a specific path for discretionary spending over the next ten years. Thereafter, the baseline long-run projections assume that real per-person discretionary funding remains constant, implying an average growth rate of 2.8 percent per year. The technical note provides additional detail on the methodology behind these projections.

---

[1] The long-run baseline projections are consistent with the Budget's baseline concept, which is explained in more detail in Chapter 21, "Current Services Estimates," in this volume. The projections assume full payment of scheduled Social Security and Medicare benefits without regard to the projected depletion of the trust funds for these programs. Additional baseline assumptions beyond the ten-year window are detailed in the technical note to this chapter.

Chart 3-1. Comparison of Annual Surplus/Deficit

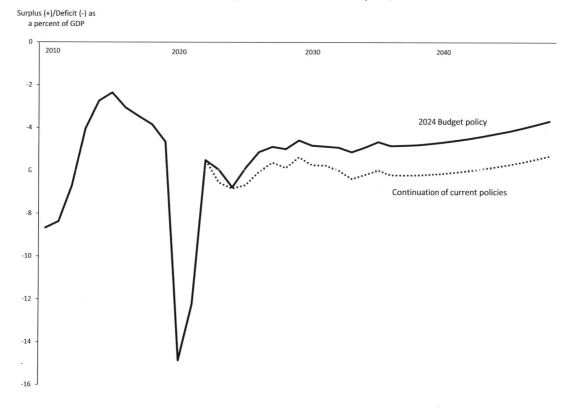

Chart 3-2. Comparison of Publicly Held Debt

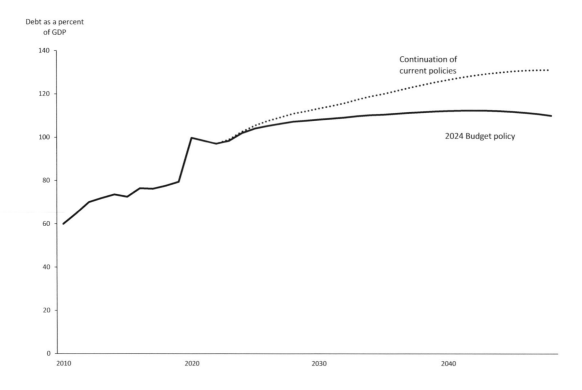

Under the baseline, the deficit is projected to average 6.0 percent of annual GDP through the ten-year window. (See Table S-2 of the main *Budget* volume.) Debt is projected to rise to 117.4 percent of GDP in 2033 under current policies. Beyond the ten-year horizon, Chart 3-1 shows that deficits under the baseline projections fall from 6.4 percent of GDP in 2033 to 5.3 percent of GDP by the end of the 25-year window. Chart 3-2 shows that debt under the baseline projections continues to rise as a share of GDP, with increases slowing in the 2040s. From 2033 to 2040, debt is projected to increase from 117.4 to 126.5 percent of GDP under the baseline projections, an increase of 1.3 percentage points per year. In contrast, from 2040 to 2048, debt is projected to increase from 126.5 to 131.2 percent of GDP under the baseline projections, an increase of 0.6 percentage points per year. By the end of the 25-year window, debt as a share of GDP in the baseline projections plateaus. Real net interest eases from 1.2 to 1.1 percent of GDP between 2033 and 2040 under the baseline projections, and then remains stable through 2048.

Debt as a share of GDP grows more slowly over time in part because of the projected slowdown in population aging from 2023 forward. Consistent with the demographic assumptions in the 2022 Social Security Trustees' report (see Chart 3-3 below), the elderly (aged 65 or older) share of the U.S. population is projected to rise from 16.7 percent in 2021 to 21.4 percent in 2038 as more baby boomers retire. This aging of the baby-boom cohorts into retirement reduces the rate of labor force growth and therefore the rate of economic growth. However, by the late 2030s, the elderly share of the U.S. population is projected to plateau. As a result, the demographic drag on economic growth from the aging of the U.S. population is projected to subside from 2030 forward, which, all else equal, reduces debt as a share of GDP.

Impact of 2024 Budget Policies on the Long-Term Fiscal Outlook

The 2024 Budget proposes major investments to grow the economy from the middle out and the bottom up, to reduce everyday costs for Americans, and to strengthen public health and improve health outcomes. These investments are coupled with major reforms to both corporate and individual taxation. Because the Budget's reforms to the tax system and reforms to reduce spending—for example, on subsidies to pharmaceutical companies—far exceed the proposed investments, the Budget substantially improves the long-term fiscal outlook.

The Budget's policies lower annual deficits compared to the baseline projections in every year, beginning immediately. To assess the long-run impact, this chapter develops 25-year projections for the impact of the Administration's policies on the Budget, as described in the technical note. The resulting projections show that the revenue increases in the President's Budget more than offset net spending increases in every year, while generating additional savings over the long run. In total, all Budget proposals are projected to reduce deficits by more than $7 trillion in the second decade and improve the fiscal outlook over the long run.

Chart 3-3. Elderly (Age 65+) Share of the U.S. Population

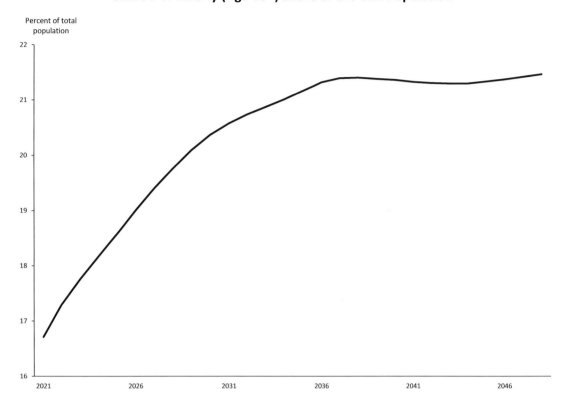

Charts 3-1 and 3-2 illustrate the improvement in deficits and debt. The Budget improves the fiscal outlook over the short and long term, with lower deficits throughout the 25-year window. Similarly, the Budget's policies significantly flatten the projected debt increase compared to the baseline, with debt as a percent of GDP falling in the 2040s, returning back to its 2034 level by 2048. Budget proposals would result in further improvement in the fiscal outlook after 25 years.

Uncertainty and Alternative Assumptions

Future budget outcomes depend on a host of unknowns: changing economic conditions, unforeseen international developments, unexpected demographic shifts, and unpredictable technological advances. The longer budget projections are extended, the more the uncertainties increase. These uncertainties make even short-run budget forecasting quite difficult. For example, the Budget's projection of the deficit in five years is 5.0 percent of GDP, but a distribution of probable outcomes ranges from a deficit of 11.2 percent of GDP to a surplus of 1.2 percent of GDP, at the 10th and 90th percentiles, respectively.[2]

This section considers some specific sources of uncertainty in the projections above, which are summarized in Table 3-1.

Climate Risk.— Real economic growth is highly uncertain. Going forward, real GDP growth is projected to be below its longer-run historical average of 2.5 percent per year, as the slowdown in population growth and the increase in the population over age 65 reduce labor supply growth. In these projections, real GDP growth averages 2.1 percent per year for the period following the end of the ten-year budget window.

Over the long run, the path of real GDP is subject to significant downside risk from climate change. Absent further action to slow the rate of greenhouse gas (GHG) emissions, global temperatures remain on pace to increase over two degrees Celcius from their pre-industrial average by the end of this century. Warming on this scale may have profound impacts on the American economy and the Federal fiscal outlook.

Table 3–1.   25-YEAR DEBT PROJECTIONS UNDER ALTERNATIVE BUDGET SCENARIOS

(Percent of GDP)

2024 Budget Policy	110.0
Real Economic Growth:	
Higher climate damages to real GDP	112.6
Intermediate climate damages to real GDP	111.9
Lower climate damages to real GDP	111.2
Health:	
Excess cost growth 0.5 ppt lower	99.2
Excess cost growth 0.5 ppt higher	123.3
Discretionary Spending:	
Grow with GDP	116.9
Grow with inflation only	107.6

---

[2] These estimates are presented in Chart 2-1 of Chapter 2, "Economic Assumptions," in this volume.

Chart 3-4. Climate Risk Alternatives

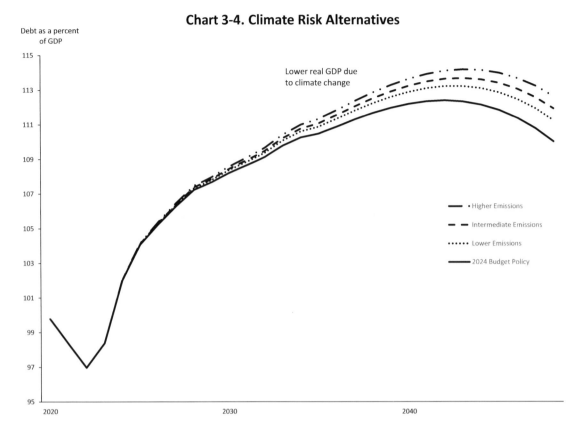

Climate change leads to physical changes that can impact the economy through a variety of pathways. Acute physical risks from an increased rate and severity of natural disasters can harm the productivity of American farms, factories, offices, and infrastructure. Chronic risks like sea level rise and warmer temperatures have the potential to do the same. The combined effects of climate change are projected to lead to lower economic output in the United States.

The severity of future climate change and U.S. vulnerability to this change will reflect past and current actions, future domestic policy and economic decisions, as well as policy choices and economic decisions made abroad. While the United States has pledged to reach net-zero GHG emissions by 2050, a primary source of uncertainty regarding physical climate risks to the United States are the GHG emission mitigation choices of other countries. To illustrate the implications of this uncertainty, we analyze the Federal budget impacts of three potential scenarios for GHG emission reductions.[3] All scenarios are consistent with the U.S. emissions reduction commitments.

Under the "lower emissions" scenario, other countries also eliminate net GHG emissions by 2050. Under the "intermediate emissions" scenario, other countries maintain their current policies. Under the "higher emissions" scenario, other countries weaken their current GHG reduction policies.

As Chart 3-4 shows, even under the lower emissions scenario, climate damages' consequences to the macroeconomy weaken the fiscal outlook. Debt to GDP under the lower emissions scenario is projected to reach 111.2 percent by 2048, compared to 110.0 percent in the policy baseline. Debt to GDP is projected to be even higher under the intermediate and higher emissions scenarios, reaching 111.9 percent and 112.6 percent, respectively, by 2048. Beyond the 25-year window considered here, the macroeconomic outlooks under these emissions scenarios diverge further over time. As a consequence, the higher emissions scenario, in particular, would lead to even further deteriorations in the longer-term fiscal outlook. This underscores both the macroeconomic and the fiscal risks posed by climate change, as well as the benefits of reducing future emissions. This is one of many reasons why there is an urgent need for continued action on climate change and why the 2024 President's Budget proposes significant investments to reduce the Federal Government's long-term fiscal exposure to climate-related financial risks and to reduce future risks for all Americans.[4]

---

[3] Specifically, these are the Shared Socioeconomic Pathways scenarios 1-.26, 2-4.5, and 3-7.0, which were developed by an international community of climate modeling experts. In contrast to the Budget policy path, each of these alternate climate scenarios accounts for the estimated effects of future emissions on future changes in temperatures, which, in turn, affect future GDP projections. The damages from these scenarios on GDP are estimated using a composite of recent, peer-reviewed models. For more detail, please see the 2023 CEA-OMB white paper on "Methodologies and Considerations for Integrating the Physical and Transition Risks of Climate Change into Macro-Economic Forecasting for the President's Budget."

[4] For more information, please see Chapter 10, "Budget Exposure to Increased Costs and Lost Revenue Due to Climate Change," in this volume.

Chart 3-5. Alternative Health Care Costs

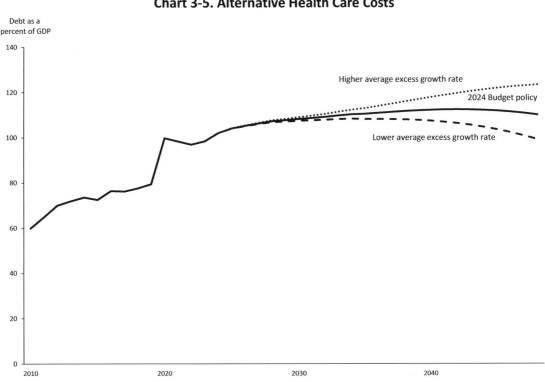

Debt as a percent of GDP

Higher average excess growth rate
2024 Budget policy
Lower average excess growth rate

Future Pandemics.— A future pandemic could also have a large impact on both the economy and the Federal balance sheet. While these impacts are not quantified here, during the COVID-19 pandemic, the U.S. Government provided around $4.6 trillion to support the American taxpayer, including expanded unemployment benefits, small business cash infusions, payments to families to cover child-related expenses, and checks to over 170 million Americans. In spite of these well-targeted investments, the lost economic output due to the pandemic could have been as high as $1.5 trillion as of the end of 2021. Globally, the estimated direct effect of a pandemic-induced economic slowdowns ranges from between 0.5 to 2.0 percent of global GDP. While harder to calculate, there were also increased indirect costs due to increased mortality and lost human capital.

To address these risks, the Budget includes transformative investments in pandemic preparedness. These investments are intended to reduce harm to lives and livelihoods. But they also could lead to better long-term economic and fiscal outcomes than what we would expect if these investments were not made.

Healthcare Cost Growth.— Another significant source of uncertainty is healthcare cost growth. As noted above, the baseline projections follow the Medicare Trustees in assuming that, on average, Medicare per-beneficiary costs annually grow about 1.2 percentage points faster than GDP per capita ("excess cost growth") over the next 25 years, starting at high excess growth rates that steadily approach zero. A primary input to these

projections is overall national health expenditures, the sum of all private and government health expenditures. In the past, especially prior to 1990, national health expenditures grew even more rapidly than the economy. For example, throughout the 1980s, national health per-beneficiary costs grew 3.1 percentage points faster than GDP per capita. However, on average since 2010, per-enrollee healthcare costs have grown roughly in line with GDP, with particularly slow growth in Federal health expenditures for Medicare and Medicaid.

Chart 3-5 shows the debt ratio in 25 years under different healthcare cost growth trajectories, reflecting the variability of recent trends in healthcare cost growth. If excess healthcare cost growth was 0.5 percentage points faster than the Medicare Trustees' projections, the debt ratio in 25 years would increase from 110.0 percent of GDP under the base case Budget policy to 123.3 percent of GDP, with larger deviations every year thereafter. In contrast, if excess healthcare cost growth was 0.5 percentage points slower than the Medicare Trustees' projections, the debt-to-GDP ratio would peak in 2034 and debt would fall to 99.2 percent of GDP by the end of the 25-year period. This slower trajectory more closely aligns with recent trends.

Tax Policy.— Policy choices will also have a large impact on long-term budget deficits and debt, as evident from the discussion of the 2024 Budget proposals. Small permanent changes can have significant long-term impacts. In the base case policy projections, revenues gradually increase with rising real income, since real bracket

Chart 3-6. Alternative Discretionary Assumptions

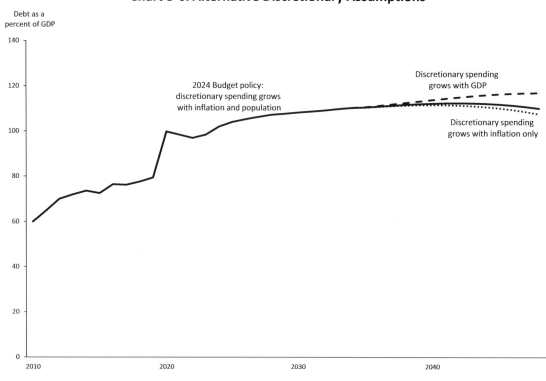

creep—the change in average tax rates as taxpayers' incomes rise faster than tax bracket thresholds—increases individual income taxes as a share of GDP. If receipts remain a constant percent of GDP after the budget window, the debt ratio would be expected to increase compared to the base case.

Discretionary Growth Rates.— The base case policy projections for discretionary programs assume that after 2033, discretionary spending grows with inflation and population (see Chart 3-6). Alternative assumptions could include growing discretionary spending with GDP or with inflation only. At the end of the 25-year horizon, the debt ratio ranges from 107.6 percent of GDP in the inflation-only case to 116.9 percent of GDP in the GDP case, with the base case falling in the middle.

Interest Rates.— A final major source of uncertainty is interest rates. A rise in real interest rates would increase the burden of debt, forcing the Federal Government to raise additional revenue, reduce spending, or increase borrowing in order to pay off old debt. Over the last two decades, interest rate projections have been, on average, too high. Chart 3-7 shows the path of actual ten-year Treasury rates from 2000 to 2022, along with previous Administration forecasts for the ten-year Treasury rate. Chart 3-8 shows the equivalent chart for CBO forecasts. Table 2-5 of Chapter 2, "Economic Assumptions," shows the average forecast errors in economic projections from past Federal budgets, CBO, and the Blue Chip panel of professional forecasters. On average, all three groups of

forecasters have been about 0.6 percentage points too high in projecting the three-month Treasury rate two years into the future and about 2.1 percentage points too high projecting the same rate six years out.

The Administration's forecast for interest rates over the next decade show the ten-year Treasury note rate stabilizing to 3.4 percent in 2033. Beyond 2033, this chapter's projections assume interest rates stay constant at the 2033 level. If the actual interest rate path were lower, this would result in a lower debt-to-GDP ratio over the long run. Alternatively, as CBO projects, interest rates could continue to rise after the ten-year budget window, which would result in a higher debt-to-GDP ratio over the long run. While rates have risen recently, the Blue Chip panel of professional forecasters, as of October 2022, has a consensus forecast for the 2033 ten-year Treasury note rate of 3.1 percent, lower than the Administration's forecast.[5]

Actuarial Projections for Social Security and Medicare

While the Administration's long-run projections focus on the unified budget outlook, Social Security Old-Age and Survivors Insurance and Disability Insurance (OASDI) and Medicare Hospital Insurance (HI) benefits are paid out of trust funds financed almost entirely by dedicated payroll tax revenues. Projected trust fund revenues fall

---

[5] Long range projections of the Blue Chip panel are only collected twice a year. As of the time of this writing, the October 2022 survey is the most current one available.

Chart 3-7. Historical Values and Budget Projections for 10-Year Treasury Rates

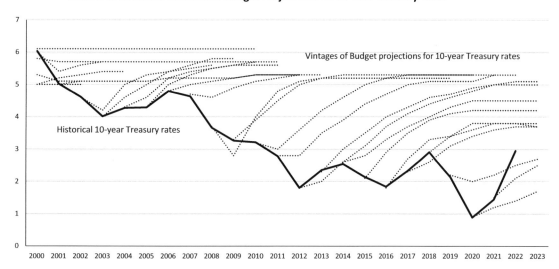

short of the levels necessary to finance projected benefits over the next 75 years.

The Social Security and Medicare Trustees' reports feature the actuarial balance of the trust funds as a summary measure of their financial status. For each trust fund, the actuarial balance is calculated as the magnitude of change in receipts or program benefits (expressed as a percentage of taxable payroll) that would be needed to preserve a small positive balance in the trust fund at the end of a specified time period. The estimates cover periods ranging in length from 25 to 75 years.

Table 3-2 shows the projected income rate, cost rate, and annual balance for the Medicare HI and combined OASDI trust funds at selected dates under the Trustees' intermediate assumptions in the 2022 reports. There is a continued imbalance in the long-run projections of the HI program due to revenues that do not match costs over time. According to the 2022 Trustees' report, the HI trust fund reserves are projected to become depleted in 2028; in that year, dedicated revenues would be expected to be able to cover 90 percent of scheduled payments. The President's Budget includes proposals that will extend the solvency of the Medicare trust fund by at least 25 years.

The 2022 Social Security Trustees' report projects that under current law, there is a long-term mismatch between program revenue and costs. Social Security is currently drawing on its trust fund reserves to cover the revenue shortfall. Over time, as the ratio of workers to retirees falls, costs are projected to rise further while revenues excluding interest are projected to rise less rapidly. In the process, the Social Security trust fund reserves, which were built up since 1983, would be drawn down and eventually become depleted in 2035, based on the projections in the 2022 report. At that point, the dedicated revenues could pay for 80 percent of program expenditures for the rest of 2035, declining to 74 percent for 2096.

Table 3–2. INTERMEDIATE ACTUARIAL PROJECTIONS FOR OASDI AND HI, 2022 TRUSTEES' REPORTS

	2021	2022	2031	2040	2090
	Percent of Payroll				
Medicare Hospital Insurance (HI):					
Income Rate	3.4	3.4	3.7	3.8	4.4
Cost Rate	3.4	3.4	4.2	4.8	4.9
Annual Balance	0.0	0.0	−0.5	−1.0	−0.5
Projection Interval:			25 years	50 years	75 years
Actuarial Balance			−0.8	−0.8	−0.7
	Percent of Payroll				
Old Age Survivors and Disability Insurance (OASDI):					
Income Rate	12.4	12.8	13.2	13.3	13.4
Cost Rate	13.9	14.1	15.9	16.7	17.8
Annual Balance	−1.5	−1.3	−2.7	−3.4	−4.4
Projection Interval:			25 years	50 years	75 years
Actuarial Balance			−2.2	−3.0	−3.4

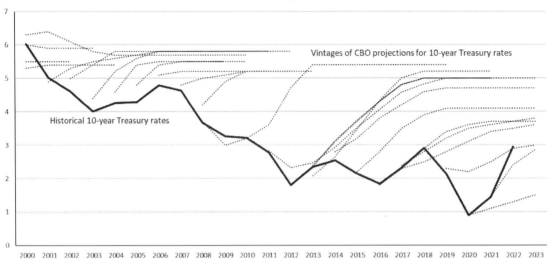

Chart 3-8. Historical Values and CBO Projections for 10-Year Treasury Rates

The long-term budget projections in this chapter assume that benefits would continue to be paid in full despite the projected depletion of the trust fund reserves through a hypothetical change in law that would provide general revenue transfers as needed.

TECHNICAL NOTE: SOURCES OF DATA AND METHODS OF ESTIMATING

The long-run budget projections are based on actuarial projections for Social Security and Medicare as well as demographic and economic assumptions. A simplified model of the Federal budget, developed at OMB, is used to compute the budgetary implications of these assumptions after the ten-year budget window.

Demographic and Economic Assumptions.— For the years 2023-2033, the assumptions are drawn from the Administration's economic projections used for the 2024 Budget. The economic assumptions are extended beyond this interval by holding the inflation rate, interest rates, and the unemployment rate constant at the levels assumed in the final year (2033) of the Budget forecast. Population growth and labor force growth are extended using the intermediate assumptions from the 2022 Social Security Trustees' report. The projected rate of growth for real GDP is built up from the labor force assumptions and an assumed rate of productivity growth. Productivity growth, measured as real GDP per hour, is assumed to equal its terminal annual rate of growth in the Budget's economic assumptions, less the short-run effects of proposed policies: 1.7 percent per year.

The CPI inflation rate is held constant at 2.3 percent per year, the unemployment rate is held constant at 3.8 percent, the yield to maturity on ten-year Treasury notes is held constant at 3.4 percent, and the 91-day Treasury bill rate is held constant at 2.5 percent. Consistent with the demographic assumptions in the Trustees' reports, U.S. population growth slows slightly from an average of about 0.5 percent per year during the budget window to about three-quarters of that rate by the end of the 25-year projection period. Real GDP growth is projected to be less than its historical average of around 2.5 percent per year, because the slowdown in population growth and the increase in the population over age 65 reduce labor supply growth. In these projections, real GDP growth averages 2.1 percent per year for the period following the end of the ten-year budget window. The economic and demographic projections described above are set exogenously and do not change in response to changes in the budget outlook across the alternate scenarios presented in this chapter.

Baseline Projections.— For the period through 2033, receipts and outlays in the baseline and policy projections follow the 2024 Budget's baseline and policy estimates respectively. Outside the budget window, discretionary spending grows at the rate of inflation and population growth. Long-run Social Security spending is projected by the Social Security actuaries using this chapter's long-run economic and demographic assumptions. Medicare benefits follow a projection of beneficiary growth and excess healthcare cost growth from the 2022 Medicare Trustees' report current law baseline. Excess cost growth for private health insurance is assumed to grow at a rate that averages the excess cost growth assumed in the Medicare actuarial assumptions and provided in their Illustrative Alternative. In these projections, private health insurance excess cost growth averages 1.0 percent after 2033. Medicaid outlays are based on the economic and demographic projections in the model, which assume average excess cost growth of approximately 0.8 percentage points above growth in GDP per capita after 2033. Other entitlement programs are projected based on rules of thumb linking program spending to elements of the economic and demographic projections such as the poverty rate. Individual income tax revenues are projected using a microsimulation model that incorporates real bracket creep. Corporate tax and other receipts are projected to grow with GDP.

SPECIAL ANALYSES AND PRESENTATIONS

4. BUDGET PROCESS

This chapter addresses several broad categories of budget process—the budget enforcement framework and related proposals, presentation, and reforms issues. First, the chapter provides a recent history on budget enforcement and discusses related proposals. The proposals and discussions include: an explanation of the discretionary levels in the 2024 Budget; adjustments to base discretionary levels including program integrity initiatives, funding requests for disaster relief and wildfire suppression; limits on advance appropriations; the proposals and explanations supporting veterans medical care and the newly enacted Cost of Toxic Exposures Fund; a discussion of the system under the Statutory Pay-As-You-Go Act of 2010 of scoring legislation affecting receipts and mandatory spending; and an extension of the spending reductions required by Section 251A of the Balanced Budget and Emergency Deficit Reduction Act (BBEDCA).

Second, this chapter describes adjustments and proposals in budget presentation. The Budget Presentation section begins with a discussion about adjustments to the BBEDCA baseline which provide for a more accurate reflection of the Administration's 2024 policy choices. It then discusses a proposed reclassification of Contract Support Costs (CSCs) and Payments for Tribal Leases accounts in the Department of the Interior's Bureau of Indian Affairs and the Department of Health and Human Services' Indian Health Service (IHS); the Pell Grant program; a discussion of how BBEDCA Section 251A sequestration is shown in the Budget; and the budgetary treatment of the housing Government-sponsored enterprises and the United States Postal Service.

Third, this chapter describes reform proposals to improve budgeting with respect to individual programs as well as across Government. These proposals include: changes to capital budgeting for large civilian Federal capital projects; protections for the rental payments made to the Federal Buildings Fund by Federal agencies; increases in funding and changes in how funding occurs for the Indian Health Service at the Department of Health and Human Services; and changes to retiree medical care for the Department of Defense. Last the Chapter introduces a discussion related to the timing of the release of the President's Budget.

I. BUDGET ENFORCEMENT FRAMEWORK AND PROPOSALS

History of Recent Budget Enforcement

The Federal Government uses statutory budget enforcement mechanisms to control revenues, spending, and deficits. The Statutory Pay-As-You-Go Act of 2010, enacted on February 12, 2010, reestablished a statutory procedure to enforce a rule of deficit neutrality on new revenue and mandatory spending legislation. The Budget Control Act of 2011 (BCA), enacted on August 2, 2011, amended BBEDCA by reinstating limits ("caps") on the amount of discretionary budget authority that could be provided through the annual appropriations process. Similar enforcement mechanisms were established by the Budget Enforcement Act of 1990 and were extended in 1993 and 1997, but expired at the end of 2002. The BCA also created a Joint Select Committee on Deficit Reduction that was instructed to develop a bill to reduce the Federal deficit by at least $1.5 trillion over a 10-year period, and imposed automatic spending cuts to achieve $1.2 trillion of deficit reduction over nine years after the Joint Committee process failed to achieve its deficit reduction goal.

The original enforcement mechanisms established by the BCA—the caps on spending in annual appropriations and instructions to calculate reductions to achieve the $1.2 trillion deficit reduction goal—expired at the end of fiscal year 2021, although the sequestration of mandatory spending has been extended through 2031 for most programs and 2032 for Medicare. Prior to the expiration of the BCA, the discretionary caps were revised upward a number of times, with changes usually occurring in the form of two-year budget agreements: the 2014 and 2015 limits were revised by the Bipartisan Budget Act of 2013 (BBA of 2013; Public Law 113-67); the 2016 and 2017 limits were revised by the Bipartisan Budget Act of 2015 (BBA of 2015; Public Law 114-74); the 2018 and 2019 limits were revised by the Bipartisan Budget Act of 2018 (BBA of 2018; Public Law 115-123); and, most recently, the 2020 and 2021 limits were revised by the Bipartisan Budget Act of 2019 (BBA of 2019; Public Law 116-37).

The threat of sequestration if the caps were breached, and the ability to adjust the caps for certain types of spending, proved sufficient to ensure compliance with these statutorily adjusted discretionary spending limits. When caps were in place, BBEDCA required OMB to adjust the caps each year for: changes in concepts and definitions; appropriations designated by the Congress and the President as emergency requirements; and appropriations designated by the Congress and the President for Overseas Contingency Operations/Global War on Terrorism (OCO/GWOT). BBEDCA also specified cap adjustments (which are limited to fixed amounts) for: appropriations for continuing disability reviews and redeterminations by the Social Security Administration; the healthcare fraud and abuse control program at the Department of Health and Human Services; appropriations designated by the Congress as being for disaster relief; appropriations for reemployment services and eligibility assessments; appropriations for wildfire suppression at the Department of Agriculture and the Department of the Interior; and, for 2020 only, appropriations provided for the 2020 Census at the Department of Commerce.

Discretionary Spending Levels

The 2024 Budget builds on the success of the 2023 Budget and appropriations process by requesting funding levels that are sufficient to protect veterans, provide for a robust national defense, and continue to build the Nation's human and physical capital through non-defense discretionary spending. The Administration intends to continue working with the Congress on reinvesting in research, education, public health, and other core functions of Government. The Budget retains many of the useful and historical mechanisms of the congressional budget process by defining base levels while allowing for adjustments to those levels above base activities, such as program integrity, disaster relief, and wildfire suppression. Additionally, it highlights veterans' healthcare by carving out the Department of Veterans Affairs (VA) medical care program to ensure the Nation meets its commitments to veterans while also providing the Congress with the appropriate tools for oversight, independent of other discretionary spending.

For base defense programs, the 2024 Budget proposes a level of $886.4 billion, which is 3.3 percent higher than the 2023 enacted level. The amounts in the 2024 Budget are based on the National Security and National Defense strategies and the Department of Defense Future Years Defense Program, which includes a five-year appropriations plan and estimated expenditures necessary to support the programs, projects, and activities of the Department of Defense. After 2028, the Budget reflects outyear growth rates consistent with the 2023 President's Budget.

For non-defense, the 2024 Budget requests $688 billion, a 7.3 percent increase over enacted levels. Non-defense receives current services growth in all years after 2024.

The 2024 Budget again proposes to separate out the Veterans Affairs (VA) medical care program from the rest of discretionary spending, and requests $121 billion. The VA medical care third category grows at the current services level subsequent to 2025 and is discussed in more detail below.

The discretionary policy levels are reflected in Table S–7 of the main *Budget* volume. The proposed adjustments to the base appropriations levels and the approach to VA medical care and the newly enacted Cost of War Toxic Exposures Fund and are described below.

ADJUSTMENTS TO BASE DISCRETIONARY FUNDING LEVELS

Program Integrity Funding

There is compelling evidence that investments in administrative resources can significantly decrease the rate of improper payments and recoup many times their initial investment for certain programs. In such programs, using adjustments to base discretionary funding for program integrity activities allows for the expansion of oversight and enforcement activities in the largest benefit programs including Social Security, Unemployment Insurance, Medicare and Medicaid. In such cases, where return on investment using discretionary dollars is proven, adjustments to base discretionary funding are a useful budgeting tool. Formerly, when statutory spending caps on the discretionary budget were in place under the BCA, the law allowed the caps to be adjusted upward to account for additional discretionary funding that supported savings in these mandatory programs. These adjustments continue in congressional budget enforcement under the Congressional Budget Act and are called allocation adjustments. Such adjustments are needed because budget scoring rules do not allow the mandatory savings from these initiatives to be credited for budget enforcement purposes.

The Administration continues to support making discretionary investments in program integrity activities and maintains the same structure in place under the BCA and enacted in both the 2022 and the 2023 appropriations processes: allocation adjustments are available only if appropriations meet a minimum amount. The Administration funds base amounts similar to base investments in previous years, and then adjusts the base discretionary spending upward for the amounts dedicated to these allocation adjustments. The treatment of this funding in the Budget is consistent with the Congress' use of congressional allocation adjustments done through the annual budget resolution process (see Chapter 8, "Budget Concepts" for more information on this process). The allocation adjustment amounts proposed extend through 2033 at the rate of inflation assumed in the 2024 Budget for the amounts dedicated to Medicare savings. Funding for the Unemployment Insurance program adopts the outyear levels adopted in the BBA of 2018 through 2027, then allows the amounts to grow with inflation through the Budget window. For Social Security the requested funding stream in the outyears reflects a full complement of program integrity activities described below.

The Budget shows the mandatory program savings derived from 10 years of discretionary program integrity funding separately in an adjustment to the baseline projections for spending in Social Security, Unemployment Insurance, Medicare, and Medicaid. This separation allows the Administration to clearly show the effects of the savings from these proposed discretionary program integrity amounts that receive special budgetary treatment, while recognizing the savings in these mandatory programs has been a historical and consistent part of program operations.

The following sections explain the benefits and budget presentation of the proposed level of allocation adjustments to base discretionary funding for program integrity activities.

Social Security Administration (SSA) Dedicated Program Integrity Activities.—SSA takes seriously its

Table 4–1. PROGRAM INTEGRITY DISCRETIONARY ADJUSTMENTS AND MANDATORY SAVINGS

(Budget authority and outlays in millions of dollars)

	2024	2025	2026	2027	2028	2029	2030	2031	2032	2033	10-year Total
Social Security Administration (SSA) Program Integrity:											
Discretionary Budget Authority (non add)[1]	*1,583*	*1,601*	*1,712*	*1,715*	*1,719*	*1,823*	*1,868*	*1,922*	*1,966*	*2,011*	*17,920*
Discretionary Outlays[1]	1,583	1,600	1,703	1,715	1,719	1,815	1,865	1,918	1,963	2,008	17,889
Mandatory Savings[2]	–94	–2,296	–3,726	–4,693	–5,955	–6,311	–7,555	–8,370	–9,270	–10,505	–58,775
Net Savings	1,489	–696	–2,023	–2,978	–4,236	–4,496	–5,690	–6,452	–7,307	–8,497	–40,886
Health Care Fraud and Abuse Control Program:											
Discretionary Budget Authority (non add)[1]	*612*	*626*	*640*	*655*	*670*	*686*	*701*	*718*	*734*	*751*	*6,793*
Discretionary Outlays[1]	442	601	620	639	658	678	698	719	741	763	6,559
Mandatory Savings[2,3]	–1,178	–1,243	–1,313	–1,383	–1,425	–1,468	–1,512	–1,557	–1,605	–1,652	–14,336
Net Savings	–736	–642	–693	–744	–767	–790	–814	–838	–864	–889	–7,777
Unemployment Insurance (UI) Program Integrity:											
Discretionary Budget Authority (non add)[1]	*433*	*533*	*608*	*633*	*648*	*662*	*678*	*693*	*709*	*726*	*6,323*
Discretionary Outlays[1]	424	528	605	631	648	661	677	692	709	725	6,300
Mandatory Savings[2]	–708	–722	–648	–621	–482	–550	–436	–616	–548	–518	–5,849
Net Savings	–284	–194	–43	10	166	111	241	76	161	207	451

[1] The discretionary costs are equal to the outlays associated with the budget authority levels proposed for adjustments to the non-defense discretionary levels in the 2024 Budget. For SSA, the costs for 2024 through 2033 reflect the costs to complete the anticipated dedicated program integrity workloads for SSA; for HCFAC the costs for each of 2024 through 2033 are equal to the outlays associated with the budget authority levels inflated from the 2024 level for HCFAC, using the 2024 Budget assumptions. The UI discretionary costs for 2024 through 2027 are equal to outlays from the budget authority amounts authorized for congressional enforcement, while the outlays from the remaining years are from the budget authority inflated off of the 2027 level.

[2] The mandatory savings from the discretionary adjustment funding are included as adjustments to baseline in the Budget and displayed as savings in the Social Security, Medicare, Medicaid, and UI programs. For the SSA, amounts are based on estimates of savings from SSA's Office of the Chief Actuarys and the Centers for Medicare and Medicaid Services' Office of the Actuary. For UI amounts are based on the Department of Labor's Division of Fiscal and Actuarial Services' estimates of savings.

[3] These savings are based on estimates from the HHS Office of the Actuary for return on investment (ROI) from program integrity activities.

responsibilities to ensure eligible individuals receive the benefits to which they are entitled, and to safeguard the integrity of benefit programs to better serve recipients. The Budget's proposed discretionary amount of $1,870 million ($287 million in base funding and $1,583 million in allocation adjustment funding) will allow SSA to conduct 575,000 full medical continuing disability reviews (CDRs) and approximately 2.5 million Supplemental Security Income (SSI) non-medical redeterminations of eligibility. The Social Security Act requires that SSA conduct medical CDRs, which are periodic reevaluations to determine whether disabled Old-Age, Survivors, and Disability Insurance (OASDI) or SSI beneficiaries continue to meet SSA's standards for disability. Redeterminations are periodic reviews of non-medical eligibility factors, such as income and resources, for the means-tested SSI program and can result in a revision of the individual's benefit level. Program integrity funds also support the anti-fraud cooperative disability investigation (CDI) units and special attorneys for fraud prosecutions. To support these important anti-fraud activities, the Budget provides for SSA to transfer $19.1 million to the SSA Inspector General to fund CDI unit activities.

The Budget includes a discretionary allocation adjustment for each year of the 10-year budget window. As a result of the discretionary funding requested in 2024, as well as the fully funded base and continued funding of allocation adjustment amounts in 2025 through 2033,

the OASDI, SSI, Medicare and Medicaid programs would recoup approximately $79 billion in gross Federal savings, including approximately $59 billion from access to adjustments, with additional savings after the 10-year period, according to estimates from SSA's Office of the Chief Actuary and the Centers for Medicare and Medicaid Services' Office of the Actuary. Access to increased adjustment amounts and SSA's commitment to fund the fully loaded costs of performing the requested CDR and redetermination volumes would produce net deficit savings of approximately $41 billion in the 10-year window, and provide additional savings in the outyears. These costs and savings are reflected in Table 4-1.

SSA is required by law to conduct medical CDRs for all beneficiaries who are receiving disability benefits under the OASDI program, as well as all children under age 18 who are receiving SSI. SSI redeterminations are also required by law. SSA uses predictive models to prioritize the completion of redeterminations based on the likelihood of change in non-medical factors. The frequency of CDRs and redeterminations relies on the availability of funds to support these activities. The mandatory savings from the base funding in every year and the discretionary allocation adjustment funding enacted for 2023 are included in the baseline, as the baseline assumes the continued funding of program integrity activities. The Budget shows the savings that would result from the increase in CDRs and redeterminations made possible by the discretionary allocation adjustment funding requested in 2024 through 2033 as an adjustment to the baseline. These amounts fully support the dedicated program integrity workloads. With access to the amounts proposed, SSA is on track to regain currency in its CDR workload in 2026 and prevent new backlogs from forming throughout the budget window.

Current estimates indicate that CDRs conducted in 2024 will yield a return on investment (ROI) of about $10 on average in net Federal program savings over 10 years per $1 budgeted for dedicated program integrity funding, including OASDI, SSI, Medicare and Medicaid program effects. Similarly, SSA estimates indicate that non-medical redeterminations conducted in 2024 will yield a ROI of about $3 on average of net Federal program savings over 10 years per $1 budgeted for dedicated program integrity funding, including SSI and Medicaid program effects. The Budget assumes the full cost of performing CDRs to ensure that sufficient resources are available. The savings from one year of program integrity activities are realized over multiple years, as some reviews find that beneficiaries are no longer eligible to receive OASDI or SSI benefits.

The savings resulting from redeterminations will be different for the base funding and the allocation adjustment funding levels in 2024 through 2033 because redeterminations of eligibility can uncover both underpayment and overpayment errors. SSI recipients are more likely to initiate a redetermination of eligibility if they believe there are underpayments, and these recipient-initiated redeterminations are included in the base program amounts provided annually. The estimated savings per dollar spent on CDRs and non-medical redeterminations in the baseline reflects an interaction with the Affordable Care Act's expansion of Medicaid to additional low-income adults, as a result of which some SSI beneficiaries, who would otherwise lose Medicaid coverage due to a medical CDR or non-medical redetermination, would continue to be covered.

Health Care Fraud and Abuse Control Program (HCFAC).—The Budget proposes base and adjustment funding levels over the next 10 years growing at the rate of inflation in the Budget. The discretionary base funding of $325 million and adjustment of $612 million for HCFAC activities in 2024 includes funding to invest in additional Medicare medical review; support Medicaid program integrity data analytics, the Medicaid and CHIP Program System (MACPro), and Medicaid error rate measurement; and data analytics and improper payment measurement work in the Marketplaces. The funding is to be allocated among the Centers for Medicare & Medicaid Services (CMS), the Administration for Community Living, the Health and Human Services Office of Inspector General, and the Department of Justice.

Over 2024 through 2033, as reflected in Table 4-1, this $6.8 billion investment in HCFAC adjustment funding will generate approximately $14.3 billion in savings to Medicare and Medicaid. This results in net deficit reduction of $7.8 billion over the 10-year period, reflecting prevention and recoupment of improper payments

made to providers, as well as recoveries related to civil and criminal penalties. For HCFAC program integrity efforts, CMS actuaries conservatively estimate at least $2 is saved or averted for every additional $1 spent.

Reemployment Services and Eligibility Assessments (RESEA).—The Bipartisan Budget Act of 2018 (BBA) established a new adjustment to discretionary base funding for program integrity efforts targeted at Unemployment Insurance through 2027. The RESEA adjustment is permitted up to a maximum amount specified in the law if the underlying appropriations bill first funds a base level of $117 million for Unemployment Insurance program integrity activities. The Budget proposes adjustment levels at the same amount enacted in the BBA. Program integrity funding in 2028 through 2033 continues to rise by the inflation estimated in the Budget. Table 4-1 shows the mandatory savings of $5.8 billion over 10 years, which includes an estimated $2.2 billion reduction in State unemployment taxes. When netted against the discretionary costs for the cap adjustment funding, the 10-year net effect for the program is $451 million.

Disaster Relief Funding

The 2024 Budget maintains the same methodology for determining the funding ceiling for disaster relief used in previous budgets and adopted in the 2022 budget resolution. For the 2024 Budget, OMB estimates the total adjustment available for disaster funding for 2024 at $20.3 billion. This ceiling estimate is based on three components: a 10-year average of disaster relief funding provided in prior years that excludes the highest and lowest years ($11.9 billion); 5 percent of Robert T. Stafford Disaster Relief and Emergency Assistance Act (Stafford Act) amounts designated as emergency requirements since 2012 ($8.3 billion); and carryover from the previous year ($0 billion). In addition, the estimate of emergency requirements for Stafford Act activities was updated based on applicable amounts provided for 2023 in the Infrastructure Investment and Jobs Act (Division B of Public Law 117-58), the Continuing Appropriations and Ukraine Supplemental Appropriations Act, 2023 (Division A of Public Law 117-180), and the Consolidated Appropriations Act, 2023 (CAA, 2023; Division N of Public Law 117-328). For 2024, the Administration is requesting $20.1 billion in funding for the Federal Emergency Management Agency's (FEMA) Disaster Relief Program, of which nearly $1 billion will go towards Building Resilient Infrastructure Communities (BRIC), and more than $0.1 billion for the Small Business Administration's Disaster Loans Program. The request covers the costs of Presidentially-declared major disasters, including identified costs for previously declared catastrophic events and the estimated annual cost of non-catastrophic events expected to be obligated in 2024.

Consistent with past practice, the 2024 request level does not seek to pre-fund anticipated needs in other programs that may arise out of disasters that have yet to occur. After 2024, the Administration does not have adequate information about known or future requirements necessary to estimate the total amount that will be requested in future years. Accordingly, the Budget does not explicitly request any disaster relief funding in any year after the budget year and includes a placeholder in each of the outyears that is equal to the 10-year average ($11.9 billion) of disaster relief currently estimated under the formula for the 2024 ceiling. This funding level does not reflect a specific request but a placeholder amount that, along with other outyear appropriations levels, will be decided on an annual basis as part of the normal budget development process.

Wildfire Suppression Operations at the Departments of Agriculture and the Interior

Wildfires naturally occur on public lands throughout the United States. The cost of fighting wildfires has increased due to landscape conditions resulting from drought, pest and disease damage, overgrown forests, expanding residential and commercial development near the borders of public lands, and program management decisions. In the past, when these costs exceeded the funds appropriated, the Federal Government covered the shortfall through transfers from other land management programs. For example, in 2018, Forest Service wildfire suppression spending of $2.6 billion required transfers of $720 million from other non-fire programs. Historically, these transfers had been repaid in subsequent appropriations; however, such "fire borrowing" impedes the missions of land management agencies to reduce the risk of catastrophic fire and restore and maintain healthy functioning ecosystems.

To create funding certainty in times of wildfire disasters, the Consolidated Appropriations Act of 2018 (CAA) enacted a new cap adjustment to BBEDCA, which began in 2020. This adjustment has been used since that time, and the Administration proposes continuing this adjustment in the Budget. The adjustment is permitted so long as a base level of funding for wildfire suppression operations is funded in the underlying appropriations bill. The base level is defined as being equal to average cost over 10 years for wildfire suppression operations that was requested in the President's 2015 Budget. These amounts have been determined to be $1,011 million for the Department of Agriculture's Forest Service and $384 million for the Department of the Interior (DOI). The 2024 Budget requests these base amounts for wildfire suppression and proposes the full $2,650 million adjustment specified in the CAA of 2018 for 2024 with $ 2,300 million included for Forest Service and $350 million included for DOI. Providing the full level will ensure that adequate resources are available to fight wildland fires, protect communities, and safeguard human life during the most severe wildland fire season.

For the years after 2024, the Administration does not have sufficient information about future wildfire suppression needs and, therefore, includes a placeholder in the 2024 Budget for wildfire suppression in each of the outyears that is equal to the current 2024 request. Actual funding levels, up to but not exceeding the authorized funding adjustments, will be decided on an annual basis as part of the normal budget process.

Limit on Discretionary Advance Appropriations

An advance appropriation first becomes available for obligation one or more fiscal years beyond the year for which the appropriations act is passed. Budget authority is recorded in the year the funds become available for obligation, not in the year the appropriation is enacted.

There are legitimate policy reasons to use advance appropriations to fund programs. For example, some education grants are forward funded (available beginning July 1 of the fiscal year) to provide certainty of funding for an entire school year, since school years straddle Federal fiscal years. This funding is recorded in the budget year because the funding is first legally available in that fiscal year. However, $22.6 billion of this education funding is advance appropriated (available beginning three months later, on October 1) rather than forward funded. Prior Congresses increased advance appropriations and decreased the amounts of forward funding as a gimmick to free up room in the budget year without affecting the total amount available for a coming school year. This approach works because the advance appropriation is not recorded in the budget year but rather the following fiscal year. However, it works only in the year in which funds switch from forward funding to advance appropriations; that is, it works only in years in which the amounts of advance appropriations for such "straddle" programs are increased.

To curtail this approach, which allows over-budget funding in the budget year and exerts pressure for increased funding in future years, congressional budget resolutions since 2001 have set limits on the amount of discretionary advance appropriations and the accounts which can receive them. By freezing the amount that had been advance appropriated to these accounts at the level provided in the most recent appropriations bill, additional room within discretionary spending limits cannot be created by shifting additional funds to future fiscal years.

The Budget includes $28,768 million in advance appropriations for 2025, consistent with limits established in recent congressional budget resolutions, and freezes them at this level in subsequent years. Outside of these limits, the Administration's Budget would request discretionary advance appropriations for veterans medical care, as is required by the Veterans Health Care Budget Reform and Transparency Act (Public Law 111-81). The Department of Veterans Affairs has included detailed information in its Congressional Budget Justifications about the overall 2025 veterans medical care funding request.

For a detailed table of accounts that have received discretionary and mandatory advance appropriations since 2022 or for which the Budget requests advance appropriations for 2025 and beyond, please refer to the Advance Appropriations chapter in the *Appendix*.

Veterans Affairs Category and the Cost of War Toxic Exposures Fund

The Budget separates VA medical care as a third category within the discretionary budget based on a recognition that VA medical care has grown much more rapidly than other discretionary spending over time, largely due to systemwide growth in healthcare costs. Additionally, recent enactment of the Sergeant First Class Heath Robinson Honoring our Promise to Address Comprehensive Toxics Act of 2022, or the Honoring our PACT Act of 2022, (Public Law 117-168; "PACT Act") created the Cost of War Toxic Exposures Fund (TEF) to ensure that there is sufficient funding available to cover costs associated with providing healthcare and benefits to veterans exposed to environmental hazards, without shortchanging other elements of veteran care and services. While the TEF requires annual appropriations, the PACT Act directs the appropriations to be considered mandatory funding, similar to the treatment of annual appropriations for Medicaid and Supplemental Nutrition Assistance Programs.

Veterans Affairs Medical Care Program, Third Category. The Administration has put forward a request for discretionary medical care services of $121 billion in 2024 and $113 billion in 2025 as a third category of discretionary spending, alongside the Defense Category and the Non-Defense Category. The Administration's proposal to create a third category of discretionary spending will allow the Congress to consider the funding needs for VA medical care holistically, taking into account both discretionary and mandatory funding streams together. Setting a separate budget allocation for VA medical care accomplishes three important goals. First, it helps ensure adequate funding for veterans' healthcare without adversely impacting other critical programs, whether inside or outside of VA. Second, it also ensures that other critical priorities--both defense and non-defense--won't adversely impact veterans medical care. And third, it prevents the use of the mandatory TEF funding as a mechanism to shift discretionary resources into the non-VA medical care categories.

Cost of War Toxic Exposures Fund. Consistent with the PACT Act, the Administration proposes mandatory medical care funding in the TEF of $17.1 billion in 2024 and $21.5 billion in 2025. The PACT Act authorized the TEF to fund the incremental costs above 2021 for healthcare associated with environmental hazards and for any expenses incident to the delivery of healthcare and benefits associated with exposure to environmental hazards, as well as medical research relating to exposure to environmental hazards. Consistent with the law, the Administration is limiting the TEF request to those increases only and excluding costs not associated with exposure to environmental hazards. It is requesting that the Congress provide all other funding needs in the traditional discretionary appropriations accounts to ensure that veterans have the care and benefits they earned. In addition to the $17.1 billion for medical care, the Administration proposes $3.2 billion of mandatory funding in the TEF for 2024 for non-medical care costs incident to the delivery of healthcare and benefits associated with exposure to environmental hazards and medical research relating to exposure to environmental hazards. Overall, the mandatory baseline reflects the estimates of TEF funding for the next 10 years, consistent with the baseline rules for mandatory funding.

VA has developed a methodology for medical care and for non-medical care incident to the delivery of veterans' healthcare and benefits that underpin the TEF request.

- Medical Care Methodology: VA used the relative share of co-payment exempt care provided to a sample of Priority Group 6[1] veterans as a proxy for the proportion of healthcare that could reasonably be associated with exposure to environmental hazards (84 percent). VA then identified the projected healthcare costs of all Vietnam, Gulf War, and Post-9/11 veterans who were assumed to have deployed to a theater of operations. VA applied the proportion of environmental hazard-associated care (84 percent) to the projected healthcare costs for these cohorts of veterans in 2021 and then further discounted for medical facility leasing costs. This approach establishes the baseline level of expenses in 2021 for providing medical care associated with exposure to environmental hazards to veterans. The PACT Act directs that all increases in these costs associated with exposure to environmental hazards above the baseline level be funded through the TEF. Consistent with that directive, VA estimated the corresponding amount projected for 2024 and 2025 and calculated the increase over 2021 baseline level to arrive at the TEF estimate. VA also estimated other non-actuarially-modeled healthcare costs that could be attributable to the TEF.

- Non-medical Care Methodology: VA identified five accounts with costs incident to the delivery of veterans' healthcare and benefits associated with exposure to environmental hazards that could be requested in the TEF. These costs include supporting the processing of new presumptive condition disability compensation claims, allocating a percentage of claims appeals workload associated with new and expanded presumptive conditions attributable to the PACT Act, and modernizing IT systems and infrastructure to support expected increased claims processing.

Statutory PAYGO

The Statutory Pay-As-You-Go Act of 2010 (PAYGO Act; Public Law 111-139) requires that new legislation changing mandatory spending or revenue must be enacted on a "pay-as-you-go" (PAYGO) basis; that is, that the cumulative effects of such legislation must not increase projected on-budget deficits. PAYGO is a permanent requirement, and it does not impose a cap on spending or a floor on revenues. Instead, PAYGO requires that legislation reducing revenues must be fully offset by cuts in mandatory programs or by revenue increases, and that any bills

---

[1] Priority Group 6 Veterans are enrolled in both Priority Group 6 and in either Priority Group 7 or Priority Group 8, as applicable, pursuant to 38 CFR § 17.38(d)(3)(iii). For any care that VA cannot find to have resulted from a cause other than the service, testing, or activity that resulted in the exposure to environmental hazards, VA furnishes this care without copayment liability pursuant to 38 U.S.C. § 1710(a)(2).

increasing mandatory spending must be fully offset by revenue increases or cuts in mandatory spending.

This requirement of deficit neutrality is not enforced on a bill-by-bill basis, but is based on two scorecards maintained by OMB that tally the cumulative budgetary effects of PAYGO legislation as averaged over rolling 5- and 10-year periods, starting with the budget year. Any impacts of PAYGO legislation on the current year deficit are counted as budget year impacts when placed on the scorecard. PAYGO is enforced by sequestration. Within 14 business days after a congressional session ends, OMB issues an annual PAYGO report. If either the 5- or 10-year scorecard shows net costs in the budget year column, the President is required to issue a sequestration order implementing across-the-board cuts to nonexempt mandatory programs by an amount sufficient to offset those net costs. The list of exempt programs and special sequestration rules for certain programs are contained in sections 255 and 256 of BBEDCA.

The PAYGO effects of legislation may be directed in legislation by reference to statements inserted into the *Congressional Record* by the chair of the House and Senate Budget Committees. Any such estimates are determined by the Budget Committees and are informed by, but not required to match, the cost estimates prepared by the Congressional Budget Office (CBO). If this procedure is not followed, then the PAYGO effects of the legislation are determined by OMB. Provisions of mandatory spending or receipts legislation that are designated in that legislation as an emergency requirement are not scored as PAYGO budgetary effects.

The PAYGO rules apply to the outlays resulting from outyear changes in mandatory programs made in appropriations acts and to all revenue changes made in appropriations acts. However, outyear changes to mandatory programs as part of provisions that have zero net outlay effects over the sum of the current year and the next five fiscal years are not considered under the PAYGO rules.

The PAYGO rules do not apply to increases in mandatory spending or decreases in receipts that result automatically under existing law. For example, mandatory spending for benefit programs, such as unemployment insurance, rises when the number of beneficiaries rises, and many benefit payments are automatically increased for inflation under existing laws.

Changes to off-budget programs (Social Security and the Postal Service) do not have budgetary effects for the purposes of PAYGO and are not counted, though they may have a real effect on the deficit. Provisions designated by the Congress in law as emergencies appear on the scorecards, but the effects are subtracted before computing the scorecard totals.

In addition to the exemptions in the PAYGO Act itself, the Congress has enacted laws affecting revenues or direct spending with a provision directing that the budgetary effects of all or part of the law be held off of the PAYGO scorecards. In the most recently completed congressional session, seven laws were enacted with such a provision.

As was the case during an earlier PAYGO enforcement regime in the 1990s, the PAYGO sequestration has not been required since the PAYGO Act reinstated the statutory PAYGO requirement. For the second session of the 117th Congress, the most recently completed session, enacted legislation placed costs of $72.5 billion in each year of the 5-year scorecard and $55.7 million in each year of the 10-year scorecard. However, the budget year balance on each of the PAYGO scorecards is zero because the CAA, 2023 (Public Law 117-328) shifted the debits on both scorecards from fiscal year 2023 to fiscal year 2025. Consequently, no PAYGO sequestration was required in 2023. The CAA, 2023, also requires that, at the end of the first session of the 118th Congress, any debit for fiscal year 2024 on the 5- and 10-year scorecards be rolled forward to 2025.[2]

BBEDCA Section 251A Reductions

In August 2011, as part of the Budget Control Act of 2011 (BCA; Public Law 112-25), bipartisan majorities in both the House and Senate voted to establish the Joint Select Committee on Deficit Reduction to recommend legislation to achieve at least $1.5 trillion of deficit reduction over the period of fiscal years 2012 through 2021 (Joint Committee sequestration). The failure of the Congress to enact such comprehensive deficit reduction legislation to achieve the $1.5 trillion goal triggered a sequestration of discretionary and mandatory spending in 2013, led to reductions in the discretionary caps for 2014 through 2021, and forced additional sequestrations of mandatory spending in each of fiscal years 2014 through 2021.

The discretionary cap regime in place under the BCA expired at the end of fiscal year 2021. Prior to the that time, various laws changed the annual reductions required to the discretionary spending limits set in the BCA through 2021. However, sequestration of mandatory resources was extended in a series of laws for each year through 2031 for most programs and the first half of 2032 for Medicare, and the Budget proposes to continue mandatory sequestration through 2033, which generates $48.9 billion in deficit reduction. This sequestration is now called the BBEDCA 251A sequestration, after the Balanced Budget and Emergency Deficit Control Act, as amended (BBEDCA), the law where mandatory sequestration continues to be extended.

Section 251A of BBEDCA requires that the same percentage reductions for non-exempt mandatory defense and non-defense spending apply each year at the rate established in 2021 for fiscal years 2022 through 2031. Those reductions are 5.7 percent for non-defense accounts, 8.3 percent for defense accounts, and 2 percent for Medicare and community and migrant health centers.[3] These reductions to mandatory programs are triggered annually by the transmittal of the President's Budget for

[2] OMB's annual PAYGO report is available on OMB's website at https://www.whitehouse.gov/omb/paygo/.

[3] The CARES Act (Public Law 116-136) suspended the 251A sequestration for Medicare programs between May 1, 2020, and December 31, 2020. This suspension was extended to March 31, 2021 by the Consolidated Appropriations Act, 2021 (Public Law 116-260); further extended to December 31, 2021, by Public Law 117-7; and extended again to March 31, 2022, by the Protecting Medicare and American Farmers from Sequester Cuts Act (Public Law 117-71).

each year and take effect on the first day of the fiscal year. Because the percentage reduction is known in advance, the Budget presents these reductions in the baseline at the account level.

The 2024 Budget shows the net effect of these mandatory sequestration reductions by accounting for reductions in 2024, and each outyear, that remain in the sequestered account and are anticipated to become newly available for obligation in the year after sequestration, in accordance with section 256(k)(6) of BBEDCA. The budget authority and outlays from these "pop-up" resources are included in the baseline and policy estimates and amount to a cost of $2.5 billion in 2024. Additionally, the Budget annually accounts for lost savings that results from the sequestration of certain interfund payments, which produces no net deficit reduction. Such amount is $1.9 billion in 2024.

II. BUDGET PRESENTATION

Adjustments to BBEDCA Baseline

In order to provide a more realistic outlook for the deficit under current legislation and policies, the Budget proposals are presented relative to a baseline that makes adjustments to the statutory baseline defined in BBEDCA. Section 257 of BBEDCA provides the rules for constructing the baseline used by the Executive and Legislative Branches for scoring and other legal purposes. The adjustments made by the Administration are not intended to replace the BBEDCA baseline for these purposes, but rather are intended to make the baseline a more useful benchmark for assessing the deficit outlook and the impact of budget proposals. The Administration's adjusted baseline makes four adjustments, each described below.

First, the Budget removes the outyear effects of emergency spending. Because this funding varies significantly from year to year, removing emergency funding provides a more consistent discretionary baseline for policy comparison. Eliminating this spending in an adjustment to the baseline, which is consistent with the historical practice of not projecting specific emergency needs in the Budget, also avoids the unintended suggestion of large savings in policy when compared to the BBEDCA baseline. Amounts that fund ongoing Government programs but that carried an emergency designation in the CAA, 2023, continue to inflate in the adjusted baseline.

Second, the Budget removes from the baseline the double count of discretionary VA spending, largely for medical care, that is requested to be appropriated as mandatory in the TEF, consistent with the directives under the PACT Act. Under BBEDCA rules, discretionary funding provided for amounts in 2023 continues into the outyears. Yet, as described above, the PACT Act created the TEF to fund the costs above the 2021 level for healthcare associated with environmental hazards and for expenses incident to the delivery of healthcare and benefits associated with environmental hazards, as well as medical research relating to exposure to environmental hazards. The increases in healthcare expenses and some of the other expenses that are expected to be provided through the TEF have, in part, been provided in other accounts in the past. The adjusted baseline removes the extension of the cost of providing this care in those accounts so that the outlays from the TEF are not double-counted in the baseline.

Third, the Budget removes the advance appropriation for 2024 for the Indian Health Service and the outyear extension of that appropriation. Because the CAA, 2023 funded appropriations for 2023, as well as provided an advance in 2024, each inflates in in the BBEDCA baseline. This significant double count of budget authority and outlays would overstate the size of the baseline dedicated to these programs. Eliminating the advance in the adjusted baseline provides a more accurate reflection of current services in the Budget.

Last, the Budget shows the continuation of mandatory savings from discretionary program integrity allocation adjustments in the adjusted baseline. The discretionary baseline continues the spending from these initiatives under BBEDCA rules, meaning much of the savings is reasonably captured in the adjusted baseline. The savings generated from the disretionary increase between the baseline and policy is also captured in the adjusted baseline to acknowledge the historical tendency to fully fund these discretionary program integrity initiatives. Thus, the adjusted baseline captures the savings generated in these mandatory entitlement programs from continuing these initiatives over 10 years at the levels requested by the Administration in the 2024 Budget. Each of the discretionary allocation adjustments for program integrity are described above under Adjustments to Base Discretionary Levels, Program Integrity.

These adjustments to baseline are detailed in this Volume in Chapter 21, "Current Services Estimates".

Reclassification of Contract Support Costs and Payments for Tribal Leases at the Department of Health and Human Services' Indian Health Service and the Department of the Interior's Bureau of Indian Affairs

The 2024 Budget proposes to reclassify Contract Support Costs (CSCs) and Payments for Tribal Leases, programs that historically have been funded as discretionary in the Department of Health and Human Services' Indian Health Service (IHS) and the Department of the Interior's Bureau of Indian Affairs, as mandatory. Specifically, the Budget proposes that, beginning in 2024, the CSCs and Payments for Tribal Leases accounts will continue to be funded through the annual appropriations process but will be reclassified as mandatory funding. The 2024 Budget requests $1.8 billion in 2024 and the reclassification totals $26.4 billion over 10 years. This shift is shown in the discretionary funding tables in the Budget by reducing the base discretionary in the amount of the 2024 Budget request, inflated into the 10-year window. Separately, the Administration is proposing broader changes to the funding of IHS starting in 2025, as described in the third section of this Chapter (Budget Reform proposals).

Pell Grants

The Pell Grant program includes features that make it unlike other discretionary programs, including that Pell Grants are awarded to all applicants who meet income and other eligibility criteria. This section provides some background on the unique nature of the Pell Grant program and explains how the Budget accommodates changes in discretionary costs.

Under current law, the Pell program has several notable features:

- The Pell Grant program acts like an entitlement program, such as the Supplemental Nutrition Assistance Program or Supplemental Security Income, in which anyone who meets specific eligibility requirements and applies for the program receives a benefit. Specifically, Pell Grant costs in a given year are determined by the maximum award set in statute, the number of eligible applicants, and the award for which those applicants are eligible based on their needs and costs of attendance. The maximum Pell award for the academic year 2024-2025 is $7,395, of which $6,335 was established in discretionary appropriations and the remaining $1,060 in mandatory funding is provided automatically by the College Cost Reduction and Access Act as amended (CCRAA).

- The cost of each Pell Grant is funded by discretionary budget authority provided in annual appropriations acts, along with mandatory budget authority provided not only by the CCRAA but also the Health

Care and Education Reconciliation Act of 2010. There is no programmatic difference between the mandatory and discretionary funding.

- If valid applicants are more numerous than expected, or if these applicants are eligible for higher awards than anticipated, the Pell Grant program will cost more than projected at the time of the appropriation. If the costs during one academic year are higher than provided for in that year's appropriation, the Department of Education funds the extra costs with the subsequent year's appropriation.[4]

- To prevent deliberate underfunding of Pell costs, in 2006 the congressional and Executive Branch scorekeepers agreed to a special scorekeeping rule for Pell. Under this rule, the annual appropriations bill is charged with the full Congressional Budget Office estimated cost of the Pell Grant program for the budget year, plus or minus any cumulative shortfalls or surpluses from prior years.

Given the nature of the program, it is reasonable to consider Pell Grants an individual entitlement for purposes of budget analysis and enforcement. The discretionary portion of the award funded in annual appropriations acts

---

[4] This ability to "borrow" from a subsequent appropriation is unique to the Pell program. It comes about for two reasons. First, like many education programs, Pell is "forward-funded"—the budget authority enacted in the fall of one year is intended for the subsequent academic year, which begins in the following July. Second, even though the amount of funding is predicated on the expected cost of Pell during one academic year, the money is made legally available for the full 24-month period covering the current fiscal year and the subsequent fiscal year. This means that, if the funding for an academic year proves inadequate, the following year's appropriation will legally be available to cover the funding shortage for the first academic year. The 2024 Budget appropriations request, for instance, will support the 2024-2025 academic year beginning in July 2023 but will become available in October 2023 and can therefore help cover any shortages that may arise in funding for the 2023-2024 academic year.

Table 4–2. DISCRETIONARY PELL FUNDING NEEDS
(Budget authority in millions of dollars)

Discretionary Pell Funding Needs (Baseline)

	2024	2025	2026	2027	2028	2029	2030	2031	2032	2033
Estimated Program Cost for $6,335 Disc. Maximum Award ..	28,517	28,786	29,175	29,552	30,910	31,257	31,640	32,046	32,420	32,883
Baseline Discretionary Appropriation - 2023 Enacted	22,475	22,475	22,475	22,475	22,475	22,475	22,475	22,475	22,475	22,475
Surplus/Funding Gap from Prior Year	13,438	8,566	3,425	−2,104	−8,011	−15,276	−22,887	−30,882	−39,283	−48,057
Mandatory Budget Authority Available	1,170	1,170	1,170	1,170	1,170	1,170	1,170	1,170	1,170	1,170
Baseline Discretionary Surplus/Funding Gap (−)	8,566	3,425	−2,104	−8,011	−15,276	−22,887	−30,882	−39,283	−48,057	−57,295

Effect of 2024 Budget Policies on Discretionary Pell Funding Needs

	2024	2025	2026	2027	2028	2029	2030	2031	2032	2033
Increase Discretionary Maximum Award to $6,835	−2,479	−2,493	−2,517	−2,538	−2,674	−2,701	−2,734	−2,769	−2,803	−2,848
Increase Mandatory Add-On to Double Grant by 2029	5	11	18	24	12	15	18	21	27	29
Mandatory Funding Shift[1]	−62	−62	−62	−66	−76	−78	−80	−82	−85	−82
Increase Discretionary Appropriation by $1.8 billion	1,800	1,800	1,800	1,800	1,800	1,800	1,800	1,800	1,800	1,800
Annual Effect of 2024 Budget Policies	−736	−744	−761	−780	−938	−964	−996	−1,030	−1,061	−1,101
Cumulative Effect of 2024 Budget Policies	−736	−1,480	−2,241	−3,021	−3,959	−4,923	−5,919	−6,949	−8,010	−9,111
2024 Budget Discretionary Surplus/Funding Gap (−)	7,830	1,945	−4,345	−11,032	−19,235	−27,810	−36,801	−46,232	−56,067	−66,406

[1] Some budget authority, provided in previous legislation and classified as mandatory but used to meet discretionary Pell grant program funding needs, will be reallocated to support new mandatory costs associated with the discretionary award increase.

counts against appropriations allocations established annually under §302 of the Congressional Budget Act.

The total cost of Pell Grants can fluctuate from year to year, even with no change in the maximum Pell Grant award, because of changes in enrollment, college costs, and student and family resources. In general, the demand for and costs of the program are countercyclical to the economy; more people go to school during periods of higher unemployment, but return to the workforce as the economy improves. During the COVID pandemic, however, enrollment continued its decline since the end of the Great Recession. The Budget projects the number of Pell recipients to increase by about one percent annually, on average, over the course of the ten-year budget window. Assuming no changes in current policy, the 2024 Budget baseline expects program costs to stay within available discretionary resources until 2026 (see Table 4-2). These estimates have changed from year to year, which illustrates difficulty in forecasting Pell program costs.

The 2024 Budget reflects a significant step in the President's goal of doubling the Pell Grant. The Budget would increase the maximum Pell Grant by $820 over the current level ($7,395) for the 2024-2025 school year, for a total award of $8,215. This increase is composed of a $500 increase to the discretionary maximum award and a $320 increase to the mandatory portion of the award. The increase to the grant would increase future discretionary Pell program costs by $26 billion over 10 years, shown in Table 4-2 by combining the increase in the discretionary maximum award and increase in the mandatory add-on, under the Effects of 2024 Budget Policies. The Budget provides $24.3 billion in discretionary budget authority in 2024 to support this increase, $1.8 billion more than 2023. The Budget projects that the Pell program will still have sufficient discretionary funds to meet program costs until 2026.

Fannie Mae and Freddie Mac

The Budget continues to present Fannie Mae and Freddie Mac, the housing Government-sponsored enterprises (GSEs) currently in Federal conservatorship, as non-Federal entities. However, Treasury equity investments in the GSEs are recorded as budgetary outlays, and the dividends on those investments are recorded as offsetting receipts. In addition, the budget estimates reflect collections from the 10-basis point increase in GSE guarantee fees that was enacted under the Temporary Payroll Tax Cut Continuation Act of 2011 (Public Law 112-78) and extended by the IIJA. The Budget also reflects collections from a 4.2 basis point set-aside on each dollar of unpaid principal balance of new business purchases authorized under the Housing and Economic Recovery Act of 2008 (Public Law 111-289) to be remitted to several Federal affordable housing programs. The GSEs are discussed in more detail in Chapter 7, "Credit and Insurance."

Postal Service Treatment

The Postal Service is designated in statute as an off-budget independent establishment of the Executive Branch. This designation and budgetary treatment was most recently mandated in 1989. To reflect the Postal Service's practice since 2012 of using defaults to on-budget accounts to continue operations, despite losses, the Administration's baseline reflects probable defaults in the on-budget account showing no payment for Civil Service Retirement and Disability. This treatment allows for a clearer presentation of the Postal Service's likely actions. See the discussion of the Postal Service in the 2024 Budget *Appendix* for further explanation of this presentation and updates for the recently enacted Postal Reform Act.

Under current scoring rules, savings from any proposals for reform of the Postal Service would affect the unified deficit but would not directly affect the PAYGO scorecard. Any savings to on-budget accounts through lower projected defaults in future legislation affect both the PAYGO scorecard and the unified deficit.

III. BUDGET REFORM PROPOSALS

Federal Capital Revolving Fund

The structure of the Federal budget and budget enforcement requirements can create hurdles to funding large-dollar capital investments that are handled differently at the State and local government levels. Expenditures for capital investment are combined with operating expenses in the Federal unified budget. Both kinds of expenditures must compete for limited funding within the discretionary funding levels. Large-dollar Federal capital investments can be squeezed out in this competition, forcing agency managers to turn to operating leases to meet long-term Federal requirements. These alternatives are more expensive than ownership over the long-term because: (1) Treasury can always borrow at lower interest rates; and (2) to avoid triggering scorekeeping and recording requirements for capital leases, agencies sign shorter-term consecutive leases of the same space. For example, the cost of two consecutive 15-year leases for a building can far exceed its fair market value, with the Government paying close to 180 percent of the value of the building. Alternative financing proposals typically run up against scorekeeping and recording rules that appropriately measure cost based on the full amount of the Government's obligations under the contract, which further constrains the ability of agency managers to meet large capital needs.

In contrast, State and local governments separate capital investment from operating expenses. They are able to evaluate, rank, and finance proposed capital investments in separate capital budgets, which avoids direct competition between proposed capital acquisitions and operating expenses. If capital purchases are financed by

Chart 4-1. Scoring of $3.5 billion GSA Construction Project using the Federal Capital Revolving Fund[*]
(Budget authority in millions of dollars)

Federal Capital Revolving Fund		
	Year 1	Years 2-15
Mandatory:		
Transfer to purchasing agency to buy building...............................	3,500	
Purchasing agency repayments............	-233	-3,267

Purchasing Agency		
	Year 1	Years 2-15
Mandatory:		
Collection of transfer from Federal Capital Revolving Fund........................	-3,500	
Payment to buy building........................	3,500	
Discretionary:		
Repayments to Federal Capital Revolving Fund........................	233	3,267

Total Government-wide Deficit Impact			
	Year 1	Years 2-15	Total
Mandatory:			
Purchase building...	3,500		3,500
Collections from purchasing agency................................	-233	-3,267	-3,500
Discretionary:			
Purchasing agency repayments..	233	3,267	3,500
Total Government-wide..	3,500	---	3,500

[*]The 2024 Budget proposes one project, the Suburban FBI Headquarters Campus, estimated project balance of $3.5 billion.

borrowing, the associated debt service is an item in the operating budget. This separation of capital spending from operating expenses works well at the State and local government levels because of conditions that do not exist at the Federal level. State and local governments are required to balance their operating budgets, and their ability to borrow to finance capital spending is subject to the discipline of private credit markets that impose higher interest rates for riskier investments. In addition, State and local governments tend to own capital that they finance. In contrast, the Federal Government does not face a balanced budget requirement, and Treasury debt has historically been considered the safest investment regardless of the condition of the Federal balance sheet. Also, the bulk of Federal funding for capital is in the form of grants to lower levels of Government or to private entities, and it is difficult to see how non-federally owned investment can be included in a capital budget.

To deal with the drawbacks of the current Federal approach, the Budget proposes: (1) to create a Federal Capital Revolving Fund (FCRF) to fund large-dollar, federally owned, civilian real property capital projects; and (2) provide specific budget enforcement rules for the FCRF that would allow it to function, in effect, like State and local government capital budgets. This proposal incorporates principles that are central to the success of capital budgeting at the State and local level—a limit on total funding for capital investment, annual decisions on the allocation of funding for capital projects, and spreading the acquisition cost over 15 years in the discretionary operating budgets of agencies that purchase the assets. The 2024 Budget proposes that that FCRF would be capitalized initially by a $10 billion mandatory appropriation, and scored with anticipated outlays over the 10-year window for the purposes of pay-as-you-go budget enforcement

rules. Balances in the FCRF would be available for transfer to purchasing agencies to fund large-dollar capital acquisitions only to the extent projects are designated in advance in appropriations Acts and the agency receives a discretionary appropriation for the first of a maximum of 15 required annual repayments. If these two conditions are met, the FCRF would transfer funds to the purchasing agency to cover the full cost to acquire the capital asset. Annual discretionary repayments by purchasing agencies would replenish the FCRF and would become available to fund additional capital projects. Total annual capital purchases would be limited to the lower of $5 billion or the balance in the FCRF, including annual repayments.

The Budget uses the FCRF concept to fund construction of a suburban FBI Headquarters campus with an estimated project balance of $3.5 billion when taking into account available GSA balances previously appropriated for this project. A project of this size and scope, if funded through the traditional discretionary appropriations process would account for potentially all GSA capital funding for consecutive fiscal years. In accordance with the principles and design of the FCRF, the 2024 budget requests appropriations language in the General Services Administration's (GSA) Federal Buildings Fund account, designating that the project to be funded out of the FCRF, which is also housed within GSA, along with 1/15 of the full purchase price, or $233 million for the first-year repayment back to the FCRF. The FCRF account is displayed funding the FBI project with additional unspecified projects being funded in future years, along with returns to the account from the annual project repayments.

The flow of funds for the FBI project is illustrated in Chart 4–1. Current budget enforcement rules would require the entire $3.5 billion building cost to be scored as discretionary budget authority in the first year, which would negate the benefit of the FCRF and leave agencies and policy makers facing the same trade-off constraints. As shown in Chart 4-1, under this proposal, transfers from the FCRF to agencies to fund capital projects, $3.5 billion in the case of the proposed project in 2024, and the actual execution by GSA would be scored as direct spending (shown as mandatory in Chart 4-1), while agencies would use discretionary appropriations to fund the annual repayments to the FCRF, or $233 million for the first-year repayment. The proposal allocates the costs between direct spending and discretionary spending—the up-front cost of capital investment would already be reflected in the baseline as direct spending once the FCRF is enacted with $10 billion in mandatory capital. This scoring approves a total capital investment upfront, keeping individual large projects from competing with annual operating expenses in the annual appropriations process. On the discretionary side of the budget the budgetary trade off would be locking into the incremental annual cost of repaying the FCRF over 15-years. Knowing that future discretionary appropriations will have to be used to repay the FCRF provides an incentive for agencies, OMB, and the Congress to select projects with the highest mission criticality and returns. In future years, OMB would review agencies' proposed projects for inclusion in the President's Budget, as shown with the GSA request, and the Appropriations Committees would make final allocations by authorizing projects in annual appropriations Acts and providing the first year of repayment. This approach would allow for a more effective capital planning process for the Government's largest civilian real property projects, and is similar to capital budgets used by State and local governments.

Protecting Funding for the Federal Buildings Fund

Since 2011, the Congress has under-funded the General Services Administration (GSA) Federal Building Fund (FBF), the primary source of maintenance, repair, and construction for GSA's federally owned building inventory. Over the last 15 years more than $11.8 billion in agency rental payments, intended to maintain and construct GSA facilities, have remained unavailable as balances in the FBF. By enacting an FBF appropriations level below the estimated annual rent collections, Congress creates an offset that allows the Appropriations Committee to fund other priorities. When that occurs, actual collections remain in the Fund as unavailable.

At the same time, the GSA inventory of federally owned buildings is seeing an increase in deferred maintenance while experiencing cost increases year over year for unfunded projects. This year, the Budget proposes a reform to ensure that all agency rental payments can be used for construction and maintenance and repair, as intended, rather than merely sitting unavailable for use in the Fund. The Budget proposes directed scoring, to take effect in fiscal year 2025, that would not credit, or score, any savings from limiting the spending in the FBF. FBF revenues would be utilized for the intended purposes of maintaining and operating the GSA owned and leased

Table 4–3. FEDERAL BUILDINGS FUND 2009–2023
(In thousands of dollars)

	President's Budget Revenue Estimate	Enacted New Obligational Authority	Net Budget Authority[1,2]
2009	8,134,239	8,427,771	350,397
2010	8,222,539	8,443,585	287,406
2011	8,870,933	7,597,540	−1,202,123
2012	9,302,761	8,017,967	−1,205,174
2013	9,777,590	8,024,967	−1,665,003
2014	9,950,560	9,370,042	−580,518
2015	9,917,667	9,238,310	−679,357
2016	9,807,722	10,196,124	388,402
2017	10,178,339	8,845,147	−1,333,192
2018	9,950,519	9,073,938	−876,581
2019	10,131,673	9,285,082	−846,591
2020	10,203,596	8,856,530	−1,347,066
2021	10,388,375	9,065,489	−1,322,886
2022	10,636,648	9,342,205	−1,294,443
2023	10,488,857	10,013,150	−475,707
Total			−11,802,436

[1] Net Budget Authority does not include rescission of prior year funding, transfers, supplemental, or emergency appropriations.
[2] Net BA for 2009–2013 includes payment to Federal Financing Bank for Redemption of Debt.

buildings portfolio. In this way, the Congress will have every incentive to set new obligational authority (NOA) at the level of the estimated collections from across Federal agencies.

The FBF has hit a tipping point with a growing backlog of deferred maintenance and an increasing number of missed opportunities to consolidate from leases into more cost effective federally-owned space – particularly given the unique opportunity to re-shape the Federal footprint post-COVID. Meanwhile, Government-wide, agencies continue to pay rent to the GSA FBF, but do not receive the commercially equivalent space and services that they pay for in accordance with the GSA statute that governs rent-setting, particularly in terms of capital reinvestment. Table 4-3, Federal Buildings Fund 2009 to 2023, shows 15 years of budget estimates of GSA rental collections (President's Budget Revenue Estimate) against the NOA enacted in the final appropriations process. The chart tells the story of years of rental payments being withheld from spending, thus creating an offset that allowed a reprioritization of spending away from the original purpose of the collections. Since 2011, the negative enacted net budget authority for the FBF for all years except one shows the annual appropriations process has gained $11.8 billion at the expense of the GSA Federal building inventory.

The Budget prioritizes FBF spending of collections, and provides the GSA with additional funding above the anticipated level of rental collections to make progress on the backlog of repairs and fund critical construction priorities. The Administration looks forward to working with the Congress to assure that the rental payments made to the FBF are prioritized for investment occupied by the agencies that paid them.

Funding for the Indian Health Service in the Department of Health and Human Services

The 2024 Budget proposes increased funding for the Department of Health and Human Services' Indian Health Service (IHS). Building on the enactment of an advance appropriation, the Budget requests additional discretionary funding for 2024 for the IHS Services and Facilities accounts. Contract Support Costs and Payments for Tribal Leases are requested as mandatory beginning in 2024. Starting in 2025, the proposal moves all of IHS out of the annual appropriations process and provides dedicated funding through multi-year authorizing legislation. For 2024, the Budget requests $9.4 billion in discretionary and mandatory funding across the IHS accounts. The Administration's base discretionary request is reduced by that amount inflated into the 10-year window to account for the shift to the mandatory side of the Budget. Overall, the Budget proposes to increase amounts for IHS annually for total funding of $288 billion with a net cost of $192 billion over the 10-year window. This proposal is presented as a part of the Administration's commitment to provide stable funding for tribal healthcare needs.

Accrual Accounting for Department of Defense Retiree Healthcare Benefits

The 2024 Budget proposes to expand accrual financing to include all DOD retiree healthcare costs, paying for this on the discretionary side of the Budget, and to move current benefits out of the discretionary budget and over to the mandatory, or direct spending, side of the Budget. Currently, healthcare for Medicare eligible military retirees and their families is funded through the Medicare-Eligible Retiree Healthcare Fund (MERHCF) via an accrual mechanism, while healthcare for non-Medicare eligible retirees and their family members is financed through discretionary annual Defense Health Program appropriations. Under this proposal, medical care funding for non-Medicare eligible retirees and their family members would be funded in the same way as medical care is funded for Medicare eligible retirees, by expanding the current MERHCF.

The current MERHCF was established by the Congress in 2001 to provide an actuarially determined, mandatory fund for military Medicare-eligible retiree healthcare. It covers Medicare-eligible DOD beneficiaries, such as military retirees, retiree family members, and 100 percent disabled retirees and survivors. The MERHCF is funded through three sources:

1. A "normal cost" contribution (percentage of basic pay) for current members, paid from the discretionary Military Personnel Accounts, based on end-strength and covering the accruing costs of future benefits;

2. A Treasury payment for the original unfunded liability, covering the costs for benefits previously earned but not previously funded, and;

3. Accrual fund investment earnings.

Under the Administration's proposal, the MERHCF would be expanded to include the costs of non-Medicare eligible military retirees. The expanded fund would also include other uniformed services (Public Health Service, Coast Guard, and NOAA Corps).

This proposal changes only the funding mechanism to recognize the full, accruing costs of military retiree healthcare benefits and does not change the benefits, or the cost of them, in any way. However, the additional accrued costs (or savings) of any change in benefits would

Table 4–4. PAYGO SCORING: EXPANDING ACCRUAL ACCOUNTING FOR DOD RETIREE HEALTHCARE BENEFITS
(Outlays in millions of dollars)

	2024	2025	2026	2027	2028	2029	2030	2031	2032	2033	10 -year Total
Discretionary Effects:											
DOD projected accrual contributions under proposal	....	11,163	11,638	12,168	12,726	13,336	13,975	14,644	15,346	16,081	121,077
Reduce cost of current law retiree health benefits for Non-MERHCF population	....	−12,540	−12,913	−13,317	−13,703	−14,093	−14,510	−14,969	−15,462	−16,007	−127,514
DOD Discretionary Savings/Cost[1]:	....	−1,377	−1,275	−1,150	−977	−757	−535	−324	−117	74	−6,438
Intragovernmental Effects:											
Treasury UFL[2] Contributions paid from General Fund to expanded MERHCF (mandatory)	....	13,402	13,804	14,218	14,644	15,083	15,536	16,002	16,482	16,977	136,148
Treasury UFL Contributions received in expanded MERHCF (mandatory)	....	−13,402	−13,804	−14,218	−14,644	−15,083	−15,536	−16,002	−16,482	−16,977	−136,148
Interest earnings paid to MERHCF from General Fund under proposal (net interest)	....	−723	−741	−5	798	595	787	1,933	2,302	2,716	7,662
Interest earnings received in MERCHF under proposal (net interest)	....	723	741	5	−798	−595	−787	−1,933	−2,302	−2,716	−7,662
Net Effects:											
Receipt of DOD accrual contributions into the MERHCF under proposal (mandatory)	....	−11,163	−11,638	−12,168	−12,726	−13,336	−13,975	−14,644	−15,346	−16,081	−121,077
Cost of retiree health benefits for Non-MERHCF population under proposal (mandatory)	....	12,540	12,913	13,317	13,703	14,093	14,510	14,969	15,462	16,007	127,514
Proposed PAYGO Effects:	....	1,377	1,275	1,149	977	757	535	325	116	−74	6,437

[1] Budget authority and outlays are equivalent amounts. The proposed DOD discretionary Five Year Defense Program, which is reflected in the 2024 Budget, inlcudes this proposal with budget effects starting in 2025.
[2] Unfunded liability

now be reflected in DOD's yearly discretionary contributions. Currently, DOD requests yearly appropriations for the cost of healthcare for eligible retirees. Under this proposal, DOD would request the cost of accruing future benefits, which would be paid into the expanded fund and the cost of healthcare would be funded on the mandatory side of the Budget, roughly doubling the current mandatory spending on DOD retiree medical care.

Also on the mandatory side of the Budget, the estimated $278 billion unfunded liability (UFL), which represents the funding required to pay the costs of all benefits already earned but not funded, would be amortized through payments from the Treasury into the expanded Fund over 15 to 30 years, determined annually by the DOD Board of Actuaries.

The proposal would shift the budget authority and outlays for current healthcare from the discretionary side to the mandatory side, increasing mandatory outlays by the amount of the benefits (paid to providers) less any collections of accrual payments made by DOD. The proposal would not be implemented until 2025. The benefit payments are expected to slightly exceed the accrual collections over the 10-year Budget window, so there would be a net increase in mandatory spending, which would be scored as a PAYGO savings of the legislation, shown in the Budget as $6.4 billion over 10 years, per Table 4-4.

Successive administrations have been supportive of accrual funding for long-term government liabilities. Accrual funding mechanisms are currently in place for, among other programs, Federal civilian and military retirement and military healthcare for Medicare-eligible retirees. This method provides funding transparency and requires agencies to immediately reflect any costs of benefit changes.

Submission Date of the President's Budget

According to the Congressional Budget and Impoundment Control Act of 1974 (Public Law 93-344), the President is required to submit a Budget for the following fiscal year no later than the first Monday in February. That date assumed a "regular order" budget formulation process, where annual appropriations bills are enacted before the start of the fiscal year, on October 1. In effect, the Congressional Budget Act envisioned a process in which the Executive Branch developed its budget request for the following year only after funding levels for the current year were established.

In practice, however, the Congress rarely enacts all appropriations before the start of the next fiscal year. Final appropriations action occurs most frequently at the end of calendar year, and often carries with it large authorizations and complex changes to a range of Government programs.

This makes it difficult for an administration to account for current year funding and policy in the next year's President's Budget and still meet the statutory deadline.

It is to the benefit of both policymakers and the public to better align the release of the President's Budget with the actual enactment of annual appropriations, as was intended by the Congressional Budget Act. The benefits of doing so include:

- Ensuring that the Congress and the public have the most recent information on the trajectory of Government spending;

- Giving administrations sufficient time to make well-informed decisions relative to the most recently enacted funding bills; and,

- Providing the Congress with the most useful and actionable information regarding Presidential priorities at the start of the annual budget process.

For these reasons, the Administration will continue to prioritize providing to the Congress and the public useful and actionable information that incorporates the most recent funding levels and policy decisions, whenever possible. The Administration looks forward to working with the Congress to ensure that the annual budget and appropriations processes better align to the vision laid out in the Congressional Budget Act.

5. FEDERAL INVESTMENT

Federal investment is the portion of Federal spending of taxpayer money intended to yield long-term benefits for the economy and the Nation. This spending promises greater benefits than if that money had been allocated in the private sector. It promotes improved efficiency within Federal agencies, as well as growth in the national economy by increasing the overall stock of capital. Investment spending can take the form of direct Federal spending or grants to State, local, tribal and territorial governments.[1] It can be designated for physical capital—a tangible asset or the improvement of that asset—that increases production over a period of years or increases value to the Government. It can also be used for research and development, education, or training, all of which are intangible, but can still increase income in the future or provide other long-term benefits.

Most presentations in the *Analytical Perspectives* volume combine investment spending with spending intended for current use. In contrast, this chapter focuses solely on Federal and federally financed investment, providing a comprehensive picture of Federal spending for physical capital, research and development, and education and training. Because the analysis in this chapter excludes spending for non-investment activities, it gives only a partial picture of Federal support for specific national needs, such as defense.

Total Federal investment spending was $1,178 billion in 2022. It is expected to decrease by 28.7 percent in 2023 to $840 billion. The Budget proposes a 2.6 percent increase from 2023 for a total of $862 billion in 2024.

---

[1] For more information on Federal grants to State and local governments see Chapter 8, "Aid to State and Local Governments," in this volume.

DESCRIPTION OF FEDERAL INVESTMENT

The Budget uses a relatively broad definition of investment. It defines Federal investment as encompassing spending for research, development, education, and training as well as physical assets such as land, structures, infrastructure, and major equipment. It also includes spending regardless of the ultimate ownership of the resulting asset or the purpose it serves. For the purposes of this definition, however, Federal investment does not include "social investment," meaning investments in healthcare or social services programs where it is difficult to separate out the degree to which the spending provides current versus future benefits. The distinction between investment spending and current outlays is a matter of judgment, but the definition used for the purposes of this analysis has remained consistent over time and is useful for historical comparisons.[2]

Investment in physical assets can be for the construction or improvement of buildings, structures, and infrastructure, including the development or acquisition of major equipment. The broader research and development category includes spending on the facilities in which these activities occur and major equipment for the conduct of research and development, as well as spending for basic and applied research, and experimental development.[3] Investment in education and training includes vocational rehabilitation, programs for veterans, funding for school systems and higher education, and agricultural extension services. This category excludes training for military personnel or other individuals in Government service.

The Budget further classifies investments as either grants to State, local, tribal and territorial governments (e.g., for highways or education) or "direct Federal programs." The "direct Federal" category consists primarily of spending for assets owned by the Federal Government, such as weapons systems and buildings, but also includes grants to private organizations and individuals for investment, such as capital grants to Amtrak, Pell Grants, and higher education loans to individuals. For grants made to State, local, tribal and territorial governments, it is the recipient jurisdiction, not the Federal Government, that ultimately determines whether the money is used to finance investment or for current use. This analysis classifies outlays based on the category in which the recipient jurisdiction is expected to spend a majority of the money. General purpose fiscal assistance is classified as current spending, although in practice, some may be spent by recipient jurisdictions on investment.

Additionally, in this analysis, Federal investment includes credit programs that are for investment purposes. When direct loans and loan guarantees are used to fund investment, the subsidy value is included as investment. The subsidies are classified according to their program purpose, such as construction, or education and training.

This discussion presents spending for gross investment, without adjusting for depreciation.

Composition of Federal Investment Outlays

Major Federal Investment

The composition of major Federal investment outlays is summarized in Table 5–1. The categories include major public physical investment, the conduct of research and

---

[2] Historical figures on investment outlays beginning in 1940 may be found in the Budget's *Historical Tables*. The *Historical Tables* are available at https://www.whitehouse.gov/omb/historical-tables/.

[3] A more thorough discussion of research and development funding may be found in Chapter 6, "Research and Development," in this volume.

development, and the conduct of education and training. Total major Federal investment outlays were $1,179 billion in 2022. They are estimated to decrease by 29.1 percent to $836 billion in 2023, and increase by 2.3 percent to $855 billion in 2024. For 2022 through 2024, defense investment outlays comprise about one-third of total major Federal investment while non-defense investment comprises around two-thirds. In 2023, defense investment outlays are expected to increase by $20.7 billion, or 8.0 percent, while non-defense investment outlays are expected to decrease by $363 billion, or 39.5 percent. In 2024, the Budget projects a defense investment increase of $46 billion, or 16.3 percent, over 2023 and a decrease in non-defense investment of $27 billion, or 4.8 percent.

Physical investment:

Outlays for major public physical capital (hereafter referred to as "physical investment outlays") were $341 billion in 2022 and are estimated to increase by 13.1 percent to $386 billion in 2023. In 2024, outlays for physical investment are estimated to increase by 12.9 percent to $436 billion. Physical investment outlays are for construction and renovation, the development or purchase of major equipment, and the purchase or sale of land and structures. Around 68 percent of these outlays are for direct physical investment by the Federal Government, with the remainder being grants to State and local governments for physical investment.

Direct physical investment outlays by the Federal Government are primarily for defense. Defense outlays for physical investment are estimated to be $222 billion in 2024, $28 billion higher than in 2023. Outlays for direct physical investment for non-defense purposes are estimated to be $73 billion in 2024, an increase of 3.4 percent from 2023.

Outlays for grants to State and local governments for physical investment are estimated to be $141 billion in 2024, a 14.6 percent increase over the 2023 estimate of $123 billion. Grants for physical investment fund transportation programs, sewage treatment plants, community and regional development, public housing, and other State and tribal assistance. Much of this investment originates from funding included in the Infrastructure Investment and Jobs Act (Public Law 117-58, "IIJA"), which was signed into law on November 15, 2021. The IIJA makes an array of transformational investments in our country's infrastructure.

Conduct of research and development:

Outlays for research and development were $153 billion in 2022. Outlays are estimated to increase by 13.6 percent to $173 billion in 2023, and increase by 13.4 percent in 2024 to $197 billion. Roughly half of research and development outlays are for defense, a trend which has remained consistent over the past decade. Physical investment for research and development facilities and equipment is included in the physical investment category.

Non-defense outlays for the conduct of research and development are estimated to be $93 billion in 2024, 6.9 percent higher than 2023. Among the sources of this increase is a roughly $18 billion investment in the research, development, and manufacturing of semiconductors as well as resources to strengthen and expand STEM opportunities, catalyze regional economic growth and development, and advance U.S. global leadership in the technologies of the future, funded partially through money from the law commonly known as CHIPS and Science Act (Public Law 117-67). Additionally, the increase reflects a nearly $2 billion investment across multiple agencies to fund the Cancer Moonshot initiative.

A discussion of research and development funding can be found in Chapter 6, "Research and Development," in this volume.

Conduct of education and training:

Outlays for the conduct of education and training were $685 billion in 2022. Outlays are estimated to decrease by 59.5 percent to $271 billion in 2023, and decrease by 19.5 percent in 2024 to $223 billion.

Grants to State, local, tribal and territorial governments for this category were $92 billion in 2022. They are estimated to decrease by 6.6 percent to $86 billion in 2023, and increase by 4.8 percent to $90 billion in 2024. In 2024, grants are estimated to be slightly over one-third of total investment in education and training. This pattern of spending on grants to State, local, tribal and territorial governments for education and training is largely explained by changes in spending levels in response to the health and economic crises caused by the COVID-19 pandemic. For example, through the Education Stabilization Fund, which received nearly $166 billion in funding from the American Rescue Plan Act of 2021 (Public Law 117-2), the Department of Education outlayed roughly $35 billion in 2022. Grants for education and training from this fund are estimated to decrease to roughly $11 billion in 2023 and increase to around $15 billion in 2024.

Direct Federal education and training outlays in 2022 were $593 billion. They are estimated to decrease by 67.8 percent to be $191 billion in 2023, and decrease by a further 30.4 percent to be $133 billion in 2024. These decreases are largely explained by changes in accounting for the Federal Direct Student Loan Program. In 2022, outlays in this account totaled $473 billion, mainly due to $436 billion in upward modifications and $27 billion in upward reestimates and interest on the reestimates. There were much smaller upward modifications and reestimates in 2023: $43 billion and $8 billion, respectively, yielding total estimated outlays for 2023 of roughly $72 billion. In 2024, outlays are estimated to be $25 billion and are only associated with loan subsidies for the 2024 cohort; no modifications or reestimates for 2024 have been made.

Programs in this category primarily consist of aid for higher education through student financial assistance, loan subsidies, and veterans' education, training, and rehabilitation. This category does not include outlays for education and training of Federal civilian and military employees. Outlays for education and training that are for physical investment and for research and development are in the categories for physical investment and the conduct of research and development.

Major Federal investment outlays will comprise an estimated 12.4 percent of total Federal outlays in 2024 and 3.1 percent of the Nation's gross domestic product. Budget authority and outlays for major Federal investment by subcategory may be found in Table 5–2 at the end of this chapter.

Miscellaneous Physical Investment

In addition to the categories of major Federal investment, miscellaneous categories of investment outlays are shown at the bottom of Table 5–1.

Outlays for commodity inventories are for the purchase or sale of agricultural products pursuant to farm price support programs and other commodities. Outlays for other miscellaneous physical investment are estimated to be $6.8 billion in 2024.

Detailed Table on Investment Spending

Table 5-2 provides data on budget authority as well as outlays for major Federal investment, divided according to grants to State and local governments and direct Federal spending. Miscellaneous investment is not included in this table.

Table 5–1.   COMPOSITION OF FEDERAL INVESTMENT OUTLAYS
(In billions of dollars)

Federal Investment	Actual 2022	Estimate	
		2023	2024
Major public physical capital investment:			
Direct Federal:			
National defense	182.8	193.5	221.9
Nondefense	45.4	69.5	72.9
Subtotal, direct major public physical capital investment	228.2	263.0	294.8
Grants to State and local governments	113.0	122.8	140.8
Subtotal, major public physical capital investment	341.2	385.8	435.6
Conduct of research and development:			
National defense	76.4	86.5	103.8
Nondefense	76.1	86.7	92.7
Subtotal, conduct of research and development	152.5	173.2	196.5
Conduct of education and training:			
Grants to State and local governments	92.0	85.9	90.0
Direct Federal	592.9	191.2	133.1
Subtotal, conduct of education and training	684.9	277.1	223.1
Total, major Federal investment outlays	**1178.6**	**836.2**	**855.2**
MEMORANDUM			
Major Federal investment outlays:			
National defense	259.3	280.0	325.8
Non-defense	919.3	556.2	529.4
Total, major Federal investment outlays	1178.6	836.2	855.2
Miscellaneous physical investment:			
Commodity inventories	–3.3	–2.1	0.0
Other physical investment (direct)	2.6	5.9	6.8
Total, miscellaneous physical investment	–0.8	3.8	6.9
Total, Federal investment outlays, including miscellaneous physical investment	1177.8	840.0	862.0

Table 5–2. FEDERAL INVESTMENT BUDGET AUTHORITY AND OUTLAYS: GRANT AND DIRECT FEDERAL PROGRAMS

(In millions of dollars)

Description	Budget Authority			Outlays		
	2022 Actual	2023 Estimate	2024 Estimate	2022 Actual	2023 Estimate	2024 Estimate
GRANTS TO STATE AND LOCAL GOVERNMENTS						
Major public physical investment:						
Construction and rehabilitation:						
Transportation:						
Highways	75,972	70,913	68,018	49,701	57,803	65,288
Mass transportation	20,945	22,080	21,901	34,032	20,192	19,819
Rail transportation	16,003	16,101	17,349	2,461	3,896	5,190
Air and other transportation	12,249	12,227	12,659	6,539	8,621	8,875
Subtotal, transportation	125,169	121,321	119,927	92,733	90,512	99,172
Other construction and rehabilitation:						
Pollution control and abatement	13,496	15,982	16,104	3,329	3,676	4,789
Community and regional development	11,922	14,797	7,120	9,266	15,967	19,373
Housing assistance	6,260	6,242	14,233	4,495	6,355	7,328
Other	45,813	1,775	1,483	942	2,217	3,649
Subtotal, other construction and rehabilitation	77,491	38,796	38,940	18,032	28,215	35,139
Subtotal, construction and rehabilitation	202,660	160,117	158,867	110,765	118,727	134,311
Other physical assets	16,343	3,856	8,566	2,214	4,090	6,453
Subtotal, major public physical investment	219,003	163,973	167,433	112,979	122,817	140,764
Conduct of research and development:						
Agriculture	380	396	414	330	393	463
Other	361	344	361	52	65	69
Subtotal, conduct of research and development	741	740	775	382	458	532
Conduct of education and training:						
Elementary, secondary, and vocational education	35,929	46,780	50,087	66,745	55,129	59,486
Higher education	3,040	3,100	3,420	2,323	2,885	3,056
Research and general education aids	997	1,111	1,151	1,170	1,318	1,236
Training and employment	3,397	3,486	3,633	3,155	4,048	3,294
Social services	15,223	17,020	18,426	14,966	18,620	18,137
Agriculture	459	471	478	373	445	566
Other	3,308	3,403	3,229	3,296	3,490	4,249
Subtotal, conduct of education and training	62,353	75,371	80,424	92,028	85,935	90,024
Subtotal, grants for investment	282,097	240,084	248,632	205,389	209,210	231,320
DIRECT FEDERAL PROGRAMS						
Major public physical investment:						
Construction and rehabilitation:						
National defense:						
Military construction and family housing	13,024	17,000	14,871	9,451	10,632	14,594
Atomic energy defense activities and other	3,847	4,842	4,771	2,977	3,794	4,587
Subtotal, national defense	16,871	21,842	19,642	12,428	14,426	19,181
Nondefense:						
International affairs	1,305	1,290	1,299	941	1,227	1,425
General science, space, and technology	3,138	2,068	2,159	1,917	2,586	2,190
Water resources projects	27,726	6,228	5,267	4,856	8,761	7,799
Other natural resources and environment	3,476	4,920	3,334	1,596	2,188	3,001
Energy	33,994	7,861	5,737	3,755	5,522	7,442
Postal service	942	2,938	754	621	1,009	945
Transportation	673	684	680	119	186	318
Veterans hospitals and other health facilities	6,552	7,350	11,870	4,541	7,281	8,537
Administration of justice	2,435	1,981	2,194	1,434	3,035	2,640
GSA real property activities	7,690	1,507	12,338	1,059	2,144	2,404
Other construction	5,618	4,696	8,526	3,755	4,556	5,963
Subtotal, nondefense	93,549	41,523	54,158	24,594	38,495	42,664
Subtotal, construction and rehabilitation	110,420	63,365	73,800	37,022	52,921	61,845

Table 5–2. FEDERAL INVESTMENT BUDGET AUTHORITY AND OUTLAYS: GRANT AND DIRECT FEDERAL PROGRAMS—Continued

(In millions of dollars)

Description	Budget Authority			Outlays		
	2022 Actual	2023 Estimate	2024 Estimate	2022 Actual	2023 Estimate	2024 Estimate
Acquisition of major equipment:						
National defense:						
Department of Defense	189,705	211,500	216,650	169,241	177,809	201,346
Atomic energy defense activities	1,799	1,678	1,792	1,204	1,306	1,440
Subtotal, national defense	191,504	213,178	218,442	170,445	179,115	202,786
Nondefense:						
General science and basic research	760	594	557	459	559	545
Postal service	4,259	4,710	4,748	1,175	1,948	3,878
Air transportation	4,818	4,740	5,209	3,881	4,471	4,808
Water transportation (Coast Guard)	2,452	1,704	1,507	1,600	3,316	2,059
Other transportation (railroads)	5	5	32	4	5	24
Hospital and medical care for veterans	4,283	3,838	4,215	3,600	6,112	4,024
Federal law enforcement activities	1,793	2,971	2,741	1,372	3,441	2,878
Department of the Treasury (fiscal operations)	5,227	412	573	498	654	1,186
National Oceanic and Atmospheric Administration	1,422	1,819	1,829	966	1,492	1,900
Other	6,222	6,773	7,872	7,039	8,747	8,292
Subtotal, nondefense	31,241	27,566	29,283	20,594	30,745	29,594
Subtotal, acquisition of major equipment	222,745	240,744	247,725	191,039	209,860	232,380
Purchase or sale of land and structures:						
National defense	–32	–33	–33	–33	–30	–29
Natural resources and environment	502	508	496	333	569	650
General government	–152	–241	....	–152	–241	....
Other	168	165	188	21	–66	–56
Subtotal, purchase or sale of land and structures	486	399	651	169	232	565
Subtotal, major public physical investment	333,651	304,508	322,176	228,230	263,013	294,790
Conduct of research and development:						
National defense:						
Defense military	78,622	92,854	95,734	71,318	81,691	98,611
Atomic energy and other	5,232	5,595	5,752	5,131	4,819	5,219
Subtotal, national defense	83,854	98,449	101,486	76,449	86,510	103,830
Nondefense:						
International affairs	231	226	226	231	226	226
General science, space, and technology:						
NASA	11,659	12,226	13,149	11,443	12,162	12,706
National Science Foundation	6,532	7,438	8,641	5,989	6,595	7,835
Department of Energy	6,448	6,397	6,821	5,472	8,160	6,981
Subtotal, general science, space, and technology	24,639	26,061	28,611	22,904	26,917	27,522
Energy	6,195	6,528	7,491	2,528	4,215	5,754
Transportation:						
Department of Transportation	1,353	1,066	1,198	797	937	1,123
NASA	720	771	833	693	739	802
Other transportation	43	41	36	28	60	43
Subtotal, transportation	2,116	1,878	2,067	1,518	1,736	1,968
Health:						
National Institutes of Health	43,588	46,341	47,700	38,962	42,310	44,417
Other health	1,378	1,289	2,738	1,033	918	1,113
Subtotal, health	44,966	47,630	50,438	39,995	43,228	45,530
Agriculture	2,618	2,497	2,576	2,062	2,701	2,933
Natural resources and environment	3,118	3,368	3,596	2,656	3,118	3,428
National Institute of Standards and Technology	5,647	2,830	2,255	773	973	1,411
Hospital and medical care for veterans	1,588	1,624	1,690	1,580	1,579	1,645
All other research and development	1,794	1,685	1,765	1,441	1,576	1,729
Subtotal, nondefense	92,912	94,327	100,715	75,688	86,269	92,146

Table 5–2.   FEDERAL INVESTMENT BUDGET AUTHORITY AND OUTLAYS: GRANT AND DIRECT FEDERAL PROGRAMS—Continued

(In millions of dollars)

Description	Budget Authority			Outlays		
	2022 Actual	2023 Estimate	2024 Estimate	2022 Actual	2023 Estimate	2024 Estimate
Subtotal, conduct of research and development	176,766	192,776	202,201	152,137	172,779	195,976
Conduct of education and training:						
Elementary, secondary, and vocational education	10,495	1,733	5,241	55,258	69,487	48,877
Higher education	518,232	104,796	69,298	516,174	98,363	60,079
Research and general education aids	2,497	2,669	3,019	2,354	2,933	2,872
Training and employment	2,654	2,704	3,091	2,176	2,454	3,099
Health	2,355	2,516	2,873	2,352	2,850	3,009
Veterans education, training, and rehabilitation	15,158	9,112	8,663	12,071	11,999	11,929
General science and basic research	1,059	1,196	1,287	936	1,116	1,170
International affairs	775	790	836	760	949	898
Other	1,088	1,040	1,307	793	1,049	1,148
Subtotal, conduct of education and training	554,313	126,556	95,615	592,874	191,200	133,081
Subtotal, direct Federal investment	**1,064,730**	**623,840**	**619,992**	**973,241**	**626,992**	**623,847**
Total, Federal investment	**1,346,827**	**863,924**	**868,624**	**1,178,630**	**836,202**	**855,167**

6. RESEARCH AND DEVELOPMENT

Science, technology, research, experimentation, and innovation have been critical to America's long standing as a global leader, to our economic strength, and to shared prosperity because they allow us to expand what is possible and to solve seemingly intractable problems. Public investment in research and development (R&D) is a critical counterpart to private investment and Federal funding, in particular, is essential to ensuring that investments in new research and technologies meet our national and global opportunities and challenges. Continued broad bipartisan support for Federal investment in cutting-edge R&D will enable the United States to achieve the greatest aspirations of this century — improved health, a stable climate, increased economic opportunity, competitive industry, global security, and a robust democracy. It will ensure that the scale of our efforts matches the magnitude of today's challenges. The Administration is building on recently enacted laws—like the CHIPS and Science Act (Public Law 117-167, "CHIPS Act") and the Inflation Reduction Act of 2022 (Public Law 117-169, "IRA")—to ensure that investment in R&D results in good jobs at home, green energy solutions, and just and equitable outcomes. The Budget proposes investments that reinforce and expand our commitment to innovation and that ensure that the benefits of scientific research and new technologies reach all people and communities.

The Administration is advancing policies to ensure that the results of federally funded research are made widely available to the public to facilitate understanding, participation, and inclusive decision-making; to the broader scientific community to promote the exchange of ideas that is key to the advancement of knowledge; and to innovators and entrepreneurs in every region of the United States, who will translate the research into world-leading businesses employing American workers. In addition to public access to research results, the Administration is placing a deliberate emphasis on ensuring that research funding extends to and can be accessed by disadvantaged communities that have been historically underserved, marginalized, and adversely affected by persistent poverty and structural inequality. The Budget continues to support funding for transformative and high-reward research approaches to tackling societal challenges. And, as we seek to make our supply chains more resilient, these R&D investments will protect intellectual property developed in the United States and help create products that are made by U.S. workers.

The President's 2024 Budget proposes an historic investment in our Nation's future, including $209.7 billion for Federal R&D[1], a $8.9 billion increase over the 2023 enacted level, including approximately $18 billion for R&D in key agencies in the CHIPS Act (the Department of Energy (DOE), the National Science Foundation (NSF), and the Department of Commerce's National Institute Standards and Technology). This Federal investment addresses societal needs in areas in which the private sector does not have sufficient economic incentive to make the required investments, particularly in the basic and applied research that has been a hallmark of the American innovation enterprise. The 2024 Budget provides $101.2 billion for basic and applied research, an increase of $3.5 billion above the 2023 enacted level.

The Budget advances the Administration's focus on the innovation ecosystem itself by targeting Federal R&D investments for maximum impact on societal needs, including for breakthroughs based on the successful Defense Advanced Research Projects Agency (DARPA) model. Building on that model, the Budget proposes support for advanced research in additional areas of focus, including:

- $2.5 billion, an increase of $1 billion over the 2023 enacted level, for the Advanced Research Projects Agency for Health (ARPA-H) to drive biomedical and health breakthroughs – ranging from molecular to societal – to deliver transformative, sustainable, and equitable health solutions for everyone;

- $650 million for the Advanced Research Projects Agency-Energy in DOE, a key element of the Administration's game changing clean energy agenda; and,

- $19 million for the new Advanced Research Projects Agency-Infrastructure in the Department of Transportation to accelerate the transformative transportation goals of the Infrastructure Investment and Jobs Act (Public Law 117-58) and conduct critical research to address the 43,000 annual roadway fatalities in the United States.

The Administration also prioritizes other potentially transformative agency approaches to investing in solutions to societal challenges, such as $1.2 billion for the recently-authorized NSF Directorate for Technology, Innovation, and Partnerships, which will focus on use-inspired and translational research to give rise to new industries and create new, high-wage jobs in STEM for a broader range of Americans. The Budget also supports efforts focused on bolstering regional innovation, including $50 million in discretionary funding for the Regional Technology and Innovation Hub program at the Department of Commerce and $300 million for NSF's Regional Innovation Engines program.

---

[1] This total includes the conduct of R&D and investments in R&D facilities and equipment (see Table 6–1). Detailed definitions and discussion are available in Section II below.

INFLATION REDUCTION ACT & CHIPS AND SCIENCE ACT

The Budget complements and builds upon the one-time funding in the IRA and the CHIPS Act. For example, the IRA provided $1.55 billion to the DOE Office of Science, which augmented investments in 17 scientific user facilities/major construction projects and 12 major items of equipment, enabling a more rapid completion. Four of these major construction projects and two major items of equipment are requesting final funding in the Budget. The IRA also provided $190 million to NOAA for the procurement of high-performance computing, data processing capacity, data management, and storage assets to improve weather, ocean, and climate modeling.

To strengthen the role of the United States in semiconductor technology, the CHIPS Act provided the Department of Commerce $11 billion to support semiconductor research and development and infrastructure investments, including programs to conduct research and prototyping of advanced semiconductor technology and to strengthen semiconductor advanced test, assembly, and packaging capability. The CHIPS Act provided NSF with $200 million over five years for semiconductors and microelectronics education and workforce development activities, which will strengthen the workforce of the future to keep the United States the leader in the industries of tomorrow, including nanotechnology, clean energy, biotechnology, quantum computing, and artificial intelligence. The aforementioned are illustrative examples of R&D supported by the IRA and the CHIPS Act and are not meant to be exhaustive.

I. PRIORITIES FOR FEDERAL RESEARCH AND DEVELOPMENT

Research investments in the most promising areas for future industry, scientific discovery, and job creation are being largely addressed through multi-agency research activities coordinated through the National Science and Technology Council and other interagency forums, like the Net-Zero Game Changers Working Group and the National Biotechnology and Biomanufacturing Initiative, since some of these challenges cannot be addressed effectively by a single agency. This section highlights the Administration's multi-agency R&D priorities and the 2024 Budget's support of those priorities.

Cutting the death rate from cancer by at least half

The President has set the ambitious goal of cutting the age-adjusted death rate from cancer by at least 50 percent over the next 25 years and improving the experience of people living with cancer, their loved ones and families. The Cancer Moonshot initiative includes developing and deploying effective ways to prevent, detect, and treat cancer through new breakthroughs and ensuring existing tools reach more Americans equitably. At nearly $2 billion in the area of R&D for Cancer Moonshot-related investments, the Budget supports laboratory, clinical, public health, and environmental health research programs that span five focus areas across more than a dozen departments and agencies, including:

- $1.7 billion at the Department of Health and Human Services and a total investment of $7.8 billion for the National Cancer Institute, plus expected critical contributions from ARPA-H to help deliver on Moonshot goals;

- $94 million at the Department of Veterans Affairs (VA), which focuses on the etiology, pathogenesis, epidemiology, diagnosis, prognosis, treatment, and prevention of cancer as well as healthcare utilization, delivery of care to cancer patients, and the delivery,

efficacy and effectiveness of therapies (incl. chemotherapy, radiation, immunotherapy, gene therapy, bone marrow transplants) for the treatment of adult leukemia/lymphoma, solid tumors and cancer pain;

- $40 million at the U.S. Department of Agriculture (USDA) for the National Institute of Food Agriculture and the Agricultural Research Service;

- $47 million for the Department of Defense's Murtha Cancer Center (up from $37 million in 2023), which supports the tri-agency Applied Proteogenomics Organizational Learning and Outcomes (APOLLO) project and its related research initiatives. The funding has expanded clinical trials, established an epidemiology division, and expanded the DOD serum repository for cancer research; and,

- $5 million at the National Aeronautics and Space Administration (NASA) to pursue cancer-related research on the International Space Station National Lab.

Close the screening gap: To reduce the deficit in cancer screenings and to expand equitable access to effective early detection, the Budget supports the development of innovative approaches to screening and early detection, including more precise, less invasive, and even at-home methods. For example, the Budget invests in the Centers for Disease Control and Prevention's (CDC) National Comprehensive Cancer Control Program, including the Cancer Genomics program, to increase the number of individuals who share information on their family history of cancer with a health care provider and are appropriately referred to genetic counseling and testing. Investment at the National Cancer Institute includes a large national trial that, if successful, will identify effective blood tests for the detection of one or more cancers, providing the opportunity for additional, less-invasive tools for early detection. The Budget also drives efforts to reach more communities with effective cancer early detection with a focus on those who are currently medically underserved, including American Indians and Alaska Natives.

Understand and address environmental and toxic exposures: To better prevent and mitigate certain types of cancers, the Budget invests in a robust scientific research agenda to enable increased understanding of the impact of environmental and toxic exposures. The Environmental Protection Agency (EPA) conducts extensive assessments to evaluate chemical hazards related to cancer outcomes. The Budget contains funding for EPA to continue investments in a variety of tools for evaluating the health hazards posed by chemicals, including the Integrated Risk Information System (IRIS), Provisional Peer-Reviewed Toxicity Values Program, and Integrated Science Assessments. The Budget also continues support for EPA to implement programs to improve air toxics data, characterize potential cancer risk, and issue regulations that result in lower emissions and reduced health risk for people across America. The Budget provides $133 million increase for FDA to bolster its regulatory capacity, to modernize its oversight of food, and reduce exposure to toxic metals and chemicals in food, dietary supplements, and cosmetics. Additional investments at CDC will enhance funding for State public health laboratories for biomonitoring programs to increase their capability and capacity to assess human exposure to environmental chemicals of concern and conduct cancer cluster investigations. The Budget also provides $68 million for military and environmental exposures research. This funding level includes $46 million in the Toxic Exposures Fund to support research required under the Sergeant First Class Heath Robinson Honoring our Promise to Address Comprehensive Toxics Act of 2022 (Public Law 117-168, "PACT Act"), which stands as the most significant expansion of benefits and services for toxic exposed veterans in more than 30 years. To better understand the impact of toxic exposures, the PACT Act requires VA to conduct new studies of veterans who served in Southwest Asia during the Gulf War and analyses of post-9/11 veterans' health trends. The Budget supports the law's requirement that the Secretary of Veterans Affairs to convene a new interagency working group to develop a five-year strategic plan on toxic exposure research. At the Department of Defense, this includes a new program, PROMETHEUS, or the PROject for Military Exposures and Toxin History Evaluation in U.S. service members, which will bring together agency and private sector innovators to understand and address cancer in exposed service members—this involves the DOD Serum Repository, which contains blood samples for all service members.

Decrease the impact of preventable cancers: The Budget supports research efforts focused on fully understanding and developing additional approaches to reach people with cancer prevention tools and to decrease the impact of nutrition- and tobacco-related cancers, including through new investments in CDC's Tobacco Prevention and Control program. The Budget also expands access to cancer-prevention approaches through evidence-based public health and community health efforts to ensure these preventative tools are reaching all U.S. populations. The Budget increases investments in CDC's National Breast and Cervical Cancer Early Detection Program to enhance breast and cervical cancer screening and diagnostic services for uninsured and underinsured American women, and supports efforts to increase HPV vaccine uptake to prevent HPV-associated cancers. Under the Budget, EPA will continue work to reduce public health risk associated with radon, the leading environmental cause of lung cancer death. Through a multi-agency effort and public private partnership, EPA co-sponsored the recent publication of The National Radon Action Plan 2021-2025, which has set a goal for the Nation to prevent at least 3,500 lung cancer deaths per year. The Budget supports EPA continuing its efforts to address radon as a health equity challenge and prioritize new strategies to reduce radon risk in underserved communities, including communities of color.

Bring cutting edge research through the pipeline to patients and communities: The Budget invests in the development and deployment of new ways to prevent, detect, and treat cancer to increase survival rates. The Budget also includes $7.8 billion for the National Cancer Institute, an increase of $500 million above the 2023 enacted level, and proposes to reauthorize the 21st Century Cures Act (Public Law 114-255) Cancer Moonshot through 2026. Investments in fundamental research would support precision medicine, target effective treatments to patients, improve cancer survivorship, and speed progress on some of the deadliest and rare cancers, including childhood cancers. Of the $40 million for USDA noted above, the Budget invests $13 million in USDA's Agriculture Science Center of Excellence for Nutrition and Diet for Better Health, or ASCEND for Better Health. ASCEND will accelerate research through partnerships with Texas A&M University and six human nutrition research centers, enable research through big data and translate research through engagement with extension and community leaders.

Support patients and caregivers: To make the experience around cancer—from screening, to getting a diagnosis, to treatment, care, and surviving—easier on those living with cancer and their caregivers, the Budget supports evidence-based and scientifically-sound public health approaches, including through investments in CDC's Cancer Survivorship Resource Center. The Budget also drives improvement in the quality of cancer care and simplifies the process for patients to identify high value cancer care.

Preparing for and preventing pandemics

The COVID-19 pandemic has claimed countless lives and cost the U.S. and global economy trillions of dollars, demonstrating our vulnerability to current and future biological threats. As COVID-19 variants and other pathogens spread globally, the Federal Government must accelerate the development of scientific and other capabilities that can stop outbreaks before they become epidemics or pandemics, regardless of natural, accidental, and deliberate origin.

Preparedness and biodefense: The Budget includes discretionary investments at HHS to better prepare the U.S. for emerging biological threats, including $1 billon for the Biomedical Advanced Research and Development Authority, of which $76 million will support the Division of Research, Innovation, and Ventures. The Budget also includes $400 million in flexible discretionary resources within the Administration for Strategic Preparedness and Response to support the development of next-generation medical countermeasures, secure the domestic medical supply chain, and adapt response efforts to stay ahead of evolving biological threats. In addition, the Budget invests in CDC's capacity to respond to emerging threats, including surveillance and laboratory capacity. The Budget also includes $20 billion in mandatory funding for HHS public health agencies in support of the Administration's pandemic preparedness and biodefense priorities as outlined in the 2022 *National Biodefense Strategy and Implementation Plan for Countering Biological Threats, Enhancing Pandemic Preparedness, and Achieving Global Health Security*. The Budget builds toward a goal of making effective vaccines, diagnostics, and therapeutics available shortly after identifying a new pathogen by investing in basic and advanced R&D of medical countermeasures for high priority viral families and biological threats, including expansion and modernization of clinical trial infrastructure necessary to inform evaluation and subsequent authorizations or approvals, as well as expansion of domestic manufacturing capacity to ensure sufficient supply is available. The Budget also invests in laboratory capacity, domestic and global threat surveillance, and biosafety and security that would enable a rapid and robust response to future threats.

Strong public health system: A crucial safeguard against pandemics is a strong, resilient, public health system. The Budget supports a rapid, scalable, and equitable public health response, with investments in R&D to develop fundamental public health capabilities such as an integrated data infrastructure, evidence-based health communication strategies, and digital health technologies needed to implement high-quality virtual healthcare. For example, VA investigators continue to publish major studies examining the relative effectiveness of different vaccines, with and without boosters, the relative protection against in-fection, re-infection, and severe disease, and the durability of that protection. DOD is committing $10 million to conduct a feasibility study on accelerating antibody and vaccine development.

Tackling Climate Change

The United States and the world face a profound climate crisis, with a narrow window to avoid the most catastrophic impacts and to seize the opportunities that tackling climate change presents. Climate change impacts are intertwined with and are exacerbated by related global change issues, such as nature and biodiversity loss, pandemics, and social inequalities. These interconnections have played out in several recent extreme-weather events; for example, Hurricane Laura had disproportionate impacts on low-income and underhoused communities,

and disaster response was hindered by the COVID-19 pandemic and an extreme heat event that immediately followed. The President has directed a whole-of-Government approach to achieve net-zero climate pollution in every sector of the economy, conserve nature, increase resilience to the impacts of climate change, drive environmental justice, support actions that protect public health and build resilience in those communities most vulnerable to climate impacts, while creating good-paying jobs that provide a free and fair chance to join a union and collectively bargain.

The 2024 Budget—with a total climate innovation investment of $16.5 billion—prioritizes multi-agency R&D investments that advance the understanding of climate change, including its interactions with nature loss and human systems; necessary innovations in clean energy, climate technology, and infrastructure; the ability to evaluate responses to climate change, including climate mitigation, resilience, and climate and ecosystem services; equity and environmental justice; and, workforce capacity to develop and effectively implement mitigation and resilience solutions including for the most vulnerable Americans.

Climate science: Advancing climate science—including physical, biological, social, and economic science—improves our understanding of our Earth and its climate and the interaction of climate change with other global changes; improves Earth system modeling capabilities and our ability to feed outputs directly into derivative risk models (i.e., flood, wildfire, drought); and improves our understanding of the changes that pose the greatest risk to communities and ecosystems, and the most promising opportunities to avoid and reduce emerging risks. Global change research investments are coordinated through the U.S. Global Change Research Program. The Budget provides $2.5 billion for NASA's Earth Science program, which will enhance our understanding of Earth systems and provide information to tackle the climate crisis and mitigate natural hazards. The Budget includes $1 billion for NSF to better understand and prepare for the adverse impacts of climate change and $8 million for a new activity that will harness the advances in computing technology to understand and analyze climate-driven problems such as extreme events that require more focused multidisciplinary research. The Budget includes $24 million for advanced grid modeling research to build electricity sector capabilities to ensure the resilience of the Nation's electric grid. It will also support the Integrative Artificial Intelligence Framework for Earth System Predictability to enable automation and learning across heterogenous data, data quality validation, and prediction. For the USDA's core climate related R&D activities, including the impacts of weather and water cycle variations on soil, air, and water resources needed for agriculture production, the Budget includes $612 million. Agriculture is faced with adapting quickly to unprecedented climate changes and weather extremes with minimal interruptions in production. The Budget includes an increase of $196 million over the 2023 enacted level for climate science, clean energy and adaptation and resilience research at the Agriculture Research Service. The Budget includes $10 million for ongoing research by the U.S. Army Corps of Engineers on forecast informed reservoir operations to improve water management at some dams based on recent advances in weather and water forecasts.

Innovation in clean energy and climate technology and infrastructure: The Budget spurs invention, development, commercialization, and deployment of clean energy and climate technologies, including those to lower costs, improve performance, and achieve net-zero emissions in the power, buildings, transportation, industrial, and agricultural sectors. The Budget invests $11.3 billion in clean energy innovation, of which $4 billion is focused on net-zero game-changer priorities that will help enable the United States to meet the President's goal of cutting greenhouse gases (GHGs) by 50-52 percent in 2030 and get to net-zero emissions by no later than 2050. Prioritized game-changing innovations include net-zero power grid and electrification, industrial products and processes for a net-zero circular economy, net-zero aviation, efficient heating and cooling, and fusion energy at scale.

CHIPS Act climate priorities: In line with the CHIPS Act, the Budget supports emerging technologies to help study and mitigate climate impacts. For example, the Budget prioritizes the use-inspired research essential for the development of future generations of climate mitigation and game-changing clean energy technologies. DOE's Office of Science will be increasing investments in fusion, requesting over $1 billion to enable advancement in the potentiality of fusion as a clean baseload energy source. The program will enable greater cooperation with the private sector through milestone-based investments and four new R&D centers. The Budget includes $1.56 million for DOE's Office of Nuclear Energy, which will continue investments in fission research and development at national laboratories, universities, and with industry partners to support the existing fleet, secure and sustainable fuel cycles, and commercial deployments of zero-carbon advanced reactors. Investments at NSF will fund an Artificial Intelligence (AI) Research Institute, bringing together academia, Government, and private industry to develop user-driven, trustworthy AI that addresses climate change issues, which will improve the Nation's understanding of severe weather and ocean phenomena, save lives and property, and increase societal resilience to climate change. In addition, NSF investments will foster transition of research by beginning work that couples climate and other priority investments to related AI institutes.

Climate change adaptation and resilience: The Budget prioritizes R&D investments that advance understanding of climate adaptation and resilience solutions. For example, NSF continues to support research that contributes to providing the scientific basis to inform and enable timely decisions on adaptation and mitigation. A key focus for NSF is developing better means of assessing and responding to the impacts of global change as well as the vulnerability and resilience of both human and natural systems to those changes, particularly in highly sensitive regions such as the Arctic and Antarctic. Activities supported by the Budget include regional climate impact integration hubs, focused on climate innovation, mitigation and adaptation, and $25 million for a new program to support resilient and adaptive collaborations for habitability, leveraging research at regional hubs more broadly applicable to other science and geographic areas.

Nature-based solutions: The Budget supports programs aimed at understanding and improving the effectiveness of nature-based solutions to achieve climate goals, improve equity and create economic prosperity. The Budget continues investment at the U.S. Geological Survey to support the development of a National Nature Assessment, which will take stock of U.S. lands, waters, wildlife and the benefits they provide to our economy, health, climate, environmental justice, and national security. The Budget also invests in greenhouse gas measurement and monitoring, including the transition of relevant research capabilities to operational use and enhancement of GHG data products to better meet user needs. The Budget supports improving visualization and accessibility of GHG data from satellites and other observing platforms as part of NASA's Earth Information Center and interagency efforts to combine atmospheric-based data with activity-based "bottom up" data to enhance the accuracy and specificity of GHG emissions information. The Budget also invests in a new annual conservation data series to fill critical data gaps in USDA's understanding of conservation data as they relate to reducing GHG emissions from agriculture.

Advancing national security and technological competitiveness

U.S. leadership in new technologies is critical to ensure future economic competitiveness and national security. The Budget builds on CHIPS Act investments in R&D to lay the foundation for the future breakthroughs that will yield new jobs, new businesses, and more exports. The Budget provides for agency investments in science, technology, and innovation to strengthen our long-term global competitiveness while reducing catastrophic risks from current and emerging technologies.

Critical and emerging technologies: The Budget invests in world-leading research and innovation in critical and emerging technologies, including: trustworthy AI aligned with the Administration's Blueprint for an AI Bill of Rights, quantum information science, advanced communications technologies, microelectronics, nanotechnology, high-performance computing, biotechnology and biomanufacturing, robotics, advanced materials and manufacturing, digital assets, undersea technologies, and space technologies. The Budget provides $96 billion for Department of Defense R&D programs. This total includes funding for the development of next generation microelectronics for defense applications, support to grow the bioeconomy, and investments in defense-related quantum R&D. To continue to recruit and train a national-security focused STEM-capable workforce, the Budget supports the National Defense Education Program. The Budget also makes strong investments in the comprehensive modernization of the strategic deterrent, providing $7.2 billion for National Nuclear Security Administration

(NNSA) research programs to sustain a safe, secure, and effective nuclear deterrent; facilitate nonproliferation efforts and arms control verification; and power the U.S. Navy. Funding for NNSA will build on recent scientific successes including the achievement of fusion ignition at the DOE's National Ignition Facility. The Budget also includes R&D needed to mitigate risks associated with nuclear nonproliferation, supporting an integrated approach to strategic arms control and treaty verification in development with allies and partners. At NSF, the Budget provides $30 million to pilot a National AI Research Resource, a shared computing and data infrastructure that will provide AI researchers across scientific disciplines with computing resources and high-quality data; and includes $8 million for multidisciplinary, multi-institution research effort in digital assets focused on examining the technical and socio-technical benefits and risks of digital assets. The Budget includes efforts to understand the holistic state of global technological competition and inform the long-term policy investments that underpin economic leadership. The Budget also supports investments in the National Biotechnology and Biomanufacturing Initiative to further U.S. economic security and supply chain resilience.

Planetary Defense: In 2022, NASA demonstrated humanity's first-ever planetary defense test with the resoundingly successful Double Asteroid Redirection Test mission. The Budget makes the critical next step in America's planetary defense capabilities by providing $210 million to the Near-Earth Objector Surveyor, an infrared space telescope that will discover and characterize potentially hazardous near-Earth objects.

Innovation for Equity

Innovative funding mechanisms and programs: The Budget supports R&D program structures and policies to equip entities which have been systemically hindered from receiving their fair share of funding – including some Historically Black Colleges and Universities (HBCU), Minority Serving Institutions (MSI), Tribal colleges, community colleges, and institutions in underserved geographic regions – to successfully compete for R&D funding. Acknowledging that funds and resources are unevenly available, often exacerbating existing disparities, stunting innovation, and building distrust of the scientific system, these investments will open new doors of opportunity and significantly strengthen the Nation's ability to compete globally and achieve U.S. strategic priorities in science and technology. Through USDA, the Budget provides $370 million for agriculture research, extension, and education to minority-serving land grant universities and Tribal colleges. At NSF, the Budget includes $397 million to broaden participation of historically underrepresented groups in STEM. NSF investments also include $281 million for the Established Program to Stimulate Competitive Research (EPSCoR) to increase geographic diversity of STEM capacity and capability. The Budget positions NASA to build on lessons from ongoing evalu-

ations to identify strategies that increase HBCU/MSI participation in NASA early stage innovation research opportunities through Small Business Innovation Research, Small Business Technology Transfer, and other NASA programs.

Equitable data infrastructure and access: The Budget supports the development of data infrastructure and data access that facilitates identification of inequities across sectors at scale, especially in underserved communities that have been systematically denied a full opportunity to participate. The Budget extends the Analytics for Equity pilot at NSF, a cutting-edge collaboration vehicle that pairs interested researchers directly with Federal agencies to produce rigorous empirical evidence and research in equity-related topics aligned to agency Learning Agendas. The initiative leverages Federal data assets and aims to broaden participation from academic institutions and researchers that may not typically have opportunities to access such data or work directly with Federal agencies.

Actionable assessments and equitable measurements: Following the Presidential Memorandum on Restoring Trust in Government Through Scientific Integrity and Evidence-based Policymaking, the U.S. Government must make evidence-based decisions guided by the best available science and data. Many R&D efforts in the Budget employ evidence-based approaches to assess and evaluate Federal investments for effectiveness and impact, as part of Government-wide efforts to ensure Federal resources are equitably and broadly disseminated.

Climate equity: Improving climate resilience requires increasing the Federal Government's effective and equitable communication of environmental and climate hazard information and various types of uncertainty in an assortment of domains to the American public. Drawing upon social and behavioral science scholarship increases the likelihood that diverse subpopulations of the American public will receive the information they need in ways that enable responses consistent with individuals' overall health and wellbeing, no matter where they live or how they identify. In line with the Justice40 initiative, the Budget supports resilience and adaptation planning, including for disadvantaged communities that are historically underserved, marginalized, and adversely affected by persistent poverty, structural racism, and systemic inequality, in order to co-create resilience solutions that address their specific long-term needs and are more just, inclusive, and equitable. The Budget provides $15 million for a new NSF fellowship that would provide researchers studying disparate impacts of climate change with a broader skillset to address the interactions of science and policy in this complex area, allowing stakeholders greater knowledge and impact into the climate effects on and methods of adaptation and resilience in their communities. The Budget also includes $35 million for an expansion of energy efficiency and renewable energy capacity at one or more Historically Black College or University or Minority Serving Institution.

Cultivating STEM education, engagement, and workforce ecosystems

The Budget supports our Nation's STEM students: the instructional, institutional, and informal environments for STEM learning; and the training and recruiting of our future STEM workforce. These investments help America to achieve its strategic priorities by tearing down institutional barriers which have long stood in the way of equitable participation in STEM fields and prevented the American innovation ecosystem from achieving its full potential.

Investments in STEM education: For NASA's Office of STEM Engagement, the Budget includes $158 million, which will allow NASA to broaden participation in STEM and expand partnerships in K-12 STEM programming. The Budget includes $155 million for DOE Office of Science's Reaching a New Energy Workforce and Funding for Accelerated Inclusive Research program. For NSF's STEM Education Directorate, the Budget proposes $1,444 million to make strategic investments in fellowships, scholarships, and traineeships to produce a diverse and well-prepared workforce in STEM for the Nation. The NSF proposal also includes $8 million to build a network of regional-scale consortia, focused on developing thriving graduate student cohorts. The Budget proposes $75 million to create the National Center for Advanced Development in Education to develop cutting-edge, transformative solutions to our Nation's most pressing education challenges.

These investments provide holistic support to students and their families, invest in a strong and diverse teacher pipeline, close the funding gap for communities historically excluded from key resources, scale solutions that root out bias, discrimination, and harassment in the classroom, laboratory, and workplace, and promote accountability across the STEM ecosystem.

II. FEDERAL RESEARCH AND DEVELOPMENT DATA

R&D is the collection of efforts directed toward gaining greater knowledge or understanding and applying knowledge toward the production of useful materials, devices, and methods. R&D investments can be characterized as basic research, applied research, development, R&D equipment, or R&D facilities. The Office of Management and Budget has used those or similar categories in its collection of R&D data since 1949. Please note that R&D crosscuts in specific topical areas as mandated by law will be reported separately in forthcoming Supplements to the President's 2024 Budget. OMB also intends to initiate an Arctic research crosscut, spanning the 2022-2024 Budgets later this year.

Background on Federal R&D Funding

More than 20 Federal agencies fund R&D in the United States. The character of the R&D that these agencies fund depends on the mission of each agency and on the role of R&D in accomplishing it. Table 6-1 shows agency-by-agency spending on basic research, applied research, experimental development, and R&D equipment and facilities.

Basic research is systematic study directed toward a fuller knowledge or understanding of the fundamental aspects of phenomena and of observable facts without specific applications toward processes or products in mind. Basic research, however, may include activities with broad applications in mind.

Applied research is systematic study to gain knowledge or understanding necessary to determine the means by which a recognized and specific need may be met.

Experimental development is creative and systematic work, drawing on knowledge gained from research and practical experience, which is directed at producing new products or processes or improving existing products or processes. Like research, experimental development will result in gaining additional knowledge.

Research and development equipment includes acquisition or design and production of movable equipment, such as spectrometers, research satellites, detectors, and other instruments. At a minimum, this category includes programs devoted to the purchase or construction of R&D equipment.

Research and development facilities include the acquisition, design, and construction of, or major repairs or alterations to, all physical facilities for use in R&D activities. Facilities include land, buildings, and fixed capital equipment, regardless of whether the facilities are to be used by the Government or by a private organization, and regardless of where title to the property may rest. This category includes such fixed facilities as reactors, wind tunnels, and particle accelerators.

Table 6–1.   FEDERAL RESEARCH AND DEVELOPMENT SPENDING
(Mandatory and discretionary budget authority[1], dollar amounts in millions)

	2022 Actual	2023 Estimate[2]	2024 Proposed	Dollar Change: 2023 to 2024	Percent Change: 2023 to 2024
By Agency					
Defense[3]	78,642	92,854	95,986	3,132	3%
Health and Human Services	45,318	48,118	50,896	2,778	6%
Energy	22,562	23,218	24,220	1,002	4%
NASA	12,479	13,105	14,022	917	7%
National Science Foundation	7,126	7,992	9,320	1,328	17%
Agriculture	3,748	3,615	3,670	55	2%
Commerce	7,214	5,114	4,388	−726	−14%
Veterans Affairs	1,588	1,624	1,690	66	4%
Transportation	1,675	1,388	1,531	143	10%
Interior	1,140	1,264	1,478	214	17%
Homeland Security	830	634	625	−9	−1%
Environmental Protection Agency	527	568	614	46	8%
Education	390	349	330	−19	−5%
Smithsonian Institution	330	341	364	23	7%
Other	554	626	589	−37	−6%
TOTAL	**184,123**	**200,810**	**209,723**	**8,913**	**4%**
Basic Research					
Defense	2,681	2,972	2,519	−453	−15%
Health and Human Services	21,991	23,377	23,207	−170	−1%
Energy	6,483	6,605	7,014	409	6%
NASA	5,718	5,627	5,820	193	3%
National Science Foundation	5,649	6,150	7,068	918	15%
Agriculture	1,464	1,398	1,415	17	1%
Commerce	270	282	309	27	10%
Veterans Affairs	619	648	701	53	8%
Transportation	....	....	....	....	....
Interior	91	101	121	20	20%
Homeland Security	88	68	60	−8	−12%
Environmental Protection Agency	....	....	....	....	....
Education	34	34	37	3	....
Smithsonian Institution	290	308	331	23	7%
Other	10	5	5	0	0%
SUBTOTAL	**45,388**	**47,575**	**48,607**	**1,032**	**2%**
Applied Research					
Defense	6,928	8,102	6,237	−1,865	−23%
Health and Human Services	22,979	24,257	27,209	2,952	12%
Energy	6,462	6,685	7,155	470	7%
NASA	2,427	2,484	2,672	188	8%
National Science Foundation	883	1,288	1,573	285	22%
Agriculture	1,602	1,525	1,614	89	6%
Commerce	1,391	1,668	1,714	46	3%
Veterans Affairs	933	940	953	13	1%
Transportation	1,358	1,055	1,206	151	14%
Interior	876	967	1,132	165	17%
Homeland Security	280	147	174	27	18%
Environmental Protection Agency	408	441	477	36	8%
Education	258	223	203	−20	−9%
Smithsonian Institution	....	....	....	....	....
Other	369	374	353	−21	−6%
SUBTOTAL	**47,154**	**50,156**	**52,672**	**2,516**	**5%**
Experimental Development					
Defense	69,013	81,780	86,978	5,198	6%
Health and Human Services	47	47	58	11	23%
Energy	4,807	5,046	5,730	684	14%

Table 6–1. FEDERAL RESEARCH AND DEVELOPMENT SPENDING —Continued

(Mandatory and discretionary budget authority [1], dollar amounts in millions)

	2022 Actual	2023 Estimate [2]	2024 Proposed	Dollar Change: 2023 to 2024	Percent Change: 2023 to 2024
NASA	4,234	4,886	5,490	604	12%
National Science Foundation	....	....	....	....	....
Agriculture	381	374	412	38	10%
Commerce	5,158	2,305	1,717	−588	−26%
Veterans Affairs	36	36	36	0	0%
Transportation	277	287	283	−4	−1%
Interior	171	194	223	29	15%
Homeland Security	449	364	312	−52	−14%
Environmental Protection Agency	119	127	137	10	8%
Education	98	92	90	−2	−2%
Smithsonian Institution	....	....	....	....	....
Other	175	247	231	−16	−6%
SUBTOTAL	**84,965**	**95,785**	**101,697**	**5,912**	**6%**
Facilities and Equipment [4]					
Defense	20	....	252	252	100%
Health and Human Services	301	437	422	−15	−3%
Energy	4,810	4,882	4,321	−561	−11%
NASA	100	108	40	−68	−63%
National Science Foundation	594	554	679	125	23%
Agriculture	301	318	229	−89	−28%
Commerce	395	859	648	−211	−25%
Veterans Affairs	....	....	....	....	....
Transportation	40	46	42	−4	−9%
Interior	2	2	2	0	0%
Homeland Security	13	55	79	24	....
Environmental Protection Agency	....	....	....	....	....
Education	....	....	....	....	....
Smithsonian Institution	40	33	33	0	0%
Other	....	....	....	....	....
SUBTOTAL	**6,616**	**7,294**	**6,747**	**−547**	**−7%**

[1] This table shows funding levels for Departments or Independent agencies with more than $200 million in R&D activities in 2024.

[2] The 2023 Estimate column applies the *Budget* volume's approach of including all 2023 enacted appropriations.

[3] DOD's contribution to the overall Federal R&D budget includes DOD Research, Development, Test, and Evaluation Budget Activities 6.1 through 6.6 (Basic Research; Applied Research; Advanced Technology Development; Advanced Component Development and Prototypes; 4 System Development and Demonstation; and Management Support).

[4] The decline in Facilities & Equipment spending in 2024 is due in some cases to the completion of large construction projects and increased funding levels in the previous two years associated with the Inflation Reduction Act of 2022 (Public Law 117-169) and the Infrastructure Investment and Jobs Act (Public Law 117-58).

7. CREDIT AND INSURANCE

The Federal Government offers direct loans and loan guarantees to support a wide range of activities including home ownership, student loans, small business, farming, energy, infrastructure investment, and exports. In addition, Government-sponsored enterprises (GSEs) operate under Federal charters for the purpose of enhancing credit availability for targeted sectors. Through its insurance programs, the Federal Government insures deposits at depository institutions, guarantees private-sector defined-benefit pensions, and insures against some other risks such as flood and terrorism. These programs are also exposed to climate-related financial risks, which the private sector is increasingly taking into account in the pricing of financial products. For a discussion of climate risks faced by Federal housing loans, please see Chapter 10, "Budget Exposure to Increased Costs and Lost Revenue Due to Climate Change."

This chapter discusses the roles of these diverse programs. The first section discusses individual credit programs and GSEs. The second section reviews Federal deposit insurance, pension guarantees, disaster insurance, and insurance against terrorism and other security-related risks. The final section includes a brief analysis of the Troubled Asset Relief Program (TARP).

I. CREDIT IN VARIOUS SECTORS

Housing Credit Programs

Through its main housing credit programs, the Federal Government promotes homeownership among various groups that may face barriers to owning a home, including low- and moderate-income people, veterans, and rural residents. By expanding affordable homeownership opportunities for underserved borrowers, these programs can advance equity. In times of economic crisis, the Federal Government's role and target market can expand dramatically.

Federal Housing Administration

The Federal Housing Administration (FHA) guarantees single-family mortgages that expand access to homeownership for households who may have difficulty obtaining a conventional mortgage. In addition to traditional single-family "forward" mortgages, FHA insures "reverse" mortgages for seniors (Home Equity Conversion Mortgages, described below) and loans for the construction, rehabilitation, and refinancing of multifamily housing, hospitals, and other healthcare facilities.

FHA Single-Family Forward Mortgages

FHA has been a primary facilitator of mortgage credit for first-time and minority homebuyers, a pioneer of products such as the 30-year self-amortizing mortgage, and a vehicle to enhance credit for many low- to moderate-income households. One of the major benefits of an FHA-insured mortgage is that it provides a homeownership option for borrowers who, though they can only make a modest down payment, can show that they are credit-worthy and have sufficient income to afford the house they want to buy. For 2022 new origination volume, 84 percent of FHA purchase mortgages were obtained by first-time homebuyers and 29 percent of all FHA loans (purchase and refinance) served minority borrowers. In addition, low-income homebuyers accounted for over 40 percent of new FHA purchase loans in calendar year 2021.

FHA Home Equity Conversion Mortgages

Home Equity Conversion Mortgages (HECMs), or "reverse" mortgages, are designed to support aging in place by enabling elderly homeowners to borrow against the equity in their homes without having to make repayments during their lifetime (unless they move, refinance, or fail to meet certain requirements). A HECM is known as a "reverse" mortgage because the change in home equity over time is generally the opposite of a forward mortgage. While a traditional forward mortgage starts with a small amount of equity and builds equity with amortization of the loan, a HECM starts with a large equity cushion that declines over time as the loan accrues interest and premiums. The risk of HECMs is therefore weighted toward the end of the mortgage, while forward mortgage risk is concentrated in the first 10 years.

FHA Mutual Mortgage Insurance (MMI) Fund

FHA guarantees for forward and reverse mortgages are administered under the Mutual Mortgage Insurance (MMI) Fund. At the end of 2022, the MMI Fund had $1.28 trillion in total mortgages outstanding and a capital ratio of 11.11 percent, an increase from the 2021 level of 8.03 percent. For more information on the financial status of the MMI Fund, please see the *Annual Report to Congress Regarding the Financial Status of the FHA Mutual Mortgage Insurance Fund, Fiscal Year 2022.*[1]

FHA's new origination volume in 2022 was $256 billion for forward mortgages and $32 billion for HECMs, and the Budget projects $206 billion and $26 billion, respectively, for 2024.

---

[1] *https://www.hud.gov/sites/dfiles/Housing/documents/2022FHA AnnualRptMMIFund.pdf*

FHA Multifamily and Healthcare Guarantees

In addition to the single-family mortgage insurance provided through the MMI Fund, FHA's General Insurance and Special Risk Insurance (GISRI) loan programs continue to facilitate the construction, rehabilitation, and refinancing of multifamily housing, hospitals, and other healthcare facilities. The credit enhancement provided by FHA enables borrowers to obtain long-term, fixed-rate financing, which mitigates interest rate risk and facilitates lower monthly mortgage payments. This can improve the financial sustainability of multifamily housing and healthcare facilities, and may also translate into more affordable rents and lower healthcare costs for consumers.

GISRI's new origination loan volume for all programs in 2022 was $26 billion and the Budget projects $21 billion for 2024. The total amount of guarantees outstanding on mortgages in the FHA GISRI Fund were $169 billion at the end of 2022.

VA Housing Loan Program

The Department of Veterans Affairs (VA) assists veterans, members of the Selected Reserve, and active duty personnel in purchasing homes in recognition of their service to the Nation. The VA housing loan program effectively substitutes a Federal guarantee for the borrower's down payment, meaning more favorable lending terms for veterans. Under this program, VA does not guarantee the entire mortgage loan, but typically fully guarantees the first 25 percent of losses upon default. In fiscal year 2022, VA guaranteed a total of 410,365 new purchase home loans, providing approximately $153.2 billion in guarantees. VA also guaranteed 127,949 Interest Rate Reduction Refinance loans and veteran borrowers lowered interest rates on their home mortgages through streamlined refinancing. VA provided approximately $257 billion in guarantees for 746,091 VA loans in fiscal year 2022. That followed $447 billion in guarantees for 1,441,745 VA loans closed in fiscal year 2021.

VA, in cooperation with VA-guaranteed loan servicers, also assists borrowers through home retention options and alternatives to foreclosure. VA intervenes when needed to help veterans and servicemembers avoid foreclosure through loan modifications, special forbearances, repayment plans, and acquired loans, as well as assistance to complete compromised sales or deeds-in-lieu of foreclosure. These standard efforts helped resolve over 96 percent of defaulted VA-guaranteed loans and assisted 205,702 veterans retain homeownership or avoid foreclosure in 2022. These efforts resulted in nearly $4 billion in avoided guaranteed claim payments. VA has responded to the COVID crisis by providing special CARES Act forbearances to support otherwise-current borrowers through the pandemic, under the Coronavirus Aid, Relief, and Economic Security Act (Public Law 116-136), colloquially referred to as the CARES Act. As of September 30, 2022, 51,222 VA borrowers were participating in a special COVID-19 forbearance.

Rural Housing Service

The Rural Housing Service (RHS) at the U.S. Department of Agriculture (USDA) offers direct and guaranteed loans to help very-low- to moderate-income rural residents buy and maintain adequate, affordable housing. RHS housing loans and loan guarantees differ from other Federal housing loan programs in that they are means-tested, making them more accessible to low-income, rural residents. The single family housing guaranteed loan program is designed to provide home loan guarantees for moderate-income rural residents whose incomes are between 80 percent and 115 percent (maximum for the program) of area median income.

RHS has traditionally offered both direct and guaranteed homeownership loans. The direct single family housing loans have been historically funded at $1 billion a year, while the single family housing guaranteed loan program, authorized in 1990 at $100 million, has grown into a $30 billion loan program annually. USDA also offers direct and guaranteed multifamily housing loans, as well as housing repair loans.

Education Credit Programs

The Department of Education (ED) direct student loan program is one of the largest Federal credit programs, with $1.34 trillion in Direct Loan principal outstanding in 2022. The Federal student loan programs provide students and their families with the funds to help meet postsecondary education costs. Because funding for the loan programs is provided through mandatory budget authority, student loans are considered separately for budget purposes from other Federal student financial assistance programs (which are largely discretionary), but should be viewed as part of the overall Federal effort to expand access to higher education.

Loans for higher education were first authorized under the William D. Ford program, which was included in the Higher Education Act of 1965 (Public Law 89-329). The direct loan program was authorized by the Student Loan Reform Act of 1993 (subtitle A of title IV of Public Law 103–66). The enactment of the SAFRA Act (subtitle A of title II of Public Law 111–152) ended the guaranteed Federal Financial Education Loan program. On July 1, 2010, ED became the sole originator of Federal student loans through the Direct Loan program.

Under the current direct loan program, the Federal Government partners with over 5,500 institutions of higher education, which then disburse loan funds to students. Loans are available to students and parents of students regardless of income, and only Parent and Graduate PLUS loans include a minimal credit check. There are three types of Direct Loans: Federal Direct Subsidized Stafford Loans, Federal Direct Unsubsidized Stafford Loans, and Federal Direct PLUS Loans, each with different terms.

The Direct Loan program offers a variety of repayment options, including income-driven repayment ones for all student borrowers. Depending on the plan, monthly payments are capped at no more than 10 or 15 percent of borrower discretionary income, with any remaining balance after 20 or 25 years forgiven. In addition, borrowers working in public service professions while making 10 years of qualifying payments are eligible for Public Service Loan Forgiveness.

The Department of Education also operates the Historically Black College and Universities (HBCU) Capital Financing Program. Since fiscal year 1996, the Program has provided HBCUs with access to low-cost capital financing for the repair, renovation, and, in exceptional circumstances, construction or acquisition of educational facilities, instructional equipment, research instrumentation, and physical infrastructure.

Small Business and Farm Credit Programs

The Government offers direct loans and loan guarantees to small businesses and farmers, who may have difficulty obtaining credit elsewhere. It also provides guarantees of debt issued by certain investment funds that invest in small businesses. Two GSEs, the Farm Credit System and the Federal Agricultural Mortgage Corporation, increase liquidity in the agricultural lending market.

Small Business Administration

The Small Business Administration (SBA) ensures that small businesses across the Nation have the tools and resources needed to start, grow, and recover their business. SBA's lending programs complement credit markets by offering creditworthy small businesses access to affordable credit through private lenders when they cannot otherwise obtain financing on reasonable terms or conditions.

In 2022, SBA provided $25.7 billion in loan guarantees to assist small business owners with access to affordable capital through its largest program, the 7(a) General Business Loan Guarantee program. This program provides access to financing for general business operations, such as operating and capital expenses. In addition, through the 504 Certified Development Company (CDC) and Refinance Programs, SBA supported $9.2 billion in guaranteed loans for fixed-asset financing and provided the opportunity for small businesses to refinance existing 504 CDC loans. These programs enable small businesses to secure financing for assets such as machinery and equipment, construction, and commercial real estate, and to free up resources for expansion. The Small Business Investment Company (SBIC) Program also supports privately-owned and -operated venture capital investment firms that invest in small businesses. In 2022, SBA supported $7.9 billion in SBIC venture capital investments. In addition to these guaranteed lending programs, the 7(m) Direct Microloan program supports the smallest of businesses, startups, and underserved entrepreneurs through loans of up to $50,000 made by non-profit intermediaries. In 2022, SBA facilitated a record $82.6 million in microlending.

Community Development Financial Institutions

Since its creation in 1994, the Department of the Treasury's Community Development Financial Institutions (CDFI) Fund has, through different grant, loan, and tax credit programs, worked to expand the availability of credit, investment capital, and financial services for underserved people and communities by supporting the growth and capacity of a national network of CDFIs, investors, and financial service providers. Today, there are more than 1,380 Certified CDFIs nationwide, including a variety of loan funds, community development banks, credit unions, and venture capital funds. CDFI certification also enables some non-depository financial institutions to apply for financing programs offered by certain Federal Home Loan Banks.

Unlike other CDFI Fund programs, the CDFI Bond Guarantee Program (BGP), enacted through the Small Business Jobs Act of 2010, does not offer grants, but is instead exclusively a Federal credit program. The BGP was designed to provide CDFIs greater access to low-cost, long-term, fixed-rate capital.

Under the BGP, the Department of the Treasury (Treasury) provides a 100 percent guarantee on long-term bonds of at least $100 million issued to qualified CDFIs, with a maximum maturity of 30 years. To date, Treasury has issued nearly $2.2 billion in bond guarantee commitments to 27 CDFIs, over $1.4 billion of which has been disbursed to help finance affordable housing, charter schools, commercial real estate, community healthcare facilities, and other eligible uses in 32 States and the District of Columbia.

Farm Service Agency

Farm operating loans were first offered in 1937 by the newly created Farm Security Administration (FSA) to assist family farmers who were unable to obtain credit from a commercial source to buy equipment, livestock, or seed. Farm ownership loans were authorized in 1961 to provide family farmers with financial assistance to purchase farmland. Presently, FSA assists low-income family farmers in starting and maintaining viable farming operations. Emphasis is placed on aiding beginning and socially disadvantaged farmers. Legislation mandates that a portion of appropriated funds are set aside for exclusive use by those underserved groups.

FSA offers operating loans and ownership loans, both of which may be either direct or guaranteed loans. Operating loans provide credit to farmers and ranchers for annual production expenses and purchases of livestock, machinery, and equipment, while farm ownership loans assist producers in acquiring and developing their farming or ranching operations. As a condition of eligibility for direct loans, borrowers must be unable to obtain private credit at reasonable rates and terms. As FSA is the "lender of first opportunity," default rates on FSA direct loans are generally higher than those on private-sector loans. FSA-guaranteed farm loans are made to more creditworthy borrowers who have access to private credit markets. Because the private loan originators must, in most situations, retain 10 percent of the risk, they exercise care in examining the repayment ability of borrowers. The subsidy rates for the direct programs fluctuate largely because of changes in the interest component of the subsidy rate.

In 2022, there were more than 24,000 direct or guaranteed loan obligations totaling over $5.8 billion. The entire portfolio of outstanding debt as of September 30, 2022 totaled $33 billion, serving 115,000 farmers and ranchers. In 2022, the amount of lending declined in both dollar and volume terms, down 13 and 16 percent, respectively. Lending in dollar terms for real estate purchases decreased 13 percent for both direct and guaranteed loans. Operating loan obligations also fell in dollar terms among direct (decreasing 15 percent) and guaranteed (decreasing 8 percent) loans. The decline in 2022 obligations was not unexpected, particularly for operating loans that provide working capital to farmers and ranchers. Rising commodity prices and Farm Program payments have contributed to an increase in farm income. Once current supply chain challenges ease, there may be pressure on farm income if commodity prices decline. This cyclicality underscores the importance of FSA's Farm Loan Programs as a safety net.

A beginning farmer is an individual or entity who: has operated a farm for not more than 10 years; substantially participates in farm operation; and, for farm ownership loans, the applicant cannot own a farm larger than 30 percent of the average size farm in the county at time of application. If the applicant is an entity, all entity members must be related by blood or marriage, and all members must be eligible beginning farmers. Beginning farmers received 53 percent of direct and guaranteed loans in 2022. Direct and guaranteed loan programs provided assistance totaling $3.1 billion to nearly 14,300 beginning farmers. Additionally in 2022, loans for socially disadvantaged farmers totaled $1.2 billion to nearly 6,000 borrowers, of which $913 million was in the farm ownership program and $321 million in the farm operating program.

The FSA Microloan program increases overall direct and guaranteed lending to small niche producers and minorities. This program dramatically simplifies application procedures for small loans and implements more flexible eligibility and experience requirements. Demand for the micro-loan program continues to grow while delinquencies and defaults remain at or below those of the regular FSA operating loan program.

Energy and Infrastructure Credit Programs

The Department of Energy (DOE) administers four credit programs: Title XVII Innovative Technology Loan Guarantee Program (Title XVII), the Advanced Technology Vehicle Manufacturing (ATVM) Loan Program, the Tribal Energy Loan Guarantee Program, and the Carbon Dioxide Transportation Infrastructure Finance and Innovation Program. Section 1703 of title XVII of the Energy Policy Act of 2005 (Public Law 109–58), as amended, authorizes DOE to issue loan guarantees for clean energy projects that employ innovative technologies or are supported by State Energy Financing Institutions to reduce, avoid, or sequester air pollutants or man-made greenhouse gases. To date, DOE has issued four loan guarantees totaling over $12 billion to support the construction of two new commercial nuclear power reactors and a clean hydrogen production and storage project. DOE has one active conditional commitment totaling $1 billion to support an advanced fossil energy project. DOE is actively working

with applicants proceeding to conditional commitment and financial close to utilize the $3.5 billion in appropriated credit subsidy and $77 billion in available loan guarantee authority currently available.

The American Recovery and Reinvestment Act of 2009 (Public Law 111–5) amended section 1705 of Title XVII and appropriated credit subsidy to support loan guarantees on a temporary basis for commercial or advanced renewable energy systems, electric power transmission systems, and leading-edge biofuel projects. Authority for the temporary program to extend new loans expired September 30, 2011. $16 billion in loans and loan guarantees was disbursed via 24 loan guarantees issued prior to the program's expiration.

Public Law 117-169, colloquially referred to as The Inflation Reduction Act of 2022 (Public Law 117-169) further amended section 1706 to the Title XVII program's authorizing statute and appropriated $4.8 billion in credit subsidy to support loan guarantees for projects that retool, repower, repurpose, or replace energy infrastructure and avoid, reduce, or sequester air pollutants or man-made greenhouse gases. Appropriated authority for the section 1706 program expires September 30, 2026. DOE is actively working to establish this new program and anticipates working with applicants toward conditional commitment and financial close starting in 2023.

Section 136 of the Energy Independence and Security Act of 2007 (Public Law 110–140) authorizes DOE to issue loans to support the development of advanced technology vehicles and qualifying components. In 2009, the Congress appropriated $7.5 billion in credit subsidy to support a maximum of $25 billion in loans under ATVM. From 2009 to 2011, DOE issued five loans totaling over $8 billion to support the manufacturing of advanced technology vehicles. Since 2021, DOE has issued five conditional commitments totaling over $5.6 billion, of which two loans have reach financial close. DOE has over $5 billion in credit subsidy balances with no loan limitation and is actively working with applicants proceeding to conditional commitment and financial close.

Title XXVI of the Energy Policy Act of 1992, as amended (Public Law 102-486) authorizes DOE to guarantee up to $20 billion in loans to Indian Tribes for energy development. The Congress has appropriated over $80 million in credit subsidy, cumulatively, to support tribal energy development. DOE issued a revised solicitation in 2022 and is actively working with applicants proceeding to conditional commitment and financial close.

Section 40304 of the Infrastructure Investment and Jobs Act (Public Law 117-58, "BIL") amended Title IX of the Energy Policy Act of 2005 by authorizing DOE to issue loans, loan guarantees, and grants to support the development of carbon dioxide transportation infrastructure (e.g., pipelines). The law provided $3 million for program start-up costs in 2022 and an advance appropriation of $2.1 billion in 2023 budget authority for the cost of loans, loan guarantees, and grants to eligible projects. DOE is actively working to establish the program.

Electric and Telecommunications Loans

Rural Utilities Service (RUS) programs of the USDA provide grants and loans to support the distribution of rural electrification, telecommunications, distance learning, and broadband infrastructure systems.

In 2022, RUS delivered $5.2 billion in direct electrification loans (including $748.3 million in Federal Financing Bank (FFB) Electric Loans, $750 million in electric underwriting, and $71.8 million rural energy savings loans), $106.3 million in direct and FFB telecommunications loans, and $939.9 million in Reconnect broadband loans. RUS also helped rural Texas electric utilities recover from the aftermath of the February 2021 winter storm. As a result, RUS made an operating loan to a local cooperative for $25 million, which also unlocked an additional $2.5 million in energy efficiency initiatives.

USDA Rural Infrastructure and Business Development Programs

USDA, through a variety of Rural Development (RD) programs, provides grants, direct loans, and loan guarantees to communities for constructing facilities such as healthcare clinics, police stations, and water systems, as well as to assist rural businesses and cooperatives in creating new community infrastructure (e.g., educational and healthcare networks) and to diversify the rural economy and employment opportunities. In 2022, RD provided $1.3 billion in Community Facility (CF) direct loans, which are for communities of 20,000 or less. The CF programs have the flexibility to finance more than 100 separate types of essential community infrastructure that ultimately improve access to healthcare, education, public safety and other critical facilities and services. RD also provided $1.3 billion in water and wastewater (W&W) direct loans, and guaranteed $1.7 billion in rural business loans, which will help create and save jobs in rural America. Since 2020, CF and W&W loan guarantees have been for communities of 50,000 or less.

Water Infrastructure

The Environmental Protection Agency's Water Infrastructure Finance and Innovation Act (Public Law WIFIA) program accelerates investment in the Nation's water infrastructure by providing long-term, low-cost supplemental loans for projects of regional or national significance. To date, WIFIA has closed 97 loans totaling $17 billion in credit assistance to help finance over $36 billion for water infrastructure projects and create 122,000 jobs. The selected projects demonstrate the broad range of project types that the WIFIA program can finance, including wastewater, drinking water, stormwater, and water reuse projects.

In addition, the WIFIA Program, authorized by the Water Resources Reform and Development Act of 2014 (Public Law 113-121), as amended, allows the U.S. Army Corps of Engineers to issue loans and loan guarantees for eligible non-Federal water resources projects. The Consolidated Appropriations Act, 2021 (Public Law 116-260) provided $12 million for the cost of loans and loan guarantees for dam safety projects at non-Federal dams identified in the National Inventory of Dams. The BIL provided an additional $64 million for this purpose. The Corps of Engineers is actively working to establish this new Federal credit program, including developing implementing regulations.

Transportation Infrastructure

The Department of Transportation (DOT) administers credit programs that fund critical transportation infrastructure projects, often using innovative financing methods. The two predominant programs are the Transportation Infrastructure Finance and Innovation Act (TIFIA) and the Railroad Rehabilitation and Improvement Financing (RRIF) loan programs. DOT's Build America Bureau administers these programs, as well as Private Activity Bonds, all under one roof. The Bureau serves as the single point of contact for States, municipalities, and other project sponsors looking to utilize Federal transportation innovative financing expertise, apply for Federal transportation credit programs, and explore ways to access private capital in public-private partnerships. The Budget reflects the TIFIA and RRIF programs' accounts in the Office of the Secretary, where the Bureau is housed.

Transportation Infrastructure Finance and Innovation Act (TIFIA)

Established by the Transportation Equity Act for the 21st Century (Public Law 105-178, "TEA-21") in 1998, the TIFIA program is designed to fill market gaps and leverage substantial private co-investment by providing supplemental and subordinate capital to transportation infrastructure projects. Through TIFIA, DOT provides three types of Federal credit assistance to highway, transit, rail, intermodal, airport, and transit-oriented development projects: direct loans, loan guarantees, and lines of credit. TIFIA can help advance qualified, large-scale projects that otherwise might be delayed or deferred because of size, complexity, or uncertainty over the timing of revenues. The Congress authorized $250 million for TIFIA in 2023. The BIL expanded incentives and support for rural transportation projects seeking financing from TIFIA. DOT launched the "TIFIA 49" initiative in 2023, which allows borrowing from TIFIA up to 49 percent of eligible project costs for transit and transit-oriented development projects.

Railroad Rehabilitation and Improvement Financing (RRIF)

Also established by TEA–21 in 1998, the RRIF program provides loans or loan guarantees with an interest rate equal to the Treasury rate for similar-term securities for terms up to 75 years. The RRIF program allows borrowers to pay the subsidy cost of a loan (a "Credit Risk Premium") using non-Federal sources, thereby allowing the program to operate without Federal subsidy appropriations. The RRIF program assists projects that further improve rail safety, promote environmental efficiency, support economic development, or increase the capacity of the national rail network. The RRIF program is a critical tool for small 'short line' railroads that routinely maintain large acquired assets with limited revenue. The BIL expanded eligible RRIF lending to include landside infrastructure at sea ports serviced by the national freight rail network.

International Credit Programs

Through 2022, seven unique Federal agencies provide or have existing portfolios of direct loans, loan guarantees, and insurance to a variety of private and sovereign borrowers: USDA, the Department of Defense, the Department of State, the Department of the Treasury, the U.S. Agency for International Development, the Export-Import Bank (ExIm), and the U.S. International Development Finance Corporation (DFC). These programs are intended to level the playing field for U.S. exporters, deliver robust support for U.S. goods and services, stabilize international financial markets, enhance security, and promote sustainable development.

Federal export credit programs provide financing support for American businesses involved in international trade and to counteract unfair foreign trade financing. Various foreign governments provide their exporters official financing assistance, usually through export credit agencies. The U.S. Government has worked since the 1970s to constrain official credit support through a multilateral agreement in the Organization for Economic Cooperation and Development (OECD). This agreement has established standards for Government-backed financing of exports. In addition to ongoing work in keeping these OECD standards up-to-date, the U.S. Government established the International Working Group on Export Credits to set up a new framework that will include China and other non-OECD countries, which were not previously subject to export credit standards. The process of establishing these new standards, which is not yet complete, advances a congressional mandate to reduce subsidized export financing programs.

Export Support Programs

When the private sector is unable or unwilling to provide financing, ExIm, the U.S. Export Credit Agency, fills the gap for American businesses by equipping them with the financing support necessary to level the playing field against foreign competitors. ExIm support includes direct loans and loan guarantees for creditworthy foreign buyers to help secure export sales from U.S. exporters. It also includes working capital guarantees and export credit insurance to help U.S. exporters secure financing for overseas sales. USDA's Export Credit Guarantee Programs (also known as GSM programs) similarly help to level the playing field. Like programs of other agricultural exporting nations, GSM programs guarantee payment from countries and entities that want to import U.S. agricultural products but cannot easily obtain credit. The GSM 102 program provides guarantees for credit extended with short-term repayment terms not to exceed 18 months.

Exchange Stabilization Fund

Consistent with U.S. obligations in the International Monetary Fund (IMF) regarding global financial stability, the Exchange Stabilization Fund (ESF) managed by the Department of the Treasury may provide loans or credits to a foreign entity or government of a foreign country. A loan or credit may not be made for more than six months in any 12-month period unless the President gives the Congress a written statement that unique or emergency circumstances require that the loan or credit be for more than six months. The CARES Act established within the ESF an Economic Stabilization Program with temporary authority for lending and other eligible investments, which included programs or facilities established by the Board of Governors of the Federal Reserve System pursuant to section 13(3) of the Federal Reserve Act. The Consolidated Appropriations Act, 2021 rescinded this authority, though loans and investments already made remain active until obligations are liquidated.

Sovereign Lending and Guarantees

The U.S. Government can extend short-to-medium-term loan guarantees that cover potential losses that might be incurred by lenders if a country defaults on its borrowings; for example, the U.S. may guarantee another country's sovereign bond issuance. The purpose of this tool is to provide the Nation's sovereign international partners access to necessary, urgent, and relatively affordable financing during temporary periods of strain when they cannot access such financing in international financial markets, and to support critical reforms that will enhance long-term fiscal sustainability, often in concert with support from international financial institutions such as the IMF. The goal of sovereign loan guarantees is to help lay the economic groundwork for the Nation's international partners to graduate to an unenhanced bond issuance in the international capital markets. For example, as part of the U.S. response to fiscal crises, the U.S. Government has extended sovereign loan guarantees to Jordan and Iraq to enhance their access to capital markets while promoting economic policy adjustment.

Development Programs

Credit is an important tool in U.S. bilateral assistance to promote sustainable development. The DFC provides loans, guarantees, and other investment tools such as equity and political risk insurance to facilitate and incentivize private-sector investment in emerging markets that will have positive developmental impact, and meet national security objectives.

The Government-Sponsored Enterprises (GSEs)

Fannie Mae and Freddie Mac

The Federal National Mortgage Association, or Fannie Mae, created in 1938, and the Federal Home Loan Mortgage Corporation, or Freddie Mac, created in 1970, were established to support the stability and liquidity of a secondary market for residential mortgage loans.

Fannie Mae's and Freddie Mac's public missions were later broadened to promote affordable housing. The Federal Home Loan Bank (FHLB) System, created in 1932, is comprised of eleven individual banks with shared liabilities. Together they lend money to financial institutions, mainly banks and thrifts, that are involved in mortgage financing to varying degrees, and they also finance some mortgages using their own funds. The mission of the FHLB System is broadly defined as promoting housing finance, and the System also has specific requirements to support affordable housing.

Together these three GSEs currently are involved, in one form or another, with approximately half of residential mortgages outstanding in the U.S. today.

History of the Conservatorship of Fannie Mae and Freddie Mac and Budgetary Effects

Growing stress and losses in the mortgage markets in 2007 and 2008 seriously eroded the capital of Fannie Mae and Freddie Mac. Legislation enacted in July 2008 strengthened regulation of the housing GSEs through the creation of the Federal Housing Finance Agency (FHFA), a new independent regulator of housing GSEs, and provided the Department of the Treasury with authorities to purchase securities from Fannie Mae and Freddie Mac.

On September 6, 2008, FHFA placed Fannie Mae and Freddie Mac under Federal conservatorship. The next day, the Treasury launched various programs to provide temporary financial support to Fannie Mae and Freddie Mac under the temporary authority to purchase securities. Treasury entered into agreements with Fannie Mae and Freddie Mac to make investments in senior preferred stock in each GSE in order to ensure that each company maintains a positive net worth. The cumulative funding commitment through these Preferred Stock Purchase Agreements (PSPAs) with Fannie Mae and Freddie Mac was set at $445.5 billion. In total, as of December 31, 2022, $191.5 billion has been invested in Fannie Mae and Freddie Mac. The remaining commitment amount is $254.1 billion.

The PSPAs also generally require that Fannie Mae and Freddie Mac pay quarterly dividends to Treasury, though the terms governing the amount of those dividends have changed several times pursuant to agreements between Treasury and Fannie Mae and Freddie Mac. Notably, changes announced on January 14, 2021 permit the GSEs to suspend dividend payments until they achieve minimum capital levels established by FHFA through regulation. The Budget projects those levels will not be reached during the Budget window and accordingly reflects no dividends through 2033. Through December 31, 2022, the GSEs have paid a total of $301.0 billion in dividend payments to Treasury on the senior preferred stock.

The Temporary Payroll Tax Cut Continuation Act of 2011 (Public Law 112–78) amended the Housing and Community Development Act of 1992 (Public Law 102-550) by requiring that Fannie Mae and Freddie Mac increase their annual credit guarantee fees on single-family mortgage acquisitions between 2012 and 2021 by an average of at least 0.10 percentage points. This sun-

set was extended through 2032 by the BIL. The Budget estimates these fees, which are remitted directly to the Treasury and are not included in the PSPA amounts, will result in deficit reduction of $77.8 billion from 2024 through 2033.

In addition, effective January 1, 2015 FHFA directed Fannie Mae and Freddie Mac to set aside 0.042 percentage points for each dollar of the unpaid principal balance of new business purchases (including but not limited to mortgages purchased for securitization) in each year to fund several Federal affordable housing programs created by the Housing and Economic Recovery Act of 2008 (Public Law 110-289), including the Housing Trust Fund and the Capital Magnet Fund. The 2024 Budget projects these assessments will generate $5.4 billion for the affordable housing funds from 2024 through 2033.

Future of the Housing Finance System

Fannie Mae and Freddie Mac are in their fourteenth year of conservatorship, and the Congress has not yet enacted legislation to define the GSEs' long-term role in the housing finance system. The Administration is committed to housing finance policy that increases the supply of housing that is affordable for low- and moderate-income households, expands fair and equitable access to homeownership and affordable rental opportunities, protects taxpayers, and promotes financial stability. The Administration has a key role in shaping, and a key interest in the outcome of, housing finance reform, and stands ready to work with the Congress in support of these goals.

The Farm Credit System (Banks and Associations)

The Farm Credit System (FCS or System) is a GSE composed of a nationwide network of borrower-owned cooperative lending institutions originally authorized by the Congress in 1916. The FCS's mission is to provide sound and dependable credit to American farmers, ranchers, producers, or harvesters of aquatic products, their cooperatives, and farm-related businesses. The institutions serve rural America by providing financing for rural residential real estate; rural communication, energy, and water infrastructure; and agricultural exports. In addition, maintaining special policies and programs for the extension of credit to young, beginning, and small farmers (YBS) and ranchers is a legislative mandate for the System.

The financial condition of the System's banks and associations remains fundamentally sound. The ratio of capital to assets was 14.9 percent on September 30, 2022, compared with 16.9 percent on September 30, 2021. An increase in interest rates, which reduced the fair value of existing fixed-rate investment securities, contributed to the decline in the capital-to-assets ratio in 2022. Capital that is available to absorb losses amounted to $62.9 billion. For the first nine months of calendar year 2022, net income equaled $5.4 billion compared with $5.2 billion for the same period of the previous year.

Over the 12-month period ending September 30, 2022, System assets grew 13.2 percent, primarily because of higher cash and investment balances and increased real estate mortgage, processing and marketing, rural infrastructure, and agricultural export loan volume. Nonperforming assets as a percentage of the dollar volume of loans and other property owned was 0.51 percent on September 30, 2022, compared with 0.55 percent on September 30, 2021.

The number of FCS institutions continues to decrease due to consolidation. As of September 30, 2022, the System consisted of four banks and 64 associations, compared with five banks and 84 associations in September 2011. Of the 67 FCS banks and associations rated under the Financial Institution Rating System (FIRS), 62 had one of the top two examination ratings (1 or 2 on a 1 to 5 scale) and accounted for 99.1 percent of gross Systems assets. Five FCS institutions had a rating of 3.

The System, while continuing to record strong earnings and capital growth, remains exposed to a variety of risks associated with its portfolio concentration in agriculture and rural America. Those risks include ongoing moderate to exceptional drought conditions in almost half of the United States, an increase in severe weather events both in number and magnitude, increases in input costs, rising interest rates, and variability in Government policies supporting U.S. producers. In addition, trade disputes, rising inflation, labor issues, variability in production levels of global agricultural products, and fluctuating COVID-19 infection rates continue to keep agricultural market volatility elevated. In this challenging economic environment, the combination of farm commodity programs, disaster assistance, and crop insurance continued to mitigate the agricultural market volatility. Because of these mitigations, in fall 2021, producers experienced improved commodity prices and higher farm incomes, despite incurring higher cash expenses.

FCS Performance and YBS Portfolio

Both the dollar volume of the System's total loans outstanding and the dollar volume of YBS loans outstanding increased in calendar year 2021. While young, beginning, and small farmers are not mutually exclusive groups, and thus cannot be added across categories, it is important to note the growth of activity within each group. For example, total System loan dollar volume outstanding increased by 10.9 percent, and loan dollar volume outstanding to young farmers increased by 10.3 percent, to beginning farmers by 18.1 percent, and to small farmers by 14.2 percent.

The number of total System loans outstanding and YBS loans outstanding increased in 2021. The number of total System loans outstanding on December 31, 2021 was up 1.8 percent from a year ago. The number of loans outstanding to young farmers increased by 2.9 percent, to beginning farmers by 4.8 percent, and to small farmers by 1.7 percent. System originations in calendar year 2021 were up 12.7 percent from the prior 12 months, by loan amount. The dollar volume of originations to young farm-

ers increased by 8.3 percent, to beginning farmers by 16.7 percent, and to small farmers by 9.3 percent.

By loan count, originations also increased for both total System lending and for each YBS category over the year ending December 31, 2021. The total number of System loans made during the year increased by 2.1 percent. The number of loans to young farmers increased by 2.8 percent, to beginning farmers by 3.0 percent, and to small farmers by 0.8 percent. The loans to young farmers originated in 2021 represented 17.9 percent of all loans the System made during the year and 11.0 percent of the dollar volume of loans made. The loans made to beginning farmers in 2021 represented 25.6 percent of all System loans made during the year and 19.2 percent of the dollar volume of loans made. The loans in 2021 to small farmers represented 44.3 percent of all loans made during the year and 18.8 percent of the dollar volume of loans made. In 2021, the System reported making a total of nearly 379,000 new loans, totaling $136.4 billion.

Federal Agricultural Mortgage Corporation (Farmer Mac)

Farmer Mac was established in 1988 by the Agricultural Credit Act of 1987 (Public Law 100-233) as a federally chartered instrumentality of the United States and an institution of the System to facilitate a secondary market for farm real estate and rural housing loans. Farmer Mac is not liable for any debt or obligation of the other System institutions, and no other System institutions are liable for any debt or obligation of Farmer Mac. The Farm Credit System Reform Act of 1996 (Public Law 104-105) expanded Farmer Mac's role from a guarantor of securities backed by loan pools to a direct purchaser of mortgages, enabling it to form pools to securitize. The Food, Conservation, and Energy Act of 2008 (Public Law 110-246) expanded Farmer Mac's program authorities by allowing it to purchase and guarantee securities backed by rural utility loans made by cooperatives.

Farmer Mac continues to meet core capital and regulatory risk-based capital requirements. As of September 30, 2022, Farmer Mac's total outstanding program volume (loans purchased and guaranteed, standby loan purchase commitments, and AgVantage bonds purchased and guaranteed) amounted to $25.3 billion, which represents an increase of 9.5 percent from the level a year ago. Of total program activity, $21.4 billion were on-balance sheet loans and guaranteed securities, and $3.9 billion were off-balance-sheet obligations. Total assets were $26.4 billion, with non-program investments (including cash and cash equivalents) accounting for $5.3 billion of those assets. Farmer Mac's net income attributable to common stockholders ("net income") for the first three quarters of calendar year 2022 was $114.4 million. Net income increased compared to the same period in 2021, during which Farmer Mac reported net income of $84.4 million.

II. INSURANCE PROGRAMS

Deposit Insurance

Federal deposit insurance promotes stability in the U.S. financial system. Prior to the establishment of Federal deposit insurance, depository institution failures often caused depositors to lose confidence in the banking system and rush to withdraw deposits. Such sudden withdrawals caused serious disruption to the economy. In 1933, in the midst of the Great Depression, a system of Federal deposit insurance was established to protect depositors and to prevent bank failures from causing widespread disruption in financial markets.

Today, the Federal Deposit Insurance Corporation (FDIC) insures deposits in banks and savings associations (thrifts) using the resources available in its Deposit Insurance Fund (DIF). The National Credit Union Administration (NCUA) insures deposits (shares) in most credit unions through the National Credit Union Share Insurance Fund (SIF). (Some credit unions are privately insured.) As of September 30, 2022, the FDIC insured $9.9 trillion of deposits at 4,746 commercial banks and thrifts, and as of September 30, 2022, the NCUA insured nearly $1.7 trillion of shares at 4,813 Federal and federally insured State-chartered credit unions.

Since its creation, the Federal deposit insurance system has undergone many reforms. As a result of the 2008 financial crisis, several reforms were enacted to protect both the immediate and longer-term integrity of the Federal deposit insurance system. The Helping Families Save Their Homes Act of 2009 (division A of Public Law 111–22) provided NCUA with tools to protect the SIF and the financial stability of the credit union system. Notably, the Act established the Temporary Corporate Credit Union Stabilization Fund, which has now been closed with its assets and liabilities distributed into the SIF. In addition, the Act:

- Provided flexibility to the NCUA Board by permitting use of a restoration plan to spread insurance premium assessments over a period of up to eight years, or longer in extraordinary circumstances, if the SIF equity ratio falls below 1.2 percent; and

- Permanently increased the Share Insurance Fund's borrowing authority to $6 billion.

The Dodd-Frank Wall Street Reform and Consumer Protection Act of 2010 (Public Law 111-203, "Dodd-Frank Act") established new DIF reserve ratio requirements. The Act required the FDIC to achieve a minimum DIF reserve ratio (ratio of the deposit insurance fund balance to total estimated insured deposits) of 1.35 percent by 2020, up from 1.15 percent in 2016. On September 30, 2018, the DIF reserve ratio reached 1.36 percent. However, as of June 30, 2020 the DIF reserve ratio fell to 1.30 percent, below the statutory minimum of 1.35 percent. The decline was a result of strong one-time growth in insured deposits. On September 15, 2020, FDIC adopted a Restoration Plan to restore the DIF reserve ratio to at least 1.35 percent by 2027.

In addition to raising the minimum reserve ratio, the Dodd-Frank Act also:

- Eliminated the FDIC's requirement to rebate premiums when the DIF reserve ratio is between 1.35 and 1.5 percent;

- Gave the FDIC discretion to suspend or limit rebates when the DIF reserve ratio is 1.5 percent or higher, effectively removing the 1.5 percent cap on the DIF; and

- Required the FDIC to offset the effect on small insured depository institutions (defined as banks with assets less than $10 billion) when setting assessments to raise the reserve ratio from 1.15 to 1.35 percent. In implementing the Dodd-Frank Act, the FDIC issued a final rule setting a long-term (i.e., beyond 2028) reserve ratio target of 2 percent, a goal that FDIC considers necessary to maintain a positive fund balance during economic crises while permitting steady long-term assessment rates that provide transparency and predictability to the banking sector.

The Dodd-Frank Act also permanently increased the insured deposit level to $250,000 per account at banks or credit unions insured by the FDIC or NCUA.

Recent Fund Performance

As of September 30, 2022, the FDIC DIF balance stood at $125.5 billion, a one-year increase of $3.5 billion. The growth in the DIF balance is primarily a result of assessment revenue inflows. The reserve ratio on September 30, 2022, was 1.26 percent.

As of September 30, 2022, the number of insured institutions on the FDIC's "problem list" (institutions with the highest risk ratings) totaled 42, which represented a decrease of 95 percent from December 2010, the peak year for bank failures during the financial crisis. Moreover, the assets held by problem institutions were 59 percent below the level in December 2009, the peak year for assets held by problem institutions.

The NCUA administered SIF ended September 2022 with assets of $20.2 billion and an equity ratio of 1.26 percent. In December 2022, NCUA maintained the normal operating level of the SIF equity ratio at 1.33 percent of insured shares, having reduced it from 1.38 percent in December 2021. If the ratio exceeds the normal operating level, a distribution is normally paid to insured credit unions to reduce the equity ratio.

The health of the credit union industry has markedly improved since the financial crisis. As of September 30, 2022, NCUA reserved $183 million in the SIF to cover potential losses, up 13.0 percent from the $162 million reserved as of December 31, 2021. The ratio of insured shares in troubled institutions to total insured shares decreased from 0.5 percent in December 2021 to 0.2 percent in September 2022. This is a significant reduction from a high of 5.7 percent in December 2009.

Budget Outlook

The Budget estimates DIF net outlays of -$51.5 billion over the current 10-year budget window (2024–2033). The Budget projects that FDIC's Restoration Plan will remain in effect until 2027, when the DIF is estimated to reach the statutory reserve ratio target of 1.35 percent. The Budget also assumes that the DIF will reach the historic long-run reserve ratio target of 1.5 percent over the 10-year budget window. Although the FDIC has authority to borrow up to $100 billion from the Department of the Treasury to maintain sufficient DIF balances, the Budget does not anticipate FDIC utilizing its borrowing authority because the DIF is projected to maintain positive operating cash flows over the entire 10-year budget horizon.

Pension Guarantees

The Pension Benefit Guaranty Corporation (PBGC) insures the pension benefits of workers and retirees in covered defined-benefit pension plans. PBGC operates two legally and financially separate insurance programs: single-employer plans and multiemployer plans.

Single-Employer Insurance Program

When an underfunded single-employer plan terminates, PBGC becomes the trustee and pays benefits, up to a guaranteed level. This typically happens when the employer sponsoring an underfunded plan goes bankrupt, ceases operation, or can no longer afford to keep the plan going. PBGC's claims exposure is the amount by which guaranteed benefits exceed assets in insured plans. In the near term, the risk of loss stems from financially distressed firms with underfunded plans. In the longer term, loss exposure also results from the possibility that well-funded plans become underfunded due to inadequate contributions, poor investment results, or increased liabilities, and that the firms sponsoring those plans become distressed.

PBGC monitors companies with large, underfunded plans and acts to protect the interests of the pension insurance program's stakeholders where possible. Under its Early Warning Program, PBGC works with companies to mitigate risks to pension plans posed by corporate transactions or otherwise protect the insurance program from avoidable losses. However, PBGC's authority to manage risks to the insurance program is limited. Most private insurers can diversify or reinsure their catastrophic risks as well as flexibly price these risks. Unlike private insurers, Federal law does not allow PBGC to deny insurance coverage to a defined-benefit plan or adjust premiums according to risk. Both types of PBGC premiums, the flat rate (a per person charge paid by all plans) and the variable rate (paid by underfunded plans), are set in statute.

Claims against PBGC's insurance programs are highly variable. One large pension plan termination may result in a larger claim against PBGC than the termination of many smaller plans. The future financial health of the PBGC will continue to depend largely on the potential termination of a limited number of very large plans.

Single-employer plans generally provide benefits to the employees of one employer. When an underfunded single-employer plan terminates, PBGC becomes trustee of the plan, applies legal limits on payouts, and pays benefits. To determine the amount to pay each participant, PBGC takes into account (a) the benefit that a participant had accrued in the terminated plan, (b) the availability of assets from the terminated plan to cover benefits, (c) how much PBGC recovers from employers for plan underfunding, and (d) the legal maximum benefit level set in statute. The guarantee limits are indexed (i.e., they increase in proportion to increases in a specified Social Security wage index) and vary based on the participant's age and elected form of payment. For plans terminating in 2023, the maximum guaranteed annual benefit payable as a single life annuity under the single-employer program is $81,000 for a retiree aged 65.

Multiemployer Insurance Program

Multiemployer plans are collectively bargained pension plans maintained by one or more labor unions and more than one unrelated employer, usually within the same or related industries. PBGC does not trustee multiemployer plans. In the Multiemployer Program, the event triggering PBGC's guarantee is plan insolvency (the inability to pay guaranteed benefits when due), whether or not the plan has terminated. PBGC provides insolvent multiemployer plans with financial assistance in the statutorily required form of loans sufficient to pay PBGC guaranteed benefits and reasonable administrative expenses. Since multiemployer plans generally do not receive PBGC assistance until their assets are fully depleted, financial assistance is almost never repaid unless the plan receives special financial assistance under the American Rescue Plan Act of 2021 (Public Law 117-2, "ARPA").

Benefits guaranteed under the multiemployer program are calculated based on (a) the benefit a participant would have received under the insolvent plan, subject to (b) the legal multiemployer maximum set in statute. The maximum guaranteed amount depends on the participant's years of service and the level of the benefit accruals. For example, for a participant with 30 years of service, PBGC guarantees 100 percent of the pension benefit up to a yearly amount of $3,960. If the pension exceeds that amount, PBGC guarantees 75 percent of the rest of the pension benefit up to a total maximum guarantee of $12,870 per year for a participant with 30 years of service. This limit has been in place since 2001 and is not adjusted for inflation or cost-of-living increases.

PBGC's FY 2021 Projections Report shows the Multiemployer Program is likely to remain solvent over the 40-year projection period. Prior to the enactment of the ARPA, PBGC's Multiemployer Program was projected to become insolvent in FY 2026. ARPA amended the Employee Retirement and Income Security Act of 1974 (Public Law 93-406) and established a new Special Financial Assistance program that provides funding from the Department of the Treasury's General Fund for lump-sum payments to eligible multiemployer plans. By providing special financial assistance to the most financially troubled multiemployer plans, ARPA significantly extends the solvency of PBGC's Multiemployer Program. ARPA also assists plans by providing funds to reinstate previously suspended benefits.

Disaster Insurance

Flood Insurance

The Federal Government provides flood insurance through the National Flood Insurance Program (NFIP), which is administered by the Department of Homeland Security Federal Emergency Management Agency (FEMA). Flood insurance is available to homeowners, renters, businesses, and State and local governments in communities that have adopted and enforce minimum floodplain management measures. Coverage is limited to buildings and their contents. As of December 2022, the program had 4.7 million policies worth $1.3 trillion in force in over 22,500 communities. The program is currently authorized until September 30, 2023.

The Congress established the NFIP in 1968 via the National Flood Insurance Act of 1968 (Title XIII of Public Law 90-448) to make flood insurance coverage widely available, to combine a program of insurance with flood mitigation measures to reduce the Nation's risk of loss from floods, and to reduce Federal disaster-assistance expenditures on flood losses. The NFIP requires participating communities to adopt certain land use ordinances consistent with FEMA's floodplain management regulations and to take other mitigation efforts to reduce flood-related losses in high flood hazard areas ("Special Flood Hazard Areas") identified through partnership with FEMA, States, and local communities. These efforts have resulted in substantial reductions in the risk of flood-related losses nationwide.

Until October 2021, flood insurance rates were based on static measurements using the Flood Insurance Rate Map. To ensure policyholders make informed decisions on the purchase of adequate insurance and on mitigation actions to protect against flood risk, in FY 2021 FEMA introduced a new pricing methodology (known as Risk Rating 2.0-Equity in Action). The new pricing methodology builds on flood hazard information and incorporates private sector datasets, catastrophe models, and evolving actuarial science. The system includes additional flood risk variables such as flood frequency, multiple flood types (riverine, storm surge, coastal, pluvial), and distance to water along with individual property characteristics. The new methodology also addresses premium inequities by taking into account the cost to rebuild as a factor in the premium, so that policyholders with low-valued home are no longer subsidizing higher-valued homes. New policies effective on or after October 1, 2021 are subject to the new pricing methodology, and existing policyholders were able to take advantage of immediate decreases in their premiums upon renewal. All remaining existing policyholders were subject to the new methodology beginning April 1, 2022 upon policy renewal.

FEMA's Community Rating System offers discounts on policy premiums in communities that adopt and enforce more stringent floodplain land use ordinances than those identified in FEMA's regulations and/or engage in mitigation activities beyond those required by the NFIP. The discounts provide an incentive for communities to implement new flood protection activities that can help save lives and property when a flood occurs. Further, NFIP offers flood mitigation assistance grants for planning and carrying out activities to reduce the risk of flood damage to structures covered by NFIP, which may include demolition or relocation of a structure, elevation or flood-proofing a structure, and community-wide mitigation efforts that will reduce future flood claims for the NFIP. In particular, flood mitigation assistance grants targeted toward repetitive and severe repetitive loss properties not only help owners of high-risk property, but also reduce the disproportionate drain these properties cause on the National Flood Insurance Fund (NFIF). The BIL provided significant additional resources of $3.5 billion over five years for the flood mitigation assistance grants. The flood grants are a Justice40 covered program.

Due to the catastrophic nature of flooding, with Hurricanes Harvey, Katrina, and Sandy as notable examples, insured flood damages can far exceed premium revenue and deplete the program's reserves. On those occasions, the NFIP exercises its borrowing authority through the Department of the Treasury to meet flood insurance claim obligations. While the program needed appropriations in the early 1980s to repay the funds borrowed during the 1970s, it was able to repay all borrowed funds with interest using only premium dollars between 1986 and 2004. In 2005, however, Hurricanes Katrina, Rita, and Wilma generated more flood insurance claims than the cumulative number of claims paid from 1968 to 2004. Hurricane Sandy in 2012 generated $8.8 billion in flood insurance claims. As a result, in 2013 the Congress increased the borrowing authority for the fund to $30.425 billion. After the estimated $2.4 billion and $670 million in flood insurance claims generated by the Louisiana flooding of August 2016 and Hurricane Matthew in October 2016, respectively, the NFIP used its borrowing authority again, bringing the total outstanding debt to the Department of the Treasury to $24.6 billion.

In the fall 2017, Hurricanes Harvey and Irma struck the southern coast of the United States, resulting in catastrophic flood damage across Texas, Louisiana, and Florida. To pay claims, NFIP exhausted all borrowing authority. The Congress provided $16 billion in debt cancellation to the NFIP, bringing its debt to $20.525 billion. To pay Hurricane Harvey flood claims, NFIP also received more than $1 billion in reinsurance payments as a result of transferring risk to the private reinsurance market at the beginning of 2017. FEMA continues to mature its reinsurance program and transfer additional risk to the private market.

In September 2022 Hurricane Ian hit the southern coast of Florida, resulting in estimated losses to the NFIP of $4.0 – 5.3 billion. Anticipating the impact of additional flood insurance claims from Hurricane Ian,

FEMA will likely have to exhaust its balances in the NFIF and Reserve Fund earlier than previously anticipated. Previous budget projections relied on both NFIF and Reserve Fund balances to make up for annual deficits between collections from policyholders and NFIF expenses, until 2027-2032 when NFIF would utilize borrowing authority for any shortfalls. However, Hurricane Ian changed the trajectory of the fiscal path, with FEMA now projecting the use of additional borrowing authority to pay claims and other expenses beginning in 2024, and resulting in spending above the current borrowing authority limit of $30.425 billion. The policy proposals in the Budget would eliminate debt and reduce borrowing to address this situation.

In July 2012, resulting largely from experiences during Hurricanes Katrina, Rita, and Wilma in 2005, the Biggert Waters Flood Insurance Reform Act of 2012 (subtitle A of title II of Public Law 112–141; BW–12) was signed into law. In addition to reauthorizing the NFIP for five years, the bill required the NFIP generally to move to full risk-based premium rates and strengthened the NFIP financially and operationally. In 2013, the NFIP began phasing in risk-based premiums for certain properties, as required by the law, and began collecting a policyholder Reserve Fund assessment that is available to meet the expected future obligations of the flood insurance program.

In March 2014, largely in reaction to premium increases initiated by BW–12, the Homeowner Flood Insurance Affordability Act of 2014 (HFIAA) (Public Law 113–89) was signed into law, further reforming the NFIP and revising many sections of BW–12. Notably, HFIAA repealed and adjusted many of the major premium increases introduced by BW–12 and required retroactive refunds of collected BW–12 premium increases, introduced a phase-in to higher full-risk premiums for structures newly mapped into the Special Flood Hazard Area until full-risk rates are achieved, and created an Office of the Flood Insurance Advocate. HFIAA also introduced a fixed annual surcharge of $25 for primary residents and $250 for all other policies to be deposited into the Reserve Fund.

The 2022-2026 FEMA Strategic Plan creates a shared vision for the NFIP and other FEMA programs to build a more prepared and resilient Nation. The Strategic Plan outlines a bold vision and three ambitious goals designed to address key challenges the agency faces during a pivotal moment in the field of emergency management: Instill Equity as a Foundation of Emergency Management, Lead Whole of Community in Climate Resilience, and Promote and Sustain a Ready FEMA and Prepared Nation. While the NFIP supports all three goals, it is central to leading whole of community in climate resilience. To that end, FEMA is pursuing initiatives including:

1. Providing products that clearly and accurately communicate flood risk;

2. Helping individuals, businesses, and communities understand their risks and the available options like the NFIP to best manage those risks;

3. Transforming the NFIP into a simpler, customer-focused program that policyholders value and trust; and

4. Increasing the number of properties covered by flood insurance (either through the NFIP or private insurance).

Crop Insurance

Subsidized Federal crop insurance, administered by USDA's Risk Management Agency (RMA) on behalf of the Federal Crop Insurance Corporation (FCIC), assists farmers in managing yield and revenue shortfalls due to bad weather or other natural disasters. The program is a cooperative partnership between the Federal Government and the private insurance industry. Private insurance companies sell and service crop insurance policies. The Federal Government, in turn, pays private companies an administrative and operating expense subsidy to cover expenses associated with selling and servicing these policies. The Federal Government also provides reinsurance through the Standard Reinsurance Agreement and pays companies an "underwriting gain" if they have a profitable year. For the 2024 Budget, the payments to the companies are projected to be $3.96 billion in combined subsidies. The Federal Government also subsidizes premiums for farmers as a way to encourage farmers to participate in the program.

The most basic type of crop insurance is catastrophic coverage (CAT), which compensates the farmer for losses in excess of 50 percent of the individual's average yield at 55 percent of the expected market price. The CAT premium is entirely subsidized, and farmers pay only an administrative fee. Higher levels of coverage, called "buy-up," are also available. A portion of the premium for buy-up coverage is paid by FCIC on behalf of producers and varies by coverage level – generally, the higher the coverage level, the lower the percent of premium subsidized. The remaining (unsubsidized) premium amount is owed by the producer and represents an out-of-pocket expense.

For 2022, the four principal crops (corn, soybeans, wheat, and cotton) accounted for over 76 percent of total liability, and approximately 89 percent of the total U.S. planted acres of the 10 principal row crops (also including barley, peanuts, potatoes, rice, sorghum, and tobacco) were covered by crop insurance. Producers can purchase both yield- and revenue-based insurance products, which are underwritten on the basis of a producer's actual production history (APH). Revenue insurance programs protect against loss of revenue resulting from low prices, low yields, or a combination of both. Revenue insurance has enhanced traditional yield insurance by adding price as an insurable component.

In addition to price and revenue insurance, FCIC has made available other plans of insurance to provide protection for a variety of crops grown across the United States. For example, "area plans" of insurance offer protection based on a geographic area (most commonly a county), and do not directly insure an individual farm. Often, the loss trigger is based on an index, such as one on rainfall, which is established by a Government entity (for example, the National Oceanic and Atmospheric Administration). One such plan is the pilot Rainfall Index plan, which insures against a decline in an index value covering Pasture, Rangeland, and Forage. These pilot programs meet the needs of livestock producers who purchase insurance for protection from losses of forage produced for grazing or harvested for hay. In 2022, there were over 54 thousand Rainfall Index policies earning premiums, covering over 252 million acres of pasture, rangeland, and forage. In 2022, there was also over $7.1 billion in liability for those producers who purchased livestock coverage and $13.9 billion in liability for those producers who purchased coverage for milk.

A crop insurance policy also contains coverage compensating farmers when they are prevented from planting their crops due to weather and other perils. When an insured farmer is unable to plant the planned crop within the planting time period because of excessive drought or moisture, the farmer may file a prevented planting claim, which pays the farmer a portion of the full coverage level. It is optional for the farmer to plant a second crop on the acreage. If the farmer does, the prevented planting claim on the first crop is reduced and the farmer's APH is recorded for that year. If the farmer does not plant a second crop, the farmer gets the full prevented planting claim, and the farmer's APH is held harmless for premium calculation purposes the following year. Buy-up coverage for prevented planting is limited to 5 percent.

RMA is continuously working to develop new products and to expand or improve existing products in order to cover more agricultural commodities. RMA issued the Pandemic Cover Crop Program, providing $5 per acre of additional premium subsidy for producers who maintained a cover cropping system and subsequently planted and insured a cash crop on the same ground. The program covered more than 20 million net acres for about $110 million over 2021 and 2022. RMA also introduced the Post-Application Coverage Endorsement, a new product concept that provides additional yield coverage to producers who split-apply nitrogen, but are unable to complete the in-season portion due to weather events. Major program changes in 2022 included allowing irrigated grain sorghum producers to used corn yields as a better index for their acreage for area plans, improve and expand the High Risk – Alternative Coverage Endorsement, as well as, numerous new improvements to livestock products. For more information and additional crop insurance program details please reference RMA's website *www.rma. usda.gov.*

Farm Credit System Insurance Corporation (FCSIC)

Although not specifically disaster-related, FCSIC, an independent Government-controlled corporation, ensures the timely payment of principal and interest on FCS obligations on which the System banks are jointly and severally liable. If the Corporation does not have sufficient funds to ensure payment on insured obligations, System

banks would be required to make payments under joint and several liability, as required by section 4.4(a)(2) of the Farm Credit Act (Public Law 92–181, as amended). The insurance provided by the Insurance Fund is limited to the resources in the Insurance Fund. System obligations are not guaranteed by the U.S. Government. On September 30, 2022, the assets in the Insurance Fund totaled $6.5 billion. As of September 30, 2022, the Insurance Fund as a percentage of adjusted insured debt was 2.01 percent. This was slightly above the statutory secure base amount of 2.00 percent. As of September 30, 2022, the principal amount of outstanding insured System obligations increased 14.9 percent compared with that of September 30, 2021, from $328.8 billion to $377.8 billion.

Insurance Against Security-Related Risks

Terrorism Risk Insurance

The Terrorism Risk Insurance Program (TRIP) was authorized by the Terrorism Risk Insurance Act of 2002 (Public Law 107-297) to ensure the continued availability of property and casualty insurance following the terrorist attacks of September 11, 2001. TRIP was originally intended to be temporary, but has been repeatedly extended. It is currently set to expire on December 31, 2027 and authorizes collections through 2029, after it was reauthorized by the Terrorism Risk Insurance Program Reauthorization Act of 2019 (title V of division I of Public Law 116–94). TRIP's initial three-year authorization established a system of shared public and private compensation for insured property and casualty losses arising from certified acts of foreign terrorism.

The prior reauthorization, the Terrorism Risk Insurance Program Reauthorization Act of 2015 (Public Law 114–1), made several program changes to reduce potential Federal liability. Over the five years after the 2015 extension, the loss threshold that triggers Federal assistance was increased by $20 million each year to $22 million in 2020, and the Government's share of losses above the deductible decreased from 85 to 80 percent over the same period. The 2015 extension also required the Department of the Treasury to recoup 140 percent of all Federal payments made under the program up to a mandatory recoupment amount, which increased by $2 billion each year until 2019 when the threshold was set at $37.5 billion. Since January 1, 2020, the mandatory recoupment amount has been indexed to a running three-year average of the aggregate insurer deductible of 20 percent of direct-earned premiums.

The Budget baseline includes the estimated Federal cost of providing terrorism risk insurance, reflecting current law. Using market data synthesized through a proprietary model, the Budget projects annual outlays and recoupment for TRIP. While the Budget does not forecast any specific triggering events, the Budget includes estimates representing the weighted average of TRIP payments over a full range of possible scenarios, most of which include no notional terrorist attacks (and therefore no TRIP payments), and some of which include notional terrorist attacks of varying magnitudes. On this basis,

Chart 7-1. Face Value of Federal Credit Outstanding

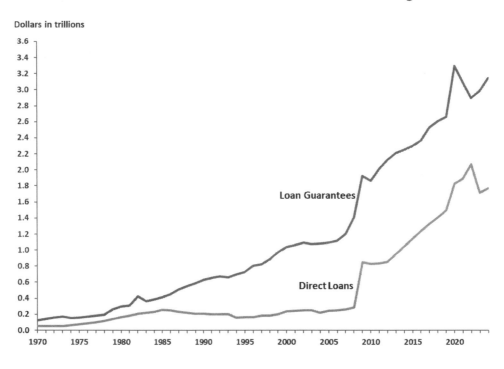

the Budget projects net spending of $473 million over the 2024–2033 period.

Aviation War Risk Insurance

In December 2014, the Congress sunset the premium aviation war risk insurance program, thereby sending U.S. air carriers back to the commercial aviation insurance market for all of their war risk insurance coverage. The National Defense Authorization Act for Fiscal Year 2020 (Public Law 116-92) authorized the non-premium program through September 30, 2023. It provides aviation insurance coverage for aircraft used in connection with certain Government contract operations by a department or agency that agrees to indemnify the Secretary of Transportation for any losses covered by the insurance.

III. BUDGETARY EFFECTS OF THE TROUBLED ASSET RELIEF PROGRAM (TARP)

This section provides analysis consistent with sections 202 and 203 of the Emergency Economic Stabilization Act of 2008 (Public Law 110-343, "EESA"), including estimates of the cost to taxpayers and the budgetary effects of TARP transactions as reflected in the Budget. This section also explains the changes in TARP costs, and includes alternative estimates as prescribed under EESA. Under EESA, the Department of the Treasury has purchased different types of financial instruments with varying terms and conditions.[2] The Budget reflects the costs of these instruments using the methodology as provided by section 123 of EESA.

The estimated costs of each transaction reflect the underlying structure of the instrument. TARP financial instruments have included direct loans, structured loans, equity, loan guarantees, and direct incentive payments. The costs of equity purchases, loans, guarantees, and loss sharing are the net present value of cash flows to and from the Government over the life of the instrument, per the Federal Credit Reform Act of 1990 (FCRA); as amended (title V of Public Law 93-344, 2 U.S.C. 661 et seq.), with an EESA-required adjustment to the discount rate for market risks. Costs for the incentive payments under TARP housing programs, other than loss sharing under the FHA Refinance program, involve financial instruments without any provision for future returns and are recorded on a cash basis.[3]

---

[2] For a more detailed analysis of the assets purchased through TARP and its budgetary effects, please see the "Budgetary Effect of the Troubled Asset Relief Program" chapter included in the *Analytical Perspectives* volume of prior budgets.

[3] Section 123 of EESA provides the Department of the Treasury the authority to record TARP equity purchases pursuant to FCRA, with required adjustments to the discount rate for market risks. The Hardest Hit Fund (HHF) and Making Home Affordable (MHA) programs involve the purchase of financial instruments that have no provision for repayment or other return on investment, and do not constitute direct loans or guarantees under FCRA. Therefore, these purchases

Tables 7–10 through 7–16 are available online. Table 7–10 summarizes the cumulative and anticipated activity under TARP, and the estimated lifetime budgetary cost reflected in the Budget, compared to estimates from the 2023 Budget. The direct impact of TARP on the deficit is projected to be $31.5 billion, down $0.2 billion from the $31.7 billion estimate in the 2023 Budget. The total programmatic cost represents the lifetime net present value cost of TARP obligations from the date of disbursement, which is now estimated to be $50.2 billion, a figure that excludes interest on reestimates.[4]

Table 7–11 shows the current value of TARP assets through the actual balances of TARP financing accounts as of the end of each fiscal year through 2022, and projected balances for each subsequent year through 2033.[5] Based on actual net balances in financing accounts at the end of 2009, the value of TARP assets totaled $129.9 billion. As of December 31, 2022, total TARP net asset value has decreased to $4 million. The overall balance of the financing accounts is estimated to continue falling as TARP investments continue to wind down.

Table 7-12 shows the estimated impact of TARP activity on the deficit, debt held by the public, and gross Federal debt following the methodology required by EESA. Direct activity under TARP is expected to increase the 2023 deficit by $2.0 billion, the major components being:

- Outlays for TARP housing programs are estimated at $132 million in 2023.

- Administrative expense outlays for TARP are estimated at $29 million in 2023.

- Outlays for the Special Inspector General for TARP are estimated at $9 million in 2023.

- Debt service is estimated at $1.8 billion for 2023 and then expected to decrease to $1.3 billion by 2033, largely due to outlays for TARP housing programs and interest effects. Total debt service will continue over time after TARP winds down, due to the financing of past TARP costs.

Debt net of financial assets due to TARP is estimated to be $38.2 billion as of the end of 2023. This is $1.4 billion higher than the projected debt held net of financial assets for 2023 that was reflected in the 2023 Budget.

Table 7-13 reflects the estimated effects of TARP transactions on the deficit and debt, as calculated on a cash basis. Under cash basis reporting, the 2023 deficit would be $4 million lower than the $2.0 billion estimate now re-

flected in the Budget. However, the impact of TARP on the Federal debt, and on debt held net of financial assets, is the same on a cash basis as under FCRA and therefore these data are not repeated in Table 7-13.

Table 7-14 shows detailed information on upward and downward reestimates to program costs. The current reestimate of $0.4 million reflects a decrease in estimated TARP costs from the 2023 Budget. This decrease was due in large part to interest effects and continued progress winding down TARP investments over the past year.

The 2024 Budget, as shown in Table 7–15, reflects a total TARP deficit impact of $31.5 billion. This is a decrease of $0.2 billion from the 2023 Budget projection of $31.7 billion. The estimated 2023 TARP deficit impact reflected in Table 7-15 differs from the programmatic cost of $50.2 billion in the Budget because the deficit impact includes $18.8 billion in cumulative downward adjustments for interest on subsidy reestimates. See footnote 2 in Table 7-15.

Table 7-16 compares the OMB estimate for TARP's deficit impact to the deficit impact estimated by CBO in its "Report on the Troubled Asset Relief Program—May 2022."[6]

CBO estimates the total cost of TARP at $31.0 billion, based on estimated lifetime TARP disbursements of $444 billion. The Budget reflects a total deficit cost of $31.5 billion, based on estimated disbursements of $449 billion. CBO and OMB cost estimates for TARP have generally converged over time as TARP equity programs have wound down.

---

[6] Available at: *https://www.cbo.gov/publication/58029.*

---

are recorded on a cash basis. Administrative expenses for TARP are recorded under the Office of Financial Stability and the Special Inspector General for TARP on a cash basis, consistent with other Federal administrative costs, but are recorded separately from TARP program costs.

[4] With the exception of MHA and HHF, all the other TARP investments are reflected on a present value basis pursuant to FCRA and EESA.

[5] Reestimates for TARP are calculated using actual data through September 30, 2022, and updated projections of future activity. Thus, the full impacts of TARP reestimates are reflected in the 2022 financing account balances.

8. AID TO STATE AND LOCAL GOVERNMENTS

The analysis in this chapter focuses on Federal spending that is provided to State and local governments, U.S. territories, and tribal governments to help fund programs administered by those entities. This type of Federal spending is known as Federal financial assistance, primarily administered as grants.

In 2022, the Federal Government spent roughly $1.2 trillion, approximately 5 percent of GDP, on aid to State, local, tribal, and territorial governments. The Budget estimates $1.1 trillion in outlays for aid to State, local, tribal, and territorial governments in both 2023 and 2024. Total Federal grant spending to State and local governments is estimated to be 4 percent of GDP in 2024.

Federal grants to State and local governments reached a historic high in 2021, at 5.5 percent of GDP, in large part due to significant Federal financial assistance provided in response to the health and economic crisis caused by the COVID-19 pandemic. Elevated outlays for aid to State, local, tribal, and territorial governments in 2022, 2023, and 2024 continue to reflect this assistance, as well as the significant infrastructure and community investments made in the Infastructure Investment and Jobs Act (Public Law 117-58, "IIJA"), the Bipartisan Safer Communities Act (Public Law 117-159), and the Inflation Reduction Act (Public Law 117-169). As explained below, the 2024 Budget builds on these successes by expanding partnerships with State and local governments to lower costs for families and grow the economy from the bottom up and middle out.

BACKGROUND AND ANALYSIS

Federal grants are authorized by the Congress in statute, which then establishes the purpose of the grant and how it is awarded. Most often Federal grants are awarded as direct cash assistance, but Federal grants can also include in-kind assistance—non-monetary aid, such as commodities purchased for the National School Lunch Program—and Federal revenues or assets shared with State and local governments.

In its 2022 State Expenditure Report, the National Association of State Budget Officers (NASBO) reports that 38 percent of total State spending, which is estimated to be about $2.86 trillion[1], in State fiscal year[2] 2022, came from Federal funds. The NASBO reports that total State expenditures (including general funds, other State funds, bonds and Federal funds) increased 9.0 percent in 2020 and 16.2 percent in 2021 and are expected to increase 7.3 percent in 2022.[3]

Table 8-1, below, shows Federal grants spending by decade, actual spending in 2022, and estimated spending in 2023 and 2024. Table 8-2 available at *https://www.whitehouse.gov/omb/analytical-perspectives/*, shows the Budget's funding level for grants in every Budget account, organized by functional category, Budget Enforcement Act (BEA) category, and by Federal Agency.

The Federal Budget classifies grants by general area or function. Of the total proposed grant spending in 2024, 55 percent is for health programs, with most of the funding for Medicaid. Beyond health programs, 15 percent of Federal aid is estimated to go to income security programs; nine percent to transportation programs; eight percent to education, training, and social services; and 12 percent for all other functions.

The Federal Budget also classifies grant spending by BEA category—discretionary or mandatory.[4] Funding for discretionary grant programs is generally determined annually through appropriations acts. Outlays for discretionary grant programs are estimated to account for 31 percent of total grant spending in 2024. Funding for mandatory programs is provided directly in authorizing legislation that establishes eligibility criteria or benefit formulas; funding for mandatory programs usually is not limited by the annual appropriations process. Outlays for mandatory grant programs are estimated to account for 69 percent of total grant spending in 2024. Section B of Table 8-1 shows the distribution of grants between mandatory and discretionary spending.

In 2024, grants provided from discretionary funding are estimated to have outlays of $336 billion, a increase of roughly 6.7 percent from 2023. The four largest discretionary programs in 2024 are estimated to be Federal-aid Highways programs, with outlays of $53 billion; Tenant Based Rental Assistance, with outlays of $33 billion; Education for the Disadvantaged (Title I), with outlays of $20 billion; and the Disaster Relief Fund, with outlays of $19 billion.

In 2024, outlays for mandatory grant programs are estimated to be $757 billion, a decrease of 5.8 percent from spending in 2023, which is estimated to be $804 billion. This estimated decline reflects the winding down of pan-

---

[1] "2022 State Expenditure Report." National Association of State Budget Officers, 2022. p. 1, 3.

[2] According to "The Fiscal Survey of States" published by the National Association of State Budget Officers (Fall 2022, p. VI), "Forty-six States begin their fiscal years in July and end them in June. The exceptions are New York, which starts its fiscal year on April 1; Texas, with a September 1 start date; and Alabama and Michigan, which start their fiscal years on October 1."

[3] "2022 State Expenditure Report." National Association of State Budget Officers, 2022. p. 2.

[4] For more information on these categories, see Chapter 15, "Budget Concepts," in this volume.

Table 8–1.   TRENDS IN FEDERAL GRANTS TO STATE AND LOCAL GOVERNMENTS

(Outlays in billions of dollars)

	Actual										Estimate	
	1960	1970	1980	1990	2000	2005	2010	2015	2020	2022	2023	2024
A. Distribution of grants by function:												
Natural resources and environment	0.1	0.4	5.4	3.7	4.6	5.9	9.1	7.0	7.2	7.6	18.9	36.0
Agriculture	0.2	0.6	0.6	1.1	0.7	0.9	0.8	0.7	0.8	0.8	1.0	1.2
Transportation	3.0	4.6	13.0	19.2	32.2	43.4	61.0	60.8	69.3	93.9	92.2	101.0
Community and regional development	0.1	1.8	6.5	5.0	8.7	20.2	18.9	14.4	52.5	43.2	57.8	58.6
Education, training, employment, and social services	0.5	6.4	21.9	21.8	36.7	57.2	97.6	60.5	67.9	95.8	90.0	92.8
Health	0.2	3.8	15.8	43.9	124.8	197.8	290.2	368.0	493.4	647.9	654.9	606.1
Income security	2.6	5.8	18.5	36.9	68.7	90.9	115.2	101.1	118.2	179.3	171.8	166.7
Administration of justice	....	0.0	0.5	0.6	5.3	4.8	5.1	3.7	9.4	5.8	12.0	8.8
General government	0.2	0.5	8.6	2.3	2.1	4.4	5.2	3.8	4.3	112.3	11.8	11.1
Other	0.0	0.1	0.7	0.8	2.1	2.6	5.3	4.3	6.1	6.9	8.6	10.8
Total	**7.0**	**24.1**	**91.4**	**135.3**	**285.9**	**428.0**	**608.4**	**624.4**	**829.1**	**1,193.3**	**1,118.9**	**1,093.0**
B. Distribution of grants by BEA category:												
Discretionary	N/A	10.2	53.4	63.5	116.7	182.3	247.4	189.6	259.4	290.8	314.4	335.6
Mandatory	N/A	13.9	38.0	71.9	169.2	245.7	361.0	434.7	569.7	902.5	804.5	757.4
Total	**7.0**	**24.1**	**91.4**	**135.3**	**285.9**	**428.0**	**608.4**	**624.4**	**829.1**	**1,193.3**	**1,118.9**	**1,093.0**
C. Composition:												
Current dollars:												
Payments for individuals [1]	2.6	9.1	33.1	77.4	186.5	278.8	391.4	463.4	608.6	790.7	815.5	760.0
Physical capital [1]	3.3	7.1	22.6	27.2	48.7	60.8	93.3	77.2	85.3	113.0	122.8	140.8
Other grants	1.1	7.9	35.8	30.7	50.7	88.4	123.7	83.7	135.2	289.7	180.6	192.3
Total	**7.0**	**24.1**	**91.4**	**135.3**	**285.9**	**428.0**	**608.4**	**624.4**	**829.1**	**1,193.3**	**1,118.9**	**1,093.0**
Percentage of total grants:												
Payments for individuals [1]	37.4%	37.7%	36.2%	57.2%	65.3%	65.1%	64.3%	74.2%	73.4%	66.3%	72.9%	69.5%
Physical capital [1]	47.3%	29.3%	24.7%	20.1%	17.0%	14.2%	15.3%	12.4%	10.3%	9.5%	11.0%	12.9%
Other grants	15.3%	33.0%	39.1%	22.7%	17.7%	20.7%	20.3%	13.4%	16.3%	24.3%	16.1%	17.6%
Total	**100.0%**	**100.0%**	**100.0%**	**100.0%**	**100.0%**	**100.0%**	**100.0%**	**100.0%**	**100.0%**	**100.0%**	**100.0%**	**100.0%**
Constant (FY 2012) dollars:												
Payments for individuals [1]	16.0	44.1	82.0	123.7	240.1	322.5	408.5	447.6	546.6	649.3	634.5	576.4
Physical capital [1]	25.1	40.1	57.6	48.0	71.9	77.8	98.5	73.4	73.1	83.9	86.1	95.4
Other grants	13.7	67.6	144.4	67.5	77.6	111.1	130.5	78.4	114.8	220.8	129.9	133.7
Total	**54.8**	**151.8**	**283.9**	**239.1**	**389.6**	**511.4**	**637.5**	**599.4**	**734.6**	**954.0**	**850.5**	**805.5**
D. Total grants as a percent of:												
Federal outlays:												
Total	7.6%	12.3%	15.5%	10.8%	16.0%	17.3%	17.6%	16.9%	12.7%	19.0%	17.6%	15.9%
Domestic programs [2]	18.0%	23.2%	22.2%	17.1%	22.0%	23.5%	23.4%	21.2%	15.0%	23.0%	22.6%	20.7%
State and local expenditures	14.2%	19.4%	26.4%	18.0%	21.0%	22.9%	25.6%	23.9%	26.5%	33.8%	N/A	N/A
Gross domestic product	1.3%	2.3%	3.3%	2.3%	2.8%	3.3%	4.1%	3.5%	3.9%	4.8%	4.2%	4.0%
E. As a share of total State and local gross investments:												
Federal capital grants	24.1%	24.6%	34.5%	21.0%	21.3%	21.2%	26.8%	21.9%	19.5%	24.2%	N/A	N/A
State and local own-source financing	75.9%	75.4%	65.5%	79.0%	78.7%	78.8%	73.2%	78.1%	80.5%	75.8%	N/A	N/A
Total	**100.0%**	**100.0%**	**100.0%**	**100.0%**	**100.0%**	**100.0%**	**100.0%**	**100.0%**	**100.0%**	**100.0%**		

N/A: Not available at publishing.

[1] Grants that are both payments for individuals and capital investment are shown under capital investment.

[2] Excludes national defense, international affairs, net interest, and undistributed offsetting receipts.

demic-related aid programs, as discussed above. Medicaid is by far the largest mandatory grant program with estimated outlays of $558 billion in 2024. After Medicaid, the four largest mandatory grant programs by outlays in 2024 are estimated to be: Child Nutrition programs, which include the School Breakfast Program, the National School Lunch Program and others, $32 billion; State and Tribal Assistance Grants, $24 billion; and Children's Health Insurance Program, $18 billion; and the Temporary Assistance for Needy Families program, $16 billion.

Federal spending by State for major grants may be found in supplemental material available on the OMB website at www.whitehouse.gov/omb/analytical-perspectives/. This material includes two tables that summarize State-by-State spending for major grant programs, one summarizing obligations for each program by agency and bureau, and another summarizing total obligations across all programs for each State, followed by 51 individual tables showing State-by-State obligation data for each grant program. The programs shown in these State-by-State tables cover the majority of total grants to State and local governments. The sections that follow include highlights of grant proposals from the Budget listed by function.

HIGHLIGHTS

Grants Management

The Administration remains committed to supporting the effective implementation and strong stewardship of the increased outlays to combat the COVID-19 pandemic discussed above, including the continued execution of the American Rescue Plan Act of 2021 (Public Law 117-2, "ARPA") as described in OMB memorandum M-21-20, "Promoting Public Trust in the Federal Government through the Effective Implementation of the American Rescue Plan and Stewardship of the Taxpayer Resources." Additionally, this Administration is committed to the continued successful execution of the IIJA, which represents a once-in-a-generation investment in our Nation's infrastructure and competitiveness. As outlined in the President's Management Agenda, the Administration will continue to take proactive steps to foster accountability, performance, and public trust in the administration of grant programs while implementing sound financial management of these resources.

Energy

Building on the more than $15 billion in Bipartisan Infrastructure Act and Inflation Reduction Act funding for the Department of Energy's Office of State and Community Energy Programs, the Administration is committed to continue creating jobs through support for State and community action to deploy clean energy infrastructure. The Budget provides more than $480 million to weatherize and decarbonize low-income homes through efficiency and electrification retrofits, including a $50 million Energy Burden Reduction pilot to retrofit up to 3,000 low-income homes with efficient electric appliances and systems that reduce energy burden to less than five percent of household income while also reducing greenhouse gas emissions. It also includes $180 million to States and communities to incubate novel approaches to clean energy technology deployment, prioritizing investments that benefit disadvantaged communities that have been marginalized or overburdened. In addition, the Budget provides $110 million to electrify tribal homes and transition tribal colleges and universities to renewable energy.

Natural Resources and Environment

The Budget commits to tackling the climate crisis with urgency by investing $100 million in Environmental Protection Agency (EPA) grants to States and Tribes that will support the implementation of on-the-ground efforts in communities across the Nation, such as reducing methane emissions.

To protect communities from hazardous waste and environmental damage, the Budget also provides $217 million for EPA's Brownfields program to provide technical assistance and grants to communities, including disadvantaged communities, so they can safely clean up and reuse contaminated properties.

Agriculture

To support tribal communities, the Budget invests $64 million for agriculture research, education and extension grants to tribal institutions and $3 million to support Native American farmers and ranchers through the Intertribal Assistance Network. It also includes $20 million at the Department of Commerce's Economic Development Administration to establish a grant program focused exclusively on the economic development needs of tribal governments and indigenous communities.

Transportation

The Budget provides robust support for transportation projects that cut commute times, improve safety, reduce freight bottlenecks, better connect communities, and reduce greenhouse gas emissions. Investments include $1.2 billion for the National Infrastructure Project Assistance ("Mega") program to deliver large transportation projects with significant benefits across multiple modes.

The Budget modernizes and upgrades roads and bridges by providing $60.1 billion for the Federal-aid Highway program, $1.3 billion above the 2023 enacted level. Together with $9.4 billion in advance appropriations provided by the IIJA for 2024, the Budget also supports: $8 billion for competitive and formula grant programs to rebuild the Nation's bridges; $1.5 billion to deploy a nationwide, publicly-accessible network of electric vehicle chargers and other alternative fueling infrastructure; $1.3 billion for the carbon reduction grant program; and $8.7 billion for the resiliency grant program to enchance the resiliance of surface transportation infrastructure to hazards and climate change.

The Budget continues support for the historic levels of Federal investment to modernize America's port and waterway infrastructure initiated under the IIJA by including $230 million for the Port Infrastructure Development Program to strengthen maritime freight capacity. The Budget also includes $1.37 billion for competitive grant programs to support passenger and frieght rail modernization, expansion, safety improvements, and $2.85 billion for the Capital Investment Grant program, which will advance the construction of new, high-quality transit corridors to reduce travel time and increase economic development.

Community and Regional Development

The Budget invests in underserved communities by providing $3.4 billion for the Community Development Block Grant program to help communities modernize infrastructure, invest in economic development, create parks and other public amenities, and provide social services.

The President is committed to ensuring that every American has access to broadband. Building on the $2 billion for the Department of Agriculture (USDA) broadband programs provided in the IIJA, the Budget provides $400 million for the ReConnect program, which provides grants and loans to deploy broadband to unserved areas, especially tribal areas. High-speed internet strengthens rural economies, and the work of installing broadband creates high-paying union jobs.

Additionally, to create jobs and drive growth in economically distressed communities across the Nation, the Budget requests more than $291 million in new base discretionary funding for the Economic Development Administration (EDA). The Budget includes a request for $200 million for the Recompete Pilot Program to address structural prime-age employment gaps and boost competitiveness in persistently distressed communities through innovative, flexible, and locally-led grants, and $100 million for the Good Jobs Challenge to fund high-quality, locally-led workforce systems that expand career opportunities for hard-working Americans. It also includes $4 billion in mandatory funding for EDA's Regional Technology and Innovation Hub Program to establish cutting-edge and strategic regional technology hubs that foster the geographic diversity of innovation and create quality jobs in underserved and vulnerable communities.

The Budget also provides $1.3 billion in discretionary grants for the Federal Emergency Management Agency to provide to States, tribes, and territories for efforts to prevent, protect against, mitigate, respond to and recover from acts of terrorism and other threats. This funding total includes $360 million for facility hardening for nonprofit organizations that are at high risk of terrorist attacks.

Education, Training, Employment, and Social Services

Disruptions caused by the COVID-19 pandemic continue to take a toll on the physical and mental health of students, teachers, and school staff. Recognizing the profound effect of physical and mental health on academic achievement, Budget includes a $550 million investment to increase the number of counselors, nurses, and mental health professionals in schools, colleges and universities. This is in addition to the $1 billion in mental health funding provided in the Bipartisan Safer Communities Act.

To advance the goal of providing a high-quality education to every student, the Budget includes $20.5 billion for Title I. Title I helps schools provide students from low-income families the learning opportunities they need to succeed. This substantial new support for the program, which serves 25 million students in nearly 90 percent of school districts across the Nation, would be a major step toward fulfilling the President's commitment to address long-standing funding disparities between under-resourced schools—which disproportionately serve students of color—and their wealthier counterparts.

The Budget also funds a Federal-State partnership providing high-quality, universal, free preschool, allowing states to expand high-quality preschool education to all four-year-olds.

The President is also committed to ensuring that children with disabilities receive the services and support they need to thrive. The Budget provides an additional $2.1 billion for Individuals with Disabilities Education Act (IDEA) Grants to States, with a total of $16.8 billion to support special education and related services for students in grades Pre-K through 12. The Budget also doubles funding to $932 million for IDEA Part C grants, which support early intervention services for infants and families with disabilities that have a proven record of improving academic and developmental outcomes.

To increase institutional capacity at Historically Black Colleges and Universities (HBCUs), Tribally Controlled Colleges and Universities (TCCUs), Minority-Serving Institutions (MSIs), and low-resourced institutions, including community colleges, the Budget provides an increase of $422 million over the 2023 enacted level for these programs. This funding includes $350 million to 4-year HBCUs, TCCUs, and MSIs to increase research and development infrastructure at these institutions.

The Budget also provides $50 million in competitive grants for States and localities to advance reforms that would reduce the overrepresentation of children and families of color in the child welfare system and address the disparate experiences and outcomes of these families, as well as $215 million for States and community-based organizations to respond to and prevent child abuse.

Health

The Budget includes increased discretionary funding to build public health capacity at the State and local government level. These resources will expand public health infrastructure in States and Territories. The United

States is facing a behavioral health crisis. The Budget provides historic investments in behavioral health, including the behavioral health workforce, youth mental health treatment, Certified Community Based Behavioral Health Clinics (CCBHCs), and Community Mental Health Centers. The Budget strengthens access to crisis services by investing in the 988 Suicide and Crisis Lifeline to address 100 percent of estimated contacts, scaling follow-up crisis services, and expanding CDC's suicide prevention program to all States, D.C., and 18 tribal and territorial jurisdictions.

The Budget invests in the treatment and prevention of infectious diseases, including Hepatitis C, HIV, and other vaccine-preventable diseases, by supporting comprehensive programs that will expand access to curative and preventive medications. The Budget includes a new mandatory proposal for a national program to significantly expand screening, testing, treatment, prevention, and monitoring of hepatitis C infections in the United States, with a specific focus on populations with high infection levels. This program will support Federal procurement of life-saving treatments, while bolstering provider capacity and related public health efforts such as testing, communication, and surveillance. The Budget invests $850 million in Ending the HIV Epidemic across HHS to aggressively reduce new HIV cases, increase access to pre-exposure prophylaxis (also known as PrEP), and ensure equitable access to services and supports for those living with HIV. The Budget also eliminates barriers to accessing PrEP for Medicaid beneficiaries and proposes a new mandatory program to guarantee PrEP at no cost for all uninsured and underinsured individuals, provide essential wraparound services through States, IHS, tribal entities, and localities, and establish a network of community providers to reach underserved areas and populations. Further, the Budget proposes a new Vaccines for Adults (VFA) program to provide uninsured adults with access to routine and outbreak vaccines at no cost and expands the VFC program to include all children under age 19 enrolled in the Children's Health Insurance Program (CHIP).

To address racial health disparities and reduce maternal mortality and morbidity rates, the Budget provides funding to create pregnancy medical home projects, expand maternal health initiatives in rural communities, implement implicit bias training for healthcare providers, and address the highest rates of perinatal health disparities, including by supporting the perinatal health workforce. To address the lack of data on health disparities and further improve access to care, the Budget strengthens collection and evaluation of health equity data. Recognizing that maternal mental health conditions are the most common complications of pregnancy and childbirth, the Budget continues to support the maternal mental health hotline and the screening and treatment for maternal mental depression and related behavioral disorders.

The Budget also provides $410 million within the Department of Housing and Urban Development (HUD), for States, local governments, and nonprofits to reduce lead-based paint and other health hazards in the homes of low-income families with young children.

Income Security

The Budget includes $104 billion in mandatory spending and tax proposals to increase the availability of affordable housing for both renters and homebuyers, most of which would be grant programs to be distributed via states and local governments. In addition to the mandatory and tax proposals, the Budget increases affordable housing supply and addresses the critical shortage of affordable housing in communities throughout the Nation by providing $1.8 billion for the HOME Investment Partnerships Program, an increase of $300 million over the 2023 enacted level, to construct and rehabilitate affordable rental housing and provide homeownership opportunities.

The Budget also provides $32.7 billion, an increase of $2.4 billion (including emergency funding) over the 2023 enacted level, for the Housing Choice Voucher (HCV) program to maintain services for all currently assisted families and to expand assistance to an additional 50,000 households, particularly those who are experiencing homelessness or fleeing, or attempting to flee, domestic violence or other forms of gender-based violence. The Budget further expands assistance to another 130,000 households with funding from HCV program reserves. To advance efforts to end homelessness, the Budget provides $3.7 billion, an increase of $116 million over the 2023 enacted level, for Homeless Assistance Grants to meet renewal needs and support survivors of domestic violence and homeless youth. Additionally, the Budget also helps address the poor housing conditions in tribal areas by providing $1.05 billion to fund tribal efforts to expand affordable housing, improve housing conditions and infrastructure, and increase economic opportunities for low-income families.

To support families struggling with home energy and water bills, the Budget provides $4.1 billion for LIHEAP. Since the Low Income Household Water Assistance Program expires at the end of 2023, the Budget proposes to expand LIHEAP to advance the goals of both programs by increasing LIHEAP funding and giving States the option to use a portion of their LIHEAP funds to provide water bill assistance to low-income households.

The Budget advances the President's goal of expanding access to affordable high-quality child care for families across the Nation, providing $9.0 billion for the Child Care and Development Block Grant, an increase of almost one billion over the 2023 enacted level. In addition, the Budget proposes a new child care program that would enable states to increase child care options and lower costs so that parents can afford to send their young children to the high-quality child care program of their choice.

The Budget supports a strong nutrition safety net by providing $7.1 billion for critical nutrition programs, including $6.3 billion for the Special Supplemental Nutrition Program for Women, Infants, and Children, to help vulnerable families put healthy food on the table and address racial disparities in maternal and child health outcomes.

Additionally, the Budget includes several investments aimed at tackling fraud in the Unemployment Insurance (UI) program, including funding to support more robust identity verification for UI applicants, help States develop and test fraud-prevention tools and strategies, and allow the Department of Labor (DOL) Office of Inspector General to increase its investigations into fraud rings targeting the UI program. Further, the Budget proposes a comprehensive package of integrity and equity focused proposals designed to provide new and expanded tools and integrity controls for States to help improve efforts to ensure entitled workers are proplerly paid and to prevent improper payments. The Budget also proposes principles to guide future efforts to reform the UI system, including improving benefit levels and access, scaling UI benefits automatically during recessions, expanding eligibility to reflect the modern labor force, improving State and Federal solvency through more equitable and progressive financing, expanding reemployment services, and safeguarding the program from fraud.

Administration of Justice

The Budget provides $4.9 billion in discretionary resources to the Department of Justice for State and local grants and $30 billion in mandatory resources to support efforts to hire police officers, reform criminal justice systems, and combat violent crime, as detailed in President Biden's Safer America Plan. In addition, the Budget proposes $760 million for juvenile justice programs, an increase of $360 million over the 2023 enacted level, to bolster decarcerative juvenile justice strategies.

OTHER SOURCES OF INFORMATION ON FEDERAL GRANTS

A number of other sources provide State-by-State spending data and other information on Federal grants but may use a broader definition of grants beyond what is included in this chapter.

The website Grants.gov is a primary source of information for communities wishing to apply for grants and other Federal financial assistance. Grants.gov hosts all competitive open notices of opportunities to apply for Federal grants.

The *System for Award Management* hosted by the General Services Administration contains detailed Assistance Listings (formerly known as the Catalog of Federal Domestic Assistance) of grant and other assistance programs; discussions of eligibility criteria, application procedures, and estimated obligations; and related information. The *Assistance Listings* are available on the internet at sam.gov.

Current and updated grant receipt information by State and local governments and other non-Federal entities can be found on USASpending.gov. This public website includes additional detail on Federal spending, including contract and loan information.

The Federal Audit Clearinghouse maintains an online database (https://harvester.census.gov/facweb/) that provides public access to audit reports conducted under OMB guidance located at 2 CFR part 200, Uniform Administrative Requirements, Cost Principles, and Audit Requirements for Federal Awards. Information is available for each audited entity, including the amount of Federal money expended by program and whether there were audit findings.

The Bureau of Economic Analysis, in the Department of Commerce, produces the monthly *Survey of Current Business*, which provides data on the National income and product accounts, a broad statistical concept encompassing the entire economy. These accounts, which are available at bea.gov/national, include data on Federal grants to State and local governments.

In addition, information on grants and awards can be found through individual Federal Agencies' websites:[5]

- USDA Current Research Information System, *https://cris.nifa.usda.gov/*
- Department of Defense Medical Research Programs, *https://cdmrp.army.mil/search.aspx*
- Department of Education, Institute of Education Sciences, Funded Research Grants and Contracts, *https://www2.ed.gov/fund/grants-apply.html*
- HHS Grants, *https://www.hhs.gov/grants/grants/index.html*
- HHS Tracking Accountability in Government Grants System, *https://taggs.hhs.gov/Advanced-Search.cfm*
- National Institutes of Health Grants and Funding, *https://grants.nih.gov/funding/index.htm*
- HUD Grants, *https://www.hud.gov/program_offices/spm/gmomgmt/grantsinfo*
- DOJ Grants, *https://www.justice.gov/grants*
- DOL Employment and Training Administration, Grants Awarded, *https://www.doleta.gov/grants/grants_awarded.cfm*
- Department of Transportation Grants, *https://www.transportation.gov/grants*
- EPA Grants, *https://www.epa.gov/grants*
- National Science Foundation Awards, *https://www.nsf.gov/awardsearch/*
- Small Business Innovation Research and Small Business Technology Transfer Awards, *https://www.sbir.gov/sbirsearch/award/all*

---

[5] *https://www.cfo.gov/wp-content/uploads/2021/Managing-for-Results-Performance-Management-Playbook-for-Federal-Awarding-Agencies.pdf*

9. LEVERAGING FEDERAL STATISTICS TO STRENGTHEN EVIDENCE-BASED DECISION-MAKING

Federal statistics have informed decision-making in the United States since its founding. The first constitutionally mandated census of population and housing in 1790 originated from "the desire of the colonists to find some equitable plan for the distribution of the burdens of the war, which proved to be one of the most perplexing questions which entered into the deliberations of the Continental Congress."[1] The 1790 Census planted the seeds for what we refer to today as *the Federal statistical system*. Over the 19th Century, the system continued to blossom into a specialized, decentralized, interconnected network addressing emerging information demands, including tax, agriculture, education, and labor, for the Nation. The 20th Century presented new policy needs leading to further expansion of the Federal statistical system that included commerce, health, energy, justice, transportation, and more. More than two decades into the 21st century, the Federal statistical system continues to provide the gold-standard for impartial, trusted Federal statistics foundational to informing decisions across the public and private sectors.

As the challenges facing the Nation continue to evolve and become more complex, so does the information required to inform decisions. Addressing the new information needs of the Nation efficiently and effectively will require even greater coordination and collaboration within the Federal statistical system and across a broad set of data partners and users in the data and evidence ecosystem. Traditionally, coordination of the decentralized system has relied heavily on the Office of the Chief Statistician of the United States and the good-faith efforts of the individual Federal statistical agencies, units, and programs. As new challenges present themselves, such as long-term downward trends in survey response,[2] increased risk of re-identification of confidential information,[3] and increased need for more blended data products,[4] it becomes increasingly difficult for Federal statistical agencies, units, and programs to meet their individual missions and serve their many stakeholders, including: Federal, State, local, territorial, and tribal governments; businesses; and individuals. While each of the Federal statistical agencies, units, and programs has found innovative ways to address challenges individually, this individual approach is proving more difficult. A successful future for the whole Federal statistical system will rely on more seamless collaboration.

The Office of the Chief Statistician of the United States, leaders across the Federal statistical system, the Administration, and the Congress have all sought ways to require, encourage, and expand coordination and collaboration across Government, recognizing the efficiencies and advancements possible when taking advantage of the whole system's statistical infrastructure and expertise. Of particular note are the requirements to adopt common frameworks for activities such as acquiring data (e.g., administrative or program data) for statistical uses, protecting identifiable data, and disseminating statistical products securely, pursuant to the Confidential Information Protection and Statistical Efficiency Act of 2018 (CIPSEA 2018),[5] as amended by Title III of the Foundations for Evidence-Based Policymaking Act of 2018 (Evidence Act).[6] The Administration understands the value of relying upon the Federal statistical system to advance key priorities such as equity, climate change, the economy, and scientific integrity. The Federal statistical system is working together to provide a strategic vision for and robust implementation of common frameworks and expanded responsibilities in support of evidence-building. It is no longer sufficient for individual statistical agencies, units, or programs to focus solely on their individual missions. And thus, *the vision for the future of the Federal statistical system is to operate as a seamless system, as stewards of much of the Nation's most sensitive data, enabling greater evidence building, civic engagement, and public and private sector decision-making.*

Operating efficiently as a seamless system requires clearly delineated roles. CIPSEA 2018 expanded the responsibilities of Federal statistical agencies and units, which serve as trusted intermediaries between data providers and evidence builders, to implement new policies and procedures for accessing, sharing, generating, protecting, and disseminating data in coordination with one another. Other provisions of the Evidence Act[7] also require agency designations of Statistical Officials, who facilitate coordination of statistical activities within and across departments and are members of the Interagency Council on Statistical Policy.

Enhanced support for the work of the Federal statistical system is needed now more than ever to ensure that Federal statistical agencies, units, and programs can meet their individual and new, collective missions. The remain-

---

[1] *https://www.census.gov/history/pdf/wright-hunt.pdf* (p. 11)

[2] *https://nces.ed.gov/fcsm/pdf/A_Systematic_Review_of_Nonresponse_Bias_Studies_Federally_Sponsored_SurveysFCSM_20_02_032920.pdf*

[3] *https://nces.ed.gov/fcsm/dpt*

[4] See for example presentations in the linked data track at the 2022 FCSM Research and Policy Conference. Available at: https://www.fcsm.gov/events/2022-fcsm-conference/.

[5] Title III of Pub. L. 115-435. Available at: *https://www.congress.gov/115/plaws/publ435/PLAW-115publ435.pdf*.

[6] Pub. L. 115-435. Available at: *https://www.congress.gov/115/plaws/publ435/PLAW-115publ435.pdf*.

[7] Title I of Pub. L. 115-435. Available at: *https://www.congress.gov/115/plaws/publ435/PLAW-115publ435.pdf*.

der of this chapter provides: (1) an overview of the Federal statistical system; (2) a discussion on the importance of trust as the backbone for the use of Federal statistics for evidence-building; (3) a description of system-wide statistical capacity and infrastructure needs and opportunities, as well as recent accomplishments that have strengthened the Federal statistical system and the broader data and evidence ecosystem required for effective evidence-based decisions; (4) highlights of new and revamped critical Government-wide statistical standards and guidance that enhance the suite of official statistics; (5) priorities and budgets of each of the 13 principal statistical agencies and units, as reflected in the 2024 President's Budget; and (6) recent achievements of Statistical Officials. For more information on the Budget's related investments in other evidence-building capacity and program evaluation, see Chapter 12, "Building and Using Evidence to Improve Government Effectiveness."

The Federal Statistical System

The Federal statistical system collects and transforms data into useful, objective information and makes it readily and equitably available to stakeholders, while protecting the responses of individual data providers. Federal, State, local, territorial, and tribal governments, as well as businesses and the public, all trust this information to be credible and reliable and use it to make informed decisions. The decentralized, interconnected network includes:

Office of the Chief Statistician of the United States (OCSOTUS). Led by the Chief Statistician of the United States (CSOTUS), this office in OMB has the statutory responsibility[8] to coordinate the Federal statistical system to ensure its efficiency and effectiveness, as well as the objectivity, impartiality, utility, and confidentiality of information collected for statistical purposes.[9] The office accomplishes its mission by: developing and maintaining statistical policies and standards; promulgating regulations from the Evidence Act; identifying priorities for improving statistical programs and methodologies; assessing statistical agency budgets; reviewing and approving collections of information from statistical agencies/units; and leading and coordinating U.S. participation in international statistical activities, among other functions.

Interagency Council on Statistical Policy (ICSP). The ICSP,[10] led by the CSOTUS, is intended to operate as a seamless system, working together to provide strategic vision and robust implementation in support of the U.S. Federal statistical system's critical longstanding—and expanding—role in supporting evidence-informed decision-making. For example, the ICSP sets strategic goals for modernizing the statistical system, ensuring data

quality and confidentiality, attaining and providing safe and appropriate data access, as well as enhancing coordination and collaboration across the system. Pursuant to the Paperwork Reduction Act of 1995 (PRA)[11] and the Evidence Act, all 24 Statistical Officials are members, as are all heads of the principal statistical agencies and units (for a total of 27 unique members, including the CSOTUS).

24 Statistical Officials. Pursuant to the Evidence Act, each Chief Financial Officers (CFO) Act agency has designated a senior staff person in the agency to be the Statistical Official with the authority and responsibility to advise on statistical policy, techniques, and procedures, and to champion statistical data quality and confidentiality. At the 11 CFO Act agencies that contain a statistical agency or unit, the head of a statistical agency or unit has been designated the Statistical Official, as required by the Evidence Act.

16 Recognized Statistical Agencies and Units. Pursuant to CIPSEA 2018, OMB currently recognizes 16 statistical agencies and units as agencies or organizational units of the Executive Branch whose activities are predominantly the collection, compilation, processing, or analysis of information for statistical purposes. These agencies cover topics such as the economy, workforce, energy, agriculture, foreign trade, education, housing, crime, transportation, and health. Of these 16 statistical agencies/units, 13 have guiding missions to produce statistics, in addition to their OMB recognition. These 13 have traditionally been referred to as the 13 principal statistical agencies/units.

Approximately 100 Other Statistical Programs. These statistical programs, beyond the 16, produce and disseminate statistics in support of other mission areas and conduct a variety of evidence-building functions, such as program evaluation, data collection, policy and program analysis, and provision of funding and other support for internal and external research.[12]

The figure below depicts each of these entities as part of the decentralized, interconnected network that is the Federal statistical system. Each provides value by advancing its specific mission and set of responsibilities. Coordination and collaboration enhance the value of each entity and the system as a whole.

Trust is the Backbone for the Use of Federal Statistics for Evidence-Building

Trust in Federal statistics and their producers underpins their value and enables improvements. It is because of the trust placed in the Federal statistical system that users derive such value from Federal statistics. Each entity within the Federal statistical system must be diligent in upholding this trust. Data providers must trust the system to protect the confidentiality and exclusively statistical use of the information they provide. Meanwhile, data users must trust that the resulting statistics are

---

[8] 44 U.S.C. 3504(e)

[9] "Statistical purpose" means "the description, estimation, or analysis of the characteristics of groups, without identifying the individuals or organizations that comprise such groups." 44 U.S.C. 3561(12)(A). It "includes the development, implementation, or maintenance of methods, technical or administrative procedures, or information resources that support the purposes described" in the preceding sentence. Id. 3561(12)(B).

[10] 44 U.S.C. 3504(e)

[11] Pub. L. 104-13. Available at: *https://www.reginfo.gov/public/reginfo/pra.pdf*

[12] A full listing is included in the Annual Reports to Congress on *Statistical Programs of the United States Government.* Available at: *https://www.whitehouse.gov/wp-content/uploads/2018/05/statistical-programs-2018.pdf*

Chart 9–1   THE DECENTRALIZED FEDERAL STATISTICAL SYSTEM

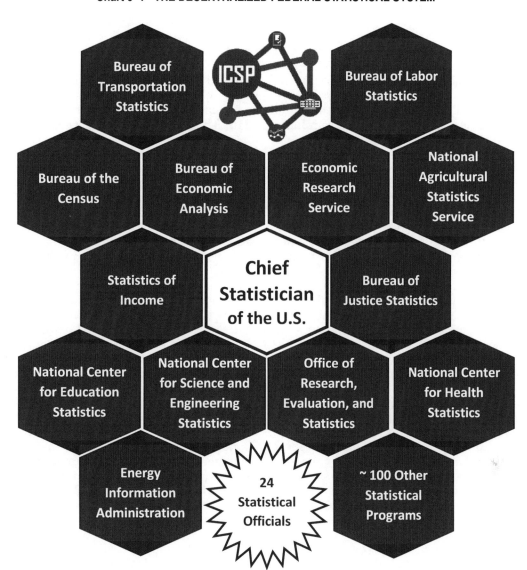

free from political bias or the perception of it, generated with quality inputs, available equitably, and reliable. OMB Statistical Policy Directive No. 1[13] identified four fundamental responsibilities that recognized statistical agencies and units must fulfill: 1) relevance and timeliness, 2) accuracy and credibility, 3) objectivity, and 4) confidentiality and exclusive statistical use of data. Importantly, it also describes how other Federal agencies, including parent departments containing statistical agencies and units, must support, enable, and facilitate statistical agencies and units to meet these responsibilities, emphasizing the importance of conducting their statistical activities autonomously to maintain trust of data providers, users, and the public.

CIPSEA 2018 incorporated those four fundamental responsibilities, and the corresponding responsibilities of other agencies, into statute. The codification of these responsibilities also signifies their criticality to the statistical infrastructure. By upholding these core responsibilities, agencies ensure the trustworthiness of the Federal statistical system—a necessity if the system is to take on an expanded role in the generation of evidence to support policy-making. Any doubts or uncertainty in the system could introduce negative effects on markets, investments, economic growth, and job creation. As required by CIPSEA 2018, OMB is committed to promulgating a regulation on the fundamental responsibilities of recognized statistical agencies and units, and to guiding and supporting agencies' fulfillment of those responsibilities. In early 2023, the Notice of Proposed Rulemaking (NPRM) was submitted for the Executive Order 12866 review process.

[13] http://www.gpo.gov/fdsys/pkg/FR-2014-12-02/pdf/2014-28326.pdf

Building Statistical Capacity and Investing in Essential Statistical Infrastructure

Statistical agency and unit—individual and collective—contributions are necessary to maintain a strong Federal statistical system and to support the broader data and evidence ecosystem as needs constantly evolve. Accurate, timely and relevant statistical products are critical inputs for other evidence builders, such as researchers and evaluators, and also for decision-making by Government programs that affect the lives and livelihoods of all people who need services and information. Statistical capacity is required to support these diverse needs efficiently, equitably, and effectively. Statistical products are also a public good; they help businesses and members of the public access services and make informed decisions, and their value increases the more they are trusted and used. Statistical infrastructure is essential to meeting agency mission delivery, enabling modernization, and promoting reliability. However, like bridges and roads, statistical infrastructure requires ongoing maintenance and updating.

Individually, Federal statistical agencies, units, and programs regularly assess their work and advance the methods used for collection, analysis, protection, and dissemination of their statistical products. They also ensure robust security and IT infrastructure is in place to facilitate their work. For example, in 2022, the National Agricultural Statistics Service (NASS) rolled out a new respondent portal aimed at reducing the time needed for agricultural producers to complete surveys and otherwise making responding more convenient. NASS will reach more producers and continue to provide data that reflect the broad diversity of America's farmers and ranchers. The new respondent portal will enable NASS to integrate new sources of data, better collect and use information, and create a more equitable, user-friendly interface for the public. Without ongoing investments in the statistical infrastructure at each of the principal statistical agencies, as well as throughout the Federal Government more broadly, the quality and relevance of Federal statistics begins to deteriorate.

Ongoing investments and advancements are needed at a system-wide level. CIPSEA 2018 contemplates advancements such as common frameworks for inventorying, protecting, acquiring from other agencies, and disseminating data securely. Executing such common frameworks requires increased interagency engagement when developing new policies or procedures.

Highlights of Recent Significant Advancements Across the Federal Statistical System

Standard Application Process (SAP). The SAP portal, which officially launched in December 2022, fundamentally improves the way researchers and other data users can find and apply for access to restricted, confidential data from any recognized statistical agency or unit for evidence-building purposes. This single "front door" will meaningfully advance evidence-building, by increasing safe access to data in a less burdensome, more transparent way for data users. Launching the SAP portal required

the Federal statistical system to work together seamlessly. This system-wide collaboration, led by ICSP, will support enhancements to the SAP process and portal over time. The National Center for Science and Engineering Statistics (NCSES) is the designated program management office for the SAP portal, and NCSES's contribution on behalf of the full Federal statistical system is one example of individual agencies supporting advancement of the expanded, system-wide mission envisioned in CIPSEA 2018. This significant achievement is a launching pad for additional collaboration in support of evidence-building—by local, tribal, territorial and State governments, researchers, businesses, community-based organizations, advocacy groups, and individual members of the public—such as those recommended by the Advisory Committee on Data for Evidence Building.[14]

Advisory Committee on Data for Evidence Building (ACDEB). In October 2022, the now-sunsetted ACDEB delivered its final report and recommendations to OMB. The ACDEB, established as required by the Evidence Act, was made up of partners across Federal, State and local governments, as well as non-governmental experts in privacy, technology, and research, among other areas. The ACDEB's primary purpose was to advise OMB on implementation of CIPSEA 2018. The OCSOTUS and the ICSP, in collaboration with other interagency councils, are thoughtfully and methodically working through the ACDEB recommendations to determine how to integrate this body of work into ongoing and complementary efforts occurring within the data and evidence ecosystem. For example, many of the ACDEB recommendations suggest frameworks and other priorities that may inform the development of regulations required by CIPSEA 2018. The final report also included a recommendation that OMB, in coordination with the ICSP, the Chief Data Officer Council, the Evaluation Officer Council, and other relevant Federal councils, develop a systematic approach to fund Evidence Act implementation. Those efforts are also highlighted in Chapter 11, "Delivering a High-Performance Government," and Chapter 12, "Building and Using Evidence to Improve Government Effectiveness." OMB will launch a cross-Government, comprehensive resource analysis, in collaboration with Council colleagues, during the remainder of 2023 and into 2024, to inform a comprehensive set of proposals to develop a consistent and sustainable mechanism for identifying and obtaining the resources needed for full Evidence Act implementation.

New Infrastructure Opportunities and Capacity-Development Needs

Envisioning a National Secure Data Service (NSDS). The 2023 President's Budget, the CHIPS and Science Act of 2022,[15] and the final ACDEB recommendations all contemplate aspects of a potential NSDS and what role it should play in the U.S. data and evidence ecosystem. Importantly, a potential NSDS will be part of this eco-

---

[14] More information on the ACDEB and its work is available at: *www.bea.gov/evidence.*

[15] Pub. L. 117-167. Available at: *https://www.congress.gov/bill/117th-congress/house-bill/4346.*

system, not a standalone activity. Much focus to date has been on early pilot projects and the capabilities such an entity will need. For example, the ACDEB final recommendations considered whether an NSDS will coordinate system-wide research on and development of privacy-preserving techniques. The CHIPS and Science Act of 2022 authorizes a 5-year Data Service Demonstration to be led by NCSES with a focus on secure data linkages. The ICSP and NCSES are collaborating to ensure implementation complements other initiatives of the Federal statistical system. This work is being informed by the ACDEB's recommendations, the SAP, and development of regulations pursuant to CIPSEA 2018.

Increasing Capacity for the Statistical Officials. Effective expansion of the U.S. statistical and evidence-building infrastructure will also require increasing the capabilities, capacity, and resources for the 24 Statistical Officials to serve their agencies. Pursuant to OMB Memorandum M-19-23, Phase 1 Implementation of the Foundations for Evidence-Based Policymaking Act of 2018: Learning Agendas, Personnel, and Planning Guidance[16] an agency's Statistical Official has the authority and responsibility to advise on, direct, and coordinate statistical policy, techniques, and procedures across the agency, and to provide leadership on confidentiality across all departmental data assets. This work is to be done in collaboration with Federal data partners, such as the Chief Data Officer, Evaluation Officer, senior agency official for privacy, and the Chief Information Officer. The Statistical Official must be an active participant on the ICSP and the agency's Data Governance Body. Specifically, within the agency, the Statistical Official is charged with overseeing:

- Development of statistical data quality standards to ensure that the agency's statistical products meet quality standards as described in the Information Quality Act and Paperwork Reduction Act, including the provision of metadata sufficient to meet stakeholder needs and to facilitate agency use of privacy-enhancing techniques; and

- Development of confidentiality standards to properly safeguard sensitive information within the agency's data assets.

To promote the ability of Statistical Officials to meet these responsibilities, agencies will pursue an initial investment of no less than 2 full-time equivalent (FTE) positions to support this work. Agencies may choose to meet this resource allocation through varied approaches, such as dedicating 2 full-time positions or spreading the work of 2 FTEs across more than 2 positions.

Expanded Partnerships and Collaboration. Beyond collaborating with each other, statistical agencies and units are also collaborating with external and internal partners, to ensure the system's future success. For example, the Statistics of Income Division (SOI) at the Department of the Treasury collaborated with a non-profit research institution to develop a synthetic individual income tax

dataset that can be shared outside of the IRS to support evidence-building. SOI also applied differential privacy techniques in the production of summarized income data for the Department of Education's College Scorecard. SOI's Joint Statistical Research Program (JSRP) continued as a critical method for enabling non-IRS staff to leverage tax data to support tax administration research. In 2023, SOI began managing JSRP applications via the Standard Application Process.

The system will also continue to rely on its traditional means of engagement with external stakeholders, such as Federal advisory committees (e.g., Federal Economic Statistics Advisory Committee,[17] Bureau of Labor Statistics Technical Advisory Committee,[18] National Center for Health Statistics Board of Scientific Counselors[19]), public comment opportunities, and focus groups or listening sessions. As a few examples, the Census Bureau created an opportunity for the public to provide input into the design of the 2030 Census via a widely advertised Federal Register Notice;[20] NCSES used feedback from multiple stakeholder engagement activities to introduce functional and usability enhancements to its website, metadata, and data tools; and OMB launched new virtual public listening sessions to hear from the public as a part of its effort to review and revise OMB's Statistical Policy Directive No. 15 (*Standards for Maintaining, Collecting, and Presenting Federal Data on Race and Ethnicity*).[21] Across the Federal statistical system, agencies, the ICSP, and the OCSOTUS are building and implementing strategies to more regularly and effectively engage and obtain critical input from members of the public on their work, including data asset needs and user-friendly, relevant data products.

Additional CIPSEA 2018 Regulations and Guidance. The future success of the Federal statistical system as the lynchpin for evidence-building will also require significant growth by recognized statistical agencies and units in how they *acquire data* and *make data safely accessible* for public and private sector uses. As required by CIPSEA 2018, OMB, through OCSOTUS, is developing regulations in these areas to promote consistent, comparable implementation of such new provisions: (1) to make more Federal data assets accessible to recognized statistical agencies and units for the purposes of developing evidence,[22] and (2) to safely and securely expand access to data assets of recognized statistical agencies and units, while protecting such assets from inappropriate access and use.[23] OMB expects to develop and issue future guidance outlining the process by which an agency may be designated a recognized statistical agency or unit. Clearer

---

[16] *https://www.whitehouse.gov/wp-content/uploads/2019/07/M-19-23.pdf*

[17] *https://apps.bea.gov/fesac/*

[18] *https://www.bls.gov/advisory/tac.htm*

[19] *https://www.cdc.gov/nchs/about/bsc.htm*

[20] *https://www.census.gov/newsroom/press-releases/2022/designing-2030-census.html*

[21] *https://www.whitehouse.gov/omb/briefing-room/2022/08/30/omb-launches-new-public-listening-sessions-on-federal-race-and-ethnicity-standards-revision/*

[22] 44 U.S.C. 3581(c)

[23] 44 U.S.C. 3582(b)

guidance is expected to encourage additional units across the Federal Government to adopt the requirements of CIPSEA 2018 and to seek designation as a recognized statistical agency or unit, thereby increasing the breadth of the system. Getting such policies and regulations right is important to the longevity and success of the Federal statistical system.

Investing in New and Revamped Critical Government-Wide Statistical Standards and Guidance

Pursuant to the PRA, the OCSOTUS develops statistical policies, guidance, standards, and best practices and maintains them through periodic review and revision, to ensure their relevance. Much of this work is accomplished through interagency coordination, including across the Federal statistical system, in collaboration with the ICSP and through public engagement.

Over the last year, the OCSOTUS disseminated several updates to and made progress on advancing other statistical policies, guidance, standards, and best practices.

Review and Revision of the Federal Standards for Collecting and Reporting Race and Ethnicity

In 2022, OMB launched a formal review of the Federal Government's Standards for Maintaining, Collecting, and Presenting Data on Race and Ethnicity (Statistical Policy Directive No. 15). Statistical Policy Directive No. 15 provides minimum standards that ensure the ability to compare information and data across Federal agencies, and also to understand how well Federal programs serve a diverse America. OMB is leading a revision process, similar to those used for other trusted statistical standards, to help ensure the rigor, validity, objectivity, and impartiality of the resulting revisions. This process includes convening an interagency technical working group to ensure perspectives from across the Executive Branch are incorporated into the recommendations for any revision to the Standards. This working group, which includes participants from more than 20 agencies across the Federal Government, began developing a set of recommendations for improving the quality and usefulness of Federal race and ethnicity data in summer 2022. Because these Standards are designed, in part, to clarify how well Federal programs serve a diverse population, this working group is broadly engaging with members of various communities and the public, and soliciting public input on the working group's recommendations. It will take the working group time to assess relevant research, engage in a meaningful way with the American public and all impacted agencies, and develop final recommendations. Given the necessary steps, the goal for completing the revision is summer 2024.

Because the revision of statistical standards takes time both to develop and to implement across all Federal agencies, in the interim in July 2022, the OCSOTUS issued a plain language discussion of the existing flexibilities available under the current Statistical Policy Directive No. 15.[24] The goal of this best practice document is to in-

crease awareness and understanding that agencies are encouraged to collect more detailed data on race and ethnicity beyond the minimum categories to better inform policy and program decisions, as long as the additional categories can be aggregated up into the minimum categories. Agencies may also add questions, separate from but beyond the required minimum questions, about an individual's race and ethnicity.

Best Practices for Collecting Sexual Orientation and Gender Identity Data on Federal Statistical Surveys

In January 2023, the OCSOTUS issued a report to spotlight current best practices in the collection and protection of sexual orientation and gender identity (SOGI) data through Federal statistical surveys,[25] in alignment with Executive Order 14075, "Advancing Equality for Lesbian, Gay, Bisexual, Transgender, Queer, and Intersex Individuals".[26] This report includes evidence-based recommendations on how to best collect the data, and includes example survey questions and advice for improving data quality and privacy protection. This report was the product of collaboration with the ICSP and the Federal Committee on Statistical Methodology (FCSM), as well as engagement with members of stakeholder communities and the public. This document complements the Federal Evidence Agenda on LGBTQI+ Equity, also required by Executive Order 14075 and released January 2023, which provides a roadmap for Federal agencies to build and use the evidence needed to advance equity for and improve the health and well-being of LGBTQI+ people.

Measurement of the Bioeconomy

In 2022, the President signed Executive Order 14081, "Advancing Biotechnology and Biomanufacturing Innovation for a Sustainable, Safe, and Secure American Bioeconomy." This Executive Order proposes to coordinate a whole-of-Government approach to advance biotechnology and biomanufacturing towards innovative solutions in health, climate change, energy, food security, agriculture, supply chain resilience, and national and economic security. Critical to this broader effort is the measurement of the bioeconomy. As such, the OCSOTUS has convened an interagency technical working group that is charged with improving and enhancing Federal statistical data collection designed to characterize the economic value of the U.S. bioeconomy, with a focus on the contribution of biotechnology.[27]

These efforts are critical for measuring the output of the U.S. economy and defining growth and change. The U.S.

[24] https://www.whitehouse.gov/wp-content/uploads/2022/07/Flexibilities-and-Best-Practices-Under-SPD-15.pdf

[25] https://www.whitehouse.gov/wp-content/uploads/2023/01/SOGI-Best-Practices.pdf

[26] https://www.whitehouse.gov/briefing-room/presidential-actions/2022/06/15/executive-order-on-advancing-equality-for-lesbian-gay-bisexual-transgender-queer-and-intersex-individuals/

[27] This Working Group, comprising experts from environmental, agricultural, economic, energy, science, and labor backgrounds, has begun the important work of developing a set of recommendations for bioeconomy-related revisions to the North American Industry Classification System (NAICS) and the North American Product Classification System (NAPCS). More information on NAICS is available at https://www.census.gov/naics/. More information on NAPCS is available at https://www.census.gov/naics/napcs/.

economy has undergone transformations over the last two centuries as it shifted from an agrarian focus to heavier reliance upon industrial, digital, and currently, bio-related sectors. As such, the working group will be developing a common understanding of the scope, composition, and relevant components of potential bioeconomy-related industries, and the requirements or parameters necessary for proposing new or revised industry or product codes. As part of this process, the working group will seek robust comment from interested communities, researchers, and the public via a Federal Register Notice in 2023, and use this to provide their formal recommendations to the CSOTUS and the Economic Classification Policy Committee (ECPC). In turn, the ECPC will use these insights in their review and revision process for the 2027 NAICS and NAPCS.

Natural Capital Accounting and
Environmental Economic Statistics

OMB, through the Office of Information and Regulatory Affairs, jointly led the development of the National Strategy for Statistics for Environmental Economic Decisions with the Office of Science and Technology Policy and the Department of Commerce. The final national strategy,[28] published in January 2023, was the product of a policy working group representing 27 agencies across the Executive Branch. This final national strategy incorporated feedback from the public received in response to a *Federal Register* notice published in August 2022. Because currently the Federal Government does not produce a core set of repeatable, reliable, environmental measures connected to the economy, this final national strategy lays out a 15-year plan to do so. This plan will initiate new, reliable, regularly updated statistical series of data that will connect the environment and the economy to better inform decisions about the environment. To meet these goals and develop comparable, consistent statistical series, the plan envisions the OCSOTUS playing a leading role in coordinating this work across the Executive Branch, as well as developing relevant statistical classification systems.

Highlights of 2024 Principal Statistical Agency and Unit Budget Proposals

Each of the 13 principal statistical agencies and units is the leader as to a subset of Federal statistical products and services, which are increasingly interdependent. The collective priorities reflected in the Budget demonstrate the commitment of those statistical agencies and units to advancing not only their own missions, but the more coordinated future of the Federal statistical system.

- *Bureau of the Census (Census Bureau), Department of Commerce.* Funding is requested to support ongoing, core programs and to: (1) continue a multiyear transformation from a survey-centric model to a model centered on blending different sources of data to benefit all Census programs and provide timelier and more relevant statistical products; (2) facilitate

data processing and data releases from the 2022 Economic Census; (3) make new investments in economic statistics for Puerto Rico, in addition to data on businesses' use of technology, post-secondary employment outcomes, and health care; (4) develop new longitudinal demographic research; (5) research innovative methods for producing data on the impacts of natural disasters on the population; (6) improve population and demographic estimates in the intercensal years and enhance the customer experience; (7) support research, design, and testing efforts for the 2030 Census; and (8) support, through both new and continued investments, the new Department of Commerce and Census Bureau strategic plans, as well as Administration priorities in the areas of equity, evaluation, and evidence-building.

- *Bureau of Economic Analysis (BEA), Department of Commerce.* Funding is requested to support core programs, including the production of some of the Nation's most critical economic statistics—such as Gross Domestic Product—and to: (1) develop a new system of U.S. Economic-Environmental Accounts to systematically measure the contributions of environmental economic activities to economic growth; and (2) modernize and expand the Travel and Tourism Satellite Account to track the continued recovery and future growth of the industry.

- *Bureau of Justice Statistics (BJS), Department of Justice.* Funding is requested to support ongoing data collections and to explore new uses of current BJS data, identify and use new administrative data sources, and create efficiencies to collect and disseminate timely and accurate data and to support new efforts to: (1) explore the feasibility of using new administrative data sources to provide more complete national-level data on key aspects of the justice system, including reinstating the Civil Justice Survey of State Courts; (2) continue the redesign of the National Crime Victimization Survey instrument to employ a split-sample design during implementation to ensure comparability of estimates between the current and redesigned instruments; (3) refresh and build upon the 2017 National Census of Victim Service Providers frame to describe the basic characteristics of all organizations and programs serving victims of crime or abuse; (4) support ongoing data modernization efforts to increase efficiencies and improve dissemination practices, including new website and data tool web designs to optimize and expand data access; (5) continue supporting DOJ's implementation of the Evidence Act through the Statistical Official's role; and (6) continue supporting BJS's implementation of the CIPSEA 2018 requirements.

- *Bureau of Labor Statistics (BLS), Department of Labor.* Funding is requested to support core programs, including for the production of principal Federal economic indicators, and to pursue new technologies and non-traditional data sources for many of them. These

---

[28] *https://www.whitehouse.gov/wp-content/uploads/2023/01/ Natural-Capital-Accounting-Strategy-final.pdf*

include: (1) integrating administrative trade data for homogenous product areas into the International Price Program; (2) releasing 2023-2033 economic and employment projections, including as part of an updated Occupational Outlook Handbook; (3) publishing the first multiyear, all-industry, nationwide estimates on occupational injuries and illnesses that result in days of job transfer or work restriction; (4) expanding data on underserved and marginalized workers and modernize data capacities in the Current Population Survey; (5) improving the timeliness of the chained Consumer Price Index; (6) releasing Job Openings and Labor Turnover Survey data early with expanded detail; (7) restoring agricultural industries to the Occupational Employment and Wage Statistics program; (8) producing production-quality thresholds to support the Supplemental Poverty Measure and researching a consumption-based poverty measure and a chained Consumer Price Index for low-income households; (9) continuing to support the future of work and production of gold-standard data and analyses with the Headquarters move to the Suitland Federal Center; and (10) continue to provide data to meet the Administration's equity goals.

- *Bureau of Transportation Statistics (BTS), Department of Transportation.* Funding is requested to support core programs and to: (1) continue the Freight Logistics Optimization Works Initiative that BTS manages for improving the effectiveness of freight transportation and to reduce supply chain disruptions; (2) fund the effort to improve the timeliness and coverage of transportation financial statistics; (3) fund the Electric Vehicle Inventory and Use Survey that would collect data on the characteristics and uses of Electric Vehicles (EVs) to better understand this emerging form of transportation; (4) develop a model with existing data sources to measure transportation cost burden and identify data gaps; (5) explore methods for capturing individual and household cost, travel time, trips not taken, accessibility, and access to key resources across different demographic groups; and (6) launch a data sharing platform for equitable data.

- *Economic Research Service (ERS), Department of Agriculture.* Funding is requested to support core programs and to: (1) fund the National Household Food Acquisition and Purchase Survey, which enables robust analysis of how food choices, nutrition security, and other important program decisions vary across different households in the United States for various racial, ethnic, and disability groups across various income classes and by participation in various food assistance programs; (2) fund the Survey of Irrigation Organizations, which is conducted by Economic Research Service (ERS) and National Agricultural Statistics Service (NASS) and provides a greater understanding of local irrigation decisions and their impact on drought resilience; and (3) conduct an in-dependent review of the methods, data construction, and model construction of the Core Food Access and Food Environment Data Systems as the food access environment evolves.

- *Energy Information Administration (EIA), Department of Energy.* Funding is requested to continue delivering the critical data, analysis, forecasts, and long-term energy outlooks on which its stakeholders rely, and to: (1) expand electric grid operations data for one-stop access to high-value, near real-time data on actual electricity demand, demand forecasts, pricing, and emissions; (2) pursue new data collection methodologies to enable EIA to track and report on short-term shifts in energy consumption patterns; (3) develop data on EV integration with the grid, including the use of existing data sources where feasible to increase understanding of EV electricity consumption and infrastructure; (4) improve analysis of international energy issues, trends, and events, such as time-sensitive assessments of significant geopolitical events; (5) modernize the National Energy Modeling System to deliver expanded scenario analysis of decarbonization pathways, for example, developing model representations for increased electrification, biofuels, hydrogen, and carbon capture, transport, and sequestration; and (6) increase information accessibility and usability by leveraging new technologies to make statistics and analyses more accessible and transparent.

- *National Agricultural Statistics Service (NASS), Department of Agriculture.* Funding is requested to improve customer service, improve access to data, and modernize IT infrastructure. NASS has identified specific actions that would provide cost savings by moving the agency towards a more modern approach in how it collects, analyzes, processes, and disseminates data. This modernization and enhancement would also lessen the digital divide between small and large producers, lower the need for producers to pay for publicly available data, and create more equitable markets by allowing all participants to easily gain insights from the key agricultural information NASS provides through their census and survey programs. This investment would facilitate cybersecurity enhancement and modernization of NASS data release and publications of the Census of Agriculture.

- *National Center for Education Statistics (NCES), Department of Education.* Funding is requested to provide support for NCES ongoing activities and to: (1) expand NCES's geospatial Education Demographic and Geographic Estimates program; (2) establish a dedicated R&D program to accelerate innovations in the National Assessment of Educational Progress (NAEP); (3) fund an NCES-wide R&D program to support research into topics such as school recruitment and partnering initiatives and data collection and reporting tools for use by entities outside of NCES; (4) build new district-level features into

NCES's monthly School Pulse Panel; (5) expand and fully implement initiatives to collect school-level finance data from elementary and secondary schools; (6) pilot work to centralize approaches to sampling across NCES studies; (7) meet obligations under the Evidence Act for the Education Department's Statistical Official, and for NCES (e.g., including the Standard Application Process and the expected increase in requests for confidential data that will result); (8) fund internal process improvement initiatives; (9) support the expansion of timely and policy relevant Diversity, Equity, Inclusion, and Accessibility initiatives; and (10) enhance outreach to parents and families by making NCES data more accessible.

- *National Center for Health Statistics (NCHS), Department of Health and Human Services.* Funding is requested to support its base programs as well as to promote modernizing data collection, accessibility, linkage, and interoperability, consistent with CDC's Data Modernization Initiative, and implement the Evidence Act. Investment areas include: (1) increasing the quality, timeliness, and scope of health data through innovative research in survey methods and new technologies for data collection, including real-time surveys; (2) generating data to understand health equity and the social determinants of health through sampling and leveraging the NCHS Data Linkage Program; (3) enhancing the value of existing health data through improved visualization and presentation tools; (4) increasing access to data through use of virtual data enclaves; (5) implementing requirements to acquire data assets for evidence-building purposes; and (6) expanding electronic health record capabilities and interoperability with vital statistics.

- *National Center for Science and Engineering Statistics (NCSES), National Science Foundation.* Funding is requested to provide support for ongoing NCSES activities and to: (1) lead and expand Government-wide development of evidence-building infrastructure activities including the Standard Application Process and the National Secure Data Service demonstration project; (2) implement mandates as part of the CHIPS and Science Act of 2022, such as the establishment of a cybersecurity workforce data initiative, collecting and reporting of Federal research award data, and expanding data collection activities for the STEM workforce; (3) further the Nation's understanding of the impact of research and development funding on the U.S. and global scientific enterprises; (4) improve the Government's classification systems for defining and measuring cybersecurity, bioeconomy, the skilled technical workforce, and data science occupations; and (5) study and expand privacy-preserving techniques to facilitate data linking in support of evidence-building.

- *Office of Research, Evaluation, and Statistics (ORES), Social Security Administration.* Funding is requested to continue core programs, including to:

(1) conduct research on Social Security programs and their beneficiaries, publishing papers in the Social Security Bulletin; (2) provide policymakers and the public with objective, scientific, and methodologically sound information and analysis; (3) automate and modernize the production of statistical publications; (4) leverage the expertise of researchers around the Nation through grants and contracts, such as the Retirement and Disability Research Consortium; (5) provide objective, secure data and statistics while protecting privacy through strict adherence to disclosure review policies; and (6) meet SSA-wide duties under the Evidence Act including as SSA Statistical Official and CIPSEA 2018 responsibilities, including active engagement in the work of the Interagency Council on Statistical Policy.

- *Statistics of Income Division (SOI), Department of the Treasury (Treasury).* Funding is requested to provide support for ongoing SOI programs and to: (1) incorporate and implement the tax law provisions of the Inflation Reduction Act of 2022; (2) implement requirements of Executive Order 13985 by collaborating with Treasury, the Equitable Data Working Group, and other Federal agencies to acquire and analyze tax data by race and ethnicity; (3) implement the Evidence Act and CIPSEA 2018, including preserving and expanding access to data for research and policy purposes when permitted by law, while preserving and increasing the confidentiality of taxpayer data, and increasing staffing to meet the new responsibilities; (4) identify additional interagency collaboration in research and data production and to bring together data from multiple tax filing populations, to develop more useful data and therefore enhance tax administration and policy evaluation; (5) explore machine learning, natural language processing, and optical character recognition, improving IRS administrative data quality and accessibility; (6) modernize SOI's processing environment by coordinating with the IRS's Enterprise Digitization team to reduce the use of paper-filed tax returns in SOI programs; (7) undertake review of processing center program completion dates and workload planning to help mitigate risks due to staffing constraints and reduce lag between tax return filings and the release of official statistics; (8) support implementation of a Federal data strategy and governance process within the IRS and Treasury; and (9) update the SOI website by improving infographics and its search function capability.

Recent Highlights and Achievements of Statistical Officials

Each Statistical Official has an important role to play not only for their own agency, but also the more coordinated future of the Federal statistical system. As noted previously, effective expansion of the U.S. statistical and evidence-building infrastructure will require increasing the capabilities, capacity, and resources for the 24

Statistical Officials to serve their agencies and departments. Some agencies may still be staffing the function to the initial, minimum investment level of 2 FTE positions. This section reflects the first-time reporting in this area, highlighting agency accomplishments, with future year reporting intended to more broadly represent key activities and accomplishments across all agencies.

- *Department of Agriculture (USDA).* The USDA Statistical Official leveraged ERS resources to establish Democratizing the Data, a pilot project that applies a natural language processing algorithm to focus on data assets as a product innovation by finding out how datasets are being used across scientific and public research. This project aims to develop a conceptual framework that describes the production, dissemination, use, and ultimately the value of data, and then apply this framework to two ERS data assets as a proof of concept for valuing public data.

- *Department of Commerce (DOC).* The DOC Statistical Official identified an opportunity for the Census Bureau and BEA to play a large role in assisting DOC with their responsibilities under the American Rescue Plan Act[29] and the Infrastructure Investment and Jobs Act.[30] To provide this leadership, DOC directed the formation of a Data Governance Working Group (DGWG) under the purview of the Commerce Data Governance Board (CDGB). The DGWG—chaired by the Census Bureau's Deputy Director who provided statistical agency and evaluation methods expertise—developed a final report titled "Best Practices for Monitoring and Evaluating the ARP, IIJA, and Other Programs." The implementation of the recommendations from this report continues in a new working group, under the purview of the CDGB and co-chaired by the Census Bureau, titled the Metrics Working Group.

- *Department of Defense (DOD).* The DOD Statistical Official was first identified and officially designated in June 2022. DOD coordinates and collaborates extensively with interagency partners on statistical initiatives. Internally, the office within DOD that includes the Statistical Official responsibilities collaborates closely with the DOD Performance Improvement Officer and the DOD Chief Digital and Artificial Intelligence Officer to centralize data for decision- and policy-making, and to improve statistical data and reporting in support of the DOD Strategic Management Plan and the National Defense Strategy.

- *Department of Education (ED).* The ED Statistical Official worked with colleagues across the Department to clarify how statistical data can be accessed for projects other offices might be considering. The Statistical Official also supported extensive engagement by NCES staff on Department-wide data governance boards and related efforts as part of its administrative data statistical work.

- *Department of Energy (DOE).* The DOE Statistical Official expanded data access, deploying dynamic user-friendly dissemination tools, promoting open-source models, and collaborating with other Federal agencies, including the United States Geological Survey, Environmental Protection Agency, and Census Bureau, to expand electricity data, provide new insights into energy usage trends, and support the development of a critical minerals demand forecast.

- *Department of Health and Human Services (HHS).* The HHS Statistical Official provided leadership across HHS for data linkage, dissemination, and curation of linked data files to better inform policies and support robust evidence-based programmatic decisions. In 2022, NCHS linked its survey data with Department of Veteran Affairs administrative records and the Centers for Medicare and Medicaid Services' Transformed Medicaid Statistical Information System administrative data to support epidemiological surveillance and policy evaluation studies for populations at risk for substance abuse disorders and other health inequities.

- *Department of Homeland Security (DHS).* The DHS Statistical Official worked with departmental and component leadership to support the Secretary's decision in September 2022 to direct the establishment of an independent Office of Homeland Security Statistics (OHSS). The office will be led by the Statistical Official and will independently report on all DHS Homeland Security data. The mission of the OHSS will be to maximize DHS data transparency and consistency, support data-driven decision-making, and improve efficiency of statistical reporting.

- *Department of Housing and Urban Development (HUD).* The HUD Statistical Official directed changes in the calculations of HUD's program parameters, namely program eligibility Income Limits and Fair Market Rents (FMRs), to account for the effects of rapid general price inflation and volatile rental prices in markets throughout the United States on the operations of HUD and other Federal housing programs. The revisions to the FMR calculations involved, for the first time, the evaluation and adoption of various private sector data sources on market rents into the estimation program.

- *Department of the Interior (DOI).* The DOI Statistical Official worked across the agency and Government to advance statistical capacity related to the mission areas of resource management, science and information, and the agency's Trust obligations to Native Americans. This included working with the DOI Data Governance Board to elevate the role of statistics in translating data to evidence for evaluation; building evidence capacity related to DOI's Infrastructure Investment and Jobs Act programs; and

---

[29] Pub. L. 117-2
[30] Pub. L. 117-58

supporting the development of the National Strategy for Natural Capital Accounts.

- *Department of Justice (DOJ).* The DOJ Statistical Official leveraged BJS resources to support DOJ with new data collection efforts, including standing up new systems to measure the incidence of particular crimes and their enforcement. The Statistical Official has also been successful in getting the word out across DOJ on BJS's role and value to DOJ programs.

- *Department of Labor (DOL).* The DOL Statistical Official worked with other DOL officials to develop an initial Capacity Assessment for Research, Evaluation, Statistics, and Analysis required under the Evidence Act, which provides a baseline for measuring future improvements to coverage, data quality, evidence-building methods, effectiveness, and independence of statistics, evaluation, research, and analysis activities. DOL's Capacity Assessment consists of a review of DOL-wide staff use of evidence (statistics, research, analysis) in decision-making, including areas of strength and opportunities for improvement. The Assessment also includes an overview of statistical capacity through the DOL statistical agency, the Bureau of Labor Statistics (BLS).

- *Department of State.* The Department of State Statistical Official holds a leadership role on the Department's Enterprise Data Council, and continued to contribute towards the implementation of the Department's newly established Enterprise Data Strategy and associated data campaigns. These campaigns focus data analytics resources toward high-level foreign policy and management priorities, including cybersecurity and multilateralism, to discover and deliver evidence-based policy and process improvements on behalf of the American People.

- *Department of Transportation (DOT).* The DOT Statistical Official led the development of common Notice of Funding Opportunity (NOFO) data language to be used in all research NOFOs. The goal of the language is to require that data resulting from grant programs (many of which are associated with the Infrastructure Investment and Jobs Act) be submitted to DOT, where these data will then be curated, federated, and accessible for internal and external communities to use. This effort takes the first step in creating a culture that is data-driven, outcomes-based, and focused on continuous learning and evidence building.

- *Department of the Treasury (Treasury).* In addition to actively contributing to Evidence Act deliverables led by others, and regularly providing advice through the Treasury Data Governance Board, the Treasury's Statistical Official led the development of the Department's draft Scientific Integrity Policy and worked with the Data Governance Board to set

up a workshop to share data literacy and training activities Department-wide.

- *Department of Veterans Affairs (VA).* The VA Statistical Official, in conjunction the VA Governance Council, developed an enterprise analytics platform to facilitate data governance, management, and analytics. The Platform supports several enterprise initiatives leveraging previously siloed datasets from across VA into authoritative, integrated data assets for evidence-building and decision support. This Platform is enabling VA to better oversee and manage the Sergeant First Class Heath Robinson Honoring our Promise to Address Comprehensive Toxics Act implementation (e.g., enabling efficient, secure information sharing and collaboration across key VA organizations).

- *Environmental Protection Agency (EPA).* The EPA Statistical Official, in collaboration with the National Center for Environmental Economics, worked to advance EPA's capacity to produce and use statistical evidence through the provision of analytical support and consulting services. This program successfully provided guidance on the development of statistical surveys to aid those offices without expertise on survey methodology, conducted statistical analyses to support agency decision-making, and developed new statistical products to support key EPA priorities of Environmental Justice and Civil Rights.

- *General Services Administration (GSA).* The GSA Statistical Official worked with the President's Management Council, OMB, the Office of Personnel Management, and others at GSA to launch the first-ever Federal employee pulse survey pilot to better understand Federal employee needs and perceptions at a time when many Federal agencies planned for a return to in-person work or navigated newly hybrid workplaces.

- *National Aeronautics and Space Administration (NASA).* The NASA Statistical Official promoted statistical principles within NASA and enabled evidence-based decision-making, particularly in the area of NASA investments by developing and promoting analyses through the Strategic Investments Division (SID) Insights Book. The SID Insights Book is a collection of executive-level summaries of analyses that provide evidence-based statistical insights for NASA leadership. It brings statistical analyses being conducted at multiple levels within the agency to a broader audience, enabling larger reach with the intent of informing NASA decisions.

- *National Science Foundation (NSF).* The NSF Statistical Official co-led Agency efforts to leverage internal data to inform NSF efforts to increase diversity, equity, inclusion, and accessibility. As a part of this effort, the Statistical Official introduced NSF colleagues tasked with developing policies to increase

STEM diversity to various Federal data sources and provided advice on the 'fitness for use' of the sources.

- *Nuclear Regulatory Commission (NRC).* The NRC Statistical Official, in collaboration with the Data Governance Board, was instrumental in the development of NRC's first Artificial Intelligence (AI) Strategic Plan, which is intended to: (1) ensure NRC readiness for regulatory decision-making, (2) establish an organizational framework to review AI applications, (3) strengthen and expand AI partnership, (4) cultivate an AI-proficient workforce, and (5) pursue use cases to build an AI foundation across the NRC. The overall goal of this strategic plan is to ensure continued staff readiness to review and evaluate AI applications effectively and efficiently.

- *Office of Personnel Management (OPM).* The OPM Statistical Official is leading the implementation of a framework to coordinate the development of human capital data analytics products across the agency to ensure it is producing accurate, relevant, and timely Federal workforce statistics to OPM leadership, Federal agencies, and the public.

- *Social Security Administration (SSA).* The SSA Statistical Official oversaw a comprehensive review of SSA's disclosure limitations policies, standards, and practices, leveraging contractor resources, to ensure SSA was using proper data protection practices. This review is helping SSA to disseminate relevant and timely statistical information.

- *Small Business Administration (SBA).* The SBA Statistical Official worked throughout SBA to assess statistical needs and priorities, and participated in working groups to promote the use of administrative data for statistical purposes. The Statistical Official championed forward thinking in development of the SBA's new integrated platform to allow for a common framework for collecting and protecting administrative data that can be used for accessing, sharing, generating, protecting, and disseminating data, while protecting confidentiality and privacy.

- *United States Agency for International Development (USAID).* In support of the U.S. Government's Initiative for Global Vaccine Access (Global VAX) led by USAID, the Agency's Statistical Official collaborated with USAID's Bureau for Global Health to deliver a solution for submitting, analyzing, and visualizing data to accelerate COVID-19 vaccine uptake in partner countries. This collaboration led to USAID launching the Global VAX Initiative Dashboards, which share COVID-19 vaccination data with USAID and other U.S. Government stakeholders. The Statistical Official also facilitated the creation of a framework for improving data quality, which included identifying priority data domains and taxonomies to standardize data use and facilitate interoperability.

Table 9–1.   2022–2024 BUDGET APPROPRIATIONS FOR PRINCIPAL STATISTICAL AGENCIES[1]
(In millions of dollars)

Agency	Actual		Estimate
	2022	2023	2024
Bureau of the Census [2]	1,369.3	1,503.9	1,626.0
Bureau of Economic Analysis	111.1	121.9	139.5
Bureau of Justice Statistics	40.0	42.0	78.0
Bureau of Labor Statistics	688.0	698.0	758.4
Bureau of Transportation Statistics [3,4]	26.0	29.3	31.7
Economic Research Service.	84.8	93.0	98.0
Enery Information Administration	129.1	135.0	149.6
National Agricultural Statistics Service [5]	190.2	211.1	240.6
National Center for Education Statistics	352.3	369.8	286.3
Statistics	127.1	138.5	148.6
Assessment.	217.5	223.5	228.4
National Assessment Governing Board	7.8	7.8	9.3
National Center for Health Statistics.	180.4	187.4	189.5
National Center for Science and Engineering Statistics, NSF	66.8	90.8	106.9
Office of Research, Evaluation, and Statistics, SSA	39.7	40.9	41.0
Statistics of Income Division, IRS	42.4	41.7	45.6

[1] Reflects any rescissions and sequestration.
[2] Agency Total includes discretionary and mandatory funds.
[3] 2022 estimates reflects an allocation account from the Highway Trust Fund.
[4] 2023 and 2024 amounts reflects an allocation account from the Highway Trust Fund a from the DOT Salaries and Expenses appropriation for the FLOW initiative.
[5] Includes funds for the periodic Census of Agriculture of $46.9, $66.4 and $80.5 respectively.

Conclusion

This Chapter highlighted exciting and impactful work underway across the Federal statistical system. Realizing the full potential of Federal statistics for effective evidence-building requires ongoing, robust investments and growth in both agency-specific and system-wide statistical capacity and infrastructure. Such investments must be made in a way that maintains the trust of State, territorial, local, and tribal governments, businesses, and the public, all of whom provide data to the Federal Government, as well as decision makers from those sectors who use the resulting statistics for developing and improving policies, including those necessary to enhance the equitable delivery of services and programs. Additional investments in system-wide statistical capacity and infrastructure must be ongoing to meet the increasing demands for data access and the new challenges to the public trust that arise in the context of the evolving data landscape.

10. BUDGET EXPOSURE TO INCREASED COSTS AND LOST REVENUE DUE TO CLIMATE CHANGE

The climate crisis poses a serious threat to the United States economy and human welfare, with a narrowing timeframe to make strategic investments to avoid the most catastrophic impacts. Acute effects such as extreme weather events, changing precipitation patterns, impacts to air quality and water quality, disruptions to supply chains, and changes to food production and supply can result in cascading impacts disrupting services.[1] Chronic physical risks from climate change also adds risks to deteriorating infrastructure, land-use changes, and populations.[2] Without action, climate change threatens the Nation's economy, national security, essential services, and the Nation's fiscal health. The Fourth National Climate Assessment (NCA4)[3] notes that:

> *Climate change is transforming where and how we live and presents growing challenges to human health and quality of life, the economy, and the natural systems that support us. Risks posed by climate variability and change vary by region and sector and by the vulnerability of people experiencing impacts.*

To help address threats that climate change poses to the economy, the President signed Executive Order 14030, "Climate-Related Financial Risk" on May 20, 2021. Section 6(b) of Executive Order 14030 directs "[t]he Director of OMB and the Chair of the Council of Economic Advisers, in consultation with the Director of the National Economic Council, the National Climate Advisor, and the heads of other agencies as appropriate, [to] develop and publish annually, within the President's Budget, an assessment of the Federal Government's climate risk exposure." This chapter meets the requirements of this section of the Executive Order.

This assessment is complementary to the analysis directed by Section 6(a) of Executive Order 14030, "[T]he Director of OMB, in consultation with the Secretary of the Treasury, the Chair of the Council of Economic Advisers, the Director of the National Economic Council, and the National Climate Advisor, shall identify the primary sources of Federal climate-related financial risk exposure and develop methodologies to quantify climate risk within the economic assumptions and the long-term budget projections of the President's Budget." The work directed by Section 6(a) takes a broad, macroeconomic view of the impact of climate risk on economic assumptions used within the President's Budget, which includes gross domestic product (GDP) and the debt based on long-term budget projections. The 6(a) analysis assesses how climate change indirectly affects Federal revenues and outlays through macroeconomic channels, whereas the analysis under Section 6(b) primarily focuses on the direct impact of climate on Federal expenditures through illustrative examples. Therefore, together the analysis of Section 6(a) and Section 6(b) show the multi-faceted impact of climate change on the Federal Budget.

This chapter is divided into two sections: 1) a review of test cases of assessments of the Federal Budget's exposure to climate risk, using the limited climate risk financial tools that are currently available; and 2) an outline of a common framework for agencies to assess the budget exposure to climate risk of federally administered programs, federally owned assets, operations, and mission. This year's chapter includes three assessments of the Federal Budget's exposure: an updated analysis on flood risk to selected Federal facilities; a summary of the work completed under Section 5(c) of Executive Order 14030 on the climate risks to Federal lending with an analysis on the exposure of the single-family housing portfolio of the Federal Government; and a new assessment on the impact of increasing temperatures due to climate change on the Low Income Home Energy Assistance Program (LIHEAP). These test cases rely on today's limited climate financial tools and as a result, can underestimate risk. Therefore, the results are intended to illustrate, but not represent, a comprehensive estimate of projected impacts. They are presented here to document methodologies to date, including the limitations of current tools, so to inform the development of the next generation of robust climate financial risk methods and tools. The section on the framework of future assessments is structured as follows: 1) current approaches used by Federal agencies for assessing climate risk; 2) climate data and modeling that is currently available to agencies; 3) a proposed common framework to assess climate-related financial risk and necessary technical inputs; and 4) a discussion of next

---

[1] Jay, A., D.R. Reidmiller, C.W. Avery, D. Barrie, B.J. DeAngelo, A. Dave, M. Dzaugis, M. Kolian, K.L.M. Lewis, K. Reeves, and D. Winner, 2018: Overview. In Impacts, Risks, and Adaptation in the United States: Fourth National Climate Assessment, Volume II [Reidmiller, D.R., C.W. Avery, D.R. Easterling, K.E. Kunkel, K.L.M. Lewis, T.K. Maycock, and B.C. Stewart (eds.)]. U.S. Global Change Research Program, Washington, DC, USA, pp. 33–71. doi: 10.7930/NCA4.2018.CH1

[2] Clarke, L., L. Nichols, R. Vallario, M. Hejazi, J. Horing, A.C. Janetos, K. Mach, M. Mastrandrea, M. Orr, B.L. Preston, P. Reed, R.D. Sands, and D.D. White, 2018: Sector Interactions, Multiple Stressors, and Complex Systems. In Impacts, Risks, and Adaptation in the United States: Fourth National Climate Assessment, Volume II [Reidmiller, D.R., C.W. Avery, D.R. Easterling, K.E. Kunkel, K.L.M. Lewis, T.K. Maycock, and B.C. Stewart (eds.)]. U.S. Global Change Research Program, Washington, DC, USA, pp. 638–668. doi: 10.7930/NCA4.2018.CH17

[3] Jay, A., D.R. Reidmiller, C.W. Avery, D. Barrie, B.J. DeAngelo, A. Dave, M. Dzaugis, M. Kolian, K.L.M. Lewis, K. Reeves, and D. Winner, 2018: Overview. In Impacts, Risks, and Adaptation in the United States: Fourth National Climate Assessment, Volume II [Reidmiller, D.R., C.W. Avery, D.R. Easterling, K.E. Kunkel, K.L.M. Lewis, T.K. Maycock, and B.C. Stewart (eds.)]. U.S. Global Change Research Program, Washington, DC, USA, pp. 33–71. doi: 10.7930/NCA4.2018.CH1

**Table 10–1.   PRELIMINARY SUMMARY OF QUANTIFIED FEDERAL CLIMATE RISK EXPOSURE
PROJECTED CHANGE IN ANNUAL EXPENDITURES OF ASSESSED PROGRAMS**

(In billions of 2021 dollars[1])

Assessment Topic	Mid-Century			Late-Century		
	Central Measure[3]	Low	High	Central Measure[3]	Low	High
Crop Insurance[2]	N/A	N/A	N/A	1.3	0.3	2.2
Coastal Disasters	15.3	4.6	34.0	51.8	22.9	98.5
Healthcare	1.0	0.2	1.9	11.9	0.9	22.9
Wildland Fire Supression	1.7	0.9	2.4	3.9	1.6	10.0
Total for Assessments[4]	**18.0**	**5.7**	**38.3**	**68.8**	**25.7**	**133.6**

N/A = Not Available

[1] The summary table of the assessments within the 2023 President's Budget used 2020 dollars, hence the values in this table, which are in 2021 dollars, are slightly higher due to inflation.

[2] The crop insurance analysis was only conducted for late century.

[3] The median of all wildland fire suppression simulations is used in the "Central Measure" column, so outliers in the "Higher" scenario are not overemphasized in the results. All other topics use the mean as the central measure.

[4] Multiple Federal financial risks are not included in this table due to the nascent ability to quantify future expenditures in this field.

steps to further develop the common framework to improve climate financial risk tools.

Update on the Federal Budget Exposure to Climate Risk

In an effort to better understand the risks that climate change poses to the Federal Budget, the Office of Management and Budget (OMB) continues to work across the Federal Government to further the assessment of climate-related financial risks. In the 2023 President's Budget, OMB published an assessment[4] that included six types of climate risks and projected a $26 billion to $134 billion (2021 dollars) increase in Federal costs, shown in Table 10-1. This is likely an underestimation of impacts due to the limitations of today's climate financial risk tools. The analyses in the 2023 President's Budget demonstrated the feasibility of conducting quantitative assessment of climate risk in the Federal Budget.

This chapter provides several updates to the Federal Budget's exposure to climate risk. The goal of the three analyses conducted this year is to advance our collective understanding of the current capabilities and limitations of available modeling tools and data, in order to generate a more representative assessment of the true cost of climate change in the Federal Budget. Through a series of illustrative analytical test cases, Federal researchers and modelers identified informative trends and identified data and modeling gaps that will inform improvements in climate financial risk modeling tools and provide a more accurate and representative estimate of the cost of climate risks for the Federal Budget in coming years. Through additional refinement of analytical tools and continued research, policy officials will be equipped with the knowledge to make more informed decisions about investing resources more efficiently to mitigate climate risk. The analysis on flood risk to Federal facilities now provides an estimate of the loss for a select set of Federal facilities and incorporates forward-looking climate scenarios for flood-

ing. The evaluation of the Federal single-family housing lending portfolio, provides insights on the current risk climate change may bring to the portfolio, while also underscoring the need for improved analytical tools to assess climate related financial risk. Lastly, LIHEAP—a Federal program that assists low-income households with heating and cooling costs—is added to the assessment of Federal fiscal climate risks.

Quantified fiscal impacts of climate change provided for the new test cases are illustrative and not suitable for decision-making due to the limitations of today's tools that are unable to provide accurate and robust projections of exposure and loss. The presented quantitative results are not official Government estimates. Rather, these results provide transparency and underscore the lack of data and modeling currently available through the Federal Government to accurately assess climate related financial risk.

Findings from the three test cases —i.e., not cost estimates, not intended for decision-making—include:

- *Federal single-family housing portfolio*: After conducting a test case exercise that analyzes past, present, and future climate risks to the Federal single-family housing portfolio, the conclusion of the agencies' analysis indicated that current climate financial risk tools underestimate climate risk. This analysis concluded that five climate hazards (hurricanes, coastal flooding, riverine flooding, wildfires, and tornadoes) examined, riverine flooding is anticipated to cause half of the annual losses of unpaid principal balances across the Department of Agriculture (USDA), the Department of Veterans Affairs (VA), and the Department of Housing and Urban Development's (HUD) single-family housing portfolio. However, when applying a proprietary climate risk model, utilized by one of the largest housing lenders in the Nation, to Federal lending data to test the model the researchers found that the model did not consider future climate projections, and therefore underestimated climate risks.

---

[4] Office of Management and Budget (2022). Climate Risk Exposure: An Assessment of the Federal Government's Financial Risks to Climate Change.

- *Replacement Cost of Federal Facilities Impacted by Sea Level Rise*: The researchers found that there is currently no public or private sector climate data available to accurately estimate the cost implications of sea level rise on Federal facilities. In an illustrative analysis using public data, noting among the multiple data limitations—including: 1) that the data used was not intended to identify site-specific risks; and 2) does not take into account the value of the services provided, the annual replacement value effected from sea level rise is projected between $72 million and $127 million for mid-century and between $449 million and $1.786 billion by the end of the century, not counting transition costs – an underestimation of climate risk due to data limitations. For example, following Hurricane Katrina, in only one year, $38 million was needed to repair more than 83 Federal facilities damaged from the hurricane.[5] This shows that better data and modeling is needed to evaluate the true cost of climate change to Federal facilities (see Table 10-3).

- *Heating and Cooling Assistance*: The 20-year average for heating degree days is projected to decline by up to 30 percent by the end of the century, while the average number of cooling degrees days in estimated to increase by 65 percent. These changes may impact energy demand for heating and cooling, and in turn, LIHEAP funding. In addition to changes in the trends of cooling degree days and heating degree days, extreme weather events induced by climate change will continue to impact the needs of cooling and heating assistance, as the frequency, duration, and intensity of extreme weather events are projected to change over time.

The analyses presented in this chapter are expected to be revised in future years as new climate and financial risk modeling capabilities are incorporated and data quality and availability are improved. The results of these assessments should be viewed as tests cases, not definitive or comprehensive results. The preparation of these illustrative test cases highlights where further research is needed to address data gaps and methodological limitations, which are discussed further in the section titled "Establishing a Common Framework for Evaluating Climate-Related Financial Risks".

Exploratory Analyses on Federal Lending Portfolio of Single-Family Housing

Executive Order 14030, Section 5(c) directs the Secretary of Agriculture, the Secretary of Housing and Urban Development, and the Secretary of Veterans Affairs, "to consider approaches to better integrate climate-related financial risk into underwriting standards, loan terms and conditions, and asset management and servicing procedures, as related to their Federal lending policies and programs". OMB established the 5c Task Force under the

Federal Credit Policy Council, with HUD, USDA, and VA (lending agencies) to conduct initial analyses and to create a replicable framework for assessing climate risk in Federal lending programs. This analysis marks the first time that the Federal Government has undertaken the task of broadly examining how climate-related financial risks could impact Federal lending across multiple agencies and evaluating the limitations of current tools used to calculate those risks.

The 5c Task Force determined that the first step to considering new approaches for integrating climate related financial risk in various lending programs is to understand the nature and extent of risks to the single-family guaranteed housing programs at each Federal agency. These programs include:

- USDA's Rural Development (RD) Single Family Housing Guaranteed Loan Program (SFHG);

- HUD's Federal Housing Administration (FHA) single-family insurance program;

- HUD's Government National Mortgage Association (Ginnie Mae) Mortgage-Backed Security (MBS) guarantee program; and

- VA's Loan Guaranty program (VA).

The Federal lending programs for single-family housing had a cumulative outstanding exposure of $2.1 trillion as of 2021, and Ginnie Mae had a similar exposure in outstanding guaranteed MBS.

In order to gain a better understanding of the cost of climate change to the Federal lending portfolio, as well as the limitations of today's climate financial risk tools, OMB and the lending agencies conducted three exploratory analyses to evaluate retrospective, current, and future climate risk. In the prospective test case, OMB and the lending agencies applied a proprietary climate risk model utilized by one of the Nation's largest housing lenders to Federal lending data in order to determine if the results would accurately value the risk that climate change poses to the Federal lending portfolio. Leveraging the existing proprietary tool, OMB's test case failed to measure substantive climate risk which is likely a gross underestimation due to the significant limitations of this climate financial risk tool. These three exploratory test cases indicate that both public and private sector models, when applied to Federal data, vastly undervalue the true cost that climate change poses to lending agencies. This finding suggests that proprietary climate models are underestimating the cost of climate change to lenders in the private housing market. Although these exploratory analyses have several shortcomings, which are summarized below, these test cases demonstrate that new tools must be developed to gauge past, present, and potential future risk to the single-family guaranteed housing programs. OMB and the lending agencies are eager to work with the private sector to develop these tools in line with detailed recommendations at the bottom of this section.

---

[5] Congressional Research Service. (2007). General Services Administration Federal Facilities Affected by Hurricane Katrina. *https://crsreports.congress.gov/product/pdf/RS/RS22281/14*

Risk Assessment

Retrospective Risk: To examine past risk, the lending agencies executed a retrospective analysis using a sample of 18 disasters that resulted in Presidentially Declared Major Disaster Areas. The agencies analyzed single-family housing borrowers and portfolio behavior for one year after these 18 extreme weather events from 2017 through 2021. This retrospective analysis demonstrated that disaster-affected areas' 90-day delinquency (DQ3) rates increase after disasters when compared to non-disaster areas, including an increase by 1.6 percentage points[6] for RD, an increase by 2.4 percentage points for VA, and an increase by 2.5 percentage points for FHA. That is, the 90-day delinquency rate for Federal mortgages was 1.6 to 2.5 percentage points higher. It was determined that using 90-day delinquency as a measure of past risk underestimates systemic portfolio-wide risk and costs to the Federal Government. Leveraging a 90-day delinquency as a measure of past risk fails to account for the role that disaster loss mitigation programs, private and Federal insurances, and Federal assistance dollars play in protecting against default, effectively shift portfolio hazard risk onto State and Federal entities. Furthermore, using the default metric in isolation was shown to ignore other systemic risks to the portfolio, such as the impact of climate risk poses to insurance carriers. This is exemplified by the 2022 bankruptcy of eight companies in Louisiana following Hurricane Ida, affecting tens of thousands of customers and forcing the State to scramble to find coverage.[7]

Current Risk: To examine current risk, the agencies developed a novel, expected annual loss (EAL) calculation using portions of the Federal Emergency Management Agency (FEMA) National Risk Index (NRI) database, as well as their own self-reported unpaid principal balance (UPB) estimates. Calculations for each agency were tabulated for five select hazards: hurricanes, coastal flooding, riverine flooding, wildfires, and tornadoes. Across all three agencies, riverine flooding posed the highest risk with UPB-EALs ranging from $160 million for RD, to $1.1 billion for VA, and $1.7 billion for FHA, which represented at least half of total UPB-EAL for each agency, indicating riverine flooding are anticipated to cause half of the expected annual losses of unpaid principal balances. Concurrently, Ginnie Mae, which guarantees MBS that utilizes the other agencies' loans as underlying collateral, calculated similar UPB-EALs for the respective portfolios. Compared to the total volume of each agency's portfolio, the sum of UPB-EALs for the five hazards mentioned above was approximately a quarter of a percent of total UPB (0.27 percent for VA and FHA, 0.23 percent for RD,

and 0.27 percent for Ginnie Mae), which underestimates climate financial risk due to modeling limitations. These results do not take into account that each program has unique coverage and policy requirements that will mitigate the Federal Government's financial loss exposure. The test case indicates the limitations of this methodology. In order to garner the most accurate current risk projections, it was determined that it would be critical to augment NRI analysis with a climate risk analytical tool that accounts for higher precision on current and near time future risk and includes additional climate modeling augmented by expanded climate hazard categories.

Future Risk: With regard to future risk, the agencies conducted preliminary and partial prospective analysis on the impact of climate events to a simulated Federal housing portfolio over the next 30 years. The agencies used a sample of publicly available Ginnie Mae data, which represented approximately 72 percent of the total FHA/VA/RD portfolio. This initial analysis uses a proprietary model common in the private sector and already available to the 5c Task Force through an existing contract with one of the lending agencies. The agencies used this model to estimate losses to each agency under two assumptions of future economic conditions (a 50th percentile baseline scenario and a 96th percentile severe adverse scenario) and then compared losses in these scenarios with and without climate shocks occurring. The proprietary model projects the expected loss in the lending agencies' mortgage portfolios that could occur for different scenarios of world events, economic trends, and some climate impacts. Federal researchers found that the model showed little risk – a vast underestimation considering a recent study published in Nature found that "residential properties exposed to flood risk are overvalued by $121 billion–$237 billion, depending on the discount rate."[8] The Federal analysis is considered preliminary and partial due to limitations in the analytical methods available. For example, the researchers found that current tools could not incorporate an adequate range of potential natural disasters, including wildfires and winter storm events, that are becoming more frequent from climate change, nor does the model incorporate a range of warming scenarios based on the best science and the most up to date climate models. Additional limitations include, but are not limited to:

- The proprietary model only includes climate shocks that are based on historical data, rather than future climate information obtained from global climate models. While this does provide a starting point for a prospective analysis on the Federal housing portfolio, future analysis should incorporate warming scenarios based on the best available science.

- The projected climate shocks are based on the FEMA-designated natural disasters for riverine and coastal floods, hurricanes, typhoons, and tornadoes, rather than global climate modeling. The magnitude of the impact of other natural disasters that are not

---

[6] A percentage point measures the difference between two percentages. For example, the difference between 5.5 percent and four percent is 1.5 percentage point. In this text, the percentage point is the change in the 90-day delinquency rates.

[7] Finch, M. (2022, Aug. 5). "Eighth Louisana homeowners insurer goes under, stranding 10,300 policyholders." *https://www.nola.com/news/business/eighth-louisiana-homeowners-insurer-goes-under-stranding-10-300-policyholders/article_74eca3b8-1502-11ed-bfc8-8f4127db48fe.html*

[8] Gourevitch, J.D., Kousky, C., Liao, Y., Nolte, C., Pollack, A.B., Porter, J.R., and Weill, J.A.. (2023) Unpriced climate risk and the potential consequences of overvaluation in US housing markets. Nature Climate Change. *https://doi.org/10.1038/s41558-023-01594-8*

accounted for in this model, such as wildfires and winter storm events, which are becoming more frequent from climate change, and earthquakes, is unknown and strongly warrants further analysis.

- The analysis only makes projections for current portfolio exposure, and the analysis does not model the addition of new mortgages to agency portfolios over the 30-year period.

- The modeling is agnostic to the varying insurance structures by program, which guarantee different amounts of losses through claims to lenders/issuers, and ignores that insurance and Federal and State disaster relief are effectively shifting portfolio hazard risk onto State and Federal entities. The analysis was conducted at the State level due to data limitations.

- Each program has unique coverage and policy requirements, which may change the overall Federal Government exposure to the respective portfolios.

The agencies' efforts to analyze the climate-related financial risks of the Federal housing portfolio has highlighted the lack of available modeling suitable for prospective analyses and the need for additional data and modeling resources to understand the future climate risk to Federal mortgage programs. The conclusion of this analysis is that current tools underestimate climate risk to the portfolio and that new tools need to be developed to gauge past, present, and potential future risk to the single-family guaranteed housing programs. In the next phase of the 5C workstream, the Task Force will define the new tools that are needed to identify, assess, and respond to the risk climate change poses to the portfolios. The Task Force is planning to engage the National Oceanic and Atmospheric Administration (NOAA) and Department of Energy (DOE) National Laboratories climate modeling experts in tool design and development, leverage the latest in climate modeling capabilities, and is eager to engage stakeholders including climate-related data and analytics providers, non-profit organizations, and academia.

To refine and expand this analysis, the 5c Task Force recommends the following key next steps:

- building expertise and learning within the interagency through a Climate Data Working Group that relies on the latest climate and hazard models and defining appropriate data sources for current and future climate risk analysis as well as relevant data sets for consideration;

- developing or procuring the necessary skills and resources in order to improve quantitative capabilities in a rapidly evolving landscape;

- determining an appropriate cadence for repeating and refining the analyses, based on the availability of budget resources and workload requirements;

- sharing lessons learned on risk analysis with other programs within the agencies, and more broadly with other Federal lending and guarantee programs;

- engaging with NOAA, the DOE National Laboratories, and private sector stakeholders through conversations on current practices and challenges posed by climate change in the financial and housing sectors;

- analyzing options suggested by academics, industry groups, and other stakeholders to managing increasing risks from climate change;

- expanding the pool of assets to be analyzed by working with Government-sponsored enterprises and appropriate agencies on identifying a pool of federally-owned or subsidized housing assets to conduct rigorous analysis of current and future climate risk; and,

- coordinating across agencies to identify programs, funding, and procedures to disclose and manage climate risk reduction for the housing pool.

Update on the Flood Risk to Federal Civilian Facilities

Federal facilities face a number of climate change-related hazards, including increased flood risks, extreme weather events, and fire. For example, flooding damage from heavy downpours is projected to increase in various regions across the Nation.[9] Sea-level rise is also expanding the coastal floodplain, causing increased frequency and magnitude of coastal flooding and compounding damages from storm surges. This increase has led to record numbers of events that cause over $1 billion in damages.[10]

OMB, the U.S. Geological Survey (USGS), and NOAA used the Federal Real Property Profile Management System (FRPP MS)[11], a public dataset to assess the flood risks of federally-owned buildings and structures. The FRPP MS public dataset is an inventory system; it was not designed nor intended to be used for flood analysis or any other complex analysis requiring precision. For that reason, there are numerous caveats to the use of the data which are documented in the white paper *Federal Budget's Climate Risk Exposure: A Preliminary Assessment and Proposed Framework for Future Assessments.*[12] These caveats underscore the limitations of the projections shared within this section. Given the current data and modeling available, the following es-

---

[9] AECOM, 2013. The Impact of Climate Change and Population Growth on the National Flood Insurance Program through 2100. Prepared for the Federal Emergency Management Agency.

[10] National Oceanic and Atmospheric Administration, National Centers for Environmental Information. (2023, Jan. 10). U.S. Billion Dollar Weather and Climate Disasters. *https://www.ncdc.noaa.gov/billions/.*

[11] General Services Administration. (n.d.). Federal Real Property Profile Management System (FRPP MS). *https://www.gsa.gov/policy-regulations/policy/real-property-policy/asset-management/federal-real-property-profile-management-system-frpp-ms*

[12] Office of Management and Budget. (2023). Federal Budget's Climate Risk Exposure: A Preliminary Assessment and Proposed Framework for Future Assessments.

Table 10–2. TEST CASE NUMERIC RESULTS: PROJECTED ANNUAL REPLACEMENT VALUE EFFECTED BY FLOODING

(In million of dollars)

	100-Year Flood Event (1% Annual Chance)			500-Year Flood Event (0.2% Annual Chance)		
	Year 2022	Year 2052	Change: 2022 To 2052	Year 2022	Year 2052	Change: 2022 To 2052
Low (Exploratory; Not For Decision-Making Purposes)	$84	$94	$10	$23	$24	$2
Midpoint (Exploratory; Not For Decision-Making Purposes)	$171	$195	$25	$46	$49	$3
High (Exploratory; Not For Decision-Making Purposes)	$258	$297	$39	$70	$74	$5

Note: Analysis is an illustrative example of the process for developing projections, rather than an official Government estimate of the projected losses. These projections are not for decision-making purposes. Estimated replacement value effected is not a financial loss to the Federal Government.

timates have significant limitations, and the projected losses and exposure should be interpreted as preliminary and partial and not for decision making purposes. We can currently state with confidence that Federal facilities are exposed to flood risk. The numeric estimates in the tables of this section are for illustrative purposes only and are not for decision-making purposes, given we currently lack the data required to make robust exposure and loss projections.

To conduct this analysis, USGS overlaid the location of federally-owned facilities with flood hazard maps provided by First Street Foundation's Flood Model for 2022 and the mid-21st century.[13] The flood hazard maps generated by the First Street Foundation's Flood Model show the locations for both the projected one percent annual probability of flooding and 0.2 percent probability of flooding with projected flood depths. These flood hazard maps differ from those used in the flood risk assessment for Federal facilities within the 2023 President's Budget, which assessed current exposure and did not examine future climate risk. Additionally, while the assessment from the 2023 President's Budget examined the impact of Sea Level Rise (SLR), using the data underlying the NOAA Sea Level Rise Viewer[14] to determine at what level of SLR Federal facilities would experience inundation, for this year's assessment, NOAA provided projections of the risk of flooding based on recently published Federal projections

of SLR.[15] These projections are provided for the years 2050 and 2100 and two SLR scenarios (Intermediate and Intermediate-High), representing potential circumstances where significant risk management and adaptation actions are necessary to avoid adverse impacts. This advances the analysis provided in last year's assessment by using the latest Federal projections for SLR for specific future time periods and identifying specific scenarios for SLR.

Table 10-2 shows the projected annual estimated replacement value effected for approximately 40 percent of Federal buildings from flooding. This table provides projected annual estimated replacement value effects for flood events that have the same annual chance of occurring in 2022 and 2052, which accordingly means that in 2052 an event with equivalent annual chance of occurring is expected to cause more flooding than in 2022. The estimated replacement value effects for a 100-year flood event are projected to increase between $10 million to $39 million annually by 2052, albeit there is immense uncertainty due to limitations of the climate financial risk models, hence the projections are not for decision-making. For a 500-year flood event, the effects are projected to increase $2 million to $5 million annually. The overall

[13] The flood hazard maps, which are for a "low" warming scenario thirty years into the future, are from a proprietary modeling.

[14] National Oceanic and Atmospheric Administration. Office of Coastal Management. (2022). Sea Level Rise Viewer. Retrieved from Digital Coast: https://coast.noaa.gov/digitalcoast/tools/slr.html

[15] Sweet, W.V., B.D. Hamlington, R.E. Kopp, C.P. Weaver, P.L. Barnard, D. Bekaert, W. Brooks, M. Craghan, G. Dusek, T. Frederikse, G. Garner, A.S. Genz, J.P. Krasting, E. Larour, D. Marcy, J.J. Marra, J. Obeysekera, M. Osler, M. Pendleton, D. Roman, L. Schmied, W. Veatch, K.D. White, and C. Zuzak, 2022: Global and Regional Sea Level Rise Scenarios for the United States: Updated Mean Projections and Extreme Waer Level Probabilities Along U.S. Coastlines. NOAA Technical Report NOS 01. National Oceanic and Atmospheric Administration, National Ocean Service, Silver Spring, MD, 111 pp. https://oceanservice.noaa.gov/hazards/sealevelrise/noaa-nostechrpt01-global-regional-SLR-scenarios-US.pdf

Table 10–3. TEST CASE NUMERIC RESULTS: ANNUAL PROJECTED REPLACEMENT VALUE EFFECTED BY SEA LEVEL RISE

(In million of dollars)

Scenario	Year	Projected Estimated Replacement Value
Intermediate (Exploratory; Not for Decision-Making Purposes)	2050	$72
	2100	$449
Intermediate High (Exploratory; Not for Decision-Making Purposes)	2050	$127
	2100	$1,786

Note: Analysis is an illustrative example of the process for developing projections, rather than an official Government estimate of the projected losses. These projections are not for decision-making purposes. Estimated replacement value effected is not a financial loss to the Federal Government.

projected estimated replacement value effect is smaller for a 500-year flood event relative to the projected effect under the 100-year flood event since the lower probability of the 500-year flood event (0.2 percent) more than offsets the greater severity and area covered of the 500-year flood relative to the 100-year flood. The estimated replacement value effect from SLR is projected between $72 million and $127 million for mid-century and between $449 million and $1.786 billion by the end of the century (see Table 10-3), albeit there is immense uncertainty due to limitations of the climate financial risk models – hence the projections are not for decision-making and are a gross underestimate of the cost. For example, following Hurricane Katrina, in only one year, $38 million was needed to repair more than 83 damaged Federal facilities. This shows that better data and modeling is needed to evaluate the true cost of climate change to Federal facilities.[16]

While this year's assessment on the flood risks to Federal facilities has made notable improvements relative to last year's assessment, there are still significant caveats to the analysis. The extent of future changes in flood risk has not been estimated across the full Federal inventory of real property. For instance, assets that were not assessed include national security-sensitive facilities and real property exempt due to the Freedom of Information Act (FOIA), which leaves approximately 40 percent of the real property in the Federal portfolio for the analysis within this assessment. Given that the FRPP MS public dataset is not intended to be used for analysis of site-specific risks and that climate science continues to evolve, there is a significant level of uncertainty in the projected flood risk and estimates. Additionally, it is noted that SLR is only one factor involved in coastal flooding, and these projections do not take into account the value of the services provided that would be impacted by flooding and SLR. As the data and science improve, future assessments will reevaluate available methods and accordingly may have substantial changes in projected exposure and estimates relative to this year's assessment.

Projected Impacts on Higher Temperatures on LIHEAP

The NCA4 examines the impacts of extreme heat on human health.[17] Extreme heat is tied to higher risks for multiple illnesses and death, especially for vulnerable populations, such as older adults, children, and pregnant women.[18] Heat-related illnesses include cardiovascular

and respiratory complications[19], electrolyte imbalance, kidney stones[20], and premature birth.[21] Although cold-related deaths are projected to decline due to climate change, heat-related deaths are expected to increase.[22] These projected impacts highlight the importance of Federal programs that help mitigate the risks of temperature-related illnesses and deaths, such as LIHEAP.[23] LIHEAP provides households with financial assistance to offset energy costs. LIHEAP benefits target households with low incomes, particularly those that have a high home energy burden (percentage of income that goes to heating and cooling bills).

Chart 10-1 highlights how heating degree days and cooling degree days have changed over the last century for the continental United States.[24] Degree days are measures of how cold or warm a location is. A degree day compares the mean (the average of the high and low) outdoor temperatures recorded for a location to a standard temperature, usually 65 degrees Fahrenheit. The more extreme the outside temperature, the higher the number of degree days. A high number of degree days generally results in higher levels of energy use for space heating or cooling.[25] Heating degree days are equal to the annual sum of the greater of: 1) 65 degrees Fahrenheit minus the daily average temperature; or 2) zero. Cooling degree days are equal to the annual sum of the greater of: 1) the daily average temperature minus 65 degrees Fahrenheit; or 2) zero. When examining the 20-year moving averages for cooling degree days and heating degree days for the years 1915 versus 2022[26], cooling degree days have already increased in the United States by 20 percent, while heating degree days have decreased 12 percent.

---

[16] Congressional Research Service. (2007). General Servies Administration Federal Facilities Affected by Hurricane Katrina. *https://crsreports.congress.gov/product/pdf/RS/RS22281/14*

[17] Ebi, K.L., J.M. Balbus, G. Luber, A. Bole, A. Crimmins, G. Glass, S. Saha, M.M. Shimamoto, J. Trtanj, and J.L. White-Newsome, 2018: Human Health. In Impacts, Risks, and Adaptation in the United States: Fourth National Climate Assessment, Volume II [Reidmiller, D.R., C.W. Avery, D.R. Easterling, K.E. Kunkel, K.L.M. Lewis, T.K. Maycock, and B.C. Stewart (eds.)]. U.S. Global Change Research Program, Washington, DC, USA, pp. 539–571. doi: 10.7930/NCA4.2018.CH14

[18] Sarofim, M. C., S. Saha, M. D. Hawkins, D. M. Mills, J. Hess, R. Horton, P. Kinney, J. Schwartz, and A. St. Juliana, 2016: Ch. 2: Temperature-related death and illness. The Impacts of Climate Change on Human Health in the United States: A Scientific Assessment., U.S. Global Change Research Program, Washington, DC, 43–68. doi:10.7930/

J0MG7MDX.

[19] Gronlund, C. J., A. Zanobetti, G. A. Wellenius, J. D. Schwartz, and M. S. O'Neill, 2016: Vulnerability to renal, heat and respiratory hospitalizations during extreme heat among U.S. elderly. Climatic Change, 136 (3), 631–645. doi:10.1007/s10584-016-1638-9.

[20] Ross, M. E., A. M. Vicedo-Cabrera, R. E. Kopp, L. Song, D. S. Goldfarb, J. Pulido, S. Warner, S. L. Furth, and G. E. Tasian, 2018: Assessment of the combination of temperature and relative humidity on kidney stone presentations. Environmental Research, 162, 97–105. doi:10.1016/j.envres.2017.12.020.

[21] Ha, S., D. Liu, Y. Zhu, S. S. Kim, S. Sherman, and P. Mendola, 2017: Ambient temperature and early delivery of singleton pregnancies. Environmental Health Perspectives, 125, 453–459. doi:10.1289/EHP97.

[22] Sarofim, M. C., S. Saha, M. D. Hawkins, D. M. Mills, J. Hess, R. Horton, P. Kinney, J. Schwartz, and A. St. Juliana, 2016: Ch. 2: Temperature-related death and illness. The Impacts of Climate Change on Human Health in the United States: A Scientific Assessment., U.S. Global Change Research Program, Washington, DC, 43–68. doi:10.7930/J0MG7MDX.

[23] 42 U.S.C. 8621 et seq.

[24] National Centers for Environmental Information, National Oceanic Atmospheric Administration, 2022. Climate at a Glance National Time Series. *https://www.ncei.noaa.gov/access/monitoring/climate-at-a-glance/national/time-series/*

[25] Energy Information Administration. (n.d.). Units and calculators explained: Degrees days. *https://www.eia.gov/energyexplained/units-and-calculators/degree-days.php*

[26] The years included in the moving averages are (1896-1915) for 1915 and (2003-2022) for 2022.

Chart 10-1. Heating Degree Days and Cooling Degree Days for the Continental United States, 1915 – 2022ᵃ

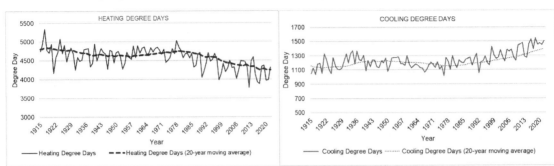

ᵃ Heating degree days are equal to the annual sum of the greater of 1) 65 degrees Fahrenheit minus the daily average temperature or 2) zero. Cooling degree days are equal to the annual sum of the greater of 1) the daily average temperature minus 65 degrees Fahrenheit or 2) zero.

Source: National Centers for Environmental Information, National Oceanic Atmospheric Administration, 2022.

The increase of cooling degree days and decrease of heating degree days are projected to continue under different warming scenarios, also referred to as Representative Concentration Pathways (RCPs),[27] as shown in Chart 10-2. Under the RCP 4.5 emissions scenario, the 20-year average for heating days is projected to decline by 13 percent between 2039[28] and 2099[29], while number of cooling degree days increases by 20 percent for the same time period. For the RCP 8.5 emissions scenario, heating degree days are projected to decline by 30 percent, while cooling degree days are projected to increase by 65 percent. These trends may impact energy demand for heating and cooling, and in turn, the needs of LIHEAP. In addition to changes in the trends of cooling degree days and heating degree days, extreme weather events induced by climate change will continue to impact the needs of cooling and heating assistance, as the frequency, duration, and intensity of extreme weather events are projected to change over time.

In order to develop expenditure projections of LIHEAP that could be used for decision-making, there are several areas of research that need further development:

1. Underpin all perils risk with the most up to date climate modeling relying on expertise from NOAA, the National Labs, and industry experts.

2. Incorporate modeling on the costs of natural gas and other residential energy sources used for residential heating, and the transition to electrification.

3. Integrate LIHEAP grantees' design decisions into modelling.

4. Incorporate assumptions regarding population growth and interstate migration.

5. Analyze electrical grid stability to understand the ability of the current framework of utility distribution to handle increased demand for cooling.

While other aspects of the modeling could be developed, these items are essential to developing informative projections.

The Need for Action

The United States and the rest of the world has a narrow moment to pursue actions to avoid the most catastrophic impacts of the climate crisis. By reducing greenhouse gas (GHG) pollution from 2005 levels by 50 to 52 percent in 2030 and reaching net-zero emissions economy-wide by no later than 2050, we can do our part to avoid the worst and irreversible impacts of climate change.[30] The Administration, in partnership with the Congress' historic action under the Inflation Reduction Act of 2022 (Public Law 117-169) and the Infrastructure Investment and Jobs Act (Public Law 117-58), is taking a whole-of-Government approach to reduce emissions in every sector of the economy; increase resilience to the impacts of climate change; protect public health; conserve our lands, waters, and biodiversity; deliver environmental justice; and spur good paying union jobs and economic growth, especially through innovation, commercializa-

---

[27] RCPs are widely used in the climate research community to describe different climate futures and are based on the volume of greenhouse gases emitted. RCPs form the foundation for the majority of recent climate-related modeling efforts.

[28] 20 year average uses the years 2020-2039.

[29] 20 year average uses the years 2070-2099.

[30] *White House Fact Sheet: President Biden Sets 2030 Greenhouse Gas Pollution Reduction Target Aimed at Creating Good-Paying Union Jobs and Securing U.S. Leadership on Clean Energy Technologies.* April 22, 2021.

Chart 10-2. PROJECTED Heating Degree Days and Cooling Degree Days for the Continental United States, 2020– 2100ᵃ

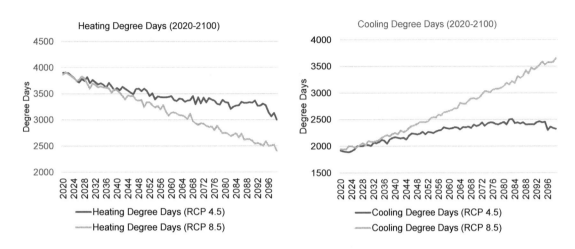

ᵃ Heating degree days are equal to the annual sum of the greater of 1) 65 degrees Fahrenheit minus the daily average temperature or 2) zero. Cooling degree days are equal to the annual sum of the greater of 1) the daily average temperature minus 65 degrees Fahrenheit or 2) zero.

Source: Coupled Model Intercomparison Project 5 (CMIP5), author's calculations

tion, and deployment of clean energy technologies and infrastructure. With that approach is a need to advance consistent, clear, intelligible, comparable, and accurate disclosure of climate-related financial risk, while taking near-term actions to reduce exposure to those risks.

The Inflation Reduction Act of 2022 is the single largest investment in climate and energy in history, delivering $370 billion in investments to tackle the climate crisis and strengthen American energy security. This law will increase U.S. clean energy deployment of solar, wind, battery storage, and more, creating good-paying jobs for American workers. A variety of rebates and tax incentives will help families save money on energy costs, including support for making home energy efficiency upgrades, installing new electric appliances or rooftop solar panels, and purchasing new or used electric vehicles. This law also provides grants, loans, and other programs to support cleaner industrial facilities, ports, and heavy-duty vehicles; community-led climate and environmental justice projects; and climate-smart agriculture and forestry. The savings, jobs, and other benefits provided by this legislation will provide tangible benefits to diverse communities across the Nation. These investments are more than paid for through this legislation, which reduces the deficit.

Additionally, the Infrastructure Investment and Jobs Act provides unprecedented levels of resources for upgrading the power grid, improving public transit and investing in zero-emission transit and school buses, installing a nationwide EV charging network, cleaning up legacy pollution, replacing lead pipes, and delivering clean water. This legislation also aims to strengthen the Nation's resilience and save taxpayer money, helping communities safeguard against extreme weather events, catastrophic wildfires, and other climate-related disasters—which last year caused more than $150 billion in damages from the biggest 20 weather and climate disasters alone.[31]

The 2024 Budget highlights several near-term budgetary needs that will both help reduce the Federal Government's long-term fiscal exposure to climate-related financial risk and reduce future climate risks for all Americans. In total, the Budget invests $52.2 billion in discretionary funding to tackle the climate crisis. This includes more than $15 billion to advance clean energy innovation and support emissions mitigation, and further U.S. competitiveness through innovative technologies that accelerate the transition to a net-zero emissions economy. $24 billion within the Budget is provided to strengthen climate resilience and adaptation efforts across the Federal Government. Investments to increase the resilience of ecosystems and communities to wildfires, flooding, and drought and better incorporate climate impacts into pre-disaster planning and infrastructure development ensure that the Nation is rebuilding smarter and safer for the future. OMB utilized the results of the FY23 Federal Budget Exposure to Climate Risk presented in Table 10-1 to sharpen our understanding of where the largest costs of climate change are to the Federal Budget. Based on the findings that crop insurance, coastal flooding, health insurance, and wildfires are expected to substantially increase the annual spending of the Government, the Budget proposes to reduce three out of four of those climate risks and in turn reduce the cost of climate change

[31] NOAA National Centers for Environmental Information (NCEI) U.S. Billion-Dollar Weather and Climate Disasters (2023). *https://www.ncei.noaa.gov/access/billions/*, DOI: *10.25921/stkw-7w73*

in the long-term. For example, the 2024 Budget includes: a new mandatory proposal to provide incentives to farmers through their crop insurance to plant cover crops to make their fields more resilient to climate change[32]; a discretionary request to provide long-term pay increases to wildland firefighters so we are better able to respond to and decrease climate risks; over \$1.9 billion for the Corps of Engineers to address coastal and inland flood risks; \$175 million for flood mitigation grants through FEMA; and a commitment to work with the Congress to determine the coastal areas most at risk of climate change where investments should be prioritized. In addition, the Budget also provides more than \$500 million for FEMA's flood hazard mapping program, which will support the implementation of the Federal Flood Risk Management Standard, as well as continued modeling and data acquisition for current and future flood conditions.

The Administration has not only taken bold action to confront the financial risks created by the climate crisis, but turned it into an opportunity to advance environmental justice. Severe harms from climate change fall disproportionally upon socially vulnerable populations, and racial and ethnic minority communities are particularly vulnerable to climate impacts. The Budget supports communities that have been left behind by targeting investments to ensure that 40 percent of the benefits from tackling the climate crisis are directed toward addressing the disproportionately high cumulative impacts on disadvantaged communities. For instance, the Budget provides \$160 million for the Demonstration of Industrial Decarbonization Technologies, which is a competitive solicitation managed by DOE to support the creation of at least two large-scale industrial decarbonization projects directly benefitting disadvantaged communities.

In summary, climate risk data shows us that if we fail to invest in climate change, we are failing at our responsibility to properly manage funding on behalf of tax payers. Near-term Federal investments to both mitigate GHG emissions and adapt to future climate scenarios can help reduce future financial burdens, but will rely on both congressional appropriations and Federal implementation to reduce those risks. Investments in climate adaptation can significantly reduce future risk exposure. Higher up-front climate adaptation costs will save taxpayers and the Federal Government in the long-term. On the other hand, business-as-usual investments could further exacerbate future climate risks. Additionally, more work is needed to identify and quantify the Federal Budget's exposure to climate change fiscal risk. For this reason, the Budget establishes a Climate-Related Risk Technical Support Center at the Department of the Treasury. The Center would develop, conduct, and integrate assessments on the Federal Government's climate-related risk exposure and facilitate climate risk data sharing across the Government and with the private sector. Better understanding and analysis is important for taking steps to

mitigate the broad and urgent financial crises the Federal Government could face.

Establishing a Common Framework for Evaluating Climate-Related Financial Risks

The assessments from the 2023 President's Budget and this year provide policymakers and stakeholders a framework for the potential monetary impacts of climate change on Federal assets and programs and can inform action that reduces the Federal Government's exposure to climate-related financial risks taking into account the current limitations on Federal data and tools.

In order to meet the requirements of Section 6(b) of Executive Order 14030, "Climate-Related Financial Risks," in future years, we need a consistent and repeatable methodology to enable year-over-year comparisons, inform action to reduce climate-related financial risk to the Federal Budget, and improve understanding of the effect of actions agencies are taking to reduce these risks. To address this challenge, the White House established the Assessments of Federal Financial Climate Risk Interagency Working Group (AFFCR), which is led by OMB. The AFFCR is working on establishing a generalized framework for how the assessments of climate-related financial risk can be conducted and identifying and coordinating climate risk data across the Federal Government. This section of the chapter is organized into the following sections: 1) summary descriptions of the current approaches used by Federal agencies to assess climate-related risk to assets and programs; 2) a description of currently available climate data and information products necessary to conduct climate-related financial risk assessments; 3) an outline of proposed common framework for use across the Federal Government to assess climate-related financial risk and necessary technical inputs; and 4) a description of next steps the AFFCR is taking to further develop the common framework and technical capabilities necessary for future annual assessments of climate-related financial risk for the Federal Budget.

Current Approaches for Assessing Climate-Related Risks

Here we present two ongoing activities across the Federal Government to assess climate risk to assets, programs, or other activities within the Government. While these approaches do not necessarily seek to quantify financial risks, the methodological approaches inform and can be incorporated into the proposed common framework for climate-related financial risks.

Assessments Required for Agency Climate Adaptation and Resilience Plans: Many agencies within the Federal Government have developed quantitative measures to assess climate vulnerabilities; however, most agencies have not developed monetized estimates of climate-related financial risks.[33] Within and outside of the Federal Government, the quantification of climate-related financial risk is a burgeoning area of research and there has

---

[32] Department of Agriculture, Climate Hubs. (n.d.). "Cover Cropping to Improve Climate Resilience." *https://www.climatehubs.usda.gov/hubs/northeast/topic/cover-cropping-improve-climate-resilience*

[33] Gade, J.T., P.M. Seman, A.O. Pinson, A.K. Jordan, J.R. Arnold, B.A. Thames, P.S. O'Brien, C.A. Hiemstra, P.M. Loechl, K.D. White, and E.E. Ritchie. (2020). Department of Defense Climate Assessment Tool. Army Corps of Engineers: Washington DC.

not been previous Federal guidance quantifying climate-related financial risks. In response to Executive Order 14008, "Tackling the Climate Crisis at Home and Abroad" and Executive Order 14030, agencies created Climate Adaptation Plans (CAPs) "to evaluate the most significant climate-related risks and vulnerabilities for agency operations and missions, and identify action to manage those risks and vulnerabilities."[34] For example, USDA and the Department of Health and Human Services (HHS) outline the vulnerabilities and climate adaptation planning for their programs, such as decreased agricultural productivity driven by climate change impacting the demand for USDA programs and expanding "existing climate change-related public health and biomedical research activities" overseen by HHS.[35, 36] As part of the CAPs, agencies also assessed the climate vulnerabilities to real property and have the development of quantitative metrics of climate vulnerabilities as part of their adaptation and resilience planning. The General Services Administration (GSA) is currently integrating environmental and climate justice factors to inform decisions related to real property. As part of GSA's climate adaptation planning, the agency also intends to quantitatively assess climate-related financial risk, and projects completion of this action by the end of 2026.[37] At many agencies, the offices responsible for developing the CAP are not necessarily connected to the offices responsible for long-term budget planning (e.g., the Office of the Chief Financial Officer (OCFO)), although some agencies—including GSA—have assigned climate risk disclosure responsibilities to the OCFO explicitly built into their CAP.[38]

Agency-Specific Qualitative Assessment Tools and Methods: In response to Executive Order 14008 and Executive Order 14057, "Catalyzing Clean Energy Industries and Jobs Through Federal Sustainability", agencies have developed qualitative tools and assessments that assist the agencies in determining their climate vulnerabilities. These tools and assessments typically either provide highly detailed analyses for individual projects or are broad screening tools. The scope of most assessments undertaken to-date have included physical risk to assets (e.g., buildings and infrastructure).

Two examples of these tools include the Department of Defense (DOD) and Department of Homeland Security's (DHS) screening tools to assess exposure to climate-related risks for their assets and facilities. The DOD Climate

Assessment Tool (DCAT) allows DOD personnel to identify the vulnerability—defined as exposure, sensitivity, and adaptive capacity—of installations. The tool makes use of both historical extreme events and climate change projections to determine the vulnerability of an asset and whether the vulnerability of the asset warrants further climate-related studies.[39] Similarly, DHS developed a qualitative questionnaire-based vulnerability assessment tool to assign vulnerability scores to agency assets.

While these tools are essential for climate adaptation and resilience planning, the tools are not designed to demonstrate the Federal Budget's exposure to climate change. In other words, while the tools assess climate risks to assets (e.g., whether a mission-critical asset is vulnerable to sea level rise), the tools do not monetize the climate risk of the agency. Further work is needed to develop this analytical capability.

Available Federal Data and Modeling – Climate Data

Federal agencies maintain a range of scientific data products that provide climate change projections for various analytical purposes and agency- or program-specific management decisions.[40] For non-Sea Level Rise projections, these products largely present statistically downscaled projections of Coupled-Model Intercomparison Project Phase 5 (CMIP5) climate model simulations.[41] Downscaling is a set of methods that translate large-scale Global Climate Models (GCMs) data into a finer spatial resolution that can be used for specific decision or management contexts.[42] The NCA4 provided a series of statistically downscaled scenario products covering the period through 2100 for the purpose of developing NCA4, and have been since used in Federal climate projection data products.[43] As noted below, GCM output, whether downscaled or not, does not provide information related to many hazards of interest, including flood, wildfire, sea

[34] Council of Environmental Quality—Office of the Chief Sustainability Officer. (n.d.). Climate Resilient Infrastructure and Operations. *https://www.sustainability.gov/federalsustainabilityplan/resilience.html*

[35] Department of Agriculture. (2021). Action Plan for Climate Adaptation and Resilience. *https://www.sustainability.gov/pdfs/usda-2021-cap.pdf*

[36] Department of Health and Human Services. (2022). 2021 Climate Action Plan. *https://www.sustainability.gov/pdfs/hhs-2021-cap.pdf*

[37] General Services Administration. (2022). GSA Climate Change Risk Management Plan: 2022 Progress Report. *https://www.sustainability.gov/pdfs/gsa-2022-cap.pdf*

[38] General Services Administration. (2022). Climate Change Risk Management Plan. *https://www.sustainability.gov/pdfs/gsa-2021-cap.pdf*

[39] Department of Defense. (n.d.) DOD Climate Assessment Tool. *https://media.defense.gov/2021/Apr/05/2002614579/-1/-1/0/DOD-CLIMATE-ASSESSMENT-TOOL.PDF*

[40] Examples include NASA Earth Exchange Downscaled Climate Projections (NEX-DCP30), DOI USBR Downscaled CMIP3 and CMIP5 Climate and Hydrology Projections (Maurer, E. P., L. Brekke, T. Pruitt, and P. B. Duffy (2007), 'Fine-resolution climate projections enhance regional climate change impact studies', Eos Trans. AGU, 88(47), 504.), US Forest Service National Forest Climate Change Maps, USACE's Climate Hydrology Assessment Tool, DOT FWHA's Climate Data Processing Tool (based on DOI USBR downscaled CMIP5 projections).

[41] Taylor, K. E., R. J. Stouffer, and G. A. Meehl, 2012: An overview of CMIP5 and the experiment design. Bulletin of the American Meteorological Society, 93 (4), 485–498. doi:10.1175/BAMS-D-11-00094.1

[42] Climate Adaptation Science Centers-U.S. Geological Survey. (2021). "Data Spotlight: Downscaled Climate Projections to Inform Climate Research in the South-Central U.S. Region." *https://www.usgs.gov/news/data-spotlight-downscaled-climate-projections-inform-climate-research-south-central-us-region*

[43] Avery, C.W., D.R. Reidmiller, M. Kolian, K.E. Kunkel, D. Herring, R. Sherman, W.V. Sweet, K. Tipton, and C. Weaver, 2018: Data Tools and Scenario Products. In Impacts, Risks, and Adaptation in the United States: Fourth National Climate Assessment, Volume II [Reidmiller, D.R., C.W. Avery, D.R. Easterling, K.E. Kunkel, K.L.M. Lewis, T.K. Maycock, and B.C. Stewart (eds.)]. U.S. Global Change Research Program, Washington, DC, USA, pp. 1413–1430. doi: 10.7930/NCA4.2018.AP3

level rise, tornadoes, or hurricanes. To assess risks related to these hazards, specialized hazard-specific models, driven by climate model output, are used.

Developing tools that support agencies' efforts to identify appropriate downscaled climate projections and the selection of climate scenarios relevant to an agency or program's specific vulnerabilities, risk profile, or planning timescale of interest remains an ongoing effort. The Consolidated Appropriations Act, 2022 (Public Law 117-103) directs the Office of Science and Technology Policy (OSTP) to develop guidance on the use of climate information and scenarios in Federal agency adaptation planning. This direction was repeated in the Consolidated Appropriations Act, 2023 (Public Law 117-328). The guidance will facilitate future updates to Federal Climate Adaptation Plans, consistent with Executive Order 14057, "Executive Order on Catalyzing Clean Energy Industries and Jobs Through Federal Sustainability"; agencies should use these tools in identifying appropriate climate projections and resources for assessing climate-related financial risk to the Federal Budget. This forthcoming guidance should be considered when identifying appropriate climate projections for assessing climate-related financial risk to the Federal Budget. One recent tool, developed largely based on the NCA4 downscaled climate projections for screening level assessment, is the Climate Mapping for Adaptation and Resilience (CMRA) Assessment Tool.[44] CMRA was released in September 2022, as a joint effort among NOAA, the Department of the Interior (DOI), and the White House. In addition to showing past and current climate risk exposure, the tool presents statistically downscaled projections of climate variables from NCA4.[45] The scenarios are based on the RCP scenarios 4.5 and 8.5. The projections are provided for three epochs: Early Century (2015-2044), Mid Century (2035-2064), and Late Century (2070-2099).[46] Projections of climate variables in CMRA include:

- temperature projections, such as annual days above 95 degrees, average minimum temperature, and average maximum temperature;

- precipitation projections, such as average annual precipitation and annual number of days with measurable precipitation; and

- coastal inundation projections based on the results of the NOAA 2022 *Technical Report of Sea Level Rise*.[47]

Other currently available downscaled climate resources and tools from Federal agencies and partner organizations include, but are not limited to, the following examples:

- *U.S. Climate Resilience Toolkit* and *Climate Explorer*
- NOAA's *Sea Level Rise Viewer*
- *2022 Sea Level Rise Technical Report*[48]
- *Climate Risk and Resilience Portal (ClimRR)*
- *Climate and Hazard Mitigation Planning (CHaMP) Tool*
- *NASA's Sea Level Change Tool*
- *NASA's NEX-GDDP-CMIP6*

Other natural hazard exposure resources are provided below, although the projected hazard exposure may not be based on downscaled global climate models:

- *Drought.gov*
- *Heat.gov*
- *FEMA's National Risk Index*

In the fall of 2023, the Fifth National Climate Assessment (NCA5) will be released and projections used in the assembly of NCA5 can be used to update Federal climate data and decision-making tools. NCA5 will use downscaled datasets for the continental U.S. that is based on CMIP6. These updated tools should be used in future climate-related financial risk assessments, including for the 2025 President's Budget.

Available Federal Data and Modeling – Facility & Program Data

Agency data on assets and outlays are essential to conducting these analyses. For example, the Federal Real Property Profile Management System (FRPP MS) contains

---

[44] Climate Mapping for Resilience and Adaptation. *https://resilience.climate.gov/*

[45] Department of Commerce, National Oceanic and Atmospheric Administration. "Biden Administration launches portal to help communities assess exposure to climate hazards" (September 8, 2022) *https://www.noaa.gov/news-release/biden-administration-launches-portal-to-help-communities-assess-exposure-to-climate-hazards*

[46] Avery, C.W., D.R. Reidmiller, M. Kolian, K.E. Kunkel, D. Herring, R. Sherman, W.V. Sweet, K. Tipton, and C. Weaver, 2018: Data Tools and Scenario Products. In Impacts, Risks, and Adaptation in the United States: Fourth National Climate Assessment, Volume II [Reidmiller, D.R., C.W. Avery, D.R. Easterling, K.E. Kunkel, K.L.M. Lewis, T.K. Maycock, and B.C. Stewart (eds.)]. U.S. Global Change Research Program, Washington, DC, USA, pp. 1413–1430. doi: 10.7930/NCA4.2018.AP3

[47] Sweet, W.V., B.D. Hamlington, R.E. Kopp, C.P. Weaver, P.L. Barnard, D. Bekaert, W. Brooks, M. Craghan, G. Dusek, T. Frederikse, G. Garner, A.S. Genz, J.P. Krasting, E. Larour, D. Marcy, J.J. Marra, J. Obeysekera, M. Osler, M. Pendleton, D. Roman, L. Schmied, W. Veatch, K.D. White, and C. Zuzak, 2022: Global and Regional Sea Level Rise Scenarios for the United States: Updated Mean Projections and Extreme Water Level Probabilities Along U.S. Coastlines. NOAA Technical Report NOS 01. National Oceanic and Atmospheric Administration, National Ocean Service, Silver Spring, MD, 111 pp. *https://oceanservice.noaa.gov/hazards/sealevelrise/noaa-nostechrpt01-global-regional-SLR-scenarios-US.pdf*

[48] Sweet, W.V., B.D. Hamlington, R.E. Kopp, C.P. Weaver, P.L. Barnard, D. Bekaert, W. Brooks, M. Craghan, G. Dusek, T. Frederikse, G. Garner, A.S. Genz, J.P. Krasting, E. Larour, D. Marcy, J.J. Marra, J. Obeysekera, M. Osler, M. Pendleton, D. Roman, L. Schmied, W. Veatch, K.D. White, and C. Zuzak, 2022: Global and Regional Sea Level Rise Scenarios for the United States: Updated Mean Projections and Extreme Water Level Probabilities Along U.S. Coastlines. NOAA Technical Report NOS 01. National Oceanic and Atmospheric Administration, National Ocean Service, Silver Spring, MD, 111 pp. *https://oceanservice.noaa.gov/hazards/sealevelrise/noaa-nostechrpt01-global-regional*

data of all Federal civilian real property owned, leased, or controlled by the Federal Government, with the exception of real property withheld for national security reason—for example, no DOD installations are included—or withheld due to a FOIA exemption.[49] The data is collected annually and provides an inventory snapshot of the real property held by the Federal Government. The FRPP MS includes data on the location of the asset, a score of the asset's condition, and replacement value.[50] While this data does provide a starting point for conducting analyses on the climate risks to Federal facilities, this data product was not established to screen federally-owned real property for physical risks. For example, accuracy of longitude and latitude are not guaranteed, as seen in the updated assessment on the flood risk to Federal Facilities. Future assessments on Federal real property may evaluate alternatives to the FRPP MS.

With respect to Federal programs, agencies maintain records of the outlays spent on individual programs, generally by fiscal year. Historical outlay data may or may not be required for projecting outlays under various climate scenarios. For example, the 2022 analysis on wildland fire suppression outlays did require historical outlays for the modeling, while the modeling for crop insurance premiums did not.[51] However, regardless of whether the historical outlays are used within the modeling directly, this data provides important context for whether or not the projected outlays are in an explicable range. In addition to the data outlined above, agency data other than expenditures and revenue may be used when conducting the analysis, such as acres burned by wildland fire published by the National Interagency Fire Center.[52]

In addition to the analysis presented earlier in this chapter, there are few sources of information on modeling the Federal Budget's exposure to climate risk. The 2022 white paper produced by OMB outlines how assessments were conducted for six programmatic areas: premium subsidies for the Federal Crop Insurance Program, Federal emergency relief for coastal disasters, Federal healthcare spending, Federal wildland fire suppression, Federal facilities' exposure to flood risk, and the National Flood Insurance Program.[53] Additionally, DOD assessed the flood risk to DOD installations, which will be included in an update to DODI 4165.70 Real Property Management.[54] While not specific to net outlays of the Federal Government, the Environmental Protection Agency's Framework for Evaluating Damages and Impacts (FrEDI) was released in 2021 and synthesizes the research of dozens of climate change studies conducted under the Climate Change Impacts and Risk Analysis (CIRA) project, which quantifies the economic damages in the U.S. by sector.[55] Economic damages by sector will not necessarily align with outlays or revenue losses of the Federal Government; however, FrEDI could be used for topics where there is compelling evidence that sectoral damages are correlated with Federal Government spending or revenues.

Proposed Common Framework to Assess Climate-Related Financial Risk for the Federal Budget

The assessment of the Federal Budget's exposure to climate change is comprised of analyses on federally-owned assets and specific Federal programs. In future years, the cost of changes in mission and operations could be further explored. These components will be assessed using a common structure and set of assumptions. The assessment will examine the impact of the physical risks of climate change. The physical risks are the direct result of the changes in climate on the current environment, such as increased frequency and intensity of natural disasters on infrastructure.[56] The other form of risk from climate change is transition risks, which are not examined in this assessment, although this is a potential area for further research.[57]

Generally, the Federal Budget's exposure to climate risk is measured as the projected change in real dollars of net outlays of the Federal Budget caused by climate change. By focusing on net outlays, this narrows the scope of what is examined relative to other economic analyses on the physical impacts of climate change. The literature on the Federal Budget exposure to climate change is limited, while there is a rich literature on the impacts of climate change on a wide variety of economic sectors. Unfortunately, there are only select programs where assuming the program's outlays will be proportional to economic losses of a particular sector is appropriate.

The Assessments of Federal Financial Climate Risks (AFFRC) Interagency Working Group is developing an overarching framework for assessing the climate-related financial risks to physical assets, programs, agency mission, or operations of the Federal Government. A common set of technical assumptions and climate data resources and climate scenarios will underpin these assessments. These common assumptions for future assessments could include common climate scenario options and time periods for assessing risks.

Physical Asset Risk: Climate change presents a significant risk to the Federal portfolio of physical assets

[49] U.S. General Services Administration. (n.d.). Federal Real Property Profile Management System (FRPP MS). *https://www.gsa.gov/policy-regulations/policy/real-property-policy/asset-management/federal-real-property-profile-management-system-frpp-ms*

[50] Ibid.

[51] Office of Management and Budget. Climate Risk Exposure: An Assessment of the Federal Government's Financial Risk to Climate Change. (April 2022) *https://www.whitehouse.gov/wp-content/uploads/2022/04/OMB_Climate_Risk_Exposure_2022.pdf*

[52] National Interagency Fire Center. (n.d.). Statistics. *https://www.nifc.gov/fire-information/statistics*

[53] Office of Management and Budget. Climate Risk Exposure: An Assessment of the Federal Government's Financial Risk to Climate Change. (April 2022) *https://www.whitehouse.gov/wp-content/uploads/2022/04/OMB_Climate_Risk_Exposure_2022.pdf*

[54] Department of Defense. (2022). DTM 20222-03 "Flood Hazard Area Management for DoD Installations" released 7 June 2022.

[55] Environmental Protection Agency. Technical Documentation on the Framework for Evaluating Damages and Impacts (FrEDI). (2021) U.S. Environmental Protection Agency, EPA 430-R-21-004. *https://www.epa.gov/cira/fredi*

[56] Financial Stability Oversight Council. Report on Climate-related Risks. (2021). *https://home.treasury.gov/system/files/261/FSOC-Climate-Report.pdf*

[57] Ibid.

(buildings, infrastructure, and other fixed capital), given the Federal Government is financially responsible for any damages from natural disasters that occur to its own assets. This also includes assets that are climate-sensitive, such as dams, irrigation infrastructure, and flood levees, that also present risks where they may under-perform (i.e., service reduction) due to a changing climate. Using an expected value approach to developing projections of annual losses to the Federal portfolio of physical assets requires three key pieces of information to formulate a dollar value of losses:

1. Exposure: Improving the estimated exposure of Federal assets requires accurate and transparent accounting of Federal real property, whether the information is held within the FRPP MS or another dataset held by individual agencies.

2. Frequency and intensity of climate-related events: The availability of widely accessible models for the frequency of climate-related events varies by the type of event and geography. For example, while the projected annual frequency of days over 100 degrees Fahrenheit under different climate scenarios is accessible from the downscaled data of NCA4, there are not easily available projections for the frequency of hurricanes under different climate scenarios.

3. Modeling of Losses: In many cases exposure to a climate stressor will not result in a complete loss of the physical asset, therefore, a model that translates the exposure and sensitivity of the asset and frequency, duration, and intensity of climate events to losses is needed. Options are currently limited in modeling of losses that could easily be applied, and this is an area in significant need of further research.

Expenditures of Federal Programs: The physical impacts of climate change on Federal programs can vary depending on the structure of the program. Certain programs experience greater outlays as a result of climate change. For example, this includes programs that respond to the physical risks of climate change, such as wildland fire suppression, Stafford Act Programs, and other Federal programs pertaining to emergency management. There are also programs that experience increased outlays, but the mission of the program is broader than responding to climate-related events. This includes Federal health care programs, which was described in last year's assessment. The NCA4 discusses the broad range of health impacts that are associated with climate change.[58] Given that in 2021, Medicare spending composed 21 percent ($900.8 billion) of total National Healthcare Expenditures and

Medicaid composed $734.0 billion (17 percent)[59], there is sufficient evidence to assume that a significant portion of the increase in national health expenditures as a result of climate change would be absorbed by Federal healthcare spending.[60, 61] For credit programs, climate change may increase default risk of direct loans from the Federal Government and loans guaranteed by the Federal Government. Borrowers being unable to sufficiently recover financially from climate-related events could result in higher rates of delinquency and default. Some Federal programs may experience decreased revenue caused by climate change, particularly given that climate change can cause disruptions to trade and may cause economic losses to a wide range of industrial sectors.[62] Ongoing work responding to Section 6(a) in Executive Order 14030 will quantify the macro-economic costs of climate change and could be used in concert with other tools, to inform revenue projections. Lastly, some programs may have their efficacy impacted by climate change, but not experience higher outlays or decreased revenues; instead, the program may experience a fall in performance metrics, such as members of the public served. Below we provide three possible methods for projecting expenditures of Federal programs.

1. Comprehensive Modeling of Physical Damages and Expenditures: For certain programs, a comprehensive modeling structure may be considered, which would build on the common framework used across agencies. This would not only provide the Federal Budget exposure, but non-monetary outcomes of climate change as well. For example, the analysis on wildland fire suppression in the 2022 white paper provided projections of acres burned by wildland fire, in addition to the projections of outlays for wildland fire suppression from the Forest Service and DOI. Developing comprehensive modeling requires substantial investment by the Federal Government for an individual program since the modeling of the program mechanics are unlikely to translate to other

[58] Ebi, K.L., J.M. Balbus, G. Luber, A. Bole, A. Crimmins, G. Glass, S. Saha, M.M. Shimamoto, J. Trtanj, and J.L. White-Newsome, 2018: Human Health. In Impacts, Risks, and Adaptation in the United States: Fourth National Climate Assessment, Volume II [Reidmiller, D.R., C.W. Avery, D.R. Easterling, K.E. Kunkel, K.L.M. Lewis, T.K. Maycock, and B.C. Stewart (eds.)]. U.S. Global Change Research Program, Washington, DC, USA, pp. 539–571. doi: 10.7930/NCA4.2018.CH14

[59] Centers for Medicare & Medicaid Services. NHE Fact Sheet. (2022) *https://www.cms.gov/Research-Statistics-Data-and-Systems/Statistics-Trends-and-Reports/NationalHealthExpendData/NHE-Fact-Sheet* accessed on February 8, 2023.

[60] EPA. 2017. Multi-model framework for quantitative sectoral impacts analysis: A technical report for the Fourth National Climate Assessment. U.S. Environmental Protection Agency, EPA 430-R-17-001. *https://www.epa.gov/cira/multi-model-framework-quantitative-sectoral-impacts-analysis*

[61] Tamma Carleton, Amir Jina, Michael Delgado, Michael Greenstone, Trevor Houser, Solomon Hsiang, Andrew Hultgren, Robert E Kopp, Kelly E McCusker, Ishan Nath, James Rising, Ashwin Rode, Hee Kwon Seo, Arvid Viaene, Jiacan Yuan, Alice Tianbo Zhang, Valuing the Global Mortality Consequences of Climate Change Accounting for Adaptation Costs and Benefits, The Quarterly Journal of Economics, Volume 137, Issue 4, November 2022, Pages 2037–2105, *https://doi.org/10.1093/qje/qjac020*

[62] Smith, J.B., M. Muth, A. Alpert, J.L. Buizer, J. Cook, A. Dave, J. Furlow, K. Preston, P. Schultz, and L. Vaughan, 2018: Climate Effects on U.S. International Interests. In Impacts, Risks, and Adaptation in the United States: Fourth National Climate Assessment, Volume II [Reidmiller, D.R., C.W. Avery, D.R. Easterling, K.E. Kunkel, K.L.M. Lewis, T.K. Maycock, and B.C. Stewart (eds.)]. U.S. Global Change Research Program, Washington, DC, USA, pp. 604–637. doi: 10.7930/NCA4.2018.CH16

Federal programs. For these models, the modeling will generally have three stages.

- Climate projections: Agencies will utilize guidance provided by the AFFCR on the selection and use of appropriate climate projections and associated variables to ensure consistency throughout the assessment.

- Physical damages of climate change: Agencies develop a model, if needed, that translates the climate projections into the physical impact of interest (e.g., acres burned by wildland fire, health impacts from poorer air quality, damage to infrastructure, buildings loss).

- Federal financial damage of climate change: Agencies develop a model that estimates the cost to the Federal Government based on the physical damages projected in the previous stage.

2. Modeling Expenditures Directly from Climate Variables: Given the resource intensity of developing comprehensive modeling for individual Federal programs, a more streamlined framework involves establishing a relationship between historical climate variables and outlays, then utilizing the relationship to develop projections of outlays under different climate change scenarios. Additionally, where there is a demonstrated relationship between program expenditures and climate variables, agencies could explore the possibility of using the correlation among Federal outlays of different programs to investigate whether the relationship between climate variables and the outlays of one Federal program can also be used to explain other programs. Method development would need to address suitable approaches for characterizing non-linear relationships between changes in climate variables and program expenditures.

3. Modeling Expenditures as a Proportion of Economic Damages: Where the outlays or losses of the Federal Program are assumed to be proportional to the sectoral damages projected in FrEDI. While this method would require the least amount of additional modeling, further research would need to be conducted to ensure that assuming outlays increase proportionally with economic damages to a particular sector included within FrEDI is reasonable.

Given the wide-diversity of Federal programs, there is no "one size fits all" approach, when developing projections of expenditure changes for individual programs, however the approaches discussed here would provide a common framework to build agency-or program-specific analyses. The AFFCR is exploring modeling approach options, including developing capability for comprehensive modeling of physical damages and expenditures, an approach to model expenditures directly from climate variables, and modeling expenditures as a proportion of economic damages.

Mission and Operational Risk: Mission and operational risk could both explicitly impact the outlays of the agency and impact performance, but rather cause the performance of the agency to decline given funding constraints. The risk to operations brought on by climate change is diverse. Impacts to mission and operations may include:

- disruptions in continuity of operation, including disruptions caused within supply chains of federally procured goods and services;

- loss of assets not owned by the Federal Government but of which the Federal Government has a vested interest in maintenance; and

- reduced ability to meet mission and functional performance. For example, climate-related risks to NASA's critical launch facilities or current technologies to assist in agricultural conservation decreasing in effectiveness due to climate change.

At this time the AFFCR is not actively establishing a framework for quantifying mission and operations risks; however, as data collection continues and research in this area may grow, the AFFCR will explore the feasibility of creating a framework for quantifying the impacts on operations and mission risk in the future.

Continued Work to Develop the Common Framework and Methodology for Future Assessments

The assessment included in this chapter presents advances in incorporating forward-looking projections of climate change and multiple approaches to estimate how changes in climate variables and natural hazards (e.g., flooding) relate to potential future risk to Federal assets and programs. This work has built on the continued growth of accessible climate information (e.g., NCA4 statistically downscaled projections, CMRA, flooding projections from Federal and external providers), and further work remains to link projections in changes to physical variables to Federal Budget decision contexts. To support future assessments, the AFFCR is working in several areas: 1) continuing to develop the common framework, provide technical guidance, and examples of implementation across a range of Federal assets and programs; 2) identifying necessary and emerging climate data and information resources, including projections of extreme weather events where information is currently unavailable (e.g., projecting physical impacts of tropical cyclones); and 3) increasing capacity and training of Federal agencies to conduct climate-related financial risk assessments.

MANAGEMENT PRIORITIES

11. DELIVERING A HIGH-PERFORMANCE GOVERNMENT

The American people deserve a high-performing, effective Government—one that sets and meets ambitious goals for protecting individuals and communities, modernizes infrastructure, invests in children, and takes care of the most vulnerable. Like all high-performing organizations, the Federal Government has developed a set of management routines that drive a results-oriented culture and help organizations deliver prioritized, transparent outcomes. Grounded in proven, evidence-based management practices of high-performing public and private sector organizations, the Federal Government's approach to delivering a more effective and efficient Government is operationalized through the ***Federal Performance Framework***, and rests on three main components: clearly defining mission success, engaging senior leaders to assess progress using data-driven reviews, and reporting results transparently to the public.

The Administration is committed to using this Framework—originally authorized by the Congress in 1993 with the Government Performance and Results Act of 1993 (GPRA)[1] and updated in 2010 with the GPRA Modernization Act of 2010 (GPRAMA)[2]—to make a difference in the lives of the American people, including disadvantaged communities that have been historically underserved, marginalized, and adversely affected by persistent poverty and structural inequality. Federal agencies use these performance planning activities, practices, and routines to shift the Government's focus from programs to people; from the means of Government to its ends; and from rules to values. Moreover, this systems-focused approach allows the Federal Government to align its budget and resources to its performance framework, helping to ensure that agencies' organizational goals and objectives are resourced effectively, efficiently, and with accountability. This commitment to good Government—using a multi-disciplinary array of management tools incorporated within the Federal Performance Framework to strive toward an equitable, effective, and accountable Government that delivers results for all—has been evident since the start of the Administration. From supporting effective implementation of major, newly enacted legislation, such as the Infrastructure and Investment and Jobs Act (Public Law 117-58, "Bipartisan Infrastructure Law"), to advancing efforts to fulfill the goals of the President's Management Agenda, the Framework and its routines are being used to improve outcomes for the American public and ensure transparency on progress through the central reporting website *Performance.gov*.

This Chapter reviews the Federal Government's Performance Framework approach to performance management, and its application to date by the Administration

to improve outcomes and deliver a high-performance Government. The Chapter begins by offering an update and overview on the 'state' of the Framework. It details some of the investments being made by the President's 2024 Budget and other actions taken to strengthen the capacity of agencies to deliver on their organizational performance commitments. The Chapter then turns to a discussion of the Federal Government's use of strategic planning and priority goal-setting to define success, and the use of regular, data-driven performance reviews to identify and address barriers proactively across a portfolio of over 400 strategic objectives and 90 Agency Priority Goals (APGs). The next two sections highlight the use of the Framework to promote and foster interagency coordination and collaboration. One section provides an update on the President's Management Agenda and Cross-Agency Priority (CAP) Goals to advance Government-wide management priorities, with a specific focus on progress made to date to improve service delivery and customer experience — a key component of this approach. Specifically, the section discusses some of the efforts, supported by over $510 million included in the President's 2024 Budget, to strengthen activities focused on modernizing programs, reducing administrative burdens, and piloting new online tools and technologies in order to deliver better customer service to the American people. The next section presents accomplishments, investments, and actions to improve the Federal Permitting process, a good example of how interagency coordination is enabling a more effective, efficient, just, and equitable Government. The Chapter concludes by previewing forthcoming efforts to ensure that leaders, managers, and supervisors across the Federal Government will be held to the highest standards of accountability for understanding how their operational units are performing, and adjusting workforce policies to maximize the organizational performance and organizational health of the agency. By establishing routines to monitor progress, diagnose issues, and identify relationships related to organizational health and organizational performance within the major operating units of an agency, agencies will build on efforts to collectively drive performance results in support of their mission, deliver programs and services, and meet stakeholder needs and priorities on an ongoing basis.

The State of the Federal Performance Framework

At its core, the Federal Performance Framework and its associated practices and routines provide a set of tools that enable organizations to ensure the means of Government are effectively and efficiently applied to deliver results for the people of the United States — the ends of Government. The 1993 GPRA framework was organized around a longer-term agency strategic plan, and

[1] *Public Law 103-62.*
[2] *Public Law 111-352.*

Chart 11-1. Federal Performance Management Cycle Policy Framework

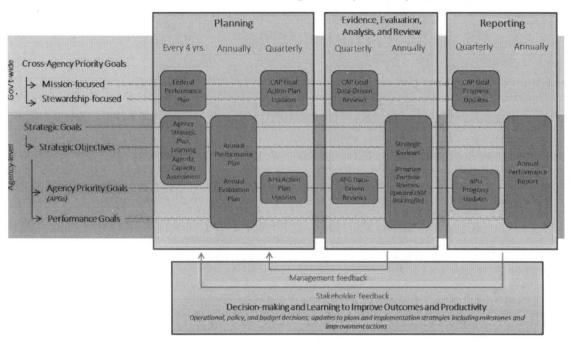

agency performance plan and report updated annually. Widely viewed at the time as landmark legislation in the public administration field, the GPRA offered a model of legislation to be exported to other countries. Its intent was simple: apply leading organizational management practices from the private sector to Government. However, too much emphasis was placed on external transparency reporting over the needs of decision-makers in the Executive Branch, creating a cycle that undermined the law's effectiveness. The GPRAMA updated and modernized the original 1993 GPRA, seeking to address this shortcoming while incorporating other lessons learned from public and private sector management practices.

The GPRAMA reinforced core organizational performance and management routines and practices for Federal agencies by creating an updated statutory framework with a renewed focused on organizational strategic planning, priority goal setting that engages leadership, and enhanced public reporting of progress and results achieved on a central website (*Performance.gov*). It shifted focus from a "supply-side" approach of producing information towards a "demand-driven" model that centered on supporting leadership in identifying and accomplishing their top priorities within the framework; clarifying roles and responsibilities of agency Chief Operating Officers (COO), Performance Improvement Officers (PIO), and Goal Leaders; aligning strategic planning with Presidential election cycles; and emphasizing the use of performance information and evidence for decision-making by agency leadership while seeking to minimize reporting and compliance burdens.

The Framework's major provisions create a cycle of performance management routines that govern organiza-

tional planning and goal-setting, data-driven reviews of progress against those goals, and reporting for agencies to use to drive organizational performance and management improvements. Importantly, its construction across four-year, annual, and quarterly cycles provides a key mechanism for maximizing the organizational learning that stems from the management routines of data-driven reviews. Agencies translate the longer-term strategic goals and objectives in their Strategic Plans to programmatic performance goals, including APGs in the Agency Performance Plan (APP). The APP communicates the agency's strategic objectives and performance goals with other elements of the agency's budget request, detailing how goals will be achieved, identifying priorities among the goals, and describing mechanisms to monitor progress, which is subsequently reported annually in the Agency Performance Report (APR) for the most recently completed organizational performance period. With a two-year coverage period that is reviewed and updated annually by the agency, the APP complements the longer-term planning in the Strategic Plan with a shorter and intermediate-term operational planning horizon for the organization. This gives agencies the opportunity to revise implementation strategies and programmatic operations in order to address and overcome identified barriers or challenges to delivering on their missions.

Moreover, since GPRAMA's enactment in 2010, the Federal Performance Framework has continued to evolve to accommodate the coordination and integration of additional Government-wide, management-focused legislation and initiatives that have been introduced to improve overall organizational performance by applying increasingly specialized decision-support functions and skillsets. Over the years, the Framework has incorporated both newly created legislative requirements (e.g., the Foundations for Evidence-Based Policymaking Act of 2018, the Program Management Improvement Accountability Act) as well as additional management initiatives (e.g., Customer Experience, Enterprise Risk Management) that address the need for increasingly sophisticated approaches to managing the organizational complexities of Federal agencies.

Evidence the Framework Is Working

Evidence from agencies and academic research shows that the routines and practices established by the GPRA Modernization Act and institutionalized into the Framework through the Office of Management and Budget's (OMB) guidance are contributing to increased use of performance information. Specifically, research by Moynihan and Kroll demonstrates that the current GPRAMA routines are not only driving greater use of performance information in decision-making by managers (2016),[3] but are doing so more effectively than earlier management reforms, which failed to show positive correlations with increased manager use of performance information (2020).[4] The Government Accountability Office (GAO) recently examined the use of performance information by Federal managers. Results from GAO's 2020 Managers Survey indicated an increase in the overall use of performance information Government-wide from 3.39 (on a scale of 5) in 2017 to 3.64 in 2020.[5] In fact, the 2020 results reflect the highest increase since the GAO developed the index in 2007. Moreover, the GAO further found that managers reported significantly greater use of performance information in decision-making when their programs were subject to data-driven reviews.[6]

Despite these promising trends and findings on the advantages the Framework can convey to overall organizational performance and data-driven decision-making, the Administration recognizes there are inherent challenges associated with the Framework — some of which are common to implementing any system for organizational performance management across complex organizations. Accumulating over several years of implementation and organizational learning, the following challenges have emerged as intrinsic to the Framework:

- Meeting the needs of separate, independent branches of the Federal Government that can at times have divergent incentive structures;

- While policies, guidance, and legislative requirements are optimized at the agency/departmental HQs-level, elongated delivery and implementation chains demand organizational processes and management tools for leading practices and routines to permeate to lower-levels of the organization;

- Balancing the value of providing transparency and maintaining management routines with the administrative burden of performance reporting;

- Facilitating collaboration and coordination in areas that require multiple organizations working together to achieve an outcome;

- Orientation toward compliance activities over usefulness to agency leadership in assessing progress toward outcomes;

- Unevenness across agencies capacity and capabilities—including technical expertise, staffing, and data—to do this work in increasingly complex organizational environments; and

- Limited tenure of leadership at agencies, and staff attrition and turnover.

Although some of these barriers are inherent to most organizational performance management systems for complex organizations, OMB and agencies nonetheless continue to make strides in addressing such challenges to improve the overall efficacy and utility of the Framework. This Chapter now turns to highlighting some of those efforts.

For example, OMB is taking steps to further coordinate and align Government-wide management efforts. In addition to implementing the Performance Framework and partnering with the Office of Personnel Management (OPM) on workforce priorities, OMB's Office of Performance and Personnel Management (OPPM) now includes the Evidence Team responsible for implementing the Learning Agendas and evaluation activities in Title I of the Foundations for Evidence Based Policymaking Act ("Evidence Act"). An OMB Customer Experience team is also now organized within OPPM, working jointly with OMB's U.S. Digital Service (USDS), Office of the Federal Chief Information Officer (OFCIO), Office of Information and Regulatory Affairs (OIRA), and Resource Management Offices (RMOs) to drive improvements in service delivery.

Proposals to Eliminate Outdated, Unnecessary, and Duplicative Reporting by Agencies

Federal agencies annually produce thousands of congressionally-mandated plans and reports. While transparency and accountability through regular public reporting are important pillars of the Framework, plans and reports that were once useful can become outdated, duplicative, or less useful over time. A provision of GPRAMA requires Federal agencies to annually identify

---

[3] Moynihan, Donald, and Alexander Kroll. (2016). "Performance management routines that work? An early assessment of the GPRA Modernization Act." *Public Administration Review*, 76(2): 314–323.

[4] Moynihan, Donald, and Alexander Kroll. (2021). "Tools of Control? Comparing Congressional and Presidential Performance Management Reforms." *Public Administration Review*, 81(4): 599–609.

[5] U.S. Government Accountability Office (GAO). (2021). *Evidence-Based Policy Making: Survey Results Suggest Increased Use of Performance Information across the Federal Government. GAO-22-103910* (November, 2021).

[6] U.S. Government Accountability Office (GAO). (2021). *Evidence-Based Policy Making: Survey Results Suggest Increased Use of Performance Information across the Federal Government. GAO-22-103910* (November, 2021).

for elimination or modification plans and reports that are outdated or duplicative, an exercise that seeks to balance the value of providing transparency with the administrative burden of performance reporting that is no longer necessary. Previous efforts have led to the repeal of several dozen plans or reports through the Government Reports Elimination Act of 2014 (Public Law 113-188), as well as varying degrees of additional congressional engagement, including most recently the passage out of committee of S.2769 (Congressional Reporting Burden Reduction Act) in the 116th Congress.

In conjunction with the President's 2024 Budget, OMB is making available a list that consolidates across Federal agencies over *50* proposals for modifying outdated or duplicative congressionally-required plans or reports. The report modification actions proposed by Federal agencies range from elimination of the plan or report, to changes that would introduce efficiencies into the reporting requirement through actions that would streamline, consolidate, or reduce reporting frequency, preserving transparency while reducing unnecessary burden. In the aggregate, these recommendations, if enacted by the Congress, would shift the administrative reporting burden of agencies towards higher-priority reporting requirements. And adoption of some of the report modification proposals put forth by the OMB specifically could have a magnified impact, given their Government-wide applicability and reach.

Building Agency Capacity and Analytical Capabilities for Practicing Data-Driven Management

To tackle the unevenness that exists across agencies to do this work, OMB continues to focus on building the analytical capacity of agencies so that they may put into practice elements of the Framework and apply its principles of data-driven management. The President's 2024 Budget proposes investments, at both the agency-HQ/enterprise and agency-component levels, to strengthen the capabilities of Federal agencies to do this work, from advancing performance management to other analytic activities supporting data-driven management.

- **$4 million in an enterprise data and analytics capability at the National Science Foundation (NSF)** to support data integration across customer experience surveys, modeling, and other program monitoring to inform agency strategy, programmatic decisions and investments needed for advancing NSF priorities and strategic goals.

- **$2.5 million and 10 staff FTEs (full-time equivalents) at the Department of the Treasury's Bureau of the Fiscal Service** to strengthen a broad complement of analytical-support activities including enterprise-strategic planning, program evaluation, data-collection, and performance analytics to support the delivery of Government payments to hard-to-reach populations as well as improving the overall capability to assess progress against outcomes.

- **$2 million and five FTEs to strengthen and expand enterprise governance support for policy and resource allocation decision-making bodies** within the Department of Veterans Affairs Office of Enterprise Integration.

- **Over $3 million at the Department of State to support the Administration's Indo-Pacific Strategy,** including over $2 million to expand data analytics for the Bureau of East Asian and Pacific Affairs and approximately $1 million for the Bureau of Global Public Affairs to strengthen strategic planning, research, and analytics capabilities of the Department's Asia Pacific Media Hub.

See the *Analytical Perspectives* Volume's companion chapter, Chapter 12 "Building and Using Evidence to Improve Government Effectiveness," for more information and a further discussion on the Budget's related investments in strengthening agency capacity for program evaluation and evidence-building.

Data-Driven Performance Reviews to Drive Results in Execution

Strategic planning and priority goal setting are common tools designed to set the direction of an organization. Research exploring the relationship of this planning to organizational performance has shown it has a positive impact on organizational performance in both public and private sectors across international settings, and is most powerful as a predictor of organizational effectiveness.[7] The Agency Strategic Plan defines the agency mission, long-term goals and objectives, strategies planned to achieve those goals, and the approaches it will use to monitor its progress in addressing specific national problems, needs, challenges, and opportunities related to its mission.

At the beginning of each new administration term, concurrent with the preparation of the President's Budget, each Federal agency produces a revised four-year Strategic Plan which sets out the long-term objectives the agency hopes to accomplish. By defining from the start of an administration what strategic priorities and objectives the agency aims to achieve, what actions the agency will take to realize those priorities, and how the agency will deal with challenges and risks that may hinder progress, a new administration can ensure the deliberateness of sound planning and resourcing that will be needed to drive effectiveness in the multi-year execution efforts to follow.

Last year, in parallel with the release of the President's 2023 Budget, Federal agencies updated their Agency Strategic Plans covering 2022-2026. Agencies identified Strategic Goals, Strategic Objectives, and APGs that reflect the bottom line of Government advancing outcomes

---

[7] George, Bert, Walker, Richard, and Monster, Joost. (2019). "Does Strategic Planning Improve Organizational Performance? A Meta-Analysis." *Public Administration Review*, 79(6): 810-819.

across key Administration priorities, including improving customer experience, advancing equity, combatting climate change, improving the Nation's infrastructure, and meeting the health, welfare, and economic challenges of the COVID-19 pandemic.

Organizational Learning and the Data-Driven Performance Review: From Strategic Planning and Goal-Setting to Implementation

Conducting routine, data-driven performance reviews led by agency leaders on a set of the agency's performance improvement priorities is a management practice proven to produce better results. Incorporating a range of quantitative and qualitative evidence with regular reviews provides a mechanism for agency leaders to review the organization's performance and bring together the people, resources, and analysis needed to drive progress on agency priorities of both mission-focused and management goals. Frequent data-driven performance reviews should reinforce the agency's priorities and establish an agency culture of continuous learning and improvement, sending a signal throughout the organization that agency leaders are focused on effective and efficient implementation to improve the delivery of results. Planning activities related to Agency Learning Agendas, Annual Evaluation Plans, and Capacity Assessments required by the Evidence Act reinforce this same culture of learning and improvement that is also cultivated by the data-driven performance review.

Research by Moynihan and Kroll (2016, 2021)[8,9] examining the impact of GPRAMA routines on a key behavioral outcome of the Federal Performance Framework—the use of performance information for decision-making—finds high positive correlations. Such findings regarding performance information use are embodied in the two primary routines of frequent, data-driven performance reviews within the Framework: the quarterly data-driven performance review of APGs, and the annual data-driven Strategic Review of Agency Strategic Objectives.

Whether they are following the quarterly cadence for APGs, or the annual cadence for strategic objectives, these practices inform strategic and operational decision-making, budget formulation, and near-term agency actions by following a few key principles. First, agencies are afforded significant flexibility in designing the performance review process to fit and accommodate a diversity of organizational attributes, including the agency's mission, leadership preferences, organizational structure, and culture. Second, data-driven performance reviews, and particularly APG quarterly reviews, are conducted with the appropriate Goal Leader to assess progress achieved during the most recent quarter, overall trend data, and the likelihood of meeting the planned level of performance. During such sessions, Goal Leaders are held accountable for knowing whether or not their performance indicators

are trending in the right direction at a reasonable speed and, if they are not, for understanding why they are not and for having a plan to accelerate progress on the goal.

Chart 11–2 offers a graphic depiction of how these principles are applied to provide a conceptual framework for the annual data-driven strategic review of strategic objectives, which are treated as the primary unit for strategic analysis and decision-making. Based on feedback, the Federal Performance Framework's Strategic Review policy continues to confer a range of benefits, including improved interagency collaboration, a chance to identify evidence gaps and opportunities to improve data quality to in-form better resource allocation decisions, and further utilizing data-driven performance reviews to improve decision-making as part of the formulation process for the budget.

2022 Strategic Reviews: Policy and Focus

Agencies' annual, internal Strategic Reviews provide a critical opportunity for management for organizational learning in the implementation of programs supporting strategic objectives. Following the agencies' internal assessments, the Strategic Review meetings provide an opportunity for agencies and OMB to discuss progress in the implementation of the Agency Strategic Plan, using recent evidence while aligning these management discussions to a timeline that informs the President's budget development and future strategic planning, evidence-building, and management efforts by agencies.

The 2022 Strategic Reviews and subsequent Agency/OMB meetings was the first year of reviews since the establishment of the new strategic goal and objectives frameworks, learning agendas, and performance and evaluation plans in March 2022. On the heels of the Administration's collective accomplishment in publishing four-year Agency Strategic Plans and two-year APGs, OMB sought to drive progress and collaborate with agencies through the annual Strategic Review process this past summer. While the 2021 Strategic Review meetings focused on the development of strategic plans and priority goals, the 2022 meetings were designed to bring together senior leadership from OMB, policy councils, and agencies to review progress towards achieving over 400 strategic goals and objectives – including assessments of the impacts from enterprise risk management reviews, and findings and contributions from agency learning agendas. These reviews played a key role in identifying the subset of over 90 strategic objectives that would be designated by agencies as either an area of Noteworthy Progress or a Focus Area for Improvement.[10] Additionally, agendas for the 2022 Strategic Review meetings also included a limited number of 'Deep Dive' topics. These topics focused on one to three substantive policy, management, or evidence-building areas in which collaboration and coordination between OMB and the agency were critical to make meaningful gains.

[8] Moynihan, Donald, and Alexander Kroll. (2016). "Performance management routines that work? An early assessment of the GPRA Modernization Act." *Public Administration Review*, 76(2): 314–323.

[9] Moynihan, Donald, and Alexander Kroll. (2021). "Tools of Control? Comparing Congressional and Presidential Performance Management Reforms." *Public Administration Review*, 81(4): 599–609.

[10] For additional information on OMB's policies governing strategic reviews and the categorization of strategic objectives, see Circular A-11, Part 6, Section 260.

Chart 11-2. Conceptual Framework for the Annual Data-driven Review of Strategic Objectives

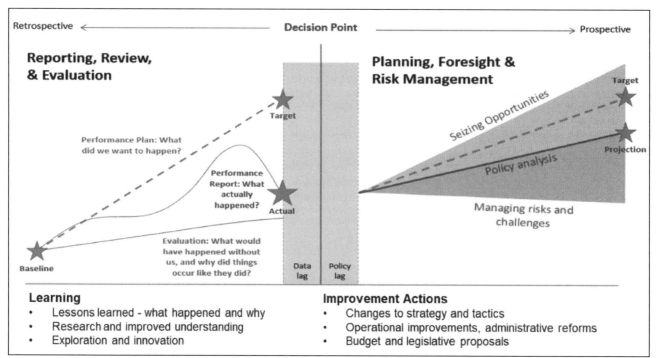

2022 Strategic Reviews: Opportunities and Leading Practices

Several leading practices emerged during the Strategic Review as tools for achieving further improvements in performance management:

- *Use analysis generated by the strategic review process and engagement with OMB/Agency leadership to propose and validate shifts in strategic direction and priorities based on new, emergent legislation or other events that significantly change the operating environment.*

  For example, the Department of the Treasury used its 2022 review to reorient strategic priorities and objectives in its 2022-2026 Strategic Plan in response to the Inflation Reduction Act of 2022. The Strategic Review meeting with the Department of Commerce facilitated similar strategic-level discussions related to the CHIPS and Science Act.

- *Overcome the potential for and challenges of "mission fragmentation" across Departmental components, bureaus, and programs by leveraging their expertise in the production of "performance dashboards" when assessing progress, and ensuring their participation in the Strategic Review meeting.*

  Agencies utilize a "performance dashboard" format for presenting their Strategic Review

Summary of Findings by Strategic Objective, the critical output of their internal strategic review process. First introduced for the 2019 Strategic Reviews, the performance dashboard requirement stemmed from a private sector best practice that first gained popularity in the early 1990s, and has since been the subject of numerous publications.[11] Findings presented in the performance dashboards reflect the agency's assessment of progress towards achieving strategic objectives and synthesize analyses by agency managers and leaders on the actions needed to sustain or improve performance and/or mitigate risks to overcome performance and evidence-building challenges. The most effective strategic review meetings included the attendance of the Bureau Administrator or program manager, able to speak to the substantive complexities of a particular implementation challenge or policy issue.

---

[11] See Kaplan, R. S., and D. P. Norton (1992). "The Balanced Scorecard: Measures That Drive Performance," *Harvard Business Review* 70(1), 71-79; Kaplan, R. S., and D. P. Norton (1993). "Putting the Balanced Scorecard to Work," *Harvard Business Review* 71(5), 134-148; Kaplan, R. S., and D. P. Norton (1996). "Using the Balanced Scorecard as a Strategic Management System," *Harvard Business Review* 74(1), 75-86; and Niven, Paul R (2008). *Balanced Scorecard for Government and Nonprofit Agencies*. 2nd ed. Hoboken, NT: Wiley.

Chart 11-3. 2022 Strategic Review Deep Dive Topics Word Cloud

Covid recovery

Evidence

Customer experience

Climate Public safety

Housing   Jobs/Employment

Oversight/fraud prevention

Federal workforce

Localization Infrastructure

Future of Work IT DEIA

Data Supply chain

New mandates/legislation

Internal reorganization

Project management

- *While the complexity of issues, asymmetry of information, and time constraints of the strategic review meeting do not always allow for final resolution, the selection of Deep Dive topics for the Agenda can be used to surface issues for the continued engagement and discussion needed to find shared policy solutions.*

  For example, Deep Dive topics were a major hallmark of the 2022 Strategic Review meetings, providing an opportunity to elevate a limited number of issues or topics that would benefit from strategic, senior leadership engagement between OMB and agencies. These topics ranged from items in the Strategic Plan and areas of emerging strategic-level import, such as implementation approaches to recently enacted or expected legislation, to issues in which no other natural channels for EOP engagement existed. Chart 11–3 depicts a word cloud that offers a visual representation summarizing Deep Dive topics across strategic review meeting agendas. Addressing persistent Workforce and Human Capital challenges and having a collaborative discussion on resources for overcoming barriers emerged as the most common Deep Dive topic, appearing on one-third of OMB/Agency strategic review meeting agendas. The second most common Deep Dive topic across meetings focused on partnering on implementation approaches to new legislation and statutory requirements.

- *Strengthen connections across performance management and budget frameworks.* The Strategic Review presents an opportunity for strengthening con-

nections across performance, budget and resource management by providing a mechanism by which agencies' organizational and programmatic performance planning activities are not occurring independent of complementary resourcing planning and discussions. It allows leadership and management to understand the current strategic or operational environments, informing shorter- and medium-term planning through the development of organizational performance and program plans to inform budget formulation and resourcing discussions, providing a strategic context. Selection of Deep Dive topics during the 2022 Strategic Review meetings offered a forum for those discussions to occur. Below is one example highlighting the connection between 2022 Strategic Review meeting topics and the 2024 Budget.

OPM's strategic review meeting included a Deep Dive topic to discuss ongoing planning and implementation efforts for the recently enacted Postal Service Reform Act of 2022, and specifically, new statutory requirements for OPM to implement the Postal Service Health Benefits Program. Implementation of this major new program, which is to be operational by January 2025, will be a multi-year, collaborative effort for the Administration, requiring additional resources in both the near-term and beyond. The 2024 Budget for OPM proposes an investment of an additional $28 million to prioritize implementation of the Postal Service Health Benefits Program and deliver this critical service to the country's Postal Service employees and retirees.

OMB began collecting internal feedback on its Strategic Review policy starting with the 2018 performance period. Since then, participants and other stakeholders participating in the process have consistently reported that the internal review and analysis being generated is valuable. As support for the internal strategic review process continues to increase, identifying more opportunities to shape and refine both its policy and implementation remain a continued focus for OMB and agencies.

2022-2023 APGs: Progress at the One-Year Mark

APGs are used to achieve an agency's near-term, implementation-focused priorities. Agencies establish Priority Goals every two years and use clearly identified Goal Leaders, Deputy Goal Leaders, and quarterly metrics and milestones to manage progress. Agency Chief Operating Officers (generally, Deputy Secretaries or Deputy Administrators) lead quarterly data-driven performance reviews to overcome barriers and accelerate performance results. Progress on APGs is updated publicly on a quarterly basis, with data and progress reported on *Performance.gov.*

Federal agencies continue to build upon the successes and performance outcomes achieved over previous two-year cycles while charting new and even more ambitious priority performance goals. Marking the seventh cohort of APGs since their initial establishment,[12] APGs reflect the Administration's commitments in near-term performance improvement outcomes that at the same time advance progress towards longer-term, outcome-focused strategic goals and objectives within each agency's four-year Strategic Plan. For the current cohort of APGs, OMB provided guidance[13] to agencies on priority goal-setting efforts, encouraging specific alignment of both strategic objectives and APGs with the Administration's policy priorities, including in particular, continued work to meet the health, welfare, and economic challenges of the COVID-19 pandemic, advance equity, and address climate change. It also encouraged agencies to set joint APGs in areas where programs from multiple agencies must work together to achieve a common outcome.

The incorporation of joint APGs into the guidance was designed as a policy response to address the simple fact that many of the most pressing challenges facing Government do not fit neatly within the boundaries of a single agency, bureau, division, or office. Yet, the routines and enabling functions of the Framework can provide a management and governance mechanism for facilitating the collaboration and coordination required in a multi-actor network of vertical hierarchies and horizontal relationships. In short, the complexities of multi-organi-zational or intra-agency efforts demand some degree of integrated governance structures if they are to be successful in orchestrating policies that drive implementation activities.

Ninety APGs covering the FYs 2022-2023 performance period are currently available on Performance.gov. Major agencies, in collaboration with OMB, have worked over the past year to deliver on the performance commitments made across a portfolio of 200+ key performance indicators and milestones. Below are some highlights at the one-year implementation mark of September 30, 2022, for the current cycle of 2022-2023 APGs.

- **Department of Commerce (DOC) / Department of Agriculture (USDA).** *Joint Goal* to expand access to affordable, reliable, high-speed broadband internet, with a focus on communities in the greatest need. At the one-year implementation mark (September 30, 2022), the Commerce and Agriculture Departments had worked together to expand affordable and reliable access to high-quality internet service with the potential ability to serve over 347,000 households, including vulnerable communities such as tribal and unserved households, and was on-track to meet their goal of 550,000 by the end of 2023.

- **Department of Energy (DOE) / Department of Transportation (DOT).** *Joint Goal* to complete the critical building blocks needed for the deployment of a national network of electric vehicle (EV) chargers under the Bipartisan Infrastructure Law. At the one-year implementation mark (September 30, 2022), the Energy and Transportation Departments had overseen and assisted with the development and review of State EV Infrastructure Deployment Plans from all 50 states, Puerto Rico, and the District of Columbia. Based on the review and recommendations of the Joint Office of Energy and Transportation, the Federal Highway Administration approved all plans in September 2022, which collectively unlock $1.5 billion in funding to begin building out convenient, reliable, affordable, and equitable EV charging corridors along over 75,000 miles of the highway system.

- **Department of Housing and Urban Development (HUD).** By September 30, 2023, protect families from lead-based paint and other health hazards by making an additional 20,000 units of at-risk housing healthy and lead-safe for residents. At the one-year implementation mark (September 30, 2022), HUD had successfully made 9,855 housing units healthy and lead-safe, and was on-track to meet its goal of 20,000 units by the end of 2023.

- **Department of Veterans Affairs (VA).** By September 30, 2023, the VA will ensure 90 percent of rural-dwelling veterans are satisfied with their access to healthcare when and where they need it. At the one-year implementation mark (September 30, 2022), the Department had achieved an 87 percent patient satisfaction score regarding access to rural

---

[12] Agency High Priority Performance Goals were the predecessor to the APG, first established in "Delivering a High Performance Government" in the *Analytical Perspectives* volume of the 2011 Budget (pp 73-90). The policy framework and requirements for High Priority Performance Goals were subsequently codified into statute through enactment of GPRAMA and expanded through OMB guidance via the Federal Performance Framework in OMB Circular A-11, Part 6, *Section 250.*

[13] OMB Memorandum M-21-22, Update to Implementation of Performance Management Statutes (Mar. 24, 2021).

health care, and was on-track to meet its goal of 90 percent patient satisfaction levels by the end of 2023.

- **Department of the Interior (DOI).** By September 30, 2023, the Department's Bureau of Reclamation will facilitate water conservation capacity of 55,236 acre-feet to help reduce the impact of drought. At the one-year implementation mark (September 30, 2022), the Department of the Interior had exceeded their goal to increase water conservation capacity to help achieve a more sustainable water supply and address the impacts of drought in the western United States. In 2022, the Bureau of Reclamation facilitated water conservation capacity of 93,449 acre-feet to help reduce the impact of drought in communities such as Big Bear Valley, Santa Ana Watershed, and the Donna Irrigation District in Southern Texas.

- **National Aeronautics and Space Administration (NASA).** By September 30, 2023, NASA will complete commissioning of the James Webb Space Telescope, the most powerful and complex space telescope ever built, and begin Webb's Cycle 2 observations. At the one-year implementation mark (September 30, 2022), NASA had successfully launched, commissioned, and began routine operations of the James Webb Space Telescope, achieving all of Webb's 2022 APG milestones. As the world's most powerful space telescope, Webb has already found the most distant objects in the universe, discovered new chemicals in the atmospheres of exoplanets, and begun generating science papers at a rate of three to four a day, fulfilling its aim to prompt the rewriting of textbooks.

- **Office of Personnel Management (OPM).** By September 30, 2023, OPM will help the Bipartisan Infrastructure Law agencies fill 75 percent of surge hiring positions identified in the first quarter of 2022. At the one-year implementation mark (September 30, 2022), OPM had successfully assisted BIL agencies to reach more than 53 percent of their hiring targets and was on track to accomplish its goal by the end of 2023.

- **Small Business Administration (SBA).** By September 30, 2023, the SBA will increase Federal contracting awards to small disadvantaged businesses (SDBs) to 12 percent, promoting diversity, equity, inclusion, and accessibility to help more Americans realize their entrepreneurial dreams while growing the U.S. industrial base. At the one-year implementation mark (September 30, 2022), the SBA had steadily increased the number of disadvantaged small businesses receiving Federal procurement contracts – up from 9 percent in 2017 to 11 percent in 2021, representing nearly 5,000 certified 8(a) firms as of 2021.

The SBA goal team was on track to reach its target of 12 percent by the end of 2023.

Facilitating Interagency Collaboration and Advancing Government-wide Management Priorities through the President's Management Agenda (PMA)

The *President's Management Agenda (PMA)* lays out a long-term vision for improving the Federal Government's ability to deliver agency mission outcomes, provide excellent service, and effectively steward taxpayer dollars. Under the leadership and direction of *Priority Area Leaders*, each priority area of the PMA is advanced through Strategies supported by Strategy Leads who oversee the development and execution of more defined goals organized into a select number of CAP Goals. Focused on implementation, defining metrics and milestones, and piloting innovative approaches to address stated goals, interagency teams work collaboratively with interagency forums, including the President's Management Council (PMC), executive management councils, and communities of practice, to ensure that collaborative, values-driven approaches developed through the PMA create lasting change.

Long-term in nature and designed to drive the cross-Government collaboration needed to tackle management challenges affecting multiple agencies, the Administration leverages the CAP Goals as a mechanism to coordinate and publicly track implementation of PMA priorities and strategies across Federal agencies—with teams reporting on progress quarterly through public updates to Performance.gov to foster accountability and build public trust. This system-wide focus affords opportunities to identify issues early, resolve conflicts across discrete lines of effort, and provide the training and guidance needed for agency practitioners while incorporating data-management and evidence-building strategies, along with other capacity-building strategies to advance the Administration's management priorities.

Updates and accomplishments to date across the PMA's three Priority Areas are provided on *Performance.gov*. A more in-depth discussion of Priority Area two—*Delivering Excellent, Equitable, and Secure Federal Services and Customer Experience*—follows in the Section below.

Improving Government Through Delivery of Secure Federal Services and Excellent Customer Experience

Federal services have not always been designed with the public's needs and priorities in mind, nor have these services always kept up with these needs. Poorly designed, out of date, and inequitable Government services are a cost to the Nation; it can mean that veterans don't get benefits they have earned, small business owners cannot access financing to grow their businesses, new mothers and infants lack critical nutrition supports, and disaster survivors face mountains of paperwork to rebuild their homes.

Just over one year ago, in December 2021, the President signed Executive Order 14058, "Transforming Federal Customer Experience and Service Delivery to Rebuild Trust in Government," directing a whole-of-Government effort to design and operate an equitable, effective, and accountable Government that delivers results for all Americans. Since then, more than 17 Federal agencies have taken actions to deliver customer experiences that are more simple, seamless, and secure. The President's 2024 Budget includes more than $510 million to strengthen activities focused on modernizing programs, reducing administrative burdens, and piloting new online tools and technologies. Importantly, the Budget targets efforts on deepening the expertise, capacity, and capabilities that Federal agencies need to meaningfully engage and better serve their customers—the American people.

The President's 2024 Budget directs funding for customer experience, including service design efforts and digital service delivery improvements, at all 17 Federal agencies that maintain the 35 High Impact Service Providers (HISPs) designated by OMB. These efforts are a continuation of Executive Order 14058 commitments, cross-agency life experience work, and core customer experience (CX) management activities as directed in OMB Circular A-11, Section 280. Specifically, the Budget supports the expansion or creation of customer experience offices at nine Federal agencies. The Departments of Homeland Security, Labor, and Interior, with four HISPs each, will establish Department-level customer experience offices to develop enterprise strategies to support customer experience performance. New CX teams at the Social Security Administration, Small Business Administration, Census Bureau, and Department of the Treasury are also supported in the President's Budget request. The Budget makes additional investments in existing CX teams at the Departments of Agriculture and Veterans Affairs. The Budget will also support more than 120 new full-time equivalent (FTEs) individuals with customer experience and digital product training, skills, and experience. This talent can lead customer experience activities across Federal agencies, including engaging and learning from customers, mapping customer journeys, identifying pain points, analyzing customer feedback, and prototyping and testing service improvements.

The Federal Government interacts with millions of people each day and provides vital services during some of the most critical moments in people's lives. Whether searching for vaccine safety information when a child is born, claiming retirement benefits, or rebuilding after a hurricane, Americans expect Government services to be responsive to their needs. But too often, people have to navigate a tangled web of Government websites, offices, and phone numbers to access the services they depend on. The "life experience" organizing framework requires a new model of the Federal delivery system working together—within agencies, across agencies, even across levels of Government—driven by customer (human-centered design) research, rather than within bureaucratic silos, to solve problems. Multiple agencies often serve the same customer in the same moment; for instance, the Transition Assistance Program for service members is administered by multiple agencies, as are multiple Disaster assistance programs that individuals may be navigating at the same time. For the first time, more than $75 million is dedicated towards interagency life experience work to enable more efficient administration of Federally-funded benefits programs, improve the journey of disaster survivors accessing Federal assistance, and streamline the Medicare enrollment process for seniors. At least 10 Federal agencies will play a role in implementing these multi-agency projects.

The President's 2024 Budget funds the development of enterprise Voice of Customer platforms at seven Federal agencies, building on the existing efforts of individual HISPs. Further investment in enterprise Voice of Customer platforms will allow Federal agencies to develop the in-house capacity to engage customers at the point of service, reaching a broad range of community voices so that agencies may consider a variety of customer perspectives and experiences in developing their customer experience strategies. For example, the Office of Federal Student Aid will leverage more robust Voice of Customer tools to better understand the needs of students, parents, and borrowers across the phases of loan management, from application through to repayment.

The President's 2024 Budget facilitates an additional $13 million for six Federal agencies to work directly with GSA's Tech-nology Transformation Services (TTS) for priority projects identified through CX Action Plans. Agencies and GSA can strategi-cally deploy talent through teams such as the Digital Corps Fellows, Presidential Innovation Fellows, Centers of Excellence, and 18F. For example, the Department of the Interior is provided $2.5 million to secure product management and develop talent to support efforts such as the Fish and Wildlife Services' digital permitting activities, and online management of Individual Indian Money accounts.

The Administration understands that regardless of their age, location, digital savvy, disability, education, or English proficiency, the American people deserve a Government that understands who they are, what they need, and how best to deliver for them. Whether during a pivotal life experience such as retiring, or a routine interaction to renew a passport, the Government must build its understanding of its customers and involve them--the people they serve--to improve benefits, services, and programs and enable the Government to deliver for all Americans. The President's 2024 Budget makes historic investments in building the capacity of Government to deliver the 21st Century services Americans expect and deserve. Efforts supported in the 2024 Budget will lay the foundation to improve interactions with Government, rebuilding trust, ensuring no one is left behind, and inspiring others to join the Government in serving future generations of Americans.

Coordinating the Federal Interagency Permitting Process to Deliver Federal Infrastructure Projects On Time, On Task, and On Budget

With the passage of the Bipartisan Infrastructure Law and the Inflation Reduction Act of 2022, the United States is making a once-in-a-generation investment in America's infrastructure, communities, and competitiveness that will create good-paying union jobs, grow the economy, and combat climate change. Long overdue improvements to the Nation's ports, airports, rail, and roads will help ease inflationary pressures, create conditions for businesses to thrive, and strengthen supply chains—which will ultimately lower costs for families. Building new clean energy generation and transmission projects will improve access to affordable clean energy that powers homes and businesses at lower costs. Responsible and sustainable domestic sourcing of critical minerals and materials will power the clean energy economy and reduce reliance on unreliable foreign supply chains. And delivering clean residential water supplies, high-speed internet, healthy forests and open space to all Americans, especially those historically underserved, is critical to make the Nation stronger.

To make the most of these historic investments and ensure the timely and sound delivery of critical infrastructure projects, the Administration released the *Permitting Action Plan* in May 2022 to strengthen and accelerate Federal environmental review and permitting and ensure processes are effective, efficient, timely, and transparent, guided by the best available science to promote positive environmental and community outcomes, and shaped by early and meaningful public engagement.The *Permitting Action Plan* and *M-23-14 implementation guidance* directs agencies to accelerate smart permitting through early cross-agency coordination; establish clear timeline goals and track key project information; engage in early and meaningful outreach and communication with States, Tribal Nations, territories, and local communities; improve agency responsiveness, technical assistance and support; and use resources and the environmental review process to improve impact.

The interagency Federal Permitting Improvement Steering Council is also leveraging its expanded authorities under the Bipartisan Infrastructure Law to work with agencies and sponsors of infrastructure projects to identify and resolve key issues that cause project review delays, bottlenecks, redundancies, and inefficiencies, improve coordination among agencies, help avoid and resolve potential conflicts, identify and share best practices, and accelerate information sharing and troubleshooting. The Administration has also convened sector-specific teams of experts that are advancing the responsible build-out and modernization of U.S. infrastructure by facilitating interagency coordination on siting, permitting, supply chain, and related issues. Federal agencies are also utilizing the *Federal Permitting Dashboard* to increase transparency and accountability by tracking key project information, including timetables and milestones, for infrastructure projects.

Taken together, these actions are helping to strengthen supply chains, lower costs for families, grow the clean energy economy, revitalize communities across the Nation, support good-paying jobs, and accelerate and deliver infrastructure investments on time, on task, and on budget without unnecessary bureaucratic delay.

Communicating Performance Results and Information Transparently

To improve the usefulness of program information through reporting modernization, a central website, *Performance.gov*, makes finding and consuming performance information easier for the public, the Congress, delivery partners, agency employees, and other stakeholders. First established in 2010, Performance.gov continues to offer an online window to Federal performance management efforts, helping to improve accountability by providing one centralized reporting location to find information on agency goals, and regular progress updates towards achieving APGs and and CAP Goals which are being used to implement and drive progress on the President's Management Agenda.

The Administration has continued to develop the Performance.gov platform as a primary means to inform the public on the management initiatives and performance improvements major Federal agencies are making, which allows for an increased and expanded ability to communicate directly with the American public. Site traffic has increased steadily over the years, even throughout Administration transitions.

Enhancements to the site continue to make agency performance information more discoverable. For example, with the release of the President's 2023 Budget last year, Agency Strategic Goals and Strategic Objectives are now posted to the site, making this information more easily viewable and accessible for users. Presented on Performance.gov, Strategic Objectives represent, in the aggregate, the 'bottom-line' the Federal Government is managing towards. More recently, in September 2022 a new feature was added to the site that allows visitors to explore Strategic Objectives and Priority Goals not just by agency, but by 'policy theme'. The ability to explore goals and objectives by policy themes that are reflective of the outcomes to be achieved illustrates a continued effort to forge greater collaboration in policy areas that cut across agency's organizational boundaries, where goal outcomes are shared. Offering increased transparency into strategic objectives both by agency and by policy theme enhances not only how agency's strategic goal frameworks are visualized, but also elevates their role and function within agency strategic planning and reviews for improving organizational performance. And it builds a more coherent picture of outcomes that spans the organizational boundaries of Federal agencies by introducing the ability to focus on both shared, common outcomes to be delivered, as well as the agency responsible for driving progress on those outcomes. Users can explore the Federal Government's strategic priorities using this feature on *performance.gov/explore/goals*.

Chart 11-4. 2022 FEVS Results for Item 37, My Organization is Successful at Accomplishing its Mission.

Item	2018	2019	2020	2021	2022
37. My organization is successful at accomplishing its mission.	77	77	81	80	78

Through these enhancements to date, along with other planned future site updates including accompanying social media channels, the Administration continues to support the evolution of Performance.gov from a site that is not just a GPRAMA-compliance tool, but also one that builds trust in Government by communicating performance results effectively and offering a cohesive, comprehensive view of Federal performance and management. A complementary site, *Evaluation.gov*, offers a comprehensive view of agency evidence-building plans and associated program evaluation activities and resources.

Framework for Measuring, Monitoring, and Assessing the Organizational Health and Organizational Performance of Federal Agencies in a Changing Work Environment

Agencies must base decisions about their work environments on how they can most effectively achieve their respective missions while strengthening their organizations to be resilient for the future, especially relating to the delivery of Federal services and programs for the people and communities they serve. Now – and over the next year and beyond – agencies are working to expand their existing management routines to incorporate more coordinated considerations and indicators of 'organizational health' and 'organizational performance' in order to better monitor progress and diagnose issues related to both, and collectively drive performance results in support of their missions. These efforts are shaped by the need to ensure that agency decisions regarding work environments are based on continual improvement of organizational health and organizational performance.

This initiative builds on principles previously set forth by OMB, OPM, and the General Services Administration (GSA) in OMB Memorandum M-21-25, Integrating Planning for A Safe Increased Return of Federal Employees and Contractors to Physical Workplaces with Post-Reentry Personnel Policies and Work Environment (June 10, 2021), which directed agencies to rely on evidence when making decisions about agency work environments. It also introduces and identifies key definitional concepts that are essential to effective implementation across the Federal Government.[14]

A major focus of efforts in implementing this initiative will be to build the management mechanisms by which agencies can access the tools and evidence needed to facilitate the development of 'Organizational Health and Organizational Performance Frameworks.' In collaboration with GSA and OPM, OMB will be establishing a Community of Practice for Organizational Health and Organizational Performance, inviting participation from officials within the major operating units at agency bureaus and components to share available, existing evidence as well as new, emerging evidence and leading practices related to establishing routines and indicators for measuring, monitoring, and improving organizational health and organizational performance.

Conclusion

The Federal Performance Framework provides the foundation of routines and practices by which management functions and skillsets supporting decision-making capabilities can be coordinated—in concert together—as part of an integrated, synchronized management system at the enterprise level for improving the organizational performance and service delivery of Federal agencies. This Chapter has offered descriptive insight into that Framework, illustrating progress that has been achieved in both its evolution and application by Federal agencies. Each year, Federal employees completing the Federal

---

Organizational Performance is defined as the effectiveness to date of an organization in delivering mission-aligned results. Such effectiveness and results can be influenced by a range of factors or dimensions, both internal and external to the organization, which themselves can be measured through an array of indicators and evidence.

Work Environment is defined as the combination of: personnel policies; talent and workforce performance management strategies; workforce capacity, workloads, and work schedules; design of workspaces and workplaces; supportive and assistive technology tools for individual and collaborative work; and integration of diversity, equity, inclusion, and accessibility (DEIA) principles across management practices and processes. Among other factors (e.g., resource allocation, workforce availability, policy or statutory constraints), work environments can impact organizational health and, in turn, performance.

Organizational Health and Organizational Performance Framework is defined as a set of validated indicators that can be routinely measured, tracked, and assessed, with which an organization's senior leadership, managers, front-line supervisors, workforce, and stakeholders can monitor the organization's effectiveness and ability (including resilience, capability, and capacity) to perform and adapt. An effective organizational health and organizational performance framework can inform agency decisions regarding a variety of factors, including empowering agency leaders and managers to make, monitor, and assess changes in the organization's work environment.

---

[14] *Organizational Health* is defined as the ability (including dimensions such as resilience, capability, and capacity) of an organization to collectively drive performance results in support of its mission, deliver programs and services, and meet stakeholder needs and priorities on an ongoing basis.

Employee Viewpoint Survey (FEVS) are asked whether their agency is successful at accomplishing its mission. Their responses help OMB gauge how well the Federal Performance Framework is working to enable mission achievement at agencies. The results displayed in Chart 11–4 from the 2022 FEVS show that, across agencies, a large percentage of employees consistently report that they "Strongly Agree or Agree" that their organization successfully accomplishes its mission.[15]

The Administration's actions and efforts reflect a concerted, coordinated management approach to achieving the outcomes of Government. By using the Federal Performance Framework to communicate its goals, showing the public its plans to get there, and then being transparent about its results, the Administration seeks to build trust with the American public. Leadership engagement, clear goals, measurement, analysis of progress, and frequent progress reviews to find and promote what works and fix or eliminate what does not are keys to improving the lives of the American people.

Implementation of the Federal Performance Framework and its application since 2010 are leading to increased use of data and performance information to drive the decision-making needed for organizational performance improvement at Federal agencies—particularly where previous systems have been less effective. As Federal managers have an important obligation to ensure that every dollar spent delivers equitable and effective results for all Americans, the Framework is a proven tool and means for achieving those ends. Looking ahead, the practices and routines of the Federal Performance Framework and their application across agencies serves to shape future initiatives in Federal organizational performance management and capitalize on these promising performance tailwinds. Specifically, expanding and developing routines around 'organizational health' and 'organizational performance' at bureaus and components will help provide Federal leaders and managers with a process that improves accountability within the organizational units of each agency. Developing 'Organizational Health and Organizational Performance Frameworks' within agencies and generating an evidence-base that establishes relationships among work environments, organizational health, and organizational performance will equip agency leadership with the tools they need to support decisions regarding work environments while continually improving delivery on agency missions that provides results to the American people.

---

[15] U.S. Office of Personnel Management (OPM), (2022). Federal Employee Viewpoint Survey Results: Governmentwide Management Report.

12. BUILDING AND USING EVIDENCE TO IMPROVE GOVERNMENT EFFECTIVENESS

The *Presidential Memorandum on Restoring Trust in Government Through Scientific Integrity and Evidence-Based Policymaking* called on Federal agencies to use the best science and data available for decision-making, and to build more evidence when it does not exist to tackle complex, dynamic public policy challenges. Efforts to restore trust in Government can succeed only if Government programs deliver results for the American people and do so effectively and equitably. The use of rigorous evidence on what works and investments that build evidence where it is lacking underpin the Federal Government's ability to design and implement programs that are equitable, effective, and accountable. To ensure that the Government delivers on its commitments to all Americans, the Federal Government has an obligation to bring evidence to bear on decision-making and to evaluate what is working, for whom, and under what circumstances.

The Foundations for Evidence-Based Policymaking Act of 2018,[1] or Evidence Act, has advanced the Federal Government's ability to produce and use data for more effective decision-making. However, the law itself did not provide agencies with funding to stand up or expand the functions or capabilities necessary to carry out its vision, nor did it clarify how agencies are expected to fund evidence-planning and building activities, including those needed to support the new statutory framework for program evaluation. The Administration has demonstrated its commitment to executing on the Evidence Act through investments in evidence and evaluation priorities. As described in this chapter, the Budget includes new and sustained investments necessary for agencies to establish and staff the evaluation function, plan and execute evidence-building activities that employ high-quality evaluation methods, and deliver on evidence-based policymaking. Chapter 9, "Leveraging Federal Statistics to Strengthen Evidence-Based Decision-Making," describes evidence-building investments in statistical infrastructure and data within the Federal statistical system.

Implementing the Evidence Act represents a fundamental shift toward a more holistic reliance on evidence across the Government; it is not a compliance or reporting exercise. This was reflected in agency development and publication of the plans and assessments required under Title I of the Evidence Act—the multiyear Learning Agenda, the Annual Evaluation Plan, and the Capacity Assessment for Statistics, Evaluation, Research and Analysis ("Capacity Assessment")—in a way that fulfills their purpose as strategic, evidence-building plans. To fully realize this shift, however, requires agencies to also develop processes and practices that establish habitual and routine reliance on evidence across agency functions and demand new or better evidence when it is needed.

Building and using evidence is most useful when done in service of other priorities, not as a separate activity distinct from core functions. The Office of Management and Budget (OMB) remains focused on delivering a future in which agencies use all available evidence to make better program, operational, and administrative decisions, build evidence where it is lacking, and ultimately serve the American people more effectively.

A key marker of a culture of evidence is thinking about evidence needs and building in data and evaluation activities from the start. This allows us to invest resources in strategies with a high likelihood of success and helps us learn from these investments to inform future decision-making. This is particularly the case for large new investments, such as those spurred by the American Rescue Plan Act of 2021 (ARP),[2] Infrastructure Investment and Jobs Act (IIJA),[3] and Inflation Reduction Act of 2022 (IRA).[4] Across Administration priorities, we aim to ensure that evidence is used during the entire lifecycle of program development and implementation, and that we generate evidence to facilitate learning and improvement from these investments.

Recent Progress in Advancing Evidence

Government-Wide Progress and Administration Accomplishments to Date

The Evidence Act recognized the need for agency-level leadership to effectively implement the law's requirements and establish evaluation as a critical agency function. CFO Act agencies, as well as many small or independent agencies and agency components, have responded by establishing Evaluation Officers in a senior leadership position with the responsibility for working with other senior leaders to implement the law's many activities. OMB has convened the *Evaluation Officer Council* (EOC) since 2019, providing a forum for these evaluation leaders to share lessons learned, exchange information, discuss challenges, and coordinate on solutions. The Council supports an annual workshop series to build evaluation capacity across the Government and contributes members' expertise to initiatives led by other evidence Councils. The Interagency Council on Evaluation Policy, a formal technical workgroup of the EOC, builds on this work by convening evaluation experts with a variety of methodological and topical expertise to support the Federal evaluation community through technical assistance, papers and tools, and professional development opportunities for staff. The OMB Evidence Team also hosts and organizes an online internal-to-Government Community

---

[1] Public Law 115-435.

[2] American Rescue Plan Act of 2021, Public Law 117-2.

[3] Infrastructure Investment and Jobs Act, Public Law 117-58 (2021).

[4] Public Law 117-169 (2022).

Key Administration accomplishments to advance evidence:

- The President issued a *Presidential Memorandum on Restoring Trust in Government Through Scientific Integrity and Evidence-based Policymaking* to reaffirm and strengthen the commitment to making decisions based on the best available evidence and data.

- Each Federal Agency has published its first-ever *Learning Agenda* and *Capacity Assessment* and a second *Annual Evaluation Plan*; these are available on *Evaluation.gov*, providing visibility and transparency for Federal evidence-building.

- OMB issued *Memorandum M-21-27, Evidence-Based Policymaking: Learning Agendas and Annual Evaluation Plans*, to strengthen guidance on Title I of the Evidence Act and highlight for agency leadership the importance of a culture of evidence.

- Many agencies established their first public-facing *Evaluation Policy* to outline how program evaluations will adhere to the Government-wide standards of relevance and utility, independence and objectivity, rigor, transparency, and ethics.

- OMB published the first-ever *President's Management Agenda Learning Agenda* in order to foster evidence-building to inform Government-wide management practices.

- OMB and the Office of Science and Technology Policy (OSTP) launched the Year of Evidence for Action, including a virtual *Evidence Summit* and eleven *Evidence Forums* in order to help bridge the gap between the Federal and external research and evaluation communities.

- In *IIJA Implementation Guidance*, OMB encouraged the use of funds for evaluation within Federal agencies and among award recipients in order to ensure that Government is measuring the effectiveness of these investments.

- OSTP published the *Federal Evidence Agenda on LGBTQI+* Equity in order to document the priority evidence questions that the Federal Government needs to answer to advance equity for and improve the well-being of LGBTQI+ people.

---

of Practice, which features curated resources—including reports, toolkits, presentations, and workshops—for the Federal evaluation community on topics related to Evidence Act Title I implementation, program evaluation, and evidence more generally. The resource page on *Evaluation.gov* provides an opportunity for the public to access many of these resources.

This year, OMB partnered with the White House Office of Science and Technology Policy (OSTP) to launch the *Year of Evidence for Action* to support agencies as they turn from planning to doing in implementing their Learning Agendas and Annual Evaluation Plans. The kickoff Summit and series of Evidence Forums brought Federal leaders together with experts from non-profits and academic organizations to share leading practices from Federal agencies to generate and use research-backed knowledge to advance better, more equitable outcomes for all of America. The discussions aimed to strengthen and develop new strategies and structures to promote consistent evidence-based decision-making inside the Federal Government, while increasing connection and collaboration among researchers, knowledge-producers and decision-makers inside and outside of the Federal Government. *Readouts* from the Forums are available on Evaluation.gov.

This year also saw the launch of a new interactive Learning Agenda Question *Dashboard* on Evaluation. gov to provide a critical first step in helping agencies and external researchers engage more effectively with one

another. While agencies are making great progress in executing their evidence-building activities, there remain many unanswered priority questions and opportunities to engage the external research community. As described in *OMB Memorandum M-21-27*, Evidence-Based Policymaking: Learning Agendas and Annual Evaluation Plans, building an evidence culture requires institutionalizing both the demand for and generation of evidence while also making the available evidence easier to find and use. The dashboard is one step in this direction by making it easy for external partners and members of the public to explore where evidence is most needed, allowing those external to Government to consider how their own research can be most policy-relevant and how they might collaborate with Federal agencies to build evidence in priority areas. Through the dashboard, users can search all agency Learning Agenda questions by agency, topic, and mission/operational focus. A forthcoming Research Portal will share concrete opportunities for the external research community to engage directly with Federal agencies in support of their evidence-building needs. This platform will facilitate collaborative applied research and evaluation while building capacities for policy-relevant evidence generation and use.

It is clear that an evidence mindset has begun to take hold, not only within agencies covered by the Evidence Act's requirements, but also for whole-of-Government priorities, including the President's Management Agenda and Executive Orders, and major crosscutting investments such as those included in ARP, IIJA, and IRA. This can be seen in the development of cross-Government Learning Agendas, including the President's Management Agenda Learning Agenda and the American Rescue Plan Equity Learning Agenda, which offer more opportunities for the external research community to contribute learning and expertise to answer priority cross-Government questions. They also provide an important venue for agencies to work together to help answer these tough questions.

The Administration has also implemented new strategies for identifying and investing in inter-agency evidence-building, through guidance that requires improved coordination and engagement across leaders and teams to ensure that evidence has a seat at the table as Government-wide initiatives are conceptualized and planned. For example, OMB's implementing guidance (*OMB Memorandum M-22-12*, Advancing Effective Stewardship of Taxpayer Resources and Outcomes in the Implementation of the Infrastructure Investment and Jobs Act) for IIJA states that "agencies must design programs with clear goals and objectives, consistent with statutory requirements and informed by an understanding of the people they are meant to serve, draw from the best available data and evidence about effective strategies for similar programs and investments." Agencies were directed to build capacity, including staff to engage in evidence-building and use, and were encouraged to include language in funding notices requesting that applicants allocate funding in their budgets for personnel and data infrastructure needs to support performance management and program evaluation.

Building Evidence Through Cross-Government Learning Agendas

The *President's Management Agenda (PMA) Learning Agenda* marks the first systematic effort to instill an evidence-informed approach to advancing the crosscutting management priorities laid out in the President's Management Agenda. The PMA Learning Agenda galvanizes the Federal evaluation community as well as external academics and public management researchers to work together to generate the evidence needed to guide PMA implementation. Specifically, the Learning Agenda raises the critical questions for building the evidence base on how to strengthen and empower the Federal workforce, how to deliver programs and services effectively and build trust, and how to advance equity and support underserved communities. By articulating these evidence needs, the PMA Learning Agenda aims to reinforce a focus on learning, bridge silos, and catalyze innovation beyond the Federal Government.

Among the many advancements the Administration has made to build evidence and evaluation planning into the core work of administering funding is the support for evidence-building and use in implementing the American Rescue Plan Act (ARP). Even as agencies moved quickly to implement ARP provisions, they took a number of steps to prioritize identifying and applying the best available evidence in designing their programs. For example, the Department of the Treasury (Treasury) integrated

clear expectations around the use of evidence and evaluation in the compliance and reporting *guidance* for the State and Local Fiscal Recovery Fund. The Department of Agriculture (USDA) conducted a robust stakeholder engagement process and drew on the strong evidence base for the Special Supplemental Nutrition Program for Women, Infants, and Children (WIC) program effectiveness to identify the specific mix of innovations to introduce or pilot as part of WIC Modernization efforts. Similarly, the ability to implement Pandemic Electronic Benefits Transfer (EBT) relied on the rigorous evaluation of summer EBT that USDA conducted in 2016. Agencies have also worked together to capitalize on their relative strengths in capacity and expertise. Treasury and the Department of Housing and Urban Development (HUD) are working collaboratively to implement an evaluation of the Emergency Rental Assistance Program, and agencies (Treasury, the Small Business Administration, the Department of Health and Human Services (HHS), US Department of Veterans Affairs (VA), and USDA) have partnered with the General Services Administration's (GSA) Office of Evaluation Sciences (OES) on ARP program evaluations, many of which bring an emphasis on equity.

To further complement this work, and contribute to a robust portfolio of evidence, the OMB Evidence Team and OES are working together to lead a national evaluation conducted by an independent contractor. The research questions driving the ARP National Evaluation are informed by the *ARP Equity Learning Agenda* and will lead to a systematic look at the contributions of over 30 selected ARP-funded programs toward achieving equitable outcomes. With the support of the White House ARP Implementation Team as well broad agency support through an Agency Expert Team, this study will describe ARP program planning, implementation, and evaluation efforts, including the integration of equity across these areas. It will also analyze the effectiveness of ARP program implementation, particularly with respect to advancing equity through both in depth evaluations and targeted analyses for a subset of selected programs.

In January 2023, the Administration released the *Federal Evidence Agenda on Lesbian, Gay, Bisexual, Transgender, Queer, and Intersex Individuals (LGBTQI+) Equity* under the auspices of the National Science and Technology Council's Subcommittee for Equitable Data in response to Executive Order 14075, "Advancing Equality for Lesbian, Gay, Bisexual, Transgender, Queer, and Intersex Individuals." This document provides a roadmap for Federal agencies to continue to build the evidence needed to advance equity for and improve the health and well-being of LGBTQI+ people. Importantly, the Federal Evidence Agenda includes a Learning Agenda to Advance LGBTQI+ Equity, which includes a series of 13 over-arching learning questions across four thematic areas (Health, Healthcare, and Access to Care; Housing Stability and Security; Economic Security and Education; and Safety, Security, and Justice) with more specific learning questions within these areas. Federal agencies will use the Federal Evidence Agenda to develop and implement their sexual orientation, gender identity, and sex characteristics (SOGI) Data Action Plans to build the evidence needed. The Federal Evidence Agenda on LGBTQI+ Equity also highlights priority questions for external researchers to contribute to the Federal Government's efforts to continue to build evidence to advance equity for LGBTQI+ people.

The Administration recognizes that an evidence-based Government must also build and use evidence across key priorities, including advancing equity, improving customer experience, developing the Federal workforce, and promoting diversity, equity, inclusion, and accessibility. Across these priorities, we need to ensure that evidence is used as efforts and approaches are developed, and that evidence is intentionally and thoughtfully generated to facilitate learning and improvement. To facilitate this work, the Administration has emphasized the importance of evidence-building, including evaluation, in its guidance and Executive Orders. For example, the Executive Order 14058, *"Transforming Federal Customer Experience and Service Delivery to Rebuild Trust in Government"* includes a specific requirement that High-Impact Service Providers conduct assessments of their work, including rigorous program evaluation (Section 6) and to engage with key evidence-building colleagues, including the Evaluation Officer Council.

Agency Progress and Accomplishments

Since the Evidence Act was enacted in January 2019, agencies have made notable progress meeting the law's requirements, including advancing their ability to build and use evidence and supporting the new statutory system for program evaluation. In spring 2022, these efforts culminated in agencies publishing their first-ever Learning Agendas and Capacity Assessments, as well as their FY 23 Annual Evaluation Plans. These evidence plans are now available on agency websites and *linked centrally* on Evaluation.gov. Whether an agency had a program evaluation function prior to the Evidence Act or not, this has resulted in transparency on evidence plans, changes and advancements to this work, and awareness of gaps that had not previously been identified.

While a few agencies had a Learning Agenda prior to the Evidence Act, these were typically not available to the public (such as in the case of the Department of Labor's (DOL) learning agenda) and did not provide detail on the proposed approaches, data, and potential challenges. These elements are now expected to be made transparent for all agencies. Some agencies have been internally planning their evaluation activities annually for decades, but none had a public Annual Evaluation Plan that outlined specifics on the anticipated evaluations that would support significant evidence-building priorities. The Evidence Act also required all agencies to conduct a Capacity Assessment to examine its capacity across evaluation, statistics, research, and other analytic functions.

As the *Capacity Assessments* demonstrate, agencies with more mature and long-standing evidence, statistical, data, and evaluation functions were better positioned to implement the Evidence Act. For example, HUD's long-

standing practice of developing and publishing their "Research Roadmap" allowed them to utilize their established practice to craft an agency-wide Learning Agenda. For a number of other agencies, the Evidence Act has catalyzed the creation of previously absent capabilities. For example, several agencies lacked a central evaluation function prior to the Evidence Act, including the Department of the Interior (DOI), Office of Personnel Management (OPM), and Department of Homeland Security (DHS), among others. Following enactment of the Evidence Act, OPM has made significant progress to stand up an evaluation function. The agency now has a full-time Evaluation Officer and two full-time equivalent (FTE) employees supporting evaluation across the agency. To support these efforts, the President's Budget includes funding for an additional FTE to further enhance OPM's capacity to build evidence around the Federal workforce and personnel policies. Other agencies, including the Department of Transportation, are in the process of establishing a central office to manage these functions and are hiring both dedicated leadership and support staff with demonstrated evaluation expertise to lead the work of Evidence Act implementation and evaluation in the coming years. The President's Budget acknowledges more investment is needed to build and strengthen evaluation capacity, and examples of other key investments are discussed in this Chapter.

The Department of Homeland Security is another leading example of agency progress. In 2022, DHS launched a pilot process to explore how the agency can use evidence planning to strengthen program design and planning. The pilot process involves DHS determining how the proposed activities are expected to lead to the anticipated goals and outcomes; where evidence exists to support the logic model; and where sufficient evidence does not exist, determine what strategies are needed to understand if results are achieved, including if it is appropriate and feasible to evaluate the program. This is an important internal DHS planning exercise that is a collaboration among the Evaluation Officer, financial assistance policy and oversight office, grants administration office, and program offices. Building this into standard operating procedures has and will continue to be instrumental in identifying Learning Agenda questions, possible areas where evaluation may be needed, and where performance management and reporting on results can be strengthened. DHS continues to replicate this practice in 2023 for the Federal Emergency Management Agency (FEMA), US Citizenship and Immigration Services, Cybersecurity and Infrastructure Security Agency (CISA), Countering Weapons of Mass Destruction Office, the Science and Technology Directorate, and for policy areas where building evidence on what works is crucial, such as grants to prevent domestic terrorism and violence.

How the 2024 Budget Advances an Evidence-Based Government in Federal Agencies

The Budget includes a number of investments to increase evidence-based policymaking, sustains critical existing evidence investments, acknowledges where there

A mature evaluation function at an agency goes above the Evidence Act requirements, and includes practices such as:

- An Agency Evaluation Officer that is a member of the Senior Executive Service or similarly situated senior leader and brings the requisite evaluation skills based in social sciences training and experience

- Evaluation-skilled staff supporting the Evaluation Officer in coordinating enterprise-wide to develop agency Learning Agendas and evaluation plans

- Funding for independent evaluation contracts, with robust and diversified funding support from departmental management and program accounts

- Active engagement in the Evaluation Officer Council, Interagency Council on Evaluation Policy, and Federal interagency evaluation communities

- Ongoing collaboration with leadership throughout the agency

- Professional development support for evaluation staff to increase and/or maintain their expertise in evaluation methodologies, tools, and theories

is a need for more evidence capacity, and supports programs that demonstrate evidence of effectiveness. The Budget makes targeted investments to support these activities; agencies must also build in costs for data collection, evidence-building, and evaluation planning and execution from the start, not as an afterthought, as they implement new and existing programs.

Sustaining or Enhancing Long-Standing Evaluation Functions

In addition to offering strong support to those agencies that are continuing to grow their evaluation functions, the Budget recognizes that the Evidence Act requirements were new for all agencies, and even those with mature evidence-building and evaluation functions in place prior to the law's enactment need continued investment and support. The Budget sustains or enhances funding for evaluation offices or units that pre-date the Evidence Act, including for evaluation activities at the Department of Education's (ED) Institute of Education Sciences; several parts of HHS, including the Office of the Assistant Secretary for Planning and Evaluation (ASPE), the Office of Planning, Research and Evaluation (OPRE), and the Centers for Disease Control and Prevention (CDC); HUD's Office of Policy Development and Research; USDA's Food and Nutrition Service; DOL's Chief Evaluation Office; GSA's OES; the Millennium Challenge Corporation; and AmeriCorps. The Budget includes an investment in dedicated staff to support the Evaluation Officer at the Social Security Administration (SSA), in order to ensure that the agency completes the activities on its Learning Agenda and Annual Evaluation Plans. It also includes modest investments to advance professional development opportunities for DOL and SSA's research and evaluation staff. At HHS, the Budget continues to support evidence and evaluation activities in ASPE. The Budget includes significant support for the research, evaluation, and demonstration activities that HUD conducts, as well as resources targeted specifically to eviction-prevention programs and

HUD-wide technical assistance. It also includes continued investments at the US Agency for International Development in the Bureau for Policy, Planning and Learning for implementation of the Evidence Act and associated evidence-building activities, including evaluation.

Investing Further in Evidence Capacity and Evaluation Officer Leadership

An evidence culture requires robust capacity across the Government and within agencies. Leadership is critical, including both leaders with evaluation expertise and the support from agency leaders focused on other programmatic or operational functions. While the Administration is making progress through Government-wide initiatives and agency-specific milestones, much work remains, in part due to a lack of highly skilled evaluators in agencies. This includes vacancies in Evaluation Officer positions or the assignment of Evaluation Officer responsibilities to a senior executive who is already responsible for multiple other roles.

As OMB Memorandum M-21-27 underscores, agencies are expected to fill the role of Evaluation Officer with someone who brings superior skills and demonstrated expertise, and who has the time and resources needed to lead and execute the Learning Agenda and evaluation activities across their agency. Without qualified Evaluation Officers who have sufficient time to devote to the role, agencies miss opportunities to leverage the value of evaluation in supporting mission-critical work. Agencies that have established this leadership position are better positioned to meet the challenges of identifying, prioritizing, and addressing their agency's most critical evidence needs. Many agencies have begun to create an evaluation function where it did not previously exist, or where it lacked the necessary capacity to even minimally execute the function. The President's Budget recognizes where increased emphasis on the evaluation function is needed at agencies to fulfill the promise of Title I of the Evidence Act and targets enhanced support to advance this work,

---

Advancing Evaluation Capacity at FEMA

The Budget includes multiple new FTEs with specialized evaluation expertise to coordinate and collaborate across FEMA in both preparedness and response program areas to maximize evidence and evaluation planning and action to inform program improvements, rigorously assess results, and identify evidence gaps and needed improvements. The vision for an evaluation function at FEMA includes staffing these positions with program evaluation experts that can plan and execute evaluations that align with program evaluation standards, as outlined in OMB Memorandum M-20-12 and DHS' agency evaluation policy. To execute on this vision, the FEMA Evaluation Officer and program offices will be coordinating closely to set aside a portion of administrative and other available funds to support priority evaluations or other evidence-building activities. The Budget includes a number of items to further establish an enterprise-wide evaluation capacity at FEMA. With the selection of a full-time evaluation expert leader to serve as the FEMA Evaluation Officer, these new positions and the current capacity lay the foundation for robust evidence and evaluation planning at FEMA. For DHS, the Budget also includes program evaluation specialists to support CISA's and DHS' Evaluation Officers.

---

institutionalize their evaluation policies, and embed rigorous evidence and evaluation planning.

Investing in Qualified Evaluators

In addition to the importance of the Evaluation Officer role, agencies need highly qualified technical evaluation staff to plan and execute priority evidence-building activities. Across agencies, evaluation staff are responsible for conceptualizing and designing evaluations, including identifying methodological options, preparing solicitation requests for third-party independent evaluations, reviewing technical proposals, overseeing contracted evaluation projects, conducting technical reviews, and interacting with technical evaluators and expert technical work group members. Federal evaluators must also build and maintain collegial relationships with other stakeholders in their agency to accomplish their goals, including career staff who lead the programs being evaluated, procurement and contracting officials, attorneys, performance and statistical staff, and career and political leadership. Maintaining relationships with staff in the Federal programs addressed by the evaluation is a particularly essential role. For these reasons, Federal evaluator positions at all professional levels need to be filled with highly capable evaluators.

To this end, the Budget provides funding to ensure that each CFO Act agency has at least some dedicated staff that have specialized evaluation experience to support the Evaluation Officer in planning and executing Learning Agendas and Annual Evaluation Plans. The Budget includes additional evaluator positions at DHS, the Department of Commerce, DOI, the Department of Justice, the Environmental Protection Agency (EPA), the National Aeronautics and Space Administration (NASA), the Nuclear Regulatory Commission, SSA, Treasury, USDA, OPM, and VA. For example, the Budget includes two full-time evaluation specialized positions at NASA in order to have dedicated staff with expertise to support enterprise-wide program evaluation planning and execution. The Budget also makes once-in-a-generation investments to stand up evaluation functions in order to provide the

infrastructure to address priority areas where evidence has been lacking for decades. For example, the President's Budget includes a direct investment to build the capacity within the Veterans Benefits Administration (VBA) to build and use evidence, including program evaluation, to ensure that VBA is effectively delivering benefits to our Nation's veterans. At EPA, the Budget includes an additional $6 million and 5 FTE above the base request for evaluation work to support the duties of the Evaluation Officer in implementing the Title I of the Evidence Act. The Administration supports EPA's efforts to structure major funding activities to incorporate evaluation from the outset of those activities, including early integration of evidence into the IRA programs and a higher degree of planning to better target resources and expertise toward evidence-building priorities. The Budget also supports much-needed investments at DOI, including funding for three qualified program evaluators and $4.5 million for an independent program evaluation fund. At Treasury, the Budget also provides new FTE to increase capacity to support the Evaluation Officer, as well as funding for new data and evaluation staff at the Alcohol and Tobacco Tax and Trade Bureau, the Bureau of the Fiscal Service, and the Community Development Financial Institutions Fund.

Investments in Evaluation-Focused Evidence-Building Activities

To fully realize the vision for evidence-based policymaking, the Federal Government requires expert and empowered leadership and staff as described above, and a robust evaluation infrastructure including dedicated funding for evaluations projects. As described in *OMB Memorandum M-20-12*, Phase 4 Implementation of the Foundations for Evidence-Based Policymaking Act of 2018: Program Evaluation Standards and Practices, Federal agencies should establish the conditions that enable evaluators to operate with an appropriate level of independence from programmatic, regulatory, and policymaking activities. In order to produce credible information and maintain high-quality processes and products, evaluations should be planned, implemented, and interpreted by qualified evaluators with relevant education, skills, and experience for the methods undertaken.

Agencies should use the variety of funding sources available across the agency for implementation of their Learning Agendas and Annual Evaluation Plans, among other evidence-building needs, including setting aside a portion of program and/or general departmental or administrative funds to plan and execute priority evaluations. One example is the proposal for the Congress to continue allowing the Department of Education to set aside funding for evaluations of higher education programs. This pooled evaluation authority, first provided in fiscal year 2022, would continue to permit ED to expand its ability to evaluate higher education programs, analogous to the evaluation set-aside in the Elementary and Secondary Education Act for K-12 programs.

The Budget also continues essential authorities for evaluating and improving Federal programs. For example, the Budget maintains the authority for DOL to set aside up to 0.75 percent of appropriations so that there may be sufficient funds for conducting significant and rigorous evaluations, and it continues to provide DOL's Chief Evaluation Office the authority to carry out grants and demonstration projects to test innovative strategies for building evidence. The Budget also includes measures to further support these offices, such as the request for the Evaluation Funding Flexibility General Provision, which would give DOL's Chief Evaluation Office and Bureau of Labor Statistics and HHS's ASPE and OPRE the ability to use evaluation funds over a greater period of time to support strategic, long-term, and flexible evaluation planning.

The President's Budget includes proposals to execute evidence-building efforts on agencies' Learning Agendas and Annual Evaluation Plans. For example, the Budget includes an investment at SSA to conduct an evaluation of the agency's outreach efforts with individuals potentially eligible for benefits. The Budget further builds on the 2023 Budget proposal for a cross-agency Equity in Procurement evaluation at the Small Business Administration, by providing $1.25 million for this project.

As is also highlighted in Chapter 9, the final report from the Advisory Committee on Data for Evidence Building included a recommendation that OMB, in coordination with the Interagency Council on Statistical Policy, the Chief Data Officer Council, the Evaluation Officer Council, and other relevant Federal councils, develop a systematic approach to funding Evidence Act implementation. OMB will launch a cross-Government, comprehensive resource analysis, in collaboration with Council colleagues, during the remainder of 2023 and into 2024 in order to inform a comprehensive set of proposals to develop a consistent and sustainable mechanism for identifying and obtaining the resources needed for full Evidence Act implementation.

Acting on Available Evidence

The President's Budget also proposes investments in those programs and areas where evidence already exists. Investing in promising and evidence-based programs is central to the Administration's commitment to an evidence-based Government. The budget highlights examples of programs and policy areas where evidence has already led to action, and where further investments are being made. For example, the Maternal, Infant, and Early Childhood Home Visiting (MIECHV) Program provides funding for States, territories, and tribal entities to implement evidence-based home visiting programs. MIECHV includes funding for evaluation to continue building the evidence base. MIECHV is a critical program serving expectant and new parents with children up to kindergarten age who live in communities at higher risk for poor maternal and child health outcomes.

The Budget also includes $165 million at ED to expand an existing postsecondary retention and completion grants program that provides competitive grants to States, tribal colleges and universities, and institutions of higher education to implement or expand evidence-based, statewide, and institutional level retention and completion reforms that improve student outcomes, including retention and completion rates, transfers from two- to four-year institutions, and employment outcomes. The requested increase would more than triple the number of grantees and would strengthen evaluation of the projects by executing the program as a tiered-evidence competition, under which interventions with a higher level of evidence could be scaled up with larger grants.

At DOL, the Budget continues to invest in evidence-based programs, including $335 million to expand investments in Registered Apprenticeship programs that have been shown to improve employment outcomes and will provide greater opportunities for women to enter Registered Apprenticeship and nontraditional occupations. In addition, the Budget includes $550 million for Reemployment Services and Eligibility Assessments (RESEA). By law, States are required to use no less than 25 percent of RESEA funds for interventions or service delivery strategies with strong causal evidence showing a demonstrated capacity to improve employment and earnings outcomes for program participants.

How the 2024 Budget Makes Government-Wide Evaluation Investments

To maximize efficient use of Federal funding available for evaluation and ensure implementation is undertaken by highly qualified staff, the Administration is taking actions to create an environment where agencies can plan and execute high-quality evaluations that align with the program evaluation standards and practices set out in OMB Memorandum M-20-12. In addition to critical investments in agency evaluation functions and evidence-building activities, the Budget includes Government-wide investments in evaluation to address unmet crosscutting needs.

Crosscutting Solutions

Even when agencies have open positions for evaluation experts, they face many barriers to hiring qualified staff. OMB and OPM continue to explore options for accelerating hiring through processes such as Subject Matter Expert

Qualification Assessment and central hiring actions. The Budget also establishes a $1 million cross-Governmental Program Evaluation Fellowship Program to be housed at the Administration for Children and Families at HHS. The Fellowship would build on successful fellowship models, such as the White House Leadership Development Program, and would place specialized evaluation experts at agencies that need support to accelerate implementation of the evaluation function. The Administration will also support efforts by the Evaluation Officer Council to plan for a Program Evaluation Corps, which would recruit program evaluators into the civil service and place them in agencies that lack sufficient evaluation capacity.

In 2014, the OMB Data-Driven Innovation (DDI) Fund received $2 million in no-year appropriations "for projects that enable Federal agencies to increase the use of evidence and innovation in order to improve program results and cost-effectiveness by utilizing rigorous evaluation and other evidence-based tools." Through the DDI fund, OMB has executed transfers to other agencies and hosted expert detailees to tackle cross-Government evidence-building priorities and advance evaluation capacity Government-wide. Examples of DDI-funded initiatives include launching and testing the Pay-for-Success funding model; identifying evaluation principles and practices in a National Academies workshop (later incorporated into OMB Memorandum M-20-12); strengthening performance management and evaluation in DOL and ED regulations and guidance for employment and training programs; establishing the Interagency Council on Evaluation Policy; and developing tools for agencies to implement Learning Agendas (a leading practice codified in the Evidence Act). The Administration is using the small amount of remaining funds to deliver new ways to benefit agencies Government-wide through high-quality evaluations. This includes enhancing the accessibility and useability of a Government-wide Federal Evaluation Toolkit, carrying out rigorous evaluations of telework and remote work, and supporting the CDC in updating its widely-used evaluation framework for public health.

Data Access and Infrastructure to Support Evidence-Buidling

Credible evidence-building, including program evaluation, requires access to data, either existing or newly collected, that accurately captures the intended information and addresses the questions of interest. Leveraging existing administrative and statistical data can provide significant cost efficiencies, but requires additional skills and capacity. Strategic, cost-efficient evidence-building relies on strong data governance that facilitates data discovery, assessing fitness/suitability of the data for the intended purpose, data access, data protection, and use of existing statistical, program, or other administrative data to enable and support secondary uses, including for program evaluation. Agencies continue to innovate, improve, and build the data infrastructure, capacity, and governance to carry out the goals of the Evidence Act. Although much progress has been made, there is still work to be done to organize evidence-building, data management,

and data access functions to ensure an integrated and direct connection to evidence needs. Chapter 9 describes how the Federal statistical system is expanding its long-standing capacity to produce and make accessible data for evidence-building as the recognized statistical agencies and units work together to implement Title III of the Evidence Act. Evaluation Officers, in collaboration with Statistical Officials, Chief Data Officers, Senior Agency Officials for Privacy, Chief lnformation Security Officers, and other relevant officials, have a role in fostering data management in order to successfully support agencies to deliver on Learning Agenda and evaluation plan priorities.

Top Implementation Priorities for the Year Ahead

Now that the Government has ambitious plans in place to build evidence in key priority areas, we must collectively turn our attention to executing on these plans. Successful execution is critical if we are to effectively build, strengthen, and empower a culture of evidence across the Federal Government. Agency leaders have a critical role in the following actions:

- *Act on evidence within agencies and across the Government.* This includes: (1) focusing agencies' attention on executing the studies identified on their multiyear Learning Agendas and Annual Evaluation Plans, (2) collaborating across agencies and Government-wide on priority, crosscutting evidence-building needs, and (3) ensuring that results are shared widely and made available in timely and useable ways for decision-makers.

- *Embed evidence use in core agency functions.* Agencies must generate high-quality evidence and ensure that evidence is brought to the decision-making table. Leaders and staff must use evidence to inform the planning and implementation of agency programs, operations, regulations, and management activities.

- *Build evaluation in from the start of new programs and identify evidence opportunities within existing programs.* Funding announcements and program implementation should not be disconnected from agency evidence-building plans. Each action agencies take to act on appropriated funds is an opportunity to assess if funding strategies are advancing agency missions and goals, and to examine what is known to work, for whom, and under what circumstances, and where critical evidence gaps still exist. Agencies should integrate a strong focus on evidence and evaluation in key Administration priorities, including equity and customer experience.

- *Increase agency capacity to build evidence for use in decision-making.* This includes: (1) acting on new and proposed investments in evaluation and other evidence-building activities, (2) prioritizing available resources for FTE to support these functions, including staff to build evidence and translate evidence for decision-makers, (3) leveraging Government-wide solutions for procuring evaluation services and hiring qualified evaluators, (4) supporting evidence and evaluation training for staff and the use of shared resources and tools, and (5) encouraging evidence training for agency executives and increased engagement by agency leaders in communicating evidence use as a priority.

- *Expand support for the Federal evaluation community through engagement and collaboration with the external research community.* This includes: (1) launching a new Research Portal on Evaluation.gov in support of both agency-specific and crosscutting Learning Agenda questions, (2) continued partnership between OMB and OSTP to further the goals of the Year of Evidence for Action, and (3) building new communities of practice between researchers and agencies to support priorities on the President's Management Agenda.

Conclusion

The past year, the Administration has made continued progress across all Federal agencies toward realizing the vision of a fully evidence-based Federal Government.

Learning Agendas and Annual Evaluation Plans are now public, and agencies are pivoting from planning to execution. The Budget makes critical investments to build evaluation capacity where it is most needed so that all agencies have at least some skilled evaluators to do this work. However, capacity remains limited in many agencies, and this is an opportune time for evaluators and similarly trained social scientists to consider a career as a Federal civil servant. The Government needs this technical expertise in order to realize the vision of routinely building and using evidence to inform mission delivery and internal operations. In addition, there has never been a better time for external academics and researchers to align their own work to the priorities that the Federal Government has laid out, and for philanthropy to consider how it can help support this work. We face many challenges as a nation, and we are asking hard and honest questions about how to best address them. Partnering together across sectors is the only way that this work can be accomplished at the scale it is needed. This is the moment to demonstrate to the American people that their Government uses data and relies on facts, and in doing so can rebuild the trust that is fundamental to our democracy.

13. STRENGTHENING THE FEDERAL WORKFORCE

"My Administration is committed to protecting, empowering, and rebuilding the career Federal workforce so they can bring more resources to bear in service of the American people."

—President Biden

More than four million dedicated individuals, civilian and military, work for the Federal Government, serving the American people, in all types of occupations and in locations across the Nation and around the world. This chapter describes the Administration's resolute commitment to rebuilding the civilian Federal workforce as it seeks to be a model employer and to enable Federal agency mission and performance, with its approximately 2.2 million employees. The chapter outlines the current state of the Federal workforce, provides both historic and contemporary analysis and data, and highlights the Administration's leading workforce priorities, strategies, and initiatives.

As the Nation looks ahead to the future, together employers and workers are striving to chart a new path forward for the American workplace. In the Federal sphere, the President's Management Agenda (PMA), with its focus on strengthening and empowering the Federal workforce, prioritizes human capital strategies designed to deliver Federal organizational performance through the successful promotion of service and delivery outcomes for our people, thereby bolstering trust in our Government. Federal offices and workers will be positioned to take on the challenges before them as they work to rebuild our Nation. This will be accomplished by creating more equitable employee engagement experiences across departments and agencies, improving the hiring experience and processes to efficiently onboard Federal talent, attracting the right talent to the right roles, and promoting diversity, equity, inclusion and accessibility across all human capital activities.

The Budget advances the PMA's workforce priorities and strategies by providing resources for Federal workforce initiatives that will aid our organizational capacity rebuilding efforts.

Namely, the Budget makes the following historic workforce investments to:

- Provide an average pay increase of 5.2 percent for both civilian and military employees, assuring fair and equitable compensation needed for recruitment and retention of skilled talent and proposes action to alleviate growing pay limitations that threaten the viability of the civilian workforce harming public access to robust, modern, and agile Federal programs;

- Promote general investment in departments and agencies to sustain well-resourced human capital

functions capable of rebuilding and strengthening the workforce;

- Expand and bolster Federal strategic agency hiring capacity by advancing "Talent Teams" and promoting the use of pooled hiring actions leveraging scalability and vigorous employee assessments including Subject Matter Expert Qualification Assessments (SMEQA);

- Promote recruitment and bring onboard the most qualified employees, including by prioritizing robust early-career and internship program pipelines;

- Prioritize implementation of agency crafted strategic diversity, equity, inclusion and accessibility (DEIA) plans designed to embed a new workplace culture in routine actions and practices; and

- Provide stable and predictable funding for reimagined and reinvigorated Federal Executive Boards (FEBs) to strengthen the Federal workforce, better communicate and execute management and workforce priorities, and encourage cross-agency local community engagement.

In addition to these investments, the PMA sets out four key strategies to strengthen and empower the Federal workforce.

Strategy 1: Attract and hire the most qualified employees, who reflect the diversity of our country, in the right roles across the Federal Government

The Administration has made significant progress putting into place key elements to drive successful hiring reforms, with a sustained focus on fostering a more resilient and inclusive workforce and building more diverse and equitable hiring pipelines that will enable agency mission and service delivery to the American public.

Recruiting Highly Qualified Talent

People are a critical ingredient in mission success for Federal agencies. The Federal workforce is the first priority of the PMA, ensuring consistent focus on investment in programs and policies that allow agencies to more easily and effectively recruit for needed talent. This work to fill talent needs includes a focus on strategic outreach to a broad set of communities across the Nation, including to those who have not yet considered Federal service; and spans internships and early career positions, through leadership levels and across mission-critical occupations.

The Administration believes one of the most impactful ways to rebuild the Federal Government's lagging early-career talent pipeline is to revive Federal internship programs. Internships and apprenticeships have been an ongoing focus of the President's Management

Council (PMC) and are called out in Strategy One of the PMA Workforce Priority. There are a number of current programs and authorities available to agencies to bring on interns and apprentices, and these opportunities are often underutilized. Benefits of paid internship and apprenticeship programs include increasing the chances of students' gaining a full-time position after graduation, improving our ability to hire diverse candidates, allowing agencies to train employees for specific business needs and critical skillsets, and serving as a trial period for agencies and interns to determine if the individual is a good fit for permanent employment. The 2023 Budget supported the hiring of 35,000 interns across the Government, and the Administration is on track to meet this goal. Key guidance has been issued to agencies on how to hire paid interns, and the Office of Personnel Management (OPM) has developed a dedicated internship portal at INTERN. USAJOBS.gov. The PMC internship working group continues to lead, guide, and refine improvements to internship policies and procedures, including working with OPM to reduce barriers to hiring a diverse group of paid interns and bolster Federal internship programs. This initiative is augmented by work in the PMA to develop a recruitment community of practice. In the Budget, the Administration proposes to further sustain and grow opportunities for interns, apprentices, and early career talent – particularly paid opportunities—to ensure equitable access and by supporting agency efforts to incorporate internships into routine workforce planning.

In addition to the heightened need and commitment to recruit interns and early career talent, Federal agencies face recruitment and retention challenges in other mission-critical skill areas, such as information technology, cyber, and digital talent, as well as human resources (HR). To support and achieve important hiring goals, we must start by bolstering our capabilities across human capital support functions—such as HR specialists, Talent Teams, learning and development professionals, and employee engagement managers. Over the last five fiscal years, retention rates for HR management professionals have consistently trailed the Government-wide average retention rate (69.7 percent compared to 77.2 percent). For the first time, the Budget supports creation of a senior executive position at OPM dedicated to the development and career pathing for the HR workforce.

In 2022, to recruit people with critical skills, agencies created over 4,000 recruitment campaigns and posted over 750 recruitment events to attract job seekers to their job opportunity announcements, and over 900,000 job seekers made their resumes searchable to hiring managers and HR professionals in the USAJOBS.gov Agency Talent Portal. OPM also expanded opportunities to retain and develop current workers by leveraging USAJOBS Open Opportunities to post nearly 700 opportunities for current Federal employees to develop and grow their professional skills and experience – all while keeping their current Federal jobs. These activities will be continued and scaled up, as a focus area in the PMA.

To help accelerate the recruitment of qualified talent into Government, OPM and the Office of Management and Budget (OMB) are supporting a number of pooled hiring initiatives across agencies and partnering with the executive councils and agencies to recruit talent for mission-critical occupations, early career opportunities, and other critical positions. In addition, the Federal network outside of Washington, D.C., will be engaged in these efforts through the FEBs, as described further below.

Improving the Effectiveness of the Hiring Process

The Federal Government relies on its workforce to deliver on its mission for the American people. To ensure a highly qualified workforce, agencies have continued to build on efforts to develop Talent Teams, develop technical assessments and use subject matter experts (SMEs) to identify talent, and leverage economies of scale through pooled hiring actions to surge talent to meet agency mission needs. Supported by the Budget, agencies will continue to build a foundation to reframe merit-based competitive hiring by focusing on streamlining applicant, hiring manager, and HR professional experience through skill-based hiring. This work is further enabled by OPM guidance on Executive Order 13932, "Modernizing and Reforming the Assessment and Hiring of Federal Job Candidates" and forthcoming technical tools in USAJOBS and USA Staffing to enable SME participation in the qualifications process, and to allow easier sharing of qualified applicant lists across agencies. In total, these efforts are designed to help managers consider the most qualified applications and hire quality candidates, while also allowing applicants who are qualified but not ultimately selected to still receive offers from other Federal agencies.

To help agencies scale these best practices, OPM created a Hiring Experience (HX) Group dedicated to providing technical resources, supporting Talent Teams, and coordinating pooled hiring actions. Throughout 2022, OPM and OMB worked with agencies to conduct Government-wide pooled hiring actions and to pilot the first use of the Competitive Service Act that allows agencies to share hiring certificates (certs). Pooled hiring actions using technical assessments have resulted in improved applicant experience as well as increased hiring manager satisfaction, as they are able to bring in the talent they need. This also helps to decrease the number of public announcements without any selections and supports swifter applicant placement. Across Government, agencies have leveraged pooled hiring to select customer experience strategists, industrial/organizational psychologists, grants management specialists, contract specialists, and data scientists. HX will continue to work with agencies to streamline the process for HR specialists, applicants, and hiring managers to ensure more pooled hiring actions and shared cert actions become part of the Government-wide hiring toolkit, along with custom assessments to identify skills and competencies.

In addition, the Budget provides for consistent support to agency Talent Teams, designed to inject targeted strategic hiring practices and operations at the employing agency level, and for agencies to adopt the use of improved assessments. As more than 26 agencies have begun standing up and hiring into Talent Teams, they can the policy of the Administration to be a model for DEIA, where all employees are treated with dignity and respect. Throughout 2022, Federal agencies built and kicked off implementation of strategic and customized action plans to drive forward the Executive Order's Federal sector goals.

In September 2022, the Chief Diversity Officers Executive Council kicked off its inaugural interagency meeting, which will facilitate sustaining a national strategy for DEIA across Federal agencies and the workforce. Chaired by OPM, and with OMB and the Equal Employment Opportunity Commission serving as Vice Chairs, the Council advises agency leadership on promising practices in DEIA. A primary function of the new Council is to monitor agency implementation of DEIA plans through progress milestones, which are holistically aligned with the Executive Order, OPM's Governmentwide DEIA Strategic Plan and the PMA. In December 2022, the first Government-wide summit for DEIA was held, titled, "A Whole-of-Government Approach to Disability Employment," featuring academia, non-profit and private sector organizations, and Federal leaders sharing promising practices and innovative strategies to improve employment for people with disabilities in the Federal workforce. By infusing robust DEIA practices into routine recruitment and retention actions and adopting these modern employer human resource techniques, the Federal Government will expand and enhance its talent pool.

The use of data to measure outcomes is essential for high-performing employers and effective performance,

with new agency metrics for pay equity, employment rates of underrepresented racial and ethnic groups and disability inclusion, as well as broader recruitment, hiring, and retention rates to be reported and analyzed to help inform prioritization of future workforce improvements. In 2022, OPM updated the Federal Employee Viewpoint Survey (FEVS), which it administers annually to solicit feedback from Federal employees regarding their views about their current work environment, management policies and other workplace initiatives, to include a new DEIA metric, along with additional, new demographic questions.

In 2022, more Federal employees identified as members of historically underrepresented groups than in prior years. According to data from OPM from September 2022, the Federal civilian workforce self-identified as 60.5 percent White; 18.2 percent Black; 9.8 percent Hispanic of all races, a slight increase from 9.54 percent last year; 6.7 percent Asian/Pacific Islander; 1.6 percent Native American/ Alaskan Native; and 2.1 percent more than one race. Men make up 55.6 percent of all permanent Federal employees, and women represent 45 percent, which is up from 43.9 percent in September 2020. Veterans make up 29.4 percent of the Federal workforce, which is significantly higher than the percentage in the private sector non-agricultural workforce. 18.4 percent of all Federal employees self-identify as having a disability, which includes the approximately 2.5 percent who have a "targeted disability," such as blindness. Table 13-1 shows the staffing trends since 2016.

The Federal workforce has an average age of 47 years. Almost 29 percent (625,828) of employees are older than

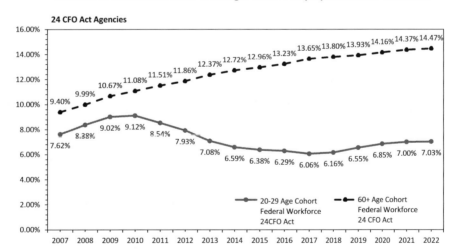

Chart 13-1. Potential Retirees to Younger than 30 Employees: Federal Workforce

60+ Age Cohort Percentage of Federal Workforce increases from 2007 to 2021 while 20-29 Age Cohort Percentage of Federal Workforce declines from 2007 to 2021.

Source: FedScope FY2007-2022 (Annual September Employment Cubes).
Data Filter: Job Series excludes nulls, Work Schedule includes only "F", Work Status includes only Non-Seasonal Full-Time Permanent, Age Cohort excludes less than 20 and unspecified, 24 CFO Act Agencies only.
Data Range: FY2007-2021, Age Cohorts 20-29, 30-39, 40-49, 50-59, and 60+.

Table 13–1. HIRING TRENDS SINCE 2016

Federal Civilian Workforce	SEP 2016	SEP 2017	SEP 2018	SEP 2019	SEP 2020	SEP 2021	SEP 2022
Total Federal Workforce Count*	2,097,038	2,087,747	2,100,802	2,132,812	2,181,106	2,191,011	2,180,296
Average Age	47.1	47.2	47.1	47.1	47.0	47.0	47.0
Total Under 30	7.88%	7.55%	7.76%	8.07%	8.39%	8.33%	8.30%
Total 55 and over	28.16%	28.79%	28.99%	29.17%	29.11%	28.98%	28.70%
Male	56.70%	56.60%	56.44%	56.27%	55.90%	55.56%	55.03%
Female	43.29%	43.38%	43.52%	43.72%	44.10%	44.44%	44.97%
All Disabilities	9.46%	10.49%	12.38%	13.89%	15.33%	17.01%	18.37%
Targeted Disabilities (These totals are included in the total disability #'s above)	1.10%	2.69%	2.66%	2.61%	2.56%	2.52%	2.54%
Veteran	29.33%	29.43%	29.34%	29.15%	28.78%	28.37%	29.35%
American Indian or Alaskan Native	1.71%	1.69%	1.66%	1.63%	1.62%	1.62%	1.62%
Asian	5.86%	5.99%	6.10%	6.01%	6.17%	6.49%	6.70%
Black/African American	17.91%	18.15%	18.21%	18.02%	18.06%	18.19%	18.25%
Native Hawaiian or Pacific Islander	0.49%	0.51%	0.52%	0.52%	0.54%	0.56%	0.57%
More Than One Race	1.47%	1.60%	1.73%	1.82%	1.91%	2.01%	2.11%
Hispanic/Latino (H/L)	8.46%	8.75%	9.08%	9.14%	9.33%	9.53%	9.75%
White	64.04%	63.26%	62.63%	61.22%	60.86%	61.20%	60.53%

Source: U.S. Office of Personnel Management
* Total count varies slightly from other sources because of date and data collection method.

further leverage these teams to develop more robust applicant assessment strategies and identify opportunities to share highly qualified applicants with other agencies when those hiring actions use a multiple-hurdle assessment approach.

The Budget continues to demonstrate the Administration's commitment to rebuilding the workforce through an improved hiring system that honors merit

system principles and provides equitable pathways into Federal service.

Civil Service Diversity, Equity, Inclusion, and Accessibility

In 2021, the President signed Executive Order 14035, "Diversity, Equity, Inclusion, and Accessibility in the Federal Workforce", followed by issuance of a Government-wide strategic plan. The Executive Order stated that it is

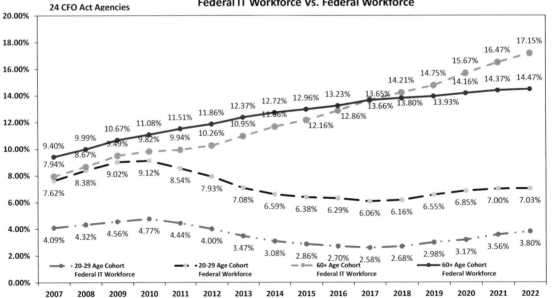

Chart 13-2. Potential Retires to Younger than 30 Employees: Federal IT Workforce Vs. Federal Workforce

60+ Age Cohort Percentage of Federal Workforce increases from 2007 to 2021 while 20-29 Age Cohort Percentage of Federal Workforce declines from 2007 to 2021.

Source: FedScope FY2007-2021 (Annual September Employment Cubes).
Data Filter: Job Series excludes nulls, Work Schedule includes only "F", Work Status includes only Non-Seasonal Full-Time Permanent, Age Cohort excludes less than 20 and unspecified, 24 CFO Act Agencies only.
Data Range: FY2007-2021, Age Cohorts 20-29, 30-39, 40-49, 50-59, and 60+.

Table 13–2. FEDERAL CIVILIAN EMPLOYMENT IN THE EXECUTIVE BRANCH

(Civilian employment as measured by full-time equivalents (FTE) in thousands, excluding the Postal Service)

Agency	Actual		Estimate		Change: 2023 to 2024	
	2021	2022	2023	2024	FTE	Percent
Cabinet agencies						
Agriculture	83.7	85.0	92.1	101.6	9.5	10.4%
Commerce	46.5	41.0	44.1	45.0	0.9	2.0%
Defense--Military Programs	783.2	772.3	787.6	794.8	7.1	0.9%
Education	4.0	4.1	4.2	4.5	0.3	6.8%
Energy	14.4	14.8	16.1	17.1	1.1	6.6%
Health and Human Services	78.4	79.2	83.3	87.6	4.3	5.2%
Homeland Security	201.6	202.8	210.4	216.3	5.9	2.8%
Housing and Urban Development	7.9	8.1	8.7	9.3	0.6	6.4%
Interior	62.0	61.9	64.3	68.3	4.0	6.2%
Justice	115.9	115.0	122.6	126.0	3.4	2.8%
Labor	14.7	14.9	16.0	18.0	2.0	12.2%
State	25.0	30.0	30.4	30.7	0.3	1.0%
Transportation	53.7	53.1	55.3	57.1	1.8	3.3%
Treasury	93.9	94.4	99.4	114.3	14.9	15.0%
Veterans Affairs	402.8	411.6	433.9	453.9	20.0	4.6%
Other agencies -- excluding Postal Service						
Bureau of Consumer Financial Protection	1.6	1.6	1.6	1.7	*	1.4%
Corps of Engineers--Civil Works	23.5	23.0	24.4	24.4	....	....
Environmental Protection Agency	14.0	14.2	14.2	15.6	1.4	10.2%
Equal Employment Opportunity Commission	1.9	2.0	2.2	2.2	....	....
Federal Communications Commission	1.5	1.4	1.6	1.6	....	....
Federal Deposit Insurance Corporation	5.9	5.9	6.3	6.3	*	0.1%
Federal Trade Commission	1.1	1.1	1.4	1.7	0.3	22.4%
General Services Administration	11.6	11.7	12.7	13.2	0.4	3.4%
International Assistance Programs	5.5	6.1	6.6	7.0	0.4	6.8%
National Aeronautics and Space Administration	16.8	17.7	18.1	17.6	−0.5	−3.0%
National Archives and Records Administration	2.7	2.7	2.9	3.0	0.1	1.9%
National Credit Union Administration	1.1	1.1	1.2	1.2	*	2.1%
National Labor Relations Board	1.2	1.2	1.3	1.5	0.1	9.2%
National Science Foundation	1.5	1.5	1.7	1.7	*	0.5%
Nuclear Regulatory Commission	2.8	2.7	2.9	3.0	0.1	3.1%
Office of Personnel Management	2.4	2.6	2.5	2.5	*	0.8%
Securities and Exchange Commission	4.5	4.5	4.7	5.1	0.5	9.7%
Small Business Administration	6.0	8.0	6.8	7.7	0.9	13.3%
Smithsonian Institution	4.9	4.7	5.0	5.1	0.1	2.5%
Social Security Administration	59.9	58.2	60.7	61.9	1.2	1.9%
Tennessee Valley Authority	10.2	10.4	10.7	10.7	....	....
U.S. Agency for Global Media	1.6	1.6	1.7	1.7	....	....
Other Defense--Civil Programs	1.1	1.1	1.1	1.2	0.1	6.1%
Total, Executive Branch civilian employment	2,183.1	2,185.8	2,274.2	2,355.9	81.7	3.6%

* 50 or less.

55, while 8.3 percent (180,933) of employees are younger than 30, an increase from 8.1 percent (compared to December 2020). Chart 13-1 shows a widening age gap at the 24 large and mid-sized agencies since 2007. This gap carries into each career field. As an example, Chart 13-2 demonstrates the growing age disparity in the information technology sector that in particular shows the drop in the percentage of the Federal workforce under the age of 30 since 2010, when Federal internships and hiring programs for recent graduates became subject to new restrictions.

Personnel Vetting Transformation

The Administration continues prioritizing improvements in how the Executive Branch vets its civilian, military, and contractor workforce through the work of the Security, Suitability, and Credentialing Performance Accountability Council (PAC). These ongoing reforms encompass the policies, processes, and tools used to

Chart 13-3. Federal vs. Private Pay Differential

(1980 normalized to 0)

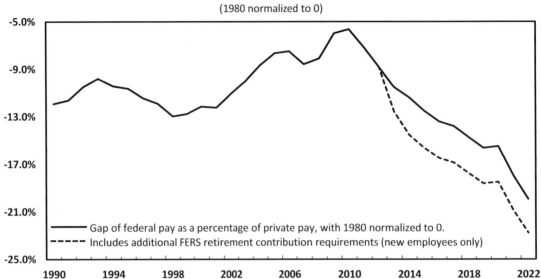

For newly hired federal employees, FERS contributions increased 2.3pp for employees hired in 2013 and an additional 1.3pp for employees hired in 2014 or after.

Sources: Public Laws, Executive Orders, Office of Personnel Management, OPM Memoranda from federal websites, Congressional Budget Office, and Bureau of Labor Statistics.

Notes: Federal pay is for civilians and includes base and locality pay. Private pay is measured by the Employment Cost Index wages and salaries, private industry workers series.

determine whether personnel should be trusted to provide needed services, be good stewards of taxpayer dollars, and protect sensitive information. During 2022, the Administration issued key policies reforming this mission space—including revised Federal Personnel Vetting Investigative Standards and new Performance Management Standards—under the Trusted Workforce 2.0 initiative. It also released an Implementation Strategy to help individual agencies develop plans for adopting reforms and facilitate their successful adoption. The Budget instructs agencies to continue preparing for the implementation of additional modernization reforms from the PAC which will require new coordination. These changes will include (1) expanding continuous vetting to non-sensitive public trust positions, (2) improving vetting processes for new personnel and those previously vetted but transferring between agencies, (3) implementing the 2022 Federal Personnel Vetting Investigative Standards, and (4) accelerating integration of personnel vetting information technology. Through these aligned policy, budget, and operational activities, the Administration is providing the American people with a workforce determined to be trustworthy.

Federal Executive Board Reform

In 1961, President Kennedy established FEBs as forums for workforce communication and regional collaboration outside of Washington, D.C. Timed with the celebration of the sixtieth anniversary of the program in 2021 and building upon the FEBs' strong foundation, the Administration launched an effort to rejuvenate the program, assure stable resources, and enhance shared governance to provide strategic direction and modernization.

The Budget assumes reforms to:

● Provide enhanced strategic workforce and management direction and expanded opportunities for engagement with local communities by establishing a new interagency forum at OPM;

● Clarify and update the internal governance structure of the program;

● Facilitate modernization and amplification of key elements of the program; and

● Bolster resources for the Federal workforce, particularly for regional Federal offices and workers outside of Washington, D.C., and agency headquarters, by enabling new opportunities for career development, human capital activities, and innovation.

A hallmark of the reform is to align strategic management and workforce priorities, and the communication and execution of those priorities, across the Federal landscape, no matter the agency or location. As an example, departments and agencies will be able to better leverage expanded Federal recruitment opportunities, including at public university systems and Minority Serving Institutions, by harnessing regional FEB representation and support.

Table 13–3. TOTAL FEDERAL EMPLOYMENT

(As measured by Full-Time Equivalents)

Description	2022 Actual	2023 Estimate	2024 Estimate	Change: 2023 to 2024	
				FTE	PERCENT
Executive Branch Civilian:					
All Agencies, Except Postal Service	2,185,751	2,274,192	2,355,917	81,725	3.5%
Postal Service [1]	667,363	563,470	554,707	−8,763	−1.6%
Subtotal, Executive Branch Civilian	2,853,114	2,837,662	2,910,624	72,962	2.5%
Executive Branch Uniformed Military:					
Department of Defense [2]	1,383,899	1,344,841	1,343,592	−1,249	−0.1%
Department of Homeland Security (USCG)	41,310	43,036	44,810	1,774	4.0%
Commissioned Corps (DOC, EPA, HHS)	6,239	6,236	6,351	115	1.8%
Subtotal, Uniformed Military	1,431,448	1,394,113	1,394,753	640	*
Subtotal, Executive Branch	4,284,562	4,231,775	4,305,377	73,602	1.7%
Legislative Branch [3]	31,662	35,257	35,718	461	1.3%
Judicial Branch	32,805	33,376	33,783	407	1.2%
Grand Total	4,349,029	4,300,408	4,374,878	74,470	1.7%

[1] Includes Postal Rate Commission.

[2] Includes activated Guard and Reserve members on active duty. Does not include Full-Time Support (Active Guard & Reserve (AGRSs)) paid from Reserve Component appropriations.

[3] FTE data not available for the Senate (positions filled were used for actual year and extended at same level).

* Non-zero less than 0.1%.

As OPM scales up transition activities to take place over calendar years 2023 and 2024 to support these reforms, OPM, OMB, and the General Services Administration are collaborating to lay the groundwork for the program's rejuvenated vision, structure, and strategic objectives.

Strategy 2: Make every Federal job a good job, where all employees are engaged, supported, heard, and empowered, with opportunities to learn, grow, join a union and have an effective voice in their workplaces through their union, and thrive throughout their careers

The Administration made significant progress in 2022 to rebuild the Federal employer-employee relationship and to invest robustly in its people.

As part of strengthening relations with Federal employee unions, in support of the strategies recommended for the Federal sector in the Vice President's Task Force on Worker Organizing and Empowerment, and to achieve the goals in Executive Order 14025, "Worker Organizing and Empowerment", in April of 2022, OPM issued guidance seeking to strengthen the management-worker relationship. To ensure relevant agencies are fulfilling their requirements under the Federal Service Labor-Management Relations Statute, the guidance outlined agency responsibilities for ensuring union organizing rights, access to and communication with bargaining unit employees, and the timely processing of bargaining unit employee payroll deduction requests for labor organization dues.

As part of the Administration's designation of 2022 as the "Year of Evidence for Action" to ensure equity in all practices[1], the Federal Government, in its pursuit to be a model employer, has prioritized the rebuilding of human capital data collection and analysis. Through thoughtful and deliberate updates to the annual Government-wide FEVS, such as a new DEIA Index to serve as a new baseline metric to assess future changes as well as benchmark comparisons for agency-specific DEIA initiatives, aligned with Executive Order 14035, and new questions to better assess evolving workplace conditions and impact on program effectiveness, agencies and employees are being enabled to engage in more informed dialogue to mutually forge a workplace culture that thrives on resilience, innovation, and customer responsiveness. As cited by Gallup, "Organizations have more success with engagement and improve business performance when they treat employees as stakeholders of their own future and the company's future. This means focusing on concrete performance management activities, such as clarifying work expectations, getting people what they need to do their work, providing development and promoting positive coworker relationships."[2] The PMA harnesses these workforce engagement strategies to help agencies rebuild and create a new Federal workplace culture.

The Administration's commitment to the civil service was further evidenced by the President's efforts to secure pay increases for Federal employees on par with private sector wage growth. The Budget will reflect an average pay increase of 5.2 percent for both civilian and military employees, honoring the pay parity principle across the combined workforce. Between 2009 and 2021, U.S. average worker pay rose by 39.9 percent while Federal civilian pay increases amounted to only 26.9 percent, yielding a pay gap of 13 percentage points. Chart 13-3 demonstrates the sustained and growing gap of Federal pay as a per-

[1] April 7, 2022, Biden Harris Administration Launches Year of Evidence for Action to Fortify and Expand Evidence-Based Policymaking (OSTP Web (whitehouse.gov).

[2] April 17, 2017, Employee Engagement vs. Employee Satisfaction and Organizational Culture, Jim Harter, Gallup (Gallup Web (gallup. com).

centage of private sector pay. The differential between Federal civilian pay and private sector pay has expanded substantially over this period, creating attrition risk within the existing workforce and reducing the competitiveness of Federal jobs. Importantly, the proposed Federal pay increase recognizes the Federal workforce's unwavering dedication to mission and service to the American people. Federal pay adjustments have not kept pace with the national labor market overall, or increases in the cost of goods, services, and benefits. The 2024 civilian pay adjustment, consistent with the Employment Cost Index, is a crucial step to addressing that imbalance.

Federal worker pay is also increasingly hamstrung by statutory and regulatory requirements and restrictions that curb the ability of agencies to reward talent, including for specialized occupations, in a national competitive job environment. As agencies confront the need for evolving digital and technological skill sets to assure service delivery for the public, their recruitment and retention toolboxes lack the means to tackle core compensation needs, particularly for senior level management officials charged with overseeing large numbers of projects, personnel, and funds. The Administration will take action to rectify long-standing white-collar Senior Executive Service and higher graded General Schedule (GS) pay compression, as well as blue-collar Federal Wage Grade pay limitations through development of a legislative proposal. The Federal Government, as a model employer, must act to enable a robust and capable civil service that is resilient to take on future challenges.

Further, the Administration worked to ensure that all Federal jobs should pay a living wage by implementing a policy in 2021 to provide that all Federal jobs are paid at a rate of at least $15 per hour, and is actively overseeing efforts to maintain this policy into 2023 for a second year. OPM has also proposed a number of changes to streamline and bolster Federal compensation to include: modifying critical position pay; establishing a critical skills incentive; increasing the special rate limitation for certain positions; updating GS pay setting for new appointments; increasing agency head awards authority; establishing a pay authority for highly qualified experts, and more recently for 2024, repealing the aggregate pay rate limitation and enhancing student loan repayments.

The Administration continues to demonstrate its publicly sustained commitment to the career workforce by opposing attempts to weaken the non-partisan, merit-based civil service. On Day One of the Administration in January 2021, the President issued Executive Order 14003, "Protecting the Federal Workforce", eliminating the Schedule F excepted service category issued during the previous Administration that undermined the foundations of the civil service and core protections for career civil servants. In 2022, the Administration stated its support for codifying in law the intent of this Executive Order, to ensure that employment in the Federal workforce remains unequivocally based on merit, skill, and experience, and does not become subject to politicization or favoritism. The Budget proposes to safeguard the Federal civilian workforce by advancing legislative changes necessary to

reinforce the underlying foundations of merit-based civilian service. The Administration looks forward to working with the Congress on this proposal. The American people deserve to be able to rely upon this expertise for program administration and delivery of services necessary for the functioning of our Government.

Strategy 3: Reimagine and build a roadmap to the future of Federal work informed by lessons from the pandemic and nationwide workforce and workplace trends

Given widely available COVID-19 vaccinations, testing, and treatments, as well as robust and responsive COVID-19 safety protocols in place across Federal agencies[3], COVID-19 is not driving agency decisions about their work environments. Now and on an ongoing basis, agencies must base decisions about their work environments on how they can most effectively achieve their respective missions while strengthening their organizations to be resilient for the future, especially relating to the delivery of Federal services and programs for the people and communities we serve.

In 2022, Federal agencies updated COVID-19 workplace safety plans in alignment with guidance from the Administration's Safer Federal Workforce Task Force and consistent with guidance from the Centers for Disease Control and Prevention, with the goal of maintaining Federal Government operations and employee safety.

In July 2022, the Administration issued forward-leaning capital planning guidance to agencies[4], encouraging increased coordination between agency strategic workforce planning and real property planning activities. When determining future physical space requirements, a critical element for agencies is their work to reimagine their workplace approaches informed by lessons learned from the pandemic, as well as from nationwide workforce and workplace 21st Century trends that include potential impacts from hybrid work, telework, remote work, alternative work schedules, and online collaboration.

Like workers across the Nation, Federal employees have continued to perform their duties, no matter the location. During 2022, Federal agencies engaged in evaluating lessons learned through the pandemic that will serve to position ongoing dialogue and future decision making relating to human capital management, facilities, and the very nature of work. Like employers around the world and across the Nation, agencies are confronting the changing nature of work, technologies, and society, and the Administration is taking steps to ensure Federal leaders are informed by evidence-based evaluation of what work will look like, what the workforce will look like, and what workplaces will look like in the years to come. The Federal Government has a wide range of occupations delivering an array of missions, including work that must be performed on the work-site, with a substantial portion

---

[3] September 15, 2022, Safer Federal Workforce Task Force Model Agency COVID-19 Safety Principles (Safer Federal Workforce Task Force (https://www.saferfederalworkforce.gov)

[4] July 20, 2022, OMB Memorandum M-22-14, FY 2024 Agency-wide Capital Planning to Support the Future of Work, (OMB Memorandum Web (whitehouse.gov).

Table 13–4. OCCUPATIONS OF FEDERAL AND PRIVATE SECTOR WORKFORCES
(Grouped by Average Private Sector Salary)

Occupational Groups	Percent	
	Federal Workers	Private Sector Workers
Highest Paid Occupations Ranked by Private Sector Salary		
Lawyers and judges	3%	1%
Engineers	4%	2%
Scientists and social scientists	5%	1%
Managers	13%	15%
Pilots, conductors, and related mechanics	3%	0%
Doctors, nurses, psychologists, etc.	9%	7%
Miscellaneous professionals	17%	10%
Administrators, accountants, HR personnel	6%	2%
Inspectors	1%	0%
Total Percentage	60%	38%
Medium Paid Occupations Ranked by Private Sector Salary		
Sales including real estate, insurance agents	1%	6%
Other miscellaneous occupations	4%	5%
Automobile and other mechanics	2%	3%
Law enforcement and related occupations	9%	1%
Office workers	2%	5%
Social workers	2%	1%
Drivers of trucks and taxis	1%	3%
Laborers and construction workers	3%	10%
Clerks and administrative assistants	12%	10%
Manufacturing	2%	7%
Total Percentage	36%	51%
Lowest Paid Occupations Ranked by Private Sector Salary		
Other miscellaneous service workers	2%	5%
Janitors and housekeepers	1%	2%
Cooks, bartenders, bakers, and wait staff	1%	4%
Total Percentage	4.1%	11.3%

Source: 2017–2022 Current Population Survey, IPUMS-CPS, University of Minnesota, www.ipums.org.
Notes: Federal workers exclude the military and Postal Service, but include all other Federal workers in the Executive, Legislative, and Judicial Branches. However, the vast majority of these employees are civil servants in the Executive Branch. Private sector workers exclude the self-employed. Neither category includes State and local government workers. This analysis is limited to full-time, full-year workers, i.e. those with at least 1,500 annual hours of work.

of the Federal workforce delivering critical services at the work site throughout the pandemic. Going forward, agencies need to be strategically prepared for evolving work environments, where teams are likely to be more distributed on a continual basis than in the past. This shift will lead to increased reliance upon enhanced technological tools, cross-collaboration, and new methods of worker engagement.

Senior Federal Government leaders and managers must monitor and assess the organizational health and organizational performance of the individual major operating units within agency bureaus and components in order to improve the ability of those units to contribute to the mission delivery of the agency. This action includes developing routines for engaging managers and staff within each such operating unit to pursue improved performance in concert with increased organizational health. These routines should be consistent with overall agency

mission and strategy, and also should be informed by a variety of indicators of organizational health and organizational performance, which can, taken together, monitor the effect of changes to workforce and workplace policies and practices.

Additional information on the Administration's efforts to inform workforce and workplace policies based on organizational performance and organizational health is included in Chapter 11, "Delivering a High-Performance Government".

Strategy 4: Build the personnel system and support required to sustain the Federal Government as a model employer able to effectively deliver on a broad range of agency missions

Rebuilding the capacity and capabilities of the Federal Government would not be possible without the more than 47,000 HR professionals in Federal service. When the

Bipartisan Infrastructure Law (Public Law 117-58) was passed at the end of 2021, Federal HR experts crafted plans to surge their hiring and quickly onboard the essential staff needed to support the implementation of the law. With coordinated, hands-on support from OPM through a cross-departmental tiger team, nearly 3,500 new public servants were hired in 90 occupations in the first year, including scientists to combat climate change, engineers to repair and rebuild our roads and bridges, and workers to help ensure that every community in America has clean water. As rebuilding efforts continue, hiring in these mission-essential functions will continue at an accelerated pace—while the Federal Government also seeks to develop its posture as a modern employer of choice, able to engage and retain the workers we hire.

The results of the surge hiring effort was incumbent on both OPM's and agency HR expertise through a close partnership including training to bring Federal HR personnel up to speed on innovative recruitment and hiring approaches, a dedicated platform for jobseekers looking for opportunities, and targeted hiring authorities and strategies to bring new talent onboard. Through this collaboration, hiring timelines were cut by an average of seven days for infrastructure-related positions proving that the Federal Government can—and must—lean into modern approaches to hiring with technology-driven process improvements that prioritize highly-skilled applicants and protect merit systems principles.

The Federal Government's success as an employer in the competition for talent calls for a vital, customer-focused OPM, Chief Human Capital Officers (CHCOs) who are partners with agency leaders, and highly-trained HR professionals able to advance the development of personnel concepts with the times. During 2022, in accordance with OPM's FY 2022-26 Strategic Plan, OPM laid the groundwork for a transformation approach to undergird OPM's organizational capacity and capability to serve as the leader in Federal human capital management with the designation of a Chief Transformation Officer. Priority focus areas include policy, research, support to agencies, and service to customers, with strategic investments in internal talent and technology made possible through increased budgetary support. With an enhanced lens on timely stakeholder engagement and improvements in data analytics to drive human capital decision-making, OPM is leading the way to scale proven enhancements to the personnel system and empower CHCOs and staff to develop human capital management approaches that enable their agencies to meet their missions.

Continued progress through a renewed vision for the Federal HR workforce is underway that will more deftly allow for enterprise-level workforce management and training approaches. Of top priority is mitigating skills gaps in the HR workforce, a perennial concern often cited by the U.S. Government Accountability Office, National Association of Public Administration, and other external entities as a critical success factor for Federal Government missions and operations. OPM and Federal agencies are working in partnership to identify and expand awareness of approaches to development to build the technical and transformational skills needed in today's HR workforce, map career pathways for current HR professionals, early career talent, and workers with transferable skills, and develop a centralized technology hub to provide access to these resources. Government-wide approaches such as these aim to yield consistently high standards for HR professional development, cost savings for agencies, and a stronger HR workforce ready to support mission needs.

Federal Workforce Trends and Updates

The total Federal workforce is comprised of approximately 4.2 million staff, with 2.2 million Federal civilian employees and 2.1 million military personnel.[5] (See Tables 13-2 and 13-3). Using data from the Bureau of Labor Statistics on full-time, full-year workers, Table 13-4 breaks out all Federal and private sector jobs into 22 occupational groups to demonstrate the differences in composition between the Federal and private workforces. Table 13-5 summarizes total pay and benefit costs. Charts 13-4 and 13-5 present trends in educational levels for the Federal and private sector workforces over the past two decades, demonstrating a continuation in the advanced educational attainment of Federal employees. Chart 13-6 shows the trends in average age in both the Federal and private sectors, reflecting the average age of Federal employees to be significantly higher than the average age of private sector employees. Charts 13-7 and 13-8 show the location of Federal employees in 1978 and again in 2022. Chart 13-9 reflects the changing nature of work, comparing the number of employees in each General Schedule grade in 1950 versus 2022, showing an almost complete shift from lower-grade to higher-grade types of work.

In calendar year 2022, USAJOBS.gov hosted over 440,000 job announcements, facilitated over 1 billion job searches, and enabled individuals to begin more than 19.5 million applications for Federal jobs. Further in calendar year 2022, over 900,000 job seekers made their resumes searchable in the USAJOBS.gov Agency Talent Portal, and agencies created over 4,800 recruitment campaigns and posted over 750 recruitment events to attract seekers to their job opportunity announcements. In calendar year 2022, USAJOBS Open Opportunities included 11 communities, and agencies posted 1,000 opportunities for current Federal employees to develop and grow their professional skills and experience – all while keeping their current Federal job. OPM's Retirement Services processed almost 110,000 new retirement cases and about 290,000 survivor claims. The Federal Employees Health Benefits Program provides benefits to more than 8.2 million Federal civilian employees, annuitants, and their families, as well as certain Tribal employees and family members through 271 plan options for the 2023 benefit year.

The Federal Government's efforts to adopt and instill long-lasting workforce strategies that promote organizational efficiency, performance, and health are intrinsically linked to a workforce that is capable of serving the American people and our Nation's evolving needs

---

[5] October 2022, Active Duty Military Personnel By Service and Selected Reserve Personnel by Reserve Component, Defense Manpower Data Center, Department of Defense (DMDC Web (osd.mil).

amid great societal and technological changes. Our people deserve nothing less than a robust and skilled Federal workforce drawing from the diversity of our Nation and equipped to navigate the course ahead and steer Federal programs and initiatives into a better tomorrow.

Table 13–5.   PERSONNEL PAY AND BENEFITS
(In millions of dollars)

Description	2022 Actual	2023 Estimate	2024 Estimate	Change: 2023 to 2024	
				Dollars	Percent
Civilian Personnel Costs:					
Executive Branch (excluding Postal Service):					
Pay	229,603	248,600	271,310	22,710	9.1%
Benefits	108,349	111,647	119,336	7,689	6.9%
Subtotal	337,952	360,247	390,646	30,399	8.4%
Postal Service:					
Pay	42,524	43,365	43,884	519	1.2%
Benefits	12,623	15,535	15,728	193	1.2%
Subtotal	55,147	58,900	59,612	712	1.2%
Legislative Branch:					
Pay	2,618	2,973	3,156	183	6.2%
Benefits	1,029	1,116	1,199	83	7.4%
Subtotal	3,647	4,089	4,355	266	6.5%
Judicial Branch:					
Pay	3,648	3,985	4,300	315	7.9%
Benefits	1,342	1,419	1,522	103	7.3%
Subtotal	4,990	5,404	5,822	418	7.7%
Total, Civilian Personnel Costs	401,736	428,640	460,435	31,795	7.4%
Military Personnel Costs					
Department of Defense--Military Programs:					
Pay	114,794	119,036	123,599	4,563	3.8%
Benefits	59,423	61,226	71,561	10,335	16.9%
Subtotal	174,217	180,262	195,160	14,898	8.3%
All other Executive Branch uniform personnel:					
Pay	4,056	4,281	4,684	403	9.4%
Benefits	748	780	877	97	12.4%
Subtotal	4,804	5,061	5,561	500	9.9%
Total, Military Personnel Costs	179,021	185,323	200,721	15,398	8.3%
Grand total, personnel costs	**580,757**	**613,963**	**661,156**	**47,193**	**7.7%**
ADDENDUM					
Former Civilian Personnel:					
Pensions	98,589	107,090	112,648	5,558	5.2%
Health benefits	13,835	15,122	15,552	430	2.8%
Life insurance	43	43	45	2	4.7%
Subtotal	112,467	122,255	128,245	5,990	4.9%
Former Military Personnel:					
Pensions	69,077	76,589	80,733	4,144	5.4%
Health benefits	11,538	12,698	13,423	725	5.7%
Subtotal	80,615	89,287	94,156	4,869	5.5%
Total, Former Personnel	193,082	211,542	222,401	10,859	5.1%

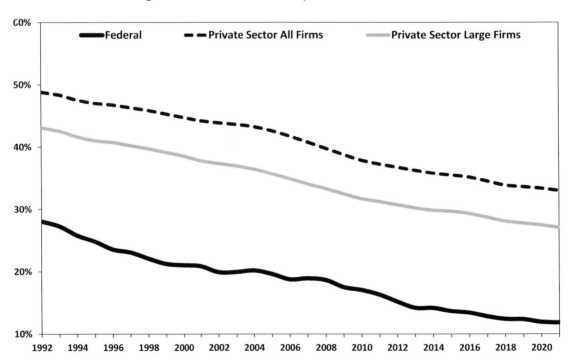

Chart 13-4. Masters Degree or Above By Year for Federal and Private Sectors

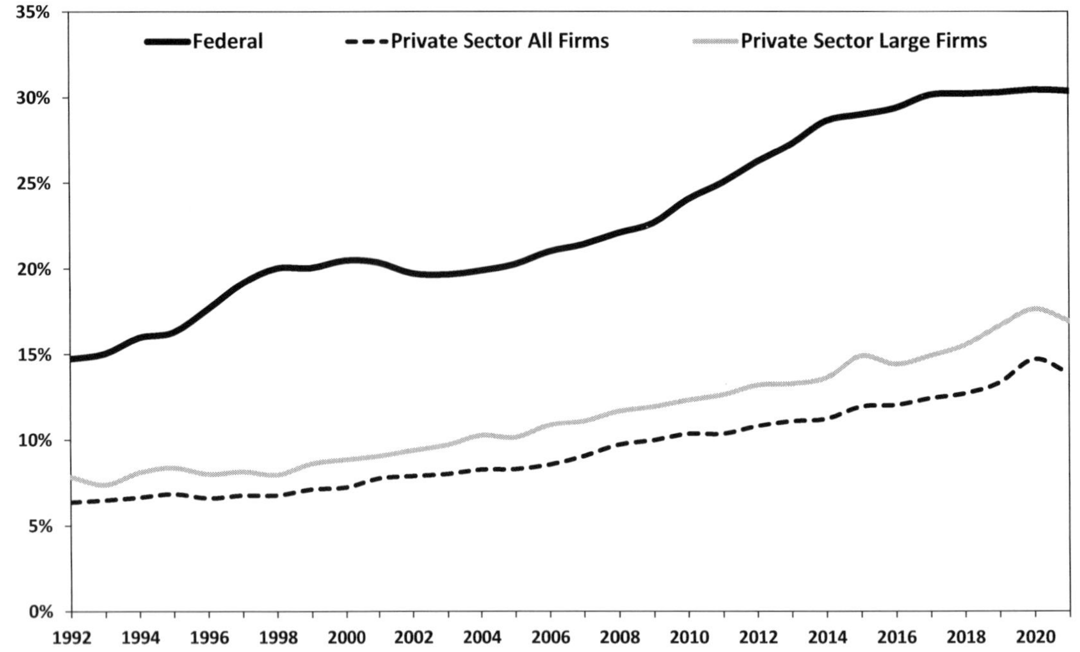

Source: 1992-2022 Current Population Survey, IPUMS-CPS, University of Minnesota, www.ipums.org.

Notes: Federal excludes the military and Postal Service, but includes all other Federal workers. Private Sector excludes the self-employed. Neither category includes State and local government workers. Large firms have at least 1,000 workers. This analysis is limited to full-time, full-year workers, i.e. those with at least 1,500 annual hours of work and presents five-year averages. Industry is from the year preceding the year on the horozontal axis.

Chart 13-5. High School Graduate or Less By Year for Federal and Private Sectors

Source: 1992-2022 Current Population Survey, IPUMS-CPS, University of Minnesota, www.ipums.org.

Notes: Federal excludes the military and Postal Service, but includes all other Federal workers. Private Sector excludes the self-employed. Neither category includes State and local government workers. Large firms have at least 1,000 workers. This analysis is limited to full-time, full-year workers, i.e. those with at least 1,500 annual hours of work and presents five-year averages. Industry is from the year preceding the year on the horozontal axis.

Chart 13-6. Average Age by Year for Federal and Private Sectors

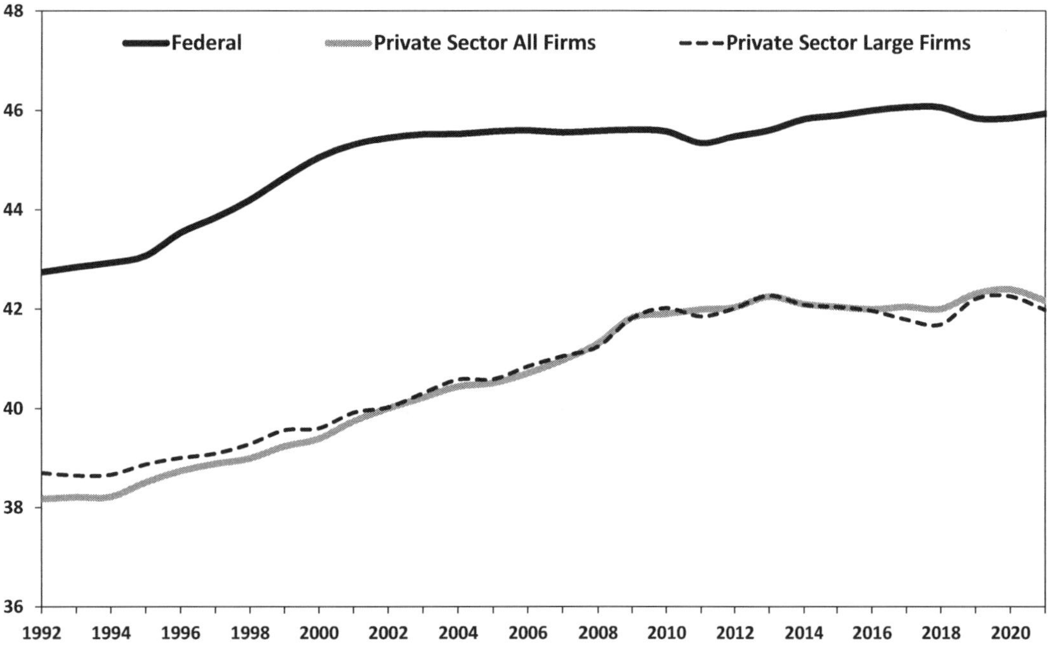

Federal — Private Sector All Firms — - - Private Sector Large Firms

Source: 1992-2022 Current Population Survey, IPUMS-CPS, University of Minnesota, www.ipums.org.

Notes: Federal excludes the military and Postal Service, but includes all other Federal workers. Private Sector excludes the self-employed. Neither category includes State and local government workers. Large firms have at least 1,000 workers. This analysis is limited to full-time, full-year workers, i.e. those with at least 1,500 annual hours of work and presents five-year averages. Industry is from the year preceding the year on the horozontal axis.

Chart 13-7. GOVERNMENT-WIDE ON-BOARD U.S. DISTRIBUTION 10–1–1978

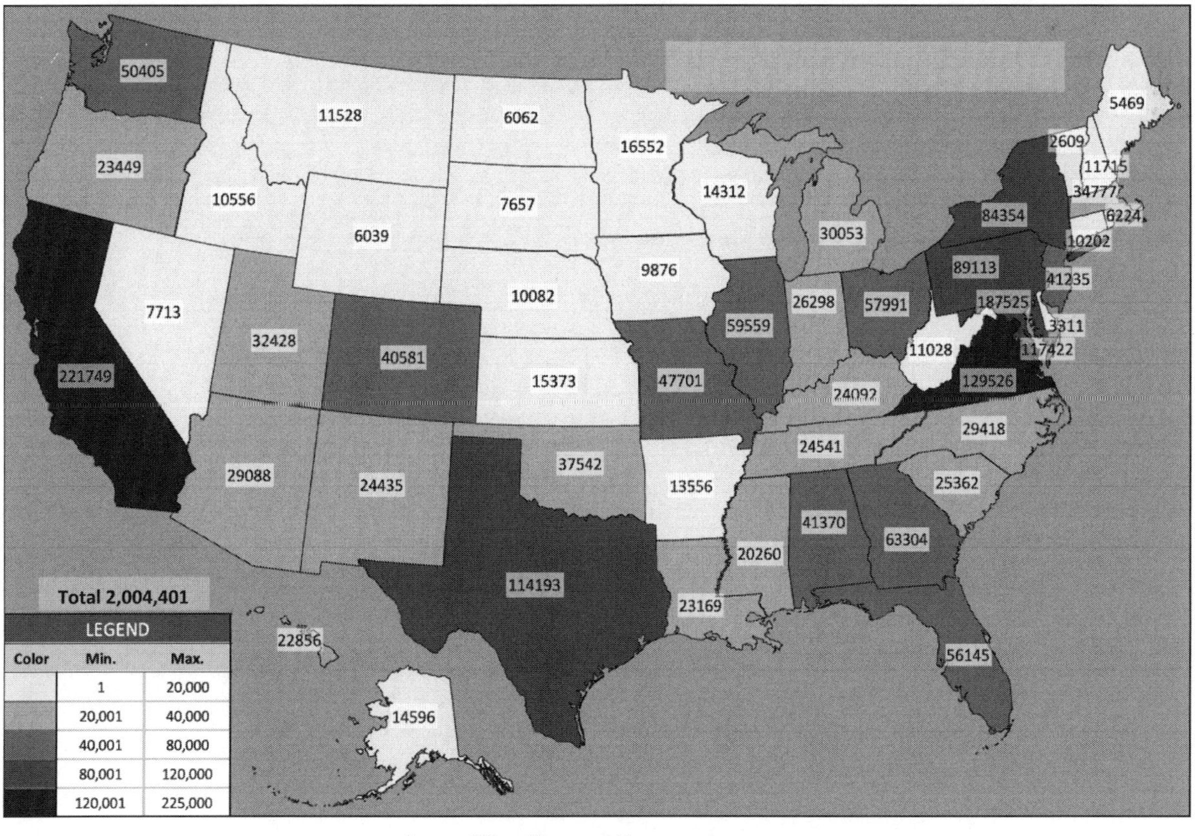

Source: Office of Personnel Management.

Chart 13-8. Government-wide On-board U.S. Distribution 9–30–2022

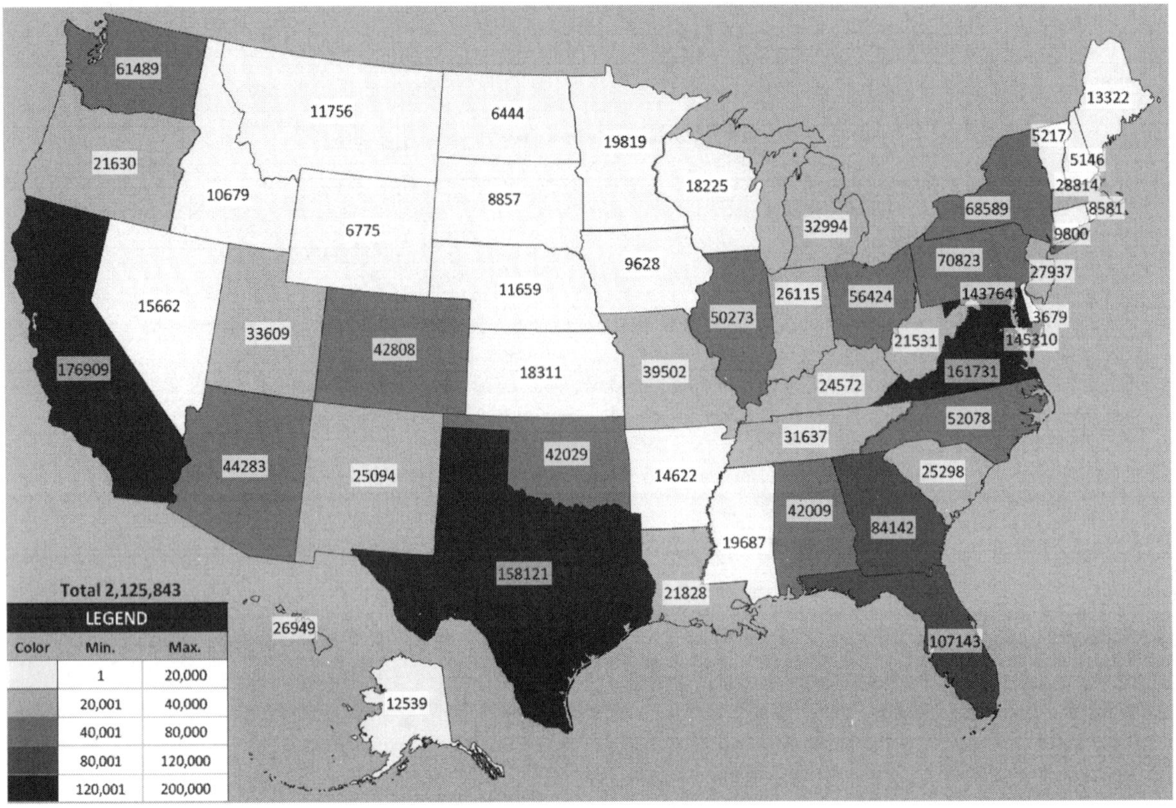

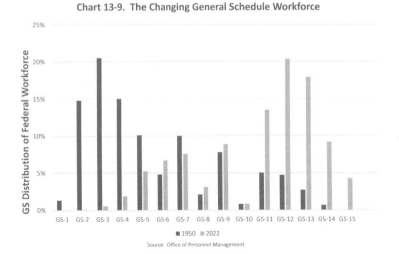

Source: Office of Personnel Management

Chart 13-9. The Changing General Schedule Workforce

Source: Office of Personnel Management

14. INFORMATION TECHNOLOGY AND CYBERSECURITY FUNDING

Information Technology Priorities

Technology serves as the foundation of the Federal Government's ability to deliver on its mission. The Administration is leading on the technology issues of our time—stopping foreign intrusions into U.S. agencies, balancing difficult trade-offs in digital identity and artificial intelligence, redefining security expectations for software and the cloud, and maximizing the impact of taxpayer dollars to drive digital transformation across the Government to deliver a better customer experience for the American people. The Budget supports launching tech policy that meets today's expectations and technology that is secure by design, allowing Federal agencies to deliver on their missions safely, reliably, and easily. The Administration is focused on understanding where agencies are on their IT modernization journeys and making the right investments at the right time to enable secure technology and innovation to advance from year to year. The Budget proposes spending $74 billion on IT at civilian agencies in 2024, which will be used to deliver simple, seamless, and secure Government services. The President's Budget also supports the implementation of Federal laws that enable agency technology planning, oversight, funding, and accountability practices, as well as Office of Management and Budget (OMB) guidance to agencies on the strategic use of IT to enable mission outcomes.

In June 2022, OMB released the "Information Technology Operating Plan" that focuses on four strategic priorities all enabled by a strong Federal workforce.[1] The priorities include:

Cybersecurity—Bolstering cybersecurity by ensuring every Department and Agency is increasing the safety and security of public services, and implementing the requirements contained in the Executive Order 14028, "Improving the Nation's Cybersecurity," as well as the Federal Zero Trust Strategy. To address this in the 24 Budget, OMB and the Office of the National Cyber Director jointly released M-22-16, Administration Cybersecurity Priorities for the FY 2024 Budget. This memo directed Federal Civilian Executive Branch (FCEB) agencies to prioritize funding in three cyber investment areas: Improving the Defense and Resilience of Government Networks; Deepening Cross-Sector Collaboration in Defense of Critical Infrastructure; and Strengthening the Foundations of Our Digitally-Enabled Future. The memo also provided additional specificity on areas such as zero trust implementation, sector risk management, and investing in a capable IT and cyber workforce.

IT Modernization—Adopting modern technologies, retiring legacy systems, employing methods of continuous improvement, and scaling them across Government, so that Government can run more effectively and improve the delivery and reliability of trusted services. The President's Budget continues to support funding for the Technology Modernization Fund (TMF), an innovative funding vehicle that gives agencies additional ways to deliver services to the American public more quickly, to better secure sensitive systems and data, and to use taxpayer dollars more efficiently. The mission of the TMF is to enable agencies to accelerate transformation of the way they use technology to deliver their mission and services to the American public in an effective, efficient, and secure manner.

Digital-First Customer Experience—Using design and technology to deliver an exceptional customer experience for the American public that demonstrably meets user needs and is on par with today's customer expectations. The President's Budget reflects funding for multi-year implementation efforts to improve service delivery under the 21st Century Integrated Digital Experience Act (Public Law 115-336). The President's Budget also supports technology resources for high impact service providers and other Government-wide customer experience improvements under Executive Order 14058, "Transforming Federal Customer Experience and Service Delivery to Rebuild Trust in Government," including increases to Government-wide common products, platforms, and services that enable interactions that are consistent across Government.

Data as a Strategic Asset—Driving key insights into the decision-making process by harnessing accurate, available, and actionable data to power intelligent Government operations and citizen experiences. OMB released the Federal Data Strategy (FDS) in 2019 as a foundational document for enabling agencies to use and manage Federal data to serve the American people. The FDS provides a consistent framework of principles and practices that are intended to guide agencies as they continue to leverage, utilize, and implement data as a resource and strategic asset. The FDS provides an overarching and iterative approach to data stewardship through the release of annual action plans that support the implementation of the strategy over an eight-year period.

Federal Spending on IT

As shown in Table 14-1, the President's Budget for IT at civilian Federal agencies is estimated to be $74 billion in 2024[2]. This figure is a 13 percent increase from the 2023 estimate. Chart 14-1 shows trending information

---

[1] https://www.whitehouse.gov/wp-content/uploads/2022/06/Federal-IT-Operating-Plan_June-2022.pdf

[2] The scope of the analysis in this chapter refers to agencies represented on the IT Dashboard, located at https://www.itdashboard.gov/. This analysis excludes the Department of Defense.

Table 14–1. ESTIMATED FY 2024 CIVILIAN FEDERAL IT SPENDING AND PERCENTAGE BY AGENCY

(In millions of dollars)

Agency	FY 2024	Percent of Total
Department of Veterans Affairs	$10,991	14.7%
Department of Health and Human Services	$10,006	13.4%
Department of Homeland Security	$9,039	12.1%
Department of the Treasury	$7,137	9.8%
Department of Justice	$4,805	6.4%
Department of Transportation	$4,079	5.6%
Department of Agriculture	$4,069	5.5%
Department of Energy	$4,024	5.4%
Department of State	$3,521	4.7%
Department of Commerce	$2,930	3.9%
Social Security Administration	$2,502	3.4%
National Aeronautics and Space Administration	$2,393	3.2%
Department of the Interior	$1,971	2.5%
Department of Education	$1,742	2.3%
General Services Administration	$1,125	1.5%
Department of Labor	$1,047	1.4%
Department of Housing and Urban Development	$526	0.7%
Environmental Protection Agency	$504	0.7%
Small Business Administration	$445	0.6%
Office of Personnel Management	$442	0.6%
U.S. Agency for International Development	$376	0.5%
U.S. Army Corps of Engineers	$285	0.4%
National Science Foundation	$192	0.3%
Nuclear Regulatory Commission	$174	0.2%
National Archives and Records Administration	$108	0.2%
Total	**$74,435**	**100%**

This analysis excludes the Department of Defense.

for Federal civilian IT spending from 2021 forward.[3] The President's Budget includes funding for 4,529 investments at 25 agencies. These investments support the three IT Portfolio areas shown in Chart 14-2. Of those 4,529 IT investments, 588 have been designated as major IT investments. As outlined in OMB Circular A-11 Section 55: IT Investments Guidance, agencies are required to determine major IT investment designations based on several factors including, but not limited to, whether the investment under consideration has significant program or policy implications; has high executive or public visibility; has high development, high operating, and/or high maintenance costs; or requires special management attention because of its importance to the agency's mission or critical functions. For each designated major IT investment, agencies are required to submit a business case analysis which provides additional transparency regarding the major investment's cost, schedule, risk, and performance. OMB also requires that each reporting agency Chief Information Officer (CIO) provide additional risk ratings for each major IT investment reported on the IT Dashboard website. Throughout the fiscal year, agency CIOs are required to continuously reassess how risks

for their major IT investments are being managed and mitigated.

Federal Spending on Cybersecurity

Cybersecurity is a top priority for this Administration. Our adversaries continue to employ novel and sophisticated methods in an effort to compromise Federal systems. With the release of *Executive Order 14028,* "Improving the Nation's Cybersecurity" on May 12, 2021, the Administration initiated a paradigm shift for cybersecurity. The Executive Order sets a framework to aggressively change the cybersecurity strategy and culture across the Federal enterprise to ultimately center around leading industry practices. Through implementation of Executive Order 14028, Federal agencies are enhancing the protection of Federal systems through modernization of cybersecurity defenses, improving information sharing between the U.S. Government and the private sector, and strengthening the United States' ability to rapidly respond to incidents when they occur. Agencies can no longer rely on a perimeter-based approach or "digital walls" to keep sophisticated actors from gaining unauthorized access to Federal systems. The Administration is focused on making Federal systems more defensible by adopting zero trust principles, a security strategy premised on the idea that trust is never granted implicitly but must be continually evaluated.

---

[3] Note that as of the 2020 CPIC guidance, IT related grants made to State and local governments are no longer included in agency IT investment submissions.

To that end, OMB has released several government-wide policies that align to the zero trust vision outlined in Executive Order 14028. On January 26, 2022, OMB released *OMB Memorandum 22-09*, Moving the U.S. Government Toward Zero Trust Cybersecurity Principles, or the Federal Zero Trust Strategy. The strategy requires agencies to invest in technology that is built and deployed with security foremost in mind and move towards a zero trust architecture that provides the vigilance to detect malicious behaviors and react quickly. The Federal Zero Trust Strategy and associated agency implementation plans delineate meaningful milestones in implementing a zero trust architecture.

In September 2022, OMB took new actions to address potential security gaps in the software supply chain. By issuing *OMB Memorandum 22-18,* Enhancing the Security of the Software Supply Chain through Secure Development Practices, the Administration focused agencies on shifting to exclusively utilizing software developed with appropriate security practices in place. This memorandum focuses on minimizing the risks associated with running unvetted technologies on agency networks, increasing the resilience of Federal technology against cyber threats.

Additionally, OMB will carry forward the vision—not just the actions—laid out in Executive Order 14028. The cyber landscape is rapidly evolving, and we will continue to discover new threats and tactics that our adversaries intend to use against us. This is why agencies must build upon the strategic direction of Executive Order 14028 and take actions to secure Federal systems against all present and future threats as they become known to us. For example, the Administration recognized the future threat that quantum computers may pose to the Federal Government, and consequently published *OMB Memorandum 23-02*, Migrating to Post-Quantum Cryptography, which establishes requirements for agencies to prioritize and identify where they are using cryptography within their most sensitive systems that are vulnerable to decryption by a future quantum computer. This guidance will help prepare our Government for an inevitable shift in security that could ultimately expose securely encrypted secrets to foreign adversaries if we do not act decisively.

In the two years since the release of Executive Order 14028, Federal agencies have made considerable progress towards a more cyber-secure future. Agencies are implementing higher levels of encryption, using the best methods in the industry to verify legitimate users, and utilizing toolsets that create constant vigilance within Federal systems. These efforts to adopt technologies and practices that enhance cybersecurity defenses and ensuring the human capital to maintain these endeavors will and must continue. The President's Budget includes approximately $12.7 billion of budget authority for civilian cybersecurity-related activities, an increase of 13 percent over the prior year.

Table 14–2. ESTIMATED CIVILIAN FEDERAL CYBERSECURITY SPENDING BY AGENCY

(In millions of dollars)

Organization	FY 2022	FY 2023	FY 2024
Civilian CFO Act Agencies	**$9,554**	**$10,700**	**$12,170**
Department of Agriculture	$269	$239	$248
Department of Commerce	$442	$478	$427
Department of Education	$194	$217	$313
Department of Energy	$785	$788	$928
Department of Health and Human Services	$695	$813	$947
Department of Homeland Security	$2,578	$2,920	$3,097
Department of Housing and Urban Development	$52	$74	$88
Department of Justice	$957	$1,174	$1,353
Department of Labor	$82	$96	$124
Department of State	$565	$570	$748
Department of the Interior	$145	$164	$192
Department of the Treasury	$749	$963	$1,042
Department of Transportation	$358	$414	$443
Department of Veterans Affairs	$645	$611	$927
Environmental Protection Agency	$58	$37	$67
General Services Administration	$103	$127	$129
National Aeronautics and Space Administration	$174	$198	$196
National Science Foundation	$278	$295	$300
Nuclear Regulatory Commission	$32	$38	$37
Office of Personnel Management	$40	$45	$53
Small Business Administration	$31	$26	$37
Social Security Administration	$254	$330	$376
U.S. Agency for International Development	$69	$82	$97
Non-CFO Act Agencies	**$459.6**	**$489.1**	**$548.5**
Access Board	$0.3	$0.8	$0.8
American Battle Monuments Commission	$1.3	$1.3	$1.3
Armed Forces Retirement Home	*	*	*
U.S. Agency for Global Media	$5.9	$6.0	$10.7
Chemical Safety and Hazard Investigation Board	$1.6	$0.7	$0.7
Commission on Civil Rights	$0.8	$0.6	$1.0
Commodity Futures Trading Commission	$12.6	$13.6	$15.4
Consumer Product Safety Commission	$3.2	$4.7	$3.8
Corporation for National and Community Service	$4.1	$6.8	$11.2
Council of the Inspectors General on Integrity and Efficiency	$0.4	$0.8	$0.8
Court Services and Offender Supervision Agency for the District	$4.0	$4.0	$4.0
Defense Nuclear Facilities Safety Board	$2.1	$3.3	$3.8
Equal Employment Opportunity Commission	$6.4	$8.8	$8.7
Export-Import Bank of the United States	$5.4	$4.6	$5.0
Farm Credit Administration	$3.8	$4.0	$4.0
Federal Communications Commission	$35.5	$27.3	$30.5
Federal Deposit Insurance Corporation	$82.6	$83.7	$83.7
Federal Election Commission	*	*	*
Federal Financial Institutions Examination Council	*	*	*
Federal Labor Relations Authority	$0.5	$0.5	$0.6
Federal Maritime Commission	$0.3	$0.3	$0.4
Federal Retirement Thrift Investment Board	$57.8	$29.0	$24.3
Federal Trade Commission	$16.0	$25.0	$41.1
Gulf Coast Ecosystem Restoration Council	*	*	*
Institute of Museum and Library Services	$0.5	$0.7	$0.9
African Development Foundation	$2.1	$2.4	$2.5
Inter-American Foundation	*	*	*
Millennium Challenge Corporation	$1.5	$2.2	$2.3
Overseas Private Investment Corporation	*	*	*
Peace Corps	$8.8	$12.3	$23.0
Trade and Development Agency	$1.3	$1.3	$1.3

Table 14–2. ESTIMATED CIVILIAN FEDERAL CYBERSECURITY SPENDING BY AGENCY—Continued
(In millions of dollars)

Organization	FY 2022	FY 2023	FY 2024
International Trade Commission	$3.4	$5.5	$6.5
Marine Mammal Commission	*	*	*
Merit Systems Protection Board	$0.5	$0.8	$1.7
Morris K. Udall and Stewart L. Udall Foundation	$0.1	$0.2	$0.2
National Archives and Records Administration	$10.0	$10.8	$21.6
National Credit Union Administration	$10.6	$13.2	$14.2
National Endowment for the Arts	$1.5	$5.2	$4.3
National Endowment for the Humanities	$1.1	$1.3	$1.6
National Labor Relations Board	$3.3	$4.1	$5.8
National Transportation Safety Board	$4.8	$5.8	$7.3
Nuclear Waste Technical Review Board	$0.4	$0.4	$0.5
Occupational Safety and Health Review Commission	$1.1	$1.1	$1.1
Office of Government Ethics	$0.3	$0.7	$3.4
Office of Special Counsel	$1.2	$1.1	$1.1
Presidio Trust	$0.6	*	*
Privacy and Civil Liberties Oversight Board	$2.1	$2.0	$2.0
Railroad Retirement Board	$5.1	$6.1	$7.6
Securities and Exchange Commission	$59.8	$58.0	$58.0
Selective Service System	$2.0	$0.5	$0.0
Smithsonian Institution	$9.8	$13.3	$14.9
Surface Transportation Board	$1.2	$1.4	$1.1
Tennessee Valley Authority	$44.9	$74.7	$57.3
U.S. Army Corps of Engineers	$4.0	$4.0	$15.0
United States Holocaust Memorial Museum	$1.7	$2.8	$3.0
United States Institute of Peace	*	*	*
National Gallery of Art	$3.7	$3.9	$4.3
Postal Regulatory Commission	$1.0	$1.1	$2.1
Pension Benefit Guaranty Corporation	$26.9	$26.6	$32.2
Total	**$10,014**	**$11,189**	**$12,718**

* $500,000 or less

CHART 14-1. TRENDS IN FEDERAL CIVILIAN IT SPENDING

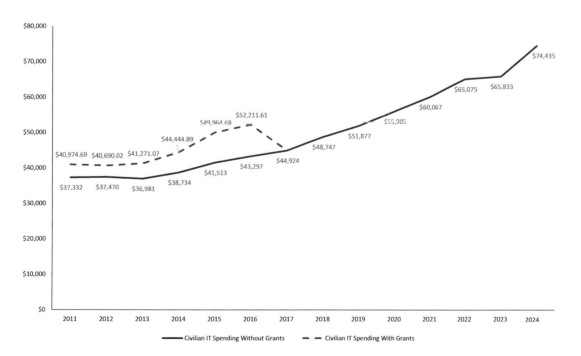

Table 14–3. NIST FRAMEWORK FUNCTION CIVILIAN CFO ACT AGENCY FUNDING TOTALS

(In millions of dollars)

NIST Framework Function	FY 2023	FY 2024
Identify	3,435	3,500
Protect	4,392	5,058
Detect	1,148	1,266
Respond	1,410	1,637
Recover	315	344
M-22-16 Priorities	....	366
Total	**10,700**	**12,170**

This analysis excludes Department of Defense spending.

CHART 14-2. FY 2024 CIVILIAN IT INVESTMENT PORTFOLIO SUMMARY

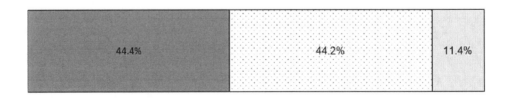

□ IT Infrastructure, IT Security, and IT Management   □ Mission Delivery   □ Administrative Services and Support Systems

TECHNICAL BUDGET ANALYSES

15. BUDGET CONCEPTS

The budget system of the United States Government provides the means for the President and the Congress to decide how much money to spend, what to spend it on, and how to raise the money they have decided to spend. Through the budget system, they determine the allocation of resources among the agencies of the Federal Government and between the Federal Government and the private sector. The budget system focuses primarily on dollars, but it also allocates other resources, such as Federal employment. Budget decisions made affect the Nation as a whole, State and local governments, and individual Americans. Many decisions have worldwide significance. The Congress and the President enact budget decisions into law. The budget system ensures that these laws are carried out.

This chapter provides an overview of the budget system and explains some of the more important budget concepts. It includes summary dollar amounts to illustrate major concepts. Other chapters of the budget documents dis-cuss these concepts and more detailed amounts in greater depth.

The following section discusses the budget process, covering formulation of the President's Budget, action by the Congress, and execution of enacted budget laws. The next section provides information on budget coverage, including a discussion of on-budget and off-budget amounts, functional classification, presentation of budget data, types of funds, and full-cost budgeting. Subsequent sections discuss the concepts of receipts and collections, budget authority, and outlays. These sections are followed by discussions of Federal credit; surpluses, deficits, and means of financing; Federal employment; and the basis for the budget figures. A glossary of budget terms appears at the end of the chapter.

Various laws, enacted to carry out requirements of the Constitution, govern the budget system. The chapter refers to the principal ones by title throughout the text and gives complete citations in the section just preceding the glossary.

THE BUDGET PROCESS

The budget process has three main phases, each of which is related to the others:

1. Formulation of the President's Budget;

2. Action by the Congress; and

3. Execution of enacted budget laws.

Formulation of the President's Budget

The Budget of the United States Government consists of several volumes that set forth the President's fiscal policy goals and priorities for the allocation of resources by the Government. The primary focus of the Budget is on the budget year—the next fiscal year for which the Congress needs to make appropriations, in this case 2024. (Fiscal year 2024 will begin on October 1, 2023, and end on September 30, 2024.) The Budget also covers the nine years following the budget year in order to reflect the effects of budget decisions over the longer term. It includes the funding levels provided for the current year, in this case 2023, which allows the reader to compare the President's Budget proposals with the most recently enacted levels. The Budget also includes data on the most recently completed fiscal year, in this case 2022, so that the reader can compare budget estimates to actual accounting data.

In a normal year (excluding transitions between administrations), the President begins the process of formulating the budget by establishing general budget and fiscal policy guidelines, usually by late spring of each year. Based on these guidelines, the Office of Management and Budget (OMB) works with the Federal agencies to establish specific policy directions and planning levels to guide the preparation of their budget requests.

During the formulation of the budget, the President, the Director of OMB, and other officials in the Executive Office of the President continually exchange information, proposals, and evaluations bearing on policy decisions with the Secretaries of the Departments and the heads of the other Government agencies. Decisions reflected in previously enacted budgets, including the one for the fiscal year in progress, reactions to the last proposed budget (which the Congress is considering at the same time the process of preparing the forthcoming budget begins), and evaluations of program performance all influence decisions concerning the forthcoming budget, as do projections of the economic outlook, prepared jointly by the Council of Economic Advisers, OMB, and the Department of the Treasury.

Agencies normally submit their budget requests to OMB, where analysts review them and identify issues that OMB officials need to discuss with the agencies. OMB and the agencies resolve many issues themselves. Others require the involvement of White House policy officials and the President. This decision-making process is usually completed by late December. At that time, the final stage of developing detailed budget data and the preparation of the budget documents begins.

The decision-makers must consider the effects of economic and technical assumptions on the budget estimates. Interest rates, economic growth, the rate of inflation, the unemployment rate, and the number of people eligible for various benefit programs, among other factors, affect Government spending and receipts. Small changes in these assumptions can alter budget estimates by many billions of dollars. (Chapter 2, "Economic Assumptions," provides more information on this subject.)

Thus, the budget formulation process involves the simultaneous consideration of the resource needs of individual programs, the allocation of resources among the agencies and functions of the Federal Government, and the total outlays and receipts that are appropriate in light of current and prospective economic conditions.

The law governing the President's Budget requires the transmittal of the following fiscal year's Budget to the Congress on or after the first Monday in January but not later than the first Monday in February of each year. The budget is usually scheduled for transmission to the Congress on the first Monday in February, giving the Congress eight months to act on the budget before the fiscal year begins. However, because a significant portion of budget formulation depends on analyzing current year funding levels, budget timing can be affected by the timing of enactment of appropriations for the current year. In addition, in years when a Presidential transition has taken place, the timeline for budget release is commonly extended to allow the new administration sufficient time to take office and formulate its budget policy. While there is no specific timeline set for this circumstance, the detailed budget is usually completed and released in April or May. However, in order to aid the congressional budget process (discussed below), new administrations often release a budget blueprint that contains broad spending outlines and descriptions of major policies and priorities earlier in the year.

Congressional Action[1]

The Congress considers the President's Budget proposals and approves, modifies, or disapproves them. It can change funding levels, eliminate programs, or add programs not requested by the President. It can add or eliminate taxes and other sources of receipts or make other changes that affect the amount of receipts collected.

The Congress does not enact a budget as such. Through the process of adopting a planning document called a budget resolution, the Congress agrees on targets for total spending and receipts, the size of the deficit or surplus, and the debt limit. The budget resolution provides the framework within which individual congressional committees prepare appropriations bills and other spending and receipts legislation. The Congress provides funding for specified purposes in appropriations acts each year. It also enacts changes each year in other laws that affect spending and receipts.

In making appropriations, the Congress does not vote on the level of outlays (spending) directly, but rather on budget authority, which is the authority provided by law to incur financial obligations that will result in outlays. In a separate process, prior to making appropriations, the Congress usually enacts legislation that authorizes an agency to carry out particular programs, authorizes the appropriation of funds to carry out those programs, and, in some cases, limits the amount that can be appropriated for the programs. Some authorizing legislation expires after one year, some expires after a specified number of years, and some is permanent. The Congress may enact appropriations for a program even though there is no specific authorization for it or its authorization has expired.

The Congress begins its work on its budget resolution shortly after it receives the President's Budget. Under the procedures established by the Congressional Budget Act of 1974 (Congressional Budget Act), the Congress decides on budget targets before commencing action on individual appropriations. The Congressional Budget Act requires each standing committee of the House and Senate to recommend budget levels and report legislative plans concerning matters within the committee's jurisdiction to the Budget Committee in each body. The House and Senate Budget Committees then each design and report, and each body then considers, a concurrent resolution on the budget. The Act calls for the House and Senate to resolve differences between their respective versions of the congressional budget resolution and adopt a single budget resolution by April 15 of each year.

In the report on the budget resolution, the Budget Committees allocate the total on-budget budget authority and outlays set forth in the resolution to the Appropriations Committees and the other committees that have jurisdiction over spending. These committee allocations are commonly known as "302(a)" allocations, in reference to the section of the Congressional Budget Act that provides for them. The Appropriations Committees are then required to divide their 302(a) allocations of budget authority and outlays among their subcommittees. These subcommittee allocations are known as "302(b)" allocations. There are procedural hurdles associated with considering appropriations bills that would breach an Appropriations subcommittee's 302(b) allocation. Similar procedural hurdles exist for considering legislation that would cause the 302(a) allocation for any committee to be breached. The Budget Committees' reports may discuss assumptions about the level of funding for major programs. While these assumptions do not bind the other committees and subcommittees, they may influence their decisions.

Budget resolutions may include "reserve funds," which permit adjustment of the resolution allocations as necessary to accommodate legislation addressing specific matters, such as healthcare or tax reform. Reserve funds are most often limited to legislation that is deficit neutral, including increases in some areas offset by decreases in others. The budget resolution may also contain "reconciliation directives" (discussed further below).

[1] For a fuller discussion of the congressional budget process, see Bill Heniff Jr., *Introduction to the Federal Budget Process* (Congressional Research Service Report 98–721), and Robert Keith and Allen Schick, *Manual on the Federal Budget Process* (Congressional Research Service Report 98–720, archived).

Since the concurrent resolution on the budget is not a law, it does not require the President's approval. However, the Congress considers the President's views in preparing budget resolutions, because legislation developed to meet congressional budget allocations does require the President's approval. In some years, the President and the joint leadership of the Congress have formally agreed on plans to reduce the deficit. These agreements were then reflected in the budget resolution and legislation passed for those years.

If the Congress does not pass a budget resolution, the House and Senate typically adopt one or more "deeming resolutions" in the form of a simple resolution or as a provision of a larger bill. A deeming resolution may serve nearly all functions of a budget resolution, except it may not trigger reconciliation procedures in the Senate.

Once the Congress approves the budget resolution, it turns its attention to enacting appropriations bills and authorizing legislation. The Appropriations Committee in each body has jurisdiction over annual appropriations. These committees are divided into subcommittees that hold hearings and review detailed budget justification materials prepared by the Executive Branch agencies within the subcommittee's jurisdiction. After a bill has been drafted by a subcommittee, the full committee and the whole House, in turn, must approve the bill, sometimes with amendments to the original version. The House then forwards the bill to the Senate, where a similar review follows. If the Senate disagrees with the House on particular matters in the bill, which is often the case, the two bodies form a conference committee (consisting of some Members of each body) to resolve the differences. The conference committee revises the bill and returns it to both bodies for approval. When the revised bill is agreed to, first in the House and then in the Senate, the Congress sends it to the President for approval or veto.

Since 1977, when the start of the fiscal year was established as October 1, there have been only three fiscal years (1989, 1995, and 1997) for which the Congress agreed to and enacted every regular appropriations bill by that date. When one or more appropriations bills are not enacted by this date, the Congress usually enacts a joint resolution called a "continuing resolution" (CR), which is an interim or stop-gap appropriations bill that provides authority for the affected agencies to continue operations at some specified level until a specific date or until the regular appropriations are enacted. Occasionally, a CR has funded a portion or all of the Government for the entire year.

The Congress must present these CRs to the President for approval or veto. In some cases, Congresses have failed to pass a CR or Presidents have rejected CRs because they contained unacceptable provisions. Left without funds, Government agencies were required by law to shut down operations—with exceptions for some limited activities—until the Congress passed a CR or appropriations bill the President would approve. Previous shutdowns have ranged in duration from just one day to several weeks.

The Congress also provides budget authority in laws other than appropriations acts. In fact, while annual appropriations acts fund the majority of Federal programs, they account for only about a third of the total spending in a typical year. Authorizing legislation controls the rest of the spending, which is commonly called "mandatory spending." A distinctive feature of these authorizing laws is that they provide agencies with the authority or requirement to spend money without first requiring the Appropriations Committees to enact funding. This category of spending includes interest the Government pays on the public debt and the spending of several major programs, such as Social Security, Medicare, Medicaid, unemployment insurance, and Federal employee retirement. Almost all taxes and most other receipts also result from authorizing laws.

Some authorizing legislation making changes to laws that affect receipts or mandatory spending may be developed under a unique set of procedures known as reconciliation. The budget resolution often includes reconciliation directives, which direct each designated authorizing committee to report amendments to the laws under the committee's jurisdiction that would achieve changes in the levels of receipts or mandatory spending controlled by those laws. These directives specify the dollar amount of changes that each designated committee is expected to achieve, but do not specify which laws are

BUDGET CALENDAR

The following timetable highlights the scheduled dates for significant budget events during a normal budget year:

Between the 1st Monday in January and the 1st Monday in February	President transmits the budget
Six weeks later	Congressional committees report budget estimates to Budget Committees
April 15	Action to be completed on congressional budget resolution
May 15	House consideration of annual appropriations bills may begin even if the budget resolution has not been agreed to.
June 10	House Appropriations Committee to report the last of its annual appropriations bills.
June 15	Action to be completed on "reconciliation bill" by the Congress.
June 30	Action on appropriations to be completed by House
July 15	President transmits Mid-Session Review of the Budget
October 1	Fiscal year begins

to be changed or the changes to be made. However, the Budget Committees' reports on the budget resolution frequently discuss assumptions about how the laws would be changed. Like other assumptions in the report, they do not bind the committees of jurisdiction but may influence their decisions. A reconciliation instruction may also specify the total amount by which the statutory limit on the public debt is to be changed.

The committees subject to reconciliation directives draft the implementing legislation. Such legislation may, for example, change the tax code, revise benefit formulas or eligibility requirements for benefit programs, or authorize Government agencies to charge fees to cover some of their costs. Reconciliation bills are typically omnibus legislation, combining the legislation submitted by each reconciled committee in a single act.

The Senate considers such omnibus reconciliation acts under expedited procedures that limit total debate on the bill. To offset the procedural advantage gained by expedited procedures, the Senate places significant restrictions on the substantive content of the reconciliation measure itself, as well as on amendments to the measure. Any material in the bill that is extraneous or that contains changes to the Federal Old-Age and Survivors Insurance and the Federal Disability Insurance programs is not in order under the Senate's expedited reconciliation procedures. Non-germane amendments are also prohibited. Reconciliation acts, together with appropriations acts for the year, are usually used to implement broad agreements between the President and the Congress on those occasions where the two branches have negotiated a comprehensive budget plan. Reconciliation acts have sometimes included other matters, such as laws providing the means for enforcing these agreements.

Budget Execution

Government agencies may not spend or obligate more than the Congress has appropriated, and they may use funds only for purposes specified in law. The Antideficiency Act prohibits agencies from spending or obligating funds in advance or in excess of an appropria-

tion, unless specific authority to do so has been provided in law. The Antideficiency Act also requires the President to apportion the budgetary resources available for most executive branch agencies. The President has delegated this authority to OMB. Some apportionments are by time periods (usually by quarter of the fiscal year), some are by projects or activities, and others are by a combination of both. Agencies may request OMB to reapportion funds during the year to accommodate changing circumstances. This system helps to ensure that funds do not run out before the end of the fiscal year.

During the budget execution phase, the Government sometimes finds that it needs more funding than the Congress has appropriated for the fiscal year because of unanticipated circumstances. For example, more might be needed to respond to a severe natural disaster. Under such circumstances, the Congress may enact a supplemental appropriation.

On the other hand, the President may propose to reduce a previously enacted appropriation, through a "rescission" or "cancellation" of those funds. How the President proposes this reduction determines whether it is considered a rescission or a cancellation. A rescission is a reduction in previously enacted appropriations proposed pursuant to the Impoundment Control Act (ICA). The ICA allows the President, using the specific authorities in that Act, to transmit a "special message" to the Congress to inform Members of these proposed rescissions, at which time the funding can be withheld from obligation for up to 45 days on the OMB-approved apportionment. Agencies are instructed not to withhold funds without the prior approval of OMB. If the Congress does not act to rescind these funds within the 45-day period, the funds are made available for obligation.

The President can also propose reductions to previously enacted appropriations outside of the ICA; in these cases, these reductions are referred to as cancellations. Cancellation proposals are not subject to the requirements and procedures of the ICA and amounts cannot be withheld from obligation. The 2024 President's Budget includes $14.3 billion in proposed cancellations.

COVERAGE OF THE BUDGET

Federal Government and Budget Totals

The budget documents provide information on all Federal agencies and programs. However, because the laws governing Social Security (the Federal Old-Age and Survivors Insurance and the Federal Disability Insurance trust funds) and the Postal Service Fund require that the receipts and outlays for those activities be excluded from the budget totals and from the calculation of the deficit or surplus, the budget presents on-budget and off-budget totals. The off-budget totals include the Federal transactions excluded by law from the budget totals. The on-budget and off-budget amounts are added together to derive the totals for the Federal Government. These are sometimes referred to as the unified or consolidated budget totals.

It is not always obvious whether a transaction or activity should be included in the budget. Where there is a question, OMB normally follows the recommendation of the 1967 President's Commission on Budget Concepts to be comprehensive of the full range of Federal agencies, programs, and activities. In recent years, for example, the budget has included the transactions of the Affordable Housing Program funds, the Universal Service Fund, the Public Company Accounting Oversight Board, the Securities Investor Protection Corporation, Guaranty Agencies Reserves, the National Railroad Retirement Investment Trust, the United Mine Workers Combined Benefits Fund, the Federal Financial Institutions Examination Council, Electric Reliability Organizations (EROs) established pursuant to the Energy Policy Act

Table 15–1. TOTALS FOR THE BUDGET AND THE FEDERAL GOVERNMENT

(In billions of dollars)

	2022 Actual	Estimate	
		2023	2024
Budget authority			
Unified	6,585	6,566	7,049
On-budget	5,488	5,340	5,721
Off-budget	1,096	1,225	1,328
Receipts:			
Unified	4,897	4,802	5,036
On-budget	3,831	3,604	3,828
Off-budget	1,066	1,198	1,208
Outlays:			
Unified	6,273	6,372	6,883
On-budget	5,192	5,160	5,567
Off-budget	1,081	1,212	1,316
Deficit (–) / Surplus (+):			
Unified	–1,376	–1,569	–1,846
On-budget	–1,361	–1,555	–1,739
Off-budget	–15	–14	–107

of 2005, the Corporation for Travel Promotion, and the National Association of Registered Agents and Brokers.

In contrast, the budget excludes tribal trust funds that are owned by Indian Tribes and held and managed by the Government in a fiduciary capacity on the Tribes' behalf. These funds are not owned by the Government, the Government is not the source of their capital, and the Government's control is limited to the exercise of fiduciary duties. Similarly, the transactions of Government-sponsored enterprises, such as the Federal Home Loan Banks, are not included in the on-budget or off-budget totals. Federal laws established these enterprises for public policy purposes, but they are privately owned and operated corporations. Nevertheless, because of their public charters, the budget discusses them and reports summary financial data in the Budget *Appendix* and in some detailed tables.

The budget also excludes the revenues from copyright royalties and spending for subsequent payments to copyright holders where 1) the law allows copyright owners and users to voluntarily set the rate paid for the use of protected material, and 2) the amount paid by users of copyrighted material to copyright owners is related to the frequency or quantity of the material used. The budget excludes license royalties collected and paid out by the Copyright Office for the retransmission of network broadcasts via cable collected under 17 U.S.C. 111 because these revenues meet both of these conditions. The budget includes the royalties collected and paid out for license fees for digital audio recording technology under 17 U.S.C. 1004, since the amount of license fees paid is unrelated to usage of the material.

The *Appendix* includes a presentation for the Board of Governors of the Federal Reserve System for information only. The amounts are not included in either the on-budget or off-budget totals because of the independent status of the System within the Government. However, the Federal Reserve System transfers its net earnings to the Treasury, and the budget records them as receipts.

Chapter 16 of this volume, "Coverage of the Budget," provides more information on this subject.

Functional Classification

The functional classification system is used to organize budget authority, outlays, and other budget data according to the major purpose served—such as agriculture, transportation, income security, and national defense. There are 20 major functions, 17 of which are concerned with broad areas of national need and are further divided into subfunctions. For example, the Agriculture function comprises the subfunctions Farm Income Stabilization and Agricultural Research and Services. The functional classification meets the Congressional Budget Act requirement for a presentation in the budget by national needs and agency missions and programs. The remaining three functions—Net Interest, Undistributed Offsetting Receipts, and Allowances—enable the functional classification system to cover the entire Federal budget.

The following criteria are used in establishing functional categories and assigning activities to them:

- A function encompasses activities with similar purposes, emphasizing what the Federal Government seeks to accomplish rather than the means of accomplishment, the objects purchased, the clientele or geographic area served (except in the cases of functions 450 for Community and Regional Development, 570 for Medicare, 650 for Social Security, and 700 for Veterans Benefits and Services), or the Federal agency conducting the activity (except in the case of subfunction 051 in the National Defense function, which is used only for defense activities under the Department of Defense—Military).

- A function must be of continuing national importance, and the amounts attributable to it must be significant.

- Each basic unit being classified (generally the appropriation or fund account) usually is classified according to its primary purpose and assigned to only one subfunction. However, some large accounts that serve more than one major purpose are subdivided into two or more functions or subfunctions.

In consultation with the Congress, the functional classification is adjusted from time to time as warranted. Detailed functional tables, which provide information on Government activities by function and subfunction, are available online at https://www.whitehouse.gov/omb/analytical-perspectives/.

Agencies, Accounts, Programs, Projects, and Activities

Various summary tables in the *Analytical Perspectives* volume of the Budget provide information on budget authority, outlays, and offsetting collections and receipts arrayed by Federal agency. A table that lists budget authority and outlays by budget account within each agency and the totals for each agency of budget authority, outlays, and receipts that offset the agency spending totals is available online at: https://www.whitehouse.gov/omb/analytical-perspectives/. The *Appendix* provides budgetary, financial, and descriptive information about programs, projects, and activities by account within each agency.

Types of Funds

Agency activities are financed through Federal funds and trust funds.

Federal funds comprise several types of funds. Receipt accounts of the *general fund*, which is the greater part of the budget, record receipts not earmarked by law for a specific purpose, such as income tax receipts. The general fund also includes the proceeds of general borrowing. General fund appropriation accounts record general fund expenditures. General fund appropriations draw from general fund receipts and borrowing collectively and, therefore, are not specifically linked to receipt accounts.

Special funds consist of receipt accounts for Federal fund receipts that laws have designated for specific purposes and the associated appropriation accounts for the expenditure of those receipts.

Public enterprise funds are revolving funds used for programs authorized by law to conduct a cycle of business-type operations, primarily with the public, in which outlays generate collections.

Intragovernmental funds are revolving funds that conduct business-type operations primarily within and between Government agencies. The collections and the outlays of revolving funds are recorded in the same budget account.

Trust funds account for the receipt and expenditure of monies by the Government for carrying out specific purposes and programs in accordance with the terms of a statute that designates the fund as a trust fund (such as the Highway Trust Fund) or for carrying out the stipulations of a trust where the Government itself is the beneficiary (such as any of several trust funds for gifts and donations for specific purposes). *Trust revolving funds* are trust funds credited with collections earmarked by law to carry out a cycle of business-type operations.

The Federal budget meaning of the term "trust," as applied to trust fund accounts, differs significantly from its private-sector usage. In the private sector, the beneficiary of a trust usually owns the trust's assets, which are managed by a trustee who must follow the stipulations of the trust. In contrast, the Federal Government owns the assets of most Federal trust funds, and it can raise or lower future trust fund collections and payments, or change the purposes for which the collections are used, by changing existing laws. There is no substantive difference between a trust fund and a special fund or between a trust revolving fund and a public enterprise revolving fund.

However, in some instances, the Government does act as a true trustee of assets that are owned or held for the benefit of others. For example, it maintains accounts on behalf of individual Federal employees in the Thrift Savings Fund, investing them as directed by the individual employee. The Government accounts for such funds in *deposit funds*, which are not included in the budget. (Chapter 22 of this volume, "Trust Funds and Federal Funds," provides more information on this subject.)

Budgeting for Full Costs

A budget is a financial plan for allocating resources—deciding how much the Federal Government should spend in total, program by program, and for the parts of each program, and deciding how to finance the spending. The budgetary system provides a process for proposing policies, making decisions, implementing these policies, and reporting the results. The budget needs to measure costs accurately so that decision makers can compare the cost of a program with its benefits, the cost of one program with another, and the cost of one method of reaching a specified goal with another. These costs need to be fully included in the budget up front, when the spending decision is made, so that executive and congressional decision makers have the information and the incentive to take the total costs into account when setting priorities.

The budget includes all types of spending, including both current operating expenditures and capital investment, and to the extent possible, both are measured on the basis of full cost. Questions are often raised about the measure of capital investment. The present budget provides policymakers the necessary information regarding investment spending. It records investment on a cash basis, and it requires the Congress to provide budget authority before an agency can obligate the Government to make a cash outlay. However, the budget measures only costs, and the benefits with which these costs are compared, based on policy makers' judgment, must be presented in supplementary materials. By these means, the budget allows the total cost of capital investment to be compared up front in a rough way with the total expected future net benefits. Such a comparison of total costs with benefits is consistent with the formal method of cost-benefit analysis of capital projects in Government, in which the full cost of a capital asset as the cash is paid out is compared with the full stream of future benefits (all in terms of present values). (Chapter 5 of this volume, "Federal Investment," provides more information on capital investment.)

RECEIPTS, OFFSETTING COLLECTIONS, AND OFFSETTING RECEIPTS

In General

The budget records amounts collected by Government agencies two different ways. Depending on the nature of the activity generating the collection and the law that established the collection, they are recorded as either:

Governmental receipts, which are compared in total to outlays (net of offsetting collections and offsetting receipts) in calculating the surplus or deficit; or

Offsetting collections or *offsetting receipts*, which are deducted from gross outlays to calculate net outlay figures. These amounts are recorded as offsets to outlays so that the budget totals represent governmental rather than market activity and reflect the Government's net transactions with the public. They are recorded in one of two ways, based on interpretation of laws and longstanding budget concepts and practice. They are offsetting collections when the collections are authorized by law to be credited to expenditure accounts. Otherwise, they are deposited in receipt accounts and called offsetting receipts.

Offsetting collections and offsetting receipts result from any of the following types of transactions:

- *Business-like transactions or market-oriented activities with the public*—these include voluntary collections from the public in exchange for goods or services, such as the proceeds from the sale of postage stamps, the fees charged for admittance to recreation areas, and the proceeds from the sale of Government-owned land; and reimbursements for damages. The budget records these amounts as *offsetting collections from non-Federal sources* (for offsetting collections) or as *proprietary receipts* (for offsetting receipts).

- *Intragovernmental transactions*—collections from other Federal Government accounts. The budget records collections by one Government account from another as *offsetting collections from Federal sources* (for offsetting collections) or as *intragovernmental receipts* (for offsetting receipts). For example, the General Services Administration rents office space to other Government agencies and records their rental payments as offsetting collections from Federal sources in the Federal Buildings Fund. These transactions are exactly offsetting and do not affect the surplus or deficit. However, they are an important accounting mechanism for allocating costs to the programs and activities that cause the Government to incur the costs.

- *Voluntary gifts and donations*—gifts and donations of money to the Government, which are treated as offsets to budget authority and outlays.

- *Offsetting governmental transactions*—collections from the public that are governmental in nature and should conceptually be treated like Federal revenues and compared in total to outlays (e.g., tax receipts, regulatory fees, compulsory user charges, custom duties, license fees) but are required by law or longstanding practice to be misclassified as offsetting. The budget records amounts from non-Federal sources that are governmental in nature as *offsetting governmental collections* (for offsetting collections) or as *offsetting governmental receipts* (for offsetting receipts).

Governmental Receipts

Governmental receipts are collections that result from the Government's exercise of its sovereign power to tax or otherwise compel payment. Sometimes they are called receipts, budget receipts, Federal receipts, or Federal revenues. They consist mostly of individual and corporation income taxes and social insurance taxes, but also include excise taxes, compulsory user charges, regulatory fees, customs duties, court fines, certain license fees, and deposits of earnings by the Federal Reserve System. Total receipts for the Federal Government include both on-budget and off-budget receipts (see Table 15–1, "Totals for the Budget and the Federal Government," which appears earlier in this chapter.) Chapter 17 of this volume, "Governmental Receipts," provides more information on governmental receipts.

Offsetting Collections

Some laws authorize agencies to credit collections directly to the account from which they will be spent and, usually, to spend the collections for the purpose of the account without further action by the Congress. Most revolving funds operate with such authority. For example, a permanent law authorizes the Postal Service to use collections from the sale of stamps to finance its operations without a requirement for annual appropriations. The budget records these collections in the Postal Service Fund (a revolving fund) and records budget authority in an amount equal to the collections. In addition to revolving funds, some agencies are authorized to charge fees to defray a portion of costs for a program that are otherwise financed by appropriations from the general fund and usually to spend the collections without further action by the Congress. In such cases, the budget records the offsetting collections and resulting budget authority in the program's general fund expenditure account. Similarly, intragovernmental collections authorized by some laws may be recorded as offsetting collections and budget authority in revolving funds or in general fund expenditure accounts.

Sometimes appropriations acts or provisions in other laws limit the obligations that can be financed by offsetting collections. In those cases, the budget records budget authority in the amount available to incur obligations, not in the amount of the collections.

Offsetting collections credited to expenditure accounts automatically offset the outlays at the expenditure account level. Where accounts have offsetting collections, the budget shows the budget authority and outlays of the account both gross (before deducting offsetting collections) and net (after deducting offsetting collections). Totals for the agency, subfunction, and overall budget are net of offsetting collections.

Offsetting Receipts

Collections that are offset against gross outlays but are not authorized to be credited to expenditure accounts are credited to receipt accounts and are called offsetting receipts. Offsetting receipts are deducted from budget authority and outlays in arriving at total net budget authority and outlays. However, unlike offsetting collections credited to expenditure accounts, offsetting receipts do not offset budget authority and outlays at the account level. In most cases, they offset budget authority and outlays at the agency and subfunction levels.

Proprietary receipts from a few sources, however, are not offset against any specific agency or function and are classified as undistributed offsetting receipts. They are deducted from the Government-wide totals for net budget authority and outlays. For example, the collections of rents and royalties from outer continental shelf lands are undistributed because the amounts are large and for the most part are not related to the spending of the agency that administers the transactions and the subfunction that records the administrative expenses.

Similarly, two kinds of intragovernmental transactions—agencies' payments as employers into Federal employee retirement trust funds and interest received by trust funds—are classified as undistributed offsetting receipts. They appear instead as special deductions in computing total net budget authority and outlays for the Government rather than as offsets at the agency level. This special treatment is necessary because the amounts are so large they would distort measures of the agencies' activities if they were attributed to the agency.

User Charges

User charges are fees assessed on individuals or organizations for the provision of Government services and for the sale or use of Government goods or resources. The payers of the user charge must be limited in the authorizing legislation to those receiving special benefits from, or subject to regulation by, the program or activity beyond the benefits received by the general public or broad segments of the public (such as those who pay income taxes or customs duties). Policy regarding user charges is established in OMB Circular A–25, "User Charges." The term encompasses proceeds from the sale or use of Government goods and services, including the sale of natural resources (such as timber, oil, and minerals) and proceeds from asset sales (such as property, plant, and equipment). User charges are not necessarily dedicated to the activity they finance and may be credited to the general fund of the Treasury.

The term "user charge" does not refer to a separate budget category for collections. User charges are classified in the budget as receipts, offsetting receipts, or offsetting collections according to the principles explained previously.

See Chapter 18, "Offsetting Collections and Offsetting Receipts," for more information on the classification of user charges.

BUDGET AUTHORITY, OBLIGATIONS, AND OUTLAYS

Budget authority, obligations, and outlays are the primary benchmarks and measures of the budget control system. The Congress enacts laws that provide agencies with spending authority in the form of budget authority. Before agencies can use these resources—obligate this budget authority—OMB must approve their spending plans. After the plans are approved, agencies can enter into binding agreements to purchase items or services or to make grants or other payments. These agreements are recorded as obligations of the United States and deducted from the amount of budgetary resources available to the agency. When payments are made, the obligations are liquidated and outlays recorded. These concepts are discussed more fully below.

Budget Authority and Other Budgetary Resources

Budget authority is the authority provided in law to enter into legal obligations that will result in immediate or future outlays of the Government. In other words, it is the amount of money that agencies are allowed to commit to be spent in current or future years. Government officials may obligate the Government to make outlays only to the extent they have been granted budget authority.

In deciding the amount of budget authority to request for a program, project, or activity, agency officials esti-mate the total amount of obligations they will need to incur to achieve desired goals and subtract the unobligated balances available for these purposes. The amount of budget authority requested is influenced by the nature of the programs, projects, or activities being financed. For current operating expenditures, the amount requested usually covers the needs for the fiscal year. For major procurement programs and construction projects, agencies generally must request sufficient budget authority in the first year to fully fund an economically useful segment of a procurement or project, even though it may be obligated over several years. This full funding policy is intended to ensure that the decision-makers take into account all costs and benefits at the time decisions are made to provide resources. It also avoids sinking money into a procurement or project without being certain if or when future funding will be available to complete the procurement or project, as well as saddling future agency budgets with must-pay bills to complete past projects.

Budget authority takes several forms:

- *Appropriations*, provided in annual appropriations acts or other laws, permit agencies to incur obligations and make payments;

- *Borrowing authority*, usually provided in permanent law, permits agencies to incur obligations but requires them to borrow funds, usually from the general fund of the Treasury, to make payments;

- *Contract authority*, usually provided in permanent law, permits agencies to incur obligations in advance of a separate appropriation of the cash for payments or in anticipation of the collection of receipts that can be used for payments; and

- *Spending authority from offsetting collections*, usually provided in permanent law, permits agencies to credit offsetting collections to an expenditure account, incur obligations, and make payments using the offsetting collections.

Because offsetting collections and offsetting receipts are deducted from gross budget authority, they are referred to as negative budget authority for some purposes, such as Congressional Budget Act provisions that pertain to budget authority.

Authorizing statutes usually determine the form of budget authority for a program. The authorizing statute may authorize a particular type of budget authority to be provided in appropriations acts, or it may provide one of the forms of budget authority directly, without the need for further appropriations.

An appropriation may make funds available from the general fund, special funds, or trust funds. An appropriations act may also authorize the spending of offsetting collections credited to expenditure accounts, including revolving funds. Borrowing authority is usually authorized for business-like activities where the activity being financed is expected to produce income over time with which to repay the borrowing with interest. The use of contract authority is traditionally limited to transportation programs.

New budget authority for most Federal programs is normally provided in annual appropriations acts. However, new budget authority is also made available through permanent appropriations under existing laws and does not require current action by the Congress. Much of the permanent budget authority is for trust funds, interest on the public debt, and the authority to spend offsetting collections credited to appropriation or fund accounts. For most trust funds, the budget authority is appropriated automatically under existing law from the available balance of the fund and equals the estimated annual obligations of the funds. For interest on the public debt, budget authority is provided automatically under a permanent appropriation enacted in 1847 and equals interest outlays.

Annual appropriations acts generally make budget authority available for obligation only during the fiscal year to which the act applies. However, they frequently allow budget authority for a particular purpose to remain available for obligation for a longer period or indefinitely (that is, until expended or until the program objectives have been attained). Typically, budget authority for current operations is made available for only one year, and budget authority for construction and some research projects is available for a specified number of years or indefinitely. Most budget authority provided in authorizing statutes,

such as for most trust funds, is available indefinitely. If budget authority is initially provided for a limited period of availability, an extension of availability would require enactment of another law (see "Reappropriation" later in this chapter).

Budget authority that is available for more than one year and not obligated in the year it becomes available is carried forward for obligation in a following year. In some cases, an account may carry forward unobligated budget authority from more than one prior year. The sum of such amounts constitutes the account's *unobligated balance*. Most of these balances had been provided for specific uses, such as the multiyear construction of a major project, and so are not available for new programs. A small part may never be obligated or spent, primarily amounts provided for contingencies that do not occur or reserves that never have to be used.

Amounts of budget authority that have been obligated but not yet paid constitute the account's *unpaid obligations*. For example, in the case of salaries and wages, one to three weeks elapse between the time of obligation and the time of payment. In the case of major procurement and construction, payments may occur over a period of several years after the obligation is made. Unpaid obligations (which are made up of accounts payable and undelivered orders) net of the accounts receivable and unfilled customers' orders are defined by law as the *obligated balances*. Obligated balances of budget authority at the end of the year are carried forward until the obligations are paid or the balances are cancelled. (A general law provides that the obligated balance of budget authority that was made available for a definite period is automatically cancelled five years after the end of the period.) Due to such flows, a change in the amount of budget authority available in any one year may change the level of obligations and outlays for several years to come. Conversely, a change in the amount of obligations incurred from one year to the next does not necessarily result from an equal change in the amount of budget authority available for that year and will not necessarily result in an equal change in the level of outlays in that year.

The Congress usually makes budget authority available on the first day of the fiscal year for which the appropriations act is passed. Occasionally, the appropriations language specifies a different timing. The language may provide an *advance appropriation*—budget authority that does not become available until one fiscal year or more beyond the fiscal year for which the appropriations act is passed. *Forward funding* is budget authority that is made available for obligation beginning in the last quarter of the fiscal year (beginning on July 1) for the financing of ongoing grant programs during the next fiscal year. This kind of funding is used mostly for education programs, so that obligations for education grants can be made prior to the beginning of the next school year. For certain benefit programs funded by annual appropriations, the appropriation provides for *advance funding*—budget authority that is to be charged to the appropriation in the succeeding year, but which authorizes obligations to be incurred in the last quarter of the current fiscal year if necessary to meet benefit payments in excess of the specific amount appropriated for the year. When such authority is used, an adjustment is made to increase the budget authority for the fiscal year in which it is used and to reduce the budget authority of the succeeding fiscal year.

Provisions of law that extend into a new fiscal year the availability of unobligated amounts that have expired or would otherwise expire are called *reappropriations*. Reappropriations of expired balances that are newly available for obligation in the current or budget year count as new budget authority in the fiscal year in which the balances become newly available. For example, if a 2024 appropriations act extends the availability of unobligated budget authority that expired at the end of 2023, new budget authority would be recorded for 2024. This scorekeeping is used because a reappropriation has exactly the same effect as allowing the earlier appropriation to expire at the end of 2023 and enacting a new appropriation for 2024.

The Federal Government uses budget enforcement mechanisms to control revenues, spending, and deficits (see Chapter 4, "Budget Process," for a detailed discussion of the budget enforcement framework). For purposes of budget enforcement, the budget classifies budget authority as *discretionary* or *mandatory*. This classification indicates whether an appropriations act or authorizing legislation controls the amount of budget authority that is available. Generally, budget authority is discretionary if provided in an appropriations act and mandatory if provided in authorizing legislation. However, the budget authority provided in appropriations acts for certain specifically identified programs is also classified as mandatory by OMB and the congressional scorekeepers. This is because the authorizing legislation for these programs entitles beneficiaries—persons, households, or other levels of government—to receive payment, or otherwise legally obligates the Government to make payment and thereby effectively determines the amount of budget authority required, even though the payments are funded by a subsequent appropriation.

Sometimes, budget authority is characterized as current or permanent. Current authority requires the Congress to act on the request for new budget authority for the year involved. Permanent authority becomes available pursuant to standing provisions of law without appropriations action by the Congress for the year involved. Generally, budget authority is current if an annual appropriations act provides it and permanent if authorizing legislation provides it. By and large, the current/permanent distinction has been replaced by the discretionary/mandatory distinction, which is similar but not identical. Outlays are also classified as discretionary or mandatory according to the classification of the budget authority from which they flow (see "Outlays" later in this chapter).

The amount of budget authority recorded in the budget depends on whether the law provides a specific amount or employs a variable factor that determines the amount. It is considered *definite* if the law specifies a dollar amount (which may be stated as an upper limit, for ex-

ample, "shall not exceed …"). It is considered *indefinite* if, instead of specifying an amount, the law permits the amount to be determined by subsequent circumstances. For example, indefinite budget authority is provided for interest on the public debt, payment of claims and judgments awarded by the courts against the United States, and many entitlement programs. Many of the laws that authorize collections to be credited to revolving, special, and trust funds make all of the collections available for expenditure for the authorized purposes of the fund, and such authority is considered to be indefinite budget authority because the amount of collections is not known in advance of their collection.

Obligations

Following the enactment of budget authority and the completion of required apportionment action, Government agencies incur obligations to make payments (see earlier discussion under "Budget Execution"). Agencies must record obligations when they incur a legal liability that will result in immediate or future outlays. Such obligations include the current liabilities for salaries, wages, and interest; and contracts for the purchase of supplies and equipment, construction, and the acquisition of office space, buildings, and land. For Federal credit programs, obligations are recorded in an amount equal to the estimated subsidy cost of direct loans and loan guarantees (see "Federal Credit" later in this chapter).

Outlays

Outlays are the measure of Government spending. They are payments that liquidate obligations (other than most exchanges of financial instruments, of which the repayment of debt is the prime example). The budget records outlays when obligations are paid, in the amount that is paid.

Agency, function and subfunction, and Government-wide outlay totals are stated net of offsetting collections and offsetting receipts for most budget presentations. (Offsetting receipts from a few sources do not offset any specific function, subfunction, or agency, as explained previously, but only offset Government-wide totals.) Outlay totals for accounts with offsetting collections are stated both gross and net of the offsetting collections credited to the account. However, the outlay totals for special and trust funds with offsetting receipts are not stated net of the offsetting receipts. In most cases, these receipts offset the agency, function, and subfunction totals but do not offset account-level outlays. However, when general fund payments are used to finance trust fund outlays to the public, the associated trust fund receipts are netted against the bureau totals to prevent double-counting budget authority and outlays at the bureau level.

The Government usually makes outlays in the form of cash (currency, checks, or electronic fund transfers). However, in some cases agencies pay obligations without disbursing cash, and the budget nevertheless records outlays for the equivalent method. For example, the budget records outlays for the full amount of Federal employees' salaries, even though the cash disbursed to employees is net of Federal and State income taxes withheld, retirement contributions, life and health insurance premiums, and other deductions. (The budget also records receipts for the amounts withheld from Federal employee paychecks for Federal income taxes and other payments to the Government.) When debt instruments (bonds, debentures, notes, or monetary credits) are used in place of cash to pay obligations, the budget records outlays financed by an increase in agency debt. For example, the budget records the acquisition of physical assets through certain types of lease-purchase arrangements as though a cash disbursement were made for an outright purchase. The transaction creates a Government debt, and the cash lease payments are treated as repayments of principal and interest.

The budget records outlays for the interest on the public issues of Treasury debt securities as the interest accrues, not when the cash is paid. A small portion of Treasury debt consists of inflation-indexed securities, which feature monthly adjustments to principal for inflation and semi-annual payments of interest on the inflation-adjusted principal. As with fixed-rate securities, the budget records interest outlays as the interest accrues. The monthly adjustment to principal is recorded, simultaneously, as an increase in debt outstanding and an outlay of interest.

Most Treasury debt securities held by trust funds and other Government accounts are in the Government account series. The budget normally states the interest on these securities on a cash basis. When a Government account is invested in Federal debt securities, the purchase price is usually close or identical to the par (face) value of the security. The budget generally records the investment at par value and adjusts the interest paid by Treasury and collected by the account by the difference between purchase price and par, if any.

For Federal credit programs, outlays are equal to the subsidy cost of direct loans and loan guarantees and are recorded as the underlying loans are disbursed (see "Federal Credit" later in this chapter).

The budget records refunds of receipts that result from overpayments by the public (such as income taxes withheld in excess of tax liabilities) as reductions of receipts, rather than as outlays. However, the budget records payments to taxpayers for refundable tax credits (such as earned income tax credits) that exceed the taxpayer's tax liability as outlays. Similarly, when the Government makes overpayments that are later returned to the Government, those refunds to the Government are recorded as offsetting collections or offsetting receipts, not as governmental receipts.

Not all of the new budget authority for 2024 will be obligated or spent in 2024. Outlays during a fiscal year may liquidate obligations incurred in the same year or in prior years. Obligations, in turn, may be incurred against budget authority provided in the same year or against unobligated balances of budget authority provided in prior years. Outlays, therefore, flow in part from budget authority provided for the year in which the money is spent and in part from budget authority provided for prior years. The ratio of a given year's outlays resulting from budget authority enacted in that or a prior year to the original amount of that budget authority is referred to as the outlay rate for that year.

As shown in the accompanying chart, $5,382 billion of outlays in 2024 (78 percent of the outlay total) will be made from that year's $7,049 billion total of proposed new budget authority (a first-year outlay rate of 76 percent). Thus, the remaining $1,501 billion of outlays in 2024 (22 percent of the outlay total) will be made from budget authority enacted in previous years. At the same time, $1,667 billion of the new budget authority proposed for 2024 (24 percent of the total amount proposed) will not lead to outlays until future years.

As described earlier, the budget classifies budget authority and outlays as discretionary or mandatory. This classification of outlays measures the extent to which actual spending is controlled through the annual appropriations process. About 27 percent of total outlays in 2022 ($1,664 billion) were discretionary and the remaining 73 percent ($4,609 billion in 2022) were mandatory spending and net interest. Such a large portion of total spending is mandatory because authorizing rather than appropriations legislation determines net interest ($476 billion in 2022) and the spending for a few programs with large amounts of spending each year, such as Social Security ($1,212 billion in 2022) and Medicare ($747 billion in 2022).

The bulk of mandatory outlays flow from budget authority recorded in the same fiscal year. This is not necessarily the case for discretionary budget authority and outlays. For most major construction and procurement projects and long-term contracts, for example, the budget authority available at the time the projects are initiated covers the entire estimated cost of the project even though the work will take place and outlays will be made over a period extending beyond the year for which the budget authority is enacted. Similarly, discretionary budget authority for most education and job training activities is appropriated for school or program years that begin in the fourth quarter of the fiscal year. Most of these funds result in outlays in the year after the appropriation.

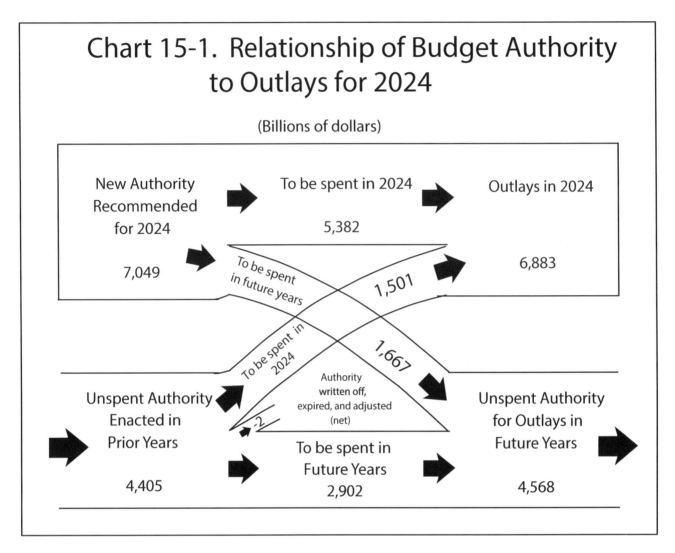

Chart 15-1. Relationship of Budget Authority to Outlays for 2024

(Billions of dollars)

New Authority Recommended for 2024 — 7,049

To be spent in 2024 — 5,382

Outlays in 2024 — 6,883

To be spent in future years — 1,501

To be spent in 2024 — 1,667

Authority written off, expired, and adjusted (net) — -2

Unspent Authority Enacted in Prior Years — 4,405

To be spent in Future Years — 2,902

Unspent Authority for Outlays in Future Years — 4,568

FEDERAL CREDIT

Some Government programs provide assistance through direct loans or loan guarantees. A ***direct loan*** is a disbursement of funds by the Government to a non-Federal borrower under a contract that requires repayment of such funds with or without interest and includes economically equivalent transactions, such as the sale of Federal assets on credit terms. A ***loan guarantee*** is any guarantee, insurance, or other pledge with respect to the payment of all or a part of the principal or interest on any debt obligation of a non-Federal borrower to a non-Federal lender. The Federal Credit Reform Act of 1990, as amended (FCRA), prescribes the budgetary treatment for Federal credit programs. Under this treatment, the budget records obligations and outlays up front, for the net cost to the Government, rather than recording the cash flows year by year over the term of the loan. FCRA treatment allows the comparison of direct loans and loan guarantees to each other, and to other methods of delivering assistance, such as grants.

The cost of direct loans and loan guarantees, sometimes called the "subsidy cost," is estimated as the present val-

ue of expected payments to and from the public over the term of the loan, discounted using appropriate Treasury interest rates.[2] Similar to most other kinds of programs, agencies can make loans or guarantee loans only if the Congress has appropriated funds sufficient to cover the subsidy costs, or provided a limitation in an appropriations act on the amount of direct loans or loan guarantees that can be made.

The budget records the subsidy cost to the Government arising from direct loans and loan guarantees—the budget authority and outlays—in ***credit program accounts***. When a Federal agency disburses a direct loan or when a non-Federal lender disburses a loan guaranteed by a Federal agency, the program account disburses or outlays an amount equal to the estimated present value cost, or subsidy, to a non-budgetary credit ***financing account***. The financing accounts record the actual transactions with the public. For a few programs, the estimated sub-

---

[2] Present value is a standard financial concept that considers the time-value of money. That is, it accounts for the fact that a given sum of money is worth more today than the same sum would be worth in the future because interest can be earned.

sidy cost is negative because the present value of expected Government collections exceeds the present value of expected payments to the public over the term of the loan. In such cases, the financing account pays the estimated subsidy cost to the program's negative subsidy receipt account, where it is recorded as an offsetting receipt. In a few cases, the offsetting receipts of credit accounts are dedicated to a special fund established for the program and are available for appropriation for the program.

The agencies responsible for credit programs must reestimate the subsidy cost of the outstanding portfolio of direct loans and loan guarantees each year. If the estimated cost increases, the program account makes an additional payment to the financing account equal to the change in cost. If the estimated cost decreases, the financing account pays the difference to the program's downward reestimate receipt account, where it is recorded as an offsetting receipt. FCRA provides permanent indefinite appropriations to pay for upward reestimates.

If the Government modifies the terms of an outstanding direct loan or loan guarantee in a way that increases the cost as the result of a law or the exercise of administrative discretion under existing law, the program account records obligations for the increased cost and outlays the amount to the financing account. As with the original subsidy cost, agencies may incur modification costs only if the Congress has appropriated funds to cover them. A modification may also reduce costs, in which case the amounts are generally returned to the general fund, as the financing account makes a payment to the program's negative subsidy receipt account.

Credit financing accounts record all cash flows arising from direct loan obligations and loan guarantee commitments. Such cash flows include all cash flows to and from the public, including direct loan disbursements and repayments, loan guarantee default payments, fees, and recoveries on defaults. Financing accounts also record intragovernmental transactions, such as the receipt of subsidy cost payments from program accounts, borrowing and repayments of Treasury debt to finance program activities, and interest paid to or received from the Treasury. The cash flows of direct loans and of loan guarantees are recorded in separate financing accounts for programs that provide both types of credit. The budget totals exclude the transactions of the financing accounts because they are not a cost to the Government. However, since financing accounts record all credit cash flows to and from the public, they affect the means of financing a budget surplus or deficit (see "Credit Financing Accounts" in the next section). The budget documents display the transactions of the financing accounts, together with the related program accounts, for information and analytical purposes.

The budgetary treatment of direct loan obligations and loan guarantee commitments made prior to 1992 was grandfathered in under FCRA. The budget records these on a cash basis in *credit liquidating accounts*, the same as they were recorded before FCRA was enacted. However, this exception ceases to apply if the direct loans or loan guarantees are modified as described above. In that case, the budget records the subsidy cost or savings of the modification, as appropriate, and begins to account for the associated transactions under FCRA treatment for direct loan obligations and loan guarantee commitments made in 1992 or later.

Under the authority provided in various acts, certain activities that do not meet the definition in FCRA of a direct loan or loan guarantee are reflected pursuant to FCRA. For example, the Emergency Economic Stabilization Act of 2008 (EESA) created the Troubled Asset Relief Program (TARP) under the Department of the Treasury, and authorized Treasury to purchase or guarantee troubled assets until October 3, 2010. Under the TARP, Treasury purchased equity interests in financial institutions. Section 123 of the EESA provides the Administration the authority to treat these equity investments on a FCRA basis, recording outlays for the subsidy as is done for direct loans and loan guarantees. The budget reflects the cost to the Government of TARP direct loans, loan guarantees, and equity investments consistent with the FCRA and Section 123 of EESA, which requires an adjustment to the FCRA discount rate for market risks. Similarly, Treasury equity purchases under the Small Business Lending Fund are treated pursuant to the FCRA, as provided by the Small Business Jobs Act of 2010. The Coronavirus Aid, Relief, and Economic Security (CARES) Act authorized certain investments in programs and facilities established by the Federal Reserve. Section 4003 of the CARES Act provided that these amounts be treated in accordance with FCRA.

BUDGET DEFICIT OR SURPLUS AND MEANS OF FINANCING

When outlays exceed receipts, the difference is a deficit, which the Government finances primarily by borrowing. When receipts exceed outlays, the difference is a surplus, and the Government automatically uses the surplus primarily to reduce debt. The Federal debt held by the public is approximately the cumulative amount of borrowing to finance deficits, less repayments from surpluses, over the Nation's history.

Borrowing is not exactly equal to the deficit, and debt repayment is not exactly equal to the surplus, because of the other transactions affecting borrowing from the public, or other means of financing, such as those discussed in this section. The factors included in the other means of financing can either increase or decrease the Government's borrowing needs (or decrease or increase its ability to repay debt). For example, the change in the Treasury operating cash balance is a factor included in other means of financing. Holding receipts and outlays constant, increases in the cash balance increase the Government's need to borrow or reduce the Government's ability to repay debt, and decreases in the cash balance decrease the need to borrow or increase the ability to repay debt. In some years, the net effect of the other means of financing is minor relative to the borrowing or debt repayment; in other years, the net effect may be significant.

Borrowing and Debt Repayment

The budget treats borrowing and debt repayment as a means of financing, not as receipts and outlays. If borrowing were defined as receipts and debt repayment as outlays, the budget would always be virtually balanced by definition. This rule applies both to borrowing in the form of Treasury securities and to specialized borrowing in the form of agency securities. The rule reflects the common-sense understanding that lending or borrowing is just an exchange of financial assets of equal value—cash for Treasury securities—and so is fundamentally different from, say, paying taxes, which involve a net transfer of financial assets from taxpayers to the Government.

In 2022, the Government borrowed $1,970 billion from the public, bringing debt held by the public to $24,252 billion. This borrowing financed the $1,376 billion deficit in that year, as well as the net impacts of the other means of financing, such as changes in cash balances and other accounts discussed below.

In addition to selling debt to the public, the Department of the Treasury issues debt to Government accounts, primarily trust funds that are required by law to invest in Treasury securities. Issuing and redeeming this debt does not affect the means of financing, because these transactions occur between one Government account and another and thus do not raise or use any cash for the Government as a whole.

(See Chapter 20 of this volume, "Federal Borrowing and Debt," for a fuller discussion of this topic.)

Exercise of Monetary Power

Seigniorage is the profit from coining money. It is the difference between the value of coins as money and their cost of production. Seigniorage reduces the Government's need to borrow. Unlike the payment of taxes or other receipts, it does not involve a transfer of financial assets from the public. Instead, it arises from the exercise of the Government's power to create money and the public's desire to hold financial assets in the form of coins. Therefore, the budget excludes seigniorage from receipts and treats it as a means of financing other than borrowing from the public. The budget also treats proceeds from the sale of gold as a means of financing, since the value of gold is determined by its value as a monetary asset rather than as a commodity.

Credit Financing Accounts

The budget records the net cash flows of credit programs in credit financing accounts. These accounts include the transactions for direct loan and loan guarantee programs, as well as the equity purchase programs under TARP that are recorded on a credit basis consistent with Section 123 of EESA. Financing accounts also record equity purchases under the Small Business Lending Fund consistent with the Small Business Jobs Act of 2010, and certain investments in programs and facilities established by the Federal Reserve consistent with Section 4003 of the CARES Act. Credit financing accounts are excluded from the budget because they are not allocations of resources by the Government (see "Federal Credit" earlier in this chapter). However, even though they do not affect the surplus or deficit, they can either increase or decrease the Government's need to borrow. Therefore, they are recorded as a means of financing.

Financing account disbursements to the public increase the requirement for Treasury borrowing in the same way as an increase in budget outlays. Financing account receipts from the public can be used to finance the payment of the Government's obligations and therefore reduce the requirement for Treasury borrowing from the public in the same way as an increase in budget receipts.

Deposit Fund Account Balances

The Treasury uses non-budgetary accounts, called deposit funds, to record cash held temporarily until ownership is determined (for example, earnest money paid by bidders for mineral leases) or cash held by the Government as agent for others (for example, State and local income taxes withheld from Federal employees' salaries and not yet paid to the State or local government or amounts held in the Thrift Savings Fund, a defined contribution pension fund held and managed in a fiduciary capacity by the Government). Deposit fund balances may be held in the form of either invested or uninvested balances. To the extent that they are not invested, changes in the balances are available to finance expenditures without a change in borrowing and are recorded as a means of financing other than borrowing from the public. To the extent that they are invested in Federal debt, changes in the balances are reflected as borrowing from the public (in lieu of borrowing from other parts of the public) and are not reflected as a separate means of financing.

United States Quota Subscriptions to the International Monetary Fund (IMF)

The United States participates in the IMF primarily through a quota subscription. Financial transactions with the IMF are exchanges of monetary assets. When the IMF temporarily draws dollars from the U.S. quota, the United States simultaneously receives an equal, offsetting, interest-bearing, Special Drawing Right (SDR)-denominated claim in the form of an increase in the U.S. reserve position in the IMF. The U.S. reserve position in the IMF increases when the United States makes deposits in its account at the IMF when the IMF temporarily uses members' quota resources to make loans and decreases when the IMF returns funds to the United States as borrowing countries repay the IMF (and the cash flows from the reserve position to the Treasury letter of credit).

The U.S. transactions with the IMF under the quota subscriptions do not increase the deficit in any year, and the budget excludes these transfers from budget outlays and receipts, consistent with the budgetary treatment for exchanges of monetary assets recommended by the President's Commission on Budget Concepts in 1967. The only exception is that interest earnings on U.S. deposits in its IMF account are recorded as offsetting receipts. Other exchanges of monetary assets, such as deposits of cash in Treasury accounts at commercial banks, are likewise not included in the Budget. However, the Congress has historically expressed interest in showing some kind of budgetary effect for U.S. transactions with the IMF.[3]

of the 2016 Budget. As discussed in that volume, the budgetary treatment of the U.S. participation in the NAB is similar to the quota. See pages 85-86 of the *Analytical Perspectives* volume of the 2018 Budget for a more complete discussion of the changes made to the budgetary presentation of quota increases in Title IX of the Department of State, Foreign Operations, and Related Programs Appropriations Act, 2016.

---

[3] For a more detailed discussion of the history of the budgetary treatment of U.S. participation in the quota and New Arrangements to Borrow (NAB), see pages 139-141 in the *Analytical Perspectives* volume

FEDERAL EMPLOYMENT

The Budget includes information on civilian and military employment. It also includes information on related personnel compensation and benefits and on staffing requirements at overseas missions. Chapter 13 of this volume, "Strengthening the Federal Workforce," provides employment levels measured in full-time equivalents (FTEs). Agency FTEs are the measure of total hours worked by an agency's Federal employees divided by the total number of one person's compensable work hours in a fiscal year.

BASIS FOR BUDGET FIGURES

Data for the Past Year

The past year column (2022) generally presents the actual transactions and balances as recorded in agency accounts and as summarized in the central financial reports prepared by the Department of the Treasury for the most recently completed fiscal year. Occasionally, the Budget reports corrections to data reported erroneously to Treasury but not discovered in time to be reflected in Treasury's published data. In addition, in certain cases the Budget has a broader scope and includes financial transactions that are not reported to Treasury (see Chapter 23 of this volume, "Comparison of Actual to Estimated Totals," for a summary of these differences).

Data for the Current Year

The current year column (2023) includes estimates of transactions and balances based on the amounts of budgetary resources that were available when the Budget was prepared. In cases where the Budget proposes policy changes effective in the current year, the data will also reflect the budgetary effect of those proposed changes.

Data for the Budget Year

The Budget year column (2024) includes estimates of transactions and balances based on the amounts of budgetary resources that are estimated to be available, including new budget authority requested under current authorizing legislation, and amounts estimated to result from changes in authorizing legislation and tax laws.

The Budget *Appendix* generally includes the appropriations language for the amounts proposed to be appropriated under current authorizing legislation. In a few cases, this language is transmitted later because the exact requirements are unknown when the budget is transmitted. The *Appendix* generally does not include appropriations language for the amounts that will be requested under proposed legislation; that language is usually transmitted later, after the legislation is enacted. Some tables in the budget identify the items for later transmittal and the related outlays separately. Estimates of the total requirements for the Budget year include both the amounts requested with the transmittal of the budget and the amounts planned for later transmittal.

Data for the Outyears

The Budget presents estimates for each of the nine years beyond the budget year (2025 through 2033) in order to reflect the effects of budget decisions on objectives and plans over a longer period.

Allowances

The budget may include lump-sum allowances to cover certain transactions that are expected to increase or decrease budget authority, outlays, or receipts but are not, for various reasons, reflected in the program details. For example, the budget might include an allowance to show the effect on the budget totals of a proposal that would affect many accounts by relatively small amounts, in order to avoid unnecessary detail in the presentations for the individual accounts.

Baseline

The Budget baseline is an estimate of the receipts, outlays, and deficits or surpluses that would occur if no changes were made to current laws and policies during the period covered by the Budget. Its construction is governed by rules codified in BBEDCA. The baseline assumes, with limited exceptions, that receipts and mandatory spending, which generally are authorized on a permanent basis, will continue in the future consistent with current law and policy. Funding for discretionary programs is inflated from the most recent enacted appropriations using specified inflation rates. In certain cases, adjustments to the BBEDCA baseline are needed to better represent the deficit outlook under current policy and to serve as a more appropriate benchmark against which to measure policy changes; this presentation is colloquially referred to as the "adjusted baseline." (Chapter 21 of this volume, "Current Services Estimates," provides more information on the baseline and adjustments in the 2024 Budget baseline.)

Baseline outlays represent the amount of resources that the Government would use over the period covered by the Budget on the basis of laws currently enacted.

The baseline serves several useful purposes:

- It may warn of future problems, either for Government fiscal policy as a whole or for individual tax and spending programs.

- It may provide a starting point for formulating the President's Budget.

- It may provide a benchmark against which the President's Budget and alternative proposals can be compared to assess the magnitude of proposed changes.

PRINCIPAL BUDGET LAWS

The Budget and Accounting Act of 1921 created the core of the current Federal budget process. Before enactment of this law, there was no annual centralized budgeting in the Executive Branch. Federal Government agencies usually sent budget requests independently to congressional committees with no coordination of the various requests in formulating the Federal Government's budget. The Budget and Accounting Act required the President to coordinate the budget requests for all Government agencies and to send a comprehensive budget to the Congress. The Congress has amended the requirements many times and portions of the Act are codified in Title 31, United States Code. The major laws that govern the budget process are as follows:

Article 1, section 8, clause 1 of the Constitution, which empowers the Congress to lay and collect taxes.

Article 1, section 9, clause 7 of the Constitution, which requires appropriations in law before money may be spent from the Treasury and the publication of a regular statement of the receipts and expenditures of all public money.

Antideficiency Act (codified in Chapters 13 and 15 of Title 31, United States Code), which prescribes rules and procedures for budget execution.

Balanced Budget and Emergency Deficit Control Act of 1985, as amended, which establishes limits on discretionary spending and provides mechanisms for enforcing mandatory spending and discretionary spending limits.

Chapter 11 of Title 31, United States Code, which prescribes procedures for submission of the President's budget and information to be contained in it.

Congressional Budget and Impoundment Control Act of 1974 (Public Law 93–344), as amended. This Act comprises the:

- *Congressional Budget Act of 1974*, as amended, which prescribes the congressional budget process;

- *Impoundment Control Act of 1974*, *as amended*, which controls certain aspects of budget execution; and

- *Federal Credit Reform Act of 1990, as amended (2 USC 661–661f)*, which the Budget Enforcement Act of 1990 included as an amendment to the Congressional Budget Act to prescribe the budget treatment for Federal credit programs.

Chapter 31 of Title 31, United States Code, which provides the authority for the Secretary of the Treasury to issue debt to finance the deficit and establishes a statutory limit on the level of the debt.

Chapter 33 of Title 31, United States Code, which establishes the Department of the Treasury as the authority for making disbursements of public funds, with the authority to delegate that authority to executive agencies in the interests of economy and efficiency.

Government Performance and Results Act of 1993 (Public Law 103–62, as amended), which emphasizes managing for results. It requires agencies to prepare strategic plans, annual performance plans, and annual performance reports.

Statutory Pay-As-You-Go Act of 2010, which establishes a budget enforcement mechanism generally requiring that direct spending and revenue legislation enacted into law not increase the deficit.

GLOSSARY OF BUDGET TERMS

Account refers to a separate financial reporting unit used by the Federal Government to record budget authority, outlays and income for budgeting or management information purposes as well as for accounting purposes. All budget (and off-budget) accounts are classified as being either expenditure or receipt accounts and by fund group. Budget (and off-budget) transactions fall within either of two fund groups: 1) Federal funds and 2) trust funds. (Cf. Federal funds group and trust funds group.)

Accrual method of measuring cost means an accounting method that records cost when the liability is incurred. As applied to Federal employee retirement benefits, accrual costs are recorded when the benefits are earned rather than when they are paid at some time in the future. The accrual method is used in part to provide data that assists in agency policymaking, but not used in presenting the overall budget of the United States Government.

Advance appropriation means appropriations of new budget authority that become available one or more fiscal years beyond the fiscal year for which the appropriation act was passed.

Advance funding means appropriations of budget authority provided in an appropriations act to be used, if necessary, to cover obligations incurred late in the fiscal year for benefit payments in excess of the amount specifically appropriated in the act for that year, where the budget authority is charged to the appropriation for the program for the fiscal year following the fiscal year for which the appropriations act is passed.

Agency means a Department or other establishment of the Government.

Allowance means a lump-sum included in the budget to represent certain transactions that are expected to increase or decrease budget authority, outlays, or receipts but that are not, for various reasons, reflected in the program details.

Balanced Budget and Emergency Deficit Control Act of 1985 (BBEDCA) refers to legislation that altered the budget process, primarily by replacing the earlier fixed targets for annual deficits with a Pay-As-You-Go requirement for new tax or mandatory spending legislation and with caps on annual discretionary funding. The Statutory Pay-As-You-Go Act of 2010, which is a standalone piece of legislation that did not directly amend the BBEDCA, reinstated a statutory pay-as-you-go rule for revenues and mandatory spending legislation, and the Budget Control Act of 2011, which did amend BBEDCA, reinstated discretionary caps on budget authority through 2021.

Balances of budget authority means the amounts of budget authority provided in previous years that have not been outlayed.

Baseline means a projection of the estimated receipts, outlays, and deficit or surplus that would result from continuing current law or current policies through the period covered by the budget.

Budget means the Budget of the United States Government, which sets forth the President's comprehensive financial plan for allocating resources and indicates the President's priorities for the Federal Government.

Budget authority (BA) means the authority provided by law to incur financial obligations that will result in outlays. (For a description of the several forms of budget authority, see "Budget Authority and Other Budgetary Resources" earlier in this chapter.)

Budget Control Act of 2011 refers to legislation that, among other things, amended BBEDCA to reinstate discretionary spending limits on budget authority through 2021 and restored the process for enforcing those spending limits. The legislation also increased the statutory debt ceiling; created a Joint Select Committee on Deficit Reduction that was instructed to develop a bill to reduce the Federal deficit by at least $1.5 trillion over a 10-year period; and provided a process to implement alternative spending reductions in the event that legislation achieving at least $1.2 trillion of deficit reduction was not enacted.

Budget resolution—see concurrent resolution on the budget.

Budget totals mean the totals included in the budget for budget authority, outlays, receipts, and the surplus or deficit. Some presentations in the budget distinguish on-budget totals from off-budget totals. On-budget totals reflect the transactions of all Federal Government entities except those excluded from the budget totals by law. Off-budget totals reflect the transactions of Government entities that are excluded from the on-budget totals by law. Under current law, the off-budget totals include the Social Security trust funds (Federal Old-Age and Survivors Insurance and Federal Disability Insurance Trust Funds) and the Postal Service Fund. The budget combines the on- and off-budget totals to derive unified (i.e. consolidated) totals for Federal activity.

Budget year refers to the fiscal year for which the budget is being considered, that is, with respect to a session of the Congress, the fiscal year of the Government that starts on October 1 of the calendar year in which that session of the Congress begins.

Budgetary resources mean amounts available to incur obligations in a given year. The term comprises new budget authority and unobligated balances of budget authority provided in previous years.

Cap means the legal limits for each fiscal year under BBEDCA on the budget authority and outlays (only if applicable) provided by discretionary appropriations.

Cap adjustment means either an increase or a decrease that is permitted to the statutory cap limits for each fiscal year under BBEDCA on the budget authority and outlays (only if applicable) provided by discretionary appropriations only if certain conditions are met. These conditions may include providing for a base level of funding, a designation of the increase or decrease by the Congress, (and in some circumstances, the President) pursuant to a section of the BBEDCA, or a change in concepts and definitions of funding under the cap. Changes in concepts and definitions require consultation with the Congressional Appropriations and Budget Committees. While there are no discretionary caps in place for 2024, the 2024 Budget retains several cap adjustments as "allocation adjustments" to be used pursuant to the Congressional Budget Act and included in the Congressional Budget Resolution.

Cash equivalent transaction means a transaction in which the Government makes outlays or receives collections in a form other than cash or the cash does not accurately measure the cost of the transaction. (For examples, see the section on "Outlays" earlier in this chapter.)

Collections mean money collected by the Government that the budget records as a governmental receipt, an offsetting collection, or an offsetting receipt.

Concurrent resolution on the budget refers to the concurrent resolution adopted by the Congress to set budgetary targets for appropriations, mandatory spending legislation, and tax legislation. These concurrent resolutions are required by the Congressional Budget Act of 1974, and are generally adopted annually.

Continuing resolution means an appropriations act that provides for the ongoing operation of the Government in the absence of enacted appropriations.

Cost refers to legislation or administrative actions that increase outlays or decrease receipts. (Cf. savings.)

Credit program account means a budget account that receives and obligates appropriations to cover the subsidy cost of a direct loan or loan guarantee and disburses the subsidy cost to a financing account.

Current services estimate—see Baseline.

Debt held by the public means the cumulative amount of money the Federal Government has borrowed from the public and not repaid.

Debt held by the public net of financial assets means the cumulative amount of money the Federal Government has borrowed from the public and not repaid, minus the current value of financial assets such as loan assets, bank deposits, or private-sector securities or equities held by the Government and plus the current value of financial liabilities other than debt.

Debt held by Government accounts means the debt the Department of the Treasury owes to accounts within the Federal Government. Most of it results from the surpluses of the Social Security and other trust funds, which are required by law to be invested in Federal securities.

Debt limit means the maximum amount of Federal debt that may legally be outstanding at any time. It includes both the debt held by the public and the debt held by Government accounts, but without accounting for offsetting financial assets. When the debt limit is reached, the Government cannot borrow more money until the Congress has enacted a law to increase the limit.

Deficit means the amount by which outlays exceed receipts in a fiscal year. It may refer to the on-budget, off-budget, or unified budget deficit.

Direct loan means a disbursement of funds by the Government to a non-Federal borrower under a contract that requires the repayment of such funds with or without interest. The term includes the purchase of, or participation in, a loan made by another lender. The term also includes the sale of a Government asset on credit terms of more than 90 days duration as well as financing arrangements for other transactions that defer payment for more than 90 days. It also includes loans financed by the Federal Financing Bank (FFB) pursuant to agency loan guarantee authority. The term does not include the acquisition of a federally guaranteed loan in satisfaction of default or other guarantee claims or the price support "loans" of the Commodity Credit Corporation. (Cf. loan guarantee.)

Direct spending—see mandatory spending.

Disaster funding means a discretionary appropriation that is enacted that the Congress designates as being for disaster relief. Such amounts are a cap adjustment to the limits on discretionary spending under BBEDCA. The total adjustment for this purpose cannot exceed a ceiling for a particular year that is defined as the total of the average funding provided for disaster relief over the previous 10 years (excluding the highest and lowest years) and the unused amount of the prior year's ceiling (excluding the portion of the prior year's ceiling that was itself due to any unused amount from the year before). Disaster relief is defined as activities carried out pursuant to a determination under section 102(2) of the Robert T. Stafford Disaster Relief and Emergency Assistance Act.

Discretionary spending means budgetary resources (except those provided to fund mandatory spending programs) provided in appropriations acts. (Cf. mandatory spending.)

Emergency requirement means an amount that the Congress has designated as an emergency requirement. Such amounts are not included in the estimated budgetary effects of PAYGO legislation under the requirements of the Statutory Pay-As-You-Go Act of 2010, if they are mandatory or receipts. Such a discretionary appropriation that is subsequently designated by the President as an emergency requirement results in a cap adjustment to the limits on discretionary spending under BBEDCA, when such limits are in place.

Entitlement refers to a program in which the Federal Government is legally obligated to make payments or provide aid to any person who, or State or local government that, meets the legal criteria for eligibility. Examples include Social Security, Medicare, Medicaid, and the Supplemental Nutrition Assistance Program (formerly Food Stamps).

Federal funds group refers to the moneys collected and spent by the Government through accounts other than those designated as trust funds. Federal funds include general, special, public enterprise, and intragovernmental funds. (Cf. trust funds group.)

Financing account means a non-budgetary account (an account whose transactions are excluded from the budget totals) that records all of the cash flows resulting from post-1991 direct loan obligations or loan guarantee commitments. At least one financing account is associated with each credit program account. For programs that make both direct loans and loan guarantees, separate financing accounts are required for direct loan cash flows and for loan guarantee cash flows. (Cf. liquidating account.)

Fiscal year means the Government's accounting period. It begins on October 1 and ends on September 30, and is designated by the calendar year in which it ends.

Forward funding means appropriations of budget authority that are made for obligation starting in the last quarter of the fiscal year for the financing of ongoing grant programs during the next fiscal year.

General fund means the accounts in which are recorded governmental receipts not earmarked by law for a specific purpose, the proceeds of general borrowing, and the expenditure of these moneys.

Government-sponsored enterprises mean private enterprises that were established and chartered by the Federal Government for public policy purposes. They are classified as non-budgetary and not included in the Federal budget because they are private companies, and their securities are not backed by the full faith and credit of the Federal Government. However, the budget presents statements of financial condition for certain Government sponsored enterprises such as the Federal National Mortgage Association. (Cf. off-budget.)

Intragovernmental fund—see Revolving fund.

Liquidating account means a budget account that records all cash flows to and from the Government resulting from pre-1992 direct loan obligations or loan guarantee commitments. (Cf. financing account.)

Loan guarantee means any guarantee, insurance, or other pledge with respect to the payment of all or a part of the principal or interest on any debt obligation of a non-Federal borrower to a non-Federal lender. The term does not include the insurance of deposits, shares, or other withdrawable accounts in financial institutions. (Cf. direct loan.)

Mandatory spending means spending controlled by laws other than appropriations acts (including spending for entitlement programs) and spending for the Supplemental Nutrition Assistance Program, formerly food stamps. Although the Statutory Pay-As-You-Go Act of 2010 uses the term direct spending to mean this, mandatory spending is commonly used instead. (Cf. discretionary spending.)

Means of financing refers to borrowing, the change in cash balances, and certain other transactions involved in financing a deficit. The term is also used to refer to the debt repayment, the change in cash balances, and certain other transactions involved in using a surplus. By definition, the means of financing are not treated as receipts or outlays and so are non-budgetary.

Obligated balance means the cumulative amount of budget authority that has been obligated but not yet outlayed. (Cf. unobligated balance.)

Obligation means a binding agreement that will result in outlays, immediately or in the future. Budgetary resources must be available before obligations can be incurred legally.

Off-budget refers to transactions of the Federal Government that would be treated as budgetary had the Congress not designated them by statute as "off-budget." Currently, transactions of the Social Security trust funds and the Postal Service are the only sets of transactions that are so designated. The term is sometimes used more broadly to refer to the transactions of private enterprises that were established and sponsored by the Government, most especially "Government-sponsored enterprises" such as the Federal Home Loan Banks. (Cf. budget totals.)

Offsetting collections mean collections that, by law, are credited directly to expenditure accounts and deducted from gross budget authority and outlays of the expenditure account, rather than added to receipts. Usually, they are authorized to be spent for the purposes of the account without further action by the Congress. They result from business-like transactions with the public, including payments from the public in exchange for goods and services, reimbursements for damages, and gifts or donations of money to the Government and from intragovernmental transactions with other Government accounts. The authority to spend offsetting collections is a form of budget authority. (Cf. receipts and offsetting receipts.)

Offsetting receipts mean collections that are credited to offsetting receipt accounts and deducted from gross budget authority and outlays, rather than added to receipts. They are not authorized to be credited to expenditure accounts. The legislation that authorizes the offsetting receipts may earmark them for a specific purpose and either appropriate them for expenditure for that purpose or require them to be appropriated in annual appropriation acts before they can be spent. Like offsetting collections, they result from business-like transactions or

market-oriented activities with the public, including payments from the public in exchange for goods and services, reimbursements for damages, and gifts or donations of money to the Government and from intragovernmental transactions with other Government accounts. (Cf. receipts, undistributed offsetting receipts, and offsetting collections.)

On-budget refers to all budgetary transactions other than those designated by statute as off-budget. (Cf. budget totals.)

Outlay means a payment to liquidate an obligation (other than the repayment of debt principal or other disbursements that are "means of financing" transactions). Outlays generally are equal to cash disbursements, but also are recorded for cash-equivalent transactions, such as the issuance of debentures to pay insurance claims, and in a few cases are recorded on an accrual basis such as interest on public issues of the public debt. Outlays are the measure of Government spending.

Outyear estimates mean estimates presented in the budget for the years beyond the budget year of budget authority, outlays, receipts, and other items (such as debt).

Overseas Contingency Operations/Global War on Terrorism (OCO/GWOT) means a discretionary appropriation that is enacted that the Congress and, subsequently, the President have so designated on an account by account basis. Such a discretionary appropriation that is designated as OCO/GWOT results in a cap adjustment to the limits on discretionary spending under BBEDCA, when such limits are in place. Funding for these purposes has most recently been associated with the wars in Iraq and Afghanistan.

Pay-as-you-go (PAYGO) refers to requirements of the Statutory Pay-As-You-Go Act of 2010 that result in a sequestration if the estimated combined result of new legislation affecting direct spending or revenue increases the on-budget deficit relative to the baseline, as of the end of a congressional session.

Public enterprise fund—see Revolving fund.

Reappropriation means a provision of law that extends into a new fiscal year the availability of unobligated amounts that have expired or would otherwise expire.

Receipts mean collections that result from the Government's exercise of its sovereign power to tax or otherwise compel payment. They are compared to outlays in calculating a surplus or deficit. (Cf. offsetting collections and offsetting receipts.)

Revolving fund means a fund that conducts continuing cycles of business-like activity, in which the fund charges for the sale of products or services and uses the proceeds to finance its spending, usually without requirement for annual appropriations. There are two types of revolving funds: Public enterprise funds, which conduct business-like operations mainly with the public, and intragovernmental revolving funds, which conduct business-like operations mainly within and between Government agencies. (Cf. special fund and trust fund.)

Savings refers to legislation or administrative actions that decrease outlays or increase receipts. (Cf. cost.)

Scorekeeping means measuring the budget effects of legislation, generally in terms of budget authority, receipts, and outlays, for purposes of measuring adherence to the Budget or to budget targets established by the Congress, as through agreement to a Budget Resolution.

Sequestration means the cancellation of budgetary resources. The Statutory Pay-As-You-Go Act of 2010 requires such cancellations if revenue or direct spending legislation is enacted that, in total, increases projected deficits or reduces projected surpluses relative to the baseline. The Balanced Budget and Emergency Deficit Control Act of 1985, as amended, requires annual across-the-board cancellations to selected mandatory programs through 2031.

Special fund means a Federal fund account for receipts or offsetting receipts earmarked for specific purposes and the expenditure of these receipts. (Cf. revolving fund and trust fund.)

Statutory Pay-As-You-Go Act of 2010 refers to legislation that reinstated a statutory pay-as-you-go requirement for new tax or mandatory spending legislation. The law is a standalone piece of legislation that cross-references BBEDCA but does not directly amend that legislation. This is a permanent law and does not expire.

Subsidy means the estimated long-term cost to the Government of a direct loan or loan guarantee, calculated on a net present value basis, excluding administrative costs and any incidental effects on governmental receipts or outlays.

Surplus means the amount by which receipts exceed outlays in a fiscal year. It may refer to the on-budget, off-budget, or unified budget surplus.

Supplemental appropriation means an appropriation enacted subsequent to a regular annual appropriations act, when the need for additional funds is too urgent to be postponed until the next regular annual appropriations act.

Trust fund refers to a type of account, designated by law as a trust fund, for receipts or offsetting receipts dedicated to specific purposes and the expenditure of these receipts. Some revolving funds are designated as trust funds, and these are called trust revolving funds. (Cf. special fund and revolving fund.)

Trust funds group refers to the moneys collected and spent by the Government through trust fund accounts. (Cf. Federal funds group.)

Undistributed offsetting receipts mean offsetting receipts that are deducted from the Government-wide totals for budget authority and outlays instead of being offset against a specific agency and function. (Cf. offsetting receipts.)

Unified budget includes receipts from all sources and outlays for all programs of the Federal Government, including both on- and off-budget programs. It is the most comprehensive measure of the Government's annual finances.

Unobligated balance means the cumulative amount of budget authority that remains available for obligation under law in unexpired accounts. The term "expired balances available for adjustment only" refers to unobligated amounts in expired accounts.

User charges are charges assessed for the provision of Government services and for the sale or use of Government goods or resources. The payers of the user charge must be limited in the authorizing legislation to those receiving special benefits from, or subject to regulation by, the program or activity beyond the benefits received by the general public or broad segments of the public (such as those who pay income taxes or custom duties).

16. COVERAGE OF THE BUDGET

The Federal budget is the central instrument of national policy making. It is the Government's financial plan for proposing and deciding the allocation of resources to serve national objectives. The budget provides information on the cost and scope of Federal activities to inform decisions and to serve as a means to control the allocation of resources. When enacted, it establishes the level of public goods and services provided by the Government.

Federal Government activities can be either "budgetary" or "non-budgetary." Those activities that involve direct and measurable allocation of Federal resources are budgetary. The payments to and from the public resulting from budgetary activities are included in the budget's accounting of outlays and receipts. Federal activities that do not involve direct and measurable allocation of Federal resources are non-budgetary and are not included in the budget's accounting of outlays and receipts. More detailed information about outlays and receipts may be found in Chapter 15, "Budget Concepts," of this volume.

The budget documents include information on some non-budgetary activities because they can be important instruments of Federal policy and provide insight into the scope and nature of Federal activities. For example, the budget documents show the transactions of the Thrift Savings Program (TSP), a collection of investment funds managed by the Federal Retirement Thrift Investment Board (FRTIB). Despite the fact that the FRTIB is budgetary and one of the TSP funds is invested entirely in Federal securities, the transactions of these funds are non-budgetary because current and retired Federal employees own the funds. The Government manages these funds only in a fiduciary capacity.

The budget also includes information on cash flows that are a means of financing Federal activity, such as for credit financing accounts. However, to avoid double-counting, means of financing amounts are not included in the estimates of outlays or receipts because the costs of the underlying Federal activities are already reflected in the deficit.[1] This chapter provides details about the budgetary and non-budgetary activities of the Federal Government.

Budgetary Activities

The Federal Government has used the unified budget concept—which consolidates outlays and receipts from Federal funds and trust funds, including the Social Security trust funds—since 1968, starting with the 1969 Budget. The 1967 President's Commission on Budget Concepts (the Commission) recommended the change to include the financial transactions of all of the Federal Government's programs and agencies. Thus, the budget includes information on the financial transactions of all 15 Executive Departments, all independent agencies (from all three branches of Government), and all Government corporations.[2]

The budget shows outlays and receipts for on-budget and off-budget activities separately to reflect the legal distinction between the two. Although there is a legal distinction between on-budget and off-budget activities, conceptually there is no difference between them. Off-budget Federal activities reflect the same kinds of governmental roles as on-budget activities and result in outlays and receipts. Like on-budget activities, the Government funds and controls off-budget activities. The "unified budget" reflects the conceptual similarity between on-budget and off-budget activities by showing combined totals of outlays and receipts for both.

Many Government corporations are entities with business-type operations that charge the public for services at prices intended to allow the entity to be self-sustaining, although some operate at a loss in order to provide subsidies to specific recipients. Often these entities are more independent than other agencies and have limited exemptions from certain Federal personnel requirements to allow for flexibility.

All accounts in Table 25-1, "Federal Budget by Agencies and Account," in the supplemental materials to this volume are budgetary. The majority of budgetary accounts are associated with the Departments or other entities that are clearly Federal agencies. Some budgetary accounts reflect Government payments to entities that the Government created or chartered as private or non-Federal entities. Some of these entities receive all or a majority of their funding from the Government. These include the Corporation for Public Broadcasting, Gallaudet University, Howard University, the Legal Services Corporation, the National Railroad Passenger Corporation (Amtrak), the Smithsonian Institution, the State Justice Institute, and the United States Institute of Peace. A related example is the Standard Setting Body, which is not a federally created entity but since 2003 has received a majority of funding through a federally mandated assessment on public companies under the Sarbanes-Oxley Act.

---

[1] For more information on means of financing, see the "Budget Deficit or Surplus and Means of Financing" section of Chapter 15, "Budget Concepts," in this volume.

[2] Government corporations are Government entities that are defined as corporations pursuant to the Government Corporation Control Act, as amended (31 U.S.C. 9101), or elsewhere in law. Examples include the Commodity Credit Corporation, the Export-Import Bank of the United States, the Federal Crop Insurance Corporation, the Federal Deposit Insurance Corporation, the Millennium Challenge Corporation, the Overseas Private Investment Corporation (now the U.S. International Development Finance Corporation), the Pension Benefit Guaranty Corporation, the Tennessee Valley Authority, the African Development Foundation (22 U.S.C. 290h-6), the Inter-American Foundation (22 U.S.C. 290f), the Presidio Trust (16 U.S.C. 460bb note), and the Valles Caldera Trust (16 U.S.C. 698v-4).

Although the Federal payments to these entities are budgetary, the entities themselves are non-budgetary.

Whether the Government created or chartered an entity does not alone determine its budgetary status. The Commission recommended that the budget be comprehensive but it also recognized that proper budgetary classification required weighing all relevant factors regarding establishment, ownership, and control of an entity while erring on the side of inclusiveness. Generally, entities that are primarily Government owned or controlled are classified as budgetary. OMB determines the budgetary classification of entities in consultation with the Congressional Budget Office (CBO) and the Budget Committees of the Congress.

One recent example of a budgetary classification was for the Puerto Rico Financial Oversight Board, created in June 2016 by the Puerto Rico Oversight, Management, and Economic Stability Act (Public Law 114–187). By statute, this oversight board is not a Department, Agency, establishment, or instrumentality of the Federal Government, but is an entity within the territorial government financed entirely by the territorial government. Because the flow of funds from the Territory to the oversight board is mandated by Federal law, the budget reflects the allocation of resources by the territorial government to the territorial entity as a receipt from the territorial government and an equal outlay to the oversight board, with net zero deficit impact. Because the oversight board itself is not a Federal entity, its operations are not included in the budget.

Another example involves the National Association of Registered Agents and Brokers (NARAB) (15 U.S.C. 6751-64), established by statute in 2015. NARAB allows for the adoption and application of insurance licensing, continuing education, and other nonresident producer qualification requirements on a multi-State basis. In other words, NARAB streamlines the ability of a nonresident insurer to become a licensed agent in another State. In exchange for providing enhanced market access, NARAB collects fees from its members. In addition to being statutorily established—which in itself is an indication that the entity is governmental for budget purposes—NARAB's board of directors is appointed by the President and confirmed by the Senate. It must also submit bylaws and an annual report to the Department of the Treasury and its primary function involves exercising a regulatory function.

Off-budget Federal activities.—Despite the Commission's recommendation that the budget be comprehensive, every year since 1971 at least one Federal program or Agency has been presented as off-budget because of a legal requirement.[3] The Government funds such off-budget Federal activities and administers them according to Federal legal requirements. However, their net costs are excluded, by law, from the rest of the budget totals, also known as the "on-budget" totals.

Off-budget Federal activities currently consist of the U.S. Postal Service and the two Social Security trust funds: Old-Age and Survivors Insurance and Disability Insurance. Social Security has been classified as off-budget since 1986 and the Postal Service has been classified as off-budget since 1990.[4] Other activities that were designated in law as off-budget at various times before 1986 have been classified as on-budget by law since at least 1985 as a result of the Balanced Budget and Emergency Deficit Control Act of 1985 (Public Law 99–177). Activities that were off-budget at one time but that are now on-budget are classified as on-budget for all years in historical budget data.

Social Security is the largest single program in the unified budget and it is classified by law as off-budget; as a result, the off-budget accounts constitute a significant part of total Federal spending and receipts. Table 16–1 divides total Federal Government outlays, receipts, and the surplus or deficit between on-budget and off-budget amounts. Within this table, the Social Security and Postal Service transactions are classified as off-budget for all years to provide a consistent comparison over time.

Non-Budgetary Activities

The Government characterizes some important Government activities as non-budgetary because they do not involve the direct allocation of resources.[5] These activities can affect budget outlays or receipts even though they have non-budgetary components.

Federal credit programs: budgetary and non-budgetary transactions.—Federal credit programs make direct loans or guarantee private loans to non-Federal borrowers. The Federal Credit Reform Act of 1990 (FCRA) (2 U.S.C. 661-661f) established the current budgetary treatment for credit programs. Under FCRA, the budgetary cost of a credit program, known as the "subsidy cost," is the estimated lifetime cost to the Government of a loan or a loan guarantee on a net present value basis, excluding administrative costs.

Outlays equal to the subsidy cost are recorded in the budget up front, as they are incurred—for example, when a loan is made or guaranteed. Credit program cash flows to and from the public are recorded in non-budgetary

---

[3] While the term "off-budget" is sometimes used colloquially to mean non-budgetary, the term has a meaning distinct from non-budgetary. Off-budget activities would be considered budgetary, absent legal requirement to exclude these activities from the budget totals.

[4] See 42 U.S.C. 911 and 39 U.S.C. 2009a, respectively. The off-budget Postal Service accounts consist of the Postal Service Fund, which is classified as a mandatory account, and the Office of the Inspector General and the Postal Regulatory Commission, both of which are classified as discretionary accounts. The Postal Service Retiree Health Benefits Fund is an on-budget mandatory account with the Office of Personnel Management. The off-budget Social Security accounts consist of the Federal Old-Age and Survivors Insurance trust fund and the Federal Disability Insurance trust fund, both of which have mandatory and discretionary funding.

[5] Tax expenditures, which are discussed in Chapter 19 of this volume, are an example of Government activities that could be characterized as either budgetary or non-budgetary. Tax expenditures refer to the reduction in tax receipts resulting from the special tax treatment accorded certain private activities. Because tax expenditures reduce tax receipts and receipts are budgetary, tax expenditures clearly have budgetary effects. However, the size and composition of tax expenditures are not explicitly recorded in the budget as outlays or as negative receipts and, for this reason, tax expenditures might be considered a special case of non-budgetary transactions.

financing accounts and the information is included in budget documents to provide insight into the program size and costs. For more information about the mechanisms of credit programs, see Chapter 15 of this volume, "Budget Concepts." More detail on credit programs is in Chapter 7 of this volume, "Credit and Insurance."

Deposit funds.—Deposit funds are non-budgetary accounts that record amounts held by the Government temporarily until ownership is determined (such as earnest money paid by bidders for mineral leases) or held by the Government as an agent for others (such as State income taxes withheld from Federal employees' salaries and not yet paid to the States). The largest deposit fund is the Government Securities Investment Fund, also known as the G-Fund, which is part of the TSP, the Government's defined contribution retirement plan. The Federal Retirement Thrift Investment Board manages the fund's investment for Federal employees who participate in the TSP (which is similar to private-sector 401(k) plans). The Department of the Treasury holds the G-Fund assets, which are the property of Federal employees, only in a fiduciary capacity; the transactions of the Fund are not resource allocations by the Government and are therefore non-budgetary.[6] For similar reasons, Native American-owned funds that are held and managed in a fiduciary capacity are also excluded from the budget.

Government-Sponsored Enterprises (GSEs).— GSEs are privately owned and therefore distinct from Government corporations. The Federal Government has chartered GSEs such as the Federal National Mortgage Association (Fannie Mae), the Federal Home Loan Mortgage Corporation (Freddie Mac), the Federal Home Loan Banks, the Farm Credit System, and the Federal Agricultural Mortgage Corporation to provide financial intermediation for specified public purposes. Although federally chartered to serve public-policy purposes, GSEs are classified as non-budgetary because they are intended to be privately owned and controlled—with any public benefits accruing indirectly from the GSEs' business transactions. Estimates of the GSEs' activities can be found in a separate chapter of the Budget *Appendix*, and their activities are discussed in Chapter 7 of this volume, "Credit and Insurance."

In September 2008, in response to the financial market crisis, the director of the Federal Housing Finance Agencies (FHFA)[7] placed Fannie Mae and Freddie Mac into conservatorship for the purpose of preserving the assets and restoring the solvency of these two GSEs. As conservator, FHFA has broad authority to direct the operations of these GSEs. However, these GSEs remain private companies with boards of directors and management responsible for their day-to-day operations. The Budget continues to treat these two GSEs as non-budgetary private entities in conservatorship rather than as Government agencies. By contrast, CBO treats these

GSEs as budgetary Federal agencies. Both treatments include budgetary and non-budgetary amounts.

While OMB reflects all of the GSEs' transactions with the public as non-budgetary, the payments from the Treasury to the GSEs are recorded as budgetary outlays and dividends received by the Treasury are recorded as budgetary receipts. Under CBO's approach, the subsidy costs of Fannie Mae's and Freddie Mac's past credit activities are treated as having already been recorded in the budget estimates; the subsidy costs of future credit activities will be recorded when the activities occur. Lending and borrowing activities between the GSEs and the public apart from the subsidy costs are treated as non-budgetary by CBO, and Treasury payments to the GSEs are intra-governmental transfers (from Treasury to the GSEs) that net to zero in CBO's budget estimates.

Overall, both the budget's accounting and CBO's accounting present Fannie Mae's and Freddie Mac's gains and losses as Government receipts and outlays, which reduce or increase Government deficits. The two approaches, however, reflect the effect of the gains and losses in the budget at different times.

Other federally created non-budgetary entities.— In addition to the GSEs, the Federal Government has created a number of other entities that are classified as non-budgetary. These include federally funded research and development centers (FFRDCs), non-appropriated fund instrumentalities (NAFIs), and other entities; some of these are non-profit entities and some are for-profit entities.[8]

FFRDCs are entities that conduct agencies-specific research under contract or cooperative agreement. Some FFRDCs were created to conduct research for the Department of Defense but are administered by colleges, universities, or other non-profit entities. Despite this non-budgetary classification, many FFRDCs receive direct resource allocation from the Government and are included as budget lines in various agencies. Examples of FFRDCs include the Center for Naval Analysis and the

---

[6] The administrative functions of the Federal Retirement Thrift Investment Board are carried out by Government employees and included in the budget totals.

[7] FHFA is the regulator of Fannie Mae, Freddie Mac, and the Federal Home Loan Banks.

[8] Although most entities created by the Federal Government are budgetary, the Congress and the President have chartered, but not necessarily created, approximately 100 non-profit entities that are non-budgetary. These include patriotic, charitable, and educational organizations under Title 36 of the U.S. Code and foundations and trusts chartered under other titles of the Code. Title 36 corporations include the American Legion, the American National Red Cross, Big Brothers—Big Sisters of America, Boy Scouts of America, Future Farmers of America, Girl Scouts of the United States of America, the National Academy of Public Administration, the National Academies of Sciences, Engineering, and Medicine, and Veterans of Foreign Wars of the United States. Virtually all of the non-profit entities chartered by the Government existed under State law prior to the granting of a Government charter, making the Government charter an honorary rather than governing charter. A major exception to this is the American National Red Cross. Its Government charter requires it to provide disaster relief and to ensure compliance with treaty obligations under the Geneva Convention. Although any Government payments (whether made as direct appropriations or through agencies appropriations) to these chartered non-profits, including the Red Cross, would be budgetary, the non-profits themselves are classified as non-budgetary. On April 29, 2015, the Subcommittee on Immigration and Border Security of the Committee on the Judiciary in the U.S. House of Representatives adopted a policy prohibiting the Congress from granting new Federal charters to private, non-profit organizations.

Jet Propulsion Laboratory.[9] Even though FFRDCs are non-budgetary, Federal payments to the FFRDC are budget outlays. In addition to Federal funding, FFRDCs may receive funding from non-Federal sources.

Non-appropriated fund instrumentalities (NAFIs) are entities that support an agencies's current and retired personnel. Nearly all NAFIs are associated with the Departments of Defense, Homeland Security (Coast Guard), and Veterans Affairs. Most NAFIs are located on military bases and include the Armed Forces exchanges (which sell goods to military personnel and their families), recreational facilities, and childcare centers. NAFIs are financed by proceeds from the sale of goods or services and do not receive direct appropriations; thus, they are characterized as non-budgetary but any agencies payments to the NAFIs are recorded as budget outlays.

A number of entities created by the Government receive a significant amount of non-Federal funding. Non-Federal individuals or organizations significantly control some of these entities. These entities include Gallaudet University, Howard University, Amtrak, and the Universal Services Administrative Company, among others. Most of these entities receive direct appropriations or other recurring payments from the Government. The appropriations or other payments are budgetary and included in Table 25-1. However, many of these entities are themselves non-budgetary. Generally, entities that receive a significant portion of funding from non-Federal sources but are not controlled by the Government are non-budgetary.

Regulation.—Federal Government regulations often require the private sector or other levels of government to make expenditures for specified purposes that are intended to have public benefits, such as workplace safety and pollution control. Although the budget reflects the Government's cost of conducting regulatory activities, the costs imposed on the private sector as a result of regulation are treated as non-budgetary and not included in the budget. The annual Regulatory Plan and the semi-annual Unified Agenda of Federal Regulatory and Deregulatory Actions describe the Government's regulatory priorities and plans.[10] OMB regularly publishes reports summarizing agency estimates of the costs and benefits of Federal regulation.[11]

Monetary policy.—As a fiscal policy tool, the budget is used by elected Government officials to promote economic growth and achieve other public policy objectives. Monetary policy is another tool that governments use to promote economic policy objectives. In the United States, the Federal Reserve System—which is composed of a Board of Governors and 12 regional Federal Reserve Banks—conducts monetary policy. The Federal Reserve Act provides that the goal of monetary policy is to "maintain long-run growth of the monetary and credit aggregates commensurate with the economy's long run potential to increase production, so as to promote effectively the goals of maximum employment, stable prices, and moderate long-term interest rates."[12] The Full Employment and Balanced Growth Act of 1978, also known as the Humphrey-Hawkins Act, reaffirmed the dual goals of full employment and price stability.[13]

By law, the Federal Reserve System is a self-financing entity that is independent of the Executive Branch and subject only to broad oversight by the Congress. Consistent with the recommendations of the Commission, the effects of monetary policy and the actions of the Federal Reserve System are non-budgetary, with exceptions for the transfer to the Treasury of excess income generated through its operations. The Federal Reserve System earns income from a variety of sources including interest on Government securities, foreign currency investments and loans to depository institutions, and fees for services (e.g., check clearing services) provided to depository institutions. The Federal Reserve System remits to Treasury any excess income over expenses annually. For the fiscal year ending September 2022, Treasury recorded $106.7 billion in receipts from the Federal Reserve System. In addition to remitting excess income to Treasury, the Dodd-Frank Wall Street Reform and Consumer Protection Act requires the Federal Reserve to transfer a portion of its excess earnings to the Consumer Financial Protection Bureau (CFPB).[14]

The Board of Governors of the Federal Reserve is a Federal Government agencies, but because of its independent status, its budget is not subject to Executive Branch review and is included in the Budget *Appendix* for informational purposes only. The Federal Reserve Banks are subject to Board oversight and managed by boards of directors chosen by the Board of Governors and member banks, which include all national banks and State banks that choose to become members. The budgets of the regional Banks are subject to approval by the Board of Governors and are not included in the Budget *Appendix*.

---

[12] See 12 U.S.C. 225a.

[13] See 15 U.S.C. 3101 et seq.

[14] See section 1017 of Public Law 111-203 (12 U.S.C. 5497).

---

[9] The National Science Foundation maintains a list of FFRDCs at https://www.nsf.gov/statistics/ffrdc/.

[10] The most recent Regulatory Plan and introduction to the Unified Agenda issued by the General Services Administration's Regulatory Information Service Center are available at https://www.reginfo.gov/ and at https://www.gpo.gov/.

[11] In the 2018, 2019, and 2020 report, OMB indicates that for the five rules for which monetized costs and benefits were estimated in 2019, the issuing agencies estimated a total of $0.2 to $3.7 billion in annual benefits and up to $0.6 billion in annual costs, in 2018 dollars. These totals include only the benefits and costs for the minority of rules for which both those categories of impacts were estimated. The most recent report is available at https://www.whitehouse.gov/omb/information-regulatory-affairs/reports/#ORC.

17. GOVERNMENTAL RECEIPTS

This chapter presents the Budget's estimates of taxes and governmental receipts including the effects of tax legislation enacted in 2022, discusses the provisions of those enacted laws, and introduces the Administration's additional receipt proposals.

ESTIMATES OF GOVERNMENTAL RECEIPTS

Governmental receipts are taxes and other collections from the public that result from the exercise of the Federal Government's sovereign or governmental powers. The difference between governmental receipts and outlays is the surplus or deficit.

The Federal Government also collects income from the public through market-oriented activities. Collections from these activities are subtracted from gross outlays, rather than added to taxes and other governmental receipts, and are discussed in Chapter 18, "Offsetting Collections and Offsetting Receipts," in this volume.

Total governmental receipts (hereafter referred to as "receipts") are estimated to be $4,802.5 billion in 2023, a decrease of $94.9 billion or 1.9 percent from 2022. The estimated decrease in 2023 is largely due to decreases in individual income taxes, as collections return to normal after historically high capital gains realizations in tax year 2021. Receipts in 2023 are estimated to be 18.2 percent of Gross Domestic Product (GDP), which is lower than in 2022 when receipts were 19.6 percent of GDP.

Receipts in the 2024 Budget are estimated to rise to $5,036.4 billion in 2024, an increase of $23.9 billion or 4.9 percent relative to 2023. Receipts are projected to grow at an average annual rate of 6.2 percent between 2024 and 2028, rising to $6,399.5 billion. Receipts are projected to rise to $7,991.3 billion in 2033, growing at an average annual rate of 4.5 percent between 2028 and 2033. This growth is largely due to assumed increases in incomes resulting from both real economic growth and inflation, along with tax reforms.

As a share of GDP, receipts are projected to increase slightly from 18.2 percent in 2023 to 18.5 percent in 2024, and to increase steadily to 20.1 percent in 2033.

Table 17–1. RECEIPTS BY SOURCE—SUMMARY
(In billions of dollars)

	2022 Actual	Estimate										
		2023	2024	2025	2026	2027	2028	2029	2030	2031	2032	2033
Individual income taxes	2,632.1	2,327.9	2,390.0	2,617.3	2,849.1	3,029.0	3,205.9	3,366.3	3,542.6	3,731.9	3,948.1	4,154.5
Corporation income taxes	424.9	546.0	666.2	733.1	733.9	740.1	759.1	763.3	763.1	771.1	778.6	803.4
Social insurance and retirement receipts	1,483.5	1,675.2	1,742.1	1,820.6	1,909.1	1,990.9	2,094.3	2,182.0	2,276.8	2,373.1	2,472.9	2,613.4
(On-budget)	(417.6)	(477.1)	(533.9)	(557.3)	(584.4)	(611.7)	(644.5)	(673.5)	(703.8)	(733.5)	(766.0)	(808.8)
(Off-budget)	(1,066.0)	(1,198.1)	(1,208.2)	(1,263.3)	(1,324.7)	(1,379.2)	(1,449.7)	(1,508.4)	(1,573.0)	(1,639.6)	(1,706.9)	(1,804.6)
Excise taxes	87.7	91.5	114.1	114.4	118.6	120.7	121.5	124.8	128.4	130.1	136.9	140.9
Estate and gift taxes	32.6	20.9	25.3	28.3	29.1	44.9	47.5	51.7	52.1	57.0	62.5	67.6
Customs duties	99.9	101.7	60.7	49.8	52.3	54.3	56.2	58.1	60.2	62.5	54.7	57.2
Miscellaneous receipts	136.7	39.4	38.0	56.0	80.5	100.6	115.2	123.2	129.5	138.5	147.4	154.4
Total, receipts	**4,897.4**	**4,802.5**	**5,036.4**	**5,419.5**	**5,772.6**	**6,080.5**	**6,399.5**	**6,669.4**	**6,952.8**	**7,264.2**	**7,601.1**	**7,991.3**
(On-budget)	(3,831.4)	(3,604.4)	(3,828.2)	(4,156.2)	(4,447.9)	(4,701.3)	(4,949.8)	(5,160.9)	(5,379.8)	(5,624.6)	(5,894.2)	(6,186.8)
(Off-budget)	(1,066.0)	(1,198.1)	(1,208.2)	(1,263.3)	(1,324.7)	(1,379.2)	(1,449.7)	(1,508.4)	(1,573.0)	(1,639.6)	(1,706.9)	(1,804.6)
Total receipts as a percentage of GDP	19.6	18.2	18.5	19.1	19.5	19.7	19.9	19.9	19.9	19.9	20.0	20.1

LEGISLATION ENACTED IN 2022 THAT AFFECTS GOVERNMENTAL RECEIPTS

Six laws were enacted during 2022 that affect receipts. The major provisions of those laws that have a significant impact on receipts are described below. [1]

ENDING IMPORTATION OF RUSSIAN OIL ACT (Public Law 117–109)

The Act, which was signed into law on April 8, 2022, prohibits the importation of energy products from Russia

---

[1] In the discussions of enacted legislation, years referred to are calendar years, unless otherwise noted.

that are classified under chapter 27 of the Harmonized Tariff Schedule.

SUSPENDING NORMAL TRADE RELATIONS WITH RUSSIA AND BELARUS ACT (Public Law 117–110)

The Act, which was signed into law on April 8, 2022, authorizes the President to proclaim increases in the rates of duty applicable to products of Russia or Belarus. This authority terminates on January 1, 2024.

FORMULA ACT (Public Law 117–160)

The Act, which was signed into law on July 21, 2022, provides through December 31, 2022, duty-free treatment to infant formula.

AN ACT MAKING APPROPRIATIONS FOR LEGISLATIVE BRANCH FOR THE FISCAL YEAR ENDING SEPTEMBER 30, 2022, AND FOR OTHER PURPOSES (Public Law 117–167)

The Act, commonly referred to as the "CHIPS and Science Act of 2022," was signed into law on August 9, 2022, and provides a 25 percent investment tax credit for investments in semiconductor manufacturing.

INFLATION REDUCTION ACT (Public Law 117–169)

The Act, which was signed into law on August 16, 2022, reduces the deficit by asking the largest corporations to pay their fair share, makes the tax code fairer, and helps families save money on their energy bills while accelerating the deployment of clean energy technology to combat the climate crisis. Major provisions of the law include:

Making corporations pay their fair share.–The Act imposes a 15 percent minimum alternative tax beginning tax years after 2022 on corporations with a three-year average income of more than $1 billion, determined on the basis of the corporation's adjusted financial statement income (i.e., book income). It imposes a one percent excise tax of the fair market value of any repurchased stock during the taxable year by a publicly traded U.S. corporation. The law imposes an excise tax on the sale by the manufacturer, producer, or importer of any selected drug who fails to enter into a drug pricing agreement.

Enforcing collection of taxes already owed.–The Act appropriates funding for Internal Revenue Service enforcement activities, operations support, business sys-

tems modernization, and taxpayer services, available through 2031, which is expected to reduce the tax gap by improving taxpayer compliance.

Lowering energy costs while reducing harmful pollution.–The Act includes various green energy tax credits and incentives for businesses and individuals, including: a production tax credit for electricity generated from renewable energy sources; a new tax credit for qualifying zero-emission nuclear power produced by facilities placed in service prior to enactment; the extension of the residential clean energy efficient credit for qualified energy efficiency improvements; an advanced manufacturing production credit for projects beginning in 2023; and new clean electricity production and investment credits; and tax credits related to electric vehicles, including credits for the purchase of clean and plug-in vehicles.

CONSOLIDATED APPROPRIATIONS ACT, 2023 (Public Law 117–328)

The Act, which was signed into law on December 29, 2022, includes the SECURE 2.0 Act of 2022, which makes numerous changes to retirement law. It requires that employee-sponsored retirement plans automatically enroll all eligible employees with a contribution rate in the first year of at least three percent up to a maximum of 10 percent, with certain exceptions for new and small businesses. It improves access to retirement accounts for part time workers who have completed 500 hours of service for two consecutive years. It increases the three-year small business startup credit from 50 to 100 percent for employers with up to 50 employees. It replaces the nonrefundable credit for qualified individuals making contributions to individual retirement accounts with a "Saver's Match" Federal contribution of up to $2,000 per year for individuals with incomes up to $71,000. It increases the age to begin mandatory distributions from retirement plans, and increases the catch-up limits beginning in 2025 for individuals ages 60 to 63. It provides for a pension-linked emergency savings account of up to $2,500, in addition to permitting employees to withdraw up to $1,000 per year for personal or family emergencies without penalty, as well as withdraw funds penalty free for those that are terminally ill, are victims of domestic abuse, or are affected by a Stafford Act disaster. The Act also treats student loan payments as elective deferrals for purposes of retirement plan matching. Further, it limits the deduction for charitable conservation easements, subject to a three-year holding period test.

BUDGET PROPOSALS

The 2024 Budget proposes a series of revenue raisers directed at wealthy individuals and large corporations. The Budget aims to replace counterproductive tax laws that reward offshoring and profit shifting with provisions that encourage job creation at home and put an end to the worldwide race to the bottom on corporate tax rates. It also includes a set of measures to make sure the wealthiest Americans and corporations pay their fair share in

taxes while ensuring that no one making $400,000 per year or less will pay more in new taxes. These proposals affecting governmental receipts are included in the table that follows. Descriptions of proposals can be found in the Department of the Treasury's *General Explanations of the Administration's Fiscal Year 2024 Revenue Proposals.* [2]

---

[2] Available at this link: *https://home.treasury.gov/policy-issues/tax-policy/revenue-proposals.*

Table 17–2. EFFECT OF BUDGET PROPOSALS

(In millions of dollars)

	2023	2024	2025	2026	2027	2028	2029	2030	2031	2032	2033	2024–2028	2024–2033
Reform business taxation:													
Raise the corporate income tax rate to 28 percent ...	89,130	137,068	126,786	125,160	129,655	137,689	137,514	133,428	133,851	131,646	132,962	656,358	1,325,759
Increase the excise tax rate on repurchase of corporate stock	3,934	20,266	20,364	21,243	22,143	23,059	24,016	25,031	26,111	27,247	28,429	107,075	237,909
Tax corporate distributions as dividends	....	69	110	123	129	136	144	152	161	169	178	567	1,371
Limit tax avoidance through inappropriate leveraging of parties to divisive reorganizations	....	250	741	1,451	2,295	3,212	4,176	5,178	6,214	7,299	8,399	7,949	39,215
Limit losses recognized in liquidation transactions ...	....	299	507	522	538	554	570	587	605	623	642	2,420	5,447
Prevent basis shifting by related parties through partnerships	....	3,442	5,893	6,150	6,408	6,670	6,905	7,083	7,195	7,270	7,336	28,563	64,352
Conform definition of "control" with corporate affiliation test	....	370	541	556	569	579	586	592	595	598	600	2,615	5,586
Strengthen limitation on losses for noncorporate taxpayers	....	....	1,185	2,241	2,519	12,571	14,373	10,268	9,533	9,371	9,282	18,516	71,343
Accelerate and tighten rules on excess employee remuneration[1]	....	2,328	792	163	1,491	2,259	1,932	1,544	1,237	1,211	1,271	7,033	14,228
Prevent prison facility rent payments from contributing to qualification as a REIT	....	....	....	....	....	....	....	....	....	....	....	....	....
Subtotal, reform business taxation	93,064	164,092	156,919	157,609	165,747	186,729	190,216	183,863	185,502	185,434	189,099	831,096	1,765,210
Reform international taxation:													
Revise the global minimum tax regime, limit inversions, and make related reforms	18,461	44,951	55,091	48,450	43,750	44,943	46,935	49,007	51,154	53,378	55,682	237,185	493,341
Adopt the undertaxed profits rule	....	....	40,219	66,414	66,022	65,205	63,540	62,897	62,360	61,559	60,821	237,860	549,037
Repeal the deduction for foreign-derived intangible income:													
Repeal the deduction for foreign-derived intangible income	....	9,800	16,627	12,619	9,994	10,294	10,602	10,920	11,248	11,585	11,932	59,334	115,621
Provide additional support for research and experimentation expenditures	....	−9,800	−16,627	−12,619	−9,994	−10,294	−10,602	−10,920	−11,248	−11,585	−11,932	−59,334	−115,621
Subtotal, repeal the deduction for foreign-derived intangible income	....	....	....	....	....	....	....	....	....	....	....	....	....
Revise the rules that allocate Subpart F income and GILTI between taxpayers to ensure that Subpart F income and GILTI are fully taxed	....	166	294	320	344	366	388	408	427	446	465	1,490	3,624
Eliminate exploited mismatch in calculation of earnings and profits of controlled foreign corporations	....	190	321	331	341	351	362	373	384	395	407	1,534	3,455
Limit foreign tax credits from sale of hybrid entities ..	....	315	492	445	410	384	365	350	340	333	328	2,046	3,762
Restrict deductions of excessive interest of members of financial reporting groups	....	2,609	4,316	4,193	4,078	4,073	4,167	4,280	4,389	4,514	4,657	19,269	41,276
Treat payments substituting for partnership effectively connected income as U.S. source dividends	....	4	9	9	9	9	10	10	10	10	10	40	90
Expand access to retroactive qualified electing fund elections	....	....	1	1	2	2	2	2	2	2	2	6	16
Reform taxation of foreign fossil fuel income:													
Modify foreign oil and gas extraction income and foreign oil related income rules	....	138	243	261	278	299	318	334	351	369	388	1,219	2,979
Modify tax rule for dual capacity taxpayers	....	2,932	5,148	5,541	5,902	6,344	6,732	7,073	7,443	7,814	8,215	25,867	63,144
Subtotal, reform taxation of foreign fossil fuel income	....	3,070	5,391	5,802	6,180	6,643	7,050	7,407	7,794	8,183	8,603	27,086	66,123
Provide tax incentives for locating jobs and business activity in the United States and remove tax deductions for shipping jobs overseas:													
Provide tax credit for inshoring jobs to the United States	....	−11	−12	−12	−13	−13	−14	−14	−15	−15	−16	−61	−135
Remove tax deductions for shipping jobs overseas	....	11	12	12	13	13	14	14	15	15	16	61	135
Subtotal, provide tax incentives for locating jobs and business activity in the United States and remove tax deductions for shipping jobs overseas	....	....	....	....	....	....	....	....	....	....	....	....	....
Subtotal, reform international taxation	18,461	51,305	106,134	125,965	121,136	121,976	122,819	124,734	126,860	128,820	130,975	526,516	1,160,724

Table 17–2. EFFECT OF BUDGET PROPOSALS—Continued

(In millions of dollars)

	2023	2024	2025	2026	2027	2028	2029	2030	2031	2032	2033	2024–2028	2024–2033
Support housing and urban development:													
Make permanent the New Markets Tax Credit	....	....	....	–97	–278	–483	–716	–990	–1,290	–1,602	–1,792	–858	–7,248
Provide a neighborhood homes credit	....	–18	–142	–534	–1,213	–1,894	–2,284	–2,391	–2,375	–2,351	–2,362	–3,801	–15,564
Expand and enhance the low-income housing credit ...	....	–38	–192	–549	–1,198	–2,041	–2,944	–3,872	–4,823	–5,799	–6,803	–4,018	–28,259
Subtotal, support housing and urban development	....	–56	–334	–1,180	–2,689	–4,418	–5,944	–7,253	–8,488	–9,752	–10,957	–8,677	–51,071
Modify energy taxes:													
Eliminate fossil fuel tax preferences:													
Repeal the enhanced oil recovery credit	....	....	....	....	....	....	....	....	....	....	....	....	....
Repeal the credit for oil and natural gas produced from marginal wells	....	....	....	....	....	....	....	....	....	....	....	....	....
Repeal expensing of intangible drilling costs	....	1,369	2,003	1,591	1,122	599	394	383	366	337	328	6,684	8,492
Repeal the deduction for costs paid or incurred for any qualified tertiary injectant used as part of tertiary recovery method [2]	....	....	....	....	....	....	....	....	....	....	....	....	....
Repeal the exception to passive loss limitations provided to working interests in oil and natural gas properties	....	5	9	9	8	8	8	8	7	7	7	39	76
Repeal the use of percentage depletion with respect to oil and natural gas wells	....	1,118	1,144	1,203	1,279	1,357	1,426	1,489	1,554	1,616	1,675	6,101	13,861
Increase geological and geophysical amortization period for independent producers	....	51	187	320	359	353	345	336	324	301	271	1,270	2,847
Repeal expensing of mine exploration and development costs	....	113	166	131	93	50	32	32	31	28	27	553	703
Repeal percentage depletion for hard mineral fossil fuels	....	78	77	78	79	81	83	86	87	89	91	393	829
Repeal capital gains treatment for royalties	....	26	54	57	62	64	66	69	71	73	75	263	617
Repeal the exemption from the corporate income tax for fossil fuel publicly traded partnerships .	....	....	....	....	....	....	80	159	199	236	271	....	945
Repeal the Oil Spill Liability Trust Fund and Superfund excise tax exemption for crude oil derived from bitumen and kerogen-rich rock [1]...	....	110	153	157	163	170	176	180	185	191	195	753	1,680
Repeal accelerated amortization of air pollution control equipment	....	13	32	50	66	82	96	110	108	98	86	243	741
Subtotal, eliminate fossil fuel tax preferences .	....	2,883	3,825	3,596	3,231	2,764	2,706	2,852	2,932	2,976	3,026	16,299	30,791
Eliminate drawbacks on petroleum taxes that finance the Oil Spill Liability Trust Fund and Superfund [1]....	....	163	220	223	225	229	231	233	236	240	242	1,060	2,242
Impose digital asset mining energy excise tax [1]	....	74	199	327	385	394	405	415	425	435	444	1,379	3,503
Subtotal, modify energy taxes	....	3,120	4,244	4,146	3,841	3,387	3,342	3,500	3,593	3,651	3,712	18,738	36,536
Strengthen taxation of high-income taxpayers:													
Apply the net investment income tax to pass-through business income of high-income taxpayers	12,342	22,839	26,245	27,381	28,606	30,298	31,589	33,004	34,162	35,348	36,472	135,369	305,944
Increase the net investment income tax rate and additional Medicare tax rate for high-income taxpayers	14,891	29,627	28,282	27,872	30,074	32,494	34,525	36,772	39,104	41,532	44,089	148,349	344,371
Increase the top marginal income tax rate for high-income earners.....................	20,063	53,029	52,206	28,716	11,963	12,757	13,571	14,422	15,271	16,191	17,137	158,671	235,263
Reform the taxation of capital income	....	2,306	13,211	19,230	21,135	22,086	23,205	24,600	26,066	27,455	34,561	77,968	213,855
Impose a minimum income tax on the wealthiest taxpayers	....	....	43,698	48,977	51,620	52,507	52,093	51,533	46,084	43,616	46,481	196,802	436,609
Subtotal, strengthen taxation of high-income taxpayers	47,296	107,801	163,642	152,176	143,398	150,142	154,983	160,331	160,687	164,142	178,740	717,159	1,536,042
Modify rules relating to retirement plans:													
Prevent excessive accumulations by high-income taxpayers in tax-favored retirement accounts and make other reforms	....	6,633	5,887	3,266	1,915	1,231	898	749	699	702	734	18,932	22,714
Subtotal, modify rules relating to retirement plans	....	6,633	5,887	3,266	1,915	1,231	898	749	699	702	734	18,932	22,714
Support workers, families, and economic security:													
Expand the child credit, and make permanent full refundability and advanceability [3]	–5,843	–259,273	–74,899	–7,864	–9,432	–12,166	–12,520	–12,792	–13,038	–13,370	–13,802	–363,634	–429,156

Table 17–2. EFFECT OF BUDGET PROPOSALS—Continued

(In millions of dollars)

	2023	2024	2025	2026	2027	2028	2029	2030	2031	2032	2033	2024–2028	2024–2033
Restore and make permanent the American Rescue Plan expansion of the earned income tax credit for workers without qualifying children [3]	−378	−13,940	−14,997	−15,354	−15,650	−15,774	−15,959	−16,027	−16,088	−16,126	−16,130	−75,715	−156,045
Make permanent the Inflation Reduction Act expansion of health insurance premium tax credits [3]	....	....	....	−14,791	−20,253	−21,057	−21,518	−20,618	−21,020	−22,098	−23,281	−56,101	−164,636
Make the adoption tax credit refundable and allow certain guardianship arrangements to qualify [3]	....	....	−1,011	−1,979	−1,704	−1,655	−1,639	−1,623	−1,602	−1,594	−1,582	−6,349	−14,389
Make permanent the income exclusion for forgiven student debt [3]	....	....	....	−1	−11	−25	−164	−180	−197	−215	−235	−37	−1,028
Extend tax-preferred treatment to certain Federal and tribal scholarship and education loan programs	....	−41	−63	−71	−78	−82	−85	−87	−89	−92	−94	−335	−782
Increase the employer-provided childcare tax credit for businesses	....	−17	−35	−35	−36	−38	−39	−39	−39	−40	−40	−161	−358
Improve the work opportunity tax credit program integrity to promote longer-term employment	....	65	134	86	27	17	13	9	8	5	4	329	368
Subtotal, support workers, families, and economic security	−6,221	−273,206	−90,871	−40,009	−47,137	−50,780	−51,911	−51,357	−52,065	−53,530	−55,160	−502,003	−766,026
Modify estate and gift taxation:													
Improve tax administration for trusts and decedents' estates	....	−3	1	1	−9	−5	−5	−1	5	12	21	−15	17
Limit duration of generation-skipping transfer tax exemption	....	....	....	....	....	....	....	....	....	....	....	....	....
Modify income, estate, gift, and generation-skipping transfer tax rules for certain trusts	....	1,052	3,157	3,710	4,999	6,506	8,480	6,063	8,480	10,343	12,355	19,424	65,145
Revise rules for valuation of certain property	....	279	789	918	1,107	1,299	1,356	1,466	1,571	1,700	1,829	4,392	12,314
Subtotal, modify estate and gift taxation	....	1,328	3,947	4,629	6,097	7,800	9,831	7,528	10,056	12,055	14,205	23,801	77,476
Close loopholes:													
Tax carried (profits) interests as ordinary income	....	398	662	661	659	657	664	677	691	705	719	3,037	6,493
Repeal deferral of gain from like-kind exchanges	....	642	1,765	1,818	1,873	1,929	1,986	2,047	2,107	2,171	2,236	8,027	18,574
Require 100 percent recapture of depreciation deductions as ordinary income for certain depreciable real property	....	39	120	249	389	540	704	881	1,073	1,279	1,502	1,337	6,776
Limit use of donor advised funds to avoid a private foundation payout requirement	....	20	19	13	8	4	3	4	4	4	4	64	83
Exclude payments to disqualified persons from counting toward private foundation payout requirement	....	1	2	1	1	1	1	....	....	....	....	6	7
Extend the period for assessment of tax for certain Qualified Opportunity Fund investors	....	5	15	18	15	11	10	8	6	2	....	64	90
Impose ownership diversification requirement for small insurance company election	....	245	797	873	975	1,046	1,109	1,171	1,228	1,302	1,383	3,936	10,129
Expand pro rata interest expense disallowance for business-owned life insurance	....	557	561	583	615	643	673	704	737	768	803	2,959	6,644
Modify rules for insurance products that fail the statutory definition of a life insurance contract	2	4	....	....	....	....	....	....	....	....	....	4	4
Correct drafting errors in the taxation of insurance companies under the Tax Cuts and Jobs Act of 2017	....	65	97	101	100	73	55	48	41	37	33	436	650
Define the term "ultimate purchaser" for purposes of diesel fuel exportation [1]	....	4	8	10	12	14	16	19	21	23	26	48	153
Subtotal, close loopholes	2	1,980	4,046	4,327	4,647	4,918	5,221	5,559	5,908	6,291	6,706	19,918	49,603
Improve tax administration:													
Enhance accuracy of tax information:													
Expand the Secretary's authority to require electronic filing for forms and returns	....	....	....	....	....	....	....	....	....	....	....	....	....
Improve information reporting for reportable payments subject to backup withholding	....	40	91	155	211	221	231	241	252	263	288	718	1,993
Subtotal, enhance accuracy of tax information	....	40	91	155	211	221	231	241	252	263	288	718	1,993
Amend the centralized partnership audit regime to permit the carryover of a reduction in tax that exceeds a partner's tax liability	....	−5	−5	−5	−6	−6	−7	−7	−7	−7	−8	−27	−63
Modify requisite supervisory approval of penalty included in notice	....	134	136	138	144	145	157	153	159	166	174	697	1,506

Table 17–2. EFFECT OF BUDGET PROPOSALS—Continued

(In millions of dollars)

	2023	2024	2025	2026	2027	2028	2029	2030	2031	2032	2033	2024–2028	2024–2033
Modify the requirement that general counsel review certain offers in compromise	....	6	14	9	2	2	2	2	2	2	2	33	43
Incorporate chapters 2/3A in centralized partnership audit regime proceedings	....	....	....	....	....	....	....	....	....	....	....	....	....
Simplify foreign exchange gain or loss rules and exchange rate rules for individuals	....	–1	–2	–2	–2	–2	–2	–2	–2	–2	–3	–9	–20
Increase threshold for simplified foreign tax credit rules and reporting	....	–10	–29	–31	–34	–34	–34	–35	–35	–36	–40	–138	–318
Authorize limited sharing of business tax return information to measure the economy more accurately	....	....	....	....	....	....	....	....	....	....	....	....	....
Expand TIN matching and improve child support enforcement	....	....	....	....	....	....	....	....	....	....	....	....	....
Clarify that information previously disclosed in a judicial or administrative proceeding is not return information	2	2	2	2	2	2	2	2	2	2	2	10	20
Subtotal, strengthen tax administration	2	166	207	266	317	328	349	354	371	388	415	1,284	3,161
Improve tax compliance:													
Address taxpayer noncompliance with listed transactions:													
Extend statute of limitations for listed transactions	....	23	52	66	79	78	76	74	73	72	70	298	663
Impose liability on shareholders to collect unpaid income taxes of applicable corporations	....	457	477	498	519	540	563	587	613	639	667	2,491	5,560
Subtotal, address taxpayer noncompliance	....	480	529	564	598	618	639	661	686	711	737	2,789	6,223
Impose an affirmative requirement to disclose a position contrary to a regulation	....	7	9	11	12	12	14	14	15	16	16	51	126
Require employers to withhold tax on failed nonqualified deferred compensation plans	....	198	207	217	226	237	247	258	270	283	295	1,085	2,438
Extend to six years the statute of limitations for certain tax assessments	....	....	....	....	....	....	....	....	....	....	....	....	....
Increase the statute of limitations on assessment of the COVID-related paid leave and employee retention tax credits [3]	....	3	39	118	96	13	....	....	....	....	....	269	269
Expand and increase penalties for noncompliant return preparation and e-filing and authorize IRS oversight of paid preparers:													
Expand and increase penalties for noncompliant return preparation and e-filing [3]	....	25	49	68	84	94	95	95	96	93	94	320	793
Grant authority to IRS for oversight of all paid preparers [3]	....	37	50	47	47	51	56	62	66	73	79	232	568
Subtotal, expand and increase penalties and oversight for return preparation and e-filing and authorize IRS oversight of paid preparers	....	62	99	115	131	145	151	157	162	166	173	552	1,361
Address compliance in connection with tax responsibilities of expatriates	....	....	1	2	3	4	5	5	4	4	4	10	32
Define control of the payment of wage	....	....	....	....	....	....	....	....	....	....	....	....	....
Subtotal, improve tax compliance	....	750	884	1,027	1,066	1,029	1,056	1,095	1,137	1,180	1,225	4,756	10,449
Modernize rules, including those for digital assets:													
Apply the wash sale rules to digital assets and address related party transactions	....	1,240	1,629	1,743	2,098	2,256	2,459	2,710	2,909	3,126	3,351	8,966	23,521
Modernize rules treating loans of securities as tax-free to include other asset classes and address income inclusion	....	....	....	....	....	....	....	....	....	....	....	....	....
Provide for information reporting by certain financial institutions and digital asset brokers for purposes of exchange of information	....	....	....	90	157	167	178	188	200	215	227	414	1,422
Require reporting by certain taxpayers of foreign digital asset accounts	....	37	75	141	165	176	187	198	211	226	239	594	1,655
Amend the mark-to-market rules to include digital assets	....	3,634	99	109	120	132	146	160	176	194	213	4,094	4,983
Subtotal, modernize rules, including for digital assets	....	4,911	1,803	2,083	2,540	2,731	2,970	3,256	3,496	3,761	4,030	14,068	31,581
Improve benefits tax administration:													

Table 17–2. EFFECT OF BUDGET PROPOSALS—Continued

(In millions of dollars)

	2023	2024	2025	2026	2027	2028	2029	2030	2031	2032	2033	2024–2028	2024–2033
Clarify tax treatment of fixed indemnity health policies	....	....	....	....	....	....	....	....	....	....	....	....	....
Rationalize funding for post-retirement medical and life insurance benefits	....	....	....	....	....	....	....	....	....	....	....	....	....
Clarify tax treatment of on-demand pay arrangements	....	....	....	....	....	....	....	....	....	....	....	....	....
Subtotal, improve benefits tax administration	....	....	....	....	....	....	....	....	....	....	....	....	....
Extend IRA funding:													
Extend mandatory funding provided to the IRS for fiscal years 2032 and 2033 [3]	....	....	....	....	....	....	....	....	....	47,121	57,883	....	105,004
Subtotal, extend IRA funding	....	....	....	....	....	....	....	....	....	47,121	57,883	....	105,004
Other initiatives:													
Require coverage of three primary care visits and three behavioral health visits without cost-sharing [3]	....	....	....	–4,622	–4,284	–1,631	–985	–1,014	–1,063	–1,116	–1,164	–10,537	–15,879
Improve access to behavioral healthcare in the private insurance market [3]	....	....	....	–2,393	–3,288	–3,409	–3,558	–3,669	–3,839	–4,018	–4,200	–9,090	–28,374
Extend surprise billing protections to ground ambulances	....	....	66	95	100	104	109	112	117	123	125	365	951
Limit cost-sharing for insulin at $35 per month	....	–545	–484	–98	....	....	....	....	....	....	....	–1,127	–1,127
Increase civil penalties for labor law violations	....	150	200	250	250	250	250	250	300	300	300	1,100	2,500
Establish Electronic Visa Update System user fee	....	52	58	64	72	79	88	108	118	130	143	325	912
Fund Unemployment Insurance (UI) program integrity	....	....	....	–11	–35	–189	–90	24	–114	–150	–163	–235	–728
Subtotal, other initiatives	....	–343	–160	–6,715	–7,185	–4,796	–4,186	–4,189	–4,481	–4,731	–4,959	–19,199	–41,745
Total, effects of budget proposals	**152,604**	**68,481**	**356,348**	**407,590**	**393,693**	**420,277**	**429,644**	**428,170**	**433,275**	**485,532**	**516,648**	**1,646,389**	**3,939,658**

[1] Net of income offsets.

[2] Effects are included in the estimate of Repeal the enhanced oil recovery credit.

[3] This proposal affects both receipts and outlays. The net effect is shown above. The outlay effects included in these estimates are as follows:

	2023	2024	2025	2026	2027	2028	2029	2030	2031	2032	2033	2024–2028	2024–2033
Expand the child credit and make permanent full refundability and advanceability	–108	–234,552	–138,503	–33,455	–9,700	–8,901	–8,990	–8,997	–8,934	–8,926	–8,989	–425,111	–469,947
Restore and make permanent the American Rescue Plan expansion of the earned income tax credit for workers without qualifying children	–2	–12,396	–13,322	–13,546	–13,527	–13,676	–13,875	–13,980	–14,064	–14,130	–14,178	–66,467	–136,694
Make permanent the Inflation Reduction Act expansion of health insurance premium tax credits	....	....	....	–9,904	–13,533	–13,955	–14,352	–14,192	–14,572	–15,199	–15,879	–37,392	–111,586
Make the adoption tax credit refundable and allow certain guardianship arrangements to qualify	....	....	–1,000	–1,937	–1,661	–1,608	–1,591	–1,575	–1,553	–1,544	–1,532	–6,206	–14,001
Make permanent the income exclusion for forgiven student debt	....	....	....	....	–1	–1	–19	–19	–20	–22	–24	–2	–106
Increase the statute of limitations on assessment of the COVID-related paid leave and employee retention tax credits	....	2	35	119	108	21	....	....	....	....	....	285	285
Expand and increase penalties for noncompliant return preparation and e-filing	....	9	15	18	20	22	22	22	22	19	19	84	188
Grant authority to IRS for oversight of all paid preparers	....	23	29	22	19	20	22	24	25	28	30	113	242
Extend mandatory funding provided to the IRS for fiscal years 2032 and 2033	....	....	....	....	....	....	....	....	....	–14,304	–14,838	....	–29,142
Require coverage of three primary care visits and three behavioral health visits without cost-sharing	....	....	....	–927	–839	–300	–165	–158	–166	–175	–178	–2,066	–2,908
Improve access to behavioral healthcare in the private insurance market	....	....	....	–560	–767	–788	–821	–805	–841	–872	–900	–2,115	–6,354
Extend surprise billing protections to ground ambulances	....	....	14	19	20	20	21	20	21	22	20	73	177
Limit cost-sharing for insulin at $35 per month	....	–135	–116	–21	....	....	....	....	....	....	....	–272	–272
Total, outlay effect of receipt proposals	–110	–247,049	–152,848	–60,172	–39,861	–39,146	–39,748	–39,660	–40,082	–55,103	–56,449	–539,076	–770,118

Table 17–3. RECEIPTS BY SOURCE

(In millions of dollars)

Source	2022 Actual	Estimate										
		2023	2024	2025	2026	2027	2028	2029	2030	2031	2032	2033
Individual income taxes:												
Federal funds..........	2,632,146	2,337,331	2,382,306	2,472,318	2,770,241	2,990,509	3,158,559	3,319,323	3,500,484	3,696,464	3,885,798	4,077,726
Legislative proposal, not subject to PAYGO	....	−21,598	−36,607	−38,130	−38,912	−40,185	−42,159	−44,340	−46,847	−49,524	−22,029	−18,125
Legislative proposal, subject to PAYGO	....	12,127	44,311	183,065	117,788	78,715	89,483	91,315	88,972	84,997	84,310	94,877
Total, Individual income taxes....	**2,632,146**	**2,327,860**	**2,390,010**	**2,617,253**	**2,849,117**	**3,029,039**	**3,205,883**	**3,366,298**	**3,542,609**	**3,731,937**	**3,948,079**	**4,154,478**
Corporation income taxes:												
Federal funds..........	424,865	438,412	470,444	485,982	466,832	474,306	485,199	488,006	489,673	495,102	471,793	488,632
Legislative proposal, not subject to PAYGO	....	....	....	....	....	....	....	....	....	....	31,168	35,615
Legislative proposal, subject to PAYGO	....	107,587	195,724	247,106	267,082	265,792	273,853	275,276	273,432	275,977	275,659	279,116
Total, Corporation income taxes...	**424,865**	**545,999**	**666,168**	**733,088**	**733,914**	**740,098**	**759,052**	**763,282**	**763,105**	**771,079**	**778,620**	**803,363**
Social insurance and retirement receipts (trust funds):												
Employment and general retirement:												
Old-age survivors insurance (off-budget)	911,191	1,024,331	1,033,840	1,080,972	1,134,596	1,181,284	1,241,174	1,291,335	1,346,598	1,403,604	1,461,228	1,544,805
Legislative proposal, not subject to PAYGO	....	−167	−1,064	−1,061	−2,214	−2,311	−1,906	−1,859	−1,937	−2,020	−2,109	−2,200
Disability insurance (off-budget)....................	154,784	173,959	175,558	183,561	192,667	200,596	210,765	219,284	228,668	238,348	248,132	262,325
Legislative proposal, not subject to PAYGO	....	−28	−180	−180	−375	−392	−323	−315	−329	−343	−358	−373
Hospital Insurance...............	339,145	357,451	369,461	386,673	406,247	424,614	447,443	467,097	488,547	510,903	534,002	566,212
Legislative proposal, not subject to PAYGO	....	21,598	36,607	38,130	38,912	40,185	42,159	44,340	46,847	49,524	52,286	55,231
Legislative proposal, subject to PAYGO	....	29,853	58,345	60,476	64,313	68,396	72,917	76,751	80,915	84,914	89,138	93,471
Railroad retirement:												
Social security equivalent account	2,366	2,723	2,495	2,537	2,575	2,614	2,655	2,695	2,737	2,785	2,835	2,886
Rail pension & supplemental annuity	3,249	3,306	3,366	3,454	3,521	3,584	3,649	3,879	3,988	4,237	4,364	4,989
Total, Employment and general retirement	1,410,735	1,613,026	1,678,428	1,754,562	1,840,242	1,918,570	2,018,533	2,103,207	2,196,034	2,291,952	2,389,518	2,527,346
On-budget..........................	(344,760)	(414,931)	(470,274)	(491,270)	(515,568)	(539,393)	(568,823)	(594,762)	(623,034)	(652,363)	(682,625)	(722,789)
Off-budget..........................	(1,065,975)	(1,198,095)	(1,208,154)	(1,263,292)	(1,324,674)	(1,379,177)	(1,449,710)	(1,508,445)	(1,573,000)	(1,639,589)	(1,706,893)	(1,804,557)
Unemployment insurance:												
Deposits by States [1]	59,294	47,854	47,493	48,693	50,320	52,552	54,955	55,954	57,261	58,057	59,244	60,674
Legislative proposal, subject to PAYGO	....	....	....	....	−11	−35	−189	−90	24	−114	−150	−163
Amounts included in the adjusted baseline [2]	....	....	....	−40	−96	−154	−312	−261	−395	−233	−321	−371
Federal unemployment receipts [1]	6,927	7,093	8,418	9,142	9,876	10,600	11,327	12,599	12,805	11,731	12,276	12,835
Railroad unemployment receipts [1]	277	321	150	36	49	90	169	222	181	126	142	202
Total, Unemployment insurance	66,498	55,268	56,061	57,831	60,138	63,053	65,950	68,424	69,876	69,567	71,191	73,177
Other retirement:												
Federal employees retirement - employee share	6,270	6,912	7,562	8,150	8,663	9,200	9,743	10,320	10,910	11,512	12,150	12,817
Non-Federal employees retirement [3]	24	30	30	30	29	29	29	28	28	27	27	27
Total, Other retirement	6,294	6,942	7,592	8,180	8,692	9,229	9,772	10,348	10,938	11,539	12,177	12,844
Total, Social insurance and retirement receipts (trust funds)....................................	**1,483,527**	**1,675,236**	**1,742,081**	**1,820,573**	**1,909,072**	**1,990,852**	**2,094,255**	**2,181,979**	**2,276,848**	**2,373,058**	**2,472,886**	**2,613,367**

17. GOVERNMENTAL RECEIPTS

Table 17–3. RECEIPTS BY SOURCE—Continued

(In millions of dollars)

Source	2022 Actual	Estimate										
		2023	2024	2025	2026	2027	2028	2029	2030	2031	2032	2033
On-budget	*(417,552)*	*(477,141)*	*(533,927)*	*(557,281)*	*(584,398)*	*(611,675)*	*(644,545)*	*(673,534)*	*(703,848)*	*(733,469)*	*(765,993)*	*(808,810)*
Off-budget	*(1,065,975)*	*(1,198,095)*	*(1,208,154)*	*(1,263,292)*	*(1,324,674)*	*(1,379,177)*	*(1,449,710)*	*(1,508,445)*	*(1,573,000)*	*(1,639,589)*	*(1,706,893)*	*(1,804,557)*
Excise taxes:												
Federal funds:												
Alcohol	10,196	10,279	10,139	10,137	10,256	10,362	10,535	10,702	10,950	11,294	11,453	11,755
Tobacco	11,259	11,582	10,571	9,186	9,161	9,042	8,920	8,830	8,712	8,599	8,484	8,353
Transportation fuels	–5,126	–4,601	–3,984	–2,430	–798	–791	–780	–765	–747	–737	–770	–814
Legislative proposal, subject to PAYGO	....	....	5	10	13	16	19	22	25	28	31	34
Telephone and teletype services	316	184	144	117	94	74	58	45	36	30	28	29
Indoor tanning services	69	66	63	60	57	54	51	48	45	42	39	36
Medical devices	–1	....	....	....	....	....	....	....	....	....	....	....
Other Federal fund excise taxes	7,351	6,050	13,212	13,378	13,885	14,412	14,959	15,524	16,127	16,764	17,432	18,129
Legislative proposal, subject to PAYGO	....	3,342	16,812	17,055	17,940	18,751	19,515	20,316	21,165	22,068	23,017	24,004
Total, Federal funds	24,064	26,902	46,962	47,513	50,608	51,920	53,277	54,722	56,313	58,088	59,714	61,526
Trust funds:												
Transportation	46,631	41,892	40,469	39,999	40,230	40,135	39,920	39,647	39,405	39,535	43,508	44,561
Airport and airway	11,377	16,084	16,700	17,944	18,675	19,376	20,099	20,861	21,694	22,600	23,571	24,548
Sport fish restoration and boating safety	634	629	632	633	637	640	645	654	663	674	683	693
Tobacco assessments	1	....	....	....	....	....	....	....	....	....	....	....
Black lung disability insurance	180	307	302	287	288	288	288	283	281	281	277	277
Inland waterway	124	118	119	119	120	120	121	121	122	122	123	124
Superfund	413	2,544	2,980	3,108	3,206	3,307	3,416	3,519	3,631	3,748	3,876	3,998
Legislative proposal, subject to PAYGO	....	....	235	321	329	338	351	360	367	375	385	393
Oil spill liability	562	622	617	617	617	618	619	619	618	618	618	617
Legislative proposal, subject to PAYGO	....	....	124	168	170	171	174	175	176	177	180	180
Vaccine injury compensation	333	315	313	314	316	319	323	328	331	335	338	342
Leaking underground storage tank	245	189	184	181	180	178	175	174	172	171	191	195
Supplementary medical insurance	2,804	1,461	4,043	2,800	2,800	2,800	1,557	2,800	4,043	2,800	2,800	2,800
Patient-centered outcomes research	360	390	409	430	452	474	499	525	549	575	603	632
Total, Trust funds	63,664	64,551	67,127	66,921	68,020	68,764	68,187	70,066	72,052	72,011	77,153	79,360
Total, Excise taxes	**87,728**	**91,453**	**114,089**	**114,434**	**118,628**	**120,684**	**121,464**	**124,788**	**128,365**	**130,099**	**136,867**	**140,886**
Estate and gift taxes:												
Federal funds	32,550	20,099	24,322	26,308	26,684	41,128	42,260	44,608	47,459	50,169	53,827	57,055
Legislative proposal, subject to PAYGO	....	....	1,016	1,978	2,413	3,791	5,200	7,103	4,662	6,880	8,677	10,594
Total, Estate and gift taxes	**32,550**	**20,899**	**25,338**	**28,286**	**29,097**	**44,919**	**47,460**	**51,711**	**52,121**	**57,049**	**62,504**	**67,649**
Customs duties and fees:												
Federal funds	97,643	99,405	58,513	47,560	49,921	51,856	53,689	55,527	57,538	59,727	51,825	54,219
Trust funds	2,265	2,251	2,173	2,262	2,375	2,451	2,532	2,609	2,694	2,789	2,891	2,997
Total, Customs duties and fees	**99,908**	**101,656**	**60,686**	**49,822**	**52,296**	**54,307**	**56,221**	**58,136**	**60,232**	**62,516**	**54,716**	**57,216**
Miscellaneous receipts:												
Federal funds:												
Miscellaneous taxes	719	737	736	735	736	737	738	732	733	732	732	734
Deposit of earnings, Federal Reserve System	106,674	....	....	14,432	35,753	54,329	65,376	69,395	72,416	78,484	85,432	90,918
Transfers from the Federal Reserve	642	653	685	703	724	746	768	791	814	838	864	890

Table 17–3.   RECEIPTS BY SOURCE—Continued

(In millions of dollars)

Source	2022 Actual	Estimate										
		2023	2024	2025	2026	2027	2028	2029	2030	2031	2032	2033
Fees for permits and regulatory and judicial services	21,179	22,470	24,606	27,740	30,864	32,353	35,798	39,692	42,902	45,629	47,834	49,449
Legislative proposal, subject to PAYGO	....	....	52	58	64	72	79	88	108	118	130	143
Fines, penalties, and forfeitures	6,142	13,848	10,333	10,835	10,846	10,785	10,867	10,940	11,005	11,076	11,150	10,971
Legislative proposal, subject to PAYGO	....	....	150	200	250	250	250	250	250	300	300	300
Refunds and recoveries	−10	−10	−10	−10	−10	−10	−10	−10	−10	−10	−10	−10
Total, Federal funds	135,346	37,698	36,552	54,693	79,227	99,262	113,866	121,878	128,218	137,167	146,432	153,395
Trust funds:												
United Mine Workers of America, combined benefit fund	11	6	6	5	4	4	3	3	3	2	2	2
Defense cooperation	294	490	252	155	159	162	165	169	172	176	180	183
Fees for permits and regulatory and judicial services	67	70	70	70	70	70	70	70	70	70	70	70
Fines, penalties, and forfeitures	957	1,116	1,132	1,094	1,038	1,065	1,088	1,081	1,072	1,068	716	708
Total, Trust funds	1,329	1,682	1,460	1,324	1,271	1,301	1,326	1,323	1,317	1,316	968	963
Total, Miscellaneous receipts	**136,675**	**39,380**	**38,012**	**56,017**	**80,498**	**100,563**	**115,192**	**123,201**	**129,535**	**138,483**	**147,400**	**154,358**
Total, budget receipts.................	**4,897,399**	**4,802,483**	**5,036,384**	**5,419,473**	**5,772,622**	**6,080,462**	**6,399,527**	**6,669,395**	**6,952,815**	**7,264,221**	**7,601,072**	**7,991,317**
On-budget............................	(3,831,424)	(3,604,388)	(3,828,230)	(4,156,181)	(4,447,948)	(4,701,285)	(4,949,817)	(5,160,950)	(5,379,815)	(5,624,632)	(5,894,179)	(6,186,760)
Off-budget............................	(1,065,975)	(1,198,095)	(1,208,154)	(1,263,292)	(1,324,674)	(1,379,177)	(1,449,710)	(1,508,445)	(1,573,000)	(1,639,589)	(1,706,893)	(1,804,557)

[1] Deposits by States cover the benefit part of the program. Federal unemployment receipts cover administrative costs at both the Federal and State levels. Railroad unemployment receipts cover both the benefits and administrative costs of the program for the railroads.

[2] For additional information on adjustments to the baseline, see Chapter 21 in this volume, "Current Services Estimates."

[3] Represents employer and employee contributions to the civil service retirement and disability fund for covered employees of Government-sponsored, privately owned enterprises and the District of Columbia municipal government.

18. OFFSETTING COLLECTIONS AND OFFSETTING RECEIPTS

I. INTRODUCTION AND BACKGROUND

The Government records money collected in one of two ways. It is either recorded as a governmental receipt and included in the amount reported on the receipts side of the budget or it is recorded as an offsetting collection or offsetting receipt, which reduces (or "offsets") the amount reported on the outlay side of the budget. Governmental receipts are discussed in the previous chapter, "Governmental Receipts." The first section of this chapter broadly discusses offsetting collections and offsetting receipts. The second section discusses user charges, which consist of a subset of offsetting collections and offsetting receipts and a small share of governmental receipts. The third section describes the user charge proposals in the 2024 Budget.

Offsetting collections and offsetting receipts are recorded as offsets to spending so that the budget totals for receipts and (net) outlays reflect the amount of resources allocated by the Government through collective political choice, rather than through the marketplace.[1] This practice ensures that the budget totals measure the transactions of the Government with the public, and avoids the double counting that would otherwise result when one account makes a payment to another account and the receiving account then spends the proceeds. Offsetting receipts and offsetting collections are recorded in the budget in one of two ways, based on interpretation of laws and longstanding budget concepts and practice. They are offsetting collections when the collections are authorized to be credited to expenditure accounts. Otherwise, they are deposited in receipt accounts and called offsetting receipts.

There are two sources of offsetting receipts and offsetting collections: from the public and from other budget accounts. Like governmental receipts, offsetting receipts and offsetting collections from the public reduce the deficit or increase the surplus. In contrast, offsetting receipts and offsetting collections resulting from transactions with other budget accounts, called intragovernmental transactions, exactly offset the payments made by these accounts, with no net impact on the deficit or surplus.[2] In 2022, offsetting receipts and offsetting collections from the public were $844 billion, while receipts and collections from intragovernmental transactions were $1,621 billion, for a total of $2,465 billion Government-wide.

As described above, intragovernmental transactions are responsible for the majority of offsetting collections and offsetting receipts, when measured by the magnitude of the dollars collected. Examples of intragovernmental transactions include interest payments to funds that hold Government securities (such as the Social Security trust funds), general fund transfers to civilian and military retirement pension and health benefits funds, and agency payments to funds for employee health insurance and retirement benefits. Although receipts and collections from intragovernmental collections exactly offset the payments themselves, with no effect on the deficit or surplus, it is important to record these transactions in the budget to show how much the Government is allocating to fund various programs. For example, in the case of civilian retirement pensions, Government agencies make accrual payments to the Civil Service Retirement and Disability Fund on behalf of current employees to fund their future retirement benefits; the receipt of these payments to the Fund is shown in a single receipt account. Recording the receipt of these payments is important because it demonstrates the total cost to the Government today of providing this future benefit.

Offsetting receipts and collections from the public comprise approximately one-third of total offsetting collections and offsetting receipts, when measured by the magnitude of the dollars collected. Most of the funds collected through offsetting collections and offsetting receipts from the public arise from business-like transactions with the public. Unlike governmental receipts, which are derived from the Government's exercise of its sovereign power, these offsetting collections and offsetting receipts arise primarily from voluntary payments from the public for goods or services provided by the Government. They are classified as offsets to outlays for the cost of producing the goods or services for sale, rather than as governmental receipts. These activities include the sale of postage stamps, land, timber, and electricity; charging fees for services provided to the public (e.g., admission to National parks); and collecting premiums for healthcare benefits (e.g., Medicare Parts B and D). As described above, treating offsetting collections and offsetting receipts as offsets to outlays ensures the budgetary totals represent governmental rather than market activity.

A relatively small portion ($102.6 billion in 2022) of offsetting collections and offsetting receipts from the public is derived from the Government's exercise of its sovereign power. From a conceptual standpoint, these should be classified as governmental receipts. However, they are classified as offsetting rather than governmental receipts either because this classification has been specified in law or because these collections have traditionally been classi-

---

[1] Showing collections from business-type transactions as offsets on the spending side of the budget follows the concept recommended by the Report of the President's Commission on Budget Concepts in 1967 and is discussed in Chapter 15 of this volume, "Budget Concepts."

[2] For the purposes of this discussion, "collections from the public" include collections from non-budgetary Government accounts, such as credit financing accounts and deposit funds. For more information on these non-budgetary accounts, see Chapter 16, "Coverage of the Budget."

196

ANALYTICAL PERSPECTIVES

Table 18–1. OFFSETTING COLLECTIONS AND OFFSETTING RECEIPTS FROM THE PUBLIC

(In billions of dollars)

	Actual 2022	Estimate 2023	Estimate 2024
Offsetting collections (credited to expenditure accounts):			
User charges:			
Postal Service stamps and other Postal Service fees (off-budget)	76.8	78.7	81.5
Sale of energy:			
Tennessee Valley Authority	60.8	57.2	56.5
Bonneville Power Administration	4.5	3.9	4.0
Deposit Insurance	8.2	10.9	28.8
Employee contributions for employees and retired employees health benefits funds	18.4	19.7	21.0
Pension Benefit Guaranty Corporation fund	10.5	12.0	13.6
Federal Crop Insurance Corporation Fund	6.3	5.8	6.7
Defense Commissary Agency	4.2	4.8	4.9
Passenger Security Fee	2.5	2.8	4.7
Patent and Trademark fees	4.1	4.1	4.2
National Flood Insurance Fund	3.5	3.6	3.7
All other user charges	40.3	37.2	36.4
Subtotal, user charges	240.2	240.8	265.9
Other collections credited to expenditure accounts:			
Commodity Credit Corporation fund	6.2	5.9	6.7
Supplemental Security Income (collections from the States)	2.8	3.4	3.5
Other collections	49.9	11.0	5.0
Subtotal, other collections	58.9	20.3	15.2
Subtotal, offsetting collections	299.1	261.1	281.1
Offsetting receipts (deposited in receipt accounts):			
User charges:			
Medicare premiums	137.4	145.3	154.5
Outer Continental Shelf rents, bonuses, and royalties	11.8	8.3	7.7
Immigration fees	5.5	5.9	6.5
Spectrum auction, relocation, and licenses	103.5	--	20.5
All other user charges	73.1	34.4	31.9
Subtotal, user charges deposited in receipt accounts	331.4	194.0	221.1
Other collections deposited in receipt accounts:			
Military assistance program sales	39.6	39.8	41.0
Interest received from credit financing accounts	45.5	46.9	48.7
Government-sponsored enterprise (GSE) guarantee fees	5.8	6.4	6.8
Student loan receipt of negative subsidy and downward reestimates	27.9	13.1	1.0
All other collections deposited in receipt accounts	92.9	56.0	42.1
Subtotal, other collections deposited in receipt accounts	214.0	164.7	142.1
Subtotal, offsetting receipts	545.4	358.7	363.2
Total, offsetting collections and offsetting receipts from the public	844.5	619.7	644.3
Total, offsetting collections and offsetting receipts excluding off-budget	767.5	541.0	562.8
ADDENDUM:			
User charges that are offsetting collections and offsetting receipts [1]	571.6	434.8	487.0
Other offsetting collections and offsetting receipts from the public	272.9	185.0	157.3

[1] Excludes user charges that are classified on the receipts side of the budget. For total user charges, see Table 18–3.

fied as offsets to outlays. Most of the offsetting collections and offsetting receipts in this category derive from fees from Government regulatory services or Government licenses, and include, for example, charges for regulating the nuclear energy industry, bankruptcy filing fees, and immigration fees.[3]

[3] This category of receipts is known as "offsetting governmental receipts." Some argue that regulatory or licensing fees should be viewed as payments for a particular service or for the right to engage in a particular type of business. However, these fees are conceptually much more similar to taxes because they are compulsory, and they fund activities that are intended to provide broadly dispersed benefits, such as protecting the health of the public. Reclassifying these fees as governmental receipts could require a change in law, and because of conventions for scoring appropriations bills, would make it impossible for fees that are controlled through annual appropriations acts to be scored as offsets to discretionary spending.

Table 18–2. SUMMARY OF OFFSETTING RECEIPTS BY TYPE
(In millions of dollars)

Receipt Type	Actual 2022	Estimate					
		2023	2024	2025	2026	2027	2028
Intragovernmental..	1,159,908	1,050,392	1,121,626	1,208,146	1,305,554	1,257,125	1,335,695
Receipts from non-Federal sources:							
Proprietary	449,836	342,623	347,135	347,960	393,273	406,109	444,756
Offsetting governmental	95,575	16,062	16,056	16,592	16,887	17,153	17,546
Total, receipts from non-Federal sources	545,411	358,685	363,191	364,552	410,160	423,262	462,302
Total, offsetting receipts..............................	1,705,319	1,409,077	1,484,817	1,572,698	1,715,714	1,680,387	1,797,997

The final source of offsetting collections and offsetting receipts from the public is gifts. Gifts are voluntary contributions to the Government to support particular purposes or reduce the amount of Government debt held by the public.

The spending associated with the activities that generate offsetting collections and offsetting receipts from the public is included in total or "gross outlays." Offsetting collections and offsetting receipts from the public are subtracted from gross outlays to the public to yield "net outlays," which is the most common measure of outlays cited and generally referred to as simply "outlays."[4] For 2022, gross outlays to the public were $7,118 billion, or 28.5 percent of GDP and offsetting collections and offsetting receipts from the public were $844 billion, or 3.4 percent of GDP, resulting in net outlays of $6,273 billion or 25.1 percent of GDP. Government-wide net outlays reflect the Government's net disbursements to the public and are subtracted from governmental receipts to derive the Government's deficit or surplus. For 2022, governmental receipts were $4,897, or 19.6 percent of GDP, and the deficit was $1,357 billion, or 5.5 percent of GDP.

Although both offsetting collections and offsetting receipts are subtracted from gross outlays to derive net outlays, they are treated differently when it comes to accounting for specific programs and agencies. Offsetting collections are usually authorized to be spent for the purposes of an expenditure account and are generally available for use when collected, without further action by the Congress. Therefore, offsetting collections are recorded as offsets to spending within expenditure accounts, so that the account total highlights the net flow of funds.

Like governmental receipts, offsetting receipts are credited to receipt accounts, and any spending of the receipts is recorded in separate expenditure accounts. As a result, the budget separately displays the flow of funds into and out of the Government. Offsetting receipts may or may not be designated for a specific purpose, depending on the legislation that authorizes their collection. If designated for a particular purpose, the offsetting receipts may, in some cases, be spent without further action by Congress. When not designated for a particular purpose, offsetting receipts are credited to the general fund, which contains all funds not otherwise allocated and which is used to finance Government spending that is not financed out of dedicated funds. In some cases where the receipts are designated for a particular purpose, offsetting receipts are reported in a particular agency and reduce or offset the outlays reported for that agency. In other cases, the offsetting receipts are "undistributed," which means they reduce total Government outlays, but not the outlays of any particular agency.

Table 18-1 summarizes offsetting collections and offsetting receipts from the public. The amounts shown in the table are not evident in the commonly cited budget measure of outlays, which is already net of these collections and receipts. For 2024, the table shows that total offsetting collections and offsetting receipts from the public are estimated to be $644 billion, or 2.4 percent of GDP. Of these, an estimated $281 billion are offsetting collections and an estimated $363 billion are offsetting

---

[4] Gross outlays to the public are derived by subtracting intragovernmental outlays from gross outlays. For 2023, gross outlays were $8,739 billion and intragovernmental outlays were $1,207 billion.

Table 18–3. GROSS OUTLAYS, USER CHARGES, OTHER OFFSETTING COLLECTIONS AND OFFSETTING RECEIPTS FROM THE PUBLIC, AND NET OUTLAYS
(In billions of dollars)

	Actual 2022	Estimate	
		2023	2024
Gross outlays to the public	7,117.8	6,991.6	7,527.0
Offsetting collections and offsetting receipts from the public:			
User charges [1]	571.6	434.8	487.0
Other	306.6	204.4	165.1
Subtotal, offsetting collections and offsetting receipts from the public	844.5	619.7	644.3
Net outlays..	6,273.3	6,371.9	6,882.7

[1] $4.9 billion of the total user charges for 2022 were classified as governmental receipts, and the remainder were classified as offsetting collections and offsetting receipts. $5.1 billion and $5.3 billion of the total user charges for 2023 and 2024 are classified as governmental receipts, respectively.

receipts. Table 18–1 also identifies those offsetting collections and offsetting receipts that are considered user charges, as defined and discussed below.

As shown in the table, major offsetting collections from the public include proceeds from Postal Service sales, electrical power sales, loan repayments to the Commodity Credit Corporation for loans made prior to enactment of the Federal Credit Reform Act, and Federal employee payments for health insurance. As also shown in the table, major offsetting receipts from the public include premiums for Medicare Parts A, B and D, proceeds from military assistance program sales, rents and royalties from Outer Continental Shelf oil extraction, and interest income.

Tables 18–2 and 18–3 provide further detail about offsetting receipts, including both offsetting receipts from the public (as summarized in Table 18–1) and intragov-

ernmental transactions. Table 18–5, "Offsetting Receipts by Type," and Table 18–6, "Offsetting Collections and Offsetting Receipts, Detail—2024 Budget," which is a complete listing by account, are available at https://www.whitehouse.gov/omb/analytical-perspectives/. In total, offsetting receipts are estimated to be $1,485 billion in 2024; $1,122 billion are from intragovernmental transactions and $363 billion are from the public. The offsetting receipts from the public consist of proprietary receipts ($347 billion), which are those resulting from business-like transactions such as the sale of goods or services, and offsetting governmental receipts, which, as discussed above, are derived from the exercise of the Government's sovereign power and, absent a specification in law or a long-standing practice, would be classified on the receipts side of the budget ($16 billion).

II. USER CHARGES

User charges or user fees[5] refer generally to those monies that the Government receives from the public for market-oriented activities and regulatory activities. In combination with budget concepts, laws that authorize user charges determine whether a user charge is classified as an offsetting collection, an offsetting receipt, or a governmental receipt. Almost all user charges, as defined below, are classified as offsetting collections or offsetting receipts; for 2024, only an estimated 1.1 percent of user charges are classified as governmental receipts. As summarized in Table 18–3, total user charges for 2024 are estimated to be $492 billion with $487 billion being offsetting collections or offsetting receipts, and accounting for more than two-thirds of all offsetting collections and offsetting receipts from the public.[6]

Definition. In this chapter, user charges refer to fees, charges, and assessments levied on individuals or organizations directly benefiting from or subject to regulation by a Government program or activity, where the payers do not represent a broad segment of the public such as those who pay income taxes.

Examples of business-type or market-oriented user charges and regulatory and licensing user charges include those charges listed in Table 18-1 for offsetting collections and offsetting receipts. User charges exclude certain offsetting collections and offsetting receipts from the public, such as payments received from credit programs, and in-

terest, and also exclude payments from one part of the Federal Government to another. In addition, user charges do not include dedicated taxes (such as taxes paid to social insurance programs or excise taxes on gasoline) or customs duties, fines, penalties, or forfeitures.

Alternative definitions. The definition for user charges used in this chapter follows the definition used in OMB Circular No. A–25, "User Charges," which provides policy guidance to Executive Branch Agencies on setting the amount for user charges. Alternative definitions may be used for other purposes. Much of the discussion of user charges below—their purpose, when they should be levied, and how the amount should be set—applies to these alternative definitions as well.

A narrower definition of user charges could be limited to proceeds from the sale of goods and services, excluding the proceeds from the sale of assets, and to proceeds that are dedicated to financing the goods and services being provided. This definition is similar to one the House of Representatives uses as a guide for purposes of committee jurisdiction. (See the Congressional Record, January 3, 1991, p. H31, item 8.) The definition of user charges could be even narrower by excluding regulatory fees and focusing solely on business-type transactions. Alternatively, the user charge definition could be broader than the one used in this chapter by including beneficiary- or liability-based excise taxes.[7]

What is the purpose of user charges? User charges are intended to improve the efficiency and equity of financing certain Government activities. Charging users for activities that benefit a relatively limited number of people reduces the burden on the general taxpayer, as

---

[5] In this chapter, the term "user charge" is generally used and has the same meaning as the term "user fee." The term "user charge" is the one used in OMB Circular No. A–11, "Preparation, Submission, and Execution of the Budget"; OMB Circular No. A–25, "User Charges"; and Chapter 15 of this volume, "Budget Concepts." In common usage, the terms "user charge" and "user fee" are often used interchangeably, and in A Glossary of Terms Used in the Federal Budget Process, GAO provides the same definition for both terms.

[6] User charge totals presented in this chapter include collections from accounts classified as containing user fee data. OMB accounts are classified as containing user fee data if more than half of collections are estimated to include user charges. Consequently, totals may include collections that are not user charges in accounts that meet the threshold and exclude user charges in accounts that do not meet the threshold.

[7] Beneficiary- and liability-based taxes are terms taken from the Congressional Budget Office, The Growth of Federal User Charges, August 1993, and updated in October 1995. Gasoline taxes are an example of beneficiary-based taxes. An example of a liability-based tax is the excise tax that formerly helped fund the hazardous substance superfund in the Environmental Protection Agency. This tax was paid by industry groups to finance environmental cleanup activities related to the industry activity but not necessarily caused by the payer of the fee.

does charging regulated parties for regulatory activities in a particular sector.

User charges that are set to cover the costs of production of goods and services can result in more efficient resource allocation within the economy. When buyers are charged the cost of providing goods and services, they make better cost-benefit calculations regarding the size of their purchase, which in turn signals to the Government how much of the goods or services it should provide. Prices in private, competitive markets serve the same purposes. User charges for goods and services that do not have special social or distributional benefits may also improve equity or fairness by requiring those who benefit from an activity to pay for it and by not requiring those who do not benefit from an activity to pay for it.

When should the Government impose a charge? Discussions of whether to finance spending with a tax or a fee often focus on whether the benefits of the activity accrue to the public in general or to a limited group of people. In general, if the benefits of spending accrue broadly to the public or include special social or distributional benefits, then the program should be financed by taxes paid by the public. In contrast, if the benefits accrue to a limited number of private individuals or organizations and do not include special social or distributional benefits, then the program should be financed by charges paid by the private beneficiaries. For Federal programs where the benefits are entirely public or entirely private, applying this principle can be relatively easy. For example, the benefits from national defense accrue to the public in general, and according to this principle should be (and are) financed by taxes. In contrast, the benefits of electricity sold by the Tennessee Valley Authority accrue primarily to those using the electricity, and should be (and predominantly are) financed by user charges.

In many cases, however, an activity has benefits that accrue to both public and private groups, and it may be difficult to identify how much of the benefits accrue to each. Because of this, it can be difficult to know how much of the program should be financed by taxes and how much by fees. For example, the benefits from recreation areas are mixed. Fees for visitors to these areas are appropriate because the visitors benefit directly from their visit, but the public in general also benefits because these areas protect the Nation's natural and historic heritage now and for posterity. For this reason, visitor recreation fees

generally cover only part of the cost to the Government of maintaining the recreation property. Where a fee may be appropriate to finance all or part of an activity, the extent to which a fee can be easily administered must be considered. For example, if fees are charged for entering or using Government-owned land then there must be clear points of entry onto the land and attendants patrolling and monitoring the land's use.

What amount should be charged? When the Government is acting in its capacity as sovereign and where user charges are appropriate, such as for some regulatory activities, current policy supports setting fees equal to the full cost to the Government, including both direct and indirect costs. When the Government is not acting in its capacity as sovereign and engages in a purely business-type transaction (such as leasing or selling goods, services, or resources), market price is generally the basis for establishing the fee.[8] If the Government is engaged in a purely business-type transaction and economic resources are allocated efficiently, then this market price should be equal to or greater than the Government's full cost of production.

Classification of user charges in the budget. As shown in the note to Table 18–3, most user charges are classified as offsets to outlays on the spending side of the budget, but a few are classified on the receipts side of the budget. An estimated $5.3 billion of user charges in 2024 are classified on the receipts side and are included in the governmental receipts totals described in the previous chapter, "Governmental Receipts." They are classified as receipts because they are regulatory charges collected by the Federal Government by the exercise of its sovereign powers. Examples include filing fees in the United States courts and agricultural quarantine inspection fees.

The remaining user charges, an estimated $487 billion in 2024, are classified as offsetting collections and offsetting receipts on the spending side of the Budget. As discussed above in the context of all offsetting collections and offsetting receipts, some of these user charges are collected by the Federal Government by the exercise of its sovereign powers and conceptually should appear on the receipts side of the budget, but they are required by law or a long-standing practice to be classified on the spending side.

---

[8] Policies for setting user charges are promulgated in OMB Circular No. A–25: "User Charges" (July 8, 1993).

III. USER CHARGE PROPOSALS

As shown in Table 18–1, an estimated $281 billion of user charges for 2024 will be credited directly to expenditure accounts and will generally be available for expenditure when they are collected, without further action by the Congress. An estimated $221 of user charges for 2024 will be deposited in offsetting receipt accounts and will be available to be spent only according to the legislation that established the charges.

As shown in Table 18–4, the Administration is proposing new or increased user charges that would, in the aggregate, increase collections by an estimated $805 mil-

lion in 2024 and an estimated total of $28 billion from 2025 through 2033. These estimates reflect only the amounts to be collected; they do not include related spending. Each proposal is classified as either discretionary or mandatory, as those terms are defined in the Balanced Budget and Emergency Deficit Control Act of 1985, as amended. "Discretionary" refers to user charges controlled through annual appropriations acts and generally under the jurisdiction of the appropriations committees in the Congress. "Mandatory" refers to user charges controlled by permanent laws and under the jurisdiction of the authorizing committees. These and other terms are discussed further in this volume in Chapter 15, "Budget Concepts."

A. Discretionary User Charge Proposals

1. Offsetting collections

Department of Health and Human Services

Food and Drug Administration (FDA): Increase export certification user fee cap. Firms exporting products from the United States are often asked by foreign customers or foreign governments to supply a "certificate" for products regulated by the FDA to document the product's regulatory or marketing status. The proposal increases the maximum user fee cap from $175 per export certification to $600 to meet FDA's true cost of issuing export certificates and to ensure better and faster service for American companies that Policies for setting user charges are promulgated in OMB Circular No. A–25: "User Charges" (July 8, 1993). request the service.

Increase tobacco product user fee. Currently, FDA's regulation of all tobacco products is financed through user fees collected from six product categories: cigarettes, roll your own tobacco, snuff, chewing tobacco, cigars, and pipe tobacco. This proposal would expand FDA's tobacco user fees and include user fee assessments on e-cigarettes and other electronic nicotine delivery systems (ENDS) manufacturers, which currently do not pay user fees, and increase the current limitation on total tobacco user fee collections by $100 million in 2024. To ensure that resources keep up with new tobacco products, the proposal would also index future collections to inflation. The expansion of tobacco user fees will strengthen FDA's ability to respond to the growth of newer products such as e-cigarettes through investments in regulatory science, enforcement, and premarket review of product applications.

Commodity Futures Trading Commission (CFTC)

Establish CFTC user fee. The Budget proposes an amendment to the Commodity Exchange Act authorizing the CFTC to collect user fees to fund the Commission's activities, like other Federal financial and banking regulators. Fee funding would shift the costs of services provided by CFTC from the general taxpayer to the primary beneficiaries of CFTC oversight. Contingent upon enactment of legislation authorizing the CFTC to collect fees, the Administration proposes that collections begin in 2023 to offset a portion of CFTC's annual appropriation.

Department of the Interior

Bureau of Land Management (BLM): Establish onshore oil and gas inspection fees. The Budget proposes new inspection fees for oil and gas leases that are subject to inspection by BLM. The fees would be based on the number of oil and gas wells per lease or unit, providing for costs to be shared equitably across the industry. In 2023, BLM will spend $51 million on managing its compliance inspection program. Inspection costs include,

among other things, the salaries and travel expenses of inspectors. The proposed fees will generate approximately $51 million in 2023, thereby fully offsetting the Bureau's cost of compliance inspections and requiring energy developers on Federal lands to fund the majority of inspection-related compliance costs incurred by BLM.

Department of State

Establish The National Museum of American Diplomacy rental fee. This new user fee will enable the Department of State to provide support, on a cost-recovery basis, to outside organizations for programs and conference activities held at The National Museum of American Diplomacy.

2. Offsetting receipts

Department of State

Extend Western Hemisphere Travel Initiative surcharge. The Administration proposes to permanently extend the authority for the Department of State to collect the Western Hemisphere Travel Initiative surcharge. The surcharge was initially enacted by the Passport Services Enhancement Act of 2005 (Public Law 109–167) to cover the Department's costs of meeting increased demand for passports, which resulted from the implementation of the Western Hemisphere Travel Initiative.

Increase Border Crossing Card (BCC) fee. The Budget includes a proposal to allow the fee charged for BCC minor applicants to be set administratively, rather than statutorily, at one-half the fee charged for processing an adult border crossing card. Administrative fee setting will allow the fee to better reflect the associated cost of service, consistent with other fees charged for consular services. As a result of this change, annual BCC fee collections beginning in 2024 are projected to increase by $5 million (from $1 million to $6 million).

Increase Machine-Readable Visa (MRV) fee. The Budget includes a proposal to authorize the Department of State to account for the cost of other consular services not otherwise subject to a fee or surcharge when setting the amount of the MRV fee.

B. Mandatory User Charge Proposals

Offsetting receipts

Department Health and Human Services

Provide Authority for the Secretary to Collect and Expend Re-Survey Fees from Long-Term Care Facilities Within the Survey and Certification Program that Require a Revisit Survey. The Budget proposes to provide CMS permanent authority to charge long-term care facilities fees for any revisits required to validate the correction of deficiencies identified during initial certification, recertification, complaint, facility-reported incident, or prior revisit surveys. The collections would supplement the CMS Program Management funding for the Survey and Certification program.

Department of Homeland Security

Extend expiring Customs and Border Protection (CBP) fees. The Budget proposes to extend the Merchandise Processing Fee beyond its current expiration date of September 30, 2031 to September 30, 2033, and makes permanent the rate increase (from 0.21 percent ad valorem to 0.3464 percent ad valorem) enacted in section 503 of the U.S.-Korea Free Trade Agreement Implementation Act (Public Law 112–41). It also proposes to extend fees statutorily set under the Consolidated Omnibus Budget Reconciliation Act of 1985 (COBRA) and the Express Consignment Courier Facilities (ECCF) fee created under the Trade Act of 2002 beyond their current expiration date of September 30, 2031 to September 30, 2033.

Customs and Border Protection (CBP) User Fee Facilities. The Budget proposes authority for CBP to recover all of its costs associated with providing immigration and agriculture services at User Fee Facilities. Current law authorizes charging a fee for customs services at User Fee Facilities; however, there is an increased need for CBP to recover the costs of immigration and agriculture services that can be clearly segregated from the customs services provided at User Fee Facilities.

Department of Labor

Expand Foreign Labor Certification fees. The Budget proposes authorizing legislation to establish and retain fees to cover the costs of operating the foreign labor certification programs, which ensure that employers proposing to bring in immigrant workers have checked to ensure that American workers cannot meet their needs and that immigrant workers are being compen- sated appropriately and not disadvantaging American workers. The ability to charge fees for these programs would give the Department of Labor (DOL) a more reliable, workload-based source of funding for this function, as the Department of Homeland Security has, and would ultimately eliminate the need for discretionary appropriations. The proposal would allow DOL to charge fees for its prevailing wage determinations, permanent labor certification program, H–2B non-agricultural workers program, and CW–1 Northern Mariana Islands transitional workers program, as well as retain and adjust the H–2A agricultural worker application fees currently deposited into the General Fund. The fee levels would be set via regulation to ensure that the amounts are subject to review. Given the DOL Inspector General's important role in investigating fraud and abuse, the proposal also includes a mechanism to provide funding for the Inspector General's work to oversee foreign labor certification programs.

C. User Charge Proposals that are Governmental Receipts

Department of Homeland Security

Establish Electronic Visa Update System user fee. The Budget proposes to establish a user fee for the Electronic Visa Update System (EVUS), a CBP program to collect biographic and travel-related information from certain non-immigrant visa holders prior to traveling to the United States. This process will complement the existing visa application process and enhance CBP's ability to make pre-travel admissibility and risk determinations. CBP proposes to establish a user fee to fund the costs of establishing, providing, and administering the system.

Table 18–4.   USER CHARGE PROPOSALS IN THE 2024 BUDGET [1]

(Estimated collections in millions of dollars)

	2024	2025	2026	2027	2028	2029	2030	2031	2032	2033	2024–2028	2024–2033
OFFSETTING COLLECTIONS AND OFFSETTING RECEIPTS												
DISCRETIONARY:												
Offsetting collections												
Department of Health and Human Services												
Food and Drug Administration (FDA): Increase export certification user fee cap	5	5	5	6	6	6	7	7	7	7	27	61
FDA: Increase tobacco product user fee	100	102	104	106	108	110	113	116	119	122	520	1,100
Department of the Interior												
Bureau of Land Management: Establish onshore oil and gas inspection fees	51	51	51	51	51	51	51	51	51	51	255	510
Department of State												
Establish The National Museum of American Diplomacy rental fee	*	*	*	*	*	*	*	*	*	....	*	*
Commodity Futures Trading Commission (CFTC)												
Establish CFTC user fee	116	119	121	124	127	130	133	136	139	142	607	1,287
Offsetting receipts												
Department of State												
Extend Western Hemisphere Travel Initiative surcharge	462	473	483	495	506	518	530	542	554	567	2,419	5,130
Increase Border Crossing Card fee	6	6	6	6	6	6	6	6	6	6	30	60
Increase Machine-Readable Visa fee	....	....	143	285	285	285	285	285	285	285	713	2,138
Subtotal, discretionary user charge proposals	740	756	913	1,073	1,089	1,106	1,125	1,143	1,161	1,180	4,571	10,286
MANDATORY:												
Offsetting receipts												
Department of Health and Human Services												
Provide Authority for the Secretary to Collect and Expend Re-Survey Fees	....	14	14	15	15	15	16	16	16	17	58	138
Department of Homeland Security												
Extend expiring Customs and Border Protection (CBP) fees	....	....	....	....	....	....	....	....	8,077	8,365	....	16,442
Expand CBP user fee facilities costs	7	7	7	7	8	8	8	8	8	9	36	77
Department of Labor												
Expand Foreign Labor Certification fees [2]	6	62	118	121	125	130	134	140	144	149	432	1,129
Subtotal, mandatory user charge proposals	13	69	125	128	133	138	142	148	8,229	8,523	468	17,648
Subtotal, user charge proposals that are offsetting collections and offsetting receipts	753	825	1,038	1,201	1,222	1,244	1,267	1,291	9,390	9,703	5,039	27,934
GOVERNMENTAL RECEIPTS												
Department of Homeland Security												
Establish Electronic Visa Update System user fee	52	58	64	72	79	88	108	118	130	143	325	912
Total, user charge proposals	805	883	1,102	1,273	1,301	1,332	1,375	1,409	9,520	9,846	5,364	28,846

[1] A positive sign indicates an increase in collections.

[2] User charge totals presented for this proposal, which will gradually replace rather than supplement annual appropriations for the foreign labor certification program, include collections from existing H–2A labor certification fees currently deposited into a separate account.

* $500,000 or less

19. TAX EXPENDITURES

The Congressional Budget Act of 1974 (Public Law 93–344) requires that a list of "tax expenditures" be included in the Budget. Tax expenditures are defined in the law as "revenue losses attributable to provisions of the Federal tax laws which allow a special exclusion, exemption, or deduction from gross income or which provide a special credit, a preferential rate of tax, or a deferral of tax liability." These exceptions may be viewed as alternatives to other policy instruments, such as spending or regulatory programs.

Identification and measurement of tax expenditures depends crucially on the baseline tax system against which the actual tax system is compared. The tax expenditure estimates presented in this document are patterned on a comprehensive income tax, which defines income as the sum of consumption and the change in net wealth in a given period of time.

An important assumption underlying each tax expenditure estimate reported below is that other parts of the Tax Code remain unchanged. The estimates would be different if tax expenditures were changed simultaneously because of potential interactions among provisions. For that reason, this document does not present a grand total for the estimated tax expenditures.

Tax expenditures relating to the individual and corporate income taxes are estimated for fiscal years 2022–2032 using two methods of accounting: current tax receipt effects and present value effects. The present value approach provides estimates of the receipt effects for tax expenditures that generally involve deferrals of tax payments into the future.

TAX EXPENDITURES IN THE INCOME TAX

Tax Expenditure Estimates

All tax expenditure estimates and descriptions presented here are based upon current tax law enacted as of July 31, 2022, and reflect the economic assumptions from the Midsession Review of the Fiscal Year 2023 Budget. In some cases, expired or repealed provisions are listed if their tax receipt effects occur in fiscal year 2022 or later. Although this chapter does not include changes in tax expenditures enacted after July 31, 2022, these changes are discussed elsewhere in the Budget. see Chapter 23 of this volume, "Comparison of Actual to Estimated Totals," for highlights of key provisions including those from the Inflation Reduction Act (IRA), as well as the CHIPS Act of 2022 and the Research and Development, Competition, and Innovation Act, both passed later in 2022.

The total receipt effects for tax expenditures for fiscal years 2022–2032 are displayed according to the Budget's functional categories in Table 19-1. Descriptions of the specific tax expenditure provisions follow the discussion of general features of the tax expenditure concept.

Two baseline concepts—the normal tax baseline and the reference tax law baseline—are used to identify and estimate tax expenditures.[1] For the most part, the two concepts coincide. However, items treated as tax expenditures under the normal tax baseline, but not the reference tax law baseline, are indicated by the designation "normal tax method" in the tables. The receipt effects for these items are zero using the reference tax law. The alternative baseline concepts are discussed in detail below.

Table 19-2 ranks the major tax expenditures by the size of their 2023–2032 receipt effect. The first column provides the number of the provision in order to cross reference this table to Table 19-1, as well as to the descriptions below. The tax expenditure tables discussed herein can be obtained for current and previous years from the Department of the Treasury website.[2]

Interpreting Tax Expenditure Estimates

The estimates shown for individual tax expenditures in Tables 19-1 and 19-2 do not necessarily equal the increase in Federal receipts (or the change in the budget balance) that would result from repealing these special provisions, for the following reasons.

First, eliminating a tax expenditure may have incentive effects that alter economic behavior. These incentives can affect the resulting magnitudes of the activity, or the consequences of other tax provisions or Government programs. For example, if capital gains were taxed at higher ordinary income tax rates, capital gain realizations would be expected to decline, which could result in lower tax receipts depending on the elasticity of the capital gains tax rates. Such behavioral effects are not reflected in the estimates.

Second, tax expenditures are interdependent even without incentive effects. Repeal of a tax expenditure provision can increase or decrease the tax receipts associated with other provisions. For example, even if behavior does not change, repeal of an itemized deduction could

---

[1] These baseline concepts are thoroughly discussed in Special Analysis G of the 1985 Budget, where the former is referred to as the pre-1983 method and the latter the post-1982 method.

[2] https://home.treasury.gov/policy-issues/tax-policy/tax-expenditures. Table numbering within this chapter may not match the primary source documentation.

increase the receipt costs from other deductions because some taxpayers would be moved into higher tax brackets. Alternatively, repeal of an itemized deduction could lower the receipt cost from other deductions if taxpayers are led to claim the standard deduction instead of itemizing. Similarly, if two provisions were repealed simultaneously, the increase in tax liability could be greater or less than the sum of the two separate tax expenditures, because each is estimated assuming that the other remains in force. In addition, the estimates reported in Table 19-1 are the totals of individual and corporate income tax receipt effects and do not reflect any possible interactions between individual and corporate income tax receipts. For this reason, the estimates in Table 19-1 should be regarded as approximations.

Present-Value Estimates

The annual value of tax expenditures for tax deferrals is reported on a cash basis in all tables except Table 19-3. Cash-based estimates reflect the difference between taxes deferred in the current year and incoming receipts that are received due to deferrals of taxes from prior years. Although such estimates are useful as a measure of cash flows into the Government, they do not accurately reflect the true economic cost of these provisions. For example, for a provision where activity levels have changed over time, so that incoming tax receipts from past deferrals are greater than deferred receipts from new activity, the cash-basis tax expenditure estimate can be negative, despite the fact that in present-value terms current deferrals have a real cost to the Government (i.e., taxpayers). Alternatively, in the case of a newly enacted deferral provision, a cash-based estimate can overstate the real effect on receipts to the Government because the newly deferred taxes will ultimately be received.

Discounted present-value estimates of receipt effects are presented in Table 19-3 for certain provisions that involve tax deferrals or other long-term receipt effects. These estimates complement the cash-based tax expenditure estimates presented in the other tables.

The present-value estimates represent the receipt effects, net of future tax payments that follow from activities undertaken during calendar year 2022 which cause the deferrals or other long-term receipt effects. For instance, a pension contribution in 2022 would cause a deferral of tax payments on wages in 2022 and on pension fund earnings on this contribution (e.g., interest) in later years. In some future year, however, the 2022 pension contribution and accrued earnings will be paid out and taxes will be due; these receipts are included in the present-value estimate. In general, this conceptual approach is similar to the one used for reporting the budgetary effects of credit programs, where direct loans and guarantees in a given year affect future cash flows.

Tax Expenditure Baselines

A tax expenditure is an exception to baseline provisions of the tax structure that usually results in a reduction in the amount of tax owed. The 1974 Congressional Budget Act, which mandated the tax expenditure budget, did not specify the baseline provisions of the tax law. As noted previously, deciding whether provisions are exceptions, therefore, is a matter of judgment. As in prior years, most of this year's tax expenditure estimates are presented using two baselines: the normal tax baseline and the reference tax law baseline. Tax expenditures may take the form of credits, deductions, special exceptions and allowances.

The normal tax baseline is patterned on a practical variant of a comprehensive income tax, which defines income as the sum of consumption and the change in net wealth in a given period of time. The normal tax baseline allows personal exemptions, a standard deduction, and deduction of expenses incurred in earning income. It is not limited to a particular structure of tax rates, or by a specific definition of the taxpaying unit.

The reference tax law baseline is also patterned on a comprehensive income tax, but it is closer to existing law. Reference tax law tax expenditures are limited to special exceptions from a generally provided tax rule that serves programmatic functions in a way that is analogous to spending programs. Provisions under the reference tax law baseline are generally tax expenditures under the normal tax baseline, but the reverse is not always true.

Both the normal tax and reference tax law baselines allow several major departures from a pure comprehensive income tax. For example, under the normal tax and reference tax law baselines:

- Income is taxable only when it is realized in exchange. Thus, the deferral of tax on unrealized capital gains is not regarded as a tax expenditure. Accrued income would be taxed under a comprehensive income tax.

- There is a separate corporate income tax.

- Tax rates on noncorporate business income vary by level of income.

- Individual tax rates, including brackets, standard deduction, and personal exemptions, are allowed to vary with marital status.

- Values of assets and debt are not generally adjusted for inflation. A comprehensive income tax would adjust the cost basis of capital assets and debt for changes in the general price level. Thus, under a comprehensive income tax baseline, the failure to take account of inflation in measuring depreciation, capital gains, and interest income would be regarded as a negative tax expenditure (i.e., a tax penalty), and failure to take account of inflation in measuring interest costs would be regarded as a positive tax expenditure (i.e., a tax subsidy).

- The base erosion and anti-abuse tax (BEAT) for multinational corporations is treated as a minimum tax and considered part of the rate structure.

Although the reference tax law and normal tax baselines are generally similar, areas of difference include:

Tax rates. The separate schedules applying to the various taxpaying units and the Alternative Minimum Tax are treated as part of the baseline rate structure under both the reference tax law and normal tax methods.

Income subject to tax. Income subject to tax is defined as gross income less the costs of earning that income. Under the reference tax law, gross income does not include gifts defined as receipts of money or property that are not consideration in an exchange nor does gross income include most transfer payments from the Government.[3] The normal tax baseline also excludes gifts between individuals from gross income. Under the normal tax baseline, however, all cash transfer payments from the Government to private individuals are counted in gross income, and exemptions of such transfers from tax are identified as tax expenditures. The costs of earning income are generally deductible in determining taxable income under both the reference tax law and normal tax baselines.[4]

Capital recovery. Under the reference tax law baseline no tax expenditures arise from accelerated depreciation. Under the normal tax baseline, the depreciation allowance for property is computed using estimates of economic depreciation.

Descriptions of Income Tax Provisions

Descriptions of the individual and corporate income tax expenditures reported on in this document follow. These descriptions relate to current law as of July 31, 2022.

National Defense

1. ***Exclusion of benefits and allowances to Armed Forces personnel.***—Under the baseline tax system, all compensation, including dedicated payments and in-kind benefits, should be included in taxable income because they represent accretions to wealth that do not materially differ from cash wages. As an example, a rental voucher of $100 is (approximately) equal in value to $100 of cash income. In contrast to this treatment, certain housing and meals, in addition to other benefits provided military personnel, either in cash or in kind, as well as certain amounts of pay related to combat service, are excluded from income subject to tax.

International Affairs

2. ***Exclusion of income earned abroad by U.S. citizens.***—Under the baseline tax system, all compensation received by U.S. citizens and residents is properly included in their taxable income. It makes no difference whether the compensation is a result of working abroad or whether it is labeled as a housing allowance. In con-

trast to this treatment, U.S. tax law allows U.S. citizens and residents who live abroad, work in the private sector, and satisfy a foreign residency requirement to exclude up to $80,000, plus adjustments for inflation since 2004, in foreign earned income from U.S. taxes. In addition, if these taxpayers are provided housing by their employers, then they may also exclude the cost of such housing from their income to the extent that it exceeds 16 percent of the earned income exclusion limit. This housing exclusion is capped at 30 percent of the earned income exclusion limit, with geographical adjustments. If taxpayers do not receive a specific allowance for housing expenses, they may deduct housing expenses up to the amount by which foreign earned income exceeds their foreign earned income exclusion.

3. ***Exclusion of certain allowances for Federal employees abroad.***—In general, all compensation received by U.S. citizens and residents is properly included in their taxable income. It makes no difference whether the compensation is a result of working abroad or whether it is labeled as an allowance for the high cost of living abroad. In contrast to this treatment, U.S. Federal civilian employees and Peace Corps members who work outside the continental United States are allowed to exclude from U.S. taxable income certain special allowances they receive to compensate them for the relatively high costs associated with living overseas. The allowances supplement wage income and cover expenses such as rent, education, and the cost of travel to and from the United States.

4. ***Reduced tax rate on active income of controlled foreign corporations (normal tax method).***—Under the baseline tax system, worldwide income forms the tax base of U.S. corporations. In contrast, U.S. tax law exempts or preferentially taxes certain portions of this income. Prior to the passage of the Tax Cuts and Jobs Act TCJA (effective January 1, 2018), active foreign income was generally taxed only upon repatriation. TCJA changed these rules, so that certain active income (called "global intangible low tax income" or "GILTI") is taxed currently, even if it is not distributed. However, U.S. corporations generally receive a 50-percent deduction from U.S. tax on their GILTI (the deduction decreases to 37.5 percent in 2026), resulting in a substantially reduced rate of tax. In addition, some active income is excluded from tax, and distributions out of active income are no longer taxed upon repatriation. These reductions and exemptions from U.S. taxation are considered tax expenditures. However, U.S. shareholders of specified foreign corporations must include their pro rata share of accumulated post-1986 deferred foreign income (as of the last taxable year before January 1, 2018) in U.S. taxable income, and this inclusion acts as an offset to the reduced tax rate on CFC income in the years in which the payments are received.

5. ***Deduction for foreign-derived intangible income derived from trade or business within the United States.***—Under the baseline tax system, the United States taxes income earned by U.S. corporations from serving foreign markets (e.g., exports and royalties)

---

[3] Gross income does, however, include transfer payments associated with past employment, such as Social Security benefits.

[4] In the case of individuals who hold "passive" equity interests in businesses, the pro-rata shares of sales and expense deductions reportable in a year are limited. A passive business activity is defined generally to be one in which the holder of the interest, usually a partnership interest, does not actively perform managerial or other participatory functions. The taxpayer may generally report no larger deductions for a year than will reduce taxable income from such activities to zero. Deductions in excess of the limitation may be taken in subsequent years, or when the interest is liquidated. In addition, costs of earning income may be limited under the Alternative Minimum Tax.

at the full U.S. rate. After the passage of TCJA, domestic corporations are allowed a deduction equal to 37.5 percent of "foreign-derived intangible income," which is essentially income from serving foreign markets (defined on a formulaic basis). The deduction falls to 21.875 percent in 2026.

6. ***Interest Charge Domestic International Sales Corporations (IC-DISCs).***—Under the baseline tax system, taxpayer earnings are subject to tax using the regular tax rates applied to all taxpayers. In contrast, IC-DISCs allow a portion of income from exports to be taxed at the qualified dividend rate which is no higher than 20 percent (plus a 3.8-percent surtax for high-income taxpayers).

General Science, Space, and Technology

7. ***Expensing of research and experimentation expenditures (normal tax method).***—The baseline tax system allows a deduction for the cost of producing income. It requires taxpayers to capitalize the costs associated with investments over time to better match the streams of income and associated costs. Research and experimentation (R&E) projects can be viewed as investments because, if successful, their benefits accrue for several years. It is often difficult, however, to identify whether a specific R&E project is successful and, if successful, what its expected life will be. Because of this ambiguity, the reference tax law baseline system would allow expensing of R&E expenditures. In contrast, under the normal tax method, the expensing of R&E expenditures is viewed as a tax expenditure. The baseline assumed for the normal tax method is that all R&E expenditures are successful and have an expected life of five years. Current law requires R&E expenditures paid or incurred in taxable years beginning after December 31, 2021, to be capitalized and amortized over 5 years, while allowing R&E expenditures paid or incurred in prior taxable years to be expensed.

8. ***Credit for increasing research activities.***— The baseline tax system would uniformly tax all returns to investments and not allow credits for particular activities, investments, or industries. In contrast, the Tax Code allows an R&E credit of up to 20 percent of qualified research expenditures in excess of a base amount. The base amount of the credit is generally determined by multiplying a "fixed-base percentage" by the average amount of the company's gross receipts for the prior four years. The taxpayer's fixed base percentage generally is the ratio of its research expenses to gross receipts for 1984 through 1988. Taxpayers can elect the alternative simplified credit regime, which equals 14 percent of qualified research expenses that exceed 50 percent of the average qualified research expenses for the three preceding taxable years.

Energy

9. ***Expensing of exploration and development costs, oil and gas.***—Under the baseline tax system, the costs of exploring and developing oil and gas wells would be capitalized and then amortized (or depreciated) over an estimate of the economic life of the property. This insures that the net income from the well is measured appropriately each year. In contrast to this treatment, current law allows immediate deduction, i.e., expensing, of intangible drilling costs for successful investments in domestic oil and gas wells (such as wages, the cost of using machinery for grading and drilling, and the cost of unsalvageable materials used in constructing wells). Because expensing allows recovery of costs sooner, it is more advantageous to the taxpayer than amortization. Expensing provisions for exploration expenditures apply only to properties for which a deduction for percentage depletion is allowable. For oil and gas wells, integrated oil companies may expense only 70 percent of intangible drilling costs and must amortize the remaining 30 percent over five years. Non-integrated oil companies may expense all such costs.

10. ***Expensing of exploration and development costs, coal.***— This is similar to the previous provision but limited to coal. Current law allows immediate deduction of eligible exploration and development costs for domestic coal mines and other natural fuel deposits.

11. ***Excess of percentage over cost depletion, oil and gas.***—The baseline tax system would allow recovery of the costs of developing certain oil and gas properties using cost depletion. Cost depletion is similar in concept to depreciation, in that the costs of developing or acquiring the asset are capitalized and then gradually reduced over an estimate of the asset's economic life, as is appropriate for measuring net income. In contrast, the Tax Code generally allows independent oil and gas producers and royalty owners to take percentage depletion deductions rather than cost depletion on limited quantities of output. Under percentage depletion, taxpayers deduct a percentage of gross income from oil and gas production. In certain cases the deduction is limited to a fraction of the asset's net income. Over the life of an investment, percentage depletion deductions can exceed the cost of the investment. Consequently, percentage depletion may provide more advantageous tax treatment than would cost depletion, which limits deductions to an investment's cost.

12. ***Excess of percentage over cost depletion, coal.***—This is similar to the previous provision but limited to coal.

13. ***Exception from passive loss limitation for working interests in oil and gas properties.***—The baseline tax system accepts current law's general rule limiting taxpayers' ability to deduct losses from passive activities against nonpassive income (e.g., wages, interest, and dividends). Passive activities generally are defined as those in which the taxpayer does not materially participate, though there are numerous additional considerations brought to bear on the determination of which activities are passive for a given taxpayer. Losses are limited in an attempt to limit tax sheltering activities. Passive losses that are unused may be carried forward and applied against future passive income. An exception from the passive loss limitation is provided for a working interest in an oil or gas property that the taxpayer holds directly or through an entity that does not limit the liability of the taxpayer with respect to the interest. Thus, taxpayers can deduct losses from such working interests against nonpassive income without regard to whether they materially participate in the activity.

14. ***Capital gains treatment of royalties on coal.***—The baseline tax system generally would tax all income under the regular tax rate schedule. It would not allow preferentially low tax rates to apply to certain types or sources of income. Current law allows capital gains realized by individuals to be taxed at a preferentially low rate that is no higher than 20 percent (plus the 3.8-percent surtax). Certain sales of coal under royalty contracts qualify for taxation as capital gains rather than ordinary income.

15. ***Exclusion of interest on energy facility bonds.***—The baseline tax system generally would tax all income under the regular tax rate schedule. It would not allow preferentially low (or zero) tax rates to apply to certain types or sources of income. In contrast, the Tax Code allows interest earned on State and local bonds used to finance construction of certain energy facilities to be exempt from tax. These bonds are generally subject to the State private-activity-bond annual volume cap.

16. ***Enhanced oil recovery credit.***—A credit is provided equal to 15 percent of the taxpayer's costs for enhanced oil recovery on U.S. projects. The credit is reduced in proportion to the ratio of the reference price of oil for the previous calendar year minus $28 (adjusted for inflation from 1990) to $6.

17. ***Energy production credit.***—The baseline tax system would not allow credits for particular activities, investments, or industries. Instead, it generally would seek to tax uniformly all returns from investment-like activities. In contrast, the Tax Code provides a credit for certain electricity produced from wind energy, biomass, geothermal energy, solar energy, small irrigation power, municipal solid waste, or qualified hydropower and sold to an unrelated party. Wind facilities must have begun construction before January 1, 2022. Facilities that began construction in 2017 receive 80 percent of the credit, facilities that begun construction in 2018 receive 60 percent of the credit, facilities that began construction in 2019 receive 40 percent of the credit, and facilities that begun construction in years 2020 through 2021 receive 60 percent of the credit. Qualified facilities producing electricity from sources other than wind must begin construction before January 1, 2022. In addition to the electricity production credit, a ten-year income tax credit is allowed for the production of refined coal for facilities placed in service before January 1, 2012. The Tax Code also provided an income tax credit for Indian coal facilities. The Indian coal facilities credit expired on December 31, 2021.

18. ***Marginal wells credit.***—A credit is provided for crude oil and natural gas produced from a qualified marginal well. A marginal well is one that does not produce more than 1,095 barrel-of-oil equivalents per year, with this limit adjusted proportionately for the number of days the well is in production. The credit is no more than $3.00 per barrel of qualified crude oil production and $0.50 per thousand cubic feet of qualified natural gas production. The credit for natural gas is reduced in proportion to the amount by which the reference price of natural gas at the wellhead for the previous calendar year exceeds $1.67 per thousand cubic feet and is zero for a reference price that

exceeds $2.00. The credit for crude oil is reduced in proportion to the amount by which the reference price of oil for the previous calendar year exceeds $15.00 per barrel and is zero for a reference price that exceeds $18.00. All dollar amounts are adjusted for inflation from 2004.

19. ***Energy investment credit.***—The baseline tax system would not allow credits for particular activities, investments, or industries. Instead, it generally would seek to tax uniformly all returns from investment-like activities. However, the Tax Code provides credits for investments in solar and geothermal energy property, qualified fuel cell power plants, stationary microturbine power plants, geothermal heat pumps, waste energy recovery property, small wind property, offshore wind, and combined heat and power property. The credit is 30 percent for property that begins construction before 2020, 26 percent for property that begins construction in years 2020 through 2022, and 22 percent for property that begins construction in 2023 and in all cases that is placed in service before January 1, 2026. The credit for offshore wind is 30 percent for facilities placed in service before January 1, 2026. A 10-percent credit is available for geothermal or qualified solar property placed in service after December 31, 2025. Owners of renewable power facilities that qualify for the energy production credit may instead elect to take an energy investment credit at a rate specified by law.

20. ***Alcohol fuel credits.***—The baseline tax system would not allow credits for particular activities, investments, or industries. Instead, it generally would seek to tax uniformly all returns from investment-like activities. In contrast, the Tax Code provides an income tax credit for qualified cellulosic biofuel production which was renamed the Second generation biofuel producer credit. This provision expired on December 31, 2021.

21. ***Bio-diesel and small agri-biodiesel producer tax credits.***—The baseline tax system would not allow credits for particular activities, investments, or industries. Instead, it generally would seek to tax uniformly all returns from investment-like activities. However, the Tax Code allows an income tax credit for biodiesel and for biodiesel derived from virgin sources. In lieu of the Bio-diesel credit, the taxpayer can claim a refundable excise tax credit. In addition, small agri-biodiesel producers are eligible for a separate income tax credit for Bio-diesel production, and a separate credit is available for qualified renewable diesel fuel mixtures. This provision expired on December 31, 2022.

22. ***Tax credits for clean-fuel burning vehicles and refueling property.***—The baseline tax system would not allow credits for particular activities, investments, or industries. Instead, it generally would seek to tax uniformly all returns from investment-like activities. In contrast, the Tax Code allows credits for plug-in electric-drive motor vehicles, alternative fuel vehicle refueling property, two-wheeled plug-in electric vehicles, and fuel cell motor vehicles. These provisions, except for the plug-in electric-drive motor vehicle credit, expired after December 31, 2017.

23. ***Exclusion of utility conservation subsidies.***—
The baseline tax system generally takes a comprehensive view of taxable income that includes a wide variety of (measurable) accretions to wealth. In certain circumstances, public utilities offer rate subsidies to non-business customers who invest in energy conservation measures. These rate subsidies are equivalent to payments from the utility to its customer, and so represent accretions to wealth, income that would be taxable to the customer under the baseline tax system. In contrast, the Tax Code exempts these subsidies from the non-business customer's gross income.

24. ***Credit for holding clean renewable energy bonds.***—The baseline tax system would uniformly tax all returns to investments and not allow credits for particular activities, investments, or industries. In contrast, the Tax Code provides for the issuance of Clean Renewable Energy Bonds that entitle the bond holder to a Federal income tax credit in lieu of interest. As of March 2010, issuers of the unused authorization of such bonds could opt to receive direct payment with the yield becoming fully taxable.

25. ***Credit for investment in clean coal facilities.***—The baseline tax system would uniformly tax all returns to investments and not allow credits for particular activities, investments, or industries. In contrast, the Tax Code provides investment tax credits for clean coal facilities producing electricity and for industrial gasification combined cycle projects.

26. ***Amortize all geological and geophysical expenditures over two years.***—The baseline tax system allows taxpayers to deduct the decline in the economic value of an investment over its economic life. However, the Tax Code allows geological and geophysical expenditures incurred in connection with oil and gas exploration in the United States to be amortized over two years for non-integrated oil companies, a span of time that is generally shorter than the economic life of the assets.

27. ***Allowance of deduction for certain energy efficient commercial building property.***—The baseline tax system would not allow deductions in lieu of normal depreciation allowances for particular investments in particular industries. Instead, it generally would seek to tax uniformly all returns from investment-like activities. In contrast, the Tax Code allows a deduction for certain energy efficient commercial building property. The basis of such property is reduced by the amount of the deduction. Starting in 2021, the maximum deduction amount per square foot will be increased by a cost-of-living adjustment.

28. ***Credit for construction of new energy efficient homes.***—The baseline tax system would not allow credits for particular activities, investments, or industries. Instead, it generally would seek to tax uniformly all returns from investment-like activities. However, the Tax Code allowed contractors a tax credit of $2,000 for the construction of a qualified new energy-efficient home that had an annual level of heating and cooling energy consumption at least 50 percent below the annual consumption under the 2006 International Energy

Conservation Code. The credit equaled $1,000 in the case of a new manufactured home that met a 30-percent standard or requirements for EPA's Energy Star homes. This provision expired on December 31, 2017.

29. ***Credit for energy efficiency improvements to existing homes.***—The baseline tax system would not allow credits for particular activities, investments, or industries. However, the Tax Code provided an investment tax credit for expenditures made on insulation, exterior windows, and doors that improved the energy efficiency of homes and met certain standards. The Tax Code also provided a credit for purchases of advanced main air circulating fans, natural gas, propane, or oil furnaces or hot water boilers, and other qualified energy efficient property. This provision expired on December 31, 2017, but legislation enacted in 2020 allowed taxpayers to claim tax credits retroactively for three years.

30. ***Credit for residential energy efficient property.***—The baseline tax system would uniformly tax all returns to investments and not allow credits for particular activities, investments, or industries. However, the Tax Code provides a credit for the purchase of a qualified photovoltaic property and solar water heating property, as well as for fuel cell power plants, geothermal heat pumps, and small wind property used in or placed on a residence. The credit is 30 percent for property placed in service before January 1, 2020, 26 percent for property placed in service in 2020–2022, and 22 percent for property placed in service in 2023.

31. ***Credit for qualified energy conservation bonds.***—The baseline tax system would uniformly tax all returns to investments and not allow credits for particular activities, investments, or industries. However, the Tax Code provides for the issuance of energy conservation bonds which entitle the bond holder to a Federal income tax credit in lieu of interest. As of March 2010, issuers of the unused authorization of such bonds could opt to receive direct payment with the yield becoming fully taxable.

32. ***Advanced energy property credit.***—The baseline tax system would not allow credits for particular activities, investments, or industries. However, the Tax Code provides a 30-percent investment credit for property used in a qualified advanced energy manufacturing project. The Department of the Treasury may award up to $2.3 billion in tax credits for qualified investments.

33. ***Advanced nuclear power facilities production credit.***—The baseline tax system would not allow credits or deductions for particular activities, investments, or industries. Instead, it generally would seek to tax uniformly all returns from investment-like activities. In contrast, the Tax Code allows a tax credit equal to 1.8 cents times the number of kilowatt hours of electricity produced at a qualifying advanced nuclear power facility. A taxpayer may claim no more than $125 million per 1,000 megawatts of capacity. The Department of the Treasury may allocate up to 6,000 megawatts of credit-eligible capacity. Any unutilized national capacity limitation shall be allocated after December 31, 2020, according to prioritization rules set forth by statute.

34. *Reduced tax rate for nuclear decommissioning funds.*—The baseline tax system would uniformly tax all returns to investments and not allow special rates for particular activities, investments, or industries. In contrast, the Tax Code provides a special 20-percent tax rate for investments made by Nuclear Decommissioning Reserve Funds.

Natural Resources and Environment

35. *Expensing of exploration and development costs, nonfuel minerals.*—The baseline tax system allows the taxpayer to deduct the depreciation of an asset according to the decline in its economic value over time. However, certain capital outlays associated with exploration and development of nonfuel minerals may be expensed rather than depreciated over the life of the asset.

36. *Excess of percentage over cost depletion, nonfuel minerals.*—The baseline tax system allows the taxpayer to deduct the decline in the economic value of an investment over time. Under current law, however, most nonfuel mineral extractors may use percentage depletion (whereby the deduction is fixed as a percentage of receipts) rather than cost depletion, with percentage depletion rates ranging from 22 percent for sulfur to 5 percent for sand and gravel. Over the life of an investment, percentage depletion deductions can exceed the cost of the investment. Consequently, percentage depletion may provide more advantageous tax treatment than would cost depletion, which limits deductions to an investment's cost.

37. *Exclusion of interest on bonds for water, sewage, and hazardous waste facilities.*—The baseline tax system generally would tax all income under the regular tax rate schedule. It would not allow preferentially low (or zero) tax rates to apply to certain types or sources of income. In contrast, the Tax Code allows interest earned on State and local bonds used to finance construction of sewage, water, or hazardous waste facilities to be exempt from tax. These bonds are generally subject to the State private-activity bond annual volume cap.

38. *Capital gains treatment of certain timber income.*—The baseline tax system generally would tax all income under the regular tax rate schedule. It would not allow preferentially low tax rates to apply to certain types or sources of income. However, under current law certain timber sales can be treated as a capital gain rather than ordinary income and therefore subject to the lower capital-gains tax rate. Current law allows capital gains to be taxed at a preferentially low rate that is no higher than 20 percent (plus the 3.8-percent surtax).

39. *Expensing of multiperiod timber growing costs.*—The baseline tax system requires the taxpayer to capitalize costs associated with investment property. However, most of the production costs of growing timber may be expensed under current law rather than capitalized and deducted when the timber is sold, thereby accelerating cost recovery.

40. *Tax incentives for preservation of historic structures.*—The baseline tax system would not allow credits for particular activities, investments, or industries. However, expenditures to preserve and restore certified historic structures qualify for an investment tax credit of 20 percent for certified rehabilitation activities. The taxpayer's recoverable basis must be reduced by the amount of the credit. The credit must be claimed ratably over the five years after the property is placed in service, for property placed in service after December 31, 2017.

41. *Carbon oxide sequestration credit.*—The baseline tax system would uniformly tax all returns to investments and not allow credits for particular activities, investments, or industries. In contrast, the Tax Code allows a credit for qualified carbon oxide captured at a qualified facility and disposed of in secure geological storage. In addition, the provision allows a credit for qualified carbon oxide that is captured at a qualified facility and used as a tertiary injectant in a qualified enhanced oil or natural gas recovery project. The credit differs according to whether the carbon was captured using equipment which was originally placed in service before February 9, 2018, or thereafter.

42. *Deduction for endangered species recovery expenditures.*—The baseline tax system would not allow deductions in addition to normal depreciation allowances for particular investments in particular industries. Instead, it generally would seek to tax uniformly all returns from investment-like activities. In contrast, under current law farmers can deduct up to 25 percent of their gross income for expenses incurred as a result of site and habitat improvement activities that will benefit endangered species on their farm land, in accordance with site specific management actions included in species recovery plans approved pursuant to the Endangered Species Act of 1973.

Agriculture

43. *Expensing of certain capital outlays.*—The baseline tax system requires the taxpayer to capitalize costs associated with investment property. However, farmers may expense certain expenditures for feed and fertilizer, for soil and water conservation measures, and certain other capital improvements under current law.

44. *Expensing of certain multiperiod production costs.*—The baseline tax system requires the taxpayer to capitalize costs associated with an investment over time. However, the production of livestock and crops with a production period greater than two years is exempt from the uniform cost capitalization rules (e.g., for costs for establishing orchards or structure improvements), thereby accelerating cost recovery.

45. *Treatment of loans forgiven for solvent farmers.*—Because loan forgiveness increases a debtors net worth the baseline tax system requires debtors to include the amount of loan forgiveness as income or else reduce their recoverable basis in the property related to the loan. If the amount of forgiveness exceeds the basis, the excess forgiveness is taxable if the taxpayer is not insolvent. For bankrupt debtors, the amount of loan forgiveness reduces carryover losses, unused credits, and then basis, with the remainder of the forgiven debt excluded from taxation.

Qualified farm debt that is forgiven, however, is excluded from income even when the taxpayer is solvent.

46. ***Capital gains treatment of certain agriculture income.***—The baseline tax system generally would tax all income under the regular tax rate schedule. It would not allow preferentially low tax rates to apply to certain types or sources of income. In contrast, current law allows capital gains to be taxed at a preferentially low rate that is no higher than 20 percent (plus the 3.8-percent surtax). Certain agricultural income, such as unharvested crops, qualify for taxation as capital gains rather than ordinary income, and so benefit from the preferentially low 20-percent maximum tax rate on capital gains (plus the 3.8-percent surtax).

47. ***Income averaging for farmers.***—The baseline tax system generally taxes all earned income each year at the rate determined by the income tax. However, taxpayers may average their taxable income from farming and fishing over the previous three years.

48. ***Deferral of gain on sale of farm refiners.***—The baseline tax system generally subjects capital gains to taxes the year that they are realized. However, the Tax Code allows a taxpayer who sells stock in a farm refiner to a farmers' cooperative to defer recognition of the gain if the proceeds are re-invested in a qualified replacement property.

49. ***Expensing of reforestation expenditures.***—The baseline tax system requires the taxpayer to capitalize costs associated with an investment over time. In contrast, the Tax Code provides for the expensing of the first $10,000 in reforestation expenditures with 7-year amortization of the remaining expenses.

Commerce and Housing

This category includes a number of tax expenditure provisions that also affect economic activity in other functional categories. For example, provisions related to investment, such as accelerated depreciation, could be classified under the energy, natural resources and environment, agriculture, or transportation categories.

50. ***Exemption of credit union income.***—Under the baseline tax system, corporations pay taxes on their profits under the regular tax rate schedule. However, in the Tax Code the earnings of credit unions not distributed to members as interest or dividends are exempt from the income tax.

51. ***Exclusion of life insurance death benefits.***—Under the baseline tax system, individuals and corporations would pay taxes on their income when it is (actually or constructively) received or accrued. Nevertheless, current law generally excludes from tax amounts received under life insurance contracts if such amounts are paid by reason of the death of the insured.

52. ***Exemption or special alternative tax for small property and casualty insurance companies.***—The baseline tax system would require corporations to pay taxes on their profits under the regular tax rate schedule. It would not allow preferentially low (or zero) tax rates to apply to certain types or sources of income. Under current law, however, stock non-life insurance companies are generally exempt from tax if their gross receipts for the taxable year do not exceed $600,000 and more than 50 percent of such gross receipts consist of premiums. Mutual non-life insurance companies are generally tax-exempt if their annual gross receipts do not exceed $150,000 and more than 35 percent of gross receipts consist of premiums. Also, non-life insurance companies with no more than a specified level of annual net written premiums generally may elect to pay tax only on their taxable investment income provided certain ownership diversification requirements are met. The underwriting income (premiums, less insurance losses and expenses) of electing companies is excluded from tax. The specified premium limit is indexed for inflation; for 2022, the premium limit is $2.45 million.

53. ***Tax exemption of insurance income earned by tax-exempt organizations.***—Under the baseline tax system, corporations pay taxes on their profits under the regular tax rate schedule. The baseline tax system would not allow preferentially low (or zero) tax rates to apply to certain types or sources of income. Generally the income generated by life and property and casualty insurance companies is subject to tax, albeit under special rules. However, income from insurance operations conducted by certain tax-exempt organizations, such as fraternal societies, voluntary employee benefit associations, and others are exempt from tax.

54. ***Exclusion of interest spread of financial institutions.***—The baseline tax system generally would tax all income under the regular tax rate schedule. It would not allow preferentially low (or zero) tax rates to apply to certain types or sources of income. Consumers pay for some deposit-linked services, such as check cashing, by accepting a below-market interest rate on their demand deposits. If they received a market rate of interest on those deposits and paid explicit fees for the associated services, they would pay taxes on the full market rate and (unlike businesses) could not deduct the fees. The Government thus foregoes tax on the difference between the risk-free market interest rate and below-market interest rates on demand deposits, which under competitive conditions should equal the value of deposit services.

55. ***Exclusion of interest on owner-occupied mortgage subsidy bonds.***—The baseline tax system generally would tax all income under the regular tax rate schedule. It would not allow preferentially low (or zero) tax rates to apply to certain types or sources of income. In contrast, the Tax Code allows interest earned on State and local bonds used to finance homes purchased by first-time, low-to-moderate-income buyers to be exempt from tax. These bonds are generally subject to the State private-activity-bond annual volume cap.

56. ***Exclusion of interest on rental housing bonds.***—The baseline tax system generally would tax all income under the regular tax rate schedule. It would not allow preferentially low (or zero) tax rates to apply to certain types or sources of income. In contrast, the Tax Code allows interest earned on State and local govern-

ment bonds used to finance multifamily rental housing projects to be tax-exempt.

57. *Deductibility of mortgage interest expense on owner-occupied residences.*—Under the baseline tax system, expenses incurred in earning income would be deductible. However, such expenses would not be deductible when the income or the return on an investment is not taxed. In contrast, the Tax Code allows an exclusion from a taxpayer's taxable income for the value of owner-occupied housing services and also allows the owner-occupant to deduct mortgage interest paid on his or her primary residence and one secondary residence as an itemized non-business deduction. In general, the mortgage interest deduction is limited to interest on debt no greater than the owner's basis in the residence, and is also limited to interest on debt of no more than $1 million. Interest on up to $100,000 of other debt secured by a lien on a principal or second residence is also deductible, irrespective of the purpose of borrowing, provided the total debt does not exceed the fair market value of the residence. As an alternative to the deduction, holders of qualified Mortgage Credit Certificates issued by State or local governmental units or agencies may claim a tax credit equal to a proportion of their interest expense. In the case of taxable years beginning after December 31, 2017, and before January 1, 2026, (1) the $1 million limit is reduced to $750,000 for indebtedness incurred after December 15, 2017, and (2) the deduction for interest on home equity indebtedness is disallowed.

58. *Deductibility of State and local property tax on owner-occupied homes.*—Under the baseline tax system, expenses incurred in earning income would be deductible. However, such expenses would not be deductible when the income or the return on an investment is not taxed. In contrast, the Tax Code allows an exclusion from a taxpayer's taxable income for the value of owner-occupied housing services and also allows the owner-occupant to deduct property taxes paid on real property. In the case of taxable years beginning after December 31, 2017, and before January 1, 2026, (1) the deduction for foreign real property taxes paid is disallowed and (2) the deduction for taxes paid in any taxable year, which includes the deduction for property taxes on real property, is limited to $10,000 ($5,000 in the case of a married individual filing a separate return).

59. *Deferral of income from installment sales.*—The baseline tax system generally would tax all income under the regular tax rate schedule. It would not allow preferentially low (or zero) tax rates, or deferral of tax, to apply to certain types or sources of income. Dealers in real and personal property (i.e., sellers who regularly hold property for sale or resale) cannot defer taxable income from installment sales until the receipt of the loan repayment. Nondealers (i.e., sellers of real property used in their business) are required to pay interest on deferred taxes attributable to their total installment obligations in excess of $5 million. Only properties with sales prices exceeding $150,000 are includable in the total. The payment of a market rate of interest eliminates the benefit of the tax deferral. The tax exemption for nondealers with total

installment obligations of less than $5 million is, therefore, a tax expenditure.

60. *Capital gains exclusion on home sales.*—The baseline tax system would not allow deductions and exemptions for certain types of income. In contrast, the Tax Code allows homeowners to exclude from gross income up to $250,000 ($500,000 in the case of a married couple filing a joint return) of the capital gains from the sale of a principal residence. To qualify, the taxpayer must have owned and used the property as the taxpayer's principal residence for a total of at least two of the five years preceding the date of sale. In addition, the exclusion may not be used more than once every two years.

61. *Exclusion of net imputed rental income.*—Under the baseline tax system, the taxable income of a taxpayer who is an owner-occupant would include the implicit value of gross rental income on housing services earned on the investment in owner-occupied housing and would allow a deduction for expenses, such as interest, depreciation, property taxes, and other costs, associated with earning such rental income. In contrast, the Tax Code allows an exclusion from taxable income for the implicit gross rental income on housing services, while in certain circumstances allows a deduction for some costs associated with such income, such as for mortgage interest and property taxes.

62. *Exception from passive loss rules for $25,000 of rental loss.*—The baseline tax system accepts current law's general rule limiting taxpayers' ability to deduct losses from passive activities against nonpassive income (e.g., wages, interest, and dividends). Passive activities generally are defined as those in which the taxpayer does not materially participate, and there are numerous additional considerations brought to bear on the determination of which activities are passive for a given taxpayer. Losses are limited in an attempt to limit tax sheltering activities. Passive losses that are unused may be carried forward and applied against future passive income. In contrast to the general restrictions on passive losses, the Tax Code exempts certain owners of rental real estate activities from "passive income" limitations. The exemption is limited to $25,000 in losses and phases out for taxpayers with income between $100,000 and $150,000.

63. *Credit for low-income housing investments.*—The baseline tax system would uniformly tax all returns to investments and not allow credits for particular activities, investments, or industries. However, under current law taxpayers who invest in certain low-income housing are eligible for a tax credit. The credit rate is set so that the present value of the credit is equal to at least 70 percent of the building's qualified basis for new construction and 30 percent for (1) housing receiving other Federal benefits (such as tax-exempt bond financing) or (2) substantially rehabilitated existing housing. The credit can exceed these levels in certain statutorily defined and State designated areas where project development costs are higher. The credit is allowed in equal amounts over 10 years and is generally subject to a volume cap.

64. *Accelerated depreciation on rental housing (normal tax method).*—Under a comprehensive economic income tax, the costs of acquiring a building are capitalized and depreciated over time in accordance with the decline in the property's economic value due to wear and tear or obsolescence. This insures that the net income from the rental property is measured appropriately each year. Current law allows depreciation that is accelerated relative to economic depreciation. However, the depreciation provisions of the Tax Code are part of the reference tax law, and thus do not give rise to tax expenditures under reference tax law. Under normal tax baseline, in contrast, depreciation allowances reflect estimates of economic depreciation.

65. *Discharge of mortgage indebtedness.*—Under the baseline tax system, all income would generally be taxed under the regular tax rate schedule. The baseline tax system would not allow preferentially low (or zero) tax rates to apply to certain types or sources of income. In contrast, the Tax Code allows an exclusion from a taxpayer's taxable income for any discharge of indebtedness of up to $750,000 ($375,000 in the case of a married individual filing a separate return) from a qualified principal residence. The provision applies to debt discharged after December 31, 2020, and before January 1, 2026.

66. *Premiums for mortgage insurance deductible as interest.*—Under the baseline tax system, expenses incurred in earning income would be deductible, but such expenses would not be deductible when the income or the return on an investment is not taxed. Because imputed rental income is not subject to tax, mortgage insurance premiums do not represent expenses incurred in earning income. In contrast, the Tax Code allows mortgage insurance premiums to be treated as deductible mortgage interest expenses. The provision applies to premiums paid in 2021.

67. *Discharge of business indebtedness.*—Under the baseline tax system, all income would generally be taxed under the regular tax rate schedule. The baseline tax system would not allow preferentially low (or zero) tax rates to apply to certain types or sources of income. In contrast, the Tax Code allows an exclusion from a taxpayer's taxable income for any discharge of qualified real property business indebtedness by taxpayers other than a C corporation. If the canceled debt is not reported as current income, however, the basis of the underlying property must be reduced by the amount canceled.

68. *Exceptions from imputed interest rules.*—Under the baseline tax system, holders (issuers) of debt instruments are generally required to report interest earned (paid) in the period it accrues, not when received. In addition, the amount of interest accrued is determined by the actual price paid, not by the stated principal and interest stipulated in the instrument. But under current law, any debt associated with the sale of property worth less than $250,000 is exempted from the general interest accounting rules. This general $250,000 exception is not a tax expenditure under reference tax law but is under normal tax baseline. Current law also includes exceptions for certain property worth more than $250,000. These are tax expenditure under reference tax law and normal tax baselines. These exceptions include, sales of personal residences worth more than $250,000, and sales of farms and small businesses worth between $250,000 and $1 million.

69. *Treatment of qualified dividends.*—The baseline tax system generally would tax all income under the regular tax rate schedule. It would not allow preferentially low tax rates to apply to certain types or sources of income. For individuals, tax rates on regular income vary from 10 percent to 39.6 percent in the budget window (plus a 3.8-percent surtax on high income taxpayers), depending on the taxpayer's income. In contrast, under current law, qualified dividends are taxed at a preferentially low rate that is no higher than 20 percent (plus the 3.8-percent surtax).

70. *Capital gains (except agriculture, timber, iron ore, and coal).*—The baseline tax system generally would tax all income under the regular tax rate schedule. It would not allow preferentially low tax rates to apply to certain types or sources of income. Under current law, capital gains on assets held for more than one year are taxed at a preferentially low rate that is no higher than 20 percent (plus the 3.8-percent surtax).

71. *Capital gains exclusion of small corporation stock.*—The baseline tax system would not allow deductions and exemptions or provide preferential treatment of certain sources of income or types of activities. In contrast, the Tax Code provided an exclusion of 50 percent, applied to ordinary rates with a maximum of a 28-percent tax rate, for capital gains from qualified small business stock held by individuals for more than 5 years; 75 percent for stock issued after February 17, 2009, and before September 28, 2010; and 100 percent for stock issued after September 27, 2010. A qualified small business is a corporation whose gross assets do not exceed $50 million as of the date of issuance of the stock.

72. *Step-up basis of capital gains at death.*—Under the baseline tax system, unrealized capital gains would be taxed when assets are transferred at death. It would not allow for exempting gains upon transfer of the underlying assets to the heirs. In contrast, capital gains on assets held at the owner's death are not subject to capital gains tax under current law. The cost basis of the appreciated assets is adjusted to the market value at the owner's date of death which becomes the basis for the heirs.

73. *Carryover basis of capital gains on gifts.*—Under the baseline tax system, unrealized capital gains would be taxed when assets are transferred by gift. In contrast, when a gift of appreciated asset is made under current law, the donor's basis in the transferred property (the cost that was incurred when the transferred property was first acquired) carries over to the donee. The carryover of the donor's basis allows a continued deferral of unrealized capital gains.

74. *Ordinary income treatment of loss from small business corporation stock sale.*—The baseline tax system limits to $3,000 the write-off of losses from capital assets, with carryover of the excess to future years. In contrast, the Tax Code allows up to $100,000 in losses from the sale of small business corporate stock (capitalization less than $1 million) to be treated as ordinary losses and fully deducted.

75. ***Deferral of capital gains from like-kind exchanges.***—The baseline tax system generally would tax all income under the regular tax rate schedule. It would not allow preferentially low (or zero) tax rates, or deferral of tax, to apply to certain types or sources of income. In contrast, current law allows the deferral of accrued gains on assets transferred in qualified like-kind exchanges.

76. ***Depreciation of buildings other than rental housing (normal tax method).***—Under a comprehensive economic income tax, the costs of acquiring a building are capitalized and depreciated over time in accordance with the decline in the property's economic value due to wear and tear or obsolescence. This insures that the net income from the property is measured appropriately each year. Current law allows depreciation deductions that differ from those under economic depreciation. However, the depreciation provisions of the Tax Code are part of the reference tax law, and thus do not give rise to tax expenditures under reference tax law. Under normal tax baseline, in contrast, depreciation allowances reflect estimates of economic depreciation.

77. ***Accelerated depreciation of machinery and equipment (normal tax method).***—Under a comprehensive economic income tax, the costs of acquiring machinery and equipment are capitalized and depreciated over time in accordance with the decline in the property's economic value due to wear and tear or obsolescence. This insures that the net income from the property is measured appropriately each year. Current law allows depreciation deductions that are accelerated relative to economic depreciation. In particular, through 2022, 100 percent of the purchase cost of qualified property is eligible to be expensed immediately; this percentage phases out to zero through 2027. The depreciation provisions of the Tax Code are part of the reference tax law, and thus do not give rise to tax expenditures under reference tax law. Under the normal tax baseline, in contrast, depreciation allowances reflect estimates of economic depreciation.

78. ***Expensing of certain small investments (normal tax method).***—Under the reference tax law baseline, the costs of acquiring tangible property and computer software would be depreciated using the Tax Code's depreciation provisions. Under the normal tax baseline, depreciation allowances are estimates of economic depreciation. However, subject to investment limitations, the Tax Code allows up to $1 million (indexed for inflation) in qualifying investments in tangible property and certain computer software to be expensed rather than depreciated over time.

79. ***Exclusion of interest on small issue bonds.***—The baseline tax system generally would tax all income under the regular tax rate schedule. It would not allow preferentially low (or zero) tax rates to apply to certain types or sources of income. In contrast, the Tax Code allows interest earned on small issue industrial development bonds (IDBs) issued by State and local governments to finance manufacturing facilities to be tax exempt. Depreciable property financed with small issue IDBs must be depreciated, however, using the straight-line method. The annual volume of small issue IDBs is subject to the unified volume cap discussed in the mortgage housing bond section above.

80. ***Special rules for certain film and TV production.***—The baseline tax system generally would tax all income under the regular tax rate schedule. It would not allow deductions and exemptions or preferentially low (or zero) tax rates to apply to certain types or sources of income. In contrast, the Tax Code allowed taxpayers to deduct up to $15 million per production ($20 million in certain distressed areas) in non-capital expenditures incurred during the year. This provision is scheduled to expire at the end of 2025.

81. ***Allow 20-percent deduction to certain pass-through income.***—The baseline tax system generally would tax all income under the regular tax rate schedule. It would not allow deductions and exemptions or preferentially low (or zero) tax rates to apply to certain types or sources of income. In contrast, for tax years 2018 to 2025, the Tax Code allows for a deduction equal to up to 20 percent of income attributable to domestic pass-through businesses, subject to certain limitations.

Transportation

82. ***Tonnage tax.***—The baseline tax system generally would tax all profits and income under the regular tax rate schedule. U.S. shipping companies may choose to be subject to a tonnage tax based on gross shipping weight in lieu of an income tax, in which case profits would not be subject to tax under the regular tax rate schedule.

83. ***Deferral of tax on shipping companies.***—The baseline tax system generally would tax all profits and income under the regular tax rate schedule. It would not allow preferentially low (or zero) tax rates to apply to certain types or sources of income. In contrast, the Tax Code allows certain companies that operate U.S. flag vessels to defer income taxes on that portion of their income used for shipping purposes (e.g., primarily construction, modernization and major repairs to ships, and repayment of loans to finance these investments).

84. ***Exclusion of reimbursed employee parking expenses.***—Under the baseline tax system, all compensation, including dedicated payments and in-kind benefits, would be included in taxable income. Dedicated payments and in-kind benefits represent accretions to wealth that do not differ materially from cash wages. In contrast, the Tax Code allows an exclusion from taxable income for employee parking expenses that are paid for by the employer or that are received by the employee in lieu of wages. In 2022, the maximum amount of the parking exclusion is $280 per month. The tax expenditure estimate does not include any subsidy provided through employer-owned parking facilities. However, beginning in 2018, parking expenses are no longer deductible to employers.

85. ***Exclusion for employer-provided transit passes.***—Under the baseline tax system, all compensation, including dedicated payments and in-kind benefits, would be included in taxable income. Dedicated payments and in-kind benefits represent accretions to wealth that do not differ materially from cash wages. In contrast, the Tax Code allows an exclusion from a taxpayer's taxable

income for passes, tokens, fare cards, and vanpool expenses that are paid for by an employer or that are received by the employee in lieu of wages to defray an employee's commuting costs. Due to a parity to parking provision, the maximum amount of the transit exclusion is $280 per month in 2022. However, beginning in 2018, transit expenses are no longer deductible to employers.

86. *Tax credit for certain expenditures for maintaining railroad tracks.*—The baseline tax system would not allow credits for particular activities, investments, or industries. However, the Tax Code allowed eligible taxpayers to claim a credit equal to the lesser of 50 percent of maintenance expenditures and the product of $3,500 and the number of miles of railroad track owned or leased. This provision applies to maintenance expenditures in taxable years beginning before January 1, 2017.

87. *Exclusion of interest on bonds for highway projects and rail-truck transfer facilities.*—The baseline tax system generally would tax all income under the regular tax rate schedule. It would not allow preferentially low (or zero) tax rates to apply to certain types or sources of income. In contrast, the Tax Code provides for $15 billion of tax-exempt bond authority to finance qualified highway projects or surface freight transfer facilities.

Community and Regional Development

88. *Exclusion of interest for airport, dock, and similar bonds.*—The baseline tax system generally would tax all income under the regular tax rate schedule. It would not allow preferentially low (or zero) tax rates to apply to certain types or sources of income. In contrast, the Tax Code allows interest earned on State and local bonds issued to finance high-speed rail facilities and Government-owned airports, docks, wharves, and sport and convention facilities to be tax-exempt. These bonds are not subject to a volume cap.

89. *Exemption of certain mutuals' and cooperatives' income.*—Under the baseline tax system, corporations pay taxes on their profits under the regular tax rate schedule. In contrast, the Tax Code provides for the incomes of mutual and cooperative telephone and electric companies to be exempt from tax if at least 85 percent of their receipts are derived from patron service charges.

90. *Empowerment zones.*—The baseline tax system generally would tax all income under the regular tax rate schedule. It would not allow preferentially low tax rates to apply to certain types or sources of income, tax credits, and write-offs faster than economic depreciation. In contrast, the Tax Code allows qualifying businesses in designated economically depressed areas to receive tax benefits such as an employment credit and special tax-exempt financing. A taxpayer's ability to accrue new tax benefits for empowerment zones expires on December 31, 2025.

91. *New markets tax credit.*—The baseline tax system would not allow credits for particular activities, investments, or industries. However, the Tax Code allows taxpayers who make qualified equity investments in a community development entity (CDE), which then make qualified investments in low-income communities, to be eligible for a tax credit that is received over 7 years. The total equity investment available for the credit across all CDEs is generally $5 billion for each calendar year 2020 through 2025, the last year for which credit allocations are authorized.

92. *Credit to holders of Gulf and Midwest Tax Credit Bonds.*—The baseline tax system would not allow credits for particular activities, investments, or industries. Instead, under current law taxpayers that own Gulf and Midwest Tax Credit bonds receive a non-refundable tax credit rather than interest. The credit is included in gross income.

93. *Recovery Zone Bonds.*—The baseline tax system would not allow credits for particular activities, investments, or industries. In addition, it would tax all income under the regular tax rate schedule. It would not allow preferentially low (or zero) tax rates to apply to certain types or sources of income. In contrast, the Tax Code allowed local governments to issue up $10 billion in taxable Recovery Zone Economic Development Bonds in 2009 and 2010 and receive a direct payment from Treasury equal to 45 percent of interest expenses. In addition, local governments could issue up to $15 billion in tax exempt Recovery Zone Facility Bonds. These bonds financed certain kinds of business development in areas of economic distress.

94. *Tribal Economic Development Bonds.*—The baseline tax system generally would tax all income under the regular tax rate schedule. It would not allow preferentially low (or zero) tax rates to apply to certain types or sources of income. In contrast, the Tax Code was modified in 2009 to allow Indian tribal governments to issue tax exempt "tribal economic development bonds." There is a national bond limitation of $2 billion on such bonds.

95. *Opportunity Zones.*—The baseline tax system generally would tax all income under the regular tax rate schedule. It would not allow deferral or exclusion from income for investments made within certain geographic regions. In contrast, the Tax Code allows the temporary deferral of the recognition of capital gain if reinvested prior to December 31, 2026, in a qualifying opportunity fund which in turn invests in qualifying low-income communities designated as opportunity zones. For qualifying investments held at least 5 years, 10 percent of the deferred gain is excluded from income; this exclusion increases to 15 percent for investments held for at least 7 years. In addition, capital gains from the sale or exchange of an investment in a qualified opportunity fund held for at least 10 years are excluded from gross income.

96. *Disaster Employee Retention Credit.*—The baseline tax system would not allow credits for particular activities, investments, or industries. In contrast, the Tax Code provides employers located in certain presidentially declared disaster areas during the years 2017 through 2020 a 40-percent credit for up to $6,000 in wages paid to each eligible employee while the business was inoperable as a result of the disaster. Only wages paid after the disaster occurred and within 150 days of the last day of the incident period are eligible for the credit. Employers must

reduce their deduction for wages paid by the amount of the credit claimed.

Education, Training, Employment, and Social Services

97. *Exclusion of scholarship and fellowship income (normal tax method).*—Scholarships and fellowships are excluded from taxable income to the extent they pay for tuition and course-related expenses of the grantee. Similarly, tuition reductions for employees of educational institutions and their families are not included in taxable income. From an economic point of view, scholarships and fellowships are either gifts not conditioned on the performance of services, or they are rebates of educational costs. Thus, under the baseline tax system of the reference tax law method, this exclusion is not a tax expenditure because this method does not include either gifts or price reductions in a taxpayer's gross income. The exclusion, however, is considered a tax expenditure under the normal tax method, which includes gift-like transfers of Government funds in gross income. (Many scholarships are derived directly or indirectly from Government funding.)

98. *Tax credits for post-secondary education expenses.*—The baseline tax system would not allow credits for particular activities, investments, or industries. Under current law in 2022, however, there are two credits for certain post-secondary education expenses. The American Opportunity Tax Credit (AOTC) allows a partially refundable credit of up to $2,500 per eligible student for qualified tuition and related expenses paid. The AOTC may be claimed during each of the first four years of the student's post-secondary education. The Lifetime Learning Credit (LLC) allows a non-refundable credit for 20 percent of an eligible student's qualified tuition and fees, up to a maximum credit of $2,000 per return. The LLC may be claimed during any year of the student's post-secondary education. Only one credit may be claimed per student per year. The combined credits are phased out for taxpayers with modified adjusted gross income between $160,000 and $180,000 if married filing jointly ($80,000 and $90,000 for other taxpayers), not indexed. Married individuals filing separate returns cannot claim either credit.

99. *Deductibility of student loan interest.*—The baseline tax system accepts current law's general rule limiting taxpayers' ability to deduct non-business interest expenses. In contrast, taxpayers may claim an above-the-line deduction of up to $2,500 on interest paid on an education loan. In 2022, the maximum deduction is phased down ratably for taxpayers with modified AGI between $140,000 and $170,000 if married filing jointly ($70,000 and $85,000 for other taxpayers). Married individuals filing separate returns cannot claim the deduction.

100. *Qualified tuition programs (includes Education IRA).*—The baseline tax system generally would tax all income under the regular tax rate schedule. It would not allow preferentially low (or zero) tax rates to apply to certain types or sources of income. Some States have adopted prepaid tuition plans, prepaid room and board plans, and college savings plans, which allow persons to pay in advance or save for college expenses for designated beneficiaries. Under current law, investment income, or the return on prepayments, is not taxed when earned, and is tax-exempt when withdrawn to pay for qualified expenses. Beginning in 2018, the definition of a qualified expense was expanded to include up to $10,000 per child per year of expenses for primary or secondary education, including tuition at religious schools.

101. *Exclusion of interest on student-loan bonds.*—The baseline tax system generally would tax all income under the regular tax rate schedule. It would not allow preferentially low (or zero) tax rates to apply to certain types or sources of income. In contrast, interest earned on State and local bonds issued to finance student loans is tax-exempt under current law. The volume of all such private activity bonds that each State may issue annually is limited.

102. *Exclusion of interest on bonds for private nonprofit educational facilities.*—The baseline tax system generally would tax all income under the regular tax rate schedule. It would not allow preferentially low (or zero) tax rates to apply to certain types or sources of income. In contrast, under current law interest earned on State and local Government bonds issued to finance the construction of facilities used by private nonprofit educational institutions is not taxed.

103. *Credit for holders of zone academy bonds.*—The baseline tax system would not allow credits for particular activities, investments, or industries. Under current law, however, financial institutions that own zone academy bonds receive a non-refundable tax credit rather than interest. The credit is included in gross income. Proceeds from zone academy bonds may only be used to renovate, but not construct, qualifying schools and for certain other school purposes. The total amount of zone academy bonds that may be issued was limited to $1.4 billion in 2009 and 2010. As of March 2010, issuers of the unused authorization of such bonds could opt to receive direct payment with the yield becoming fully taxable. An additional $0.4 billion of these bonds with a tax credit was authorized to be issued each year in 2011 through 2016.

104. *Exclusion of interest on savings bonds redeemed to finance educational expenses.*—The baseline tax system generally would tax all income under the regular tax rate schedule. It would not allow preferentially low (or zero) tax rates to apply to certain types or sources of income. Under current law, however, interest earned on U.S. savings bonds issued after December 31, 1989, is tax-exempt if the bonds are transferred to an educational institution to pay for educational expenses. The tax exemption is phased out for taxpayers with AGI between $128,650 and $156,650 if married filing jointly ($83,200 and $98,200 for other taxpayers) in 2022.

105. *Parental personal exemption for students age 19 or over.*—Under the baseline tax system, a personal exemption would be allowed for the taxpayer, as well as for the taxpayer's spouse and dependents who do not claim a personal exemption on their own tax returns. These exemptions are repealed for taxable years beginning after December 31, 2017, and before January 1, 2026.

However, the definitions regarding eligibility for dependent exemptions for children (and qualifying relatives), which determine eligibility for a number of family-related provisions, remain in place. These provisions include the new $500 credit for dependents other than qualifying children (Other Dependent Credit, or ODC). In general, to be considered a dependent child, a child would have to be under age 19. In contrast, the Tax Code allows taxpayers to consider their children aged 19 to 23 as dependents, as long as the children are full-time students and reside with the taxpayer for over half the year (with exceptions for temporary absences from home, such as for school attendance). Absent this provision, children over 18 would need to meet the more stringent rules for qualified relatives in order to qualify the taxpayer for certain benefits, including the ODC.

106. ***Deductibility of charitable contributions (education).***—The baseline tax system would not allow a deduction for personal expenditures. In contrast, the Tax Code provides taxpayers a deduction for contributions to nonprofit educational institutions that are similar to personal expenditures. Moreover, taxpayers who donate capital assets to educational institutions can deduct the asset's current value without being taxed on any appreciation in value. An individual's total charitable contribution generally may not exceed 50 percent (60 percent for tax years 2018 through 2025) of adjusted gross income; a corporation's total charitable contributions generally may not exceed 10 percent of pre-tax income.

107. ***Exclusion of employer-provided educational assistance.***—Under the baseline tax system, all compensation, including dedicated payments and in-kind benefits, should be included in taxable income because it represents accretions to wealth that do not materially differ from cash wages. Under current law, however, employer-provided educational assistance is excluded from an employee's gross income, even though the employer's costs for this assistance are a deductible business expense. The maximum exclusion is $5,250 per taxpayer. From March 27, 2020, through December 31, 2025, employer-provided student loan payments are considered eligible educational assistance.

108. ***Special deduction for teacher expenses.***—The baseline tax system would not allow a deduction for personal expenditures. In contrast, the Tax Code allowed educators in both public and private elementary and secondary schools, who worked at least 900 hours during a school year as a teacher, instructor, counselor, principal or aide, to subtract up to $250 of qualified expenses, indexed to 2014, when determining their adjusted gross income (AGI).

109. ***Discharge of student loan indebtedness.***—Under the baseline tax system, all compensation, including dedicated payments and in-kind benefits, should be included in taxable income. In contrast, the Tax Code allows certain professionals who perform in underserved areas or specific fields, and as a consequence have their student loans discharged, not to recognize such discharge as income.

110. ***Qualified school construction bonds.***—The baseline tax system would not allow credits for particular activities, investments, or industries. Instead, it generally would seek to tax uniformly all returns from investment-like activities. In contrast, the Tax Code was modified in 2009 to provide a tax credit in lieu of interest to holders of qualified school construction bonds. The national volume limit is $22.4 billion over 2009 and 2010. As of March 2010, issuers of such bonds could opt to receive direct payment with the yield becoming fully taxable.

111. ***Work opportunity tax credit.***—The baseline tax system would not allow credits for particular activities, investments, or industries. Instead, it generally would seek to tax uniformly all returns from investment-like activities. In contrast, the Tax Code provides employers with a tax credit for qualified wages paid to individuals. The credit applies to employees who began work on or before December 31, 2025, and who are certified as members of various targeted groups. The amount of the credit that can be claimed is 25 percent of qualified wages for employment less than 400 hours and 40 percent for employment of 400 hours or more. Generally, the maximum credit per employee is $2,400 and can only be claimed on the first year of wages an individual earns from an employer. However, the credit for long-term welfare recipients can be claimed on second year wages as well and has a $9,000 maximum. Also, certain categories of veterans are eligible for a higher maximum credit of up to $9,600. Employers must reduce their deduction for wages paid by the amount of the credit claimed.

112. ***Employer-provided child care exclusion.***—Under the baseline tax system, all compensation, including dedicated payments and in-kind benefits, should be included in taxable income. In contrast, current law allows up to $5,000 of employer-provided child care to be excluded from an employee's gross income even though the employer's costs for the child care are a deductible business expense. The amount was temporarily increased to $10,500 for 2021.

113. ***Employer-provided child care credit.***—The baseline tax system would not allow credits for particular activities, investments, or industries. In contrast, current law provides a credit equal to 25 percent of qualified expenses for employee child care and 10 percent of qualified expenses for child care resource and referral services. Employer deductions for such expenses are reduced by the amount of the credit. The maximum total credit is limited to $150,000 per taxable year.

114. ***Assistance for adopted foster children.***—Under the baseline tax system, all compensation, including dedicated payments and in-kind benefits, should be included in taxable income. Taxpayers who adopt eligible children from the public foster care system can receive monthly payments for the children's significant and varied needs and a reimbursement of up to $2,000 for nonrecurring adoption expenses; special needs adoptions receive the maximum benefit even if that amount is not spent. These payments are excluded from gross income under current law.

115. ***Adoption credit and exclusion.***—The baseline tax system would not allow credits for particular activities. In contrast, taxpayers can receive a tax credit for qualified adoption expenses under current law. Taxpayers may also exclude qualified adoption expenses provided or reimbursed by an employer from income, subject to the same maximum amounts and phase-out as the credit. The same expenses cannot qualify for tax benefits under both programs; however, a taxpayer may use the benefits of the exclusion and the tax credit for different expenses.

116. ***Exclusion of employee meals and lodging (other than military).***—Under the baseline tax system, all compensation, including dedicated payments and in-kind benefits, should be included in taxable income. All compensation would generally be deductible by the employer. In contrast, under current law employer-provided meals and lodging are excluded from an employee's gross income. Beginning in 2018, employers are allowed a deduction for only 50 percent of the expenses of employer-provided meals, except that in 2021 and 2022, employers are eligible for a full deduction on restaurant meals provided to employees. Employer-provided lodging is fully deductible by the employer, in general.

117. ***Credit for child and dependent care expenses.***—The baseline tax system would not allow credits for particular activities or targeted at specific groups. In contrast, the Tax Code provides a tax credit to parents who work or attend school and who have child and dependent care expenses. In taxable year 2022, expenditures up to a maximum $3,000 for one dependent and $6,000 for two or more dependents are eligible for a nonrefundable credit. The credit is equal to 35 percent of qualified expenditures for taxpayers with incomes of up to $15,000. The credit is reduced to a minimum of 20 percent by one percentage point for each $2,000 of income in excess of $15,000.

118. ***Credit for disabled access expenditures.***—The baseline tax system would not allow credits for particular activities, investments, or industries. In contrast, the Tax Code provides small businesses (less than $1 million in gross receipts or fewer than 31 full-time employees) a 50-percent credit for expenditures in excess of $250 to remove access barriers for disabled persons. The credit is limited to $5,000.

119. ***Deductibility of charitable contributions, other than education and health.***—The baseline tax system would not allow a deduction for personal expenditures including charitable contributions. In contrast, the Tax Code provides taxpayers a deduction for contributions to charitable, religious, and certain other nonprofit organizations. Taxpayers who donate capital assets to charitable organizations can deduct the assets' current value without being taxed on any appreciation in value. An individual's total charitable contribution generally may not exceed 50 percent (60 percent between 2018 and 2025) of adjusted gross income; a corporation's total charitable contributions generally may not exceed 10 percent of pre-tax income.

120. ***Exclusion of certain foster care payments.***—The baseline tax system generally would tax all income under the regular tax rate schedule. It would not allow preferentially low (or zero) tax rates to apply to certain types or sources of income. Foster parents provide a home and care for children who are wards of the State, under contract with the State. Under current law, compensation received for this service is excluded from the gross incomes of foster parents; the expenses they incur are nondeductible.

121. ***Exclusion of parsonage allowances.***—Under the baseline tax system, all compensation, including dedicated payments and in-kind benefits, would be included in taxable income. Dedicated payments and in-kind benefits represent accretions to wealth that do not differ materially from cash wages. In contrast, the Tax Code allows an exclusion from a clergyman's taxable income for the value of the clergyman's housing allowance or the rental value of the clergyman's parsonage.

122. ***Indian employment credit.***—The baseline tax system would not allow credits for particular activities, investments, or industries. Instead, it generally would seek to tax uniformly all returns from investment-like activities. In contrast, the Tax Code provides employers with a tax credit for qualified wages paid to employees who are enrolled members of Indian tribes. The amount of the credit that could be claimed is 20 percent of the excess of qualified wages and health insurance costs paid by the employer in the current tax year over the amount of such wages and costs paid by the employer in 1993. Qualified wages and health insurance costs with respect to any employee for the taxable year could not exceed $20,000. Employees have to live on or near the reservation where they work to be eligible for the credit. Employers must reduce their deduction for wages paid by the amount of the credit claimed. The credit does not apply to taxable years beginning after December 31, 2021.

Health

123. ***Exclusion of employer contributions for medical insurance premiums and medical care.***—Under the baseline tax system, all compensation, including dedicated payments and in-kind benefits, should be included in taxable income. In contrast, under current law, employer-paid health insurance premiums and other medical expenses (including long-term care or Health Reimbursement Accounts) are not included in employee gross income even though they are deducted as a business expense by the employee.

124. ***Self-employed medical insurance premiums.***—Under the baseline tax system, all compensation and remuneration, including dedicated payments and in-kind benefits, should be included in taxable income. In contrast, under current law self-employed taxpayers may deduct their family health insurance premiums. Taxpayers without self-employment income are not eligible for this special deduction. The deduction is not available for any month in which the self-employed individual is eligible to participate in an employer-subsidized health plan and the deduction may not exceed the self-employed individual's earned income from self-employment.

125. ***Medical Savings Accounts and Health Savings Accounts.***—Under the baseline tax system, all compensation, including dedicated payments and in-kind benefits, should be included in taxable income. Also, the baseline tax system would not allow a deduction for personal expenditures and generally would tax investment earnings. In contrast, individual contributions to Archer Medical Savings Accounts (Archer MSAs) and Health Savings Accounts (HSAs) are allowed as a deduction in determining adjusted gross income whether or not the individual itemizes deductions. Employer contributions to Archer MSAs and HSAs are excluded from income and employment taxes. Archer MSAs and HSAs require that the individual have coverage by a qualifying high deductible health plan. Earnings from the accounts are excluded from taxable income. Distributions from the accounts used for medical expenses are not taxable. The rules for HSAs are generally more flexible than for Archer MSAs and the deductible contribution amounts are greater (in 2019, $3,500 for taxpayers with individual coverage and $7,000 for taxpayers with family coverage). Thus, HSAs have largely replaced MSAs.

126. ***Deductibility of medical expenses.***—The baseline tax system would not allow a deduction for personal expenditures. In contrast, under current law personal expenditures for medical care (including the costs of prescription drugs) exceeding 7.5 percent of the taxpayer's adjusted gross income are deductible. For tax years beginning after 2012, only medical expenditures exceeding 10 percent of the taxpayer's adjusted gross income are deductible. However, for the years 2013, 2014, 2015 and 2016, if either the taxpayer or the taxpayer's spouse turned 65 before the end of the taxable year, the threshold remained at 7.5 percent of adjusted income. Beginning in 2017, the 10-percent threshold applied to all taxpayers, including those over 65.

127. ***Exclusion of interest on hospital construction bonds.***—The baseline tax system generally would tax all income under the regular tax rate schedule. It would not allow preferentially low (or zero) tax rates to apply to certain types or sources of income. In contrast, under current law interest earned on State and local government debt issued to finance hospital construction is excluded from income subject to tax.

128. ***Refundable Premium Assistance Tax Credit.***—The baseline tax system would not allow credits for particular activities or targeted at specific groups. In contrast, for taxable years ending after 2013, the Tax Code provides a premium assistance credit to any eligible taxpayer for any qualified health insurance purchased through a Health Insurance Exchange. In general, an eligible taxpayer is a taxpayer with annual household income between 100 percent and 400 percent of the Federal poverty level for a family of the taxpayer's size and that does not have access to affordable minimum essential health care coverage. The amount of the credit equals the lesser of (1) the actual premiums paid by the taxpayer for such coverage or (2) the difference between the cost of a statutorily-identified benchmark plan offered on the exchange and a required payment by the taxpayer that increases with income. The American Rescue Plan Act of 2021 (P.L. 117-2) temporarily increased the Premium Tax Credit in three ways. For 2021 and 2022, the legislation increased the Premium Tax Credit for currently eligible individuals and families, providing access to free plans for those earning 100 to 150 percent of the Federal poverty level, and expanded eligibility to newly include individuals and families with income above 400 percent of the Federal poverty level. The legislation also expanded eligibility in 2021 to individuals who receive unemployment insurance for any week in 2021. The legislation also eliminated the requirement for individuals to repay any excess advance payments of the Premium Tax Credit for 2020.

129. ***Credit for employee health insurance expenses of small business.***—The baseline tax system would not allow credits for particular activities or targeted at specific groups. In contrast, the Tax Code provides a tax credit to qualified small employers that make a certain level of non-elective contributions towards the purchase of certain health insurance coverage for its employees. To receive a credit, an employer must have fewer than 25 full-time-equivalent employees whose average annual full-time-equivalent wages from the employer are less than $50,000 (indexed for taxable years after 2013). However, to receive a full credit, an employer must have no more than 10 full-time employees, and the average wage paid to these employees must be no more than $25,000 (indexed for taxable years after 2013). A qualifying employer may claim the credit for any taxable year beginning in 2010, 2011, 2012, and 2013 and for up to two years for insurance purchased through a Health Insurance Exchange thereafter. For taxable years beginning in 2010, 2011, 2012, and 2013, the maximum credit is 35 percent of premiums paid by qualified taxable employers and 25 percent of premiums paid by qualified tax-exempt organizations. For taxable years beginning in 2014 and later years, the maximum tax credit increases to 50 percent of premiums paid by qualified taxable employers and 35 percent of premiums paid by qualified tax-exempt organizations.

130. ***Deductibility of charitable contributions (health).***—The baseline tax system would not allow a deduction for personal expenditures including charitable contributions. In contrast, the Tax Code provides individuals and corporations a deduction for contributions to nonprofit health institutions. Tax expenditures resulting from the deductibility of contributions to other charitable institutions are listed under the education, training, employment, and social services function.

131. ***Tax credit for orphan drug research.***—The baseline tax system would not allow credits for particular activities, investments, or industries. In contrast, under current law drug firms can claim a tax credit of 25 percent of the costs for clinical testing required by the Food and Drug Administration for drugs that treat rare physical conditions or rare diseases.

132. ***Special Blue Cross/Blue Shield tax benefits.***—The baseline tax system generally would tax all profits under the regular tax rate schedule using broadly applicable measures of baseline income. It would not al-

low preferentially low tax rates to apply to certain types or sources of income. In contrast, certain Blue Cross and Blue Shield (BC/BS) health insurance providers and certain other health insurers are provided with special tax benefits, provided that their percentage of total premium revenue expended on reimbursement for clinical services provided to enrollees or for activities that improve health care quality is not less than 85 percent for the taxable year. A qualifying insurer may take as a deduction 100 percent of any net increase in its unearned premium reserves, instead of the 80 percent allowed other insurers. A qualifying insurer is also allowed a special deduction equal to the amount by which 25 percent of its health-claim expenses exceeds its beginning-of-the-year accounting surplus. The deduction is limited to the insurer's taxable income determined without the special deduction.

133. ***Distributions from retirement plans for premiums for health and long-term care insurance.***—Under the baseline tax system, all compensation, including dedicated and deferred payments, should be included in taxable income. In contrast, the Tax Code provides for tax-free distributions of up to $3,000 from governmental retirement plans for premiums for health and long term care premiums of public safety officers.

134. ***Credit for family and sick leave taken by self-employed individuals.***—The baseline tax system would not allow credits for particular activities or targeted as specific groups. Under current law, however, self-employed individuals are allowed a refundable credit equal for certain family or sick leave taken. In general, the sick leave credit is equal to 100 percent of daily self-employment income (equal to self-employment income divided by 260) during a period of qualified sick leave, up to $511 per day for 10 days. The family leave credit is equal to two thirds of daily self-employment income (but no greater than two thirds of $200) during a period of qualified family leave for up to 10 weeks. Under current law, the credit applies to leave taken prior to October 1, 2021.

Income Security

135. ***Child tax credit.***—The baseline tax system would not allow credits for particular activities or targeted at specific groups. Under current law, however, taxpayers with children under age 18 can qualify for a child tax credit. In taxable years 2022 through 2025, taxpayers may claim a $2,000 per child partially refundable child tax credit. Up to $1,500 per child of unclaimed credit due to insufficient tax liability may be refundable—taxpayers may claim a refund for 15 percent of earnings in excess of a $2,500 floor, up to the lesser of the amount of unused credit or $1,500 per child. A taxpayer may also claim a nonrefundable credit of $500 for each qualifying child not eligible for the $2,000 credit (those over sixteen and those without SSNs) and for each dependent relative. The total combined child and other dependent credit is phased out for taxpayers at the rate of $50 per $1,000 of modified AGI above $400,000 if married filing jointly ($200,000 for all other filers). For tax years beginning after December 31, 2025, the credit returns to its pre-TCJA value of $1,000.

At that time, up to the full value of the credit (subject to a phase-in of 15 percent of earnings in excess of $3,000) will be refundable and the $500 other dependent credit will expire. The credit will once again phase out at the rate of $50 per $1,000 of modified AGI above $110,000 if married filing jointly ($75,000 for single or head of household filers and $55,000 for married taxpayers filing separately).

136. ***Exclusion of railroad (Social Security equivalent) benefits.***—Under the baseline tax system, all compensation, including dedicated and deferred payments, should be included in taxable income. In contrast, the Social Security Equivalent Benefit paid to railroad retirees and the disabled is not generally subject to the income tax unless the recipient's modified gross income reaches a certain threshold under current law. See provision number 156, Social Security benefits for retired and disabled workers and spouses, dependents, and survivors, for a discussion of the threshold.

137. ***Exclusion of workers' compensation benefits.***—Under the baseline tax system, all compensation, including dedicated payments and in-kind benefits, should be included in taxable income. However, workers compensation is not subject to the income tax under current law.

138. ***Exclusion of public assistance benefits (normal tax method).***—Under the reference tax law baseline, gifts and transfers are not treated as income to the recipients. In contrast, the normal tax method considers cash transfers from the Government as part of the recipients' income, and thus, treats the exclusion for public assistance benefits under current law as a tax expenditure.

139. ***Exclusion of special benefits for disabled coal miners.***—Under the baseline tax system, all compensation, including dedicated payments and in-kind benefits, should be included in taxable income. However, disability payments to former coal miners out of the Black Lung Trust Fund, although income to the recipient, are not subject to the income tax.

140. ***Exclusion of military disability pensions.***—Under the baseline tax system, all compensation, including dedicated payments and in-kind benefits, should be included in taxable income. In contrast, most of the military disability pension income received by current disabled military retirees is excluded from their income subject to tax.

141. ***Defined benefit employer plans.*** Under the baseline tax system, all compensation, including deferred and dedicated payments, should be included in taxable income. In addition, investment income would be taxed as earned. In contrast, under current law certain contributions to defined benefit pension plans are excluded from an employee's gross income even though employers can deduct their contributions. In addition, the tax on the investment income earned by defined benefit pension plans is deferred until the money is withdrawn.

142. ***Defined contribution employer plans.***—Under the baseline tax system, all compensation, including deferred and dedicated payments, should be included in taxable income. In addition, investment income would be taxed as earned. In contrast, under current law individual

taxpayers and employers can make tax-preferred contributions to employer-provided 401(k) and similar plans (e.g. 403(b) plans and the Federal Government's Thrift Savings Plan). In 2022, an employee could exclude up to $20,500 of wages from AGI under a qualified arrangement with an employer's 401(k) plan. Employees age 50 or over could exclude up to $27,000 in contributions. The defined contribution plan limit, including both employee and employer contributions, is $61,000 in 2022. The tax on contributions made by both employees and employers and the investment income earned by these plans is deferred until withdrawn.

143. *Individual Retirement Accounts (IRAs).*— Under the baseline tax system, all compensation, including deferred and dedicated payments, should be included in taxable income. In addition, investment income would be taxed as earned. In contrast, under current law individual taxpayers can take advantage of traditional and Roth IRAs to defer or otherwise reduce the tax on the return to their retirement savings. The IRA contribution limit is $6,000 in 2022; taxpayers age 50 or over are allowed to make additional "catch-up" contributions of $1,000. Contributions to a traditional IRA are generally deductible but the deduction is phased out for workers with incomes above certain levels if the workers or their spouses are active participants in an employer-provided retirement plan. Contributions and account earnings are includible in income when withdrawn from traditional IRAs. Roth IRA contributions are not deductible, but earnings and withdrawals are exempt from taxation. Income limits also apply to Roth IRA contributions.

144. *Low- and moderate-income savers' credit.*—The baseline tax system would not allow credits for particular activities or targeted at specific groups. In contrast, the Tax Code provides an additional incentive for lower-income taxpayers to save through a nonrefundable credit of up to 50 percent on IRA and other retirement contributions of up to $2,000. This credit is in addition to any deduction or exclusion. The credit is completely phased out by $68,000 for joint filers, $51,000 for head of household filers, and $34,000 for other filers in 2022.

145. *Self-employed plans.*—Under the baseline tax system, all compensation, including deferred and dedicated payments, should be included in taxable income. In addition, investment income would be taxed as earned. In contrast, under current law self-employed individuals can make deductible contributions to their own retirement plans equal to 25 percent of their income, up to a maximum of $61,000 in 2022. Total plan contributions are limited to 25 percent of a firm's total wages. The tax on the investment income earned by self-employed SEP, SIMPLE, and qualified plans is deferred until withdrawn.

146. *Premiums on group term life insurance.*— Under the baseline tax system, all compensation, including deferred and dedicated payments, should be included in taxable income. In contrast, under current law employer-provided life insurance benefits are excluded from an employee's gross income (to the extent that the employer's share of the total costs does not exceed the cost of $50,000 of such insurance) even though the employer's costs for the insurance are a deductible business expense.

147. *Premiums on accident and disability insurance.*—Under the baseline tax system, all compensation, including dedicated payments and in-kind benefits, should be included in taxable income. In contrast, under current law employer-provided accident and disability benefits are excluded from an employee's gross income even though the employer's costs for the benefits are a deductible business expense.

148. *Exclusion of investment income from Supplementary Unemployment Benefit Trusts.*— Under the baseline tax system, all compensation, including dedicated payments and in-kind benefits, should be included in taxable income. In addition, investment income would be taxed as earned. Under current law, employers may establish trusts to pay supplemental unemployment benefits to employees separated from employment. Investment income earned by such trusts is exempt from taxation.

149. *Exclusion of investment income from Voluntary Employee Benefit Associations trusts.*— Under the baseline tax system, all compensation, including dedicated payments and in-kind benefits, should be included in taxable income. Under current law, employers may establish associations, or VEBAs, to pay employee benefits, which may include health benefit plans, life insurance, and disability insurance, among other employee benefits. Investment income earned by such trusts is exempt from taxation.

150. *Special Employee Stock Ownership Plan (ESOP) rules.*— Under the baseline tax system, all compensation, including dedicated payments and in-kind benefits, should be included in taxable income. In addition, investment income would be taxed as earned. In contrast, employer-paid contributions (the value of stock issued to the ESOP) are deductible by the employer as part of employee compensation costs. They are not included in the employees' gross income for tax purposes, however, until they are paid out as benefits. In addition, the following special income tax provisions for ESOPs are intended to increase ownership of corporations by their employees: (1) annual employer contributions are subject to less restrictive limitations than other qualified retirement plans; (2) ESOPs may borrow to purchase employer stock, guaranteed by their agreement with the employer that the debt will be serviced by the payment (deductible by firm) of a portion of wages (excludable by the employees) to service the loan; (3) employees who sell appreciated company stock to the ESOP may defer any taxes due until they withdraw benefits; (4) dividends paid to ESOP-held stock are deductible by the employer; and (5) earnings are not taxed as they accrue.

151. *Additional deduction for the blind.*—Under the baseline tax system, the standard deduction is allowed. An additional standard deduction for a targeted group within a given filing status would not be allowed. In contrast, the Tax Code allows taxpayers who are blind to claim an additional $1,750 standard deduction if single or $1,400 if married in 2022.

152. ***Additional deduction for the elderly.***— Under the baseline tax system, the standard deduction is allowed. An additional standard deduction for a targeted group within a given filing status would not be allowed. In contrast, the Tax Code allows taxpayers who are 65 years or older to claim an additional $1,750 standard deduction if single or $1,400 if married in 2022.

153. ***Deductibility of casualty losses.***—Under the baseline tax system, neither the purchase of property nor insurance premiums to protect the property's value are deductible as costs of earning income. Therefore, reimbursement for insured loss of such property is not included as a part of gross income, and uninsured losses are not deductible. In contrast, the Tax Code provides a deduction for uninsured casualty and theft losses of more than $100 each, to the extent that total losses during the year exceed 10 percent of the taxpayer's adjusted gross income. In the case of taxable years beginning after December 31, 2017, and before January 1, 2026, personal casualty losses are deductible only to the extent they are attributable to a Federally declared disaster area.

154. ***Earned Income Tax Credit (EITC).***—The baseline tax system would not allow credits for particular activities or targeted at specific groups. In contrast, the Tax Code provides an EITC to low-income workers at a maximum rate of 45 percent of income. In 2022, for a family with one qualifying child, the credit is 34 percent of the first $10,980 of earned income. The credit is 40 percent of the first $14,950 of income for a family with two qualifying children, and it is 45 percent of the first $15,410 of income for a family with three or more qualifying children. Low-income workers with no qualifying children are eligible for a 7.65-percent credit on the first $7,320 of earned income. The credit plateaus and then phases out with the greater of AGI or earnings at income levels and rates which depend upon how many qualifying children are eligible and marital status. In 2022, the phase-down for married filers begins at incomes $6,130 greater than for otherwise similar unmarried filers. Earned income tax credits in excess of tax liabilities owed through the individual income tax system are refundable to individuals. Beginning in 2018, the parameters of the EITC are indexed by the chained CPI, which results in a smaller inflation adjustment than previously. This change is permanent.

155. ***Recovery rebate credits.***—The baseline tax system would not allow credits for particular activities or targeted at specific groups. In contrast, the Coronavirus Aid, Relief, and Economic Security (CARES) Act provided rebates of $1,200 ($2,400 for married couples filing jointly) and $500 per child. The total rebate amount begins phasing out at adjusted gross income over $75,000 ($150,000 for married couples filing jointly, $112,500 for heads of household). This was followed by the Consolidated Appropriations Act which provided rebates of $600 per eligible taxpayer ($1,200 for married couples filing jointly) plus an additional $600 per child, with phase-out features similar to the CARES Act. The American Rescue Plan act provided another rebate credit of $1,400 ($2,800 for married couples filing jointly) and $1,400 per dependent in 2021. The phase out begins at the same thresholds as the CARES Act, but the full credit is phased out proportionately by $80,000 of AGI ($160,000 for married couples filing jointly, $120,000 for heads of household).

Social Security

156. ***Social Security benefits for retired and disabled workers and spouses, dependents, and survivors.***—The baseline tax system would tax Social Security benefits to the extent that contributions to Social Security were not previously taxed. Thus, the portion of Social Security benefits that is attributable to employer contributions and to earnings on employer and employee contributions (and not attributable to employee contributions which are taxed at the time of contribution) would be subject to tax. In contrast, the Tax Code may not tax all of the Social Security benefits that exceed the beneficiary's contributions from previously taxed income. Actuarially, previously taxed contributions generally do not exceed 15 percent of benefits, even for retirees receiving the highest levels of benefits. Therefore, up to 85 percent of recipients' Social Security and Railroad Social Security Equivalent retirement benefits are included in (phased into) the income tax base if the recipient's provisional income exceeds certain base amounts. (Provisional income is equal to other items included in adjusted gross income plus foreign or U.S. possession income, tax-exempt interest, and one half of Social Security and Railroad Social Security Equivalent retirement benefits.) The untaxed portion of the benefits received by taxpayers who are below the income amounts at which 85 percent of the benefits are taxable is counted as a tax expenditure. Benefits paid to disabled workers and to spouses, dependents, and survivors are treated in a similar manner. Railroad Social Security Equivalent benefits are treated like Social Security benefits. See also provision number 136, Exclusion of railroad (Social Security equivalent) benefits.

157. ***Credit for certain employer contributions to Social Security.***—Under the baseline tax system, employer contributions to Social Security represent labor cost and are deductible expenses. Under current law, however, certain employers are allowed a tax credit, instead of a deduction, against taxes paid on tips received from customers in connection with the providing, delivering, or serving of food or beverages for consumption. The tip credit equals the full amount of the employer's share of FICA taxes paid on the portion of tips, when added to the employee's non-tip wages, in excess of $5.15 per hour. The credit is available only with respect to FICA taxes paid on tips.

Veterans Benefits and Services

158. ***Exclusion of veterans death benefits and disability compensation.***—Under the baseline tax system, all compensation, including dedicated payments and in-kind benefits, should be included in taxable income because they represent accretions to wealth that do not materially differ from cash wages. In contrast, all compensation due to death or disability paid by the Veterans Administration is excluded from taxable income under current law.

159. ***Exclusion of veterans pensions.***—Under the baseline tax system, all compensation, including dedicated payments and in-kind benefits, should be included in taxable income because they represent accretions to wealth that do not materially differ from cash wages. Under current law, however, pension payments made by the Veterans Administration are excluded from gross income.

160. ***Exclusion of G.I. Bill benefits.***—Under the baseline tax system, all compensation, including dedicated payments and in-kind benefits, should be included in taxable income because they represent accretions to wealth that do not materially differ from cash wages. Under current law, however, G.I. Bill benefits paid by the Veterans Administration are excluded from gross income.

161. ***Exclusion of interest on veterans housing bonds.***—The baseline tax system generally would tax all income under the regular tax rate schedule. It would not allow preferentially low (or zero) tax rates to apply to certain types or sources of income. In contrast, under current law, interest earned on general obligation bonds issued by State and local governments to finance housing for veterans is excluded from taxable income.

General Government

162. ***Exclusion of interest on public purpose State and local bonds.***—The baseline tax system generally would tax all income under the regular tax rate schedule. It would not allow preferentially low (or zero) tax rates to apply to certain types or sources of income. In contrast, under current law interest earned on State and local government bonds issued to finance public-purpose construction (e.g., schools, roads, sewers), equipment acquisition, and other public purposes is tax-exempt. Interest on bonds issued by Indian tribal governments for essential governmental purposes is also tax-exempt.

163. ***Build America Bonds.***—The baseline tax system would not allow credits for particular activities or targeted at specific groups. In contrast, the Tax Code in 2009 allowed State and local governments to issue taxable bonds through 2010 and receive a direct payment from Treasury equal to 35 percent of interest expenses. Alternatively, State and local governments could issue taxable bonds and the private lenders receive the 35-percent credit which is included in taxable income.

164. ***Deductibility of nonbusiness State and local taxes other than on owner-occupied homes.***—Under the baseline tax system, a deduction for personal consumption expenditures would not be allowed. In contrast, the Tax Code allows taxpayers who itemize their deductions to claim a deduction for State and local income taxes (or, at the taxpayer's election, State and local sales taxes) and property taxes, even though these taxes primarily pay for services that, if purchased directly by taxpayers, would not be deductible. (The estimates for this tax expenditure do not include the estimates for the deductibility of State and local property tax on owner-occupied homes. See number 58, Deductibility of State and local property tax on owner-occupied homes.) In the case of taxable years beginning after December 31, 2017, and before January 1, 2026, (1) the deduction for foreign real property taxes paid is disallowed and (2) the deduction for taxes paid in any taxable year, which includes the deduction for property taxes on real property, is limited to $10,000 ($5,000 in the case of a married individual filing a separate return).

Interest

165. ***Deferral of interest on U.S. savings bonds.***—The baseline tax system would uniformly tax all returns to investments and not allow an exemption or deferral for particular activities, investments, or industries. In contrast, taxpayers may defer paying tax on interest earned on U.S. savings bonds until the bonds are redeemed.

APPENDIX

Performance Measures and the Economic Effects of Tax Expenditures

The Government Performance and Results Act of 1993 (GPRA) directs Federal agencies to develop annual and strategic plans for their programs and activities. These plans set out performance objectives to be achieved over a specific time period. Most of these objectives are achieved through direct expenditure programs. Tax expenditures—spending programs implemented through the tax code by reducing tax obligations for certain activities—contribute to achieving these goals in a manner similar to direct expenditure programs.

Tax expenditures by definition work through the tax system and, particularly, the income tax. Thus, they may be relatively advantageous policy approaches when the benefit or incentive is related to income and is intended to be widely available. Because there is an existing public administrative and private compliance structure for the tax system, income-based programs that require little oversight might be efficiently run through the tax system. In addition, some tax expenditures actually simplify the operation of the tax system. Tax expenditures also implicitly subsidize certain activities in a manner similar to direct expenditures. For example, exempting employer-sponsored health insurance from income taxation is equivalent to a direct spending subsidy equal to the forgone tax obligations for this type of compensation. Spending, regulatory or tax-disincentive policies can also modify behavior, but may have different economic effects. A variety of tax expenditure tools can be used, e.g., deductions, credits, exemptions, deferrals, floors, ceilings, phase-ins, phase-outs, and these can be dependent on income, expenses, or demographic characteristics (age, number of family members, etc.). This wide range of policy instruments means that tax expenditures can be flexible and can have very different economic effects.

Tax expenditures also have limitations. In many cases they add to the complexity of the tax system, which raises both administrative and compliance costs. For example, exemptions, deductions, credits, and phase-outs can complicate filing and decision-making. The income tax system may have little or no contact with persons who have no or very low incomes, and does not require information on certain characteristics of individuals used in some spending programs, such as wealth or duration of employment. These features may reduce the effectiveness of tax expenditures for addressing socioeconomic disparities. Many tax expenditures, particularly those that are structured as deductions or exemptions, also deliver higher benefits to taxpayers in higher tax brackets, an outcome that may not be desireable or intentional in some contexts, and which could be avoided if the benefit was structured as an outlay program. Relatedly, tax expenditures generally do not enable the same degree of agency discretion as an outlay program. For example, grant or direct Federal service delivery programs can prioritize activities to be addressed with specific resources in a way that is difficult to emulate with tax expenditures.

Outlay programs have advantages where the direct provision of Government services is particularly warranted, such as equipping and maintaining the Armed Forces, administering the system of justice, building and maintaince of public infrastructure, and other provision of clear public goods. Outlay programs may also be specifically designed to meet the needs of low-income families who would not otherwise be subject to income taxes or need to file a tax return. Outlay programs may also receive more year-to-year oversight and fine tuning through the legislative and executive budget process. In addition, many different types of spending programs include direct Government provision; credit programs; and payments to State and local governments, the private sector, or individuals in the form of grants or contracts, which provide flexibility for policy design. On the other hand, certain outlay programs may rely less directly on economic incentives and private-market provision than tax incentives, which could reduce the relative efficiency of spending programs for some goals. Spending programs, particularly on the discretionary side, may respond less rapidly to changing activity levels and economic conditions than tax expenditures.

Regulations may have more direct and immediate effects than outlay and tax-expenditure programs because regulations apply directly and immediately to the regulated party (i.e., the intended actor), generally in the private sector. Regulations can also be fine-tuned more quickly than tax expenditures because they can often be changed as needed by the Executive Branch without legislation. Like tax expenditures, regulations often rely largely on voluntary compliance, rather than detailed inspections and policing. As such, the public administrative costs tend to be modest relative to the private resource costs associated with modifying activities. Historically, regulations have tended to rely on proscriptive measures, as opposed to economic incentives. This reliance can diminish their economic efficiency, although this feature can also promote full compliance where (as in certain safety-related cases) policymakers believe that trade-offs with economic considerations are not of paramount importance. Also, regulations generally do not directly affect Federal outlays or receipts. Thus, like tax expenditures, they may escape the degree of scrutiny that outlay programs receive.

A Framework for Evaluating the Effectiveness of Tax Expenditures

Across all major budgetary categories—from housing and health to space, technology, agriculture, and national defense—tax expenditures make up a significant portion of Federal activity and affect every area of the economy. For these reasons, a comprehensive evaluation framework that examines incentives, direct results, and spillover effects will benefit the budgetary process by informing decisions on tax expenditure policy.

As described above, tax expenditures, like spending and regulatory programs, have a variety of objectives and economic effects. These include encouraging certain types of activities (e.g., saving for retirement or investing in certain sectors); increasing certain types of after-tax income (e.g., favorable tax treatment of Social Security income) and preferencing other types of pre-tax income (e.g. preferential rates on capital gains); and reducing private compliance costs and Government administrative costs (e.g., the exclusion for up to $500,000 of capital gains on home sales). Some of these objectives are well-suited to quantitative measurement and evaluation, while others are less well-suited.

Performance measurement is generally concerned with inputs, outputs, and outcomes. In the case of tax expenditures, the principal input is usually the revenue effect. Outputs are quantitative or qualitative measures of goods and services, or changes in income and investment, directly produced by these inputs. Outcomes, in turn, represent the changes in the economy, society, or environment that are the ultimate goals of programs. Evaluations assess whether programs are meeting intended goals, but may also encompass analyzing whether initiatives are superior to other policy alternatives.

Similar to prior years, the Administration is working towards examining the objectives and effects of the wide range of tax expenditures in the President's Budget, despite challenges related to data availability, measurement, and analysis. Evaluations include an assessment of whether tax expenditures are achieving intended policy results in an efficient manner, with minimal burdens on individual taxpayers, consumers, and firms, and an examination of possible unintended effects and their consequences.

As an illustration of how evaluations can inform budgetary decisions, consider education, and research investment credits.

Education. There are millions of individuals taking advantage of tax credits designed to help pay for educational expenses. There are a number of different credits available as well as other important forms of Federal support for higher education such as subsidized student loans and grants. An evaluation would explore the possible relationships between use of the credits and the use of student loans and grants, seeking to answer, for example, whether the use of credits reduces or increases the likelihood of students applying for loans. Such an evaluation would allow stakeholders to determine the need for programs—whether they involve tax credits, subsidized loans, or grants.

Investment. A series of tax expenditures reduce the cost of investment, both in specific activities such as research and experimentation, extractive industries, and certain financial activities, and more generally throughout the economy, through accelerated depreciation for plant and equipment. These provisions can be evaluated along a number of dimensions. For example, it is useful to consider the strength of the incentives by measuring their effects on the cost of capital (the return which investments must yield to cover their costs) and effective tax rates. The impact of these provisions on the amount of corresponding forms of investment (e.g., research spending, exploration activity, equipment) might also be estimated. In some cases, such as research, there is evidence that this private investment can provide significant positive externalities—that is, economic benefits that are not reflected in the market transactions between private parties. It could be useful to quantify these externalities and compare them with the size of tax expenditures. Measures could also indicate the effects on production from these investments such as numbers or values of patents, energy production and reserves, and industrial production. Issues to be considered include the extent to which the preferences increase production (as opposed to benefiting existing output) and their cost-effectiveness relative to other policies. Analysis could also consider objectives that are more difficult to measure but could be ultimate goals, such as promoting energy security or economic growth. Such an assessment is likely to involve tax analysis as well as consideration of non-tax matters such as market structure, scientific, and other information.

The tax proposals subject to these analyses include items that indirectly affect the estimated value of tax expenditures (such as changes in income tax rates), proposals that make reforms to improve tax compliance and administration, as well as proposals which would change, add, or delete tax expenditures.

Barriers to Evaluation. Developing a framework that is sufficiently comprehensive, accurate, and flexible is a significant challenge. Evaluations are constrained by the availability of appropriate data and challenges in economic modeling:

- Data availability—Data may not exist, or may not exist in an analytically appropriate form, to conduct rigorous evaluations of certain types of expenditures. For example, measuring the effects of tax expenditures designed to achieve tax neutrality for individuals and firms earning income abroad, and foreign firms could require data from foreign governments or firms which are not readily available.

- Analytical constraints—Evaluations of tax expenditures face analytical constraints even when data are available. For example, individuals might have access to several tax expenditures and programs aimed at improving the same outcome. Isolating the effect of a single tax credit is challenging absent a well-specified research design.

- Resources—Tax expenditure analyses are seriously constrained by staffing considerations. Evaluations typically require expert analysts who are often engaged in other areas of work related to the budget.

The Executive Branch is focused on addressing these challenges to lay the foundation for the analysis of tax expenditures comprehensively, alongside evaluations of the effectiveness of direct spending initiatives.

Table 19–1. ESTIMATES OF TOTAL INCOME TAX EXPENDITURES FOR FISCAL YEARS 2022–2032

(In millions of dollars)

	Total from corporations and individuals											
	2022	2023	2024	2025	2026	2027	2028	2029	2030	2031	2032	2023–2032
National Defense												
1 Exclusion of benefits and allowances to Armed Forces personnel	14,830	15,380	15,970	16,600	15,370	15,560	16,130	16,840	17,620	18,450	19,350	167,270
International affairs:												
2 Exclusion of income earned abroad by U.S. citizens	6,700	7,160	7,560	7,950	8,360	8,790	9,250	9,740	10,250	10,780	11,340	91,180
3 Exclusion of certain allowances for Federal employees abroad	260	280	290	310	320	340	360	380	400	420	450	3,550
4 Reduced tax rate on active income of controlled foreign corporations (normal tax method)	30,540	32,840	35,110	37,200	33,200	30,910	31,870	32,520	33,270	34,080	34,910	335,910
5 Deduction for foreign-derived intangible income derived from trade or business within the United States ...	11,900	12,790	13,680	14,490	9,130	9,590	9,890	10,090	10,330	10,580	10,840	111,410
6 Interest Charge Domestic International Sales Corporations (IC-DISCs)	1,140	1,780	1,880	1,980	2,190	2,410	2,570	2,690	2,820	2,950	3,110	24,380
General science, space, and technology:												
7 Expensing of research and experimentation expenditures (normal tax method)	–19,820	–35,610	–25,800	–15,690	–4,950	0	0	0	0	0	0	–82,050
8 Credit for increasing research activities ...	23,260	24,980	26,530	28,060	29,590	31,140	32,730	34,380	36,110	37,920	39,790	321,230
Energy:												
9 Expensing of exploration and development costs, oil and gas	720	470	300	180	160	240	330	350	340	330	300	3,000
10 Expensing of exploration and development costs, coal	60	40	30	10	10	20	30	30	30	30	30	260
11 Excess of percentage over cost depletion, oil and gas	910	1,040	1,100	1,130	1,180	1,260	1,340	1,410	1,470	1,530	1,590	13,050
12 Excess of percentage over cost depletion, coal	50	60	80	80	80	80	80	80	80	90	90	800
13 Exception from passive loss limitation for working interests in oil and gas properties	10	10	10	10	10	10	10	10	10	10	10	100
14 Capital gains treatment of royalties on coal	50	50	50	50	60	60	60	70	70	70	70	610
15 Exclusion of interest on energy facility bonds	10	10	10	10	10	10	10	10	10	10	10	100
16 Enhanced oil recovery credit	390	240	200	140	40	0	0	0	0	0	0	620
17 Energy production credit	4,160	4,540	4,830	4,970	4,630	4,330	3,930	3,510	2,860	2,260	1,560	37,420
18 Marginal wells credit	280	190	80	20	0	0	0	0	0	0	0	290
19 Energy investment credit	7,340	9,490	11,160	8,320	6,260	5,170	3,710	3,430	3,150	3,890	3,760	58,340
20 Alcohol fuel credits [1]	0	0	0	0	0	0	0	0	0	0	0	0
21 Bio-Diesel and small agri-biodiesel producer tax credits [2]	30	20	0	0	0	0	0	0	0	0	0	20
22 Tax credits for clean-fuel burning vehicles and refueling property	1,082	1,076	1,005	956	917	829	769	754	749	690	591	8,337
23 Exclusion of utility conservation subsidies	50	50	50	40	40	40	30	30	30	30	20	360
24 Credit for holding clean renewable energy bonds [3]	70	70	70	70	70	70	70	70	70	70	70	700
25 Credit for investment in clean coal facilities	0	10	20	40	40	40	30	30	20	20	40	290
26 Amortize all geological and geophysical expenditures over two years	120	140	150	150	150	150	150	140	140	120	120	1,410
27 Allowance of deduction for certain energy efficient commercial building property	160	140	140	150	160	170	170	170	170	170	170	1,610
28 Credit for construction of new energy efficient homes	120	100	100	100	100	60	20	10	0	0	0	490
29 Credit for energy efficiency improvements to existing homes	450	0	0	0	0	0	0	0	0	0	0	0

Table 19–1.   ESTIMATES OF TOTAL INCOME TAX EXPENDITURES FOR FISCAL YEARS 2022–2032—Continued

(In millions of dollars)

		Total from corporations and individuals											
		2022	2023	2024	2025	2026	2027	2028	2029	2030	2031	2032	2023–2032
30	Credit for residential energy efficient property	2,700	2,380	680	220	0	0	0	0	0	0	0	3,280
31	Credit for qualified energy conservation bonds [4]	30	30	30	30	30	30	30	30	30	30	30	300
32	Advanced energy property credit	10	10	10	10	10	10	10	10	0	0	0	70
33	Advanced nuclear power facilities production credit	0	60	180	220	240	270	280	280	280	230	100	2,140
34	Reduced tax rate for nuclear decommissioning funds	110	120	120	130	130	140	150	150	160	170	170	1,440
Natural resources and environment:													
35	Expensing of exploration and development costs, nonfuel minerals	70	40	30	10	10	20	30	40	40	30	30	280
36	Excess of percentage over cost depletion, nonfuel minerals	190	220	230	230	250	260	280	280	300	310	330	2,690
37	Exclusion of interest on bonds for water, sewage, and hazardous waste facilities	370	380	360	350	340	340	390	370	380	410	430	3,750
38	Capital gains treatment of certain timber income	150	160	160	170	180	200	210	220	230	240	250	2,020
39	Expensing of multiperiod timber growing costs	230	240	260	260	270	290	300	320	330	350	350	2,970
40	Tax incentives for preservation of historic structures	580	660	790	890	950	970	970	970	980	990	980	9,150
41	Carbon oxide sequestration credit	360	310	370	570	740	1,890	2,470	2,740	5,760	7,660	7,790	30,300
42	Deduction for endangered species recovery expenditures	30	30	40	40	40	60	60	60	70	70	80	550
Agriculture:													
43	Expensing of certain capital outlays ...	120	120	120	130	150	160	170	180	190	190	200	1,610
44	Expensing of certain multiperiod production costs	260	260	260	270	330	370	390	400	420	430	450	3,580
45	Treatment of loans forgiven for solvent farmers	60	60	60	60	70	70	70	70	70	70	70	670
46	Capital gains treatment of certain agriculture income	1,500	1,580	1,600	1,670	1,830	1,980	2,060	2,160	2,260	2,360	2,470	19,970
47	Income averaging for farmers	200	210	210	220	230	230	230	230	230	230	230	2,250
48	Deferral of gain on sale of farm refiners	15	15	20	20	20	20	20	20	25	25	25	210
49	Expensing of reforestation expenditures	60	60	70	70	80	80	80	80	80	80	90	770
Commerce and housing:													
	Financial institutions and insurance:												
50	Exemption of credit union income ...	3,070	2,910	2,960	3,110	3,310	3,480	3,590	3,700	3,850	3,880	3,930	34,720
51	Exclusion of life insurance death benefits	16,020	17,560	18,760	19,270	20,000	21,090	21,430	21,900	22,480	23,040	23,560	209,090
52	Exemption or special alternative tax for small property and casualty insurance companies	1,220	1,310	1,340	1,370	1,430	1,460	1,490	1,550	1,590	1,650	1,700	14,890
53	Tax exemption of insurance income earned by tax-exempt organizations	350	370	380	390	390	400	410	420	430	430	440	4,060
54	Exclusion of interest spread of financial institutions	7,330	8,670	7,790	7,620	7,990	8,200	8,170	8,310	8,440	8,540	8,660	82,390
	Housing:												
55	Exclusion of interest on owner-occupied mortgage subsidy bonds	1,130	1,140	1,070	1,060	1,030	1,030	1,150	1,090	1,150	1,220	1,280	11,220
56	Exclusion of interest on rental housing bonds	2,090	2,090	1,980	1,950	1,900	1,900	2,100	2,010	2,120	2,230	2,360	20,640
57	Deductibility of mortgage interest on owner-occupied residences	34,430	35,660	36,820	38,730	107,230	113,890	120,340	127,360	134,670	142,440	149,370	1,006,510

Table 19–1. ESTIMATES OF TOTAL INCOME TAX EXPENDITURES FOR FISCAL YEARS 2022–2032—Continued

(In millions of dollars)

		Total from corporations and individuals											
		2022	2023	2024	2025	2026	2027	2028	2029	2030	2031	2032	2023–2032
58	Deductibility of State and local property tax on owner-occupied homes [17]	5,110	7,420	7,290	7,440	41,360	60,900	64,490	67,960	71,660	75,640	79,860	484,020
59	Deferral of income from installment sales	1,720	1,700	1,720	1,780	1,850	1,920	2,000	2,090	2,180	2,270	2,370	19,880
60	Capital gains exclusion on home sales	49,200	50,540	52,260	54,120	61,890	64,490	67,140	69,540	72,520	75,730	78,840	647,070
61	Exclusion of net imputed rental income	128,950	133,660	134,950	135,950	163,430	169,360	175,230	181,470	188,130	195,360	202,010	1,679,550
62	Exception from passive loss rules for $25,000 of rental loss	4,970	5,120	5,260	5,590	6,130	6,280	6,410	6,580	6,740	6,890	7,040	62,040
63	Credit for low-income housing investments	11,280	10,550	10,390	10,360	10,440	10,750	11,060	11,390	11,720	12,040	12,390	111,090
64	Accelerated depreciation on rental housing (normal tax method)	3,490	2,560	2,560	3,260	4,170	5,080	5,920	6,790	7,420	8,050	8,640	54,450
65	Discharge of mortgage indebtedness	380	320	330	340	0	0	0	0	0	0	0	990
66	Premiums for mortgage insurance deductible as interest	150	0	0	0	0	0	0	0	0	0	0	0
	Commerce:												
67	Discharge of business indebtedness	40	70	50	40	40	30	40	40	40	40	60	450
68	Exceptions from imputed interest rules	30	50	60	60	70	70	80	80	80	80	80	710
69	Treatment of qualified dividends	33,290	34,830	36,440	38,140	41,880	45,600	47,430	49,500	51,660	53,890	56,230	455,600
70	Capital gains (except agriculture, timber, iron ore, and coal)	112,050	118,340	119,820	124,780	136,680	148,170	154,180	161,180	168,490	176,240	184,520	1,492,400
71	Capital gains exclusion of small corporation stock	1,680	1,770	1,850	1,930	2,000	2,070	2,150	2,240	2,330	2,430	2,530	21,300
72	Step-up basis of capital gains at death	46,750	49,240	51,860	53,570	56,430	61,630	65,950	70,340	75,400	80,860	86,810	652,090
73	Carryover basis of capital gains on gifts	2,700	2,960	3,310	3,830	4,020	4,490	4,890	4,700	4,630	4,620	4,920	42,370
74	Ordinary income treatment of loss from small business corporation stock sale	70	70	80	80	80	90	90	90	100	100	110	890
75	Deferral of capital gains from like-kind exchanges	3,830	4,020	4,230	5,430	5,569	4,870	5,130	5,380	5,640	5,940	6,240	52,449
76	Depreciation of buildings other than rental housing (normal tax method)	2,720	490	–470	–470	–480	–650	–460	–10	310	700	1,070	30
77	Accelerated depreciation of machinery and equipment (normal tax method)	22,780	6,100	–8,220	–18,560	–28,460	–39,050	–30,300	–15,830	–7,290	–1,990	1,470	–142,130
78	Expensing of certain small investments (normal tax method)	–910	4,300	8,240	10,330	13,100	16,420	15,150	12,530	11,080	10,380	10,130	111,660
79	Exclusion of interest on small issue bonds	320	300	280	280	200	140	250	190	230	310	300	2,480
80	Special rules for certain film and TV production	0	100	180	240	–390	–530	–260	–120	–50	–20	0	–850
81	Allow 20-percent deduction to certain pass-through income	51,070	50,230	50,770	53,010	21,720	0	0	0	0	0	0	175,730
Transportation:													
82	Tonnage tax	90	100	100	100	100	100	110	110	110	110	120	1,060
83	Deferral of tax on shipping companies	10	10	10	10	10	10	10	10	10	10	10	100
84	Exclusion of reimbursed employee parking expenses	1,707	2,066	2,124	2,193	2,304	2,413	2,521	2,641	2,822	3,011	3,212	25,307
85	Exclusion for employer-provided transit passes	341	407	428	450	490	522	563	603	686	774	870	5,793
86	Tax credit for certain expenditures for maintaining railroad tracks	170	130	80	60	40	30	30	20	10	10	0	410
87	Exclusion of interest on bonds for Highway Projects and rail-truck transfer facilities	160	140	140	130	130	120	110	110	100	100	140	1,220
Community and regional development:													

Table 19–1.   ESTIMATES OF TOTAL INCOME TAX EXPENDITURES FOR FISCAL YEARS 2022–2032—Continued

(In millions of dollars)

		Total from corporations and individuals											
		2022	2023	2024	2025	2026	2027	2028	2029	2030	2031	2032	2023–2032
88	Exclusion of interest for airport, dock, and similar bonds	1,350	1,350	1,280	1,260	1,220	1,230	1,360	1,300	1,370	1,440	1,530	13,340
89	Exemption of certain mutuals' and cooperatives' income	100	100	100	110	110	110	110	110	120	120	120	1,110
90	Empowerment zones	90	90	90	110	90	60	40	20	20	20	20	560
91	New markets tax credit	1,170	1,210	1,250	1,310	1,360	1,340	1,230	1,060	870	640	410	10,680
92	Credit to holders of Gulf and Midwest Tax Credit Bonds.	150	140	120	110	90	90	80	80	70	60	50	890
93	Recovery Zone Bonds [5]	130	130	110	100	90	80	80	70	60	50	50	820
94	Tribal Economic Development Bonds ..	10	10	10	10	10	10	10	10	10	10	20	110
95	Opportunity Zones	3,740	2,080	2,160	1,990	−6,400	−12,400	670	880	1,130	1,320	1,550	−7,020
96	Disaster Employee Retention Credit	110	140	60	60	50	40	40	30	30	20	10	480
Education, training, employment, and social services:													
	Education:												
97	Exclusion of scholarship and fellowship income (normal tax method)	4,110	4,230	4,460	4,720	5,270	6,090	6,430	6,780	7,160	7,540	7,960	60,640
98	Tax credits for postsecondary education expenses [6]	15,460	14,820	14,580	14,380	14,270	14,250	13,970	13,680	13,380	13,030	12,660	139,020
99	Deductibility of student loan interest	2,340	2,230	2,350	2,470	2,640	3,010	3,040	3,140	3,160	3,170	3,260	28,470
100	Qualified tuition programs (includes Education IRA)	2,790	2,960	3,280	3,730	4,550	5,470	6,550	7,980	9,860	12,370	15,700	72,450
101	Exclusion of interest on student-loan bonds	190	200	190	190	180	180	200	190	200	210	220	1,960
102	Exclusion of interest on bonds for private nonprofit educational facilities	2,960	2,960	2,790	2,750	2,680	2,680	2,970	2,840	3,000	3,170	3,330	29,170
103	Credit for holders of zone academy bonds [7]	110	90	80	60	50	50	40	40	40	30	30	510
104	Exclusion of interest on savings bonds redeemed to finance educational expenses	40	40	40	40	50	50	50	50	50	50	60	480
105	Parental personal exemption for students age 19 or over	1,910	2,930	2,890	2,770	4,650	5,580	5,490	5,420	5,320	5,160	5,050	45,260
106	Deductibility of charitable contributions (education)	7,270	7,730	8,170	8,600	10,260	13,220	13,820	14,480	14,720	14,970	15,230	121,200
107	Exclusion of employer-provided educational assistance	1,510	1,630	1,730	1,840	1,630	1,530	1,610	1,680	1,760	1,850	1,930	17,190
108	Special deduction for teacher expenses	180	180	180	180	190	210	210	210	210	220	220	2,010
109	Discharge of student loan indebtedness	80	90	110	120	140	170	190	210	230	260	290	1,810
110	Qualified school construction bonds [8]	520	490	470	440	410	390	360	330	320	290	260	3,760
	Training, employment, and social services:												
111	Work opportunity tax credit	1,730	1,790	1,840	1,900	1,270	520	350	270	210	150	120	8,420
112	Employer-provided child care exclusion	550	740	810	860	1,110	1,250	1,300	1,360	1,430	1,510	1,580	11,950
113	Employer-provided child care credit	20	20	20	20	20	20	20	30	40	40	40	270
114	Assistance for adopted foster children	670	810	940	1,020	1,100	1,210	1,330	1,460	1,600	1,770	1,960	13,200
115	Adoption credit and exclusion	870	900	920	930	940	950	960	970	980	990	990	9,530
116	Exclusion of employee meals and lodging (other than military)	6,440	6,800	6,680	6,840	8,080	8,820	9,070	9,360	9,650	9,960	10,290	85,550
117	Credit for child and dependent care expenses [9]	5,850	3,570	3,720	3,820	3,920	3,980	4,040	4,090	4,140	4,200	4,280	39,760
118	Credit for disabled access expenditures	10	10	10	10	10	10	10	10	10	10	10	100
119	Deductibility of charitable contributions, other than education and health	55,500	58,860	62,250	65,550	79,070	103,560	108,430	113,540	118,890	124,490	130,170	964,810

Table 19–1.   ESTIMATES OF TOTAL INCOME TAX EXPENDITURES FOR FISCAL YEARS 2022–2032—Continued

(In millions of dollars)

		Total from corporations and individuals											
		2022	2023	2024	2025	2026	2027	2028	2029	2030	2031	2032	2023–2032
120	Exclusion of certain foster care payments	480	570	660	710	790	860	940	1,030	1,130	1,250	1,390	9,330
121	Exclusion of parsonage allowances	970	1,020	1,070	1,130	1,190	1,260	1,320	1,390	1,460	1,540	1,620	13,000
122	Indian employment credit	50	30	30	20	20	20	20	10	10	10	10	180
Health:													
123	Exclusion of employer contributions for medical insurance premiums and medical care [10]	224,520	237,400	252,430	266,010	308,280	338,270	354,440	372,310	391,600	412,050	433,530	3,366,320
124	Self-employed medical insurance premiums	8,200	8,440	8,840	9,580	11,860	13,560	14,430	15,230	15,960	16,780	17,690	132,370
125	Medical Savings Accounts and Health Savings Accounts	13,000	13,890	14,150	14,760	16,840	18,270	18,860	19,500	20,210	20,760	21,420	178,660
126	Deductibility of medical expenses	9,910	10,900	11,350	12,170	18,390	22,760	24,640	26,630	28,700	30,900	33,280	219,720
127	Exclusion of interest on hospital construction bonds	4,040	4,050	3,830	3,760	3,680	3,680	4,060	3,890	4,100	4,330	4,570	39,950
128	Refundable Premium Assistance Tax Credit [11]	14,730	9,830	7,380	8,330	9,570	9,930	10,570	11,540	11,900	12,400	13,110	104,560
129	Credit for employee health insurance expenses of small business	40	30	10	10	0	0	0	0	0	0	0	50
130	Deductibility of charitable contributions (health)	10,570	11,170	11,770	12,350	14,090	17,030	17,820	18,620	19,470	20,330	21,210	163,860
131	Tax credit for orphan drug research	1,970	2,300	2,680	3,120	3,640	4,250	4,960	5,790	6,760	7,900	9,220	50,620
132	Special Blue Cross/Blue Shield tax benefits	320	370	380	400	420	440	460	490	530	570	610	4,670
133	Distributions from retirement plans for premiums for health and long-term care insurance	460	470	490	500	590	630	650	660	670	670	680	6,010
134	Credit for family and sick leave taken by self-employed individuals [12]	2,790	760	0	0	0	0	0	0	0	0	0	760
Income security:													
135	Child tax credit [13]	66,840	67,520	68,130	48,680	18,760	18,310	17,890	17,460	17,040	16,640	16,440	306,870
136	Exclusion of railroad retirement (Social Security equivalent) benefits	300	260	240	220	220	210	180	150	120	90	50	1,740
137	Exclusion of workers' compensation benefits	9,020	9,030	9,040	9,040	9,050	9,060	9,070	9,080	9,080	9,090	9,100	90,640
138	Exclusion of public assistance benefits (normal tax method)	670	670	660	690	730	760	800	820	810	860	880	7,680
139	Exclusion of special benefits for disabled coal miners	20	20	20	20	20	10	10	10	10	10	10	140
140	Exclusion of military disability pensions...	180	180	180	190	210	230	230	240	250	250	260	2,220
	Net exclusion of pension contributions and earnings:												
141	Defined benefit employer plans	69,340	69,560	69,950	69,340	77,660	76,780	76,650	76,270	76,350	75,110	74,180	741,850
142	Defined contribution employer plans	106,710	115,490	117,830	122,100	146,190	153,200	160,100	167,700	176,330	184,010	192,750	1,535,700
143	Individual Retirement Accounts (IRAs)	23,600	24,430	25,020	26,630	32,940	35,690	38,310	40,540	43,380	46,430	49,560	362,930
144	Low- and moderate-income savers' credit	1,260	1,380	1,440	1,460	1,570	1,540	1,520	1,490	1,450	1,440	1,410	14,700
145	Self-employed plans	34,420	37,250	38,000	39,380	47,150	49,410	51,640	54,090	56,870	59,350	62,170	495,310
	Exclusion of other employee benefits:												
146	Premiums on group term life insurance	3,330	3,390	3,480	3,590	4,090	4,360	4,500	4,650	4,810	4,970	5,130	42,970
147	Premiums on accident and disability insurance	340	340	350	350	350	350	350	350	350	350	360	3,500
148	Exclusion of investment income from Supplementary Unemployment Benefit Trusts	20	30	40	40	40	40	50	50	50	50	50	440
149	Exclusion of investment income from Voluntary Employee Benefit Associations trusts	1,240	1,310	1,400	1,490	1,670	1,730	1,820	1,920	2,010	2,110	2,210	17,670
150	Special Employee Stock Ownership Plan (ESOP) rules	210	220	220	230	230	240	240	260	270	270	280	2,460

Table 19–1. ESTIMATES OF TOTAL INCOME TAX EXPENDITURES FOR FISCAL YEARS 2022–2032—Continued

(In millions of dollars)

		Total from corporations and individuals										
		2022	2023	2024	2025	2026	2027	2028	2029	2030	2031	2032	2023–2032
151	Additional deduction for the blind	40	40	50	50	40	50	50	50	60	60	60	510
152	Additional deduction for the elderly	6,300	6,920	7,430	7,970	6,580	7,030	7,540	7,940	8,490	9,050	9,640	78,590
153	Deductibility of casualty losses	0	0	0	0	720	1,090	1,130	1,170	1,220	1,290	1,350	7,970
154	Earned income tax credit (EITC) [14]	2,410	2,700	3,010	3,230	3,340	5,030	5,200	5,340	5,540	5,690	5,890	44,970
155	Recovery rebate credits [15]	19,320	770	0	0	0	0	0	0	0	0	0	770
Social Security:													
	Exclusion of Social Security benefits:												
156	Social Security benefits for retired and disabled workers and spouses, dependents, and survivors	29,760	31,350	31,730	31,870	36,830	42,970	44,940	47,000	49,070	51,160	53,450	420,370
157	Credit for certain employer contributions to Social Security ..	1,170	1,300	1,390	1,480	1,570	1,660	1,750	1,840	1,930	2,020	2,110	17,050
Veterans benefits and services:													
158	Exclusion of veterans death benefits and disability compensation	10,430	11,260	11,780	12,050	12,980	14,680	15,270	15,870	16,490	17,140	17,830	145,350
159	Exclusion of veterans pensions	250	220	210	200	210	220	220	220	220	210	210	2,140
160	Exclusion of G.I. Bill benefits	1,540	1,500	1,510	1,530	1,630	1,820	1,880	1,930	1,980	2,040	2,100	17,920
161	Exclusion of interest on veterans housing bonds	100	100	100	100	90	100	110	100	100	110	120	1,030
General purpose fiscal assistance:													
162	Exclusion of interest on public purpose State and local bonds	38,610	38,650	36,550	35,970	35,070	35,090	38,800	37,200	39,220	41,380	43,640	381,570
163	Build America Bonds [16]	0	0	0	0	0	0	0	0	0	0	0	0
164	Deductibility of nonbusiness State and local taxes other than on owner-occupied homes [17]	5,750	8,200	7,950	7,980	90,040	127,850	131,020	138,470	146,370	155,060	164,400	977,340
Interest:													
165	Deferral of interest on U.S. savings bonds	830	820	810	800	800	790	780	770	760	750	750	7,830
Addendum: Aid to State and local governments:													
	Deductibility of:												
	Property taxes on owner-occupied homes	5,110	7,420	7,290	7,440	41,360	60,900	64,490	67,960	71,660	75,640	79,860	484,020
	Nonbusiness State and local taxes other than on owner-occupied homes	5,750	8,200	7,950	7,980	90,040	127,850	131,020	138,470	146,370	155,060	164,400	977,340
	Exclusion of interest on State and local bonds for:												
	Public purposes	38,610	38,650	36,550	35,970	35,070	35,090	38,800	37,200	39,220	41,380	43,640	381,570
	Energy facilities	10	10	10	10	10	10	10	10	10	10	10	100
	Water, sewage, and hazardous waste disposal facilities	370	380	360	350	340	340	390	370	380	410	430	3,750
	Small-issues	90	90	90	90	80	80	90	90	90	100	100	900
	Owner-occupied mortgage subsidies ...	1,130	1,140	1,070	1,060	1,030	1,030	1,150	1,090	1,150	1,220	1,280	11,220
	Rental housing	2,090	2,090	1,980	1,950	1,900	1,900	2,100	2,010	2,120	2,230	2,360	20,640
	Airports, docks, and similar facilities ...	1,350	1,350	1,280	1,260	1,220	1,230	1,360	1,300	1,370	1,440	1,530	13,340
	Student loans	190	200	190	190	180	180	200	190	200	210	220	1,960
	Private nonprofit educational facilities	2,960	2,960	2,790	2,750	2,680	2,680	2,970	2,840	3,000	3,170	3,330	29,170
	Hospital construction	4,040	4,050	3,830	3,760	3,680	3,680	4,060	3,890	4,100	4,330	4,570	39,950
	Veterans' housing	100	100	100	100	90	100	110	100	100	110	120	1,030

Table 19-1. ESTIMATES OF TOTAL INCOME TAX EXPENDITURES FOR FISCAL YEARS 2022–2032—Continued

(In millions of dollars)

	Total from corporations and individuals											
	2022	2023	2024	2025	2026	2027	2028	2029	2030	2031	2032	2023–2032

[1] The alternative fuel mixture credit results in a reduction in excise tax receipts (in millions of dollars) as follows: 2022 $310; and $0 thereafter.

[2] In addition, the biodiesel producer tax credit results in a reduction in excise tax receipts (in millions of dollars) as follows: 2022 $3,660; 2023 $1,890; and $0 thereafter.

[3] In addition, the credit for holding clean renewable energy bonds has outlay effects of (in millions of dollars): 2022 $40; 2023 $40; 2024 $40; 2025 $40; 2026 $40; 2027 $40; 2028 $40; 2029 $40; 2030 $40; 2031 $40; and 2032 $40.

[4] In addition, the qualified energy conservation bonds have outlay effects of (in millions of dollars): 2022 $40; 2023 $40; 2024 $30; 2025 $30; 2026 $30; 2027 $30; 2028 $30; 2029 $30; 2030 $30; 2031 $30; and 2032 $30.

[5] In addition, recovery zone bonds have outlay effects (in millions of dollars) as follows: 2022 $110; 2023 $110; 2024 $110; 2025 $110; 2026 $110; 2027 $100; 2028 $100; 2029 $100; 2030 $100; 2031 $100; and 2032 $100.

[6] In addition, the tax credits and deductions for postsecondary education expenses have outlay effects of (in millions of dollars): 2022 $4,020; 2023 $3,060; 2024 $3,030; 2025 $3,000; 2026 $2,980; 2027 $2,950; 2028 $2,910; 2029 $2,870; 2030 $2,820; 2031 $2,770; and 2032 $2,710.

[7] In addition, the credit for holders of zone academy bonds has outlay effects of (in millions of dollars): 2022 $40; 2023 $40; 2024 $40; 2025 $40; 2026 $40; 2027 $40; 2028 $40; 2029 $40; 2030 $40; 2031 $40; and 2032 $40.

[8] In addition, the provision for school construction bonds has outlay effects of (in millions of dollars): 2022 $560; 2023 $560; 2024 $560; 2025 $550; 2026 $550; 2027 $550; 2028 $540; 2029 $540; 2030 $540; 2031 $530; and 2032 $560.

[9] In addition, the child and dependent care credit is refundable for one year with outlay effects of (millions of dollars): 2022 $7,790; 2023 $50; and $0 thereafter.

[10] In addition, the employer contributions for health have effects on payroll tax receipts (in millions of dollars) as follows: 2022 $136,990; 2023 $149,180; 2024 $159,420; 2025 $168,350; 2026 $176,710; 2027 $184,450; 2028 $192,430; 2029 $201,100; 2030 $210,610; 2031 $220,800; and 2032 $231,700.

[11] In addition, the premium assistance credit provision has outlay effects (in millions of dollars) as follows: 2022 $61,580; 2023 $45,010; 2024 $39,900; 2025 $41,220; 2026 $42,440; 2027 $43,840; 2028 $46,270; 2029 $49,690; 2030 $52,790; 2031 $55,410; and 2032 $57,980.

[12] In addition, the effect of the credit for sick leave has outlay effects of (in millions of dollars): 2022 $930; 2023 $130; and $0 thereafter.

[13] In addition, the effect of the child tax credit on receipts has outlay effects of (in millions of dollars): 2022 $158,940; 2023 $40,840; 2024 $41,340; 2025 $41,170; 2026 $41,150; 2027 $24,800; 2028 $24,570; 2029 $24,480; 2030 $24,440; 2031 $24,460; and 2032 $23,350.

The child tax credit line also includes the credit for other dependents (in millions of dollars): 2022 $10,870; 2023 $9,700; 2024 $9,770; 2025 $9,760; 2026 $5,640; and $0 thereafter.

[14] In addition, the earned income tax credit on receipts has outlay effects of (in millions of dollars): 2022 $77,290; 2023 $59,780; 2024 $63,920; 2025 $66,730; 2026 $67,570; 2027 $67,080; 2028 $67,960; 2029 $69,220; 2030 $70,640; 2031 $71,960; and 2032 $73,400.

[15] In addition, the recovery rebate credits have outlay effects of (in millions of dollars): 2022 $13,620; 2023 $360; and $0 thereafter.

[16] In addition, the Build America Bonds have outlay effects of (in millions of dollars): 2022 $2,500; 2023 $2,470; 2024 $2,440; 2025 $2,420; 2026 $2,390; 2027 $2,360; 2028 $2,340; 2029 $2,310; 2030 $2,280; 2031 $2,250; and 2032 $2,360.

[17] Because of interactions with the $10,000 cap on State and local tax deductions for the years 2018 through 2025, these estimates understate the combined effects of repealing deductions for both property taxes on owner occupied housing and other non-business taxes. The estimate of repealing both is (in millions of dollars): 2022 $18,080; 2023 $26,580; 2024 $26,340; 2025 $26,950; 2026 $135,670; 2027 $188,800; 2028 $195,460; 2029 $206,830; 2030 $218,990; 2031 $232,280; and 2032 $246,290.

Table 19–2.   INCOME TAX EXPENDITURES RANKED BY TOTAL FISCAL YEAR 2023–2032 PROJECTED REVENUE EFFECT

(In millions of dollars)

	Provision	2022	2023	2023–2032
123	Exclusion of employer contributions for medical insurance premiums and medical care [10]	224,520	237,400	3,366,320
61	Exclusion of net imputed rental income	128,950	133,660	1,679,550
142	Defined contribution employer plans	106,710	115,490	1,535,700
70	Capital gains (except agriculture, timber, iron ore, and coal)	112,050	118,340	1,492,400
57	Deductibility of mortgage interest on owner-occupied residences	34,430	35,660	1,006,510
164	Deductibility of nonbusiness State and local taxes other than on owner-occupied homes [17]	5,750	8,200	977,340
119	Deductibility of charitable contributions, other than education and health	55,500	58,860	964,810
141	Defined benefit employer plans	69,340	69,560	741,850
72	Step-up basis of capital gains at death	46,750	49,240	652,090
60	Capital gains exclusion on home sales	49,200	50,540	647,070
145	Self-employed plans	34,420	37,250	495,310
58	Deductibility of State and local property tax on owner-occupied homes [17]	5,110	7,420	484,020
69	Treatment of qualified dividends	33,290	34,830	455,600
156	Social Security benefits for retired and disabled workers and spouses, dependents, and survivors	29,760	31,350	420,370
162	Exclusion of interest on public purpose State and local bonds	38,610	38,650	381,570
143	Individual Retirement Accounts (IRAs)	23,600	24,430	362,930
4	Reduced tax rate on active income of controlled foreign corporations (normal tax method)	30,540	32,840	335,910
8	Credit for increasing research activities	23,260	24,980	321,230
135	Child tax credit [13]	66,840	67,520	306,870
126	Deductibility of medical expenses	9,910	10,900	219,720
51	Exclusion of life insurance death benefits	16,020	17,560	209,090
125	Medical Savings Accounts and Health Savings Accounts	13,000	13,890	178,660
81	Allow 20-percent deduction to certain pass-through income	51,070	50,230	175,730
1	Exclusion of benefits and allowances to Armed Forces personnel	14,830	15,380	167,270
130	Deductibility of charitable contributions (health)	10,570	11,170	163,860
158	Exclusion of veterans death benefits and disability compensation	10,430	11,260	145,350
98	Tax credits for postsecondary education expenses [6]	15,460	14,820	139,020
124	Self-employed medical insurance premiums	8,200	8,440	132,370
106	Deductibility of charitable contributions (education)	7,270	7,730	121,200
7	Expensing of research and experimentation expenditures (normal tax method)	−910	4,300	111,660
78	Expensing of certain small investments (normal tax method)	−910	4,300	111,660
5	Deduction for foreign-derived intangible income derived from trade or business within the United States	11,900	12,790	111,410
63	Credit for low-income housing investments	11,280	10,550	111,090
128	Refundable Premium Assistance Tax Credit [11]	14,730	9,830	104,560
2	Exclusion of income earned abroad by U.S. citizens	6,700	7,160	91,180
137	Exclusion of workers' compensation benefits	9,020	9,030	90,640
116	Exclusion of employee meals and lodging (other than military)	6,440	6,800	85,550
54	Exclusion of interest spread of financial institutions	7,330	8,670	82,390
152	Additional deduction for the elderly	6,300	6,920	78,590
100	Qualified tuition programs (includes Education IRA)	2,790	2,960	72,450
62	Exception from passive loss rules for $25,000 of rental loss	4,970	5,120	62,040
97	Exclusion of scholarship and fellowship income (normal tax method)	4,110	4,230	60,640
19	Energy investment credit	7,340	9,490	58,340
64	Accelerated depreciation on rental housing (normal tax method)	3,490	2,560	54,450
75	Deferral of capital gains from like-kind exchanges	3,830	4,020	52,449
131	Tax credit for orphan drug research	1,970	2,300	50,620
105	Parental personal exemption for students age 19 or over	1,910	2,930	45,260
154	Earned income tax credit (EITC) [14]	2,410	2,700	44,970
146	Premiums on group term life insurance	3,330	3,390	42,970
73	Carryover basis of capital gains on gifts	2,700	2,960	42,370
127	Exclusion of interest on hospital construction bonds	4,040	4,050	39,950
117	Credit for child and dependent care expenses [9]	5,850	3,570	39,760
17	Energy production credit	4,160	4,540	37,420
50	Exemption of credit union income	3,070	2,910	34,720
41	Carbon oxide sequestration credit	360	310	30,300

Table 19–3. INCOME TAX EXPENDITURES RANKED BY TOTAL FISCAL YEAR 2023–2032 PROJECTED REVENUE EFFECT—Continued

(In millions of dollars)

	Provision	2022	2023	2023–2032
102	Exclusion of interest on bonds for private nonprofit educational facilities	2,960	2,960	29,170
99	Deductibility of student loan interest	2,340	2,230	28,470
84	Exclusion of reimbursed employee parking expenses	1,707	2,066	25,307
6	Interest Charge Domestic International Sales Corporations (IC-DISCs)	1,140	1,780	24,380
71	Capital gains exclusion of small corporation stock	1,680	1,770	21,300
56	Exclusion of interest on rental housing bonds	2,090	2,090	20,640
46	Capital gains treatment of certain agriculture income	1,500	1,580	19,970
59	Deferral of income from installment sales	1,720	1,700	19,880
160	Exclusion of G.I. Bill benefits	1,540	1,500	17,920
149	Exclusion of investment income from Voluntary Employee Benefit Associations trusts	1,240	1,310	17,670
107	Exclusion of employer-provided educational assistance	1,510	1,630	17,190
157	Credit for certain employer contributions to Social Security	1,170	1,300	17,050
52	Exemption or special alternative tax for small property and casualty insurance companies	1,220	1,310	14,890
144	Low- and moderate-income savers' credit	1,260	1,380	14,700
88	Exclusion of interest for airport, dock, and similar bonds	1,350	1,350	13,340
114	Assistance for adopted foster children	670	810	13,200
11	Excess of percentage over cost depletion, oil and gas	910	1,040	13,050
121	Exclusion of parsonage allowances	970	1,020	13,000
112	Employer-provided child care exclusion	550	740	11,950
55	Exclusion of interest on owner-occupied mortgage subsidy bonds	1,130	1,140	11,220
91	New markets tax credit	1,170	1,210	10,680
115	Adoption credit and exclusion	870	900	9,530
120	Exclusion of certain foster care payments	480	570	9,330
40	Tax incentives for preservation of historic structures	580	660	9,150
111	Work opportunity tax credit	1,730	1,790	8,420
22	Tax credits for clean-fuel burning vehicles and refueling property	1,082	1,076	8,337
153	Deductibility of casualty losses	0	0	7,970
165	Deferral of interest on U.S. savings bonds	830	820	7,830
138	Exclusion of public assistance benefits (normal tax method)	670	670	7,680
133	Distributions from retirement plans for premiums for health and long-term care insurance	460	470	6,010
85	Exclusion for employer-provided transit passes	341	407	5,793
132	Special Blue Cross/Blue Shield tax benefits	320	370	4,670
53	Tax exemption of insurance income earned by tax-exempt organizations	350	370	4,060
110	Qualified school construction bonds [8]	520	490	3,760
37	Exclusion of interest on bonds for water, sewage, and hazardous waste facilities	370	380	3,750
44	Expensing of certain multiperiod production costs	260	260	3,580
3	Exclusion of certain allowances for Federal employees abroad	260	280	3,550
147	Premiums on accident and disability insurance	340	340	3,500
30	Credit for residential energy efficient property	2,700	2,380	3,280
9	Expensing of exploration and development costs, oil and gas	720	470	3,000
39	Expensing of multiperiod timber growing costs	230	240	2,970
36	Excess of percentage over cost depletion, nonfuel minerals	190	220	2,690
79	Exclusion of interest on small issue bonds	320	300	2,480
150	Special Employee Stock Ownership Plan (ESOP) rules	210	220	2,460
47	Income averaging for farmers	200	210	2,250
140	Exclusion of military disability pensions	180	180	2,220
33	Advanced nuclear power facilities production credit	0	60	2,140
159	Exclusion of veterans pensions	250	220	2,140
38	Capital gains treatment of certain timber income	150	160	2,020
108	Special deduction for teacher expenses	180	180	2,010
101	Exclusion of interest on student-loan bonds	190	200	1,960
109	Discharge of student loan indebtedness	80	90	1,810
136	Exclusion of railroad retirement (Social Security equivalent) benefits	300	260	1,740
27	Allowance of deduction for certain energy efficient commercial building property	160	140	1,610
43	Expensing of certain capital outlays	120	120	1,610
34	Reduced tax rate for nuclear decommissioning funds	110	120	1,440

Table 19–3. INCOME TAX EXPENDITURES RANKED BY TOTAL FISCAL YEAR 2023–2032 PROJECTED REVENUE EFFECT—Continued

(In millions of dollars)

Provision	2022	2023	2023–2032
26 Amortize all geological and geophysical expenditures over two years	120	140	1,410
87 Exclusion of interest on bonds for Highway Projects and rail-truck transfer facilities	160	140	1,220
89 Exemption of certain mutuals' and cooperatives' income	100	100	1,110
82 Tonnage tax	90	100	1,060
161 Exclusion of interest on veterans housing bonds	100	100	1,030
65 Discharge of mortgage indebtedness	380	320	990
74 Ordinary income treatment of loss from small business corporation stock sale	70	70	890
92 Credit to holders of Gulf and Midwest Tax Credit Bonds.	150	140	890
93 Recovery Zone Bonds [5]	130	130	820
12 Excess of percentage over cost depletion, coal	50	60	800
49 Expensing of reforestation expenditures	60	60	770
155 Recovery rebate credits [15]	19,320	770	770
68 Exceptions from imputed interest rules	30	50	710
24 Credit for holding clean renewable energy bonds [3]	70	70	700
45 Treatment of loans forgiven for solvent farmers	60	60	670
16 Enhanced oil recovery credit	390	240	620
14 Capital gains treatment of royalties on coal	50	50	610
90 Empowerment zones	90	90	560
42 Deduction for endangered species recovery expenditures	30	30	550
134 Credit for family and sick leave taken by self-employed individuals [12]	2,790	760	760
103 Credit for holders of zone academy bonds [7]	110	90	510
151 Additional deduction for the blind	40	40	510
28 Credit for construction of new energy efficient homes	120	100	490
96 Disaster Employee Retention Credit	110	140	480
104 Exclusion of interest on savings bonds redeemed to finance educational expenses	40	40	480
67 Discharge of business indebtedness	40	70	450
148 Exclusion of investment income from Supplementary Unemployment Benefit Trusts	20	30	440
86 Tax credit for certain expenditures for maintaining railroad tracks	170	130	410
23 Exclusion of utility conservation subsidies	50	50	360
31 Credit for qualified energy conservation bonds [4]	30	30	300
18 Marginal wells credit	280	190	290
25 Credit for investment in clean coal facilities	0	10	290
35 Expensing of exploration and development costs, nonfuel minerals	70	40	280
113 Employer-provided child care credit	20	20	270
10 Expensing of exploration and development costs, coal	60	40	260
48 Deferral of gain on sale of farm refiners	15	15	210
122 Indian employment credit	50	30	180
139 Exclusion of special benefits for disabled coal miners	20	20	140
94 Tribal Economic Development Bonds	10	10	110
13 Exception from passive loss limitation for working interests in oil and gas properties	10	10	100
15 Exclusion of interest on energy facility bonds	10	10	100
83 Deferral of tax on shipping companies	10	10	100
118 Credit for disabled access expenditures	10	10	100
32 Advanced energy property credit	10	10	70
129 Credit for employee health insurance expenses of small business	40	30	50
76 Depreciation of buildings other than rental housing (normal tax method)	2,720	490	30
21 Bio-Diesel and small agri-biodiesel producer tax credits [2]	30	20	20
20 Alcohol fuel credits [1]	0	0	0
29 Credit for energy efficiency improvements to existing homes	450	0	0
66 Premiums for mortgage insurance deductible as interest	150	0	0
163 Build America Bonds [16]	0	0	0
80 Special rules for certain film and TV production	0	100	−850
95 Opportunity Zones	3,740	2,080	−7,020
77 Accelerated depreciation of machinery and equipment (normal tax method)	22,780	6,100	−142,130

See Table 19-1 footnotes for specific table information.

Table 19–3.   PRESENT VALUE OF SELECTED TAX EXPENDITURES FOR ACTIVITY IN CALENDAR YEAR 2022

(In millions of dollars)

	Provision	2022 Present Value of Revenue Loss
	Expensing of exploration and development costs—fuels [1]	750
35	Expensing of exploration and development costs—nonfuels	70
39	Expensing of multiperiod timber growing costs	170
44	Expensing of certain multiperiod production costs—agriculture	70
43	Expensing of certain capital outlays—agriculture	40
49	Expensing of reforestation expenditures	40
64	Accelerated depreciation on rental housing (normal tax method)	−3,900
76	Depreciation of buildings other than rental housing (normal tax method)	−150
77	Accelerated depreciation of machinery and equipment (normal tax method)	−17,770
78	Expensing of certain small investments (normal tax method)	0
63	Credit for low-income housing investments	9,680
100	Qualified tuition programs (includes Education IRA)	6,960
141	Defined benefit employer plans	81,081
142	Defined contribution employer plans	184,560
143	Exclusion of IRA contributions and earnings	2,390
143	Exclusion of Roth earnings and distributions	430
143	Exclusion of non-deductible IRA earnings	420
145	Exclusion of contributions and earnings for Self-Employed plans	7,660
162	Exclusion of interest on public-purpose bonds	11,930
	Exclusion of interest on non-public purpose bonds [2]	4,710
165	Deferral of interest on U.S. savings bonds	130

[1] Includes oil, gas, and coal.

[2] Includes all components, other than public purpose, listed under 'Exclusion of interest on State and local bonds' in the Addendum to Table 1

20. FEDERAL BORROWING AND DEBT

Debt is the largest legally and contractually binding obligation of the Federal Government. At the end of 2022, the Government owed $24,252 billion of principal to the individuals and institutions who had loaned it the money to fund past deficits. During that year, the Government paid the public approximately $534 billion of interest on this debt.[1] At the same time, the Government also held financial assets, net of financial liabilities other than debt, of $2,204 billion. Therefore, debt held by the public net of financial assets was $22,049 billion.

The $24,252 billion debt held by the public at the end of 2022 represents an increase of $1,970 billion over the level at the end of 2021. This increase is the result of the $1,376 billion deficit in 2022 and other financing transactions that increased the need to borrow by $594 billion. The $594 billion borrowing due to other financing transactions reflects a $421 billion increase in Treasury's operating cash balance (discussed in more detail below), as well as other factors. Although debt held by the public grew in dollar terms in 2022, debt held by the public as a percent of Gross Domestic Product (GDP) fell from 98.4 percent of at the end of 2021 to 97.0 percent of GDP at the end of 2022 due to the economy growing at a significantly faster rate than the debt. The deficit is estimated to increase to $1,569 billion in 2023 and to $1,846 billion in 2024, and then to fall in 2025 and 2026. After 2026, the deficit is projected to remain relatively steady at roughly 5 percent of GDP. Debt held by the public is projected to grow to $25,910 billion (98.4 percent of GDP) at the end of 2023 and $27,783 billion (102.0 percent of GDP) at the end of 2024. After 2024, debt held by the public as a percent of GDP is projected to gradually increase, reaching 109.8 percent in 2033. Debt net of financial assets is expected to grow to $23,619 billion (89.7 percent of GDP) at the end of 2023 and $25,465 billion (93.5 percent of GDP) at the end of 2024. After 2024, debt net of financial assets is projected to continue to gradually increase, to 102.4 percent of GDP at the end of 2033.

Trends in Debt Since World War II

Table 20–1 depicts trends in Federal debt held by the public from World War II to the present and estimates from the present through 2033. (It is supplemented for earlier years by Tables 7.1–7.3 in the Budget's *Historical Tables*, available as supplemental budget material.[2]) Federal debt peaked at 106.1 percent of GDP in 1946, just after the end of the war. From that point until the 1970s, Federal debt as a percentage of GDP decreased almost every year because of relatively small deficits, an expanding economy, and unanticipated inflation. With households borrowing large amounts to buy homes and consumer durables, and with businesses borrowing large amounts to buy plant and equipment, Federal debt also decreased almost every year as a percentage of total credit market debt outstanding. The cumulative effect was impressive. From 1950 to 1975, debt held by the public declined from 78.6 percent of GDP to 24.6 percent, and from 53.3 percent of credit market debt to 17.9 percent. Despite rising interest rates during this period, interest outlays became a smaller share of the budget and were roughly stable as a percentage of GDP.

Federal debt relative to GDP is a function of the Nation's fiscal policy as well as overall economic conditions. During the 1970s, large budget deficits emerged as spending grew faster than receipts and as the economy was disrupted by oil shocks and rising inflation. Federal debt relative to GDP and credit market debt stopped declining for several years in the middle of the decade. Federal debt started growing again at the beginning of the 1980s, and increased to almost 48 percent of GDP by 1993. The ratio of Federal debt to credit market debt also rose during this period, though to a lesser extent. Interest outlays on debt held by the public, calculated as a percentage of either total Federal outlays or GDP, increased as well.

The growth of Federal debt held by the public was slowing by the mid-1990s. In addition to a growing economy, two major budget agreements were enacted in the 1990s, implementing revenue increases and spending reductions and significantly reducing deficits. The debt declined markedly relative to both GDP and total credit market debt, with the decline accelerating as budget surpluses emerged from 1998 to 2001. Debt fell from 47.9 percent of GDP in 1993 to 31.5 percent of GDP in 2001. Over that same period, debt fell from 26.2 percent of total credit market debt to 17.3 percent. Interest as a share of outlays peaked at 16.5 percent in 1989 and then fell to 8.9 percent by 2002; interest as a percentage of GDP fell by a similar proportion.

The progress in reducing the debt burden stopped and then reversed course beginning in 2002. The attacks of September 11, 2001, a recession, two major wars, and tax cuts all contributed to increasing deficits, causing debt to rise, both in nominal terms and as a percentage of GDP. Following the recession that began in December 2007, the deficit increased rapidly in 2008 and 2009, as the Government intervened in the potential collapse of several major corporations and financial institutions as well as enacting a major stimulus bill. Additional tax cuts enacted in 2017 also contributed to higher deficits. Debt as a percent of GDP grew from 35.2 percent at the end of

---

[1] This is 2022 nominal interest on debt held by the public. For a discussion of real net interest, see Chapter 3, "Long-Term Budget Outlook."

[2] The *Historical Tables* are available at *https://www.whitehouse.gov/omb/historical-tables/*.

Table 20–1. TRENDS IN FEDERAL DEBT HELD BY THE PUBLIC AND INTEREST ON THE DEBT HELD BY THE PUBLIC

(Dollar amounts in billions)

Fiscal Year	Debt held by the public — Current dollars	Debt held by the public — FY 2022 dollars [1]	Debt held by the public as a percent of — GDP	Debt held by the public as a percent of — Credit market debt [2]	Interest on the debt held by the public [3] — Current dollars	Interest on the debt held by the public [3] — FY 2022 dollars [1]	Interest on the debt held by the public as a percent of [3] — Total outlays	Interest on the debt held by the public as a percent of [3] — GDP
1946	241.9	2,916.7	106.1	N/A	4.2	50.4	7.6	1.8
1950	219.0	2,133.8	78.6	53.3	4.8	47.2	11.4	1.7
1955	226.6	1,940.5	55.8	42.1	5.2	44.4	7.6	1.3
1960	236.8	1,797.3	44.3	33.1	7.8	59.3	8.5	1.5
1965	260.8	1,854.6	36.8	26.4	9.6	68.1	8.1	1.4
1970	283.2	1,678.5	27.1	20.3	15.4	91.1	7.9	1.5
1975	394.7	1,723.2	24.6	17.9	25.0	109.2	7.5	1.6
1980	711.9	2,161.0	25.5	18.4	62.8	190.5	10.6	2.2
1985	1,507.3	3,487.1	35.3	22.2	152.9	353.8	16.2	3.6
1990	2,411.6	4,793.5	40.9	22.4	202.4	402.3	16.2	3.4
1995	3,604.4	6,319.0	47.7	26.2	239.2	419.4	15.8	3.2
2000	3,409.8	5,509.3	33.7	18.7	232.8	376.2	13.0	2.3
2005	4,592.2	6,629.5	35.8	17.0	191.4	276.2	7.7	1.5
2010	9,018.9	11,799.1	60.6	24.9	228.2	298.5	6.6	1.5
2015	13,116.7	15,733.0	72.5	30.2	260.6	312.6	7.1	1.4
2016	14,167.6	16,854.1	76.4	31.2	283.8	337.7	7.4	1.5
2017	14,665.4	17,140.0	76.2	31.2	309.9	362.2	7.8	1.6
2018	15,749.6	17,985.2	77.6	31.7	371.4	424.1	9.0	1.8
2019	16,800.7	18,817.0	79.4	32.3	423.3	474.1	9.5	2.0
2020	21,016.7	23,229.2	99.8	36.0	387.4	428.2	5.9	1.8
2021	22,282.8	23,826.9	98.4	36.2	412.8	441.4	6.1	1.8
2022	24,252.4	24,252.4	97.0	36.7	533.6	533.6	8.5	2.1
2023 estimate	25,909.8	24,718.1	98.4	N/A	720.6	687.5	11.3	2.7
2024 estimate	27,782.7	25,892.9	102.0	N/A	846.2	788.6	12.3	3.1
2025 estimate	29,591.7	27,005.0	104.1	N/A	887.3	809.7	12.5	3.1
2026 estimate	31,232.8	27,919.0	105.2	N/A	930.1	831.4	12.8	3.1
2027 estimate	32,850.6	28,760.7	106.3	N/A	978.2	856.4	12.9	3.2
2028 estimate	34,516.8	29,598.6	107.2	N/A	1,031.7	884.7	12.9	3.2
2029 estimate	36,106.1	30,324.8	107.7	N/A	1,096.7	921.1	13.4	3.3
2030 estimate	37,837.8	31,126.9	108.2	N/A	1,170.9	963.2	13.6	3.3
2031 estimate	39,650.0	31,946.1	108.7	N/A	1,251.8	1,008.6	13.8	3.4
2032 estimate	41,553.5	32,790.2	109.1	N/A	1,321.7	1,043.0	14.0	3.5
2033 estimate	43,619.2	33,711.4	109.8	N/A	1,399.9	1,081.9	14.0	3.5

N/A = Not available.

1 Amounts in current dollars deflated by the GDP chain-type price index with fiscal year 2022 equal to 100.

2 Total credit market debt owed by domestic nonfinancial sectors. Financial sectors are omitted to avoid double counting, since financial intermediaries borrow in the credit market primarily in order to finance lending in the credit market. Source: Federal Reserve Board flow of funds accounts. Projections are not available.

3 Interest on debt held by the public is estimated as the interest on Treasury debt securities less the "interest received by trust funds" (subfunction 901 less subfunctions 902 and 903). The estimate of interest on debt held by the public does not include the comparatively small amount of interest paid on agency debt or the offsets for interest on Treasury debt received by other Government accounts (revolving funds and special funds).

2007 to 79.4 percent in 2019. However, due to a decline in interest rates, despite the rising debt, net interest as a share of GDP dropped from 1.8 percent of GDP in 2007 to as low as 1.4 percent of GDP in 2015, before rising again to 2.0 percent by 2019.

As a result of the COVID-19 pandemic and the Government's actions to address the pandemic and support the economy, debt held by the public increased sharply in 2020, growing from 79.4 percent of GDP at the end of 2019 to 99.8 percent at the end of 2020. In 2021, a $1,567 billion decrease in the Treasury operating cash balance offset a significant portion of the $2,775 billion deficit. Although debt held by the public grew by $1,266 billion in 2021, it fell as a percent of GDP, to 98.4 percent, due to economic growth that outpaced the growth of the debt. In 2022, debt held by the public similarly grew in dollar terms, by $1,970 billion, but fell as a percent of GDP, to 97.0 percent.

In 2023, the deficit is projected to grow to $1,569 billion. As a result of the $1,569 billion deficit and $88 billion in borrowing due to other financing transactions (discussed in more detail below), debt held by the public is projected to grow to $25,910 billion, or 98.4 percent of GDP. The deficit is projected to grow to $1,846 billion in 2024, and debt held by the public is projected to grow to $27,783 billion, or 102.0 percent of GDP. As a percent of GDP, the deficit is projected to fall in 2025 and 2026 and then remain fairly stable at roughly 5 percent of GDP. Debt held by the public is expected to gradually increase, reaching 109.8 percent of GDP by 2033. Debt net of financial assets is estimated to grow to $23,619 billion, or 89.7 percent of GDP, at the end of 2023 and $25,465 billion, or 93.5 percent of GDP, at the end of 2024, then continue to increase gradually in subsequent years, reaching 102.4 percent of GDP by the end of 2033.

Debt Held by the Public and Gross Federal Debt

The Federal Government issues debt securities for two main purposes. First, it borrows from the public to provide for the Federal Government's financing needs, including both the deficit and the other transactions requiring financing, most notably disbursements for direct student loans and other Federal credit programs.[3] Second, it issues debt to Federal Government accounts, primarily trust funds, that accumulate surpluses. By law, trust fund surpluses must generally be invested in Federal securities. The gross Federal debt is defined to consist of both the debt held by the public and the debt held by Government accounts. Nearly all the Federal debt has been issued by the Treasury and is sometimes called "public debt," but a small portion has been issued by other Government agencies and is called "agency debt."[4]

---

[3] For the purposes of the Budget, "debt held by the public" is defined as debt held by investors outside of the Federal Government, both domestic and foreign, including U.S. State and local governments and foreign governments. It also includes debt held by the Federal Reserve.

[4] The term "agency debt" is defined more narrowly in the budget than customarily in the securities market, where it includes not only the debt of the Federal agencies listed in Table 20-4, but also certain Government-guaranteed securities and the debt of the Government-sponsored enterprises listed in Table 7–7 in the supplemental materials to the "Credit and Insurance" chapter. (Table 7–7 is available at: *https://www.whitehouse.gov/omb/analytical-perspectives/*.)

Borrowing from the public, whether by the Treasury or by some other Federal agency, is important because it represents the Federal demand on credit markets. Regardless of whether the proceeds are used for tangible or intangible investments or to finance current consumption, the Federal demand on credit markets has to be financed out of the saving of households and businesses, the State and local sector, or the rest of the world. Borrowing from the public can thus affect the size and composition of assets held by the private sector and the amount of saving imported from abroad and increase the amount of future resources required to pay interest to the public on Federal debt. Borrowing from the public is therefore an important consideration in Federal fiscal policy. Borrowing from the public, however, is an incomplete measure of the Federal impact on credit markets. Different types of Federal activities can affect the credit markets in different ways. For example, under its direct loan programs, the Government uses borrowed funds to acquire financial assets that might otherwise require financing in the credit markets directly. (For more information on other ways in which Federal activities impact the credit market, see the discussion at the end of this chapter.) By incorporating the change in direct loan and other financial assets, debt held by the public net of financial assets adds useful insight into the Government's financial condition.

Issuing debt securities to Government accounts performs an essential function in accounting for the operation of these funds. The balances of debt represent the cumulative surpluses of these funds due to the excess of their tax receipts, interest receipts, and other collections over their spending. The interest on the debt that is credited to these funds accounts for the fact that some earmarked taxes and user fees will be spent at a later time than when the funds receive the monies. The debt securities are assets of those funds but are a liability of the general fund to the funds that hold the securities, and are a mechanism for crediting interest to those funds on their recorded balances. These balances generally provide the fund with authority to draw upon the Treasury in later years to make future payments on its behalf to the public. Public policy may result in the Government's running surpluses and accumulating debt in trust funds and other Government accounts in anticipation of future spending.

However, issuing debt to Government accounts does not have any of the current credit market effects of borrowing from the public. It is an internal transaction of the Government, made between two accounts that are both within the Government itself. Issuing debt to a Government account is not a current transaction of the Government with the public; it is not financed by private savings and does not compete with the private sector for available funds in the credit market. While such issuance provides the account with assets—a binding claim against the Treasury— those assets are fully offset by the increased liability of the Treasury to pay the claims, which will ultimately be covered by the collection of revenues or by borrowing. Similarly, the current interest earned by the Government account on its Treasury securities does not need to be financed by other resources.

Table 20–2. FEDERAL GOVERNMENT FINANCING AND DEBT

(In billions of dollars)

	Actual 2022	Estimate										
		2023	2024	2025	2026	2027	2028	2029	2030	2031	2032	2033
Financing:												
Unified budget deficit	1,375.9	1,569.3	1,846.4	1,671.5	1,521.0	1,508.9	1,603.6	1,535.7	1,686.5	1,775.5	1,870.8	2,034.7
Other transactions affecting borrowing from the public:												
Changes in financial assets and liabilities: [1]												
Change in Treasury operating cash balance	420.8	14.0	....	....	....	....	....	....	....	....	....	....
Net disbursements of credit financing accounts:												
Direct loan and Troubled Asset Relief Program (TARP) equity purchase accounts	–256.1	43.5	21.7	133.5	117.7	109.4	64.4	55.6	47.0	38.0	33.5	31.7
Guaranteed loan accounts	205.2	31.2	5.9	6.0	4.2	1.4	*	–0.2	–*	0.2	0.7	0.5
Subtotal, net disbursements	–50.9	74.7	27.6	139.4	122.0	110.8	64.4	55.4	46.9	38.2	34.2	32.2
Net purchases of non-Federal securities by the National Railroad Retirement Investment Trust	–5.0	–0.2	–0.8	–1.5	–1.4	–1.4	–1.4	–1.3	–1.2	–1.1	–1.1	–0.6
Net change in other financial assets and liabilities [2]	229.0	....	....	....	....	....	....	....	....	....	....	....
Subtotal, changes in financial assets and liabilities .	594.0	88.5	26.9	137.9	120.6	109.4	63.0	54.1	45.7	37.1	33.1	31.6
Seigniorage on coins	–0.4	–0.4	–0.4	–0.4	–0.4	–0.4	–0.4	–0.4	–0.5	–0.5	–0.5	–0.5
Total, other transactions affecting borrowing from the public	593.6	88.1	26.5	137.5	120.2	109.0	62.6	53.6	45.2	36.7	32.6	31.1
Total, requirement to borrow from the public (equals change in debt held by the public)	1,969.5	1,657.5	1,872.8	1,809.0	1,641.1	1,617.9	1,666.2	1,589.3	1,731.7	1,812.2	1,903.5	2,065.8
Changes in Debt Subject to Statutory Limitation:												
Change in debt held by the public	1,969.5	1,657.5	1,872.8	1,809.0	1,641.1	1,617.9	1,666.2	1,589.3	1,731.7	1,812.2	1,903.5	2,065.8
Change in debt held by Government accounts	483.5	196.9	242.0	204.3	212.1	59.4	–41.5	77.3	–40.1	–70.8	–121.5	–240.1
Less: change in debt not subject to limit and other adjustments	14.8	0.6	–0.2	–1.3	–0.7	0.2	0.8	0.4	–0.6	–0.4	–0.6	–0.3
Total, change in debt subject to statutory limitation	2,467.8	1,855.0	2,114.6	2,011.9	1,852.5	1,677.5	1,625.5	1,667.0	1,691.0	1,741.0	1,781.3	1,825.4
Debt Subject to Statutory Limitation, End of Year:												
Debt issued by Treasury	30,818.2	32,671.9	34,785.6	36,797.5	38,649.6	40,326.3	41,951.0	43,617.4	45,308.4	47,049.3	48,830.7	50,656.0
Less: Treasury debt not subject to limitation (-) [3]	–5.3	–4.1	–3.2	–3.2	–2.8	–2.0	–1.1	–0.5	–0.5	–0.5	–0.5	–0.5
Agency debt subject to limitation	*	*	*	*	*	*	*	*	*	*	*	*
Adjustment for discount and premium [4]	56.4	56.4	56.4	56.4	56.4	56.4	56.4	56.4	56.4	56.4	56.4	56.4
Total, debt subject to statutory limitation [5]	30,869.3	32,724.2	34,838.8	36,850.8	38,703.2	40,380.7	42,006.2	43,673.3	45,364.3	47,105.3	48,886.6	50,711.9
Debt Outstanding, End of Year:												
Gross Federal debt: [6]												
Debt issued by Treasury	30,818.2	32,671.9	34,785.6	36,797.5	38,649.6	40,326.3	41,951.0	43,617.4	45,308.4	47,049.3	48,830.7	50,656.0
Debt issued by other agencies	20.4	21.0	22.1	23.4	24.5	25.2	25.2	25.4	25.9	26.3	26.9	27.2
Total, gross Federal debt	30,838.6	32,692.9	34,807.7	36,821.0	38,674.1	40,351.4	41,976.1	43,642.7	45,334.3	47,075.6	48,857.6	50,683.3
As a percent of GDP	123.4%	124.1%	127.8%	129.5%	130.3%	130.5%	130.4%	130.1%	129.6%	129.0%	128.3%	127.6%
Held by:												
Debt held by Government accounts	6,586.2	6,783.1	7,025.0	7,229.3	7,441.4	7,500.8	7,459.3	7,536.6	7,496.5	7,425.6	7,304.1	7,064.0
Debt held by the public [7]	24,252.4	25,909.8	27,782.7	29,591.7	31,232.8	32,850.6	34,516.8	36,106.1	37,837.8	39,650.0	41,553.5	43,619.2
As a percent of GDP	97.0%	98.4%	102.0%	104.1%	105.2%	106.3%	107.2%	107.7%	108.2%	108.7%	109.1%	109.8%

*$50 million or less.

[1] A decrease in the Treasury operating cash balance (which is an asset) is a means of financing a deficit and therefore has a negative sign. An increase in checks outstanding (which is a liability) is also a means of financing a deficit and therefore also has a negative sign.

[2] Includes checks outstanding, accrued interest payable on Treasury debt, uninvested deposit fund balances, allocations of special drawing rights, and other liability accounts; and, as an offset, cash and monetary assets (other than the Treasury operating cash balance), other asset accounts, and profit on sale of gold.

[3] Consists primarily of debt issued by the Federal Financing Bank.

[4] Consists mainly of unamortized discount (less premium) on public issues of Treasury notes and bonds (other than zero-coupon bonds) and unrealized discount on Government account series securities.

[5] The statutory debt limit is $31,381 billion, as enacted on December 16, 2021.

[6] Treasury securities held by the public and zero-coupon bonds held by Government accounts are almost all measured at sales price plus amortized discount or less amortized premium. Agency debt securities are almost all measured at face value. Treasury securities in the Government account series are otherwise measured at face value less unrealized discount (if any).

[7] At the end of 2022, the Federal Reserve Banks held $5,634.9 billion of Federal securities and the rest of the public held $18,617.4 billion. Debt held by the Federal Reserve Banks is not estimated for future years.

The debt held by Government accounts may differ from the estimated amount of the account's obligations or responsibilities to make future payments to the public. For example, if the account records the transactions of a social insurance program, the debt that it holds does not necessarily represent the actuarial present value of estimated future benefits (or future benefits less taxes) for the current participants in the program; nor does it necessarily represent the actuarial present value of estimated future benefits (or future benefits less taxes) for the current participants plus the estimated future participants over some stated time period. The future transactions of Federal social insurance and employee retirement programs, which own 87 percent of the debt held by Government accounts, are important in their own right and need to be analyzed separately. This can be done through information published in the actuarial and financial reports for these programs.[5]

This Budget uses a variety of information sources to analyze the condition of Social Security and Medicare, the Government's two largest social insurance programs. The excess of future Social Security and Medicare benefits relative to their dedicated income is very different in concept and much larger in size than the amount of Treasury securities that these programs hold.

For all of these reasons, debt held by the public and debt held by the public net of financial assets are both better gauges of the effect of the budget on the credit markets than gross Federal debt.

Government Deficits or Surpluses and the Change in Debt

Table 20–2 summarizes Federal borrowing and debt from 2022 through 2033.[6] In 2022, the Government borrowed $1,970 billion, increasing the debt held by the public from $22,283 billion at the end of 2021 to $24,252 billion at the end of 2022. The debt held by Government accounts grew by $483 billion, and gross Federal debt increased by $2,453 billion to $30,839 billion.

Debt held by the public.—The Federal Government primarily finances deficits by borrowing from the public, and it primarily uses surpluses to repay debt held by the public.[7] Table 20–2 shows the relationship between the Federal deficit or surplus and the change in debt held by

the public. The borrowing or debt repayment depends on the Government's expenditure programs and tax laws, on the economic conditions that influence tax receipts and outlays, and on debt management policy. The sensitivity of the budget to economic conditions is analyzed in Chapter 2, "Economic Assumptions," in this volume.

The total or unified budget consists of two parts: the on-budget portion; and the off-budget Federal entities, which have been excluded from the budget by law. Under present law, the off-budget Federal entities are the two Social Security trust funds (Old-Age and Survivors Insurance and Disability Insurance) and the Postal Service Fund.[8] The on-budget and off-budget surpluses or deficits are added together to determine the Government's financing needs.

Over the long run, it is a good approximation to say that "the deficit is financed by borrowing from the public" or "the surplus is used to repay debt held by the public." However, the Government's need to borrow in any given year has always depended on several other factors besides the unified budget surplus or deficit, such as the change in the Treasury operating cash balance. These other factors—"other transactions affecting borrowing from the public"—can either increase or decrease the Government's need to borrow and can vary considerably in size from year to year. The other transactions affecting borrowing from the public are presented in Table 20–2 (where an increase in the need to borrow is represented by a positive sign, like the deficit).

In 2022 the deficit was $1,376 billion while these other factors increased the need to borrow by $594 billion, or 30 percent of total borrowing from the public. As a result, the Government borrowed $1,970 billion from the public. The other factors are estimated to increase borrowing by $88 billion (5 percent of total borrowing from the public) in 2023, and by $26 billion (1 percent) in 2024. In 2025–2033, these other factors are expected to increase borrowing by annual amounts ranging from $31 billion to $138 billion.

Three specific factors, presented in Table 20–2 and discussed below, have historically been especially important.

Change in Treasury operating cash balance.—In 2022, the cash balance increased by $421 billion, to $636 billion, returning to more typical levels after sizable fluctuations in the preceding two years. The cash balance had increased by $1,399 billion in 2020, to $1,782 billion, and decreased by $1,567 billion in 2021, to $215 billion. Over the 10 years prior to 2020, annual increases and decreases in the cash balance ranged from $2 billion to $252 billion. The higher 2020 cash balance was needed to manage the changes to outlays and receipts associated with the COVID-19 impacts and the Federal response. The large 2021 reduction in the cash balance was largely due to two factors. First, throughout 2021, the cash balance was gradually decreasing from its elevated end-of-2020 level. Second, due to the July 31 end of the debt limit suspension, the cash balance was reduced as a result of Treasury's actions to continue to finance Federal Government operations while not

---

[5] Extensive actuarial analyses of the Social Security and Medicare programs are published in the annual reports of the boards of trustees of these funds. The actuarial estimates for Social Security, Medicare, and the major Federal employee retirement programs are summarized in the *Financial Report of the United States Government*, prepared annually by the Department of the Treasury in coordination with the Office of Management and Budget, and presented in more detail in the financial statements of the agencies administering those programs.

[6] For projections of the debt beyond 2033, see Chapter 3, "Long-Term Budget Outlook."

[7] Treasury debt held by the public is measured as the sales price plus the amortized discount (or less the amortized premium). At the time of sale, the book value equals the sales price. Subsequently, it equals the sales price plus the amount of the discount that has been amortized up to that time. In equivalent terms, the book value of the debt equals the principal amount due at maturity (par or face value) less the unamortized discount. (For a security sold at a premium, the definition is symmetrical.) For inflation-protected notes and bonds, the book value includes a periodic adjustment for inflation. Agency debt is generally recorded at par.

[8] For further explanation of the off-budget Federal entities, see Chapter 16, "Coverage of the Budget."

exceeding the debt ceiling. (The debt limit is discussed in further detail elsewhere in this chapter.) For prudent risk management purposes, Treasury seeks to maintain a cash balance at least equal to projected Government outflows, including maturing securities, over the following week, subject to a $150 billion floor. The operating cash balance is projected to increase by $14 billion, to $650 billion, at the end of 2023. Changes in the operating cash balance, while occasionally large, are inherently limited over time. Decreases in cash—a means of financing the Government—are limited by the amount of past accumulations, which themselves required financing when they were built up. Increases are limited because it is generally more efficient to repay debt.

Net financing disbursements of the direct loan and guaranteed loan financing accounts.—Under the Federal Credit Reform Act of 1990 (FCRA),[9] the budgetary program account for each credit program records the estimated subsidy costs—the present value of estimated net losses—at the time when the direct or guaranteed loans are disbursed. The individual cash flows to and from the public associated with the loans or guarantees, such as the disbursement and repayment of loans, the default payments on loan guarantees, the collection of interest and fees, and so forth, are recorded in the credit program's non-budgetary financing account. Although the non-budgetary financing account's cash flows to and from the public are not included in the deficit (except for their impact on subsidy costs), they affect Treasury's net borrowing requirements.[10]

In addition to the transactions with the public, the financing accounts include several types of intragovernmental transactions. They receive payment from the credit program accounts for the subsidy costs of new direct loans and loan guarantees and for any upward reestimate of the costs of outstanding direct and guaranteed loans. They also receive interest from Treasury on balances of uninvested funds. The financing accounts pay any negative subsidy collections or downward reestimate of costs to budgetary receipt accounts and pay interest on borrowings from Treasury. The total net collections and gross disbursements of the financing accounts, consisting of transactions with both the public and the budgetary accounts, are called "net financing disbursements." They occur in the same way as the "outlays" of a budgetary account, even though they do not represent budgetary costs, and therefore affect the requirement for borrowing from the public in the same way as the deficit.

The intragovernmental transactions of the credit program, financing, and downward reestimate receipt accounts do not affect Federal borrowing from the public. Although the deficit changes because of the budgetary account's outlay to, or receipt from, a financing account, the net financing disbursement changes in an equal amount with the opposite sign, so the effects are cancelled out.

On the other hand, financing account disbursements to the public increase the requirement for borrowing from the public in the same way as an increase in budget outlays that are disbursed to the public in cash. Likewise, receipts from the public collected by the financing account can be used to finance the payment of the Government's obligations, and therefore they reduce the requirement for Federal borrowing from the public in the same way as an increase in budgetary receipts.

Credit net financing disbursements reduced borrowing by $51 billion in 2022. Credit financing accounts are projected to increase borrowing by $75 billion in 2023 and by $28 billion in 2024. From 2025 to 2033, the credit financing accounts are expected to increase borrowing by amounts ranging from $32 billion to $139 billion.

In some years, large net upward or downward reestimates in the cost of outstanding direct and guaranteed loans may cause large swings in the net financing disbursements. In 2023, upward reestimates for Small Business Administration COVID Economic Injury Disaster Loans are partly offset by downward reestimates for Department of Education student loans and Federal Housing Administration (FHA) guarantees, resulting in a net upward reestimate of $17 billion. In 2022, there was a net downward reestimate of $9 billion.

Net purchases of non-Federal securities by the National Railroad Retirement Investment Trust (NRRIT).—This trust fund, which was established by the Railroad Retirement and Survivors' Improvement Act of 2001,[11] invests its assets primarily in private stocks and bonds. The Act required special treatment of the purchase or sale of non-Federal assets by the NRRIT trust fund, treating such purchases as a means of financing rather than as outlays. Therefore, the increased need to borrow from the public to finance NRRIT's purchases of non-Federal assets is part of the "other transactions affecting borrowing from the public" rather than included as an increase in the deficit. While net purchases and redemptions affect borrowing from the public, unrealized gains and losses on NRRIT's portfolio are included in both the "other transactions" and, with the opposite sign, in NRRIT's net outlays in the deficit, for no net impact on borrowing from the public. In 2022, net decreases, including redemptions and losses, were $5.0 billion. A $0.2 billion net decrease is projected for 2023 and net annual decreases ranging from $0.6 billion to $1.5 billion are projected for 2024 and subsequent years.[12]

Net change in other financial assets and liabilities.—In addition to the three factors discussed above, in 2021 and 2022, the net change in other financial assets and liabilities was also particularly significant. Generally, the amounts in this category have relatively small impacts on total borrowing from the public. For example, this category decreased the need to borrow by $14 billion in 2020 and increased the need to borrow by $1 billion in 2019. However, this "other" category reduced the need to borrow

---

[9] Title V of Public Law 93-344.

[10] The FCRA (sec. 505(b)) requires that the financing accounts be non-budgetary. They are non-budgetary in concept because they do not measure cost. For additional discussion of credit programs, see Chapter 7, "Credit and Insurance," and Chapter 15, "Budget Concepts."

[11] Title I of Public Law 107-90.

[12] The budget treatment of this fund is further discussed in Chapter 15, "Budget Concepts."

by a net $235 billion in 2021 and increased the need to borrow by a net $229 billion in 2022.

Of the net $229 billion increase to borrowing in 2022, $157 billion was due to net investment of the Thrift Savings Plan (TSP) Government Securities Investment Fund (G-Fund).[13] The Department of the Treasury is authorized to suspend the issuance of obligations to the TSP G-Fund as an "extraordinary measure" if issuances could not be made without causing the public debt of the United States to exceed the debt limit. The 2021 debt-limit-related suspension of the daily reinvestment of the TSP G-Fund resulted in the amounts being moved from debt held by the public to deposit fund balances, an "other" financial liability. Once Treasury is able to do so without exceeding the debt limit, Treasury is required to fully reinvest the TSP G-Fund and restore any foregone interest. Accordingly, the TSP G-Fund was fully reinvested in December 2021, returning the amount from deposit fund balances to debt held by the public. The debt ceiling and the use of the TSP G-Fund are discussed in further detail below.

In addition, in March 2021, the Federal Communications Commission (FCC) received $81 billion in spectrum auction proceeds, which were initially recorded in a deposit fund. In 2022, FCC moved the auction proceeds from the deposit fund to an on-budget offsetting receipt account. The transfer out of the deposit fund was exactly offset by the collection in the receipt account, for no net impact on 2022 borrowing from the public.

Debt held by Government accounts.—The amount of Federal debt issued to Government accounts depends largely on the surpluses of the trust funds, both on-budget and off-budget, which owned 87 percent of the total Federal debt held by Government accounts at the end of 2022. Net investment may differ from the surplus due to changes in the amount of cash assets not currently invested. In 2022, there was a total trust fund surplus of $375 billion,[14] while trust fund investment in Federal securities grew by $398 billion. The remainder of debt issued to Government accounts is owned by a number of special funds and revolving funds. The debt held in major accounts and the annual investments are shown in Table 20–5, available online.

Debt Held by the Public Net of Financial Assets and Liabilities

While debt held by the public is a key measure for examining the role and impact of the Federal Government in the U.S. and international credit markets and for other purposes, it provides incomplete information on the Government's financial condition. The U.S. Government holds significant financial assets, which can be offset against debt held by the public and other financial liabilities to achieve a more complete understanding of the Government's financial condition. The acquisition of those financial assets represents a transaction with the

credit markets, broadening those markets in a way that is analogous to the demand on credit markets that borrowing entails. For this reason, debt held by the public is also an incomplete measure of the impact of the Federal Government in the United States and international credit markets.

One transaction that can increase both borrowing and assets is an increase to the Treasury operating cash balance. When the Government borrows to increase the Treasury operating cash balance, that cash balance also represents an asset that is available to the Federal Government. Looking at both sides of this transaction—the borrowing to obtain the cash and the asset of the cash holdings—provides much more complete information about the Government's financial condition than looking at only the borrowing from the public. Another example of a transaction that simultaneously increases borrowing from the public and Federal assets is Government borrowing to issue direct loans to the public. When the direct loan is made, the Government is also acquiring an asset in the form of future payments of principal and interest, net of the Government's expected losses on the loan. Similarly, when NRRIT increases its holdings of non-Federal securities, the borrowing to purchase those securities is offset by the value of the asset holdings.

The acquisition or disposition of Federal financial assets very largely explains the difference between the deficit for a particular year and that year's increase in debt held by the public. Debt held by the public net of financial assets is a measure that is conceptually closer to the measurement of Federal deficits or surpluses; cumulative deficits and surpluses over time more closely equal the debt held by the public net of financial assets than they do the debt held by the public.

Table 20–3 presents debt held by the public net of the Government's financial assets and liabilities. Treasury debt is presented in the Budget at book value, with no adjustments for the change in economic value that results from fluctuations in interest rates. The balances of credit financing accounts are based on projections of future cash flows. For direct loan financing accounts, the balance generally represents the net present value of anticipated future inflows such as principal and interest payments from borrowers. For guaranteed loan financing accounts, the balance generally represents the net present value of anticipated future outflows, such as default claim payments net of recoveries, and other collections, such as program fees. NRRIT's holdings of non-Federal securities are marked to market on a monthly basis. Government-sponsored enterprise stock, Air carrier worker support warrants and notes, and Emergency capital investment fund securities are measured at market value.

Due largely to the $421 billion increase in the Treasury operating cash balance, net financial assets increased by $596 billion, to $2,204 billion, in 2022. This $2,204 billion in net financial assets included a cash balance of $636 billion, net credit financing account balances of $1,384 billion, and other assets and liabilities that aggregated to a net asset of $183 billion. At the end of 2022, debt held by the public was $24,252 billion, or 97.0 percent of GDP.

---

[13] The TSP is a defined contribution pension plan for Federal employees. The G-Fund is one of several components of the TSP.

[14] For further discussion of trust funds, see Chapter 22, "Trust Funds and Federal Funds."

Table 20–3.   DEBT HELD BY THE PUBLIC NET OF FINANCIAL ASSETS AND LIABILITIES

(Dollar amounts in billions)

	Actual 2022	Estimate										
		2023	2024	2025	2026	2027	2028	2029	2030	2031	2032	2033
Debt Held by the Public:												
Debt held by the public	24,252.4	25,909.8	27,782.7	29,591.7	31,232.8	32,850.6	34,516.8	36,106.1	37,837.8	39,650.0	41,553.5	43,619.2
As a percent of GDP	97.0%	98.4%	102.0%	104.1%	105.2%	106.3%	107.2%	107.7%	108.2%	108.7%	109.1%	109.8%
Financial Assets Net of Liabilities:												
Treasury operating cash balance	636.0	650.0	650.0	650.0	650.0	650.0	650.0	650.0	650.0	650.0	650.0	650.0
Credit financing account balances:												
Direct loan and TARP equity purchase accounts	1,338.9	1,382.5	1,404.2	1,537.7	1,655.4	1,764.8	1,829.1	1,884.7	1,931.7	1,969.7	2,003.2	2,034.9
Guaranteed loan accounts	45.4	76.6	82.5	88.5	92.7	94.2	94.2	94.0	94.0	94.2	94.9	95.4
Subtotal, credit financing account balances	1,384.4	1,459.1	1,486.7	1,626.1	1,748.1	1,858.9	1,923.3	1,978.7	2,025.6	2,063.9	2,098.1	2,130.3
Government-sponsored enterprise stock [1]	223.7	223.7	223.7	223.7	223.7	223.7	223.7	223.7	223.7	223.7	223.7	223.7
Air carrier worker support warrants and notes [2]	12.1	11.5	11.4	10.7	10.1	9.7	9.3	8.9	4.5	0.2	....	....
Emergency capital investment fund securities	2.5	2.2	2.2	2.0	1.9	1.8	1.7	1.6	1.5	1.5	1.4	1.3
Non-Federal securities held by NRRIT	22.6	22.4	21.6	20.1	18.7	17.3	15.9	14.6	13.4	12.3	11.2	10.6
Other assets net of liabilities	−77.7	−77.7	−77.7	−77.7	−77.7	−77.7	−77.7	−77.7	−77.7	−77.7	−77.7	−77.7
Total, financial assets net of liabilities	2,203.5	2,291.2	2,318.0	2,455.1	2,574.9	2,683.8	2,746.2	2,799.9	2,841.1	2,873.8	2,906.7	2,938.2
Debt Held by the Public Net of Financial Assets and Liabilities:												
Debt held by the public net of financial assets	22,048.8	23,618.6	25,464.7	27,136.6	28,657.9	30,166.9	31,770.5	33,306.3	34,996.8	36,776.2	38,646.8	40,681.0
As a percent of GDP	88.2%	89.7%	93.5%	95.4%	96.6%	97.6%	98.7%	99.3%	100.1%	100.8%	101.5%	102.4%

[1] Treasury's warrants to purchase 79.9 percent of the common stock of the enterprises expire after September 7, 2028. The warrants were valued at $4 billion at the end of 2022.

[2] Portions of the notes and warrants issued under the Air carrier worker support program (Payroll support program) are scheduled to expire in 2025, 2026, 2030, and 2031.

Therefore, debt held by the public net of financial assets was $22,049 billion, or 88.2 percent of GDP. As shown in Table 20–3, the value of the Government's net financial assets is projected to grow to $2,291 billion in 2023. The projected 2023 increase is due to the anticipated $75 billion increase in the value of the credit financing accounts and $14 billion increase in the Treasury operating cash balance. While debt held by the public is expected to increase from 97.0 percent to 98.4 percent of GDP during 2023, debt net of financial assets is expected to increase from 88.2 percent to 89.7 percent of GDP.

Debt securities and other financial assets and liabilities do not encompass all the assets and liabilities of the Federal Government. For example, accounts payable occur in the normal course of buying goods and services; Social Security benefits are due and payable as of the end of the month but, according to statute, are paid during the next month; and Federal employee salaries are paid after they have been earned. Like debt securities sold in the credit market, these liabilities have their own distinctive effects on the economy. The Federal Government also has significant holdings of non-financial assets, such as land, mineral deposits, buildings, and equipment. The different types of assets and liabilities are reported annually in the financial statements of Federal agencies and in the *Financial Report of the United States Government*, prepared by the Treasury in coordination with OMB.

Treasury Debt

Nearly all Federal debt is issued by the Department of the Treasury. Treasury meets most of the Federal Government's financing needs by issuing marketable securities to the public. These financing needs include both the change in debt held by the public and the refinancing—or rollover—of any outstanding debt that matures during the year. Treasury marketable debt is sold at public auctions on a regular schedule and, because it is very liquid, can be bought and sold on the secondary market at narrow bid-offer spreads. Treasury also sells to the public a relatively small amount of nonmarketable securities, such as savings bonds and State and Local Government Series (SLGS) securities.[15] Treasury nonmarketable debt cannot be bought or sold on the secondary market.

Treasury issues marketable securities in a wide range of maturities, and issues both nominal (non-inflation-protected) and inflation-protected securities. Treasury's marketable securities include:

Treasury Bills—Treasury bills have maturities of one year or less from their issue date. In addition to the regular auction calendar of bill issuance, Treasury issues cash management bills on an as-needed basis for various reasons such as to offset the seasonal patterns of the Government's receipts and outlays. In 2020, Treasury began issuing four different maturities of cash management bills on a weekly basis in relation to the financing needed due to the impacts of the COVID-19 pandemic and the Government's response. Treasury phased out three of the four maturities of these weekly cash management bills in 2021. In 2023, Treasury added the 17-week bill—the

---

[15] Under the SLGS program, the Treasury offers special low-yield securities to State and local governments and other entities for temporary investment of proceeds of tax-exempt bonds.

remaining of these four maturities—to its regular weekly auction calendar.

Treasury Notes—Treasury notes have maturities of more than one year and up to 10 years.

Treasury Bonds—Treasury bonds have maturities of more than 10 years. The longest-maturity securities issued by Treasury are 30-year bonds.

Treasury Inflation-Protected Securities (TIPS)— Treasury inflation-protected—or inflation-indexed—securities are coupon issues for which the par value of the security rises with inflation. The principal value is adjusted daily to reflect inflation as measured by changes in the Consumer Price Index (CPI-U-NSA, with a two-month lag). Although the principal value may be adjusted downward if inflation is negative, at maturity, the securities will be redeemed at the greater of their inflation-adjusted principal or par amount at original issue.

Floating Rate Securities—Floating rate securities have a fixed par value but bear interest rates that fluctuate based on movements in a specified benchmark market interest rate. Treasury's floating rate notes are benchmarked to the Treasury 13-week bill. Currently, Treasury is issuing floating rate securities with a maturity of two years.

Historically, the average maturity of outstanding debt issued by Treasury has been about five years. The average maturity of outstanding debt was 74 months at the end of 2022.

In addition to quarterly announcements about the overall auction calendar, Treasury publicly announces in advance the auction of each security. Individuals can participate directly in Treasury auctions or can purchase securities through brokers, dealers, and other financial institutions. Treasury accepts two types of auction bids: competitive and noncompetitive. In a competitive bid, the bidder specifies the yield. A significant portion of competitive bids are submitted by primary dealers, which are banks and securities brokerages that have been designated to trade in Treasury securities with the Federal Reserve System. In a noncompetitive bid, the bidder agrees to accept the yield determined by the auction.[16] At the close of the auction, Treasury accepts all eligible noncompetitive bids and then accepts competitive bids in ascending order beginning with the lowest yield bid until the offering amount is reached. All winning bidders receive the highest accepted yield bid.

Treasury marketable securities are highly liquid and actively traded on the secondary market, which enhances the demand for Treasuries at initial auction. The demand for Treasury securities is reflected in the ratio of bids received to bids accepted in Treasury auctions; the demand for the securities is substantially greater than the level of issuance. Because they are backed by the full faith and credit of the United States Government, Treasury marketable securities are considered to be credit "risk-free." Therefore, the Treasury yield curve is commonly used as a

benchmark for a wide variety of purposes in the financial markets.

Whereas Treasury issuance of marketable debt is based on the Government's financing needs, Treasury's issuance of nonmarketable debt is based on the public's demand for the specific types of investments. Decreases in outstanding balances of nonmarketable debt, such as occurred in 2022, increase the need for marketable borrowing.[17]

Agency Debt

A few Federal agencies other than Treasury, shown in Table 20–4 (available online), sell or have sold debt securities to the public and, at times, to other Government accounts. At the end of 2022, agency debt was $20.4 billion, less than one-tenth of one percent of total Federal debt held by the public. Agency debt is estimated to grow to $21.0 billion at the end of 2023 and to $22.1 billion at the end of 2024.

The predominant agency borrower is the Tennessee Valley Authority (TVA), which had borrowings of $20.3 billion from the public as of the end of 2022, or over 99 percent of the total debt of all agencies other than Treasury. TVA issues debt primarily to finance capital projects.

TVA has traditionally financed its capital construction by selling bonds and notes to the public. Since 2000, it has also had available two types of alternative financing methods, lease financing obligations and prepayment obligations. Under the lease financing obligations method, TVA signs long-term contracts to lease some facilities and equipment. The lease payments under these contracts ultimately secure the repayment of third-party capital used to finance construction of the facility. TVA retains substantially all of the economic benefits and risks related to ownership of the assets.[18] At the end of 2022, lease financing obligations were $1.0 billion. Table 20–4 presents lease financing obligations separately from TVA bonds and notes to distinguish between the types of borrowing. As of the end of 2019, there are no outstanding obligations for prepayments.[19]

OMB determined that each of the two alternative financing methods is a means of financing the acquisition of assets owned and used by the Government, or of refinancing debt previously incurred to finance such assets. They are equivalent in concept to other forms of borrowing from the public, although under different terms and conditions. The budget therefore records the upfront cash proceeds from these methods as borrowing from the pub-

---

[16] Noncompetitive bids cannot exceed $10 million per bidder.

[17] Detail on the marketable and nonmarketable securities issued by Treasury is found in the *Monthly Statement of the Public Debt,* published on a monthly basis by the Department of the Treasury.

[18] This arrangement is at least as governmental as a "lease-purchase without substantial private risk." For further detail on the current budgetary treatment of lease-purchase without substantial private risk, see OMB Circular No. A–11, Appendix B.

[19] Under the prepayment obligations method, TVA's power distributors prepay a portion of the price of the power they plan to purchase in the future. In return, they obtain a discount on a specific quantity of the future power they buy from TVA. The quantity varies, depending on TVA's estimated cost of borrowing.

lic, not offsetting collections.[20] The budget presentation is consistent with the reporting of these obligations as liabilities on TVA's balance sheet under generally accepted accounting principles.

Although the Federal Housing Administration generally makes direct disbursements to the public for default claims on FHA-insured mortgages, it may also pay claims by issuing debentures. Issuing debentures to pay the Government's bills is equivalent to selling securities to the public and then paying the bills by disbursing the cash borrowed, so the transaction is recorded as being simultaneously an outlay and borrowing. The debentures are therefore classified as agency debt.

A number of years ago, the Federal Government guaranteed the debt used to finance the construction of a building for the Architect of the Capitol and subsequently exercised full control over the design, construction, and operation of the building. This arrangement is equivalent to direct Federal construction financed by Federal borrowing. The construction expenditures and interest were therefore classified as Federal outlays, and the borrowing was classified as Federal agency borrowing from the public. This borrowing is scheduled to mature by the end of 2024.

Several Federal agencies borrow from the Bureau of the Fiscal Service (Fiscal Service) or the Federal Financing Bank (FFB), both within the Department of the Treasury. Agency borrowing from the FFB or the Fiscal Service is not included in gross Federal debt. It would be double counting to add together: (a) the agency borrowing from the Fiscal Service or FFB; and (b) the Treasury borrowing from the public that is needed to provide the Fiscal Service or FFB with the funds to lend to the agencies.

Debt Held by Government Accounts

Trust funds, and some special funds and public enterprise revolving funds, accumulate cash in excess of current needs in order to meet future obligations. These cash surpluses are generally invested in Treasury securities.

The total investment holdings of trust funds and other Government accounts increased by $483 billion in 2022. Net investment by Government accounts is estimated to be $197 billion in 2023 and $242 billion in 2024, as shown in Table 20–5. The holdings of Federal securities by Government accounts are estimated to grow to $7,025 billion by the end of 2024, or 20 percent of the gross Federal debt. The percentage is estimated to decrease gradually over the next 10 years.

The Government account holdings of Federal securities are concentrated among a few funds: the Social Security Old-Age and Survivors Insurance and Disability Insurance trust funds; the Medicare Hospital Insurance and Supplementary Medical Insurance trust funds; and four Federal employee retirement funds. These Federal employee retirement funds include two trust funds, the Military Retirement Fund and the Civil Service Retirement and Disability Fund (CSRDF), and two special funds, the Department of Defense Medicare-Eligible Retiree Health Care Fund (MERHCF) and the Postal Service Retiree Health Benefits Fund (PSRHBF). At the end of 2024, these Social Security, Medicare, and Federal employee retirement funds are estimated to own 77 percent of the total debt held by Government accounts. During 2022–2024, the Military Retirement Fund has a large surplus and is estimated to invest a total of $481 billion, 52 percent of total net investment by Government accounts. Some Government accounts are projected to have net disinvestment in Federal securities during 2022–2024.

Technical note on measurement.—The Treasury securities held by Government accounts consist almost entirely of the Government account series. Most were issued at par value (face value), and the securities issued at a discount or premium are traditionally recorded at par in the OMB and Treasury reports on Federal debt. However, there are two kinds of exceptions.

First, Treasury issues zero-coupon bonds to a very few Government accounts. Because the purchase price is a small fraction of par value and the amounts are large, the holdings are recorded in Table 20–5 at par value less unamortized discount. The only Government accounts that held zero-coupon bonds during 2022 are the Nuclear Waste Disposal Fund in the Department of Energy, the Military Retirement Fund, and the MERHCF. The unamortized discount on zero-coupon bonds held by these three funds was $21.2 billion at the end of 2022.

Second, Treasury subtracts the unrealized discount on other Government account series securities in calculating "net Federal securities held as investments of Government accounts." Unlike the discount recorded for zero-coupon bonds and debt held by the public, the unrealized discount is the discount at the time of issue and is not amortized over the term of the security. In Table 20–5 it is shown as a separate item at the end of the table and not distributed by account. The amount was $6.8 billion at the end of 2022.

Debt Held by the Federal Reserve

The Federal Reserve acquires marketable Treasury securities as part of its exercise of monetary policy. For purposes of the Budget and reporting by the Department of the Treasury, the transactions of the Federal Reserve are considered to be non-budgetary, and accordingly the Federal Reserve's holdings of Treasury securities are included as part of debt held by the public.[21] Federal

---

[20] This budgetary treatment differs from the treatment in the *Monthly Treasury Statement of Receipts and Outlays of the United States Government* (Monthly Treasury Statement) Table 6 Schedule C, and the *Combined Statement of Receipts, Outlays, and Balances of the United States Government* Schedule 3, both published by the Treasury. These two schedules, which present debt issued by agencies other than Treasury, exclude the TVA alternative financing arrangements. This difference in treatment is one factor causing minor differences between debt figures reported in the Budget and debt figures reported by Treasury. The other factors are: adjustments for the timing of the reporting of Federal debt held by NRRIT; treatment of the Federal debt held by the Securities Investor Protection Corporation and the Public Company Accounting Oversight Board; and reclassification of Federal debt held by the Tennessee Valley Authority.

---

[21] For further detail on the monetary policy activities of the Federal Reserve and the treatment of the Federal Reserve in the Budget, see Chapter 16, "Coverage of the Budget."

Reserve holdings were $5,635 billion (23 percent of debt held by the public) at the end of 2022. Over the last 10 years, the Federal Reserve holdings have averaged 19 percent of debt held by the public. The historical holdings of the Federal Reserve are presented in Table 7.1 in the Budget's *Historical Tables*. The Budget does not project Federal Reserve holdings for future years.

Limitations on Federal Debt

Definition of debt subject to limit.—Statutory limitations have usually been placed on Federal debt. Until World War I, the Congress ordinarily authorized a specific amount of debt for each separate issue. Beginning with the Second Liberty Bond Act of 1917, however, the nature of the limitation was modified in several steps until it developed into a ceiling on the total amount of most Federal debt outstanding. This last type of limitation has been in effect since 1941. The limit currently applies to most debt issued by the Treasury since September 1917, whether held by the public or by Government accounts; and other debt issued by Federal agencies that, according to explicit statute, is guaranteed as to principal and interest by the U.S. Government.

The third part of Table 20–2 compares total Treasury debt with the amount of Federal debt that is subject to the limit. Nearly all Treasury debt is subject to the debt limit.

A large portion of the Treasury debt not subject to the general statutory limit was issued by the Federal Financing Bank. The FFB is authorized to have outstanding up to $15 billion of publicly issued debt. The FFB has on occasion issued this debt to CSRDF in exchange for equal amounts of regular Treasury securities. The FFB securities have the same interest rates and maturities as the Treasury securities for which they were exchanged. Most recently, the FFB issued: $9 billion to the CSRDF on October 1, 2013, with maturity dates from June 30, 2015, through June 30, 2024; and $3 billion of securities to the CSRDF on October 15, 2015, with maturity dates from June 30, 2026, through June 30, 2029. The outstanding balance of FFB debt held by CSRDF was $5 billion at the end of 2022 and is projected to be $4 billion at the end of 2023.

The other Treasury debt not subject to the general limit consists almost entirely of silver certificates and other currencies no longer being issued. It was $478 million at the end of 2022 and is projected to gradually decline over time.

The sole agency debt currently subject to the general limit, $209 thousand at the end of 2022, is certain debentures issued by the Federal Housing Administration.[22]

Some of the other agency debt, however, is subject to its own statutory limit. For example, the Tennessee Valley Authority is limited to $30 billion of bonds and notes outstanding.

The comparison between Treasury debt and debt subject to limit also includes an adjustment for measurement differences in the treatment of discounts and premiums. As explained earlier in this chapter, debt securities may be sold at a discount or premium, and the measurement of debt may take this into account rather than recording the face value of the securities. However, the measurement differs between gross Federal debt (and its components) and the statutory definition of debt subject to limit. An adjustment is needed to derive debt subject to limit (as defined by law) from Treasury debt. The amount of the adjustment was $56 billion at the end of 2022 compared with the total unamortized discount (less premium) of $111 billion on all Treasury securities.

Changes in the debt limit.—The statutory debt limit has been changed many times. Since 1960, the Congress has passed 87 separate acts to raise the limit, revise the definition, extend the duration of a temporary increase, or temporarily suspend the limit.[23]

Prior to October 2021, the seven most recent laws addressing the debt limit had each provided for a temporary suspension followed by an increase in an amount equivalent to the debt that was issued during that suspension period in order to fund commitments requiring payment through the specified end date. Most recently, the Bipartisan Budget Act of 2019[24] suspended the $21,988 billion debt ceiling from August 2, 2019, through July 31, 2021, and then raised the debt limit on August 1, 2021, by $6,414 billion to $28,401 billion. On October 14, 2021, enacted legislation[25] increased the dollar debt ceiling by $480 billion, to $28,881 billion. On December 16, 2021, enacted legislation[26] further increased the dollar debt ceiling by $2,500 billion, to $31,381 billion.

At many times in the past several decades, including 2018, 2019, 2021, and 2023, the Government has reached the statutory debt limit before an increase has been enacted. When this has occurred, it has been necessary for the Treasury to take "extraordinary measures" to meet the Government's obligation to pay its bills and invest its trust funds while remaining below the statutory limit. On January 13, 2023, as the debt subject to limit neared the $31,381 billion ceiling, the Secretary of the Treasury sent a letter to the Congress announcing that Treasury would begin to take extraordinary measures on January 19, 2023.

One such extraordinary measure is the partial or full suspension of the daily reinvestment of the TSP G-Fund. The Treasury Secretary has statutory authority to suspend investment of the G-Fund in Treasury securities as needed to prevent the debt from exceeding the debt limit. Treasury determines each day the amount of investments that would allow the fund to be invested as fully as possible without exceeding the debt limit. The TSP G-Fund had an outstanding balance of $169 billion at the end of January 2023. The Treasury Secretary is also authorized to suspend investments in the CSRDF and to declare a debt issuance suspension period, which allows the redemption of a limited amount of securities held by the

---

[22] At the end of 2022, there were also $18 million of FHA debentures not subject to limit.

[23] The Acts and the statutory limits since 1940 are listed in Table 7.3 of the Budget's *Historical Tables*, available at *https://www.whitehouse.gov/omb/historical-tables/*.

[24] Title III of Public Law 116-37.

[25] Public Law 117-50.

[26] Public Law 117-73.

CSRDF. The Postal Accountability and Enhancement Act[27] provides that investments in the PSRHBF shall be made in the same manner as investments in the CSRDF.[28] Therefore, Treasury is able to take similar administrative actions with the PSRHBF. The law requires that when any such actions are taken with the G-Fund, the CSRDF, or the PSRHBF, the Treasury Secretary is required to make the fund whole after the debt limit has been raised by restoring the forgone interest and investing the fund fully. Another measure for staying below the debt limit is disinvestment of the Exchange Stabilization Fund. The outstanding balance in the Exchange Stabilization Fund was $17 billion at the end of January 2023.

As the debt has neared the limit, including in 2019 and 2021, Treasury has also suspended the issuance of SLGS to reduce unanticipated fluctuations in the level of the debt. At times, Treasury has also adjusted the schedule for auctions of marketable securities.

In addition to these steps, Treasury has previously exchanged Treasury securities held by the CSRDF with borrowing by the FFB, which, as explained above, is not subject to the debt limit. This measure was most recently taken in October 2015.

The debt limit has always been increased prior to the exhaustion of Treasury's limited available administrative actions to continue to finance Government operations when the statutory ceiling has been reached. Failure to enact a debt limit increase before these actions were exhausted would have significant and long-term negative consequences. The Federal Government could be forced to delay or discontinue payments on its broad range of obligations, including Social Security and other payments to individuals, Medicaid and other grant payments to States, individual and corporate tax refunds, Federal employee salaries, payments to vendors and contractors, principal and interest payments on Treasury securities, and other obligations. If Treasury were unable to make timely interest payments or redeem securities, investors would cease to view Treasury securities as free of credit risk and Treasury's interest costs would increase. Because interest rates throughout the economy are benchmarked to the Treasury rates, interest rates for State and local governments, businesses, and individuals would also rise. Foreign investors would likely shift out of dollar-denominated assets, driving down the value of the dollar and further increasing interest rates on non-Federal, as well as Treasury, debt.

The debt subject to limit is estimated to increase to $32,724 billion by the end of 2023 and to $34,839 billion by the end of 2024. The Budget anticipates timely congressional action to address the statutory limit as necessary before exhaustion of Treasury's extraordinary measures.

Federal funds financing and the change in debt subject to limit.—The change in debt held by the public, as shown in Table 20–2, and the change in debt held by the public net of financial assets are determined primarily by the total Government deficit or surplus. The debt subject to limit, however, includes not only debt held by the public but also debt held by Government accounts. The change in debt subject to limit is therefore determined both by the factors that determine the total Government deficit or surplus and by the factors that determine the change in debt held by Government accounts. The effect of debt held by Government accounts on the total debt subject to limit can be seen in the second part of Table 20–2. The change in debt held by Government accounts is equal to 11 percent of the estimated total 2023 increase in debt subject to limit.

The Budget is composed of two groups of funds, Federal funds and trust funds. The Federal funds, in the main, are derived from tax receipts and borrowing and are used for the general purposes of the Government. The trust funds, on the other hand, are financed by taxes or other receipts dedicated by law for specified purposes, such as for paying Social Security benefits or making grants to State governments for highway construction.[29]

A Federal funds deficit must generally be financed by borrowing, which can be done either by selling securities to the public or by issuing securities to Government accounts that are not within the Federal funds group. Federal funds borrowing consists almost entirely of Treasury securities that are subject to the statutory debt limit. Very little debt subject to statutory limit has been issued for reasons except to finance the Federal funds deficit. The change in debt subject to limit is therefore determined primarily by the Federal funds deficit, which is equal to the difference between the total Government deficit or surplus and the trust fund surplus. Trust fund surpluses are almost entirely invested in securities subject to the debt limit, and trust funds hold most of the debt held by Government accounts. The trust fund surplus reduces the total budget deficit or increases the total budget surplus, decreasing the need to borrow from the public or increasing the ability to repay borrowing from the public. When the trust fund surplus is invested in Federal securities, the debt held by Government accounts increases, offsetting the decrease in debt held by the public by an equal amount. Thus, there is no net effect on gross Federal debt.

Table 20–6 derives the change in debt subject to limit. In 2022 the Federal funds deficit was $1,751 billion, and other factors increased financing requirements by $599 billion. In addition, special funds and revolving funds, which are part of the Federal funds group, invested a net of $90 billion in Treasury securities. Adjustments are also made for the difference between the trust fund surplus or deficit and the trust funds' investment or disinvestment in Federal securities (including the changes in NRRIT's investments in non-Federal securities) and for the change in unrealized discount on Federal debt held by Government accounts. As a net result of all these factors, $2,453 billion in financing was required, increasing gross Federal debt by that amount. Since Federal debt not subject to limit fell by $1.4 billion and the adjustment for discount and premium changed by $13.4 billion, the

---

[27] Title VIII of Public Law 109-435.

[28] Both the CSRDF and the PSRHBF are administered by the Office of Personnel Management.

[29] For further discussion of the trust funds and Federal funds groups, see Chapter 22, "Trust Funds and Federal Funds."

Table 20–6. FEDERAL FUNDS FINANCING AND CHANGE IN DEBT SUBJECT TO STATUTORY LIMIT
(In billions of dollars)

Description	Actual 2022	Estimate										
		2023	2024	2025	2026	2027	2028	2029	2030	2031	2032	2033
Change in Gross Federal Debt:												
Federal funds deficit	1,751.0	1,811.2	2,074.3	1,821.3	1,670.7	1,501.2	1,500.2	1,551.3	1,577.5	1,629.7	1,681.1	1,719.2
Other transactions affecting borrowing from the public -- Federal funds [1]	598.6	88.3	27.2	139.0	121.6	110.4	64.0	54.9	46.5	37.8	33.7	31.7
Increase (+) or decrease (-) in Federal debt held by Federal funds	89.5	42.4	41.9	54.0	61.8	66.7	61.6	61.3	68.5	74.6	67.9	75.2
Adjustments for trust fund surplus/deficit not invested/ disinvested in Federal securities [2]	17.5	−87.6	−28.7	−1.0	−1.0	−1.0	−1.0	−0.9	−0.9	−0.8	−0.8	−0.4
Change in unrealized discount on Federal debt held by Government accounts	−3.6	....	....	....	....	....	....	....	....	....	....	....
Total financing requirements	2,453.0	1,854.3	2,114.8	2,013.3	1,853.2	1,677.3	1,624.7	1,666.6	1,691.6	1,741.3	1,781.9	1,825.7
Change in Debt Subject to Limit:												
Change in gross Federal debt	2,453.0	1,854.3	2,114.8	2,013.3	1,853.2	1,677.3	1,624.7	1,666.6	1,691.6	1,741.3	1,781.9	1,825.7
Less: increase (+) or decrease (-) in Federal debt not subject to limit	−1.4	−0.6	0.2	1.3	0.7	−0.2	−0.8	−0.4	0.6	0.4	0.6	0.3
Less: change in adjustment for discount and premium [3]	−13.4	....	....	....	....	....	....	....	....	....	....	....
Total, change in debt subject to limit	2,467.8	1,855.0	2,114.6	2,011.9	1,852.5	1,677.5	1,625.5	1,667.0	1,691.0	1,741.0	1,781.3	1,825.4
Memorandum:												
Debt subject to statutory limit [4]	30,869.3	32,724.2	34,838.8	36,850.8	38,703.2	40,380.7	42,006.2	43,673.3	45,364.3	47,105.3	48,886.6	50,711.9

[1] Includes Federal fund transactions that correspond to those presented in Table 20–2, but that are for Federal funds alone with respect to the public and trust funds.

[2] Includes trust fund holdings in other cash assets and changes in the investments of the National Railroad Retirement Investment Trust in non-Federal securities.

[3] Consists of unamortized discount (less premium) on public issues of Treasury notes and bonds (other than zero-coupon bonds).

[4] The statutory debt limit is $31,381 billion, as enacted on December 16, 2021.

debt subject to limit increased by $2,468 billion, while debt held by the public increased by $1,970 billion.

Debt subject to limit is estimated to increase by $1,855 billion in 2023 and by $2,115 billion in 2024. The projected increases in the debt subject to limit are caused by the continued Federal funds deficit, supplemented by the other factors shown in Table 20–6. While debt held by the public increases by $19,367 billion from the end of 2022 through 2033, debt subject to limit increases by $19,843 billion,.

Foreign Holdings of Federal Debt

Foreign holdings of Federal debt are presented in Table 20–7. During most of American history, the Federal debt was held almost entirely by individuals and institutions within the United States. In the late 1960s, foreign holdings were just over $10 billion, less than 5 percent of the total Federal debt held by the public. Foreign holdings began to grow significantly in the early 1970s, and then remained about 15–20 percent of total Federal debt until the mid-1990s. During 1995–97, growth in foreign holdings accelerated, reaching 33 percent by the end of 1997. From 2004 to 2019, foreign holdings of Federal debt generally represented around 40 percent or more of outstanding debt. Foreign holdings increased to 48 percent by the end of 2008 and then remained relatively stable through 2015. After 2015, foreign holdings began to decline as a percent of total Federal debt held by the public,

falling from 47 percent at the end of 2015 to 40 percent at the end of 2018. In 2019, foreign holdings increased slightly, to 41 percent.

Although foreign holdings of Treasury debt continued to grow in dollars, by the end of 2020, foreign holdings had fallen to 34 percent of the total debt held by the public. In 2022, foreign holdings fell in both dollar terms, to $7,252 billion, and as a percent of total debt held by the public, to 30 percent.[30] The dollar decrease in foreign holdings was about 16 percent of net total Federal borrowing from the public in 2022. Changes in foreign holdings have been almost entirely due to decisions by foreign central banks, corporations, and individuals, rather than the direct marketing of these securities to foreign investors. All of the foreign holdings of Federal debt are denominated in dollars.

In 2022, foreign central banks and other foreign official institutions owned 51 percent of the foreign holdings of Federal debt; private investors owned the rest. At the end of 2022, the nations holding the largest shares of U.S. Federal debt were Japan, which held 15 percent of all foreign holdings, and China, which held 12 percent.

Foreign holdings of Federal debt are around 20-25 percent of the foreign-owned assets in the United States, depending on the method of measuring total assets. The foreign purchases of Federal debt securities do not mea-

---

[30] The debt calculated by the Bureau of Economic Analysis is different, though similar in size, because of a different method of valuing securities.

Table 20–7.   FOREIGN HOLDINGS OF FEDERAL DEBT
(Dollar amounts in billions)

Fiscal Year	Debt held by the public			Change in debt held by the public [2]	
	Total	Foreign [1]	Percentage foreign	Total	Foreign
1965	260.8	12.2	4.7	3.9	0.3
1970	283.2	14.0	4.9	5.1	3.7
1975	394.7	66.0	16.7	51.0	9.1
1980	711.9	126.4	17.8	71.6	1.3
1985	1,507.3	222.9	14.8	200.3	47.3
1990	2,411.6	463.8	19.2	220.8	72.0
1995	3,604.4	820.4	22.8	171.3	138.4
2000	3,409.8	1,038.8	30.5	-222.6	-242.6
2005	4,592.2	1,929.6	42.0	296.7	135.1
2010	9,018.9	4,316.0	47.9	1,474.2	745.4
2011	10,128.2	4,912.1	48.5	1,109.3	596.1
2012	11,281.1	5,476.1	48.5	1,152.9	564.0
2013	11,982.7	5,652.8	47.2	701.6	176.7
2014	12,779.9	6,069.2	47.5	797.2	416.4
2015	13,116.7	6,104.0	46.5	336.8	34.8
2016	14,167.6	6,155.9	43.5	1,050.9	51.9
2017	14,665.4	6,301.9	43.0	497.8	146.0
2018	15,749.6	6,225.9	39.5	1,084.1	-76.0
2019	16,800.7	6,923.5	41.2	1,051.1	697.6
2020	21,016.7	7,069.2	33.6	4,216.0	145.7
2021	22,282.8	7,570.9	34.0	1,266.1	501.7
2022	24,252.4	7,251.5	29.9	1,969.5	-319.4

[1] Estimated by Department of the Treasury. These estimates exclude agency debt, the holdings of which are believed to be small. The data on foreign holdings are recorded by methods that are not fully comparable with the data on debt held by the public. Projections of foreign holdings are not available.

[2] Change in debt held by the public is defined as equal to the change in debt held by the public from the beginning of the year to the end of the year.

sure the full impact of the capital inflow from abroad on the market for Federal debt securities. The capital inflow supplies additional funds to the credit market generally, and thus affects the market for Federal debt. For example, the capital inflow includes deposits in U.S. financial intermediaries that themselves buy Federal debt.

Federal, Federally Guaranteed, and Other Federally Assisted Borrowing

The Government's effects on the credit markets arise not only from its own borrowing but also from the direct loans that it makes to the public and the provision of assistance to certain borrowing by the public. The Government guarantees various types of borrowing by individuals, businesses, and other non-Federal entities, thereby providing assistance to private credit markets.

The Government is also assisting borrowing by States through the Build America Bonds program, which subsidizes the interest that States pay on such borrowing. In addition, the Government has established private corporations—Government-sponsored enterprises—to provide financial intermediation for specified public purposes; it exempts the interest on most State and local government debt from income tax; it permits mortgage interest to be deducted in calculating taxable income; and it insures the deposits of banks and thrift institutions, which themselves make loans.

Federal credit programs and other forms of assistance are discussed in Chapter 7, "Credit and Insurance," in this volume. Detailed data are presented in tables accompanying that chapter.

21. CURRENT SERVICES ESTIMATES

Current services, or "baseline," estimates are designed to provide a benchmark against which Budget proposals can be measured. A baseline is not a prediction of the final outcome of the annual budget process, nor is it a proposed budget. However, it can still be a useful tool in budgeting. It can be used as a benchmark against which to measure the magnitude of the policy changes in the President's Budget or other budget proposals, and it can also be used to warn of future problems if policy is not changed.

Ideally, a current services baseline would provide a projection of estimated receipts, outlays, deficits or surpluses, and budget authority reflecting this year's enacted policies and programs for each year in the future. Defining this baseline is challenging because funding for many programs in operation today expires within the 10-year budget window. Most significantly, funding for discretionary programs is typically provided one year at a time in annual appropriations acts. Mandatory programs are not generally subject to annual appropriations, but many operate under multiyear authorizations that expire within the budget window. The framework used to construct the baseline must address whether and how to project forward the funding for these programs beyond their scheduled expiration dates.

Since the early 1970s, when the first requirements for the calculation of a "current services" baseline were enacted, OMB has constructed the baseline using a variety of concepts and measures. Throughout the 1990s, OMB calculated the baseline using a detailed set of rules in the Balanced Budget and Emergency Deficit Control Act of 1985 (BBEDCA), as amended by the Budget Enforcement Act of 1990 (BEA; Public Law 101-508). Although BBEDCA's baseline rules lapsed for a period when the enforcement provisions of the BEA expired in 2002, budget practitioners continued to adhere to them. The Budget Control Act of 2011 (BCA; Public Law 112-25) formally reinstated the BEA's baseline rules.

The Administration believes certain adjustments to the BBEDCA baseline are needed to better represent the deficit outlook under current policy and to serve as a more appropriate benchmark against which to measure policy changes. The baseline adjustments are discussed in more detail below. Table 21–1 shows estimates of re-

Table 21–1. CATEGORY TOTALS FOR THE ADJUSTED BASELINE
(In billions of dollars)

	2022	2023	2024	2025	2026	2027	2028	2029	2030	2031	2032	2033
Receipts	4,897	4,650	4,721	4,910	5,305	5,647	5,940	6,200	6,485	6,791	7,060	7,418
Outlays:												
Discretionary:												
Defense	752	800	880	902	912	926	944	965	988	1,010	1,034	1,058
Non-defense	912	936	992	986	1,011	1,024	1,028	1,047	1,072	1,093	1,117	1,141
Subtotal, discretionary	1,664	1,736	1,872	1,888	1,923	1,950	1,972	2,012	2,059	2,103	2,151	2,199
Mandatory:												
Social Security	1,212	1,346	1,459	1,553	1,646	1,742	1,842	1,943	2,046	2,152	2,261	2,371
Medicare	747	821	842	959	1,033	1,117	1,276	1,223	1,388	1,482	1,596	1,844
Medicaid and CHIP	609	625	574	600	638	674	716	756	798	841	889	942
Other mandatory	1,565	1,182	1,041	967	981	971	1,040	1,014	1,068	1,095	1,135	1,205
Subtotal, mandatory	4,133	3,975	3,916	4,078	4,298	4,503	4,874	4,935	5,300	5,570	5,881	6,361
Net interest	476	665	796	842	882	929	984	1,053	1,133	1,220	1,310	1,393
Total, outlays	6,273	6,376	6,584	6,808	7,103	7,382	7,830	8,000	8,493	8,894	9,342	9,954
Unified deficit(+)/surplus(−)	1,376	1,726	1,863	1,897	1,798	1,735	1,890	1,800	2,008	2,103	2,282	2,535
(On-budget)	(1,361)	(1,712)	(1,757)	(1,757)	(1,637)	(1,541)	(1,670)	(1,539)	(1,709)	(1,762)	(1,901)	(2,139)
(Off-budget)	(15)	(14)	(106)	(141)	(161)	(195)	(221)	(261)	(299)	(340)	(380)	(396)
Memorandum:												
Adjusted baseline deficit	1,376	1,726	1,863	1,897	1,798	1,735	1,890	1,800	2,008	2,103	2,282	2,535
Savings from proposed discretionary program integrity adjustments	....	....	2	4	6	7	8	8	10	11	11	13
Extension of emergency funding	....	....	30	59	78	92	100	103	105	108	111	113
Indian Health Service	....	....	4	5	5	5	6	6	6	6	6	6
Veterans healthcare and other expenses	....	....	13	19	22	23	24	25	27	29	32	34
Related debt service	....	....	1	3	6	8	11	15	20	25	30	35
BBEDCA baseline deficit	1,376	1,726	1,913	1,988	1,914	1,871	2,039	1,957	2,175	2,281	2,471	2,737

ceipts, outlays, and deficits under the Administration's baseline for 2022 through 2033.[1] The table also shows the Administration's estimates by major component of the budget. The estimates are based on the economic assumptions underlying the Budget, which, as discussed later in this chapter, were developed on the assumption that the Administration's budget proposals will be enacted. The memorandum bank on Table 21-1 provides additional detail about the effects of the adjustments made to the BBEDCA baseline to produce the adjusted baseline.

Conceptual Basis for Estimates

Receipts and outlays are divided into two categories that are important for calculating the baseline: those controlled by authorizing legislation (receipts and direct or mandatory spending) and those controlled through the annual appropriations process (discretionary spending). Different estimating rules apply to each category.

Direct spending and receipts.—Direct spending includes the major entitlement programs, such as Social Security, Medicare, Medicaid, Federal employee retirement, unemployment compensation, and the Supplemental Nutrition Assistance Program (SNAP). It also includes such programs as deposit insurance and farm price and income supports, where the Government is legally obligated to make payments under certain conditions. Taxes and other receipts are like direct spending in that they involve ongoing activities that generally operate under permanent or long-standing authority, and the underlying statutes generally specify the tax rates or benefit levels that must be collected or paid, and who must pay or who is eligible to receive benefits.

The baseline generally—but not always—assumes that receipts and direct spending programs continue in the future as specified by current law. The budgetary effects of anticipated regulatory and administrative actions that are permissible under current law are also reflected in the estimates. BBEDCA requires several exemptions to this general rule. Exceptions in BBEDCA are described below:

- Expiring excise taxes dedicated to a trust fund are assumed to be extended at the rates in effect at the time of expiration. During the projection period of 2023 through 2033, the taxes affected by this exception are:

  — taxes deposited in the Airport and Airway Trust Fund, which expire on September 30, 2023;

  — taxes deposited in the Oil Spill Liability Trust Fund, which expire on December 31, 2025;

  — taxes deposited in the Patient-Centered Outcomes Research Trust Fund, which expire on September 30, 2029;

  — taxes deposited in the Sport Fish Restoration and Boating Trust Fund, which expire on September 30, 2028;

— taxes deposited in the Highway Trust Fund and the Leaking Underground Storage Tank Trust Fund, which expire on September 30, 2028; and

— taxes deposited in the Hazardous Substances Superfund, which expire on December 31, 2031.

— Expiring authorizations for direct spending programs that were enacted on or before the date of enactment of the Balanced Budget Act of 1997 are assumed to be extended if their current year outlays exceed $50 million. For example, even though the Environmental Quality Incentives Program, which was authorized prior to the Balanced Budget Act of 1997, continues only through 2023 under current law, the baseline estimates assume continuation of this program through the projection period, because the program's current year outlays exceed the $50 million threshold.[2]

The baseline also includes an adjustment to reflect savings to mandatory entitlement programs due to the activities funded by proposed discretionary program integrity allocation adjustments. Given the history of consistent enactment of these adjustments, the Administration believes that this presentation provides a more accurate representation of expected mandatory outlays for these programs.[3]

Discretionary spending.—Discretionary programs differ in one important aspect from direct spending programs: the Congress provides spending authority for almost all discretionary programs one year at a time. The spending authority is normally provided in the form of annual appropriations. Absent appropriations of additional funds in the future, discretionary programs would cease to operate after existing balances were spent. If the baseline were intended strictly to reflect current law, then a baseline would reflect only the expenditure of remaining balances from appropriations laws already enacted. Instead, the BBEDCA baseline provides a mechanical definition to reflect the continuing costs of discretionary programs. Under BBEDCA, the baseline estimates for discretionary programs in the current year are based on that year's enacted appropriations, or on the annualized levels provided by a continuing resolution if final full-year appropriations have not been enacted. For the budget year and beyond, the spending authority in the current year is adjusted for inflation, using specified inflation rates.[4] The definition attempts to keep discretionary spending for each program roughly level in real terms.

---

[1] The estimates are shown on a unified budget basis; i.e., the off-budget receipts and outlays of the Social Security trust funds and the Postal Service Fund are added to the on-budget receipts and outlays to calculate the unified budget totals.

[2] If enacted after the Balanced Budget Act of 1997 (Public Law 105-33), programs that are expressly temrary in nature expire in the baseline as provided by current law, even if their current year outlays exceed the $50 million threshold.

[3] See Chapter 4, "Budget Process," of this volume for a more thorough discussion of program integrity initiatives.

[4] The Administration's baseline uses the inflation rates for discretionary spending required by BBEDCA. This requirement results in an overcompensation in the calculation for Federal pay as a result of the calendar-year timing of Federal pay adjustments. Updating the calculation to address this annual timing discrepancy would have only a small effect on the discretionary baseline.

As noted above, the Administration believes adjustments to the BBEDCA baseline are needed to serve as a more appropriate benchmark against which to measure policy changes. Adjustments to discretionary spending are described below:

- Funding that was provided for 2023 and designated as emergency funding[5] has been removed from the baseline beginning in 2024. Removing the extension and inflation of this funding allows the baseline to provide a more meaningful benchmark for discretionary spending than a baseline strictly following the BBEDCA rules.

- The Sergeant First Class Heath Robinson Honoring our Promise to Address Comprehensive Toxics Act of 2022 (Public Law 117-168; PACT Act) created the Department of Veterans Affairs Cost of War Toxic Exposures Fund to fund the costs above the 2021 funding level for healthcare associated with environmental hazards and for expenses incident to the delivery of healthcare and benefits associated with environmental hazards, as well as medical research relating to exposure to environmental hazards. The increases in healthcare expenses and some of the other expenses that are expected to be provided through the Cost of War Toxic Exposures Fund have, in part, been provided in other accounts in the past. The adjusted baseline removes the extension of the cost of providing this care in those accounts so that the outlays from the Fund are not double-counted in the baseline.

- Public Law 117-328 pre-funded a portion of 2024 Indian Health Service for the Indian Health Services and Indian Health Facilities accounts through an advance appropriation for 2024. The adjusted baseline removes the advanced appropriation from the baseline so as not to double-count enacted Indian Health Service spending.[6]

BBEDCA § 251A sequestration.— BBEDCA § 251A requires reductions to non-exempt mandatory spending through 2031 for most programs and through 2032 for Medicare.[7] The BBEDCA baseline includes the effects of the across-the-board reductions ("sequestration") already invoked by the BBEDCA § 251A sequestration orders for 2013 through 2023, the BBEDCA § 251A sequestration

order for mandatory spending for 2024 issued with the transmittal of the 2024 Budget, and the extension of sequestration of mandatory spending through 2031 for most programs or through 2032 for Medicare.[8] Amounts that are sequestered in the baseline but return in the subsequent year as available (pop-up) are shown through 2032.

Economic Assumptions

As discussed above, an important purpose of the baseline is to serve as a benchmark against which policy proposals are measured. By convention, the President's Budget constructs baseline and policy estimates under the same set of economic and technical assumptions. These assumptions are developed on the basis that the President's Budget proposals will be enacted.

Of course, the economy and the budget interact. Government tax and spending policies can influence prices, economic growth, consumption, savings, and investment. In turn, changes in economic conditions due to the enactment of proposals affect tax receipts and spending, including for unemployment benefits, entitlement payments that receive automatic cost-of-living adjustments (COLAs), income support programs for low-income individuals, and interest on the Federal debt.

Because of these interactions, it would be reasonable, from an economic perspective, to assume different economic paths for the baseline projection and the President's Budget. However, this would greatly complicate the process of producing the Budget, which normally includes a large number of proposals that could have potential economic feedback effects. Agencies would have to produce two sets of estimates for programs sensitive to economic assumptions even if those programs were not directly affected by any proposal in the Budget. Using different economic assumptions for baseline and policy estimates would also diminish the value of the baseline estimates as a benchmark for measuring proposed policy changes, because it would be difficult to separate the effects of proposed policy changes from the effects of different economic assumptions. Using the same economic assumptions for the baseline and the President's Budget eliminates this potential source of confusion.

The economic assumptions underlying the Budget and the Administration's baseline are summarized in Table 21–2. The economic outlook underlying these assumptions is discussed in greater detail in Chapter 2 of this volume.

Major Programmatic Assumptions

A number of programmatic assumptions must be made to calculate the baseline estimates. These include assumptions about annual cost-of-living adjustments in the indexed programs and the number of beneficiaries who will receive payments from the major benefit programs. Assumptions about various automatic cost-of-living-adjustments are shown in Table 21–2, and assumptions about baseline caseload projections for the major benefit

---

[5] A subset of appropriations in Public Law 117-328 that were intended to be base appropriations in the 2023 appropriations process were designated by the Congress as emergency requirements for purposes of the 2023 Omnibus agreement. This subset of appropriations is extended in the baseline since they are counted as base funds in the Administration's discretionary presentation.

[6] The Budget also proposes to shift funding for the Indian Health Services and Indian Health Facilities accounts from discretionary to mandatory.

[7] Since enactment of the BCA, the Congress has extended sequestration of mandatory spending through a series of amendments to section 251A of BBEDCA (2 U.S.C. 901a). Most recently, the Infrastructure Investment and Jobs Act (Public Law 117-58) extended sequestration for most programs through 2031 and the Consolidated Appropriations Act, 2023 (Public Law 117-328) extended sequestration for Medicare through the first half of sequestration year 2032.

[8] The effects of the sequestration reductions are reflected in the detailed schedules for the affected budget accounts for all years. See Chapter 15, "Budget Concepts," of this volume for a more thorough discussion of sequestration procedures.

Table 21–2. SUMMARY OF ECONOMIC ASSUMPTIONS

(Fiscal years; in billions of dollars)

	2022	2023	2024	2025	2026	2027	2028	2029	2030	2031	2032	2033
Gross Domestic Product (GDP):												
Levels, in billions of dollars:												
Current dollars	25,000	26,336	27,238	28,432	29,679	30,909	32,188	33,534	34,968	36,489	38,076	39,732
Real, chained (2012) dollars	19,962	20,072	20,280	20,728	21,195	21,618	22,051	22,500	22,981	23,487	24,003	24,531
Percent change, year over year:												
Current dollars	10.4	5.3	3.4	4.4	4.4	4.1	4.1	4.2	4.3	4.3	4.3	4.3
Real, chained (2012) dollars	3.2	0.6	1.0	2.2	2.2	2.0	2.0	2.0	2.1	2.2	2.2	2.2
Inflation measures (percent change, year over year):												
GDP chained price index	6.9	4.8	2.4	2.1	2.1	2.1	2.1	2.1	2.1	2.1	2.1	2.1
Consumer price index (all urban)	7.9	5.5	2.6	2.3	2.3	2.3	2.3	2.3	2.3	2.3	2.3	2.3
Unemployment rate, civilian (percent)	3.8	4.1	4.6	4.5	4.3	4.2	4.2	4.1	3.9	3.8	3.8	3.8
Interest rates (percent):												
91-day Treasury bills	1.0	4.7	4.1	3.2	2.6	2.3	2.2	2.2	2.4	2.4	2.5	2.5
10-year Treasury notes	2.4	3.9	3.6	3.5	3.4	3.4	3.4	3.4	3.4	3.4	3.5	3.5
MEMORANDUM:												
Related program assumptions:												
Automatic benefit increases (percent):												
Social security and veterans pensions	5.9	8.7	3.6	2.3	2.3	2.3	2.3	2.3	2.3	2.3	2.3	2.3
Federal employee retirement	5.9	8.7	3.6	2.3	2.3	2.3	2.3	2.3	2.3	2.3	2.3	2.3
Supplemental Nutrition Assistance Program	22.8	12.5	5.2	2.4	2.3	2.3	2.3	2.3	2.3	2.3	2.3	2.3
Insured unemployment rate	1.16	1.37	1.57	1.53	1.50	1.46	1.42	1.39	1.34	1.30	1.30	1.28

programs are shown in Table 21–3, available at *https://www.whitehouse.gov/omb/analytical-perspectives/*. These assumptions affect baseline estimates of direct spending for each of these programs, and they also affect estimates of the discretionary baseline for a limited number of programs. For the administrative expenses for Medicare, Railroad Retirement, and unemployment insurance, the discretionary baseline is increased (or decreased) for changes in the number of beneficiaries in addition to the adjustments for inflation described earlier. It is also necessary to make assumptions about the continuation of expiring programs and provisions. As explained above, in the baseline estimates provided here, expiring excise taxes dedicated to a trust fund are extended at current rates. In general, mandatory programs with spending of at least $50 million in the current year are also assumed to continue, unless the programs are explicitly temporary in nature. Table 21–4, available at *https://www.whitehouse.gov/omb/analytical-perspectives/*, provides a listing of mandatory programs and taxes assumed to continue in the baseline after their expiration.[9] Many other important assumptions must be made in order to calculate the baseline estimates. These include the timing and content of regulations that will be issued over the projection period, the use of administrative discretion under current law, and other assumptions about the way programs operate. Table 21–4 lists many of these assumptions and their effects on the baseline estimates. The list is not intended to be exhaustive; the

variety and complexity of Government programs are too great to provide a complete list. Instead, the table shows some of the more important assumptions.

Current Services Receipts, Outlays, and Budget Authority

Receipts.—Table 21–5 shows the Administration's baseline receipts by major source. Table 21–6 shows the scheduled increases in the Social Security taxable earnings base, which affect both payroll tax receipts for the program and the initial benefit levels for certain retirees.

Outlays.—Table 21–7 shows the growth from 2023 to 2024 and average annual growth over the five-year and ten-year periods for certain discretionary and major mandatory programs. Tables 21–8 and 21–9 show the Administration's baseline outlays by function and by agency, respectively. A more detailed presentation of these outlays (by function, category, subfunction, and program) is provided as part of Table 21–12. The last three of these tables are available on the internet at *https://www.whitehouse.gov/omb/analytical-perspectives/*.

Budget authority.—Tables 21–10 and 21–11 show estimates of budget authority in the Administration's baseline by function and by agency, respectively. A more detailed presentation of this budget authority with program-level estimates is provided as part of Table 21–12. These tables are available on the internet at *https://www.whitehouse.gov/omb/analytical-perspectives/*.

---

[9] Unless otherwise described in this chapter, all discretionary programs are assumed to continue, and are therefore not presented in Table 21-4.

Table 21–5. RECEIPTS BY SOURCE IN THE PROJECTION OF ADJUSTED BASELINE

(In billions of dollars)

	2022 Actual	Estimate										
		2023	2024	2025	2026	2027	2028	2029	2030	2031	2032	2033
Individual income taxes	2,632.1	2,337.3	2,382.3	2,472.3	2,770.2	2,990.5	3,158.6	3,319.3	3,500.5	3,696.5	3,885.8	4,077.7
Corporation income taxes	424.9	438.4	470.4	486.0	466.8	474.3	485.2	488.0	489.7	495.1	471.8	488.6
Social insurance and retirement receipts	1,483.5	1,624.0	1,648.4	1,723.2	1,808.4	1,885.0	1,981.6	2,063.2	2,151.3	2,241.1	2,334.1	2,467.4
(On-budget)	(417.6)	(425.7)	(439.0)	(458.7)	(481.2)	(503.1)	(529.7)	(552.5)	(576.1)	(599.1)	(624.7)	(660.3)
(Off-budget)	(1,066.0)	(1,198.3)	(1,209.4)	(1,264.5)	(1,327.3)	(1,381.9)	(1,451.9)	(1,510.6)	(1,575.3)	(1,642.0)	(1,709.4)	(1,807.1)
Excise taxes	87.7	88.1	96.9	96.9	100.2	101.4	101.4	103.9	106.6	107.5	113.3	116.3
Estate and gift taxes	32.6	20.9	24.3	26.3	26.7	41.1	42.3	44.6	47.5	50.2	53.8	57.1
Customs duties	99.9	101.7	60.7	49.8	52.3	54.3	56.2	58.1	60.2	62.5	54.7	57.2
Miscellaneous receipts	136.7	39.4	37.8	55.8	80.2	100.2	114.9	122.9	129.2	138.1	147.0	153.9
Total, receipts	4,897.4	4,649.8	4,720.9	4,910.3	5,304.9	5,646.9	5,940.1	6,200.0	6,485.0	6,790.9	7,060.4	7,418.2
(On-budget)	(3,831.4)	(3,451.5)	(3,511.5)	(3,645.7)	(3,977.6)	(4,265.0)	(4,488.2)	(4,689.4)	(4,909.7)	(5,148.9)	(5,351.1)	(5,611.1)
(Off-budget)	(1,066.0)	(1,198.3)	(1,209.4)	(1,264.5)	(1,327.3)	(1,381.9)	(1,451.9)	(1,510.6)	(1,575.3)	(1,642.0)	(1,709.4)	(1,807.1)

Table 21–6. EFFECT ON RECEIPTS OF CHANGES IN THE SOCIAL SECURITY TAXABLE EARNINGS BASE

(In billions of dollars)

Social security (OASDI) taxable earnings base increases:	2024	2025	2026	2027	2028	2029	2030	2031	2032	2033
$160,200 to $168,600 on Jan. 1, 2024	5.0	12.5	13.6	14.8	16.2	17.7	19.2	20.8	22.5	24.8
$168,600 to $177,900 on Jan. 1, 2025	....	5.4	13.5	14.8	16.2	17.5	19.0	20.7	22.5	24.8
$177,900 to $185,100 on Jan. 1, 2026	....	....	4.1	10.4	11.4	12.3	13.4	14.5	15.8	17.5
$185,100 to $192,300 on Jan. 1, 2027	....	....	....	4.1	10.5	11.4	12.4	13.4	14.6	16.2
$192,300 to $199,800 on Jan. 1, 2028	....	....	....	....	4.4	11.0	11.9	12.9	14.1	15.6
$199,800 to $207,600 on Jan. 1, 2029	....	....	....	....	....	4.6	11.4	12.4	13.5	15.0
$207,600 to $216,000 on Jan. 1, 2030	....	....	....	....	....	....	5.0	12.4	13.5	14.9
$216,000 to $224,400 on Jan. 1, 2031	....	....	....	....	....	....	....	5.0	12.4	13.7
$224,400 to $232,800 on Jan. 1, 2032	....	....	....	....	....	....	....	....	5.0	12.7
$232,800 to $242,400 on Jan. 1, 2033	....	....	....	....	....	....	....	....	....	5.9

Table 21–7.   CHANGE IN OUTLAY ESTIMATES BY CATEGORY IN THE BASELINE

(In billions of dollars)

	2023	2024	2025	2026	2027	2028	2029	2030	2031	2032	2033	Change 2023 to 2024		Change 2023 to 2028		Change 2023 to 2033	
												Amount	Percent	Amount	Average annual rate	Amount	Average annual rate
Outlays:																	
Discretionary:																	
Defense	800	880	902	912	926	944	965	988	1,010	1,034	1,058	80	10.0%	144	3.4%	258	2.8%
Non-defense	936	992	986	1,011	1,024	1,028	1,047	1,072	1,093	1,117	1,141	56	6.0%	92	1.9%	205	2.0%
Subtotal, discretionary	1,736	1,872	1,888	1,923	1,950	1,972	2,012	2,059	2,103	2,151	2,199	136	7.8%	236	2.6%	463	2.4%
Mandatory:																	
Farm programs	29	23	20	18	19	23	24	21	19	20	20	–6	–22.0%	–6	–4.7%	–10	–3.9%
Medicaid	608	556	581	617	652	693	731	774	826	874	926	–52	–8.5%	85	2.7%	319	4.3%
Other health	187	171	159	148	148	154	161	160	152	159	165	–16	–8.7%	–33	–3.8%	–22	–1.2%
Medicare	821	842	959	1,033	1,117	1,276	1,223	1,388	1,482	1,596	1,844	20	2.4%	455	9.2%	1,023	8.4%
Federal employee retirement and disability	179	183	196	202	208	221	214	227	234	241	255	4	2.2%	42	4.3%	76	3.6%
Unemployment compensation	34	51	45	46	45	44	46	53	54	56	58	18	51.8%	10	5.2%	24	5.5%
Food and nutrition assistance	184	156	157	163	167	171	176	179	183	183	186	–28	–15.3%	–12	–1.4%	2	0.1%
Other income security programs	294	217	196	203	188	198	192	203	208	214	227	–76	–26.0%	–95	–7.5%	–67	–2.5%
Social Security	1,346	1,459	1,553	1,646	1,742	1,842	1,943	2,046	2,152	2,261	2,371	113	8.4%	496	6.5%	1,025	5.8%
Veterans programs ...	174	186	218	234	248	280	260	295	312	331	371	12	6.9%	106	10.0%	198	7.9%
Other mandatory programs	254	217	145	142	136	134	131	125	122	128	122	–37	–14.4%	–120	–12.0%	–132	–7.1%
Undistributed offsetting receipts	–134	–144	–149	–153	–167	–162	–165	–169	–173	–181	–185	–10	7.5%	–27	3.8%	–50	3.2%
Subtotal, mandatory	3,975	3,916	4,078	4,298	4,503	4,874	4,935	5,300	5,570	5,881	6,361	–59	–1.5%	899	4.2%	2,386	4.8%
Net interest	665	796	842	882	929	984	1,053	1,133	1,220	1,310	1,393	131	19.7%	320	8.2%	729	7.7%
Total, outlays	6,376	6,584	6,808	7,103	7,382	7,830	8,000	8,493	8,894	9,342	9,954	209	3.3%	1,455	4.2%	3,578	4.6%

22. TRUST FUNDS AND FEDERAL FUNDS

As is common for State and local government budgets, the budget for the Federal Government contains information about collections and expenditures for different types of funds. This chapter presents summary information about the transactions of the two major fund groups used by the Federal Government, trust funds and Federal funds. It also presents information about the income and outgo of the major trust funds and certain Federal funds that are financed by dedicated collections in a manner similar to trust funds.

The Federal Funds Group

The Federal funds group includes all financial transactions of the Government that are not required by law to be recorded in trust funds. It accounts for a larger share of the budget than the trust funds group.

The Federal funds group includes the "general fund," which is used for the general purposes of Government rather than being restricted by law to a specific program. The general fund is the largest fund in the Government and it receives all collections not dedicated for some other fund, including virtually all income taxes and many excise taxes. The general fund is used for all programs that are not supported by trust, special, or revolving funds.

The Federal funds group also includes special funds and revolving funds, both of which receive collections that are dedicated by law for specific purposes. Where the law requires that Federal fund collections be dedicated to a particular program, the collections and associated disbursements are recorded in special fund receipt and expenditure accounts.[1] An example is the portion of the Outer Continental Shelf mineral leasing receipts deposited into the Land and Water Conservation Fund. Money in special fund receipt accounts must be appropriated before it can be obligated and spent. The majority of special fund collections are derived from the Government's power to impose taxes or fines, or otherwise compel payment, as in the case of the Crime Victims Fund. In addition, a significant amount of collections credited to special funds is derived from certain types of business-like activity, such as the sale of Government land or other assets or the use of Government property. These collections include receipts from timber sales and royalties from oil and gas extraction.

Revolving funds are used to conduct continuing cycles of business-like activity. Revolving funds receive proceeds from the sale of products or services, and these proceeds finance ongoing activities that continue to provide products or services. Instead of being deposited in receipt accounts, the proceeds are recorded in revolving fund expenditure accounts. The proceeds are generally available for obligation and expenditure without further legislative action. Outlays for programs with revolving funds are reported both gross and net of these proceeds; gross outlays include the expenditures from the proceeds and net program outlays are derived by subtracting the proceeds from gross outlays. Because the proceeds of these sales are recorded as offsets to outlays within expenditure accounts rather than receipt accounts, the proceeds are known as "offsetting collections."[2] There are two classes of revolving funds in the Federal funds group. Public enterprise funds, such as the Postal Service Fund, conduct business-like operations mainly with the public. Intragovernmental funds, such as the Federal Buildings Fund, conduct business-like operations mainly within and between Government agencies.

The Trust Funds Group

The trust funds group consists of funds that are designated by law as trust funds. Like special funds and revolving funds, trust funds receive collections that are dedicated by law for specific purposes. Some of the larger trust funds are used to budget for social insurance programs, such as Social Security, Medicare, and unemployment compensation. Other large trust funds are used to budget for military and Federal civilian employees' retirement benefits, highway and transit construction and maintenance, and airport and airway development and maintenance. There are a few trust revolving funds that are credited with collections earmarked by law to carry out a cycle of business-type operations. There are also a few small trust funds that have been established to carry out the terms of a conditional gift or bequest.

There is no substantive difference between special funds in the Federal funds group and trust funds, or between revolving funds in the Federal funds group and trust revolving funds. Whether a particular fund is designated in law as a trust fund is, in many cases, arbitrary. For example, the National Service Life Insurance Fund is a trust fund, but the Servicemen's Group Life Insurance Fund is a Federal fund, even though both receive dedicated collections from veterans and both provide life insurance payments to veterans' beneficiaries.

The Federal Government uses the term "trust fund" differently than the way in which it is commonly used. In common usage, the term is used to refer to a private fund that has a beneficiary who owns the trust's income and may also own the trust's assets. A custodian or trustee manages the assets on behalf of the beneficiary according to the terms of the trust agreement, as established

---

[1] There are two types of budget accounts: expenditure (or appropriation) accounts and receipt accounts. Expenditure accounts are used to record outlays and receipt accounts are used to record governmental receipts and offsetting receipts. For further detail on expenditure and receipt accounts, see Chapter 15, "Budget Concepts," in this volume.

[2] See Chapter 18 in this volume for more information on offsetting collections and offsetting receipts.

by a trustor. Neither the trustee nor the beneficiary can change the terms of the trust agreement; only the trustor can change the terms of the agreement. In contrast, the Federal Government owns and manages the assets and the earnings of most Federal trust funds, and can unilaterally change the law to raise or lower future trust fund collections and payments or change the purpose for which the collections are used. Only a few small Federal trust funds are managed pursuant to a trust agreement whereby the Government acts as the trustee; even then, the Government generally owns the funds and has some ability to alter the amount deposited into or paid out of the funds.

Deposit funds, which are funds held by the Government as a custodian on behalf of individuals or a non-Federal entity, are similar to private-sector trust funds. The Government makes no decisions about the amount of

money placed in deposit funds or about how the proceeds are spent. For this reason, these funds are not classified as Federal trust funds, but are instead considered to be non-budgetary and excluded from the Federal budget.[3]

The income of a Federal Government trust fund must be used for the purposes specified in law. The income of some trust funds, such as the Employees and Retired Employees Health Benefits Fund, is spent almost as quickly as it is collected. In other cases, such as the military and Federal civilian employees' retirement trust funds, the trust fund income is not spent as quickly as it is collected. Currently, these funds do not use all of their annual income (which includes intragovernmental interest income). This surplus of income over outgo adds to the trust fund's balance, which is available for

---

[3] Deposit funds are also discussed in Chapter 16 of this volume, "Coverage of the Budget."

Table 22–1.   RECEIPTS, OUTLAYS, AND SURPLUS OR DEFICIT BY FUND GROUP
(In billions of dollars)

| | 2022 Actual | Estimate | | | | | |
		2023	2024	2025	2026	2027	2028
Receipts:							
Federal funds cash income:							
From the public	3,897.7	3,430.6	3,609.4	3,910.5	4,213.1	4,446.0	4,678.1
From trust funds	2.0	2.3	2.4	2.3	2.2	2.1	2.0
Total, Federal funds cash income	3,899.8	3,432.9	3,611.8	3,912.8	4,215.3	4,448.1	4,680.1
Trust funds cash income:							
From the public	1,844.1	1,991.6	2,071.3	2,166.3	2,276.4	2,379.9	2,505.8
From Federal funds:							
Interest	184.0	177.1	160.8	157.1	171.1	179.6	180.0
Other	914.6	816.2	904.6	971.6	1,048.1	986.6	1,061.5
Total, Trust funds cash income	2,942.7	2,984.9	3,136.6	3,295.1	3,495.5	3,546.2	3,747.4
Offsetting collections from the public and offsetting receipts:							
Federal funds	−553.1	−374.2	−388.3	−384.4	−423.4	−431.0	−446.8
Trust funds	−1,391.9	−1,241.2	−1,323.8	−1,404.0	−1,514.8	−1,482.8	−1,581.1
Total, offsetting collections from the public and offsetting receipts	−1,945.1	−1,615.4	−1,712.1	−1,788.4	−1,938.2	−1,913.8	−2,027.9
Unified budget receipts:							
Federal funds	3,346.6	3,058.8	3,223.5	3,528.4	3,791.9	4,017.1	4,233.2
Trust funds	1,550.8	1,743.7	1,812.8	1,891.1	1,980.7	2,063.4	2,166.3
Total, unified budget receipts	4,897.4	4,802.5	5,036.4	5,419.5	5,772.6	6,080.5	6,399.5
Outlays:							
Federal funds cash outgo	5,650.8	5,244.1	5,686.1	5,734.0	5,886.0	5,949.3	6,180.2
Trust funds cash outgo	2,567.6	2,743.1	2,908.7	3,145.3	3,345.8	3,553.8	3,850.8
Offsetting collections from the public and offsetting receipts:							
Federal funds	−553.1	−374.2	−388.3	−384.4	−423.4	−431.0	−446.8
Trust funds	−1,391.9	−1,241.2	−1,323.8	−1,404.0	−1,514.8	−1,482.8	−1,581.1
Total, offsetting collections from the public and offsetting receipts	−1,945.1	−1,615.4	−1,712.1	−1,788.4	−1,938.2	−1,913.8	−2,027.9
Unified budget outlays:							
Federal funds	5,097.7	4,870.0	5,297.8	5,349.7	5,462.6	5,518.3	5,733.4
Trust funds	1,175.7	1,501.8	1,584.9	1,741.3	1,831.0	2,071.0	2,269.7
Total, unified budget outlays	6,273.3	6,371.8	6,882.7	7,090.9	7,293.6	7,589.4	8,003.1
Surplus or deficit(–):							
Federal funds	−1,751.0	−1,811.2	−2,074.3	−1,821.3	−1,670.7	−1,501.2	−1,500.2
Trust funds	375.1	241.9	227.9	149.8	149.8	−7.7	−103.4
Total, unified surplus/deficit(–)	−1,375.9	−1,569.3	−1,846.4	−1,671.5	−1,520.9	−1,508.9	−1,603.6

Note: Receipts include governmental, interfund, and proprietary, and exclude intrafund receipts (which are offset against intrafund payments so that cash income and cash outgo are not overstated).

future expenditures. Trust fund balances are generally required by law to be invested in Federal securities issued by the Department of the Treasury.[4] The National Railroad Retirement Investment Trust is a rare example of a Government trust fund authorized to invest balances in equity markets.

A trust fund normally consists of one or more receipt accounts (to record income) and an expenditure account (to record outgo). However, a few trust funds, such as the Veterans Special Life Insurance fund, are established by law as trust revolving funds. Such a fund is similar to a revolving fund in the Federal funds group in that it may consist of a single account to record both income and outgo. Trust revolving funds are used to conduct cycle of business-type operations; offsetting collections are credited to the funds (which are also expenditure accounts) and the funds' outlays are displayed net of the offsetting collections.

Income and Outgo by Fund Group

Table 22–1 shows income, outgo, and the surplus or deficit by fund group and in the aggregate (netted to avoid double-counting) from which the total unified budget receipts, outlays, and surplus or deficit are derived. Income consists mostly of governmental receipts (derived from governmental activity, primarily income, payroll, and excise taxes). Income also includes offsetting receipts, which include proprietary receipts (derived from business-like transactions with the public), interfund collections (derived from payments from a fund in one fund group to a fund in the other fund group), and gifts. Outgo consists of payments made to the public or to a fund in the other fund group.

Two types of transactions are treated specially in the table. First, income and outgo for each fund group exclude all transactions that occur between funds within the same fund group.[5] These intrafund transactions constitute outgo and income for the individual funds that make and collect the payments, but they are offsetting within the fund group as a whole. The totals for each fund group measure only the group's transactions with the public and the other fund group. Second, outgo is calculated net of the collections from Federal sources that are credited to expenditure accounts (which, as noted above, are referred to as offsetting collections); the spending that is financed

by those collections is included in outgo and the collections from Federal sources are subsequently subtracted from outgo.[6] As a result, both interfund and intrafund offsetting collections from Federal sources are offset against outgo in Table 22–1 and are not shown separately.

The vast majority of the interfund transactions in the table are payments by the Federal funds to the trust funds. These payments include interest payments from the general fund to the trust funds for interest earned on trust fund balances invested in interest-bearing Treasury securities. The payments also include payments by Federal agencies to Federal employee benefits trust funds and Social Security trust funds on behalf of current employees and general fund transfers to employee retirement trust funds to amortize the unfunded liabilities of these funds. In addition, the payments include general fund transfers to the Supplementary Medical Insurance (SMI) trust fund for the cost of Medicare Parts B (outpatient and physician benefits) and D (prescription drug benefits) that is not covered by premiums or other income from the public. The Budget includes proposals to extend the solvency of the Medicare Hospital Insurance (HI) trust fund by at least 25 years, by increasing the net investment income tax (NIIT) rate and additional Medicare tax rate for high-income taxpayers, and directing the revenue from the NIIT to the trust fund. The Budget also directs the savings from proposed Medicare drug reforms into the HI trust fund.

In addition to investing their balances with the Treasury, some funds in the Federal funds group and most trust funds are authorized to borrow from the general fund of the Treasury.[7] Similar to the treatment of funds invested with the Treasury, borrowed funds are not recorded as receipts of the fund or included in the income of the fund. Rather, the borrowed funds finance outlays by the fund in excess of available receipts. Subsequently, any excess fund receipts are transferred from the fund to the general fund in repayment of the borrowing. The repayment is not recorded as an outlay of the fund or included in fund outgo. This treatment is consistent with the broad principle that borrowing and debt redemption are not budgetary transactions but rather a means of financing deficits or disposing of surpluses.[8]

---

[4] Securities held by trust funds (and by other Government accounts), debt held by the public, and gross Federal debt are discussed in Chapter 20 of this volume, "Federal Borrowing and Debt."

[5] For example, the railroad retirement trust funds pay the equivalent of Social Security benefits to railroad retirees in addition to the regular railroad pension. These benefits are financed by a payment from the Federal Old-Age and Survivors Insurance trust fund to the railroad retirement trust funds. The payment and collection are not included in Table 22–1 so that the total trust fund income and outgo shown in the table reflect transactions with the public and with Federal funds.

[6] Collections from non-Federal sources are shown as income and spending that is financed by those collections is shown as outgo. For example, postage stamp fees are deposited as offsetting collections in the Postal Service Fund. As a result, the Fund's income reported in Table 22–1 includes postage stamp fees and the Fund's outgo is gross disbursements, including disbursements financed by those fees.

[7] For example, the Unemployment Trust Fund is authorized to borrow from the general fund for unemployment benefits; the Bonneville Power Administration Fund, a revolving fund in the Department of Energy, is authorized to borrow from the general fund; and the Black Lung Disability Trust Fund, a trust fund in the Department of Labor, is authorized to receive appropriations of repayable advances from the general fund, which constitute a form of borrowing.

[8] Borrowing and debt repayment are discussed in Chapter 20 of this volume, "Federal Borrowing and Debt," and Chapter 15 of this volume, "Budget Concepts."

Table 22–2. COMPARISON OF TOTAL FEDERAL FUND AND TRUST FUND RECEIPTS TO UNIFIED BUDGET RECEIPTS, FISCAL YEAR 2022
(In billions of dollars)

Gross Federal fund and Trust fund cash income:	
Federal funds	4,354.4
Trust funds	3,008.3
Total, gross Federal fund and Trust fund cash income	7,362.7
Deduct: intrabudgetary offsetting collections (from funds within same fund group):	
Federal funds	–402.8
Trust funds	–58.1
Subtotal, intrabudgetary offsetting collections	–460.9
Deduct: intrafund receipts (from funds within same fund group):	
Federal funds	–51.9
Trust funds	–7.4
Subtotal, intrafund receipts	–59.3
Federal fund and Trust fund cash income net of intrabudgetary offsetting collections and intrafund receipts:	
Federal funds	3,899.8
Trust funds	2,942.7
Total, Federal fund and Trust fund cash income net of intrafund receipts	6,842.5
Deduct: offsetting collections from the public:	
Federal funds	–275.2
Trust funds	–23.9
Subtotal, offsetting collections from the public	–299.1
Deduct other offsetting receipts:	
Federal fund receipts from Trust funds	–2.0
Trust fund receipts from Federal funds:	
Interest in receipt accounts	–184.0
General fund payments to Medicare Parts B and D	–435.0
Employing agencies' payments for pensions, Social Security, and Medicare	–110.0
General fund payments for unfunded liabilities of Federal employees' retirement funds	–161.6
Transfer of taxation of Social Security and RRB benefits to OASDI, HI, and RRB	–82.1
Other receipts from Federal funds	–126.0
Subtotal, Trust fund receipts from Federal funds	–1,098.6
Proprietary receipts:	
Federal funds	–180.4
Trust funds	–269.4
Subtotal, proprietary receipts	–449.8
Offsetting governmental receipts:	
Federal funds	–95.6
Trust funds	–*
Subtotal, offsetting governmental receipts	–95.6
Subtotal, other offsetting receipts	–1,646.0
Unified budget receipts:	
Federal funds	3,346.6
Trust funds	1,550.8
Total, unified budget receipts	4,897.4
Memoradum:	
Gross receipts: [1]	
Federal funds	3,676.5
Trust funds	2,926.2
Total, gross receipts	6,602.7

* $50 million or less.
[1] Gross income excluding offsetting collections.

Some income in both Federal funds and trust funds consists of offsetting receipts.[9] Offsetting receipts are not considered governmental receipts (such as taxes), but they are instead recorded on the outlay side of the budget.[10] Expenditures resulting from offsetting receipts are recorded as gross outlays and the collections of offsetting receipts are then subtracted from gross outlays to derive net outlays. Net outlays reflect the Government's net transactions with the public.

As shown in Table 22–1, 32 percent of all governmental receipts were deposited in trust funds in 2022 and the remaining 68 percent of governmental receipts were deposited in Federal funds, which, as noted above, include the general fund. As noted above, most outlays between the trust fund and Federal fund groups (interfund outlays) flow from Federal funds to trust funds, rather than from trust funds to Federal funds. As a result, while trust funds accounted for 19 percent of total 2022 outlays, they accounted for 23 percent of 2022 outlays net of interfund transactions.

Because the income for Federal funds and trust funds recorded in Table 22–1 includes offsetting receipts and offsetting collections from the public, offsetting receipts and offsetting collections from the public must be deducted from the two fund groups' combined gross income in order to reconcile to total governmental receipts in the unified budget. Similarly, because the outgo for Federal funds and trust funds in Table 22–1 consists of outlays gross of offsetting receipts and offsetting collections from the public, the amount of the offsetting receipts and offsetting collections from the public must be deducted from the sum of the Federal funds' and the trust funds' gross outgo in order to reconcile to total (net) unified budget outlays. Table 22–2 reconciles, for fiscal year 2022, the gross total of all trust fund and Federal fund receipts with the receipt total of the unified budget.

Income, Outgo, and Balances of Trust Funds

Table 22–3 shows, for the trust funds group as a whole, the funds' balance at the start of each year, income and outgo during the year, and the end-of-year balance. Income and outgo are divided between transactions with the public and transactions with Federal funds. Receipts from Federal funds are divided between interest and other interfund receipts.

The definitions of income and outgo in this table differ from those in Table 22–1 in one important way. Trust fund collections that are offset against outgo (offsetting collections from Federal sources) within expenditure accounts instead of being deposited in separate receipt accounts are classified as income in this table, but not in Table 22–1. This classification is consistent with the definitions of income and outgo for trust funds used elsewhere in the budget. It has the effect of increasing both income and outgo by the amount of the offsetting collections from

---

[9]   Interest on borrowed funds is an example of an intragovernmental offsetting receipt and Medicare Part B's premiums are an example of offsetting receipts from the public.

[10]   For further discussion of offsetting receipts, see Chapter 18 of this volume, "Offsetting Collections and Offsetting Receipts."

Federal sources. The difference was approximately $58 billion in 2022. Table 22–3, therefore, provides a more complete summary of trust fund income and outgo.

In 2022, the trust funds group ran a surplus of $375 billion. The trust fund group is expected to run a $242 billion surplus in 2023 and a $228 billion surplus in 2024.

The size of the trust fund balances is largely the consequence of the way some trust funds are financed. Some of the larger trust funds (primarily Social Security and the Federal retirement funds) are fully or partially advance funded, with collections on behalf of individual participants received by the funds years earlier than when the associated benefits are paid. For example, under the Federal military and civilian retirement programs, Federal agencies and employees together are required to pay the retirement trust funds an amount equal to accruing retirement benefits. Since many years pass between the time when benefits are accrued and when they are paid, the trust funds accumulate substantial balances over time. [11]

---

[11] Until the 1980s, most trust funds operated on a pay-as-you-go basis as distinct from a pre-funded basis. Taxes and fees were set at levels sufficient to finance current program expenditures and administrative expenses, and to maintain balances generally equal to one year's worth of expenditures (to provide for unexpected events). As a result, trust fund balances tended to grow at about the same rate as the funds' annual expenditures. In the 1980s, pay-as-you-go financing was replaced by full or partial advance funding for some of the larger trust funds. The Social Security Amendments of 1983 (P.L. 98-21) raised payroll taxes above the levels necessary to finance then-current expenditures. Legislation enacted in the mid-1980s established the requirement for full accrual basis funding of Federal military and civilian retirement benefits.

Due to advance funding and economic growth (both real and nominal), trust fund balances increased from $205 billion in 1982 to $5.8 trillion in 2022. Based on the estimates in the 2024 Budget, which include the effect of the Budget's proposals, the balances are estimated to be $6.4 trillion at the end of 2028. Almost all of these balances are invested in Treasury securities and earn interest.

From the perspective of the trust fund, these balances are assets that represent the value, in today's dollars, of past taxes, fees, and other income from the public and from other Government accounts that the trust fund has received in excess of past spending. Trust fund assets held in Treasury securities are legal claims on the Treasury, similar to Treasury securities issued to the public. Like all other fund assets, these are available to the fund for future benefit payments and other expenditures. From the perspective of the Government as a whole, however, the trust fund balances do not represent net additions to the Government's balance sheet. The trust fund balances are assets of the agencies responsible for administering the trust fund programs and liabilities of the Department of the Treasury. These assets and liabilities cancel each other out in the Government-wide balance sheet. The effects of Treasury debt held by trust funds and other Government accounts are discussed further in Chapter 20 of this volume, "Federal Borrowing and Debt."

Table 22–4, available online, shows estimates of income, outgo, surplus or deficit, and balances for 2022 through 2028 for the major trust funds. With the exception of transactions between trust funds, the data for the individual trust funds are conceptually the same as the

Table 22–3. INCOME, OUTGO, AND BALANCES OF TRUST FUNDS GROUP
(In billions of dollars)

	2022 Actual	Estimate					
		2023	2024	2025	2026	2027	2028
Balance, start of year	5,408.2	5,783.7	6,027.2	6,255.7	6,405.5	6,555.3	6,547.6
Adjustments to balances	–*	....	....	....	....	....	....
Total balance, start of year	5,408.2	5,783.7	6,027.2	6,255.7	6,405.5	6,555.3	6,547.6
Income:							
Governmental receipts	1,550.8	1,743.7	1,812.8	1,891.1	1,980.7	2,063.4	2,166.3
Offsetting governmental	*	*	*	*	*	*	*
Proprietary	295.8	244.8	256.4	273.9	294.4	315.4	338.5
From Federal funds:							
Interest	182.9	182.2	166.0	161.7	175.5	184.0	184.0
Other	971.3	878.8	967.3	1,036.5	1,116.0	1,057.7	1,135.8
Total income during the year	3,000.9	3,049.5	3,202.5	3,363.2	3,566.7	3,620.4	3,824.6
Outgo (–)	–2,625.7	–2,807.7	–2,974.6	–3,213.4	–3,417.0	–3,628.1	–3,928.1
Change in fund balance:							
Surplus or deficit(–):							
Excluding interest	192.2	59.7	61.9	–11.9	–25.8	–191.6	–287.5
Interest	182.9	182.2	166.0	161.7	175.5	184.0	184.0
Subtotal, surplus or deficit (–)	375.1	241.9	227.9	149.8	149.8	–7.7	–103.4
Borrowing, transfers, lapses, & other adjustments	0.3	1.6	0.7	....	....	....	....
Total change in fund balance	375.5	243.5	228.6	149.8	149.8	–7.7	–103.4
Balance, end of year	5,783.7	6,027.2	6,255.7	6,405.5	6,555.3	6,547.6	6,444.2

* $50 million or less.

Note: In contrast to Table 22–1, income also includes income that is offset within expenditure accounts as offsetting collections from Federal sources, instead of being deposited in receipt accounts.

data in Table 22–3 for the trust funds group. As explained previously, transactions between trust funds are shown as outgo of the fund that makes the payment and as income of the fund that collects it in the data for an individual trust fund, but the collections are offset against outgo in the data for the trust fund group as a whole.

As noted above, trust funds are funded by a combination of payments from the public and payments from Federal funds, including payments directly from the general fund and payments from agency appropriations. Similarly, the fund outgo amounts in Table 22–4 represent both outflows to the public—such as for the provision of benefit payments or the purchase of goods or services—and outflows to other Government accounts—such as for reimbursement for services provided by other agencies or payment of interest on borrowing from Treasury. The outgo amounts reflect the Budget's assumption that all obligations of the trust funds are met.

Because trust funds and Federal special and revolving funds conduct transactions both with the public and with other Government accounts, the surplus or deficit of an individual fund may differ from the fund's impact on the surplus or deficit of the Federal Government. Transactions with the public affect both the surplus or deficit of an individual fund and the Federal Government surplus or deficit. Transactions with other Government accounts affect the surplus or deficit of the particular fund. However, because that same transaction is offset in another Government account, there is no net impact on the total Federal Government surplus or deficit.

A brief description of the major trust funds is given below; additional information for these and other trust funds can be found in the Status of Funds tables in the Budget *Appendix*.

- Social Security Trust Funds: The Social Security trust funds consist of the Old Age and Survivors Insurance (OASI) trust fund and the Disability Insurance (DI) trust fund. The trust funds are funded by payroll taxes from employers and employees, interest earnings on trust fund balances, Federal agency payments as employers, and a portion of the income taxes paid on Social Security benefits.

- Medicare Trust Funds: Like the Social Security trust funds, the Medicare HI trust fund is funded by payroll taxes from employers and employees, Federal agency payments as employers, and a portion of the income taxes paid on Social Security benefits. The HI trust fund also receives transfers from the general fund of the Treasury for certain HI benefits and premiums from certain voluntary participants. The other Medicare trust fund, SMI, finances Part

B (outpatient and physician benefits) and Part D (prescription drug benefits). SMI receives premium payments from covered individuals, transfers from States toward Part D benefits, excise taxes on manufacturers and importers of brand-name prescription drugs, and transfers from the general fund of the Treasury for the portion of Part B and Part D costs not covered by premiums or transfers from States. In addition, like other trust funds, these two trust funds receive interest earnings on their trust fund balances.

- Highway Trust Fund: The fund finances Federal highway and transit infrastructure projects, as well as highway and vehicle safety activities. The Highway Trust Fund is financed by Federal motor fuel taxes and associated fees, and, in recent years, by general fund transfers, as those taxes and fees have been inadequate to support current levels of spending.

- Unemployment Trust Fund: The Unemployment Trust Fund is funded by Federal and State taxes on employers, payments from Federal agencies, taxes on certain employees, and interest earnings on trust fund balances. Unemployment insurance is administered largely by the States, following Federal guidelines. The Unemployment Trust Fund is composed of individual accounts for each State and several Federal accounts, including accounts related to the separate unemployment insurance program for railroad employees.

- Civilian and military retirement trust funds: The Civil Service Retirement and Disability Fund is funded by employee and agency payments, general fund transfers for the unfunded portion of retirement costs, and interest earnings on trust fund balances. The Military Retirement Fund likewise is funded by payments from the Department of Defense, general fund transfers for unfunded retirement costs, and interest earnings on trust fund balances.

Table 22–5, available online, shows income, outgo, and balances of two Federal funds that are designated as special funds. These funds are similar to trust funds in that they are financed by dedicated receipts, the excess of income over outgo is invested in Treasury securities, the interest earnings add to fund balances, and the balances remain available to cover future expenditures. The table is illustrative of the Federal funds group, which includes many revolving funds and special funds.

23. COMPARISON OF ACTUAL TO ESTIMATED TOTALS

The Budget is required by statute to compare budget year estimates of receipts and outlays with the subsequent actual receipts and outlays for that year. This chapter meets that requirement by comparing the actual receipts, outlays, and deficit for 2022 with the current services estimates shown in the 2022 Budget, published in May 2021.[1] It also presents a more detailed comparison for mandatory and related programs, and reconciles the actual receipts, outlays, and deficit totals shown here with the figures for 2022 previously published by the Department of the Treasury.

Receipts

Actual receipts for 2022 were $4,897 billion, $909 billion more than the $3,988 billion current services estimate in the 2022 Budget, which was published in May 2021. As shown in Table 23-1, this increase was the net effect of legislative changes, economic conditions that differed from what had been expected, and technical factors that resulted in different tax liabilities and collection patterns than had been assumed.

Policy differences. Legislated tax changes enacted after the May 2021 estimates were finalized reduced 2022 receipts by a net $4 billion relative to the 2022 Budget current services estimate.

The Infrastructure Investment and Jobs Act (P.L. 117-58) reauthorized transportation programs, including the excise tax on motor fuels through 2028, and the tax on heavy use vehicles through 2029; reauthorized the Sport Fish Restoration and Boating Trust Fund; and extended and modified certain excise taxes dedicated to the Hazardous Substance Superfund. It also provided a tax exemption for private activity bonds for qualified broadband projects and carbon dioxide capture facilities; modified the tax treatment of contributions to the capital of a corporation; provided the extension of tax rules for stabilizing interest rates on contributions amounts to defined benefit plans, modified information reporting requirements and definitions for brokers and digital assets for returns and information statements required after 2023; terminated the employee retention tax credit after 2021, except for start-up businesses which terminated on December 31, 2021; and extended customs user fees. The Act was signed into law on November 15, 2021 and increased 2022 receipts by an estimated $1 billion.

The Suspending Normal Trade Relations with Russia and Belarus Act (P.L. 117-110) authorized the President to proclaim increases in the rates of duty applicable to products of Russia or Belarus; this authority terminates on January 1, 2024. This Act was signed into law on April 8, 2022, and increased 2022 receipts by an estimated $24 million.

The Formula Act (P.L. 117-160) provided, through December 31, 2022, duty-free treatment to infant formula. This Act was signed into law on July 21, 2022, and decreased 2022 receipts by $2 million.

Public Law 117-167, commonly referred to as the CHIPS and Science Act of 2022, established a 25 percent investment tax credit for investments in semiconductor manufacturing. The Act was signed into law on August 9, 2022, and reduced 2022 receipts by an estimated $1 billion.

The Inflation Reduction Act (P.L. 117-169) imposed a 15 percent minimum alternative tax beginning tax years

---

[1] The current services concept is discussed in Chapter 21, "Current Services Estimates." For mandatory programs and receipts, the May 2021 current services estimate was based on laws then in place, adjusted for certain expiring provisions. For discretionary programs, the current services estimate was based on appropriations enacted for 2021 adjusted for inflation, except that funding that was provided and designated as emergency funding for 2021 in division M of Public Law 116-260 to address the public health and economic effects of the COVID-19 public health emergency was removed from the baseline beginning in 2022. The current services estimates also reflected the effects of mandatory sequestration as required by the Balanced Budget and Deficit Control Act (BBEDCA) section 251A. For a detailed explanation of the 2022 estimate, see "Current Services Estimates," Chapter 17 in *Analytical Perspectives, Budget of the United States Government, Fiscal Year 2022.*

Table 23–1.   COMPARISON OF ACTUAL 2022 RECEIPTS WITH THE INITIAL CURRENT SERVICES ESTIMATES
(In billions of dollars)

	Estimate (May 2021)	Changes			Total Changes	Actual
		Policy	Economic	Technical		
Individual income taxes	2,005	–*	172	454	627	2,632
Corporation income taxes	266	–4	18	145	159	425
Social insurance and retirement receipts	1,417	....	26	41	67	1,484
Excise taxes	82	*	–2	7	6	88
Estate and gift taxes	21	....	3	9	12	33
Customs duties	57	*	4	38	43	100
Miscellaneous receipts	140	....	–28	24	–4	137
Total receipts	3,988	–4	194	719	909	4,897

* $500 million or less

after 2022 on corporations with a three-year average income of more than \$1 billion, determined on the basis of the corporation's adjusted financial statement income (i.e., book income). It imposed a one percent excise tax of the fair market value of any repurchased stock during the taxable year by a publicly traded U.S. corporation. It also appropriated funding for Internal Revenue Service enforcement activities, operations support, business systems modernization, and taxpayer services, available through 2031, which is expected to reduce the tax gap by improving taxpayer compliance. The law imposed an excise tax on the sale by the manufacturer, producer, or importer of any selected drug who fails to enter into a drug pricing agreement. Further, it included various green energy tax credits and incentives for businesses and individuals, including: a production tax credit for electricity generated from renewable energy sources; a new tax credit for qualifying zero-emission nuclear power produced by facilities placed in service prior to enactment; the extension of the residential clean energy efficient credit for qualified energy efficiency improvements; an advanced manufacturing production credit for projects beginning in 2023; and new clean electricity production and investment credits; and tax credits related to electric vehicles, including credits for the purchase of clean and plug-in vehicles. The Act was signed into law on August 16, 2022, and decreased 2022 receipts by an estimated \$3 billion.

Economic differences. Differences between the economic assumptions upon which the current services estimates were based and actual economic performance increased 2022 receipts by a net \$194 billion above the May 2021 current services estimate. The economic recovery after the COVID-19 crisis meant that wage and salary income was higher in 2022 than initially projected, which was the primary driver of increased individual income tax and social insurance receipts by \$172 billion and \$26 billion above the May 2021 estimate, respectively, and accounted for most of the net increase in receipts attributable to economic differences. Higher interest rates than initially projected reduced deposits of earnings by the Federal Reserve System by \$28 billion below the May 2021 estimate. Different economic factors than those assumed in

May 2021 had a smaller effect on other sources of receipts, increasing collections by a net \$23 billion.

Technical factors. Technical factors increased receipts by a net \$719 billion relative to the May 2021 current services estimate. These factors had the greatest effect on individual and corporation income tax receipts, increasing collections by \$454 billion and \$145 billion, respectively. The models used to prepare the May 2021 estimates of individual income taxes were based on historical economic data and then-current tax and collections data that were all subsequently revised and account for the net increase in this source of receipts attributable to technical factors. New tariffs imposed on imports accounted for the increase in customs duties.

Outlays

Outlays for 2022 were \$6,273 billion, \$567 billion more than the \$5,707 billion current services estimate in the 2022 Budget. Table 23–2 distributes the \$567 billion net increase in outlays among discretionary and mandatory programs and net interest.[2] The table also shows rough estimates according to three reasons for the changes: policy; economic conditions; and technical estimating differences, a residual.

Policy differences. Policy changes are the result of legislative actions that change spending levels, primarily through higher or lower appropriations or changes in authorizing legislation, which may themselves be in response to changed economic conditions. For 2022, policy changes increased outlays by \$118 billion relative to the initial current services estimates. Policy changes increased discretionary outlays by \$126 billion, largely due to the Infrastructure Investment and Jobs Act (P.L. 117-58); the Consolidated Appropriations Act, 2022 (P.L. 117-103); the Bipartisan Safer Communities Act (P.L. 117-159); and several emergency supplemental appropriations. Policy changes decreased mandatory outlays by a net \$9 billion. Debt service costs associated with all policy changes increased outlays by less than \$1 billion.

---

[2] Discretionary programs are controlled by annual appropriations, while mandatory programs are generally controlled by authorizing legislation. Mandatory programs are primarily formula benefit or entitlement programs with permanent spending authority that depends on eligibility criteria, benefit levels, and other factors.

Table 23–2. COMPARISON OF ACTUAL 2022 OUTLAYS WITH THE INITIAL CURRENT SERVICES ESTIMATES

(In billions of dollars)

| | Estimate (May 2021) | Changes | | | Total Changes | Actual |
		Policy	Economic	Technical		
Discretionary:						
Defense	754	30	....	–32	–2	752
Nondefense	913	96	....	–97	–1	912
Subtotal, discretionary	1,667	126	....	–129	–3	1,664
Mandatory:						
Social Security	1,196	....	31	–14	17	1,212
Other programs	2,539	–9	88	302	381	2,921
Subtotal, mandatory	3,735	–9	119	288	398	4,133
Net interest	305	*	154	17	171	476
Total outlays	5,707	118	273	176	567	6,273

* \$500 million or less

Table 23–3.   COMPARISON OF THE ACTUAL 2022 DEFICIT WITH THE INITIAL CURRENT SERVICES ESTIMATE

(In billions of dollars)

	Estimate (May 2021)	Changes			Total Changes	Actual
		Policy	Economic	Technical		
Receipts	3,988	–4	194	719	909	4,897
Outlays	5,707	118	273	176	567	6,273
Deficit	1,719	121	79	–543	–343	1,376

Note: Deficit changes are outlays minus receipts. For these changes, a positive number indicates an increase in the deficit.

Economic and technical factors. Economic and technical estimating factors resulted in a net increase in outlays of $449 billion. Technical changes result from changes in such factors as the number of beneficiaries for entitlement programs, crop conditions, or other factors not associated with policy changes or economic conditions. Defense and non-defense discretionary spending decreased relative to the current services estimate largely due to slower-than-estimated spending of both new and prior-year authority. In addition to the increases in discretionary outlays due to legislation, as discussed above, technical factors led to $129 billion in decreased spending. Outlays for mandatory programs increased $407 billion due to economic and technical factors. There was a net increase in outlays of $119 billion as a result of differences between actual economic conditions versus those forecast in May 2021.

Outlays for Social Security were $17 billion higher than anticipated in the 2022 Budget mainly due to a higher than projected cost-of-living adjustment, which was partially offset by a lower than estimated number of beneficiaries. Mandatory human resources programs including health programs and higher education programs were $513 billion higher than anticipated; the remaining changes were spread throughout government programs and lowered outlays by $115 billion. Outlays for net interest were approximately $171 billion higher due to economic and technical factors, primarily due to higher interest rates than originally assumed.

Deficit

The preceding two sections discussed the differences between the initial current services estimates and the actual Federal Government receipts and outlays for 2022. This section combines these effects to show the net deficit impact of these differences.

As shown in Table 23–3, the 2022 current services deficit was initially estimated to be $1,719 billion. The actual deficit was $1,376 billion, which was a $343 billion decrease from the initial estimate. Receipts were $909 billion higher and outlays were $567 billion higher than the initial estimate. The table shows the distribution of the changes according to the categories in the preceding two sections. The net effect of policy changes for receipts and outlays increased the deficit by $121 billion. Economic conditions that differed from the initial assumptions in May 2021 increased the deficit by $79 billion. Technical factors decreased the deficit by an estimated $543 billion.

Comparison of the Actual and Estimated Outlays for Mandatory and Related Programs for 2022

This section compares the original 2022 outlay estimates for mandatory and related programs in the current services estimates of the 2022 Budget with the actual outlays. Major examples of these programs include Social Security and Medicare benefits, Medicaid and unemployment compensation payments, and deposit insurance for banks and thrift institutions. This category also includes net interest outlays and undistributed offsetting receipts.

A number of factors may cause differences between the amounts estimated in the Budget and the actual mandatory outlays. For example, legislation may change benefit rates or coverage, the actual number of beneficiaries may differ from the number estimated, or economic conditions (such as inflation or interest rates) may differ from what was assumed in making the original estimates.

Table 23–4 shows the differences between the actual outlays for these programs in 2022 and the current services estimates included in the 2022 Budget. Actual outlays for mandatory spending and net interest in 2022 were $4,609 billion, which was $569 billion more than the current services estimate of $4,040 billion in May 2021.

As Table 23–4 shows, actual outlays for mandatory human resources programs were $4,210 billion, $513 billion higher than originally estimated. This increase was the net effect of legislative action, differences between actual and assumed economic conditions, differences between the anticipated and actual number of beneficiaries, and other technical differences.

Outlays in higher education programs were $474 billion higher than estimates primarily due to loan modification costs largely related to emergency COVID-19 relief. Health program outlays were $94 billion higher than estimates, driven mainly by a $74 billion increase in Medicaid outlays. The increase in Medicaid outlays were a result of ongoing costs associated with the legislative response to the COVID-19 pandemic, as well as differences in assumed economic conditions and number of beneficiaries. In addition, income security, veterans benefits and services programs, and other functions accounted for a decrease of outlays of $60 billion. Outlays for net interest were $476 billion, or $171 billion higher than the original estimate. As shown on Table 23–4, interest payments on Treasury debt securities increased by $237 billion. Interest earnings of trust funds increased by $59 billion, decreasing net outlays, while net outlays for other interest further decreased net outlays by $7 billion.

Reconciliation of Differences with Amounts Published by the Treasury for 2022

Table 23-5 provides a reconciliation of the receipts, outlays, and deficit totals for 2022 published by the Department of the Treasury in the September 2022 Monthly Treasury Statement (MTS) and those published in this Budget. The Department of the Treasury made adjustments to the estimates for the Combined Statement of Receipts, Outlays, and Balances that increased outlays by $50 million. Additional adjustments for the 2024 Budget increased receipts by $1,281 million and increased outlays by $1,766 million. Some of these adjustments were for financial transactions that are not reported to the Department of the Treasury but are included in the Budget, including those for the Affordable Housing Program, the Electric Reliability Organization, the Federal Financial Institutions Examination Council Appraisal Subcommittee, Federal Retirement Thrift Investment Board Program Expenses, the National Oilheat Research Alliance, the Public Company Accounting Oversight Board, the Puerto Rico Oversight Board, the Securities Investor Protection Corporation, fees and payments related to the Standard Setting Body, and the United Mine Workers of America benefit funds. There was also an adjustment for the National Railroad Retirement Investment Trust (NRRIT), which relates to a conceptual difference in reporting. NRRIT reports to the Department of the Treasury with a one-month lag so that the fiscal year total provided in the Treasury Combined Statement covers September 2021 through August 2022. The Budget has been adjusted to reflect NRRIT transactions that occurred during the actual fiscal year, which begins October 1. In addition, the Budget also reflects agency adjustments to 2022 outlays reported to Treasury after preparation of the Treasury Combined Statement. Notably, the Department of Transportation reported Governmental receipts of $60 million as offsetting receipts due to an inadvertent misclassification by the Department of the Treasury. The Budget reconciles this account as Governmental receipts, as shown in Table 23-5.

Table 23–4. COMPARISON OF ACTUAL AND ESTIMATED OUTLAYS FOR MANDATORY AND RELATED PROGRAMS UNDER CURRENT LAW

(In billions of dollars)

	2022		
	Estimate	Actual	Change
Mandatory outlays:			
Human resources programs:			
Education, training, employment, and social services:			
Higher Education	17	491	474
Other	68	53	−15
Total, education, training, employment, and social services	84	543	459
Health:			
Medicaid	518	592	74
Other	161	181	19
Total, health	679	773	94
Medicare	767	747	−20
Income security:			
Retirement and disability	218	180	−38
Unemployment compensation	50	33	−17
Food and nutrition assistance	157	187	31
Other	370	372	2
Total, income security	795	773	−21
Social security	1,196	1,212	17
Veterans benefits and services:			
Income security for veterans	148	140	−9
Other	28	22	−7
Total, veterans benefits and services	177	161	−15
Total, mandatory human resources programs	3,697	4,210	513
Other functions:			
Agriculture	20	17	−3
International	−2	1	3
Mortgage credit	−5	−33	−28
Deposit insurance	−5	−12	−6
Other advancement of commerce	25	26	1
Other functions	149	159	10
Total, other functions	182	158	−23
Undistributed offsetting receipts:			
Employer share, employee retirement	−118	−120	−2
Rents and royalties on the outer continental shelf	−5	−12	−7
Other undistributed offsetting receipts	−21	−104	−82
Total, undistributed offsetting receipts	−144	−235	−91
Total, mandatory	3,735	4,133	398
Net interest:			
Interest on Treasury debt securities (gross)	480	718	237
Interest received by trust funds	−125	−184	−59
Other interest	−51	−58	−7
Total, net interest	305	476	171
Total, outlays for mandatory and net interest	4,040	4,609	569

Table 23–5. RECONCILIATION OF FINAL AMOUNTS FOR 2022

(In millions of dollars)

	Receipts	Outlays	Deficit
Totals published by Treasury (September MTS)	4,896,119	6,271,508	1,375,389
Miscellaneous Treasury adjustments	....	50	50
Totals published by Treasury in Combined Statement	4,896,119	6,271,558	1,375,439
Department of Transportation	60	60	....
Affordable Housing Program	277	277	....
Electric Reliability Organization	89	89	....
Federal Financial Institutions Examination Council Appraisal Subcommittee	16	16	....
Federal Retirement Thrift Investment Board Program Expenses	....	−45	−45
National Oilheat Research Alliance	8	6	−2
National Railroad Retirement Investment Trust	....	836	836
Public Company Accounting Oversight Board	299	295	−4
Puerto Rico Oversight Board	60	60	....
Securities Investor Protection Corporation	416	70	−346
Standard Setting Body	41	41	....
United Mine Workers of America benefit funds	11	12	1
Other	4	49	45
Total adjustments, net	1,281	1,766	485
Totals in the Budget	4,897,400	6,273,324	1,375,924
MEMORANDUM:			
Total change since year-end statement	1,281	1,816	535